Mass Communication
IN CANADA

FIFTH EDITION
Rowland Lorimer and Mike Gasher

OXFORD
UNIVERSITY PRESS
1904 ❖ 2004
100 YEARS OF
CANADIAN PUBLISHING

OXFORD

UNIVERSITY PRESS

70 Wynford Drive, Don Mills, Ontario M3C 1J9
www.oup.com/ca

Oxford University Press is a department of the University of Oxford.
It furthers the University's objective of excellence in research, scholarship,
and education by publishing worldwide in

Oxford   New York

Auckland   Cape Town   Dar es Salaam   Hong Kong   Karachi
Kuala Lumpur   Madrid   Melbourne   Mexico City   Nairobi
New Delhi   Shanghai   Taipei   Toronto

With offices in

Argentina   Austria   Brazil   Chile   Czech Republic   France   Greece
Guatemala   Hungary   Italy   Japan   Poland   Portugal   Singapore
South Korea   Switzerland   Thailand   Turkey   Ukraine   Vietnam

Oxford is a trade mark of Oxford University Press
in the UK and in certain other countries

Published in Canada
by Oxford University Press

Statistics Canada information is used with the permission of the Minister of Industry, as Minister
responsible for Statistics Canada. Information on the availability of the wide range of data
from Statistics Canada can be obtained from Statistics Canada's Regional offices,
its World Wide Web site at http://www.statcan.ca, and its toll-free access number 1-800-263-1136

National Library of Canada Cataloguing in Publication

Lorimer, Rowland, 1944- Mass communication in Canada/
Rowland Lorimer and Mike Gasher. —5th ed.

Includes bibliographical references and index.

ISBN-10: 0-19-541804-2   ISBN-13: 978-0-19-541804-0

1.Mass media.   2. Mass media—Canada.   I. Gasher, Mike, 1954-   II. Title/

P92.C3L672003   302.23   C2003-904604-4

Cover and Text Design: Brett J. Miller
Cover Image: Mark Owen/Getty Images

5 6 – 07 06
This book is printed on permanent (acid-free) paper ∞.
Printed in Canada

Table of Contents

Preface

In the Preface to the fourth edition of *Mass Communication in Canada* we noted that, between 1986 and 2000, 'vast changes in the communications infrastructure have taken place around the world.' Truly, this can still be said, as changes in technology and access draw ever more people into the global web of mass and public communication. As we stated in the previous edition, 'specialized mass media products are designed to compete with person-to-person communication and to make person-to-person communication an unpreferred alternative in filling one's leisure time. To emphasize the expansion of public communication is to take seriously the vast numbers of hours people are spending, at work and at play, using the public communications system that the Internet represents.'

In retrospect, however, one might say that we did not take the Internet seriously enough. In this edition we redefine 'mass communication' to include public communication. There is no need to confine the definition of 'mass communication' to the centralized production and wide dissemination of products. Rather, as we explain in Chapter 2, mass communication can be defined in terms of three types of activities: centralized production with wide dissemination; decentralized production (i.e., production of content by many more people) with wide accessibility; and individuals interacting with one another on a wide scale, within the world, within a nation, within a widespread community.

Other changes introduced to the fifth edition include the following. In Chapter 1, we have strengthened the discussion of communication as both transmission and transformation by introducing Shannon and Weaver's mathematical model of communication and our social model of communication. We have undertaken a general updating, especially in Chapters 6 and 7 on policy, in Chapter 8 on ownership, and in Chapters 10 and 11 on technology and globalization. In Chapter 4, we have dropped conversational analysis, and in Chapter 5 we have reorganized our discussion of theoretical perspectives on the audience to fit a more chronological sequence and have separated British cultural studies from Marxism and the Frankfurt School.

As a whole, this book can be thought of as having four parts. Understanding those parts should help readers to assimilate more readily the ideas of the book as a whole.

Part I: Communication and Society

The first part is meant to orient the reader to the major elements of the field of mass communication: Chapter 1 speaks of communication and its importance to the creation and maintenance of society; Chapter 2 defines mass communication and the mass media (as part of communication as a whole); and Chapter 3 discusses the role of the mass media in society in the context of history, political values, and cultural dynamics.

Chapter 1 introduces communication and discusses how it affects society in three ways. The first is the breadth of its influence. Communication is involved in all social acts and we discuss nine dimensions of social activity and how communication affects them. The second way in which communication affects society is in the dual role as a conduit or transmitter of information and as a transformative agent. And the third way communication affects society is through the transformative dynamics of the dominant communication forms—oral speech, written language, visual imagery, and electronic communication.

Chapter 2 defines mass communication and the mass media. The richness and complexity of the concepts of mass communication and the mass media are discussed here and a foundation for understanding is laid down.

Having thoroughly discussed the mass media both as facilitators of information transmission among members of society and as institutions that disseminate information and entertainment products to audiences, we turn in Chapter 3 to the historical and political context of the media. This chapter examines the development of the press out of Enlightenment values and presents the press as both a contributor to and a result of the evolution of democracy. The chapter also introduces ways in which the media have been conceptualized and the distinctive characteristics of the Canadian mass media and their operation within Canadian society. It pays particular attention to the interaction between the media and Canada's political system and culture.

Part II: Content and Audiences

A McLuhanite might suggest that our first three chapters are a beginning discussion of how the medium is the message, in other words, how the structure of the media, quite apart from content, influences society. While at one level of analysis the organization of the media is more important than many realize, it would be folly to suggest that content and the interaction between content and members of various audiences is unimportant. Chapter 4 examines content and the various ways in which content is discussed by communication theorists. It begins with consideration of a concept called 'indeterminacy of representation'. Essentially, this means that an idea may be represented in many different ways. Fifteen different people would probably summarize a television program or a real event in 15 different ways. The greater the complexity of what they were describing, or the greater the difference between the backgrounds of the people doing the describing, probably the more significant would be the variability in the descriptions. Take this multiplicity one step further. The various representations are not more or less correct. Rather, the nature of representation is that one invents a reality on the foundation of, for instance, the material world. A glass is not a glass until it is created into a glass by a person who perceives it as a container from which to drink. Communications studies are concerned with the dynamics of the invention of meaning, what some call symbolic production. Indeterminacy of representation distinguishes communication studies from studies that attempt to find definitive answers, as science does.

Chapter 4, then, reviews various theoretical approaches to the study of content. Some look at the context in which the content was created; some, the intent of the author; some, the structure of ideas; some, the assumptions behind the structure of ideas; some, the frequency of concepts and expressions; some, the economic interests of those involved; and some examine genres and other defining elements of a media form. With these theoretical perspectives in place the chapter takes a closer look at the interaction between media content and society.

Chapter 5 explores the role of the audience. The beginning of the chapter offers an overview on how to conceive audiences—not as consumers of produced content but rather as individuals who engage with newspapers, magazines, books, television, movies, and music to a greater or lesser extent and interpret them according to context, their background, their desire to find something meaningful, elements of the content that may speak loudly to them, and so on. In the same way that the media invent meaning, so, as in our example of the glass, individual members of the audience invent meaning from media content, as do cultures in creating social systems within which the media operate. The chapter continues with a review of the various theoretical perspectives frequently used for scholarly research on audiences.

The remainder of the chapter examines what information the media industries collect on audiences and how they use that information. While we use the Print Measurement Bureau's data on Canadian magazines and their audiences, as we point out, other organizations, such as the Bureau of Broadcast Measurement, provide the same types of data for the broadcasting industries. Certain communication scholars tend to demean these types of data by claiming that what scholars study treats audience members as thinking citizens with certain needs and wants, while industry-based research treats audiences as commodities to be bought and sold and, at best, as consumers of content. The two approaches are quite different. But this does not mean that a scholar or student cannot gain valuable insights from examining industry-generated audience figures. By examining certain statistical data on the magazine industry—who reads what magazines, which are on upward and which are on downward trends, which have large circulations and in what parts of the country, what the age and gender mix of readership is—one can appreciate some of the changing dynamics of society, and not just for the purpose of selling audience attention to advertisers.

Part III: Major Influences on Media Functioning

Law, policy, ownership, content production, and technology are *all* part of the institutional structure of mass communication; they shape the contexts in which mass communication occurs and they all continue to evolve. And because they are mutually constitutive, it is not easy to decide which should come first. Some students better appreciate the significance of law and policy *after* they have come to grips with ownership structures and the various tensions between owners, content producers, and technology. On the other hand, others appreciate that law and policy set the rules of the game within which owners, content producers, and technology make their influence felt, and thus it is with law and policy that we begin this section.

At a time of considerable resistance to state intervention in all areas of the economy—usually regarded as state *interference*—it is important for readers to understand that laws and policies, discussed in Chapter 6, are not simply reactions or afterthoughts that address already existing economic and technological determinants. Rather, laws and policies help constitute media environments and are, when well-conceived, designed to anticipate future directions in ownership, content production, and technology. Media environments are not primarily the products of free-market economics and technology; they are socially constructed environments in which laws, policies, the goals and ideals of content producers, and economic and technological forces all come into play.

The laws and policies established by each national government determine how the media operate within that nation. Further, international laws and policies govern how the media operate at the international level, how, for instance, copyright applies across many countries, how the broadcast spectrum is allocated to various countries and to various user groups, and how places for communication satellites in geostationary orbit are allocated to various countries. This structure and these rules are created by formal statutes, in which case they are laws, and/or in government plans of action, in which case they are policy. And while laws derive from statutes, regulations derive from policy.

After discussing how policy is developed, Chapter 6 examines telecommunications policy and then broadcasting policy. Telecommunications policy, based in Canada on the Telecommunications Act, governs the technological infrastructure upon which are based all of broadcasting and land-line telephones, cellphones and other wireless communication devices, emergency communication, military communication, taxis, and other point-to-point communications systems. With the expansion of the Internet, telecommunications law will only increase in importance. In addition, who controls the hardware infrastructure can be critically important to a nation's affairs.

Broadcasting policy is determined by the Broadcasting Act. Historically, Canadian broadcasting policy has been implicated in the nation-building project of the federal government. If originally that meant linking the far reaches of the country into a national public radio network, today it means providing content that speaks to the broad diversity of the Canadian people and providing access to the radio and television airwaves for journalists, creators, and performers of all backgrounds.

Chapter 7 examines the cultural industries, film and video, music recording, book publishing, magazine publishing, newspaper publishing (which also receives greater attention in Chapters 8 and 9), and new media. In contrast to broadcasting, there are no overarching statutes to determine policy direction for these media. Yet, government does play a role in each of these cultural industries. To ensure that Canadians have a presence in film, books, magazines, music, and newspapers, policy must be put in place to ensure that the dynamics of the marketplace do not silence Canadian voices. In a marketplace dominated by US producers who have the advantages of an English-speaking market more than 10 times the size of Canada's, a government determined to advance the interests of its producers, and an ideology that denies the integrity of collectivities in favour of the rights of individuals, the distribution systems for Canadian cultural products, as well as the opportunities for creating content in the first place, could easily be overwhelmed. Chapter 7 delves into the basic policies that have encouraged Canadian cultural expression and have given Canada a place on the world stage in music, book authorship, film, and television programming. It also discusses how legislation has ensured that Canadian magazines and newspapers have been strengthened over the years and how that legislation has been challenged and renewed.

With the policy framework for the media laid out in Chapters 6 and 7, Chapter 8 goes on to discuss the structure and role of media ownership. Here, our point about the social construction of the media environment is reinforced. From the outset, the chapter establishes that there is no natural or inevitable way to structure the media economically—every society adapts its own media to its own needs, and ownership forms can be quite distinct from medium to medium within the same country. The chapter describes the two principal types of media ownership—public (or government-owned) and private—but notes that all media participate in the Canadian economy and that no media industry operates exclusively on the basis of free-market principles. The restructuring of the media economy by large, converging conglomerates is also addressed.

Chapter 9 brings content producers into the picture, concentrating on the example that journalists provide. Journalists do not simply *gather* news, nor do they simply *mirror* society. Instead, like other kinds of cultural workers—filmmakers, fiction writers, photographers, and musicians—they actively produce their material by seeking out and presenting the stories they believe are the most important, most relevant, and most interesting to their audiences' daily lives. Although journalism is similar to other forms of content production because it is produced and because news is told in story form, journalists are expected to adhere to certain well-known ideals, such as objectivity, fairness, balance, and accuracy, all in the service of their quest for truth. The pursuit of these ideals by journalists is set in the actual political, legal, and economic contexts of Canadian society for the purpose of underlining the structural tensions inherent to its practice.

Chapter 10 introduces technology as the third of the three major factors that influence how the media operate. Technology is seen to be not merely devices that can be used in this or that instance. Rather, it encompasses machinery, professional practice, and social institutions. A machine without a person who knows how to use it is inert. Even defining technology as somehow intrinsically connected to a material artifact is problematic. As the chapter also points out, neither can technology be classified as good or bad: technology introduces change; it redefines society and social relationships. Chapter 10 begins with an examination of these issues and then explores how communications technology is affecting society in Canada and around the world. Major issues such as technological convergence, the interaction between technology and policy, and technological transfer are considered. The chapter concludes with an overview of recent technological developments and how they are changing the manner in which society operates.

Part IV: Our Evolving Communications World

Both Chapters 11 and 12 look back over the phenomena discussed in the previous chapters. Chapter 11 is conceptual and focused in its overview. Chapter 12 is descriptive.

Chapter 11 has both an empirical and a theoretical foundation. When policy, ownership, content production, and technology come together, the most noticeable direction in which they take society is towards global integration. Electronic communications technology allows for instantaneous transmission of content around the world. Economies of scale encourage concentration of ownership and hence the creation of larger and larger enterprises. Facilitated by technology and increasingly larger transnational corporations whose reach is global, content production takes place with an eye on many national markets. Even in law and policy, governments have seen it as desirable over the past decade or so to create laws and policies in the form of international trade regimes to facilitate the flow of media products. And, of course, the Internet is a global communications system.

The dynamics of globalization are both positive and negative. While bringing technically sophisticated and aesthetically pleasing cultural products to broader audiences and a wider variety of locations, individuals may benefit. They gain information; they are amused; they are enlightened. But by the same token, this wide distribution carries with it the material realities, cultural values, and even the language of the producing culture. Simultaneously, globalization produces gratitude and resentment, sometimes in the mind of the same person, sometimes gratitude in the minds of some and resentment in the minds of others. In a world of vast differences in standards of living, we ignore this double reality at our peril, as the attacks on New York and Washington on 11 September 2001 illustrated. As Marshall McLuhan would say, and this is the theoretical foundation of the chapter, through electronic communication we have created a global village that has brought us all into each others' backyards, with all the difficulties as well as advantages that this entails.

Chapter 12 is a descriptive overview of the book. It follows through each of the chapters, describes what each contributes to our overall understanding of mass communication, and looks forward to the future.

Rowland Lorimer, Vancouver
Mike Gasher, Montreal

Acknowledgements

We owe particular thanks to Anne Carscallen, Richard Smith, David Mitchell, David Skinner, Stefan Lorimer, Conor Lorimer, Dianne Arbuckle, Michael Craig, Enn Raudsepp, and our anonymous readers for their comments and contributions to this edition. We also would like to thank the editorial, management, and sales teams at Oxford University Press Canada for their work and support.

PART ONE

Communication and Society

CHAPTER 1

Communication and Society

Introduction

This first chapter outlines the nature of the interaction between communication and society. After an overview that provides a sense of the quickly expanding communications universe as well as both optimistic and pessimistic views of that universe, the chapter proceeds to its three main points: (1) communication is part of all social behaviour; (2) communication encompasses both transmission and transformation; and (3) at the highest level of generality, the transformational dynamics of communication can be described by orality, literacy, and electronic processes.

A Quickly Expanding Communications Universe

We are living through monumental changes in communications. Broadcasting and film, until now the two major broadcast industries, are being challenged by multicasting via the Internet and home entertainment systems. We are seeing the creation and growth of a vast telecommunications infrastructure designed to make all types and amounts of information, entertainment, and services instantly available anywhere in the developed world and in some parts of the developing world. In joining computing power with transmission capacity, thousands of hitherto unimaginable services have become available, from banking and investing to medical diagnosis, distance-delivered education, and telecommuting (working at home for a company that may be located halfway around the world).

The knocking of broadcasting and film off their pedestals as the focal points of mass communication has disrupted both the media and society. True, national broadcasting **networks** still exist and there are plenty of them: CBC, CTV, ABC, NBC, CBS, PBS, Fox, BBC, RAI (Italy), NHK (Japan), to name only a few. Now, however, they are in direct competition with their own offshoots—the specialty channels. By concentrating on one genre or one type of content, these specialty channels are transforming our television sets from mainstream general-interest news and entertainment organs, which contribute to an overall coherence in society, into distributors of fragmented con-

tent in a manner emulating magazine racks. Specialty channels such as CNN, YTV, Bravo, the Discovery Channel, MuchMusic, CBC Newsworld, provincial educational networks, the Learning Channel, TSN, Vision TV, W Network, and so forth are the new kids on the block. Gone are the days when whoever was watching television at 6 p.m. or 11 p.m. was watching the news. The now-fragmented audience assembles only for the most unusual of circumstances, as when suicide bombers crashed airliners into the World Trade Center in New York and the Pentagon in Arlington, Virginia, on 11 September 2001, or when major natural, technological, or political disasters occur, such as the sudden death of loved celebrities like Princess Diana or the Queen Mum, the mysterious failures of planes and rockets, the collapse of political regimes, or the recent Anglo-American war on Iraq.

The film industry, television networks, cable companies, and broadcast television itself are also being unceremoniously drained of their share of our leisure time. Home computers, video games, the Internet, hand-held communications devices, and other emerging services of the telephone companies are the challengers. Nowadays, individuals can actively involve themselves in games or, through the Internet, seek out information on every conceivable subject and explore it, voice an opinion on it, and usually obtain some kind of reaction within a day, a few hours, sometimes even seconds. Already, 10 hours of monthly long-distance telephone service cost less than one month of cable service. Compare that to a decade ago when a three-minute call from Vancouver to St John's cost almost as much as a month of cable!

The technology available is wonderful. For instance, you can take a phone on your trek to the South (or North) Pole, or anywhere else in the world, and for about $2.50 per minute talk to the rescue agency of your choice. With a GPS unit attached to your watch and a cellphone you can call for help and give your exact location. Soon you will be able to see television from any country in the world virtually anywhere, providing you can afford the receiving technology. The issue is, who controls the use of the technology and how? On the one hand, governments invest in the technological infrastructure with the knowledge that it will generate sufficient economic activity to earn back that investment in tax revenues. On the other, all this new technology demands vast amounts of capital. Capital can best be raised by large business. And more capital can be raised by larger businesses.

The temptation of new technologies diverts public investment from national public broadcasters to technological infrastructure and stimulation of its use. The goal is to provide Canadians with a comparative advantage by creating support and opportunities for a wide range of commercial information, entertainment, and communications enterprises serving every conceivable audience and taking advantage of every possible technological permutation. The motivation of government is that once this is accomplished, and even as it is being implemented, the resulting communication system will be transformed from a public expenditure into revenue and employment. The temptation of new technologies also encourages concentration of ownership not only to raise the needed capital but also to allow firms to take advantage of convergence: the multiple exploitation of research and content, for example, for both a newspaper article and a television news item.

There is only one problem: a communications system designed on the basis of marketplace principles serves producers. This is because of the overarching need to make a profit. Raymond Williams, a British media scholar, once noted that people are free to say anything as long as they say it profitably. Because new communications enterprises seek revenue from advertisers, they must serve the needs of these advertisers. Advertisers need to sell goods and services to people. They have an interest in certain audiences (those with disposable incomes) and in particular content (that which encourages product consumption). Their interest in supporting content that makes a positive contribution to society or that is well produced is secondary. If advertisers' support of such programming generates goodwill for advertisers or a richer society, then they will support it because, ultimately, it generates increased consumption. If there is no long- or short-term payoff then advertisers will withdraw. The matter for communications corporations is one of fiduciary responsibility—the requirement of a publicly traded corporation to look after the economic interests of its shareholders. Some may argue that such a system also serves consumers—note, not people, not citizens, not children growing up who need care and nurturing,

but consumers—those who have money to spend and whom advertisers wish to reach.

The net result is that what commercial communications enterprises serve up—whether a celebration of plurality, a balancing of the rights of the individual with the rights of the community, or considerations of social values like medicare—is all subject to a commercial equation. A television program appears because that program makes commercial sense. To be sure, commercial sense has wide parameters, because audience members have a wide range of tastes. But, in all cases, for the commercial sector, the bottom line is profit. So much is this the case that the claim of Hollywood that it provided 'pure entertainment' has been silenced. Movies, for instance, have become purveyors of placed products. While they deliver content to the audience, they deliver the attention of the audience to firms that have paid for product placement (see Wasko et al., 1983). Some movies are little more than a launching pad for derivative records, toys, books, and T-shirts. Others are merely excuses to sell overpriced popcorn and candy.

And so the market is coming to reign supreme. Sell, sell, sell, and get rich quick! Sell the funky boots

The marriage between Hollywood movies and consumer products is a very profitable one. Jennifer Lopez, American film star, television star, and pop singer, now sells perfume. (Winfried Rothermel/CP)

made in Newfoundland. Sell the beer that will surround you with every person and object you ever dreamed of. Sell the politician who is going to build Camelot, create lots of jobs, and get rid of the debt—all painlessly. Sell the law that is going to rid the streets of criminals. Sell the drug that will rid you of all pain, worry, or inconvenient personality traits. Sell the operation that will create for you the ideal body, complete with self-selected race and gender characteristics. Sell the investigative reporter who will reveal the hidden truth. Sell the evangelist who is going to extract money from lonely and well-meaning people who have a genuine desire to help others. Sell, sell, sell.

Or are we being too jaded?

The promoters of communication technology present an alternative view of the communications landscape: they claim that it is only at the beginning of the third millennium that true democracy on a global scale is becoming possible in mass society. The Internet and home computers can bring the entire world into every home and every country. They can also turn every home and every country into an information or entertainment production centre. Informed citizens, the technology enthusiasts argue, are the foundation of democracy. True, they admit, our past communications accomplishments have been no mean feat. Our media systems have been able to bring us the best actors, locations, and information and analysis the world had to offer. We have experienced television and radio programs created by the world's greatest producers. Books written by the greatest authors, past and present, have been available in every language with interpretations by the world's best literary critics for some time. Movies by the world's greatest directors have been visiting our neighbourhoods for decades. In terms of the right 'to receive information from any source', as outlined in paragraph 19 of the United Nations Universal Declaration of Human Rights, we have been well served.

But bringing the best to our neighbourhood or our living rooms puts audience members in a passive position. The Internet and the computer in its many forms (from cellphones to desktop computers) allow citizens to participate in making meaning, making programs, compiling songs, or writing books. In other words, while we have been able to receive the best available from any source, our ability to 'seek and impart information', the two other elements of para-

Queen's University is among a number of Canadian universities that offer distance education programs. The following ad, adapted to local markets, appeared in Montreal, Toronto, and Vancouver newspapers in the spring of 2003.

graph 19 of the Declaration of Human Rights, has been considerably more constrained. Now, with Internet technology, not only are we able to explore the masterpieces of civilization according to our individual tastes, but also we can share our insights about that exploration, or anything else, with anyone in the world who might be interested. Today a universe of information and entertainment, instantaneously available everywhere and produced by anyone, is at hand—at least for those who have the time, equipment, and knowledge to use the Internet.

Want to know what feminists or environmentalists think about a specific issue? Look it up on the Web. Want to set up an exchange of views between Canada and Turkey? Put the word out on the Net and wait a few days for an answer. Want to share your insights on viticulture with the vintners of France, Chile, California, Australia, or Bulgaria? Join the International Viticulture Association and its on-line discussion group. It's all possible for next to nothing—once you have a computer, Internet access, and no time charges on your data line.

How about extending your education? Over the past decade numerous universities, such as Queen's, University of Toronto, Athabasca, Simon Fraser, and Waterloo, have developed distance education programs, which you can undertake without having to leave your home. You may enrol in a variety of courses and will be provided with reading lists, lists of lectures, lecture notes and transcripts, video recordings of lectures and special presentations, and access to on-line tutorials and discussion groups. In some programs the instructors make visits to locations that have class-sized enrolments. They hold formal and informal discussions and provide social and intellectual stimulation.

In the library world it is usually possible for anyone anywhere to obtain access to the best collections

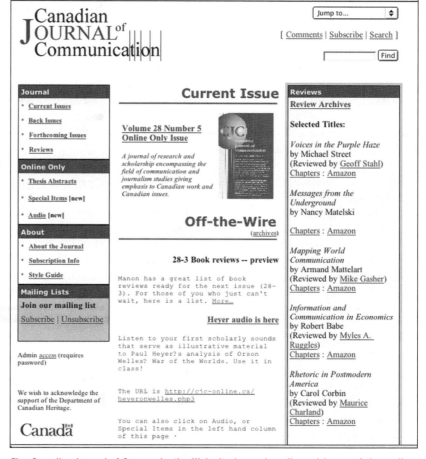

The *Canadian Journal of Communication* Web site (www.cjc-online.ca) is one of the earliest scholarly journal sites, made possible largely as a result of the efforts of Professor Richard Smith at Simon Fraser University and his students, particularly Paul Wolstenholme.

through direct document delivery service. In Canada, CISTI, the Canada Institute for Scientific and Technical Information, serves the needs of scientific researchers and in fact provides access to its 15 different journals to anyone with a dot.ca address free of charge (http://www.nrc.ca/cgi-bin/cisti/journals/rp/rp2_jour_e). The *Canadian Journal of Communication* has been on-line for nearly a decade and makes all but the most recent content available freely (www.cjc-online.ca).

Thus, one can just as well speak of technological promise as about the downgrading of social services. And arguably that investment in technology can increase the ability of our national communication system to address public interest goals.

So, are we winning or losing? Is technology going to help in creating a better, more equitable world? Or is it going to increase the gap between the rich and the poor? Ultimately, what are the implications of the current monumental changes in communications? Are we collapsing into a totally commercialized society that insufficiently differentiates between the worthwhile and the trivial, or are we evolving into a more equitable, freer, information-rich, and exciting society?

It is very difficult to say. Certainly, plenty of triviality is to be found in all media—triviality in books, magazines, newspapers, radio, television, movies, sound recording, and personal communication can be seen in spades on the Internet. But quite significant communication is also taking place.

In the late spring of 1998 a proposal brought forward by the United States to the Organization for Economic Co-operation and Development (OECD) was defeated by a coalition of public interest groups. The Multilateral Agreement on Investment (MAI) was essentially an international bill of rights for corporations that would have placed the right to do business ahead of the rights of individual governments to set rules for doing business within their jurisdictions. The defeat of the MAI was made possible by a combination of resistance within OECD countries, resistance by certain members of the OECD, and the sharing of information over the Internet by anti-MAI groups. The ability of groups to obtain information and share it quickly was an obvious contributing factor to the defeat of this agreement.

Nearly every international meeting of heads of state and finance ministers is challenged by protesters who use the Internet to inform and organize. And as we saw from the seizure of the computers of members of Al-Qaeda, they, too, used the Internet to organize and co-ordinate their 11 September offensive against the United States.

In short, even with the passing of the dot-com bubble, when any Internet company could get started with several million dollars, when firms such as Nortel overbuilt the glass fibre networks, and when the cowboy capitalism of such firms as WorldCom sought to control Internet access, we are nonetheless going through a technological revolution in communication. The technology at the base of this revolution is integrating the information and entertainment systems of the world. Whether the net result is for good or for ill remains to be seen. And whether it is for good or ill, in part, depends on the resolve of those who have the power to insist that the communications infrastructure we create will be for good.

Communication and Social Behaviour

Communication in general, and mass communication in particular, affects every dimension of society. Communication does not simply carry content; it also transforms the content it carries. More than the message matters. The medium through which a message is expressed transforms the content. As McLuhan stated it, *the medium is the message.*

The All-Pervasive Range of Influence of Communication

How communication permeates virtually every aspect of our lives was outlined in a report commissioned by the United Nations Educational, Scientific, and Cultural Organization (UNESCO). The report, often called the MacBride Report (after the commission chairman), discussed how communication impinges on our lives along six dimensions: the social, political, economic, educational, cultural, and technological (UNESCO, 1980). To that list of six we add two more dimensions: the familial and individual.

THE SOCIAL DIMENSION

Communication fills a *social need*. It provides an information base around which a society, community, or group can coalesce and interact, ideally contributing to social cohesion, a sense of belonging on the part of all members of society. All Canadians in communities of 500 persons or more have access to CBC radio and television and usually at least one commercial station. Thanks to communications satellites, families with receiving dishes have gained access to additional Canadian programming. The existence of this Canadian communication system, augmented by telephones, newspapers, books, magazines, videos, films, and the Internet, provides a context within which Canadians can see themselves as a single nation.

Canada's modern communications system is historically rooted in transportation. While it is true that Sir John A. Macdonald had the CPR built primarily to ensure the flow of goods, with the flow of goods came the flow of information—through the mail and the telegraph. The post office instituted inexpensive second-class mail rates to encourage the circulation of newspapers and magazines to help knit the country together. These, and other commercial communications—for example, Eaton's catalogue—gave Canadians a sense of connection with their compatriots elsewhere in the country. Ordering a pump organ from Berlin or Clinton, Ontario, or a wood stove from Sackville, New Brunswick, or Elmira, Ontario, for instance, gave western Canadians both an economic link and a social connection to eastern Canada. However, even then, as today, Canadian communications carried a great deal of foreign content, especially from the UK and the US. This foreign content has always been a part of the social fabric of the Canadian nation and though it has been the subject of controversy, it has given Canadians a certain worldliness that Americans seem to lack.

THE POLITICAL DIMENSION

Communication is a *political instrument*. Probably the most famous English-Canadian example of communication being used as a political instrument is of William Lyon Mackenzie politicizing Upper Canadians through his newspaper, the *Colonial Advocate*, and eventually leading them into rebellion in 1837. Similarly, Pierre Bédard spread his political ideas in *Le Canadien*, the newspaper he helped to establish. As the leader of the Parti Canadien (later the Parti Patriote), Bédard used *Le Canadien* as a nationalist party organ to oppose the Château Clique, the ruling **elite** group of Lower Canada. Even earlier, in 1778, through *La Gazette littéraire* (precursor to *La Gazette de Montréal* [1785]), Fleury Mesplet, a colleague of Benjamin Franklin, spread the ideals of the American Revolution in French Canada.

This overt political influence of communication, especially through newspapers, has remained. For instance, the controlling shareholder of Southam, the Asper family of Winnipeg, has made it clear that they see control of editorial perspective as a privilege of ownership (see Chapter 8). As well, in Quebec, *Le Devoir* is a staunch supporter of Quebec sovereignty, whereas *La Presse* supports the federal Liberals. Governments also employ the press to advance their own interests. For instance, the federal government frequently announces initiatives that will benefit one or another group and claims the credit for making any positive change. And when governments become dissatisfied with normal media coverage, they create media events to orchestrate the release of significant information, or they advertise in order to speak directly to the public.

The political role of communication, however, is constrained on the one side by a concern with **freedom of information** and on the opposite by a concern for **privacy**. For instance, governments collect vast amounts of information through surveys, censuses, satellites, clandestine activities, and mandatory reporting mechanisms such as income-tax statements. Certain parties, usually businesses trying to sell products, wish to have access to this information, and they often argue in favour of the free circulation of government information. Yet, those same companies and many individuals have concerns over the circulation of information they regard as private. Why should anyone have access to your medical record without your permission, even if your name is removed? How much power should the state have to collect information about individuals? The risk is that information collected can be disseminated, whether intentionally or not. Certainly there has been abuse. For example, the RCMP has had illegal or unexpected access to some individuals' tax records, as well as health records. In Vancouver in 1995 an anti-abortionist was obtaining, apparently from police sources, the names of the owners of vehicles parked near abortion clinics (Bolan, 1995).

Privacy concerns have led the government to keep information to itself in order to protect individual rights. In doing so, the government also protects itself against political scandal or accusations of ineptitude. However, it also jeopardizes the ability of its citizens to use this information to their advantage, whether that advantage is accumulation of wealth, political reform, or cultural development.

In short, communication can be a political instrument working in the interests of reform, in the effort to suppress individuals and information, or in a myriad of other ways. It can benefit the state, the community, the individual, commerce, and culture all at the same time or it can work for one or more of these to the detriment of the others.

THE ECONOMIC DIMENSION

Communication is an *economic force*. It makes itself felt in various ways. As described above, the information a government collects has potential economic benefit for groups and individuals. The collection of information about markets or weather conditions, for instance, can be useful to certain groups, such as agricultural producers. For example, a violent storm hit Britain in the late 1980s causing death and destruction. The storm was described as having arrived without warning—this was not true. It turned out that the weather service had been recently **privatized** and only those who subscribed to a top level of service were aware of the coming storm. The nation as a whole was not aware because certain institutions, including the media, subscribed to a lower level of service. This disaster was a result of Margaret Thatcher's attempts to create private knowledge-based industries on a foundation of public-sector information with no safeguards for public emergencies.

Because of the enhanced availability of information, nations and companies producing goods for export can gain knowledge of market trends as sophisticated as that available to domestic producers. Exporters are no longer confined to producing basic products with characteristics that change very slowly and for which there is a steady, predictable demand. They can now participate in markets where yearly trends determine which products will sell for a premium price and which will be down-market items. In fact, as demonstrated in the electronics industry, foreign producers like Sony can lead the industry, introducing new products and new styles of products—for example, the Walkman, Discman, and so forth. The severe loss of market share by North American car producers in the 1970s and 1980s is another example of how foreign producers can not only participate in a market determined by style but can even set the style. During these decades, Japanese car producers seized the small-car industry of North America through sound market analysis and quality products.

Similarly, a number of 'colonial upstarts', such as Canadians Roy Thomson and Conrad Black, as well as Australian Rupert Murdoch, seized control of a variety of British money-losing newspapers and turned them into cash cows. Knowing the size and stability of the market and the necessary costs of production, they purchased the papers and turned red ink to black—mainly by firing sometimes more than half the labour force. Automation helped, but more important were knowledge of market and production costs and a willingness to confront the unions. From a communications perspective the information a foreign producer can access matches what any local producer has, as long as the producer can pay for the information.

The economic force of communications also depends on one's ability to analyze it. The MacBride Report recommended that each nation achieve a capability to take available information and analyze it from its own national or industrial perspective. For example, planning on the basis of weather forecasts only makes sense if you can predict for your precise area and your precise activity.

THE EDUCATIONAL DIMENSION

Communication has *educational potential*. New communications technologies or facilities are customarily announced in the context of the humanitarian benefits they can contribute. These benefits are of two types: medical and educational. In countries such as Canada new developments in communications are described in terms of enhanced opportunities for people in outlying regions. For example, satellites currently facilitate both medical diagnosis and the delivery of educational courses to outlying areas. In countries with high rates of illiteracy the educational potential of communications is even greater. Telemedicine exemplifies how doctors are able to spread their expertise within the profession. In Montreal, for example, Info-Santé allows people to contact health professionals by telephone 24 hours a day, seven days a week. Other projects are developing on-line diagnostic services. Already, medical diagnostic packages have been developed and sold to interested buyers. And medical services in the developing world have been enhanced via telemedicine.

However, the educational potential of communication has, in some cases, the power to exclude. For instance, the professions—engineering, medicine, law—have access to information and a knowledge of the procedures for using that information that are not readily accessible to others. They also have permission to use that information in certain crucial settings, such as hospitals or the courts. As media expert Joshua Meyrowitz has stated, 'The information possessed by very high status people must appear to be not only unknown, but unknowable, creating in the general population both mystery and mystification' (1985: 64–5). The power of computers to store such information and retrieve it in a selective and flexible manner could open that knowledge to a much larger group of individuals (see Lorimer and Webber, 1987). But as we are seeing on the Internet, once an open information system is created, determining veracity becomes essential.

THE CULTURAL DIMENSION

Communication is both *an impulse and a threat to culture*. As the MacBride Report phrased it, communication systems have the ability to distribute information or items of quality (rich visual, audio, and dramatic presentations) widely. At the same time communication has the potential to threaten or eclipse local culture. Lavish entertainment productions and educational programs can provide the basis for invidious comparisons of the quality of life. Hollywood cinema is the norm. Rather than being evaluated on its own merits, local cinema is compared to that norm, as implied by names such as Hollywood North for Canadian film and Bollywood for Indian film. Cultural content in films is largely dominated by an American world view rather than a homegrown vision. Movies of local culture are generally rejected. Audiences tend to see movies as an escape from reality rather than an inspiration to present one's own reality as a dream for others (Knelman, 1977). Nonetheless, the myth and the reality of children in Canada striving from early childhood to become as accomplished as someone heard on radio or seen on television is powerful.

THE TECHNOLOGICAL DIMENSION

Communication also represents a *technological dilemma.* Many imagine that technological advance is rapid and independent of society, that society has a difficult time keeping up with technological change. As we point out in later chapters, technological advance does not occur as a beneficial side effect in the pursuit of scientific knowledge. Communications technology—from radios to **videotex** to satellites—is not a spinoff but an extension of conceptual thought to create devices that are technologically feasible and have a market value. Radio, television, Walkmans—in fact, books, newspapers, and magazines—are all examples of intentionally created communications devices that gained a place and survived in the marketplace.

The introduction of new technology usually provides a wider range of access to services. However, with it come both industrial and cultural repercussions. For example, Direct Broadcast Satellites (DBS), now more commonly called **Direct to Home (DTH) satellites** (hence the cable industry term 'd[ea]th stars'), are capable of providing digital, high-quality signals that can be received by a flat round antenna the size of a large pizza pan. Canadian companies include Bell Expressvu, Shaw's, and Star Choice. These satellites offer the viewer a lot more channels than do the cable companies. DTH services have had two industrial consequences: they have decreased the market share of the cable companies, and, consequently, they have forced cable companies to increase viewer choice. The immediate cultural result has been to fragment the audience for Canadian programming, lowering the market share for Canada's traditional broadcasters. To compete, Canadians have developed specialty channels and thus helped to maintain Canadian audiences for Canadian channels, if not programs.

THE FAMILIAL OR PRIMARY SOCIAL GROUP DIMENSION

The penetration of communications into family living rooms in developed countries and into the communities and villages of developing countries *changes the dynamics of the group.* Children are exposed to a much wider range of information and sometimes to a whole different language from that of their parents' generation. Children are also exposed to potential role models who may behave in ways quite contradictory to what their parents or community see as desirable. For instance, in cultures that favour clothing promoting physical modesty, parents may have a very difficult time if their teenage daughters prefer tight clothes and bare midriffs. As well, programs designed explicitly for children can encourage consumption far beyond the financial ability of the family. Christmas toy season can be especially anxiety provoking.

Just as societies must cope with communications, so must small social groups and families. The difference in the amount and the perspective of the information received by children and their elders can contribute to a lack of understanding between generations.

THE INDIVIDUAL DIMENSION

Communication both aids and constrains the development of *individual identity.* On the one hand, communication provides us with models of behaviour and helps us shape our 'selves'. On the other hand, by reinforcing certain character types and simplifying non-mainstream lifestyles, it actually may narrow the choices people tend to make in the roles they will adopt. In the arena of new communications devices, people's patterns of use can define who they are. For example, searching out and finding favourite Web sites via computers can transform what information people have and what perspective they take on certain issues. Cellphone users can be 'in touch' with anyone, all day, every day, or at least until the batteries need a recharge. Commuters often catch up on messages on the way to work while families and young people take over the cellphone frequencies in the free-time evenings.

Communication as Transmission and as Transformation

It goes almost without saying that communication involves the **transmission** or **carriage** of information. To communicate is to extend knowledge, to transfer meaning from one sentient entity to another. As a phrase from the 1960s had it, *one person* cannot communicate.

The best model for thinking about the transmission characteristics of communication was proposed in 1949, by Claude Shannon and Warren Weaver. Shannon and Weaver's so-called mathematical model of communication makes reference to the basic technical characteristics of communications technology. In this model, seen in Figure 1.1, a person, the encoder, formulates a message, for example, by putting an idea into words. Words are symbols for ideas: the word 'chair' represents the object 'chair'. The person (or device) receiving the message, the decoder, unravels the signals and, on the basis of the symbols

sent, formulates meaningful content. In this example, the decoder would formulate an idea of the object 'chair' and code it into speech or writing by making a sound or typing a word on a keyboard.

The 'channel' is the medium through which the message is conducted, for example, a human voice in air or print on paper. The decoder may then give the encoder 'feedback', that is, let the encoder know that she or he has understood the message. By virtue of sending a message back, the decoder becomes an encoder. This feedback might be produced by means of a simple non-verbal nod of the head and a smile. Or, the decoder might carry on the discourse, taking it in a new direction, for example, 'Which chair?' All these responses are feedback and they are also new messages soliciting feedback from the original encoder (or others).

Any interference in the transmission of the intended message (signified by the lightning bolts in the diagram) is referred to as noise. Noise may be loud background noise that makes it difficult to hear,

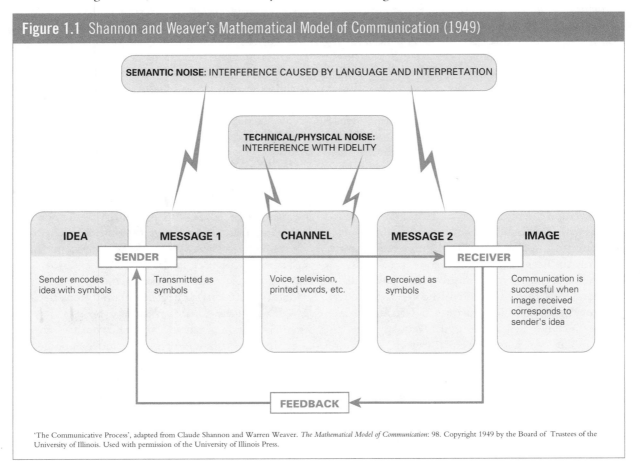

Figure 1.1 Shannon and Weaver's Mathematical Model of Communication (1949)

SEMANTIC NOISE: INTERFERENCE CAUSED BY LANGUAGE AND INTERPRETATION

TECHNICAL/PHYSICAL NOISE: INTERFERENCE WITH FIDELITY

IDEA	MESSAGE 1	CHANNEL	MESSAGE 2	IMAGE
SENDER			RECEIVER	
Sender encodes idea with symbols	Transmitted as symbols	Voice, television, printed words, etc.	Perceived as symbols	Communication is successful when image received corresponds to sender's idea

FEEDBACK

'The Communicative Process', adapted from Claude Shannon and Warren Weaver. *The Mathematical Model of Communication*: 98. Copyright 1949 by the Board of Trustees of the University of Illinois. Used with permission of the University of Illinois Press.

a heavy unfamiliar accent, the snow on a television screen, static on the radio, a misplaced paragraph in a newspaper, or the imperfect encoding into words of the idea that the encoder has in his or her mind.

Shannon and Weaver's model works well for engineers and technicians who speak in terms of fidelity and message transmission. But it works less well for sociologists and others concerned with the social nature of communication, as we are in this book. In fact, it banishes consideration of the transformative element of communication.

TRANSFORMATION

To communicate is also to transform. Writing a poem about a person represents that person differently than does a photograph or a biography. Films adapted from books transform the works on which they are based—authors often point out that their books are ruined when made into movies.

While transformation is accepted by communication theorists and sociologists, and many involved with the social nature of communication have moved on from Shannon and Weaver's (1949) model, there does not yet exist a commonly accepted model of communication that deals with the transformation inherent in communication. Therefore we have developed a simple social model of communication that can be seen in Figure 1.2. The social model emphasizes social and media-related variables that account for the transformative nature of communication. For example, the social context within which message formulation takes place is termed the 'encoding envelope'. At the

other end, the 'decoding envelope' represents the context of ideas and understandings that the decoder brings to deciphering of the encoded message. (The nature of these envelopes of understanding and meaning exchange is the stuff of semiotics, as well as of discourse analysis and other theories of meaning generation and communicative interaction that we will explore in Chapters 4 and 5.)

In between the encoding and decoding process, the social model turns away from the transmission channel and the distortion that noise introduces and focuses on the transformation of any message that any medium (or channel) introduces. For instance, to put an idea into words is not the same as painting a picture in an attempt to communicate the same idea. Or, a news story on television is not the same as a newspaper write-up of the same story. Similarly, a novel differs from its movie adaptation. In fact, talking to a child, a friend, or a person in a position of authority transforms both the content of the message and the choice of media as well as the manner in which the chosen media are used. In encoding, the envelope of activities in which the person doing the encoding engages includes taking into account the physical and social context as well as the person for whom the message is intended. In transmitting, the media transform the message by encouraging a certain structure in the encoding process, and they further transform it by making certain elements predominant for decoding. Television emphasizes the picture. Writing emphasizes linearity and logic. Oral speech emphasizes social context and body language, the individual instance rather

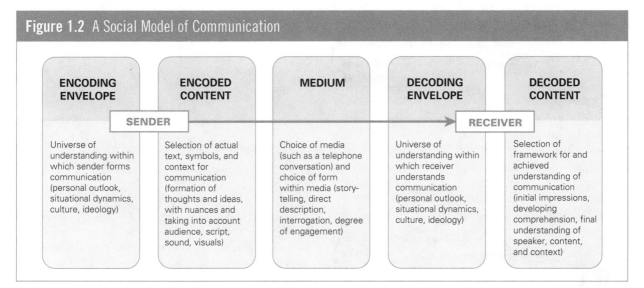

Figure 1.2 A Social Model of Communication

ENCODING ENVELOPE	ENCODED CONTENT	MEDIUM	DECODING ENVELOPE	DECODED CONTENT
Universe of understanding within which sender forms communication (personal outlook, situational dynamics, culture, ideology)	Selection of actual text, symbols, and context for communication (formation of thoughts and ideas, with nuances and taking into account audience, script, sound, visuals)	Choice of media (such as a telephone conversation) and choice of form within media (story-telling, direct description, interrogation, degree of engagement)	Universe of understanding within which receiver understands communication (personal outlook, situational dynamics, culture, ideology)	Selection of framework for and achieved understanding of communication (initial impressions, developing comprehension, final understanding of speaker, content, and context)

SENDER → RECEIVER

Harold Innis had a broad and profound impact on Canadian scholarship—his ideas have been applied in various disciplines, from communications to political science and economics. (Courtesy National Archives of Canada/C-003407)

than the general case. Although feedback is not indicated in this model, it contributes through the encoding envelope. An immediately preceding message would obviously be a predominant element in the formation of a new message.

This model provides a foundation for a simple social definition of communication. Viewed from a social perspective, communication is the process by which a message (content, meaning) is encoded, transmitted, and decoded and the manner in which a message (content, meaning) is transformed by that three-part process.

Two Canadians, Harold Innis and Marshall McLuhan, were the first scholars to bring serious attention to the transformative elements of communication. They approached the issue in broad terms, arguing that the dominant forms of communication shape a society, its economic life, politics, and culture. Innis (1950) was the first to articulate this perspective. He claimed that oral communication tends to maintain cultural practices while written communication favours the establishment and maintenance of empires—power blocs spread over large geographic

areas and across many different cultures. He used the Roman Empire as his example. To conquer and then co-ordinate, administer, and police such a vast empire required a written system for recording and communicating messages on a portable medium. Laws were created, written down accurately, and transported to the far reaches of the Empire. As well, from this communication system emerged an educated elite to maintain the system.

Innis wrote about the **media bias** of each communications medium and its transformative properties. For instance, he claimed that oral communication and early hieroglyphic writing on clay emphasized the preservation of outlooks, values, and understanding over long periods of time. Later, written communication, using the phonetic alphabet on papyrus and paper, emphasized basic social control (the rule of Roman law) across space (the entirety of the Empire). Such biases of the dominant media a society uses shape the characteristics of that society.

McLuhan, a scholar of English literature, took up Innis's ideas and extended them to the modern period. McLuhan first studied the impact of printing, capturing its influence on society by coining the term

Marshall McLuhan was one of Canada's most prominent intellectuals of the twentieth century. (©1973, Mohan Juneja. Reprinted by permission.)

Inventor of the telephone (and various other things) Alexander Graham Bell patented his invention for transmitting speech over wires in 1876. (Courtesy National Archives of Canada/C-017335)

'typographical man', which referred to humanity after the invention of printing with movable type (in the West) by Johann Gutenberg in 1454. McLuhan and many scholars since have demonstrated how the printed book transformed humanity so that all Western societies came to accept logical, linear thought, as well as individualism, conceptuality, science, and indeed monotheism. The printed book was a tremendously powerful means of communicating ideas and knowledge in early modern Europe (McLuhan, 1962). (However, David Ze [1995] and others have argued that printing with movable type had no parallel effect in Korea and China, where it had been invented several hundred years earlier.) Printing with movable type created print culture, which dominated the Western world until electronic communication was developed and harnessed by such men as Guglielmo Marconi (radio transmission) and Canadians Reginald Fessenden (radio transmission) and Alexander Graham Bell (telephone).

After examining print culture, McLuhan turned to electronic society (1964), revealing its dynamics to an unbelieving world. He was the first real analyst of the impact of the new media of communication (radio, TV,

photography, film) on what we think of as modern societies, although certain British modernists, such as Wyndham Lewis, preceded him and had a parallel concern (Tiessen, 1993). McLuhan expressed his ideas in a distinctive, aphoristic way, referring to them as **probes**. And while many scholars dismissed them, his ideas had a great impact in the 1960s in North America and Europe, spreading to politics, the advertising world, even the media. McLuhan's observations made the media and their influence an important issue. In the same way that Sigmund Freud identified the unconscious as an unknown force affecting our behaviour and that Albert Einstein posited interactions at the level of atoms that were awesomely powerful, so McLuhan was telling us that the media were transforming society before our very eyes though we couldn't observe it—until his theory revealed it. As the quintessentially sophisticated US journalist of the period, Tom Wolfe, observed, 'What if he's right?'

McLuhan argued that the electronic media created, for the very first time in history, the possibility of instant communication between any two points on the globe: he referred to this reality as the **global village**. Although now, in the age of the Internet and the World Wide Web, we are beginning to understand the significance of instant worldwide communication and electronic communication as an 'outered nervous system', in the 1960s, when hardly a single computer existed and not a single non-military communications satellite flew above us, McLuhan's writing was particularly prescient.

Like print, electronic media have powerful transforming effects on the social character of time and space. It is increasingly difficult not to have some knowledge of what is happening elsewhere in the world today. Global television, a global telephone and fax network, and the Internet are all very real. When hundreds of millions of people scattered all over the world have simultaneous access to an event, such as the recent Iraq War or the Olympic Games (Dayan and Katz, 1992), or when certain television programs are watched in over a hundred different countries around the world (see Silj, 1988; Liebes and Katz, 1986; and Ang, 1985, for their analyses of the TV program *Dallas*), it is clear that electronic media contribute to the formation of a global culture, underpinned by global capitalism. Similarly, when 20 people around the world who share a common interest or expertise can be in daily e-mail contact, or when anyone anywhere can access a Web site with no thought whatsoever of location, a different globalism can emerge, but one that is somewhat freer from global capitalism.

Both Innis (1950) and McLuhan (1962), as well as the **Toronto School** that followed in their wake (for example, Ong [1982] and Goody [1977]), placed their emphasis on media writ large. However, it is useful to explore the dynamics of oral, literate, and electronic societies in some detail in order to understand the influence of communication overall.

Oral Society

Innis claimed that the means of communication set the basic parameters for the functioning of any society. As such, in oral societies people are governed by the knowledge vested in the community and specifically preserved by certain members of society. For instance, in classical Greece, such individuals maintained and transmitted their knowledge by means of epic poems and what Innis called epic technique (1951). Epic technique involved creating poems in rhythmic six-beat lines—hexameters—that had certain rigidities and elasticities. The rigidities were the parts that were memorized. The elasticities permitted the adaptation of certain elements according to time and place. Forms, words, stock expressions, and phrases acted as aids, while the local language and situation provided the basis for ornamental gloss. The development of such techniques meant that epic poetry was in the hands of persons with excellent memories and poetic and linguistic abilities. The techniques for memorizing and reciting epics were often passed on within families of professional storytellers and minstrels. According to Innis, such families probably built up a system of memory aids that were private and carefully guarded. Catholic priest and linguist Walter Ong has described the oral process in greater detail:

> You have to do your thinking in mnemonic patterns, shaped for ready oral recurrence. Your thought must come into being in heavily rhythmic balanced patterns, in repetitions or antitheses, in alliterations and assonances, in epithetic and other formulary expression, in standard thematic settings, in proverbs, or in other mnemonic form. Mnemonic needs determine even syntax. (Ong, 1982: 34)

The epics permitted constant adaptation, as required by the oral tradition, and also allowed for the emergence of completely new content to describe conditions of social change. What was socially relevant was remembered, what was not was forgotten. As well, the flexibility permitted the incorporation of sacred myths from other civilizations, with these myths being transformed and humanized as they were turned into the content of an epic poem. The Greeks could thereby foster the development of an inclusive ideology as they expanded their empire, and this ideology could serve colonizing efforts extremely well.

While the above description may seem attractive, there are those who have viewed oral societies as especially vulnerable to power politics. Karl Popper (1945, 1962) referred to them as closed societies and saw the transformation to literate society as a movement from a closed to an open society—open to the expression of individual freedoms.

The dynamics of the oral tradition in a modern context are illustrated in the *Delgamuukw* decision, a landmark decision of the Supreme Court of Canada in which Aboriginal oral history has been accepted as a legally valid foundation for pursuing land claims. While such a decision may seem only right and proper, it has taken centuries for our literate culture to accept the veracity and authority of oral culture. In part, that acceptance has come about because of our understanding of oral communication and oral culture (see, for example, *Globe and Mail*, 15 Dec. 1997, A23, for an illustration of how we now understand oral culture).

Oral history has also been shown to be quite accurate. For instance, according to Maori oral history, New Zealand was settled by their Polynesian ancestors about 800 years ago, when eight to ten canoes of settlers set out in December from Eastern Polynesia to establish themselves in New Zealand. Recent genetic research confirms the oral history. Tracing changes in mitochondrial DNA, a genetic researcher has found that, in all likelihood, New Zealand was indeed settled by about 70 women (mitochondrial DNA is passed from mother to daughter) and their men approximately 800 years ago. Since the large canoes of the Polynesians carried about 20 people and there would have been approximately 150 settlers (not counting children) it appears they would have needed about eight to ten canoes (see *Globe and Mail*, 5 Sept. 1998).

Providing a sense of the difference between oral and literate societies, anthropologist A.B. Lord explores in *The Singer of Tales* (1964) the dynamics of a modern oral tradition (rural Yugoslavia, 1937–59).

Lord notes that, for the oral bard, the recording of the words of a song is a totally foreign experience. It preserves a particular performance at a particular time in a particular setting, in a dead, utterly useless form. It does not represent the correct or best version because there is no correct or best version. Rather like Grateful Dead concerts, each performance is unique in itself. The Canadian pianist Glenn Gould's 'literate' perspective was the antithesis of this: he believed a perfect performance, especially of the work of a composer such as Bach, could be created in the recording studio by splicing the best bits from many different performances (Payzant, 1984). He believed the concert stage merely interfered with musical perfection. Communications theorist Simon Frith (1988) carries the literate perspective one step further. He notes that whereas the record used to be a reminder of a performance, today the live performance (complete with taped inputs and pre-programmed amp settings) is a simulacrum of the record.

TIME BIAS

Societies have both history and geography—or, as Harold Innis would put it, societies occupy both time (history) and space (geography). One way societies occupy time and space is through their communications media, which, Innis argued, are characterized by biases of time or space. For now, let us address the notion of a time bias. The media can bind us historically by providing connections to our society's past. The best example of these connections are commemorative films, TV programs, radio documentaries, and books that recount important episodes in Canada's past. Think of news coverage of Remembrance Day ceremonies or other historical anniversaries, such as 6 December vigils that commemorate the 14 women who were killed at l'École polytechnique in Montreal in 1989. Communities use other markers of time bias. The slogan 'Je me souviens' on Quebec licence plates, for example, encourages Quebecers to remember their particular history as a French-speaking people within English-speaking North America. Historical murals, such as those in Vankleek Hill, Ontario, give both residents and visitors a sense of the town's past.

(Mike Gasher)

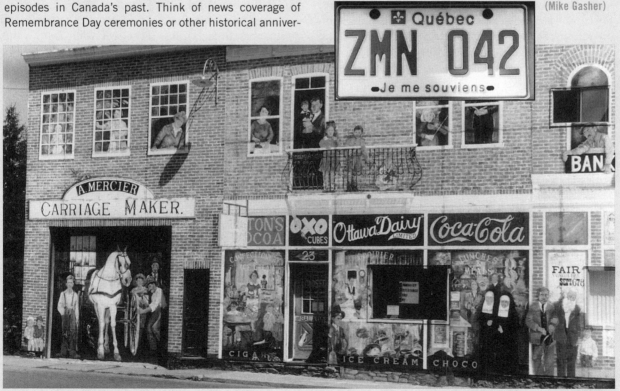

(Photograph by Mike Gasher. Reprinted with permission from artist, Elizabeth Skelly.)

The oral tradition and its ability to preserve the past, to transform that past as necessary, to base law in custom, and to explain all events within a natural cosmology point to the stability of oral societies and their tendency to preserve, extend, and adapt culture. Rather than being concerned with the continued existence of formal structures and institutions, oral societies are most successful at extending the dynamics of interaction. As Innis phrased it, they have a **time bias**, that is, they tend to extend themselves over the centuries. Change in such societies often induces an adaptation that preserves ways of acting, but in new circumstances. The ancient Greeks, for example, established a stable, continuous, but adapting culture.

Today, every community has its oral processes. Music seems to play an especially strong catalytic role in helping oral societies bond. For instance, in Eastern European countries under Communist rule, jazz music was both popular and suppressed. Communist governments were especially frightened of jazz. Perhaps it was because of the African-American roots of jazz, or perhaps it was because it seemed so uncontrolled and expressive of basic emotions. Whatever the reason, jazz was often banned. In Western countries today, there are restrictions instead of absolute bans. For example, rock-music stations and television broadcast channels do not play certain songs and videos, many of which are oral expressions of youth culture, although these may be available through record and video stores.

'WRITTEN ORALITY'

Found orality in written form (on a birthday card to a 14-year-old Canadian girl from another).

Booface (Granny P, Judie)

Hey Granny, I may not be your sister but I think I'm your third cousin twice removed then re-added by your mom's aunt's cousin's sister's brother. In other words you're my grandma. (Don't pinch my cheeks) HAHAHAHA!!!!!!

–Lots of love. Lesbo.

The word and relationship play in the above passage is more typical of speaking than writing. In speaking, the passage generates good-natured confusion and bonding. In writing, on a birthday card, the context maintains that bonding. Here, in a textbook, it invites analysis for logical sense.

The ways in which oral societies preserve knowledge and cultural integrity are fundamentally different from those of literate society. Where literate cultures emphasize the 'letter of the law', oral cultures emphasize its meaning. In an oral society organizing and originating myths serve to justify present-day reality rather than a chronology of historical events. In literate cultures, where the meaning of history can go unstated even though it is recorded in detail, history eventually becomes both synchronic and diachronic—ideas that span time and narratives that are faithful to chronology can exist simultaneously. The result, in literate society, is that each generation remakes its history in the light of the ideas of the day, but also within the chronology of recorded events. As such, history is continually rewritten in literate societies.

Literate Society

Whereas Greece, for Innis, represented an oral society, Rome represented a literate society. It was not that Greece was unaffected by writing. On the contrary, a number of authors, notably Eric Havelock (1976), claim that the basis of the enormous contribution Greek civilization made to modern civilization is to be found in writing, in their invention of the phonetic alphabet. In fact, Innis cites Greek sources from the period when writing emerged that express the significance of the change from oral to written modes. For example, in Plato's *Phaedrus* Socrates reports a conversation between the Egyptian god Thoth, the inventor of letters, and the god Amon. Amon says:

> This discovery of yours will create forgetfulness in the learners' souls, because they will not use their memories; they will trust to the external written characters and not remember of themselves. The specific you have discovered is an aid not to memory, but to reminiscence, and you give your disciples not truth but only the semblance of truth; they will be bearers of many things and will have learned nothing; they will appear to be omniscient and will generally know nothing; they will be tiresome company, having the show of wisdom without the reality.

After relaying the conversation, Socrates states:

> I cannot help feeling, Phaedrus, that writing is unfortunately like painting; for the creations of

the painter have the attitude of life, and yet if you ask them a question, they preserve a solemn silence, and the same may be said of speeches. You would imagine that they had intelligence, but if you want to know anything and put a question to one of them, the speaker always gives one unvarying answer. (Plato, 1973: 84)

This conversation resembles discussions of television, especially those that focus on its numbing effect on the mind. This is not surprising, for the transformation from an oral to a literate society was as major a change as from a literate to an electronic society. The discourse also points out the degree to which knowledge and wisdom were negotiated in oral discourse, rather than derived from a linear conceptual exposition.

Rome and the Roman Empire represent the origin of literate society because the operating concepts and processes of Rome were derived from the written rather than the spoken word. In legal proceedings, for example, the influence of writing can be seen in the fact that trained lawyers were responsible for defining the exact nature of a dispute within written laws (a literate function). Nonetheless, once the dispute was defined, the case was handed to laymen (a jury) to determine a settlement among the claimants (an oral community function). The development of contract law illustrates the Romans' ability to supplant oral practices with written ones. A contract changes an oral pact into a legal obligation and permits a much more complex and contingent agreement. It is a precise written record of an agreed obligation between persons or other legal entities. Such literate inventions allowed for both an orderly and a vast expansion of the Roman Empire. As Innis (1950, 1951) phrased it, the Roman Empire had a **space bias**, that is, a tendency to extend itself over a larger and larger territory. At the greatest extent of the Empire, in the third century AD, the Romans maintained control of the lands and people around the entire perimeter of the Mediterranean, from Southern and Central Europe to

WHO SAYS TV IS BAD FOR YOU ANYWAY?

The following historical anecdotes are meant to underline that, just like newspapers and books, television is an important medium that brings valuable information and perspectives to members of society.

Like Moses Znaimer, *Globe and Mail* TV critic John Doyle is a person who harbours no prejudice against television. In fact, it is hugely important and, Doyle figures, can be good for you. His argument runs in a four-part series that began on 26 May 2001. Behind his argument were a number of milestones that highlighted the contribution of television to modern history. Some of those milestones were:

May 1939 RCA broadcast the first live sports event, a baseball game. The broadcast laid the foundation of sports television and the new sports economy.

Fall 1951 *I Love Lucy* establishes a whole new pop culture comedy genre.

March 1954 Television cameras capture the bullying of Sen. Joseph McCarthy with contemptuous narration by Edward R. Murrow, thereby hastening an end to the Senator's witch-hunting career.

Fall 1960 Television watchers are convinced that John F. Kennedy wins his television debate against Richard Nixon. Radio listeners are of the opposite opinion. The TV politician has arrived.

Fall 1966 *W-Five* is launched by CTV as a detective-style public affairs show exposing corruption in politics and business.

July 1969 Humanity walks on the moon and is linked to earth by live broadcast.

November 1969 *Sesame Street* is created and is enormously popular for its role in helping children to learn.

September, 1972 Paul Henderson scores the TV-captured winning goal in the Canada-Russia hockey series.

June 1985 The rock concert Live Aid links two concerts in London and Philadelphia and raises millions for famine relief in Africa.

Fall 1996 CBC airs *The Newsroom*, created by Winnipegger Ken Finkleman, which satirizes the network. Finkleman becomes a television auteur.

SPACE BIAS

The notion of space bias does not come easily to some, perhaps because the word 'bias' most commonly has negative connotations. Innis used the word to mean tendency or emphasis. Thus, literacy favours or promotes the development of cultures spanning large geographic spaces.

The following footprint diagram illustrates the space bias of satellite technology. By beaming down a signal to a particular area of the earth's surface, a satellite creates, at least to some degree, a community—a community of all those receiving the same signal. Of course, people choose whether to watch and which channel to watch, and different satellite footprints can carry the same content. However, the broadcast of a news program from a particular city to widespread geographic

areas creates an artificial spatial extension of that city. To take another example, in some ways CNN and the BBC are extensions of Atlanta, Georgia, and London, England, just as the *Globe and Mail* is an extension of Toronto. These are all instances of space bias.

Canadian satellite Anik C's spotbeams create two spatial communities: one in western Canada, from Vancouver Island to northwest Ontario, the other from the top of Lake Superior east to Newfoundland. Source: Telesat Canada.

the Middle East, North Africa, and the Iberian Peninsula, and on to the north and west through present-day France and Great Britain. Crucial to the exercise of administrative power in the Roman Empire was the formation of abstract laws to apply in all situations, which were then written down on a portable medium, such as parchment, so they could be consulted in any location.

The development of literate society in Western civilization reflected an attempt to replace spoken, poetic, emotive language with clear, ordered, unambiguous, logical, written prose. This, in turn, led to the emergence of new ideas and concepts. For instance, in their writings, Cicero (106–43 BC) and other Stoic philosophers invented ideas that are now fundamental to modern thought, including the notions of a world state, natural law and justice, and universal citizenship. All these became characteristics of literate societies, as did libraries, which were scattered throughout the Roman Empire. Such ideas and institutions were nurtured by writing—a technology that allows the static

representation of ideas, so that the eye can juxtapose and compare two ideas, and that allows one to see many individual instances and abstract the general case.

Most other writings about literate societies focus on modern societies. While they discuss the influence of writing they do so within a context of an evolved technology and developed social, political, and legal institutions (see, for example, McLuhan, 1962; Goody, 1977; Olson, 1980). The basic claim of these authors is that writing has favoured the development of logical, linear, sequential, and conceptual thinking. Written discourse is logical because it is presented in such a way that anyone can understand the meaning of a written passage without the benefit of knowing the context within which the passage was written and without the possibility of further reference to the author. It can stand by itself as a statement that is consistent both internally and with reference to other common knowledge. Literate thought is conceptual because it encourages the abstraction of salient variables within a framework of analysis and can present

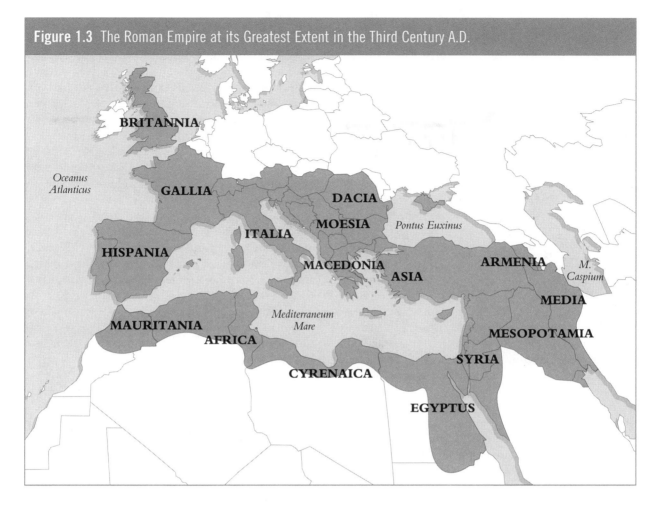

Figure 1.3 The Roman Empire at its Greatest Extent in the Third Century A.D.

both the specific and general. Literate thought is linear and sequential because only one idea can be presented at a time, followed by another, and then another, each building on its predecessor. This contrasts with what can be done in some electronic media such as television, where a picture can provide context while a spoken text presents other aspects of meaning. It also contrasts with what is available to a speaker, who can communicate, with facial or bodily gesture, certain aspects of a message while communicating other aspects in words.

Electronic Society

So central are literate dynamics to modern society that when Marshall McLuhan introduced his notion of electronic society in the early 1960s, it seemed both audacious and trivial to claim that somehow television, telephones, radio, and telex (the technologies that predominated in this period) were going to be as influential as writing, print, and literacy had been. It has taken a long time for academic discourse to fully incorporate McLuhan's ideas about the transformations in our society that result from a growing reliance on electronic communications. Perhaps because scholars depend so heavily on what we associate with writing, that is, the ability to write clearly and think logically and conceptually, we have not been able to imagine how electronic information processes can change society so dramatically. In trying to understand electronic society, McLuhan introduced the notion of a global village. By that he meant that electronic society has vast information-gathering and transmission capacities sufficient to make us intimately (perhaps too intimately) aware of the goings-on of people in every kind of situation all around the world. Though our linkage with the whole world is always incomplete, it becomes steadily more inclusive as technology and communications organizations and professionals extend our realm of knowledge, thereby transforming our local and global environments. That capacity for awareness and information-processing is fundamentally affecting our society.

Joshua Meyrowitz (1985) has argued that electronic media, above all TV, weaken the once strong link between physical place and social space. Whereas previously, place and space were inseparable, communications technologies, such as the telephone and e-mail, allow two people in distant physical places to share the same social, communicative space (for example, love on the Internet). Drawing heavily on the perspectives of McLuhan and American sociologist Erving Goffman (1959), Meyrowitz has argued that electronic media tend to undermine traditional settings of social interaction that maintained distinct and separate social identities, for instance, the boundaries between children and adults or men and women. By invading social spaces hitherto undisturbed, broadcasting affects the character of social relationships. For instance, in India the social organization of domestic space in the household tended to keep men, women, and children apart for much of the time, thereby maintaining their distinct and traditional social roles and identities. The arrival of TVs in the households of rural India has considerably disturbed traditional relations between the sexes and between young and old by breaking segregation barriers in the family (Malik, 1989). Electronic media's influence on social space is not confined to societies such as India's. In North America, for example, TV ads for feminine hygiene products take men and children into a world from which they were previously separated.

Television has become a medium that demands both the enactment of a small drama and visual interest. British theatre critic Martin Eslin (1980) has argued that, with the advent of television, dramatization has become the predominant mode of argumentation or presentation of facts. Theatricality has replaced reasoned analysis. Information is not collected and later transformed into a form presentable through television; rather, events are often staged, and TV crews select short 'clips' for television use. Indeed, this was even the case in the Iraq War of 2003, where television reporters 'embedded' with American and British troops often presented a narrow, selected view of a broad and politically complex crisis. The presentation of news on television is a matter of careful selection. Those who can create good television are

those who become newsworthy. The idea of newsworthiness itself shifts the focus away from logically or politically interesting items to the visually or dramatically interesting.

Another feature of television that has affected our electronic society can be captured in the following, recast phrase: *the camera never tells the whole truth.* We never know what is going on outside the frame. As media analyst Antonia Zerbisias (2003: A14) wrote of the widely and repeatedly broadcast toppling, by American troops, of a Saddam Hussein statue in Baghdad, 'Never mind how that video was tightly framed, showing a chanting crowd, when wider shots would have revealed a very different picture: a very large, mostly empty square surrounded by U.S. tanks.' We never know what happened the instant before the camera was turned on or the instant after it was turned off. We never know if what was filmed is typical or atypical. And while we never know 'what is not said or printed' in any means of communication, we are much more apt to feel with visual communication that we can 'trust our own eyes'. In short, the camera never presents the temporal or spatial frame.

This trust was further undermined with the development of digital technology that allows film and television producers to make the person on camera look as if he is saying what is being said—it is the same technology that is used to make animals appear as if they are speaking.

In an effort to combat the 'bad press' that television sometimes gets, Moses Znaimer, of CityTV in Toronto, created a documentary, *TVTV: The Television Revolution*, to challenge what he calls 'print dogma'. Some communication scholars took his challenge seriously: they created a McLuhanesque-style book, *TVTV: The Debate*, in which they challenged Znaimer's 'television dogma' and gave him a chance to reply (Anderson et al., 1996). The book and the documentary together provide a foundation for an in-depth discussion of the nature and influence of print and television.

From the publication of McLuhan's book, *Understanding Media* (1964), to the 1990s, discussions of electronic society were focused on television because television was the dominant medium of this period. With the development of and widespread access to personal computers and then the Internet, everyone, from communications scholars to government planners and members of the general public, has begun to realize just how profound are the social

TV AS RELIGION?

Moses Znaimer's Ten Commandments of television are:

1. Television is the triumph of the image over the printed word.
2. Print created illiteracy. TV is democratic. Everybody gets it.
3. The true nature of television is flow, not show; process, not conclusion.
4. As worldwide television expands, the demand for local programming increases.
5. The best TV tells me what happened to me, today.
6. TV is as much about the people bringing you the story as the story itself.
7. In the past, TV's chief operating skill was political. In the future it will be, it will have to be, mastery of the craft itself.
8. TV creates immediate consensus, subject to immediate change.
9. There was never a mass audience, except by compulsion.
10. Television is not a problem to be managed, but an instrument to be played.

Source: Anderson, et al. (1996: 14).

changes being brought about by electronic communications. The nature of education, e-commerce, electronic publication of scientific journals, and direct communication with friends and those from around the world we have never met all reflect that how we do things and the dynamics of cultures, political systems, and markets are being changed fundamentally by electronic communications.

Today, the basic principles of electronic communication, above and beyond television, are essentially as McLuhan outlined. Communication is instantaneous. Therefore, location and distance decrease in their importance. Electronic communication can encompass images, sound, and text. Therefore, we are far less restricted to one mode of expression. Electronic communication is as powerful as, if not more powerful than, print—because access to it is less restricted. Therefore, determining who controls it is of increased importance. This is why the fate of Microsoft is so very important to everyone, not just Bill Gates and his competitors. It is also why so many are determined to preserve part of the Internet as a place for public discourse, not merely as a medium for business.

Modes of Communication

Given the historical development of communication—from oral to literate to electronic society—as well as the theories and analysis of this development, we now turn to the underlying features of each of these communication modes. The following provides an overview of the characteristics of oral and literate forms of communication, as well as the different kinds of electronic communication: oral, audiovisual, and digital.

ORAL AND LITERATE COMMUNICATION

As anthropologist E.T. Hall (1980) has so vividly explained, oral communication incorporates lived cultural patterns—how close we stand to one another, how much inflection we put into our words through facial and bodily gesture, how we use our eyes, and so forth. The radical side of oral communication is conversation: anyone may say anything in any manner and thereby accomplish anything, from entirely preserving the achieved social relations to disrupting them completely. Investigations in a variety of disciplines, including anthropology (Goody, 1977), communications (McLuhan, 1962, 1964; Innis, 1950, 1951; Ong, 1982), and classics (Havelock, 1976), have also shown that when people engage in conversation, they focus on the intent of the person with whom they are speaking or listening to, whether those conversationalists are human beings or gods. Oral communication leads to belief systems in which environmental constants, such as the sun, moon, stars, earth, air, seas, rivers, trees, rocks, animals, and so forth, are made into persons or metaphors of persons. Oral communication also favours the formation of groups of like-minded people. The pluralism inherent in this system of environmental constants, all with their own dynamics,

TWO EXPERIMENTS IN ORAL COMMUNICATION

You can test out one of the variables surrounding oral communication. E.T. Hall called it social distance. Pick out a place near to where you are having your conversation and see if you can move the person with whom you are speaking to that spot. You can use one of two methods. One is to stand closer than usual to your fellow conversationalist. The other is to stand slightly further away. Either way, you can usually push or pull them to that spot as long as they are not conscious of your intent.

Ethnomethodologists such as Garfinkel (1984) were intent on demonstrating that conversation, at least in certain social settings, has implicit rules. They would take a behaviour from one social setting and insert it into another, such as getting up in the middle of a dinner and warmly greeting the hostess of the dinner as if one were first arriving at a dinner party. The surprised reactions of the other dinner guests confirmed, for Garfinkel, that there were implicit rules in such social situations. Notwithstanding this, conversation is a form of communication with radical potential. You can try an ethnomethodological experiment such as this, but for it to work you must not insert a behaviour that others might think you wanted to do anyway, such as planting a drive-by passionate kiss. The Quebec-produced no-dialogue TV program, *Just for Laughs,* is a marvellous source of such experiments.

provides for a variety of interpretative structures that vie for allegiance and are not necessarily consistent with one another.

Oral chants are the conservative side of oral communication. By means of exact repetition they affirm the fundamental shared realities of a community. They utilize voice and body, often adding adornments to the voice—rhythm, music, tone of voice—and adornments to the person, such as items of symbolic significance—masks, speaking sticks, incense burners. Such adornments heighten various senses, such as sight, smell, touch, hearing, as well as the overall perception and conception of the chant. Oral chants encourage affirmation of the group through an emergent sense of the whole being greater than the sum of its parts. The orientation is one of consolidation, of affirming the whole community, and of its constituent members playing out their various established roles.

Literate communication is also divided into two forms, the prosaic and the poetic. The prose text must have internal consistency and comprehensiveness. It must be capable of standing apart from its author as a meaningful statement in and by itself. Its associated analysis framework is linear—moving from one logical point to the next. It is not situationally contextualized, for example, by body language and tone of voice. Contextualization must be inherent in the text through the use of modifying words or the creation of images. Prosaic literate communication leads to the development of general and specific explanatory concepts. These explanatory concepts have a hierarchical relation to one another and, over the course of time, form an explanatory framework. Such a framework can be, for instance, a scientific theory. For example, the behaviour of objects relative to other objects was defined by a number of specific laws until Newton suggested the notion of gravity to explain such behaviour. Later, Einstein proposed his general theory of relativity, and Newton's notions were recast as specific instances within Einstein's more encompassing framework. In such a case, old concepts were eclipsed by new ones.

The hierarchical nature of prosaic literate communication results from a focus on producing and testing conceptual constants to prove the supremacy of single general concepts that seem to explain all related phenomena. Consistent with this tendency, literate societies are less amenable than are oral societies to a plurality of explanatory frameworks that gain or lose apparent validity, and hence the allegiance of followers, as events unfold. They favour a single, logically supportable, perspective.

Written poetry diverges from written prose in the analytical framework it encourages. Rather than encouraging logical and hierarchical thinking, poets strive to evoke images in the mind of the reader and, through those images, to provide insight into the real or the imaginary. The social philosophy consistent with poetic mode focuses on both the created images and the poet. On the one hand it may encourage elitism (few have the talent to work with words to produce images that resonate with an audience of any size), and on the other hand it may encourage plurality as a result of the multiplicity of images that the poets create. In addition, how poets are cast in society—as agents of the court, voices of the people, or as noble instead of corrupt—constrains both their role and the power of their images.

ELECTRONIC ORAL COMMUNICATION

Electronic society is complex and needs to be divided up to be understood. First are electronic oral communication and its two submodes, *broadcast* and *point-to-point* systems. Radio typifies the broadcast mode, while the telephone typifies point-to-point. Ironically, cellphones are really a restricted broadcast form, which is why (in analogue versions at least) they can be monitored. Cellphones are more accurately called cellular radio.

Electronic oral communication is not closely confined by space but it is confined by time. Radio waves reach many listeners, depending on their power and depending on which part of the radio spectrum they use—short-wave signals can bounce more than halfway around the world, especially at night. Telephone similarly reaches around the world. Even more than oral communication, electronic oral communication is focused on speaking, that is, the rhetorical structure of the message, and the human voice itself—there is nothing else, no person, no gestures. Like oral communication, electronic oral communication exists in the passing moment and is not preserved except in the memory of the listener and, at times, in electronic archives. It relies for its effect on immediate impression and the echoes of that impression in the listener's mind. Oral broadcasts often mimic the giving of speeches or lectures in that they may be created first in written form and then delivered orally, as in newscasts. In other instances, oral broadcasts are confined to a particular topic, or only certain individuals speak (for example, a host and a panel of experts), and certain distinctive rules are observed (see Scannell, 1991). Point-to-point electronic oral communication (the telephone in various forms) usually provides access to everyone and replaces face-to-face communication.

Electronic oral communication is affected by: (1) voice modulation (radio professionals are trained to speak in a certain manner); (2) the choice of words and whether the ideas are expressed within a narrative mode; and (3) the sequencing of ideas or, for example, the opposing ideas of different speakers. To some degree electronic oral communication is narrative or dramatic performance. It is impressionistic of both the message and the messenger. As the words go by, some phrases stick in your mind, not just their meaning but also the exact words. And the exact words are framed both more broadly in the vaguely remembered whole and more vividly in the imputed personality of the

TRANSFORMING THE MESSAGE

A cartoonist for the Los Angeles Times Syndicate, Jeff Danzinger, captured the transformative aspects of communication in a cartoon which shows Monica Lewinsky telling her story to a would-be ghost writer. There are two ways of reading this description of a cartoon. The one probably intended by the cartoonist was the scattered nature of supposed oral discourse of Monica Lewinsky and the ordered logical thought of the ghost writer. A far different reading is possible insofar as much of anyone's talk is neither strictly logical nor linear and it does not follow along a single track.

So then I said to my mother . . . 'Oh! I know what I wanted to tell you. Like yesterday? I was shopping my brains out and I remembered that the creep like, you know, no wait, it was the otherr day, not the otherr day you know. And, so I bought this, this, this thing thing, a kind of whatever thing and then I thought, well sure, like so what, I can win. Nah-uh, so Vernon said Monica, he said fine like whatever. Do you know what I mean? I mean.

The cartoon shows the balding, middle-aged writer typing into his laptop with a title-page on his left reading Butthead's Ashes by Monica Lewinsky. He translates as he types:

My mother was a great comfort to me during those challenging days, and often when I reminisce, while shopping or just letting my thoughts roam about the cards life has dealt me and the way others treated me . . .

speaker—the kind of person that would speak that way on that subject. Understanding is nuanced by perceived and projected interpretations consistent with the inferred character of the speaker.

The effectiveness of electronic oral communication can rest on the ability of certain speakers to capture, in ringing tones, the often unarticulated attitudes and understandings of the audience—sometimes called the **Zeitgeist**. The phrase 'does it ring true' is often operative. This perspective can lead to a view of certain speakers, such as talk-show hosts or investigative reporters, as believable whether or not their content stands up to detailed scrutiny. Smooth-talking politicians, especially those who wear the mantle of power well, can use this media 'bias' to their advantage. The phrases 'he sounds sincere' and 'you can tell she knows just from the sound of her voice' are germane to understanding how people evaluate electronic oral performance.

ELECTRONIC AUDIOVISUAL COMMUNICATION

Electronic audiovisual communication is most obviously exemplified by television, including both national network broadcasting and **narrowcasting**, that is, television focusing on a sector of the audience (though, in some cases, such as CNN or BBC World, this audience may stretch around the world). It also includes community television or, more accurately, community-access television. This form of television usually consists of a local cable channel made available to the public so they can make their voices heard. And while to include film would be technologically anomalous and impure according to McLuhanites, film does fit here the best. (Some would argue that film is not an electronic medium but rather, in its method of projecting images, an extension of painting.)

Electronic audiovisual communication attempts to 're-create' or 're-present' the social through its moving pictures and spoken words. In broadcasting, it combines access to special people (celebrities) in special settings (famous, meaningful, opulent) under special circumstances (orchestras in the wings). Based on its orientation to visual images, which convey its power and also allow mediated intimate contact, electronic audiovisual communication can be said to be an iconic or image-oriented medium (see Bruner, 1978). It shares with electronic oral communication the characteristic of being a narrative and dramatic medium. It presents stories of people usually within the context of

a given problem and its resolution.

The production of audiovisual images is a process that, in the final analysis, is usually directed by a single individual but involves a large and diverse team of specialists. Each member contributes to a complement of images through lighting, framing, dialogue, ambience, or editing style, which combine to create the intended impression. In some sense, electronic audiovisual communication is the re-creation of face-to-face communication in a fully visualized context conceived by the literate mind.

The cost of the creative process marks the major difference between community television and its rich sisters. The low production values of resource-starved community television contrasts with the glossy output of mainstream channels. This contrast provides daily legitimization of the position of power that the commercial channels occupy. High production values imbue media celebrities with an aura of legitimacy. Indeed, the supreme position of authority on television is that of the news anchor.

The investment demanded for the production of sophisticated audiovisual images has meant that television has fallen under the control of two types of owners: governments and large commercial organizations. Even community stations have been given over to the commercial sector, which provides access to groups and individuals as a kind of freebie in exchange for its monopoly position.

Because an infinite number of images and impressions can be created by even slight variations—the way a camera frames a person—the derivative analytic framework for this form of communication emphasizes flexibility and room for difference of opinion. In general, the television-based perspective on the world is pluralistic: it involves an acceptance of variety, particularity, and novelty. However, it is a restricted pluralism. It is peopled by a feudal court of celebrity personalities. It also has the dubious power to command the forces of communication so effectively that visual rhetoric prevails as the foundation of effective communication. The attractiveness of the image plays a very large part in determining the effectiveness of the communication of the message.

ELECTRONIC DIGITAL COMMUNICATION

Now here is a problem. If radio is electronic oral, and television is electronic audiovisual, what is the proper term for information transmission and telecommunications, exclusive of broadcasting? Until this edition, we have called it what the heading says, electronic digital communication. But everything—radio, television, sound, video—is going digital. All Web technologies are digital. To consider information transmission and telecommunications, exclusive of broadcasting, as electronic data communication is also a problem because digital data are exactly what are created in all electronic digital forms, whether images, sounds, text, or instances of purchasing. As recently as 1995, data communication was dominated by large organizations—banks, travel agents, hotel chains, central governments, stock analysts, global ad agencies, even large urban public libraries. Now, with the burgeoning of Web sites and the digitizing of broadcasting, 'digital electronic communication' is an all-encompassing term.

This said, what we used to mean by the term 'electronic digital communication' involved the communication of data that could involve an individual creating input and another or that same individual doing some final interpretations of output. However, programmed computers can suffice for all aspects—inputting, reception, and analysis. The information typical to this mode of communication is monitored (the number of items sold at a particular cash register, the number of hits to a Web site) or sampled (a market or political poll). The communicators involved—both information creators and receivers—have the capacity to analyze and benefit from vast quantities of detailed information. At its most sophisticated level, descriptive and inferential mathematical analysis and statistics can be used for summarizing data patterns, thereby revealing the secrets of brainwaves or weather patterns. Such possibilities encourage the ascendancy of planners and strategists and expert interpreters knowledgeable of both trends and trend analysis.

But what to call it? Perhaps we will have to live with ambiguity. In the same way that telecommunication encompasses broadcasting, so 'electronic data communication' seems the most suitable term, even if, strictly speaking, it encompasses digital broadcasting and Web activity.

Other Derivative and Different Viewpoints

Though Innis and McLuhan were the first to theorize on communication and its transformative effects, the shortcoming of their frameworks is that they tend towards a **technological determinism**. In other words, they tend to make us think that technology is the fundamental shaping variable and society is a mere expression of the dynamics of technology (a phenomenon explored in greater detail in Chapters 10 and 11). It is not that either author was an avowed technological determinist. McLuhan, for instance, once noted: 'we shape our tools; thereafter our tools shape us.' Thus it might be claimed that McLuhan begins his analysis with **human agency**, not technology. But it might also be claimed that McLuhan had very little to say about the 'we' in that statement (the nature of human agency). Certainly McLuhan inspired others, notably Elizabeth Eisenstein (1985), to place technology at the centre of their explanatory frameworks. They, too, deny that they are technological determinists. But rather than emphasizing human agency and social interaction, which shape both technology and the uses made of it, they slide into technologically derived descriptions of the social process. They fail to portray technology as a tool employed by those with power to advance their own interests.

Other viewpoints address and examine communications media. They are mainly rooted in material realities. They range from pure **Marxism** to current cultural theories and audience theories. (Such perspectives are introduced in later chapters, especially Chapters 4 and 5.) Raymond Williams (1974), for example, notes that communications technologies arise from the organization of society and reflect that organization. In his doctoral dissertation, 'Printing as an Agent of Stability in China', David Ze (1995) challenges Elizabeth Eisenstein's (1983) thesis in her book, *The Printing Press as an Agent of Change*. Ze makes the case that it is not technology that is important but its social organization. He argues that even though the Chinese invented movable type before it was invented in Europe, printing was an agent of social stability rather than change. The basic points of his argument are that: printing was controlled by Chinese emperors; it was used to transmit official versions of a limited number of texts; printers had everything to lose and nothing to gain in printing original material; and wood blocks were the most efficient means of reproducing texts as demand emerged. He concludes that the existence of a technology does not necessarily affect society significantly. However, if society can benefit from a technology, and people can see that benefit, then technology can speed and consolidate the evolution of a new social organization.

Summary

The purpose of this chapter has been to convey the importance of communication in the affairs of society. We did so, first, by introducing some current elements of communications: the rapidly changing technology; the growing trend of supporting communication that is financially lucrative; and the exercise of control over technology (particularly the 'who' and 'how' of control). We then discussed the extensive range of influence of communication, how communication is bound up in all social activity. We summarized eight dimensions of its influence on human activity: the social, political, economic, educational, cultural, technological, familial, and individual.

After a brief nod to the obvious fact that communication transmits content, we discussed how communication transforms the content it carries. We reviewed how oral, literate, and various modes of electronic communication have affected the basic functioning of all societies throughout history and prehistory.

The importance of communication in society cannot be overestimated. We have argued that communication is a force that contributes to social cohesion and is therefore a structuring force in society, both facilitating and constraining. Human affairs cannot be divorced from the communication system used to represent or discuss them. The design of our communication systems impinges on every element of our present and future lives.

RELATED WEB SITES

Council of Canadians: www.canadians.org
  The Council of Canadians involves itself in a wide range of issues where it feels that Canadians have a distinct set of interests.
Harold Innis Research Foundation: www.utoronto.ca/hirf
  The Harold Innis Research Foundation at the University of Toronto fosters research and other activities, including a research bulletin that focuses on the theories of Harold Innis. The University of Toronto also has a college named Innis College.
McLuhan Research Centre: www.mcluhan.utoronto.ca/
  The McLuhan Centre has quite a dynamic Web site. It

runs courses and a Web log along with many other McLuhanesque and McLuhan-oriented activities.
Canadian Journal of Communication: www.cjc-online.ca
  The *Canadian Journal of Communication* is Canada's principal communication journal. Students can make good use of it by accessing the site and searching on essay topics. The *CJC* is a leading proponent of on-line journal publishing and makes its back issues accessible on the Internet.
MZTV museum: www.mztv.com
  Broadcaster and TV mogul Moses Znaimer is founder of the MZTV museum.

FURTHER READINGS

Canadian Journal of Communication, Special Issue, 1996. 'TVTV: The Television Revolution, The Debate', eds Robert Anderson, Richard Gruneau, and Paul Heyer. This special issue offers a number of essays critical of Moses Znaimer's ideas, as presented in the documentary *TVTV: The Television Revolution*. Znaimer's ideas could be called McLuhanesque.

Eisenstein, Elizabeth. 1979. *The Printing Revolution in Early Modern Europe*. New York: Cambridge University Press. Eisenstein examines the role of the printing press and movable type.

McLuhan, Marshall. 1962. *The Gutenberg Galaxy: The Making of Typographic Man*. Toronto: University of Toronto Press. This was the first of McLuhan's two major works. It

outlines orality and literacy and their historical development. Its key thesis is that typography created the world as we know it.

———. 1964. *Understanding Media: The Extensions of Man*. Toronto: McGraw-Hill. Here McLuhan focuses on the influence of the media on the modern world. The various essays that make up the text explore the implications of (largely) electronic information systems. The book is interesting for both its insight and its foresight.

Ong, Walter. 1982. *Orality and Literacy: The Technologizing of the Word*. London: Methuen. Following McLuhan's basic ideas plus ideas from classicists, Walter Ong examines the nature of orality in greater depth than did McLuhan.

STUDY QUESTIONS

1. Communication affects the full range of human activity, from how we think about ourselves and how we act in the world to the interaction between nations. Describe the range of influence of communication and its significance for the evolution of society.
2. The influence of communication is not confined to its capacity to transfer information. Explain.
3. What are the fundamental differences between the mathematical and the social models of communication?
4. Summarize the path-breaking writings of Marshall McLuhan and the characteristics he attributes to oral societies, literate societies, and electronic societies.
5. In some sense, electronic audiovisual communication is the re-creation of face-to-face communication in a fully visualized context conceived by the literate mind. Explain.
6. How are new media influencing the structure of our society?
7. The current mass media system serves consumers, not people, not citizens, not children, not all groups within society, but consumers. Discuss.

LEARNING OUTCOMES

- To provide the understanding that communication is part of virtually every aspect of our lives, including our ideas of ourselves.
- To introduce the notion that communication is transmissive and transformative in its functioning.
- To outline the characteristics of a mathematical or technical model of communication.
- To introduce Canadians Marshall McLuhan and Harold Innis as major communication theorists.
- To provide a basic sense of the varying transformative natures of oral, literate, and electronic media and their influence on society.
- To introduce Innis's notions of space bias and time bias.
- To illustrate the dynamics of electronic communication and how it encompasses oral and electronic communication.
- To explain briefly the technological emphasis inherent in the frameworks discussed.

Mass Communication and Modern Society

Introduction: Definitions

Chapter 1 explored the influence of communication on society. It noted that communication influences the whole of the social world as a result of its transmission function and also through the transformative influences of oral, literate, and electronic communication processes. Each media form has a distinctive influence on the social process. This chapter narrows the focus from communication of all types to mass communication and from society through the ages to modern society.

The second chapter in the previous edition of this book explored the same topics as we do here—mass communication and modern society—but in this edition we introduce a new definition of 'mass communication'. Mass communication encompasses the traditional mass communication industries such as broadcasting and newspapers, the more recent decentralized mass communication that now takes place via the Internet, and third, the vastly expanded world of person-to-person communication on a mass scale that also takes place via the Internet, phone systems, and postal systems. Technology has finally brought forward worldwide communication by all members of society as the defining criterion of the field of mass communication. The Internet has joined with the postal system and the phone system to make communication between members of society on a wide scale as important to, and as influential on, society as the mass distribution of centrally produced information and entertainment products by broadcasters, newspaper, magazine, and book publishers, and the like.

This chapter begins by discussing the word 'mass' and by adding to an understanding of 'communication' as outlined in the first chapter. It then examines mass communication (and also public communication) and the nature and operation of the mass media.

THE MEANING OF 'MASS'

The *Concise Oxford Dictionary* (ninth edn, p. 838) offers various meanings of the noun 'mass'. Included are: a coherent body of matter of indefinite shape; a dense aggregation of objects; a large number or amount; the majority; the ordinary people (in the plural); affecting a large number of people or things; large scale. The purpose of our including so many definitions is to point out, moving into semiotics for a moment, that the word 'mass' is complex and extensive, truly polysemic. And, extensive as the definitions of 'mass' are, the *Concise Oxford* does not wholly recognize the use of 'mass' by social theorists. The closest it comes is to provide an example of large scale: '(mass audience, mass action, mass murder)'.

Sociologist and media theorist Herbert Blumer provides further context to the use of the word 'mass' in a communication context. In an early article, Blumer (1939) contrasted a number of different kinds of collectivities to arrive at a meaning for 'mass'. Simplifying and adapting Blumer's ideas somewhat, we can say that in a small group all members know each other and are aware of their common membership. The crowd is limited to a single physical space, is temporary in its existence and composition, and if it acts as a unit it rarely does so rationally. The public is customarily large and widely dispersed. It is often represented by largely self-appointed, 'informed' people who speak publicly and in rational discourse to validate their statements and appointment.

Denis McQuail (1983: 36) has summarized the meaning Blumer arrived at for 'mass':

> The term 'mass' captures several features of the new audience for cinema and radio which were missing or not linked together by any of these three existing concepts. It was often very large— larger than most groups, crowds or publics. It was very widely dispersed and its members were usually unknown to each other or to whoever brought the audience into existence. It lacked self-awareness and self-identity and was incapable of acting together in an organized way to secure objectives. It was marked by a shifting composition within changing boundaries. It did not act for itself, but was rather 'acted upon'. It was heterogeneous, in consisting of large numbers from

all social strata and demographic groups, but homogeneous in its behaviour of choosing a particular object of interest and in the perception of those who would like to 'manipulate' it.

McQuail, in each edition of his introduction to mass communication (1983, 1987, 1994), and Tim O'Sullivan and his colleagues, writing in 1983 in *Key Concepts in Communication,* note what they term 'mass society theory' of the early twentieth century. This model of industrialist/capitalist societies portrayed them as composed of elites (capitalist owners, politicians, the clergy, landowners, artists, intellectuals) and workers, 'a vast work-force of atomized, isolated individuals without traditional bonds of locality or kinship, who were alienated from their labour by its repetitive, unskilled tendencies and by their subjection to the vagaries of the market. Such individuals were entirely at the mercy of (i) totalitarian ideologies and propaganda; (ii) influence by the mass media (comprising, in this period, the emergent cinema and radio)' (O'Sullivan et al., 1983: 131). No mention is made of Marx or the Frankfurt School (see Chapter 4) but, presumably, the authors had these theorists in mind when they were writing. O'Sullivan et al. point out that 'Mass society theory has been refuted by historical evidence' but that the concept of the alienated majority of society has survived. Indeed, it appears to have survived the 20 years since the publication of the work of O'Sullivan and his colleagues. The moral force of such a view, which espouses such values as altruism and a sense of belonging, seems to have invested itself in much social commentary on the evils of globalization.

However, as the *Concise Oxford* attests and O'Sullivan and his colleagues point out, one need not imbue the word 'mass' with a sense of alienation or totalitarian tendencies. It can indeed mean, simply, large scale. This is how we mean it.

MASS COMMUNICATION

In Chapter 1, we defined **communication** as the process by which a message (content, meaning) is encoded, transmitted, and decoded and the manner in which a message (content, meaning) is transformed by that three-part process. If we were to carry forward the above definition of communication, we would see mass communication as communication on a mass scale, in other words, a lot of messages being encoded, transmitted, and decoded.

Some of mass communication is exactly that—many people talking on the telephone, sending and receiving e-mail, and writing and receiving letters. Interestingly, however, until very recently the accepted meaning of 'mass communication' did not describe that process at all. What was, and still is, more often termed 'mass communication' is the communication that happens by means of movies, large daily newspapers, and broadcasting, that is, the centralized creation, production, and mass distribution of information and entertainment. O'Sullivan and his colleagues captured that type of mass communication quite well:

> Mass communication is the practice and product of providing leisure entertainment and information to an unknown audience by means of corporately financed, industrially produced, state regulated, high-technology, privately consumed commodities in the modern print, screen, audio and broadcast media. (O'Sullivan et al., 1983: 131)

This definition, written prior to the development of the Internet and CD-ROM games, therefore does not encompass them.

O'Sullivan et al. pointed out that this usage of the term 'mass communication' had the potential to mislead. They advised that, following in the after currents of mass society theory, the word 'mass' encourages many to think of the audience as a vast, undifferentiated agglomeration of unthinking individuals, likely to behave in a non-rational, if not irrational, manner. This conception of the audience is misleading, they noted. In reality, those who watch television, read newspapers, or go to movies are a heterogeneous group who bring many different contexts (encoding envelopes) to any message. Moreover, they added, the word 'communication' tends to mask the industrial nature of the media and promotes a tendency to think of them as analogous to interpersonal communication, that is, person-to-person communication on a mass scale. Back in 1983, with these caveats in place, the O'Sullivan definition was generally accepted and used. Parallel definitions were put forward by others, including DeFleur and Ball-Rokeach (1989). These definitions are still in use today.

However, times and technology have changed. Beginning about 1990, when Internet usage began to be embraced by the wider world, the possibilities for person-to-person communication on a mass scale expanded dramatically. Suddenly, it became possible to post an e-mail to an address anywhere in the world that had an e-mail system, where the message would await access by the user. The transmission was instantaneous and free—no writing paper, envelope, postage stamp, mailbox, mail pickup, imperfect post office sorting and handling, travel by air, land, or sea, resorting, and delivery; nor, alternatively, any dictation over a phone to a telegrapher at an exorbitant charge per word; nor, alternatively again, any need for a dedicated machine to create a graphic to be sent over phone lines to arrive in fuzzy facsimile form at the other end.

In quick succession, a number of technologies were added to text-exchange protocols so that by 2000, digital files of any type—text, sound, image—could be exchanged between any computer user and any other computer user for an insignificant cost. Moreover, with the deployment of World Wide Web technology, alongside platform-independent file writing and reading, the foundations of centralized mass communication (that is, corporately financed, industrially produced, state-regulated, high-technology institutions) as the only form of mass communication began to unravel. By 2000, it had also become possible for any person, with a bit of effort and little more expense than a computer, some software, and Internet access, to create a Web site that was accessible around the world.

In other words, while the Internet started off as a means for person-to-person communication (on a mass scale), with the success of www technology and its increasing use by the business community and other organizations, the Internet has become both a mass person-to-person communication system and a mass (decentralized) broadcast system. The Internet has quickly evolved into a large-scale communication system open to and welcoming (by its affordability) the public. It allows anyone, in Canada or in many other countries, to create content for next to nothing and make that content available (i.e., broadcast it) to the world. Given that millions are anxious to do just that (and for other reasons as well), search engines have been developed to facilitate finding information, thereby increasing substantially the effectiveness of the technology as a means of mass communication.

These developments change the nature of mass communication fundamentally. O'Sullivan et al. described what they saw in the context of their time. What they could not imagine was a complete reorganization of mass communication or, put in different

terms, the development of technology that would allow interpersonal communication on a mass scale so easily that it would transform our social contacts and society as a whole. No one else could imagine this either, except Marshall McLuhan, and few understood fully or believed what McLuhan actually claimed.

So, reflective of their time (and then current usage of the term), O'Sullivan and his colleagues defined 'mass communication' *not as mass communication at all but rather as the mass distribution of information and entertainment products.* Looked at today, such a definition appears to carry echoes of mass society theory: not its moral, anti-alienating force, but its view of mass communication as controlled by elites, or, stated differently, centralized production and widespread distribution of communication products. We are now at a point to put forward a new definition of mass communication: *mass communication is transmission and transformation of meaning on a large scale.* (It happens that the systems for this to take place are organized by nations and international bodies but we will leave that special element to the side.)

To elaborate, mass communication has three distinct forms.

- *Mass communication is the centralized production and dissemination of mass information and entertainment.* This form of communication involves the corporately financed industrial production of entertainment and information to large, unknown audiences by means of print, screen, audio, broadcast, audiovisual, and Internet technologies or public performance for both private and public consumption. In certain instances (e.g., broadcasting and, less often, print) it is state-regulated. Some examples are: radio, television, newspapers, film, magazines, books, recorded and performed music, and advertising.
- *Mass communication is also the decentralized production and wide accessibility of information and entertainment, primarily by means of public access to the Internet.* The best example here is Web sites, but this type of mass communication can also include some books, magazines, scholarly journals, cable TV, and community radio.
- *Mass communication is the exchange of information that takes place among individuals and groups by means of public access to communication channels,* for example, wired and wireless phone, the mail, e-mail, pagers, two-way radio, and fax.

Such a three-part definition, with the public access component built into the definition, makes centralized production and dissemination of information and entertainment products a special case rather than the central feature of mass communication. This is significant because it shifts the industrialization of mass communication to one of three types of activities. It emphasizes and gives greater prominence to the provision of information, accessible on a large scale, by members of society. And it brings what we previously have called 'public communication', that is, public access to mass communication technologies, into mass communication itself, thereby reclaiming mass communication for the masses, for society as a whole.

The focus of attention in the above definition is on how certain communications activities are organized. When we turn to the mass media, we first discuss institutions, then the activity behind those institutions. Finally, it should be noted that the world communication system is based on an integration of national or state communication systems. Individual nations exert varying degrees of control over who communicates and what is communicated.

DEFINING 'MASS MEDIA'

The term 'mass media' is really a contraction of mass communication media. O'Sullivan et al. (1983: 130) define mass media by providing a list: 'Usually understood as newspapers, magazines, cinema, television, radio and advertising; sometimes including book publishing (especially popular fiction) and music (the pop industry)'. However, in the context of technological change and the three-part definition of mass communication introduced above, the **mass media** can be redefined. *The traditional mass media are technologies, practices, and institutions that make possible information and entertainment production and dissemination through newspapers, magazines, cinema, television, radio, advertising, book publishing, music publishing, recording, and performance.* These products are sold or given away to large, unknown audiences for both private and public consumption.

Other traditional mass media forms are worthy of note but not encompassed by the above definition. They include buildings, pictures, statues, coins, banners, stained glass, songs, medallions, and rituals of all kinds (see Curran, 1982: 202). They are mass media in that they involve institutions communicating with members of society. While they are media of centralized mass communication we tend not talk about them as mass media.

The new mass media are technologies, practices, and institutions accessible to the general public, designed to make information and entertaining content widely accessible. Their dominant form is the Web site. The interactive media are yet another set of technologies, practices, and institutions that allow communicative interaction on a mass scale—phones, faxes, postal services, cellphones, and other hand-held communications devices and the like. As the above list indicates, some of these are older technologies while others are new.

One point of clarification. Web sites are clearly interactive; as a result, one might question the distinction between the new mass media and interactive media. While a Web site is interactive insofar as a person can explore the content as he or she sees fit, that sort of interactivity is different in extent but not in structure from the interaction possible with a channel changer for a TV set connected to a multiplicity of channels. The interactive media are those devices and that structure that allow for the generation of original content by the user. By distinguishing among the traditional mass media, the new mass media, and the interactive media, we recapture the mass media as institutions that are part and parcel of the social process and wrest the term away from sole ownership of the industrial producers and disseminators of products.

The three-part distinction in the mass media also brings forward another important point. We are accustomed to thinking of the traditional mass media as a group of technologies, practices, and institutions that are integrated into a single effort, i.e., television broadcasting or newspaper publishing. In other words, in the traditional mass media 'content' and 'carriage', that is, the creation of content and the means of delivery, are combined. For the new and interactive mass media, so far in history at least, content and carriage are quite separate. Thus, the institutions that provide the technology for the Internet, together with those that sell or otherwise provide Internet access, are the carriers. Those who provide the content, the owners of Web sites or the senders of e-mail, are the content providers.

In the remainder of this chapter, we will elaborate on the functioning of the traditional mass media, the new mass media, and the interactive media in an attempt to provide a thorough understanding of their dynamics. The purpose of this elaboration is to give a sense of the nature and operation of all modern mass media and to lay the foundation for later chapters.

THE VARIOUS WAYS WE COMMUNICATE

Architecture, graffiti, memorial sculptures, public art, even clothing can be perceived as media of communication, even if their language isn't always accessible and their message isn't always clear. In some cases, these media evoke memories. The names of city streets—Papineau in Montreal, Granville in Vancouver, Yonge in Toronto—recall historical and political figures. Every town in Canada has some sort of war memorial serving as a symbol of personal remembrance and as a reminder to passersby of the sacrifice the town's citizens have made to Canada's past war efforts.

Building styles, too, can recall specific historical periods or they can make a statement about the community, or part of town, they inhabit. The number, size, and structural splendour of Montreal's churches speak to the power the Roman Catholic Church once wielded in Quebec. The new Vancouver Public Library's obvious architectural reference to the Roman Coliseum (see photo) remains controversial because it privileges the city's

European roots over its Asian heritage. Besides its phallic symbolism, the CN Tower (see photo) is a clear reminder that Toronto is the country's communications centre—it's a telecommunications tower serving 16 Canadian television and radio stations—as well as a major rail, air, and road transportation hub.

If these media draw much of their authority by being sanctioned, permanent community symbols, graffiti draw their communicative efficacy from their ephemeral and rebellious qualities. Often dismissed simply as vandalism, graffiti nonetheless speak to people. Sometimes the message is a straightforward 'I was here', as in the 'tags' or signatures we see on city buildings, or in the names of people spray-painted on rock faces at various spots along the Trans-Canada Highway. Or the message—often profane—can be one of protest or dissent. Whatever the case, graffiti serve very much as a 'voice of the voiceless' (see photo).

Table 2.1 A Summary of Differences between the Traditional Mass Media, the New Mass Media, and Interactive Media

	Traditional Mass Media	New Mass Media	Interactive Media
Distinct set of activities	Creation and production of content to sell to audiences or to garner income from governments and advertisers that, because they are centralized and have large audiences, help create a social meaning system	Creation and production of content by many people, provision of wide accessibility, with the intent of attracting users	Provision of communication services to many members of many societies worldwide that allow members of society to communicate with others
Particular technological configurations	Invented techno/social forms such as newspapers, books, magazines, TV, radio	Invented techno/social forms such as Web sites, broadcast messages to text devices such as cellphones and hand held communication devices	Invented techno/social forms such as phones, mail, e-mail, chat groups, etc.
Formally constituted institutions	Media outlets such as daily newspapers, radio and TV stations, book and magazine publishers, film production companies, cable companies	A great variation of providers of content, including established businesses, media businesses, individuals, organizations, governments	Post office, ISPs (Internet service providers), phone and cable companies, telecommunication companies
Laws, rules, and understandings	Broadcasting Acts, Telecom Acts, newspaper Acts (if any), CRTC rules, e.g., Canadian content, journalistic ideal	Extension of laws governing citizen and organizational behaviour such as copyright law, privacy law, anti-hate laws	Same as new mass media but more focused on individuals
Persons occupying certain roles	Journalists, editors, producers, owners, interviewees, lawyers, etc.	Site architects, content developers, programmers, owners, designers	Individuals, organizations, businesses, all engaged in sending and receiving messages
Information, entertainment, images, and symbols	Centralized packaged symbolic products carrying explicit and implicit content	Content with varying levels of sophistication, a broader spectrum than the traditional mass media	Usually ephemeral content created usually for relatively quick response
A mass audience	Members of society who interpret media messages according to their own priorities and needs	Members of society who seek to make content widely accessible or seek out content provided	Members of society who wish to communicate with others

The Mass Media

In 1983, British media researcher Denis McQuail provided a detailed overview of the traditional mass media. We will use McQuail's overview to discuss the three types of mass media. Table 2.1 summarizes the differences among these three types: traditional, new, and interactive. According to McQuail (1983), the mass media:

1. are *a distinct set of activities*;
2. involving *particular technological configurations*;
3. associated with *formally constituted institutions*;
4. acting according to *certain laws, rules, and understandings*;
5. carried out by *persons occupying certain roles*;
6. which, together, convey *information, entertainment, images, and symbols*;
7. to *the mass audience*.

A DISTINCT SET OF ACTIVITIES

From a technical perspective that concentrates on transmission or carriage, following Shannon and Weaver's mathematical model of communication, the mass media are indeed a distinct set of activities in their communicative form and function. The mass media, for example, ensure that a device, such as a microphone, is connected to a transmission device, a carrier, conduit, or **conductor**. The signal—analogue or digital—travels along the conduit either as light in a glass fibre or as electricity in a copper wire or coaxial cable. Mass media carriers ensure that, at the receiving end, the signal is decoded and reconstituted into sound, usually amplified and made available to an audience, members of which make meaning out of these transmitted sounds.

Moving beyond this model to include content and the social organization of these distinctive activities, we find that, besides the technicians and engineers, other people are involved at each of these stages—program producers who do research, professional speakers such as Peter Mansbridge, professional actors such as Megan Follows, professional experts on certain topics, and so on. In other words, there are multiple layers of content and carriage—the encoding of thoughts to words to electrical signals to light pulses and the decoding of light pulses to electrical signals to sounds to words and meaning. Each of these elements separately or grouped together is a distinctive activity of communication. The mass media organize all of these layers of encoding and decoding and their distribution or accessibility to audiences.

The social model of communication, with its greater focus on content, stresses that the transmission function (moving meaning from one place or one person to another) is also transforming. The social model stresses the role of both the encoders/decoders and the media themselves as active symbol- or meaning-producing agents that contribute to defining key and subordinate characteristics of reality, that is, what is important and what is not.

Two media theorists, Peter Berger and Thomas Luckmann (1966), describe this transforming function in the operation of the traditional mass media as a construction function. Through representing objects, events, and ideas in certain ways, the mass media 'construct' images and encourage certain perceptions in the same way as builders using bricks and mortar to construct a house. The media use the elements at hand—people, events, objects, settings—to create a meaningful whole. Semioticians use the word 'signify' to mean much the same thing as Berger and Luckmann's 'construct'. As Chapter 4 explains in more detail, semioticians, who are also media theorists, work with *signifiers*, that is, symbols or sounds (for example, words); *signifieds*, that is, objects or events to which the words refer; and *signs*, the totality of meanings we associate with the signifiers and signifieds.

A good example is a photograph. For many, a photograph represents what is, or was, there. This undervalues the work of professional photographers because they go to considerable effort to compose their work, taking into account light, background, foreground, the mood of the subject, and so on. Faced with a professional photograph, a person may describe the photographer as lucky to have captured the scene in the way he or she did. Such a statement effectively denies the construction function of the photographer. As Stephen Osborne says, even when we say 'smile for the camera' we are engaging in the construction of the visual object. We are creating a reality for a viewer. This concept is explained more fully in the box, opposite.

In summary, the mass media are a distinct set of activities because they are the primary tools societies use to make or manufacture meaning and to signify or construct reality. The traditional mass media are major contributors to our perceptions because of

CONSTRUCTING THE VISUAL OBJECT

Photographs offer an imprint of the world, a trace of things that were; as rubbings taken from gravestones attest to the authenticity of an original, so photographs attest to the authenticity of the past. This is the forensic dimension of photography, embedded in what John Berger calls the 'enigma of the visual'. Two men in a photograph stare at a TV set at the edge of a river. They are sitting on the end of a log partially hidden by thick grass; they may have had to clear away the grass in order to sit down. The TV set is a wooden cabinet model, built in an age when television sets were trying to look like real furniture. A television expert might name an epoch, a time when people were likely to be throwing away obsolete TVs like this one, even carrying them down to the riverbank. The TV in the photograph seems to have been carefully positioned on its mound of grass. The men in the photograph could be inhabiting any moment in the last 50 years: their clothing and outward aspect suggest little more. Above them a ghostly limb resembling a tree trunk leans impossibly into the space of the photograph: it casts no reflection in the water, and then we see that it is not in the photograph at all: it is a crease in its paper surface, a trace of the object that provided the original of this image. The television screen is blank. The surface of the river is limpid, as flat as the sky, and utterly still; the silhouette of scrubby trees drips into the river like ink. The two men are certainly aware of the camera (a photographer—unknown to us today—accompanies them), and, although they cannot see what we see, they anticipate us looking at them now, in the future.

—Mandelbrot, *Geist* no. 43 (Winter 2001): 3.

both the information they carry (transmission) and the interpretation they place on that information (transformation). However, our own constructions of reality and the constructions of the mass media are both important.

The notion that communication and the mass media are a distinct set of activities applies equally to the traditional mass media, the new mass media, and the interactive media. All three are involved in various ways in creating meaning. The traditional mass media make meaning to disperse to society as whole. The new mass media allow greater numbers of society to make meaning and make it available to society. The interactive media are used by and belong to society, members of which create meaning and messages for each other.

PARTICULAR TECHNOLOGICAL CONFIGURATIONS

The ideas of Marshall McLuhan and Harold Innis, especially their emphasis on oral, literate, and electronic communication processes, illustrate how the means of communication affect how a message is formed or constructed and then communicated. By examining the particular technological configurations used by the mass media (as we do in this section) we are extending the ideas of Innis and McLuhan and focusing on the mass media.

Raymond Williams (1974) has pointed out that technologies do not arise from the brain of a genius working in isolation from any social context. For example, television did not emerge as an inevitable offshoot of the search for scientific knowledge. Rather, it emerged from the interests and conceptions of technical investigators and industrial entrepreneurs who were able to imagine an electronic medium of sound and visual communication for use in the home. Inventors such as Marconi, Edison, and Bell were more driven by the idea of inventing something that would be used by many people in a social context than by intellectual curiosity. Their aggressive registration of patents is evidence of this.

Just as the inventions of new technology are shaped by societal forces, how they are used is also shaped by society. The typewriter was originally built as a toy. The original fax machine was a flop—no one could see any use for it.

The current technological configuration of television allows owners, actors, advertisers, technicians, actors, and many others to make money.

Commercial television allows the creation and production of content to be delivered almost free, subsidized as it is by the price we pay for advertised products. TV also allows large, established companies that manufacture brand-name goods to keep their products at the forefront of people's minds. It serves the capitalist system by providing jobs in the entertainment sector. It also serves mass society by allowing for atomized diversion, entertainment, and a bit of education for people during their leisure time. So television, as it is now used, is well entrenched in society. But that does not mean that this particular technological configuration could not be changed so that television could serve an entirely different purpose.

Television is but one example of a modern mass medium. A more recent example is the digital camera. For years it has languished as an inadequate device with insufficient processing power. In 2002, it left those inadequacies behind with affordable cameras and sufficient resolution to replace film cameras. A less obvious example is the increasingly ubiquitous cellphone. In 1990 a cellphone had the weight necessary to double as a club. Today, however, its light weight, together with the capacity of its microphone to pick up the voice of the user and not a lot of surrounding ambience, has played a large part in it becoming the contact instrument of choice among people from all walks of life.

In summary, the modern mass media are a set of technological configurations that bring us information in a variety of forms. In the print medium there are broadsheet and tabloid newspapers, magazines, journals, and books—mass paperbacks, quality paperbacks, hardcovers, textbooks, school books, limited editions, coffee-table books, talking books, large-print books, children's literature. In the electronic media we have public, community, educational, and commercial television, and radio is delivered by broadcast, cable, and satellite. In addition, there are both feature films and non-theatrical films. Sound recordings are available on vinyl, audio cassettes, CDs, MP3s, and DVDs as well as, in their promotional version, on video cassettes. The recent technological configurations that allow for interactivity are particularly significant because such technology transforms the communications system from a carrier of cultural and commercial products to audiences to a mode whereby individuals can communicate with one another.

In another Canadian communications first, in 1973, while working at Motorola in New York, Canadian-born Martin Cooper developed the first modern cellphone (weight 1.2 kilograms) based on technology developed by Bell labs in 1945. Twelve years after its invention, there were 6,000 registered cellphones in Canada. Ten years later, in 1995 there were 2.6 million, and in 2002, 11.5 million. Worldwide there are 1.5 billion users, a number that supersedes land-line users. China alone has 210 million users and some developing countries, especially in rural areas, have forgone land-line phones for cellular systems.

FORMALLY CONSTITUTED INSTITUTIONS

The traditional mass media capture distinct meaning-making activities, using particular technologies operating within formally constituted industrial structures for the production, processing, carriage, and marketing of content. Traditional media institutions may be under **private ownership** (commercial institutions owned by shareholders) or **public ownership**—in Canadian terms, **Crown corporations**.

Commercial Institutions

Traditional **commercial media institutions** may be defined as corporations owning media enterprises for profit. Their primary purpose is to optimize revenues and minimize costs. This principle of action guides the entire scope of their operations. However, that principle must be and is applied in a sophisticated manner that enhances the opportunities for survival and expansion.

Traditional commercial media institutions use content (delivered by means of high-fidelity technology) to build audiences. They do so by spending money to provide content that will interest their target audi-ences. Revenues come from the sale of content to audiences (newspaper subscriptions and newsstand sales) and/or from the sale of audiences to advertisers (newspaper and TV ads). Revenue is also generated through the sale of content to other organizations that must similarly build audiences (network TV **syndication**).

While the focus of a broadcasting station, newspaper, book publishing house, or film studio is creating or purchasing content, only about 10 to 15 per cent of expenditures are directly attributable to that function. Other activities, such as maintaining a physical plant, administration, sales of advertising space/time, subscriptions, and distribution, take up the remaining 85 to 90 per cent of costs. This means, for instance, that the cost to produce an episode of a TV serial, keeping in mind all the overhead costs stated above, can run over $1 million. On the other hand, game shows can be made and imported programs, especially old reruns, can be purchased for about $10,000. Similarly, for newspapers, copy from news wire is inexpensive, though syndicated material costs a little more. Employing a columnist for a year, including expenses, can easily run to $200,000—a major outlay for an individual paper, but much more affordable for a newspaper **conglomerate**.

All traditional commercial media outlets, as social and socializing institutions, must weigh their costs and profits against their perceived responsibility to the community. This is especially true for broadcasters, who, as a condition for obtaining a broadcasting licence, must outline how their programming will contribute to the community. They must also take into account audience sensitivity. For instance, for specific types of programs, such as news and public affairs programs, most audiences prefer local and national production. In most countries this preference is not as strong for dramatic productions and sitcoms.

In a few cases, privately owned media emphasize their social contribution over the bottom line. In the case of newspapers, *The Times* (London) is an example, as are *Le Monde* (Paris), the *New York Times*, *Le Devoir*

(Montreal), and, at certain points in their histories, the *Globe and Mail* (Toronto) and the *Jerusalem Post*. In their glory days, each of these papers was able to trade on its prestige as the paper of the elite to support its service to the community. More recently, such papers have either become prestige papers or flagship dailies of conglomerates, which maintain them as prestige outlets and for the generation of content that can then be used throughout the conglomerate. (*Le Devoir* is the exception here—it remains independent of a larger chain and is managed by its employees under the oversight of an outside board of directors.) Such papers might also be seen as loss leaders in a conglomerate's attempt to maintain its hold on the consuming public.

Public–Sector Institutions

The other major type of formally constituted traditional media institution is the **public-sector institution**, which, in most Western countries, is owned and/or regulated but not controlled by the state. In other words, the directors of the institution are not employees of a government ministry, nor are they responsible for carrying out the minister's orders.

In Western nations, public-sector media corporations usually operate at 'arm's length' from control of the government (although the length of the arm varies greatly). In socialist countries, public ownership of the mass media is achieved by means of state institutions not unlike government departments—a structure that is also emerging in developing countries. In various countries of Eastern Europe, for instance, commercial media operations often exist at the pleasure of the state, usually the president, and within a set of constraints defined in the constitution. (See the discussion of public media in various countries in *Canadian Journal of Communication* 20, 1 [1995].) It remains to be seen whether these media will evolve into reasonably independent institutions. Two types of institutions appear to be evolving: commercial enterprises featuring entertainment and co-owned by old Communists or media moguls like Rupert Murdoch, and state corporations operating under the watchful eye of either the president or the parliament.

Public-sector media corporations in Canada, like commercial institutions, must balance their revenues and costs. The advantage public-sector institutions have is the revenues they receive from government. These revenues, however, are not unconditional gifts. They are funds to help them fulfill the special public-service responsibilities they have been assigned in the Broadcasting Act. For example, the CBC must attempt to make its signals available to all Canadians in both languages. Its programs must appeal to all ages, not just those audiences in which advertisers have an interest. As a result of government grants, which can be generous or miserly, the publicly owned media have a greater but still limited freedom to produce programming of value to the community.

Public versus Commercial Institutions

Whether the media are owned publicly or commercially is obviously a major factor affecting the relationship between the media and the state. Where private ownership is dominant, considerations of profit-making and advertiser interests prevail over considerations of **public service**. (It is, of course, possible for private ownership of a mass media system to be organized on a non-profit basis. It occurs in the Netherlands, but it is relatively rare.) Where public ownership prevails completely and accepts no advertising, potential advertisers complain of an inability to get information to consumers, while consumers sometimes complain of the lack of escapist programming that allows them to forget the issues and concerns of the day. We will explore state-controlled broadcasting, a wholly different form of broadcasting, in Chapter 6.

The Institutions of the New Mass Media

There are really two separate tiers of institutions of the new mass media and the interactive media. One tier, the carriers, consists of service institutions that provide the needed postal or telecommunications services for users. The other tier includes the content providers. In some cases the content providers are indeed institutions, for example, businesses that wish to operate on-line such as Indigo.ca or Amazon.com, or institutions such as governments and universities that make information available via the Internet. Other content providers are not institutions at all but those who put up Web sites or who use the Internet, the phone, or the postal service to communicate with other individuals (or with institutions).

Just as the traditional mass media are regulated to ensure social service and/or are structured to avoid excessive government control, so in the provision of communication services there has been a need for the regulation of institutions once they were set up and operating. What has distinguished telecommunications and postal regulation is an absence of a need to be concerned with both content creation and its distribution because content is generated by users, not the services themselves.

The vastly increased access provided by Internet technology and the decentralized architecture of the Internet—there is no central controlling system; rather, it is a network of computing and transmission capacity—have persuaded governments, for the time being, that there is no need to regulate the first tier of carrying institutions or the second tier of content-providing institutions of the Internet beyond using laws already in existence, such as those governing libel, hate, privacy, pornography, and fraud. Even the collapse of WorldCom, a major contributor to the backbone of the Internet, has not brought forward a call for regulation of the institutions of the Internet. However, as these institutions become more critical to the functioning of society, such regulation may emerge. Certainly, the collapse of Internet services would create havoc. Future regulation may take a form similar to that used to regulate institutions, such as banks, that society depends on for stability and basic functioning.

CERTAIN LAWS, RULES, AND UNDERSTANDINGS

The traditional mass media systems operate within specific national societies. Thus, they are subject to formal legal constraints as well as less formal patterns of expectation. For years Canada has been a partial exception to this rule, in that US signals from border stations have circulated within the country and yet are not controlled by Canadian law (except insofar as they are carried by Canadian cable companies who must act within Canadian law). With the deployment of communication satellites, the Canadian exception is becoming the rule around the world. Signals are made available in countries that do not regulate their circulation.

In terms of formal laws, in the case of broadcasting the relatively limited radio frequencies available to each country oblige national governments to exercise some control, in the form of licensing requirements, over the frequencies used within their borders. In the case of newspaper and magazine publishing, most developed countries exercise little overt control. No licences are required and media content is not restricted, except by broad laws directed at libel, sedition, hate, and pornography. However, various indirect controls, such as taxation, subsidies, business policies, and distribution subsidies, can be and are employed. France is a good example of a country that uses such devices.

The laws or statutes of a country have a major impact on the traditional mass media (see Chapters 6 and 7 for a fuller discussion). In Canada, the Broadcasting Act (1991) is the pre-eminent statute controlling broadcasting. There are no equivalent statutes for Canadian newspapers, magazines, books, or recorded music. The reasons why broadcasting has received such particular attention in legislation are partly constitutional (the federal government has clear, undivided power over 'radio communication', which includes broadcasting) and partly social (a widely held belief in Canada is that centralized broadcasting is particularly important to nation-building). In addition to other formalities, such as defining broadcast undertakings, who can own outlets, and technical matters, the Broadcasting Act outlines what broadcasting should do for society. In other words, it provides a framework for policy. The Act addresses the tacitly accepted values and ideals of Canadian society and the means by which broadcasting can contribute to their achievement.

The Broadcasting Act also provides for the existence of an agency to ensure adherence to the Act. This organization, the Ottawa-based Canadian Radio-television and Telecommunications Commission (CRTC), administers the policies and provisions enunciated in the Broadcasting Act. The CRTC translates the principles of the Act into rules for broadcasters. It mediates between the ideals and values outlined in the Act and the practical realities of running broadcasting undertakings. This mediation has led to the development of many issues of concern, some short-lived and others recurring. As will become apparent throughout this book, and especially in Chapter 6, the recurring issues are valuable indicators of critical points of tension in Canada's broadcasting system.

A second key statute is the Copyright Act, which creates **intellectual property**. It transforms the expression of one's intellectual efforts, for example a script or a movie, into a piece of property that can be owned. Moreover, it attaches certain rights and privileges to that ownership. **Copyright** law stimulates creators to create by providing a means for them to require payment for their efforts and by prohibiting the use of their creation without their permission and/or payment. Copyright does not protect ideas; it protects the expression of ideas. The Copyright Act provides a framework for the way in which publishers pay royalties to authors in return for the right to publish and distribute their books. It also affects how persons who make movies based on books buy the movie rights for the book.

Other statutes also influence how the media operate, but the Copyright and Broadcasting Acts are of primary importance. Both of these Acts have resulted in the creation of certain concrete rules that are consistent with the principles of the legislation. Radio provides a good example of the effects of the Copyright Act and the Broadcasting Act and of how Canadian artists are remunerated for their intellectual property according to how often their songs are played. To comply with the Copyright Act, radio stations pay songwriters (and others) for the right to play their songs. To administer the royalty system for the performing rights of musical compositions, the Society of Composers, Authors, and Musicians of Canada (SOCAN) surveys each radio station five to six times a year. These surveys are undertaken on different days for different stations, so that sampling is occurring at all times. The radio station is required to submit a complete playlist of all songs played over a three-day period. SOCAN analyzes the playlist to determine what songs by which artists have been played, and then, based on the relative number of times a song has been played, distributes the money to the song's creators, music composer, lyricist, performer, and publishing company. No more than 50 per cent of performing rights royalties are paid to the music publisher, and SOCAN works with any relative division of royalties it is informed of between the song's various creators. Each radio station must also contribute 3.2 per cent of its gross advertising revenue to SOCAN. In general, SOCAN 'licenses the public performance and telecommunication of the world's repertoire of copyright-protected musical works in Canada and then distributes royalties to its members and affiliated international societies' (http://www.socan.ca/jsp/en/about/).

With the authority provided to it through the Broadcasting Act, the CRTC determines content rules. For example, the CRTC requires AM and FM radio stations that specialize in popular music to devote at least 35 per cent of their play time to Canadian selections. This **Canadian content** rule has had a positive impact on a number of Canadian recordings and artists, as seen by the number of them making it to radio 'top 10' charts.

The laws and rules that govern the behaviour of the mass media have developed from society's under-

Shania Twain is one of many Canadian music artists who are increasingly gaining in popularity, both domestically and internationally. (Dave Martin/CP)

standing of the potential value of a centralized, content-producing media. At a most general level, the media in Western societies are encouraged to provide 'continuity, order, integration, motivation, guidance and adaptation' (McQuail, 1983: 64). More recently, the media have been seen as contributors to social cohesion in heterogeneous societies within a globalizing world. A special issue of the *Canadian Journal of Communication* (27, 2–3), titled 'Making Connections: Culture and Social Cohesion in the New Millennium', provides interesting explorations of social cohesion from around the world. In a complex, liberal democracy, where the values and goals of society are both known in general terms and a matter of continuing debate, the media have substantial latitude for making their social contributions. Of course, that debate also encompasses whether the media are contributing appropriately. Certain media spokespersons claim that if people are watching television (since they have the freedom *not* to watch), the television station is obviously making an appropriate contribution to

INTERPRETING THE BROADCASTING ACT

As time passes societies change. Less frequently do statutes change. And so it is important to write statutes in such a way that they can be interpreted within the context of the time. For example, Section 3d(iii) of the Broadcasting Act declares that 'the Canadian broadcasting system should through its programming and the employment opportunities arising out of its operations, serve the needs and interests and reflect the circumstances and aspirations, of Canadian men, women and children, including equal rights, the linguistic duality and multicultural and multiracial nature of Canadian society and the special place of aboriginal people within

that society.' And Section 3i(i) notes that 'the programming providing by the Canadian broadcasting system should be varied and comprehensive, providing a balance of information, enlightenment and entertainment for men, women and children of all ages, interests and tastes.'

These two clauses address directly two basic differences in society, race and gender, and less directly a third, class. All three are often associated with inequality. The Act provides the framework and the media strive to address the changing norms and ideals of society with respect to race, class, and gender.

the enjoyment of their leisure time. At the other end of the spectrum, others claim that the media should set for themselves much more ambitious goals—to provide, for example, enlightening rather than escapist entertainment. This debate, which will receive further attention in later chapters, is over what constitutes the **public interest**. The point here is that both the spirit and the exact content of laws matter. On the basis of those laws certain rules are developed, and the laws themselves are founded on certain broad understandings of the role of a centralized media in a democratic society.

In addition to the Broadcasting and Copyright Acts, an important communications statute that receives less attention in discussions of the mass media is the Telecommunications Act. This is because, in the social operation of the mass media, telecommunications is an infrastructural transmission element that exists behind the scenes. It is the carriage alone, not the content. Within a social context, telecommunications is generally discussed in terms of the provision of equitable access for all citizens to telephone services. The Telecommunications Act gives the common carriers, for example, phone companies that serve everyone, the responsibility to average out their costs so that people in rural areas, on islands, or in the Far North do not end up paying dearly for phone service while city dwellers bask in low prices. They are charged not necessarily an equal monthly fee but an equitable fee, one that balances cost against the social goal of providing inexpensive access to all citizens.

The social dynamics of telecommunications service provision increases in importance when we consider the new mass media and the interactive media. Who owns and controls service provision, who they sell to, and on what terms all have an impact over the long term. For example, one need only travel from Vancouver to the south end of Salt Spring Island to lose both cellphone service and broad-band Internet access. Clearly, the provision of telecommunications services has social impact just as did the provision of postal and telephone service over our history. Currently, the laws, and especially the rules and understandings that apply to the telecommunication services that are the backbone of both the new mass media and the interactive media, are much less extensive than those that apply to the traditional mass media. As stated previously, the two main reasons for this are that the service providers are carriers who lack control over content and there is greater public access to content creation and distribution—content is not centrally produced by a few for the many.

Intellectual property and privacy laws are also applicable to the new mass media, as are laws related to speech regulation, liability, jurisdiction, domain name governance, and Internet commerce. The US has passed the Digital Millennium Copyright Act in an attempt to claim jurisdiction over any Internet content that reaches the US.

Other actions by government that affect the new mass media and the interactive media tend to be supportive of its development, rather than regulatory or restrictive. In an attempt to secure a Canadian on-line presence, various departments in government have sought to stimulate and support Canadian participation in the development of the Internet. For example, the Department of Canadian Heritage has a number of support programs and Industry Canada has invested substantially in stimulating on-line business activity. Generally speaking, and following the recommendations of the Information Highway Advisory Council, neither informal understandings nor actual restrictive or regulatory laws and rules have been developed. This is why there is an ongoing debate about on-line pornography.

PERSONS OCCUPYING CERTAIN ROLES

The number of people involved in the traditional mass media and the number of roles people play are vast.

VIEWING HOURS AND THE CBC

Commercial broadcasters worry about competition in the marketplace, about the total programs available to viewers, and about other media. As a public enterprise with a cultural and political mandate, the CBC often considers the total programming and other types of programming available out of a concern to provide a wide range of information and entertainment to all Canadians. For example, the CBC asks questions like how many hours of programming are available for every hour of television watched? It turns out to be 120 hours. In 1999 the CBC sought out the available hours of English-language programming over the previous 15 years and compared them with the per-capita hours of viewing per week. As shown in Figure 2.1 the number of TV viewing hours per week has remained fairly steady. On the other hand, the number of available hours of viewing increased steadily until 1995–6, when, with the explosion of specialty channels, it rose quite sharply. However, this increase in available viewing hours has had relatively no impact on viewing.

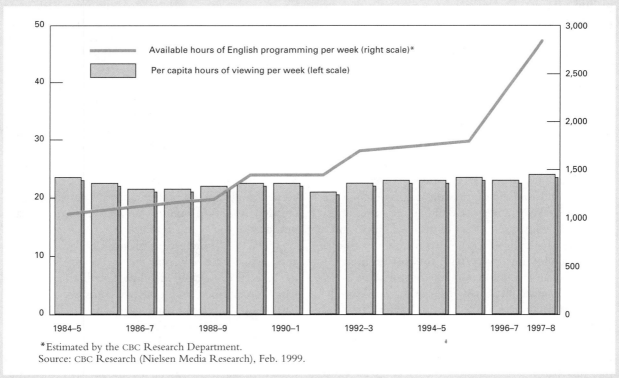

*Estimated by the CBC Research Department.
Source: CBC Research (Nielsen Media Research), Feb. 1999.

Source: *Globe and Mail*, 22 Feb., 1999. Reprinted by permission of CBC Research.

The most obvious players are the journalists. But there are also owners, editors, printers, producers, studio technicians, actors, administrators, designers, advertisers, members of regulatory bodies like the CRTC, politicians who control the purse strings (of public-sector companies), lawyers, public-interest groups, and the audience. These various players can be divided into six major groups, four operating outside the structure of the mass media—business, government, the legal system, and the audience—and two operating inside— owners and media professionals.

Business Influences from outside the Media

The influence of business on the traditional mass media is exercised through ownership and advertising. We will deal with owners, who are insiders, later. With regard to advertisers, decisions by businesses on where to advertise and how much to spend affect the fortunes of individual media enterprises. To attract advertisers, media managers are careful to ensure that content does not clash with advertisers' messages. Such clashes may be specific, such as a consumer-oriented article or program that criticizes the products of a particular advertiser; or they may be more diffuse, such as descriptions of a non-consumer or anti-consumer lifestyle. Neither would fit well with the consumerism promoted in advertising. The video *Pack of Lies* (Foundation for Media Education, 1992) discusses the relationship between content and advertising, taking a *Newsweek* story on cancer as an example. The gist of their argument is that the commercial media cannot be trusted to tell the whole truth about companies who advertise on their pages or during their programming.

To avoid offending advertisers, media enterprises normally tailor their content to correspond to advertisers' interests. Generally speaking, mass media content encourages consumption, especially of nice clothes, fancy cars, travel, liquor, and entertainment. More specifically, media enterprises may make a special effort to avoid offending certain constituencies. It is not uncommon for the media to notify advertisers, through their advertising agency, that they might not want to advertise in a particular issue (because of an editorial message that conflicts with their product). As a matter of routine, airline commercials will not be placed anywhere near stories of an airline hijacking or of an airplane crash. Drug abuse stories will not be found next to drug company ads. Ads for designer clothes will not be found next to stories on the exploitation of offshore labour. This live-and-let-live philosophy is an accommodation that allows for a range of opinion without confrontation of interests.

It is a myth that the two types of material—content and ads—are managed quite separately and that journalists or program producers are insulated from advertiser influence. In reality, as the *Report of the Royal Commission on Newspapers* (Canada, 1981) points out, it does not work that way. For instance, in the summer and fall of 1990 an informal but determined boycott of the *Kingston Whig-Standard* by local real-estate agents took place in response to one of the newspaper's articles, which outlined the advantages of self-selling by owners. Such events are unusual because the rules of the game are generally known within the industry. (The general operation of the *Kingston Whig-Standard*, an important small paper until it was taken over by Thomson and subsequently Southam, has been documented by Fetherling [1993].)

Outside business influence on the new mass media

NEWSPAPER CREDIBILITY

Every year in September, NADbank (National Audience Databank Inc.) releases annual readership figures. Funnily enough, each paper appears to be a winner over its competition, at least this was the case in 2001. The headline in the *Globe and Mail* was, 'Readership success for *The Globe*'. The headline in the *National Post* was 'Over 2 million read the *Post*'. The story in the *Post* noted that over two million Canadians read the *Post* every week (not every day) and, it boasted, the *Post* had achieved a stunning growth of 18 per cent in Toronto while the comparable figure for the *Globe and Mail* was a 10 per cent loss.

The story in the *Globe* had the following lead sentence: 'With 1,006,000 readers a day and 2.5 million a week, the *Globe and Mail* continues to be Canada's largest and most influential national newspaper. . . . Cumulative weekly readership has risen sharply over the year, up 15 per cent across Canada.'

This magazine, in which the above ad arguing against the privatization of Canada's health-care system, provides a friendly media environment for the social activist agenda of the Canadian Auto Workers and the Centre for Social Justice. (CAW Communications Department)

that these are not business influences from outside, neither are they subtle influences on how news is structured or how dramas are enacted. On-line businesses engage in commercial discourse, directly promoting products and telling the user how to buy them. As such, they are far different from the phenomenon of media self-censorship in the coverage of news based on a perceived need not to offend advertisers.

Government Influences from outside the Media

The influence of government on the traditional mass media has several dimensions (see Chapter 3 for a more detailed discussion). In a federal state such as Canada, more than one level of government influence is at work. Within any one government, we can also distinguish between bureaucratic (or departmental) structures and political structures. At the bureaucratic level, the government is a major source of information for the mass media; it is often the only source for specific types of information. The flow of information from government to the mass media benefits both parties. To inform the general public of its programs and expenditures, the government needs access to media outlets. The mass media need the information supplied by governments as a readily usable source of content for news, current affairs, and public affairs items.

The relationship between the media and government, however, has its drawbacks. For instance, because of time constraints and limited resources, media workers tend to rely heavily on the news releases and handouts prepared by the government, but, by failing to look behind these announcements, the media outlets run the risk of acting as the propaganda arm of the government. The drawback for the government is in the sheer volume of materials pumped out by numerous departments, agencies, and ministries. The mass media cannot publish or broadcast all of it, and from the government's viewpoint the selection of items can be quite arbitrary.

Related to both the bureaucratic and political lev-

and the interactive media is confined mainly to the content layer and is further restricted to commercial Web sites or commercially sponsored services such as free e-mail. So close is the relationship that the existence of these services very much depends on the ability of the commercial sites to demonstrate advertiser impact. That said, vast numbers of Web sites and all kinds of e-mail services are not influenced by business.

Inside business influences are quite another thing. As is obvious to everyone, a great many Web sites exist as on-line retail or wholesale businesses. Some are extensions of bricks-and-mortar businesses. Some exist solely on-line. But here, in addition to the fact

ACCESS TO GOVERNMENT INFORMATION

In an attempt to increase access to information that governments want citizens to have, all federal government departments have created their own Web sites. A good example is that of the Department of Canadian Heritage. The English-language address for the cultural part of the site is <www.pch.gc.ca/culture/english.htm>. An interesting exercise in examining the impact of government information, and especially press releases, is to go to the section labelled 'press releases', find one or two, and then try to find stories that built from those releases on radio and television or in the newspapers. For newspapers, in addition to purchasing a copy, you can go to the Web sites of the *Globe and Mail* (www.globeandmail.com) or the *National Post* (www.nationalpost.com) and try to find resulting articles. You will see how little some information is followed up, the angle or perspective taken by the newspapers, and the degree to which they rely on the supplied government information.

els of government is the phenomenon of government advertising. Government advertisements come in many forms: they can provide information on government programs; they can be straightforward political campaigning; or they can be in the grey area of general promotion of a given federal or provincial government. Total advertising revenues from government sources form a substantial part of the media's advertising revenues, especially for Canadian newspapers; the federal government outspends any one commercial advertiser. As well, a number of government-funded organizations also spend liberally on advertising.

In addition to being a source of information, the subject of news, and the source of advertising revenues, government also influences the mass media through its power to regulate and control them. Both at the federal and provincial levels, government has the authority to approve legislation, to impose taxes, and, in various other ways, to affect the manner in which mass media organizations conduct their operations. Commercial enterprises have a strong tendency to resist or seek to reduce government control over their operations by raising the banners of 'freedom of the press' and 'freedom of the marketplace'. However, constraints on their freedom, under legislation related to restriction of competition, for example, are more apparent than real. In recent history no successful prosecutions of media companies have occurred under Canada's competition legislation. However, the Bureau of Competition Policy has managed to restrain certain media buyouts, notably by Southam Inc., Rogers, Hollinger, and Quebecor, to prevent absolute monopolies in markets that have supported competition. Nevertheless, mass media owners continue to argue that the freedom essential to a democratic press is threatened by excessive use of government power.

In the past decade, concern about government interference appears to have settled considerably. To a large extent, this diminished concern seems to have been brought about by a new attitude on the part of the Competition Bureau as a result of new media. The best example of this new attitude is the lack of interference by the Bureau in the takeover by Israel Asper's Winnipeg-based CanWest Global of many of the major daily newspapers owned by Hollinger and its CEO, Conrad Black. At the time of the takeover, CanWest was Canada's third largest national television network chain. With the acquisition of the papers, it became the predominant information source in several major Canadian cities. Hardly a peep was heard from the Competition Bureau. Only when CanWest fired Russell Mills, publisher of the *Ottawa Citizen*, did concern about government influence emerge. As one commentator noted, CanWest was playing into the hands of those who would like government intervention by throwing its corporate weight around.

The conflicts between commercial mass media institutions and government exist at many levels and are not resolvable by allowing commercial corporations a free hand to operate mass media outlets. As for public corporations, their relationships to government are also complex. Tensions tend not to focus on issues of freedom of the press, but on issues related to public funding and accountability. The CBC in particular has a long history of difficulties in ensuring its ability to maintain the proper balance between political freedom and public accountability.

The point with respect to these government/business/media relationships is not that these issues can be resolved. Rather, they are continuing healthy tensions

Patents will be pending

Some of Canada's brightest minds are converging in Saskatoon, Saskatchewan. The Canadian Light Source synchrotron project at the University of Saskatchewan is Canada's largest science project in decades. Synchrotron light lets scientists analyse matter at the atomic level. This promises exciting breakthroughs in pharmaceuticals, computer microchips, new metal alloys, and environmental clean-up to name a few. There's a lot of science to discover in Saskatchewan. To learn how resourceful we are, visit our Web site or call 1-866-SASK-HAS.

Saskatchewan
Our Future is Wide Open ™

wideopenfuture.ca

Dr. Bill Thomlinson, Executive Director of the Canadian Light Source, Saskatoon
"The Canadian Light Source will take its place among the great synchrotrons of the world and provide a tool that will help Canada maintain its position as an innovative technological nation."

The Canadian Light Source, opening in January 2004, will use brilliant light, millions of times brighter than sunlight, in diverse fields of research ranging from medical radiation therapy to cleaner-burning fossil fuels.

Government of Saskatchewan

Advertising allows governments to reach the public and accounts for a substantial portion of media advertising revenues. (Saskatchewan Industry and Resources)

and freedom provided to the new mass media and the interactive media. In Europe, for example, where local calls are timed and cost on a per-minute basis, Internet usage is costly. In other parts of the world it is virtually unaffordable. In China, Internet access is controlled. In still other countries, infrastructure development has been slow because it has been left totally in the hands of business.

Legal Influences

In addition to the impact of laws and policies affecting the mass media, lawyers, judges, and others in the legal profession play certain roles and thereby influence the media. The courts must interpret existing statutes in instances where specific mass media practitioners or owners are thought to have operated outside the law. A much more widespread influence on content, however, is exercised with various sections of the Criminal Code that cover offences such as sedition, promulgating obscenity, propagating hate literature, issuing false messages, and interfering with the rights of an accused to a fair trial. Court decisions on cases of these kinds tend to influence all mass media practitioners—particularly journalists—and are used as indicators to guide future actions taken in the selection of media content. These influences extend to the new mass media and the interactive media. On-line seduction of people below the age of consent has created a certain number of headlines, especially when followed by actual meetings of the participants.

Legislatures have a special influence on the new and interactive media through their enactment of new laws to cover new realities. For example, copyright legislation assists those who undertake intellectual work by allowing them to receive payment for that

that must be managed in the context of the time and of democratic values.

Government influence on both the new mass media and the interactive media, at least in Canada, tends to be through investment in the infrastructure and assisting with the provision of on-line services, not least of which is government on-line. While the government has yet to commit to the provision of broadband services for all Canadians, it is only a matter of time before that point is reached. The Canadian government has also invested in all sorts of projects to assist businesses and social organizations to go on line. Canadians can count themselves lucky for the support work. While much discussion has taken place about copyright being outdated in the age of the Internet, most of it is naive and often stimulated by the excessive profits reaped by some of those who control copyright, such as the recording industry. How aggressively a country moves in what direction with respect to copyright, or privacy, or libel can determine whether a country will be a major or minor player in the Internet world.

Audience Influences from outside the Media

The fourth outside influence on the mass media is the audience. Denis McQuail (1983: 168–70) has suggested that the audience can influence media content in six different ways (what follows is his list with our discussion).

1. As critics and fans, audience members can comment (with both approval and disapproval) on the nature of specific content pieces or content producers. Numerous publications and opportunities exist to reflect critics' opinions and the preferences of fans regarding media content. The extent to which critics or fans influence future programming is debatable. Allowing audiences to voice their opinions, it would seem, serves more as endorsement or lack of endorsement and as a discharge of discontent than as a determining factor in program design.
2. Through institutionalized accountability, audience members can seek to influence mass media organizations. This is often easier to do with public corporations than with commercial enterprises. In Canada, the CRTC is obliged to regulate the broadcasting system 'in the public interest' and, in doing so, seeks the opinions and preferences of viewers and listeners across the country. For the printed media, press councils—made up of representatives of owners, journalists, and the public—can act on behalf of readers who complain about specific content in newspapers. Some media outlets also have ombudspersons who mediate between the audience and the outlet.
3. Through the market, audience members can choose among media outlets and, through such choices (revealed in ratings data), exert some influence on the mass media. However, an individual audience member acting simply as a single member of the audience cannot exert much influence by this means. So far, it has proven impossible for

audiences to organize collectively and speak with a united voice on their preferences.
4. Through direct feedback to mass media outlets audiences can make their views known and hope to influence future actions. 'Letters to the editor' are the standard form of feedback for the press, while broadcasting stations rely on phone calls and e-mail messages. The representative character of this feedback to indicate overall audience satisfaction or dissatisfaction must be questioned, however. For instance, editors select the letters to be published, and radio talk-show hosts or producers choose who will get on the air and who will not.
5. Through the use of audience images formed in the minds of content producers, the audience can influence media content. However, these images are constructs formed by the producers out of what may be very limited or non-existent contact with significant numbers of audience members. Producers may construct images of audiences comprised of those similar to themselves and thus take insufficient account of the needs or preferences of other kinds of people.
6. Through audience research, mass media practitioners can gain a more precise idea of audience interests and responses to specific media content. However, as McQuail points out, the type of audience most likely to be influential is that which can be delineated with statistical findings (audience size and breakdown) and that which matches the practitioners' own views about audience preferences.

The whole notion of the audience, especially the mass audience, is open to question when we consider the new mass media and especially the interactive media. At the first or carriage tier, services are being provided—for example, cellphone plans, phone or Internet access, and so on. There is no audience, just purchasers of those services.

At the second or content tier, Web site users seek information, but they are not so much an audience as a user group. Also on the second content tier are the producers and exchangers of information. Neither are they members of what we would call an audience.

Audience Influences on the New Mass Media and the Interactive Media

When we apply McQuail's six different ways in which the audience can influence media content and apply them to the new mass media and the interactive media, critics and fans of Web sites become *critics and users*. They may also become *producers* of their own Web sites. Critics and fans morph into *participants* in using e-mail and chatrooms. As producers or participants they control content rather than influence it. Through tracking site usage, users give evidence of sticking to the same sites for a long period of time, while critics play their normal role. However, having said this, so decentralized is Web site production and so multifarious are the reasons why people and groups create Web sites, e-mail, or chatrooms, one could hardly say that such activities are user-driven.

There is very little *institutionalized accountability* in the new mass media because, as we have explained, there is very little centralized production of content. Of course, general laws relating to the restriction of hate literature, the invasion of privacy, and the like still apply, but if any institutionalized accountability does operate, it derives from attempts by on-line firms to gain consumer trust. For example, a firm such as Torstar has an interest in ensuring that its Workopolis site is credible and Amazon has an interest in ensuring that you receive your ordered book in a timely fashion. Small on-line businesses also have an interest in forming associations and agreeing to certain standards so that the public will learn to trust doing business on the Internet. They can then advertise adherence to certain codes and gain consumer trust.

The *market*, as measured by the number of hits and the amount of time spent on the site, is perhaps the most talked-about way in which members of the public influence Internet content. Of course, this is restricted to Web sites and does not apply to use of services such as phones and e-mail. However, what equipment and what 'bundle packages' people purchase, especially for their cellphones, are influential. But this is consumer behaviour, not audience dynamics.

Direct feedback is greatly facilitated by the new mass media and plays a significant role in influencing Web sites. Direct feedback is what e-mail and chatrooms are all about! Feedback is content.

The *image* Web site producers have *of users* and their tastes is clearly influential on content produced and services made available. Web site producers can see clearly where users go, how much time they spend where they are, whether they retrieve available files for download, etc. On the basis of this information, site managers can understand their audience. However, Web site producers are not in the business of creating content to flatter the audience. It will be interesting to see how Web site content evolves.

Through tracking users and sending out cookies, *audience research* is ongoing. Notwithstanding the ability to track user behaviour, an infrastructure of user definition and measurement is not in place, nor is there much measurement of the connection between purchasing behaviour and exposure to advertising. These standards may evolve if commercial or political gain is to be had from their existence.

Several points come forward from this translation of McQuail's concepts into the new and interactive media. First is that the old mass media are in the business of ratings and the vast majority sell their audiences either to advertisers or, if they are publicly funded, to politicians or to funding bodies such as governments. The new media are attempting to establish social behaviour so that Internet usage becomes part of our lives. They are seeking stable user groups. While many thought it would be a simple matter to sell the passing attention of users to advertisers, and they did so, purchasers of user attention have backed off somewhat because they are not convinced their attempt to persuade Internet users to buy their products through such devices as banner ads is paying off. It turns out that pop-up ads and pop-under ads can build brand awareness, but they also build consumer resentment, especially when they have nothing to do with the content that a Web user is viewing. Also, because access to production is so easy, the separation of users and producers becomes a little amorphous. If one point can summarize the situation, it is that the new mass media are quite a different game and the rules of that game are just beginning to be established.

The Inside Influences of Owners and Media Professionals

Thus far, we have been looking at outside influences on the operation of both new and traditional mass media organizations. The internal structures of these organizations and the people who work in them also exert considerable influence. In the traditional mass media, journalists and other media professionals are directly engaged in the production and processing of media content. They do this within an organizational structure operated by media management, which may have several levels to it (see Chapter 9 for more on this).

Above the managerial levels are the ultimate owners of the media corporations (or the owners' representatives). In the case of public corporations, the owners are the taxpaying public, but through Parliament and other governmental bodies responsibility is vested in a governing board of some type—usually a board of directors. In the case of commercial corporations, the owners are shareholders or individual entrepreneurs (usually the former). Shares may be widely held among many investors or closely held by the members of a particular family. Owners may be actively involved in managing the media corporation or may rely largely or even entirely on senior managers. Internally, media corporations can be viewed as social systems with their own structures and history.

Moving beyond the general parameters of the ownership and management of media outlets, a number of professionals influence media operations through the roles they play. The program directors, producers, executive producers, program assistants, editors, technical people, and sales managers all have at least a dual allegiance to their profession and to the company for which they work. How they play out these roles and the social system that emerges within the corporation can greatly influence the resulting output of the station, network, magazine, or newspaper. Of particular interest is the way creative people are attracted to organizations in which they may thrive but that inevitably place some restrictions on their creativity. British media professor Margaret Gallagher (1982) provides an insightful account of how these individuals and their organizations negotiate in such a way that there is not only control and predictability over programs but also room for creativity.

Another type of owner influence has begun to assert itself more strongly with the increased concentration of ownership and hence cross-ownership of different media—the ideological interests of the owner. For many years it has been recognized that the major business interests of a media owner are either off limits or treated with kid gloves in the reporting of that owner's media. Currently in Canada, the ideological and political inclinations and aspirations of owners such as Izzy Asper and his sons have begun to influence editorial content, as we will see in Chapter 8. For now, it is sufficient to note that while owners have the power to exert editorial control, the exertion of that power may diminish the size of the audience and undermine the owner's own financial interests.

The provision of carriage is not influenced by anyone other than owners, who decide what markets they will serve, and governments, who oversee the development and maintenance of the telecommunications infrastructure and who may provide incentives for businesses to serve certain markets in certain ways. To some degree, their activities are regulated as part of the telecommunications infrastructure, but neither the owners nor the overseers affect content. With regard to content production, this area is so new and the content producers are so numerous that they are not organized into fully defined professional roles. Some differentiation is evolving, however. Information architecture is seen as something separate from Web site design, and programmers obviously differ from writers who specialize in the Internet. But such roles are just beginning to be fleshed out.

Information, Entertainment, Images, and Symbols

The terms 'information', 'entertainment', 'images', and 'symbols' cover what is otherwise known as content. Television provides information programming (news, current affairs, documentaries) and entertainment programming (sitcoms, music, drama, sports). In newspapers, information is included in news and sports, opinions in editorials and columns, advertisements, and even cartoons, while entertainment is provided in travel, leisure, gossip columns, the comics, and sports. Similarly, information and entertainment are provided by the fiction and non-fiction in magazines such as *Maclean's*, *Saturday Night*, *Canadian Living*, *Canadian Geographic*, and *This* magazine. The content of the mass media brings us direct reports of the world through information programming and indirect reports of the state of living through entertainment programs.

To say that the mass media convey images and symbols is to look at content from a different angle. Whether through words or pictures, in print or electronically, the mass media present us with images of the world—images that fall into two classes (discussed in greater detail in Chapter 4). The first is denotative, that is, those images that are explicit, objective, there for anyone to see. A descriptive analysis of a photograph that identifies its various elements or a rational argument—each presents us with denotative images. The second class of images is connotative: they are associations that are implied and/or that we infer from the context that surrounds the denotative images. Take, for instance, a travel advertisement: the photo of a boat sailing on a calm lake on a sunny day would be the denotative image, whereas the peacefulness and enjoyment implied and inferred from such an image is connotative. The focus of our discussion, and the emphasis in communications literature, is on connotative images, which may derive from very different sources. Connotative images may arise from rhetorical argument. They may have a visual base and derive from the composition of a still photograph, or from the timing and juxtaposition of a series of video shots, or even from the layout of a printed page.

Symbols can include anything, from letters of the alphabet to something as complex as a religious icon directly related to a biblical story, which, in turn, has a particular meaning. Here we use the term in a general sense, stressing the interpretive tendencies of the audience. Thus, at every level of our existence, from the biological to the psychological—the social, the cultural, the political—the meaning of a symbol is an interaction between the composition of the image and the interpretive predispositions of the audience. A death mask has a biological base; a flag has a socio-cultural as well as an aesthetic base and, perhaps, a political base. Symbolic meaning can also be understood to have connotative value.

The images the media present are rich in their symbolic meaning or connotative value, whether or not the media intend them to be. To some degree, the success of all media products, from movies and books to television programs and newspapers, depends on the presentation of images that are layered with symbolic meaning. The sum of the meaning of the images and symbols presented to us by the media represents the ideological currents and community norms of society. In this way, the media play a fundamental role in articulating and consolidating ideological control and community behaviour in society.

In the content tier of the new mass media and the interactive media, the parameters of information, entertainment, images, and symbols are far wider than in the traditional mass media essentially because of the decentralization of production. On the Web can be found content that is extending current knowledge. NASA has some of it; scientific and scholarly journals have more. At the same time, other content—art and writing—is breaking the bonds of our perceptual and conceptual frameworks and habits. In addition, the Internet spews forth the marginal—porn, hate literature, terrorism. As well, the new mass media provide the politically but responsibly radical and offer users the opportunity to exchange messages directly. It is indeed a brave new communications world.

The Mass Audience

As well as increasing the possibilities for participation in defining the representational world, the new mass media and the interactive media challenge the longevity if not the existence of the mass audience.

As noted at the beginning of this chapter, a **mass audience** is not to be thought of as a seething mass of unthinking automatons vulnerable to the intentional or unintentional manipulations of media practitioners. Rather, it is a convenient shorthand term for the great number of people who constitute the mass entertainment and information audience. And, rather than being homogeneous, vulnerable, and passive, the mass audience is better conceived as consisting of individuals who, from their diverse backgrounds, bring a variety of readings to media content—readings that are derived from their psychological, social, economic, political, cultural, and spiritual roots, as well as their age, region, and gender. The mass audience should also be distinguished from both the 'populace' (all members of society) and the public (in the sense of the 'public good', those members of society who have an interest in its order and evolution towards greater equity and justice).

Mass audiences are still a reality. They form around certain events or international spectacles like the Olympics or the soccer World Cup. They watch *Friends* and *ER* but after that the audience fragments, as it does in watching the various reality TV programs. But the new mass media so facilitate easy communication by members of the public that not only can we amuse ourselves (rather than being amused by others) but we can take strong and concerted action to take governments and corporations to task. We can organize with effectiveness against international government/business coalitions that are good for business and weigh heavily on citizens. Information can be so much more easily copied and distributed that the foundational notion of copyright is challenged. In short, our participation through communication media with the world as a whole is no longer confined to assembling together or individually in our atomized spaces for the delivery of packaged entertainment and information products. We can now engage in person-to-person communication with others from around the world in real time or not, and organize and participate in defining and acting on our own realities.

The power this has put into the hands of citizens

has fundamentally realigned the social world and the representational world, that is, the creation and production of interpretations of the social. In short, we must now begin to rethink what constitutes mass communication and how these evolving forms of mass communication are likely to affect society.

An Overview of the New Mass Media and the Interactive Media

The new mass media and the interactive media provide public access to modern communication facilities. In following McQuail's seven-point overview of the mass media, we find various changes in how these media are perceived and used.

1. The new mass media and the interactive media involve a distinct set of activities. Tier-one services allow widespread public access to electronic and other means of communication for carrying messages and meanings far and wide. Examples include the telephone and its derivatives, the Internet, and the post office and other carrier services. Tier-two content generation provides as wide a variety of content as the world wishes to produce.

2. At the tier-one level, the electronic new mass media and the interactive media involve particular technological configurations in that they are based primarily on a digital input or encoding device (a computer with modem), a means of transmission (copper wire, coaxial cable, or glass fibre), and a digital receiving or decoding device (another computer with modem). The post office's requirements for envelopes, stamps, and certain types of packaging are the print equivalent. Tier-two technology combines software with content to produce content displayed in a certain manner.

3. The new mass media and the interactive media provide general or common access to all who wish it, usually for a fee. The associated formally constituted institutions at the tier-one level provide access and transmission. They provide access to the public, that is, to any member or organization of society. Members of the public may use the new mass media and the interactive media for a variety of reasons: to send a message to an individual recipient, to send a message to a group of recipients, and to set up (and perhaps manage) a discussion group or Web site.

4. The new mass media and the interactive media operate within certain laws. At the tier-one level telecommunications law is the primary regulating influence. At the tier-two level the legal regime consists of copyright, privacy, libel, and censorship laws (restricting, for example, hate literature or pornography). Web sites often work within the norms of society and they can contain extremely valuable content, for example, reports of new scientific discoveries. Others challenge society's norms. Groups commonly generate their own rules of discussion, usually following certain understandings of conduct that are not directly imposed by society. (Hackers, of course, respect neither these nor other rules basic to the operation of the system.) The new mass media appear to operate because it is technologically possible for them to do so. We do not understand how such communication will contribute to society, though we tend to assume that this communication will generate economic activity in the form of information services. We also appear to assume that increased communication is a basic good that can contribute to democracy and to an open and dynamic society. For instance, in June 1999, the CRTC decided that it was unnecessary to regulate the Internet, in part because other Canadian laws, such as anti-pornography and anti-hate laws, were already in place and could be applied.

5. The new mass media and the interactive media allow a range of production values in the creation of messages and, as carriers, exert no control over what is or is not transmitted. In content generation in certain instances, such as electronic magazines, or in the creation of Web sites, persons occupy certain roles but formal professional roles are still evolving.

6. The new mass media and the interactive media carry content for a fee with whatever meaning the sender intends—information, entertainment, images, and/or symbols. The content may take the form of data, text, photos, sound—anything that can be digitized, anything that can fit inside an envelope or postal package. It may be encrypted or not.

7. It is probably more accurate, in relation to the new mass media and the interactive media, to say that there are users and user groups rather than simply audiences. The greater the interactivity, the more users are producers of messages.

IDENTIFICATION AND INTERACTION

Notwithstanding the definitions introduced in this chapter, it is a good experiment to try to think of counter examples. At a communications conference held in Salvador, Brazil, a number of papers discussed soap operas. It was apparent that the Brazilian academics saw Brazilian soap operas (*telenovelas*) as very much their product and their export success to the rest of the world.

At the same conference, a number of Canadian academics spoke of interactive media, the Web, and video games.

The question arose, if an audience identifies very strongly with the content of a TV format, or an individual show, in what way is this not 'interaction', while pressing buttons or looking up information on the Internet is?

The new mass media and the interactive media organize technical resources to facilitate short- and long-distance, real-time and time-delayed messages among members of society about matters they themselves define. The new mass media and the interactive media contribute to society by facilitating the flow of information and are negligibly affected by distance. They increase access to information and, at times, decrease the cost of information dissemination. They appear to be opening a new service economy just as the post office did years ago.

Summary

This chapter began with a series of definitions—'mass'; 'communication' in both technical and social senses; 'mass communication'; and 'mass media'. Most importantly, it introduced a new definition of 'mass communication' encompassing three elements:

- the centralized production and dissemination of information and entertainment products;
- the decentralized production and provision of access to information and entertainment; and
- the exchange of intelligence on a mass scale by members of society.

It then offered some definitions of the traditional centralized and industrialized mass media, the new mass media, and the interactive media. Following that the chapter explored the nature of those three types of media by means of a seven-part outline. All three types of mass media were discussed in terms of a distinct set of activities involving:

- particular technological configurations;
- associated with formally constituted institutions;
- acting according to certain laws, rules, and understandings;
- carried out by persons occupying certain roles;
- which together convey information, entertainment, images, and symbols;
- to the mass audience.

In discussing the major elements of all three types of mass media several points were stressed. The first point is how media of communication are woven into the societies of which they are a part through a legal and regulatory framework, certain types of proprietorship, professions, associated institutions, particular technology, available leisure time, and content—the images and symbols employed and the information and entertainment provided.

The second point is that if the media did not build on established modes of communication—words, images, narrative, drama, analysis, personalities—they would fail for lack of understanding or lack of audience engagement.

The third point is that society is being changed fundamentally by the new mass media and the interactive media, which are open to far greater participation by all. While this participation opens up flows of information and allows members of society to enhance their participation in social and political affairs, it also transforms the mass media from being socializing institutions to being, more simply, reflections of human activity at work and at play.

RELATED WEB SITES

CBC: www.cbc.ca

The CBC site highlights CBC programs and issues dealt with on the CBC. The site changes continuously. An interesting alternative site directed primarily at people in their twenties and thirties is www.cbcradio3.com.

Berne Convention (copyright):
www.law.cornell.edu/treaties/berne/overview.html

This is the pre-eminent world statute dealing with copyright. Its various clauses and levels are to be found at this site.

Canada's Copyright Act: http://laws.justice.gc.ca/en/C-42/text.html

Canadian legislation on copyright conforms to the Berne Convention and provides the foundation for copyright protection in Canada for both Canadian and foreign creators. This is the site of the statute.

Canadian Association of Journalists: www.eagle.ca/caj/

This site provides journalists with professional information and, from time to time, it takes up issues that are of interest to all Canadian journalists.

Canadian Broadcast Standards Council: www.cbsc.ca

The CBSC sets broadcasting standards such as how much advertising broadcasters should put in a half-hour of programming.

CBC Journalistic Standards and Practices: http://www.cbc.radio-canada.ca/accountability/journalistic/index.shtml

This code of conduct is not only a guide to journalists but also an indication to the public that CBC journalists work within a set of standards.

CBC Corporate Documents and Policies: http://www.cbc.radio-canada.ca/docs/index.shtml

The policy framework within which the CBC operates is found here.

CBC's *The National*: www.tv.cbc.ca/national

This site provides headlines of the day's news as it is carried on the program, features, further elaboration on certain stories, and even a subscription service.

Canadian Radio-television and Telecommunications Commission (CRTC): www.crtc.gc.ca

The CRTC provides everything you might want to know about its activities regulating Canada's media.

Society of Composers, Authors, and Musicians of Canada (SOCAN): www.socan.ca

The SOCAN site presents information for musicians, users of music, and the general public.

FURTHER READINGS

O'Sullivan, T., J. Hartley, D. Saunders, and J. Fiske. 1983. *Key Concepts in Communication*. Toronto: Methuen. While somewhat dated, this work provides a very useful listing of critical terms—not quite a dictionary but almost.

Curran, James. 1982. 'Communications, power, and social order', in Michael Gurevitch, Tony Bennett, James Curran, and Jane Woollacott, eds, *Culture, Society and the Media*. Toronto: Methuen. Curran discusses the historical elements of the mass media from an interesting, and wider, perspective.

McQuail, Denis. 1983. *Mass Communication Theory: An Introduction*. Beverly Hills, Calif.: Sage Publications. McQuail has written over a dozen books on the media. He is now emeritus professor at the University of Amsterdam. Some notes about his latest work on media accountability can be found at: <http://www.grady.uga.edu/coxcenter/activities/activities0102/act042.htm>.

STUDY QUESTIONS

1. Define 'communication' and 'mass' (as used in this chapter).
2. Outline the characteristics of a social model of communication.
3. Define mass communication and its three parts.
4. Define and distinguish between the mass media, the new mass media, and the interactive media.
5. How do publicly owned broadcast institutions differ in their basic purpose and mission from commercial or private broadcast institutions?
6. Define, in a few words for each, the roles played by owners, media professionals, advertisers, politicians, interest groups, the legal system, and audience members in influencing the media.
7. Discuss how definitions structure our understanding.

- To provide an understanding of the mass distribution of centrally produced symbolic or communication products, i.e., the traditional mass media.
- To explain and define the mass distribution of decentralized production of information and entertainment, i.e., the new mass media.
- To explain and define the interactive mass media as consisting of communication on a mass scale.
- To explain how traditional, interactive, and new mass media are all part of what can be considered mass communication.
- To explain how the Internet has fundamentally transformed mass communication and therefore the modern mass media and consequently is in the process of fundamentally changing society.
- To outline the many roles of those associated with the media.
- To illustrate how definitions structure understanding.

Democracy, Politics, Culture, and the Media

Introduction

The mass media are far more than activities that generate information and entertainment. They are foundational elements of democracy. This chapter examines the historical and current role of communication and information in democratic societies. It introduces three perspectives for understanding the role media play in various societies, and then examines the development and distinctive characteristics of the Canadian media and how they reflect and nurture Canadian culture and political values. The chapter ends with a comment on Canadian concerns in an international context.

European Roots: Information and Democracy

It might be said that the modern mass media began to emerge in the mid-fifteenth century with the development of printing by means of movable type—a process first employed by Johann Gutenberg in Mainz, Germany, in 1454. This advance in technology is often used to designate the end of the Middle Ages and the beginning of the Renaissance—a transition from a social order where people were subservient to the powerful Church and monarch, to a social order more sympathetic to the freedom of both individuals and ideas. The Renaissance and the movements and conceptual developments that followed it—humanism, the Reformation, the Counter-Reformation, and the Enlightenment—paved the way for the existence of free societies and modern forms of mass media.

A major aspect of the Renaissance was a rediscovery and revival of literature and learning from antiquity, especially of the Greek and Roman Empires, which had been lost and suppressed during the Middle Ages. This recovered knowledge helped to re-establish faith in humanity and nature. Led by Italian thinkers and artists, the Renaissance was the beginning of a reassertion of reason and the senses that had characterized classical Greece. Underlying the Renaissance was humanism, a conceptual approach that focused on the significance of the human being in society. In short, the Italian Renaissance began to re-establish reason and democracy with a humanism that revolved around secularized society, was infused with a love of learning and the fine arts, and committed to education for both sexes.

The successful dissemination of humanist ideas was made possible through the technologies of writing and printing, which allowed individuals to develop and record their ideas and communicate them in a manner understandable by many. Printing presses were established throughout Europe over the next centuries, which would encourage the spread of literacy. As literacy spread, so, too, did the thirst for ideas, encouraged by existing rivalries and tensions between European states. Ideas rejected by the ruling elite in one regime could be exported into others, leading to a destabilization in these states. As American historian Robert Darnton (1982) has demonstrated, a regular business of printing in Switzerland and smuggling books into France was an important precursor to the French Revolution.

The following passage from the writings of Italian printer Aldus Manutius (1450–1515) gives a sense of the times and the significance of early printers in their societies.

ALDUS MANUTIUS BASIANAS ROMANUS
gives his most devoted greetings to all students

Ever since I started this enterprise seven years ago, I have not had a single quiet hour, this I can swear. Everyone without exception says our discovery is most useful & beautiful, & it is widely praised & admired. To me, however, this striving for perfection & the eagerness to be of service to you, to supply you with the best books, has developed into an instrument of torture. I tell my friends, when they come to see me, two Greek proverbs which most aptly describe my situation. The first is: 'The thrush drops its own misfortune', or, more elegantly, as Plautus expresses it: 'The bird is father to its own death.' For it is said that bird lime (for trapping birds) is produced entirely from bird

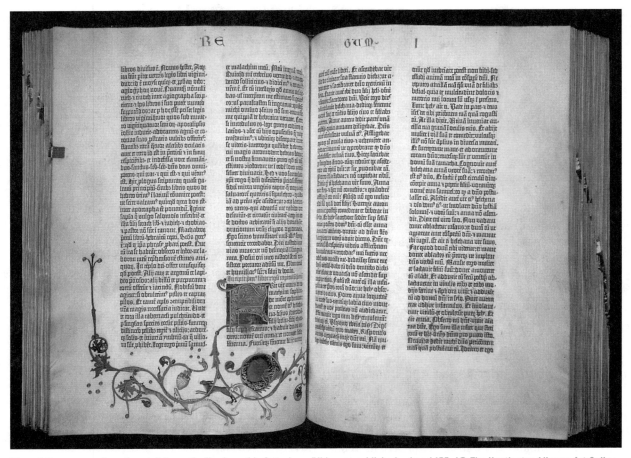

The printing process has changed dramatically since this Gutenberg Bible was published, *circa* 1455. (© The Huntington Library, Art Collections, and Botanical Gardens, San Marino, California/SuperStock)

droppings, especially those of pigeons & thrushes. . . . The second proverb is: 'We draw ills upon ourselves like Caecias the clouds.' Aristotle tells us that Caecias, the wind, blows in such a way that the clouds are not driven away, as they are in other winds, but rather that he draws & summons them toward himself. This is exactly what happened to me: I have begot my own misfortune. I have provided myself with trouble & over burdened myself with great labours. My only consolation is the assurance that my labours are helpful to all, & that the fame & the use of my books increase from day to day, so even the 'book-buriers' are now bringing their books out of their cellars and offering them for sale.

The transposition of Renaissance ideas from Italy to Germany led to a quite different manifestation of the search for knowledge, affirmation of the human spirit, and exploration of ideas. Whereas the Italians, with help from printers like Aldus Manutius, focused on the classics of antiquity, the Germans, also with assistance from such printers as Johann Gutenberg of Mainz, came to focus on the Catholic Church. This focus evolved into what we call the Reformation. To capture the matter in a few words, the Italian Renaissance overcame what had been an avenging Church (which for centuries had taken vengeance against individuals for actions deemed not in keeping with the Church's preferred rules of living) and established a freedom of intelligence that led to a vibrant culture. The German Reformation followed with a freedom of conscience from institutionalization (the Roman Catholic Church)—arguing that each individual could come to know God directly—and attempted to redefine religion and morality on a more individual basis. The Reformation began in earnest with Martin Luther's nailing of his 95 theses to the castle church door in

1517 in Wittenberg to protest against the selling of indulgences. The theses, written in Latin, were quickly translated into German, printed, and circulated throughout Germany. Luther also translated the Bible into German, making it more accessible to all. These acts of protest, delivered in a manner that brought knowledge and information to many people, led to mounting support for reformation of Church doctrine and to the development of Protestantism.

Both the Reformation and the Renaissance were brought to a close in Europe during the sixteenth and seventeenth centuries by the Counter-Reformation, a conservative backlash that re-established monarchical absolutism in both Church and state. Its most extreme manifestation was the Spanish Inquisition. During the Counter-Reformation, European states, recognizing the powerful role of ideas, writing, printing, and communication in general, put in place severe controls on printing to limit the dissemination of ideas. Various printers and writers were branded as heretics and were tortured and executed. Nevertheless, writers and printers persisted. In 1644 in England, writer John Milton penned his anti-censorship essay, *Areopagitica*, advocating the free flow of ideas. His essay was motivated by a 1643 decree that renewed a ban on type founding and maintained the monopoly of Oxford, Cambridge, and London over printing. Only in 1695, with the lapse of the Licensing Act, did printing in England gain its freedom—a freedom later confirmed in the first copyright act, the Statute of Anne, in 1710. Nonetheless, attempts to restrict publishing continued for some time after. For instance, freedom to publish in France was granted with the Revolution in 1793 but was lost under Napoleon and not restored until 1870.

After the Renaissance, Reformation, and Counter-Reformation came the Age of Reason, ushering in the eighteenth century. With the freedom to print and publish, the Age of Reason—a new try at humanism based on a combination of logic and empiricism—introduced the Enlightenment. The Enlightenment, an intellectual approach based on a scientific and rational view of the world, succeeded in establishing the ideological foundations for modern democracy and a free press. One of the main ideas of the Enlightenment came from the English philosopher John Locke (1632–1704), who argued that the authority of government or any ruler comes from the *consent of the governed*, not from some claimed connection to God (the divine right of kings).

Once the authority (divine right) of regents and popes came into question and was found to be built on tenuous foundations, it then logically fell to individuals to take the responsibility for creating a right and just world. For societies to have faith that individuals could create such a world required the development of a philosophy or world view that supported the notion that certain individuals, in consultation with society at large, and subject to the will of 'the people', could take on such a task. Moreover, for such a system to work, certain tools were required. Those tools include the right of free speech, freedom of assembly (to consult), the creation of parliaments and elections, the formation of political parties, and the development of means to communicate and disseminate information broadly.

The change in the concept of the right to govern—from divine right to the consent of the governed—was made possible not only by facilitating political and communication frameworks, but also by the existence of an emerging elite competing for power with the established landowners. An expanding, materialist, prosperous, and educated bourgeoisie gathered resources as well as articulate adherents to increase their power and push aside the landed gentry. Their power and activities, combined with a thirst for knowledge (especially scientific knowledge) and technological invention, led to manufacturing and an expansion of wealth. The result was a massive upheaval in European society as it evolved from an agrarian to an industrial society—a transformation that was, again, fertilized by communication.

From the invention of the printing press onward, the spread of knowledge laid the foundation for the profound political and social change from feudalism to democracy, from farming to industry, from medieval to Renaissance and then to Enlightenment world view. In the realm of politics, the acquisition of knowledge in the context of humanism and reason allowed certain citizens to gain enough education to govern in the name of their peers and enabled other citizens (voters) to make an informed decision on who ought to rule. Similarly, in culture, talented and knowledgeable creative artists brought forward more secular literary, musical, and artistic works that were to be appreciated by the viewer for their manifest beauty. Knowledge, reason, and information institutions became, and have remained, essential to democracies because they inform the public about the important issues of the day and the various solutions proposed by the competing elites who wish to govern.

In summary, the printing press served a key role in informing citizens on matters both important and trivial. Printers were one of the first groups of early capitalists—skill-based entrepreneurs who took the risk to print news sheets, pamphlets, and books and then to sell them to booksellers and the public. At first printers busied themselves with the dissemination of ancient wisdom, but as that wisdom was assimilated, and individualism began to take hold, authorship by living people emerged. With the emergence of contemporary authorship, the already established struggle between those in power and those who wished to gain power was intensified. A wealth of documentation prior to and including the beginnings of copyright tells us much about the various attempts by those in power to control the output of information by their rivals, especially when it was directed at the general population. In the main, those who wished to gain power spoke in the name of the bourgeoisie or the manufacturers who required greater freedoms to operate. As they achieved these freedoms others began to speak in the interests of workers. A great cacophony of voices emerged.

The Beginnings of the Modern Press

In the eighteenth and nineteenth centuries, some degree of organization was brought to the cacophony of voices through a growing trend for newspapers to be owned and aligned with political parties. This pattern—the emergence of many voices and their reduction to a few, often politically aligned, newspapers—has been repeated in most nations at various points in their histories. And just as this pattern has repeated itself, so has the subsequent transition of control of newspapers from political parties to business. In books and magazines a variation on the same pattern can be seen, with control first being established in the hands of wealthy patrons, then among liberal members of the elite, and finally passing, sometimes first through political hands, to the hands of business enterprises.

In the newspaper world, control migrated from the proponents of ideas and ideology to business interests because printing and publishing are costly affairs, and they have become more costly as time has passed. In the case of newspapers, by the twentieth century in Britain political parties had, for the most part, sought out rich party supporters in the business world and handed over operations to them, hoping they would

maintain both the paper and the political slant, often in exchange for peerages. As a result the news media have evolved into somewhat separate institutions with allegiance to a set of principles rather than to the platform, policies, and pronouncements of a particular political party. Often they see themselves as guiding both the party and the populace. In Britain, for example, the *Mirror* is still seen as a socialist paper while others, such as the *Daily Telegraph*, are staunchly conservative. In Canada and the United States, dailies have often been traditionally aligned with one or other of the two main parties—for example, the *Toronto Star* with the Liberals and Southam newspapers, such as the *Ottawa Citizen* and the *Calgary Herald*, with the Conservatives. Interestingly, whereas tabloid papers in Britain often, but not consistently, represent working-class interests, the tabloids that have evolved in Canada, such as the *Sun* publications, are reactionary and hence conservative and anti-intellectual.

In taking over the press, the business sector has promoted its own interests by emphasizing the freedom to pursue profitability in the marketplace unencumbered by state restrictions (see Chapter 8). For the most part, journalists have developed a complementary ethic by stressing the need for independence from the state for reportage and analysis. This dual business and journalistic thrust has allowed the press to establish some distance from the politicians of the day and maintain profitable operations. This is not to say that in claiming their independence newspapers, and the media as a whole, represent the interests of society. In fact, generally, the media represent the interests of the power elites in society—mostly business interests, but also the interests of the political and intellectual elites.

From the Press to the Media

Throughout history the print media have been nurtured by various interests within nations and by nations themselves, by the metropolises in which they operate, and by the liberal, eighteenth-century, social and political concepts of nationalism and individual freedom. (The concepts are social in that they outline how to organize society. They are political in that they are organized to allocate power in a certain way.) It is in the service of nationalism and individualism, and largely within liberal ideology, that the print-based news operations have reported facts and commented on matters domestic and international, social and spiritual, scientific, economic, and political.

The legislators of the early twentieth century used the ideological underpinnings of the press as a framework for the development of electronic media. As radio began to take hold, legislation in various countries extended individualism by taking the principle of **freedom of speech**, already extended as **freedom of the press**, to create freely operating electronic media, that is, media that would operate independently, in their day-to-day affairs, from government. They also extended nationalism by defining specific social and cultural goals in the founding statutes of both broadcasting and telecommunications. For instance, in Canada the goals defined for broadcasting were made explicit: in the 1968 Broadcasting Act. They were to stimulate national development, to promote unity and identity, and to showcase national talent. In telecommunications, the goals were most often facilitative: to provide for business, institutions, and the public to communicate quickly, effectively, and inexpensively (see Chapter 6).

Early on, Canadian legislators recognized radio's ability to operate on the principle of free speech and its potential to create a national community. (Courtesy National Archives of Canada/C-080917)

An example that illustrates the focus on freedom and nationalism is the use of the radio spectrum. Faced with the almost complete monopoly held by Guglielmo Marconi, the nations of the world came together and organized the fundamental of broadcasting, the radio spectrum. They formally declared the radio spectrum to be a public resource and assumed responsibility for its allocation and management. Segments of the radio spectrum were then allocated to various nations for their use, and frequencies would be assigned for various purposes—radio, television, cable, taxis, walkie-talkies, short-wave radio, cellular phones, marine radio, emergency communications, police radio, the military. But because the radio spectrum knows no national boundaries, there was and is an inevitable spillover of programs and signals.

In overview, broadcasting and telecommunications (including the Internet) constitute a global communication system organized as an assembly of national parts, with a growing international component. The national component consists of broadcast frequencies allocated to each nation and their management by various national agencies. It also consists of the telecommunications services provided to citizens and residents of each nation. The international component is comprised of broadcast signals meant to be received in countries other than those of the broadcasters, signals beamed from satellites to more than one country and interconnected services so that a phone call or a data packet can be easily sent from a location in one country to a location in another. The international component also is composed of international trade in cultural and communications-related goods and services. Both sectors are expanding, but the international component is expanding faster. This international trade in cultural products is ever more strongly challenging the economic, cultural, and political interests of individual nations in the name of consumer access. The national and international components of communications have long been played out in Canada. Our size, our (largely) shared language with the US, the location of our population (90 per cent within 100 kilometres of the US border), and cultural similarities have led Canada to provide access for its citizens to a large quantity of US programming. The legitimacy and influence of foreign content, often seen as an invasion, have been an ongoing source of intense debate in Canadian circles. These and other debates can best be understood within an overall consideration of the ownership and control of the media.

The Ownership and Control of the Traditional Mass Media

Western press traditions and liberal political theory speak of the traditional mass media as the **fourth estate**, following the first three estates of the realm. There is actually some debate on the identity of the first three estates. The term Estates General can be traced back to the *ancien régime* of France, and to its reference to the lords spiritual (the bishops), the lords temporal (the nobility), and the bourgeoisie and/or commoners. In Britain the three estates came to be seen as the Crown, the House of Lords, and the House of Commons. In the US, the first three estates have been defined as the government, the judiciary, and the clergy, and the executive, the legislative, and the judiciary (although these configurations leave out the common people and the business world, both of which are clearly major forces in US society). In Canada, the estates of the realm might be considered to be the Crown, the Senate, and the Commons, or, government (including the Crown, the PMO and Privy Council, and both the Senate and the House of Commons), business, and church and civil society. Luckily, to pull away from this fascinating plurality of opinion, we really only have to remember that the fourth estate is the media.

Notwithstanding the historical sketch provided earlier in this chapter, the interest of the fourth estate is purported to be the active pursuit of information in the name of the public good (see Boyce, 1978, for a critical history of the term). In liberal theory the function of the mass media is to preserve liberal democracy—in other words, the political system within which they now exist. The media are portrayed as watchdogs. They monitor abuse of power and attempt to ensure that the will of the people is carried out. They assist in ensuring that governments and institutions are flexible and sensitive to the changing needs and desires of society. According to this theory, the media provide the information necessary for public participation in the political process and aid in the dissemination of information about public programs and services. In short, they provide citizens with information about matters that are part of the political and socio-economic system in which they live—information that most citizens do not otherwise receive.

In contrast to liberal political theory, the neo-Marxist approach describes the media's activities not as working on behalf of the community as a whole, but rather, as promoting the already dominant ideology and the dominant classes of society. This view is based on the belief, inherent in Marxism, that capitalists add nothing of value to society but merely live off the excess productivity of labour. Neo-Marxists point out that though the media may propose revisions and small reforms, such as the election of an opposition party in place of a continuation of a current government, they do so to preserve the existing political system rather than opting for a new, more equitable system. In putting forward a limited range of ideas and analysis, the media present different manifestations of the same basic ideology and thus reinforce existing power relations and ideology. In short, the media reflect the interests of their capitalist owners in maintaining a politically stable society.

Scholars such as James Curran (1990) and John Fiske (1987, 1989a, 1989b, 1989c) have carved out a middle ground in describing the role of the media in Western society. They claim that the media contribute information and analysis on a wide variety of subjects from a fairly broad set of perspectives. The media do so in the context of a variety of competing groups and individuals, all seeking to interpret the real meaning of events. For example, in the case of Aboriginal land claims one can, at various times, see the point of view of First Nations, the provincial and federal governments, business, residents on the land, or ordinary Canadians. At times the contributions of the media are made with the interests of the public in mind; at other times they are more self-interested or represent the interests of a particular group. If major reforms are called for on a particular issue, the media eventually present and discuss that possibility. Otherwise, Fiske and Curran claim, the media generally entrench the status quo.

Given the various conceptions of the media, considerable attention and debate have been directed at the ownership and control of the media: where does it or should it rest? Analysts have identified four different sites where the power of media ownership and control are located in society:

- within the state;
- as part of social or political movements or parties;
- as private enterprises; and
- as public enterprises at arm's length from the state.

Each of these locations tilts the interests and the orientation of the media in a particular direction. Each introduces a bias focused on the interests of those who control the site in question.

Various scholars have discussed the implications of the media operating from each site, in terms of ownership, content production, and societal functioning. In the hands of the state the media strengthen state control, as has been the case in one-party totalitarian states and in certain developing countries where the state maintains close control over the media. In the hands of social and political movements they tend to fragment and politicize society, as in Italy, unless there is both a delicate balance of interests and a calm political climate, as in the Netherlands. In the hands of business, business interests are advanced at the expense of the interests of the community as a whole. In the hands of public enterprise, education, enlightenment, and, sometimes, talent development tend to become the primary values, with the interests of advertisers becoming secondary.

Siebert, Peterson, and Schramm's *Four Theories of the Press* (1971 [1956]) is the most often cited discussion of the placement of the media in society and how that affects their functioning. They identify four theories or philosophies that are meant to be descriptive of the social arrangements behind press functioning. *Authoritarian theory* assumes that all power should rest with those who rule. *Soviet Communist press theory* sees the press as supportive of government and the ruling party. *Libertarian theory* sees the press as a bastion of free speech. *Social responsibility theory* arises from the failure of the libertarian arrangement to produce a press that is of benefit to society. It places a self-consciousness and desire for the greater good of society alongside the ideal of free speech as guiding principles. We offer a slightly different alternative framework for understanding the general role of the media in society. In overview, in terms of structure and function, the media can be viewed in three ways.

1. The media further the interests of the owning/controlling entity, whether the medium is a state-controlled or party-owned press, a commercial press, a radical press, or a special-interest publication. In the case of arm's-length public institutions, the interests advanced are the values defined in the related statute (specifying roles and responsibilities) as well as the interests of the bureaucracy set up to operate the institution. The theoretical perspective that best outlines these dynamics is **political economic theory**.

2. When placed in the hands of private enterprise, the media most often pursue free speech unencum-bered by other considerations. This is usually called **libertarian theory** for its exclusive emphasis on individual liberty and free speech.

3. When placed in the hands of a public corporation or institution, the media most often inform the public by freely and widely seeking and considering information and opinion on behalf of and in response to audiences. This is commonly called **social responsibility theory**.

POLITICAL ECONOMIC THEORY

Before economics became a free-standing social science, it was seen by early proponents, such as Adam Smith (1723–90), as inexorably tied to politics. In the same way that the management of a family's resources and the power dynamics associated with it might be called domestic political economy, so the organization of a nation's resources, involving as it does both overall political decisions and economic management, could be called national political economy. As capitalism became entrenched in the nations of the West, capitalist political economy first came to be called 'capitalist economics' and then, simply 'economics'. The argument for separating politics and economics, to oversimplify matters, was that rational resource allocation was a science unto itself that operated independently of political systems. Hence, we have economics *tout seul*.

Political economy has evolved from Smith's time to become a field focused on the power dynamics associated with ownership and control. Political economists tend to be critics of the capitalist system. In contrast, capitalist economists focus on the allocation of resources through the operation of the market. They are only interested in power dynamics in special instances (such as when businesses gain **monopoly** control).

With respect to the media, political economists undertake analyses to reveal the interests and judge the performance of media owners and media-owning entities. Political economic theory argues that media ownership clearly benefits owners and other controlling entities. The owners set an editorial agenda; they allocate resources to cover certain categories of news and not others; they see that certain perspectives are represented and not others; they hire senior management and make known their priorities, which they expect employees to follow; and, in general, they make their presence and perspective known throughout their firm. Just as states can exercise tight control so can media owners, especially those who have political interests and/or other large corporate holdings.

LIBERTARIAN THEORY

Libertarian theory of the press is based on the concepts of liberty and the free will of individuals, which are derived from such liberal philosophers as John Locke (1632–1704), John Stuart Mill (1806–73), and David Hume (1711–76). The fundamental assumption of liberal philosophy is that individual freedom is the first and foremost goal to be sought, and that society should impede the freedom of the individual as little as possible. The state gains its legitimacy in its service to individuals rather than the reverse. In serving the freedom of the individual, so the liberal philosophers maintain, the state will create the most advantageous situation for all.

Libertarian theory sees the mass media as an extension of an individual's right to freedom of expression and hence as an independent voice that makes government responsible to the people. The media do so by feeding information to people so that, come election time, performance can be rewarded or punished. In a non-political context, libertarians see the mass media as assiduous pursuers of free speech. Should that pursuit result in commercial gain, or in exposing the lives of some people, such as public figures, victims of crime, or the families of criminals, so be it.

In striving to ensure distance between the government and the mass media, the libertarian concept of the media places the media in the hands of the private sector. In the course of media production and operation, the private sector has its own interests—developing markets and accruing profits—to consider above the interests of the people, of society, or of the government of the day. As a consequence, rather than allowing journalists to dedicate themselves to 'serving the people', the privately controlled media have sought to maximize their interests as private-sector corporations in order to survive and grow. An extreme example of a libertarian media practice is the exploitation of sex to sell news.

SOCIAL RESPONSIBILITY THEORY

Social responsibility theory arises from the perception that the libertarian arrangement fails to produce a press that is generally of benefit to society. The concept was originally named and put forward by a non-governmental US commission, the (Hutchins) Commission on the Freedom of the Press (1947).

In Canada, the Kent Royal Commission on Newspapers (Canada, 1981) explained the social responsibility theory well, pointing out that as newspaper publishing began to be taken over by big business, the notion of social responsibility was born of a need to fight against the potential of a new authoritarianism by big-business ownership of the press. The Kent Commission defined the concept of social responsibility as follows:

> The conjoined requirements of the press, for freedom and for legitimacy, derive from the same basic right: the right of citizens to information about their affairs. In order that people be informed, the press has a critical responsibility. In order to fulfill that responsibility it is essential that the press be free, in the traditional sense, free to report and free to publish as it thinks; it is equally essential that the press's discharge of its responsibility to inform should be untainted by other interests, that it should not be dominated by the powerful or be subverted by people with concerns other than those proper to a newspaper serving a democracy. 'Comment is free', as C.P. Snow, one of the greatest English-speaking editors, wrote, 'but facts are sacred.' The right of information in a free society requires, in short, not only freedom of comment generally but, for its news media, the freedom of a legitimate press, doing its utmost to inform, open to all opinions and dominated by none. [C.P. Snow was, for years, editor of *The Manchester Guardian*.] (Canada, 1981: 235)

Ironically, while an American commission into press freedom led by university president Clayton Hutchins coined the term, 'social responsibility' is much more accepted in Canada and in Europe than in the US. This is because, in the US, the First Amendment to the Constitution states that 'Congress shall make no law ... abridging the freedom of speech, or of the press.' Being the first of the constitutional amendments it sits at the top of the hierarchy of rights. The Canadian Constitution does not allow for such a hierarchy of rights whereby one right takes precedence over another, for instance, the freedom of the press versus the right to a fair trial. Thus, in Canada and Europe it is perfectly possible to limit free speech based on a consideration of the consequences of free speech. Routinely, in Canada, reporters must be careful not to discuss a crime in such detail as to jeopardize a person's right to a fair trial. (See Chapter 9 for a further discussion of press freedom.)

Canada: Liberal Principles in a Conservative State

While, in theory, freedom of the press is founded on the notion of free speech, in practice, it derives from the desires of competing elites—the business community, government, intellectuals, the church—to have access to the general audience. From an audience perspective, freedom of the press translates into exposure to an ideological spectrum within which individual ideas and policies are normally considered. As we have pointed out, freedom of the press developed in Europe from a power struggle between the nobility and the church on the one side and printers and manufacturers on the other side. Canadian press history is distinctive because of the acceptance of liberal principles of press operation and press freedom prior to the evolution of various separate interest groups. Thus, while printers were dependent on government printing contracts, the colonial government tolerated, to some degree, their printing anti-government commentary.

Oddly enough, Canada's tolerance was founded both on its colonial status and on the country's proximity to the United States. That is, as a colony of Great Britain, the Canadian political elite were enfranchised by their class connections to the mother country. Hence, Canada and Canadians strived to remain abreast of changes in the United Kingdom, which, when the Canadian press was developing, were towards modern liberal democracy. When the enactment of liberal principles became too slow in Britain, Canada turned to the United States for models, which were even more radically focused on the rights of individuals and freedom of enterprise without state interference.

In taking their lead from outside the country, Canadian media pioneers created a press and media culture strong on the individualism inherent in liberal principles and weak on the cultural or nationalist ideas inherent in the same theory. In more concrete terms, the Canadian media were and are strong supporters of freedom of speech. They are much less strong in their understanding of themselves as supporting institutions of Canadian society. Certainly, many journalists and media managers would claim that in bringing forward political and financial scandal, in exposing criminals, in praising heroes, they fill that role admirably. But when

the sense of individualism clashes with the need to support distinctive Canadian institutions, almost without exception, the media can be found on the side of individualism. The support of the media for free trade and against regulation of the economy in the interests of Canadians and Canadian institutions is a case in point.

It could be argued that this theme of the media neglecting to support Canadian institutions is present throughout the history of Canadian broadcasting. For instance, support of cultural distinctiveness was written into successive Broadcasting Acts, only to be gradually worn away by the media, which, with the exception of the CBC, were more interested in importing and distributing programs than in producing Canadian programs. Certainly, there is evidence to support such a viewpoint in various broadcasting histories (see, for example, Vipond, 1992; Weir, 1965; Babe, 1990; Rutherford, 1990). Robert Babe (1990), a communications political economist, identifies an additional factor that contributed to this scenario. He argues that the configuration of our broadcasting and telecommunications systems is a direct result of deals made in the US to split patents there among companies in such a way that telecommunications became a separate industry from broadcasting. Patents for radio and telephone transmission in Canada were split in the same way, and hence Canadian subsidiaries of US telecommunication companies controlled the same patents as did their parent companies in the US and operated in parallel with them. In broadcasting, ownership restrictions prevented parallel home-office/branch-plant operations. But they did not stop broadcasters from continually pushing for the right to import US programs in bulk and run essentially parallel operations.

The Traditional Mass Media and Canadian Realities

In assessing the role of the traditional mass media in Canadian society it is useful to examine the set of distinctive characteristics within which Canada's communication system operates. The first characteristic is the *vastness of the country*, which is tied to a second feature, the *small size of Canada's population*. These two variables have meant that Canada has had to invest in expensive per-capita transmission systems so that Canadians can stay in touch with each other. This investment, however, has paid off, keeping Canada at the forefront of telecommunications development and implementation. Figure 3.1 provides a chronology of dates of important communications achievements, including many Canadian firsts.

Each of these developments was cause for some rejoicing and some sense of pride. Each in its own way

Figure 3.1:	Some Important Achievements in Canadian Communication History
1885	—A transcontinental railway
1901	—A transatlantic radio link
1927	—A trans-Canada radio network
1932	—A trans-Canada telephone network
1948	—World's first commercial microwave link
1956	—World's first tropospheric scatter transmission system
1958	—A transcontinental television service
1958	—A trans-Canada microwave network
1959	—First Canadian communications satellite experiment including use of the moon as reflector
1970	—Beginning of fibre optic research
1972	—A domestic geostationary communications satellite
1973	—First nationwide digital data system
1973	—World's first digital transmission network (Dataroute)
1990	—Completion of a 7,000-kilometre coast-to-coast fibre optic network—the longest terrestrial fibre network in the world
1996	—Launch of the first North American, commercial, digital radio service

Sources: *The Challenge of Communication* (Ottawa: Department of Communications); Stentor Canadian Network Management.

strengthened east-west links from the Atlantic to the Pacific and was a factor in nation-building and cohesion. Perhaps a cause for greater celebration has been the commitment by Parliament through the CBC to provide Canadian broadcasting for all Canadians in communities of more than 500, whether east, west, or north. More recently, satellite communications have extended television and radio services to anywhere in the country.

A third significant characteristic, derived in part from the size of the country, is Canada's *regionalism*. Canada is not just a country of physical geographic variety; it is a country of various regional cultures. From the many disparate French and British colonies scattered throughout what is now Canada grew a 'con-federation'. This nation required means of internal communication, but not those in which messages would be generated from a central point and merely fed to outlying regions. Each region needed to generate its own information such that the region's particularities would be reflected. This would edify the country as a whole, or such was the ideal.

Canada is also a nation of *two official languages*. The right to speak either English or French is now enshrined in our Constitution. But Canadians have committed themselves to more than a freedom of language choice for individuals. They have committed themselves to providing various federal government services, including broadcasting, in both official languages even though in certain communities it is impossible for the audience to bear the cost of service in its own official language. Bilingual government services and bilingual broadcasting channels (not just programs) are a symbol of the right of any Canadian to live and work wherever he or she may wish. They are also a continual reminder to all that we are a bilingual country.

In 1971, during Pierre Trudeau's first term as Prime Minister, Canada also officially became a *multicultural country*. Although it was long in coming, we are beginning to see an acceptance of the desirability of tailoring programming to various ethnic communities. Multicultural television services are mostly distributed by cable rather than broadcast (and are therefore not available to everyone). In contrast, multicultural radio services are broadcast.

A final, never-to-be-forgotten characteristic of Canada's communications environment is its *proximity to the US*. Together with our acceptance of much the same basic political and economic philosophies and the fairly open border, this proximity has led to a massive penetration of US products and ideas into Canada. The counter-flow—Canadian ideas into the US—has been very limited. In Canada, more American television programming is available to the vast majority of Canadians than is Canadian programming. On most Canadian commercial radio stations, more American material is available to listeners than Canadian material. On virtually all magazine racks in Canada more American magazines are available to the reader than Canadian magazines, in spite of the fact that about 2,000 magazines are published in Canada (Statistics Canada, 2001). More American authors than Canadian authors are read by the average Canadian schoolchild. Our proximity to the US and the resultant spillover of American cultural products comprise a major factor to be taken into account in considering Canada's communications environment.

The Mass Media and Canadian Culture

We can now turn to examining the relationship between Canadian culture and Canada's mass media—including government's administration and regulation of them. This relationship is both interesting and complex. As Babe (1990) and others have argued, Canadian governments have not been consistent protectors and supporters of Canadian culture. They have risen to that role from time to time, but they have also enacted policies that have stunted the growth of cultural industries, such as film, sound recording, and publishing. Canadian government investment in communications has traditionally stressed telecommunications transmission and technology to serve the broadcasting system and interactive media, from the telephone to the Internet. In the 1990s, amid cuts to public broadcasting, the federal government spent millions on upgrading transmission networks. In 1998 Canada announced that CA★net 3—a national optical network partly funded by the federal government—would be introduced in October of that same year and would be able to deliver the entire contents of the US Library of Congress in one second. The press release announcing this noted that a parallel network in the US would require one minute. In 2003, Canada moved onto CA★net 4. The point, government spokespeople noted, was to emphasize Canadian technological leadership.

This commitment to current technology and effective, rapid transmission, marvellous though it may be, has been a mixed blessing. It has not necessarily served the cultural needs of Canada and Canadians, in spite of rhetoric used to justify each new major expenditure, because it has provided a conduit for foreign television and radio programs to reach Canadian audiences. Within Canada, it has served private-sector growth not just in broadcasting but also in the formation of national newspapers such as the *Globe and Mail* and the *National Post*. In the case of broadcasting, through the insistence of the CRTC, some cultural benefits have emerged from private-sector growth, but the private broadcasters have been reluctant contributors to cultural goals.

The usual rationale for investment in infrastructure is that technological development creates jobs, and numerous spinoff technologies lead to the creation of new industries, products, and hence jobs in the information sector. (The jargon is that there are significant **multiplier effects**, meaning that such investment leads to both direct and indirect jobs.) Not insignificantly, Canada's advanced communications infrastructure is also a vivid demonstration to the average Canadian that he or she has access to an equal or superior range of programs and services than does the average American (Charland, 1986).

It is certainly the case that a ready infrastructure has assisted Canadian business to embrace the Internet as a business tool. Not only have new Internet businesses been founded, but also traditional businesses have been able to take advantage of Canada's robust technological infrastructure.

Historically, the difficulty with investing in the technological infrastructure of communications is that Canadians have never been in a position to produce enough programs to fill the transmission capacity we have developed. And even if Canadian producers could somehow produce the programs, there would not be enough money in the pockets of advertisers, the public, and governments to pay for the full range of choice we created through the years. In other words, we have created an information environment that at once keeps us abreast industrially of the most advanced nations and also opens us to inundation by foreign cultural products. We neglected to design a system that would guarantee the development of Canadian culture and cultural production. The reason, it would seem, is our belief in individualism—in this case manifested as freedom of enterprise. This commitment has outstripped our concern for Canadian culture.

Figure 3.2 Top 20 Canadian English-Language Drama/Comedy Series Aired by Canadian Conventional Networks in 2001–2 (excluding Quebec)

Rank	Network	Program	Average audience (thousands)
1	CBC	Royal Canadian Air Farce	997
2	CBC	This Hour Has 22 Minutes	768
3	CBC	Da Vinci's Inquest	738
4	CBC	Red Green Show	730
5	CTV	Degrassi: Next Generation	576
6	CBC	Tom Stone	518
7	CTV	Cold Squad	507
8	CBC	Just For Laughs (Mondays)	467
9	CTV	The Associates	458
10	CBC	Made in Canada	457
11	CBC	Emily of New Moon	449
12	CBC	This Hour Has 22 Minutes (repeat)	399
13	CBC	Royal Canadian Air Farce (repeat)	390
14	CTV	Comedy Now	372
15	CBC	Just For Laughs (Fridays)	358
16	Global	No Boundaries	331
17	Global	Popstars	327
18	Global	Supermodels	230
19	Global	Psi Factor	186
20	Global	Andromeda	170

Figure 3.3 Top 15 Canadian English-Language Special Event Programs Aired by Canadian Conventional Networks in 2001–2 (excluding Quebec)

Rank	Network	Program	Average audience (thousands)
1	CBC	Olympics Closing Ceremony	4,601
2	CBC	Olympics Opening Ceremony	2,986
3	CBC	Grey Cup Game 2001	2,390
4	CBC	Olympics Prime Time	2,305
5	CBC	Trudeau	1,879
6	CTV	Tagged: The Johnathan Wamback Story	1,522
7	CBC	Royal Canadian Air Farce: Best of 2001	1,388
8	CTV	Stolen Miracle	1,329
9	CBC	Random Passage	1,198
10	CTV	Torso: The Evelyn Dick Story	1,191
11	CBC	Talking to Americans (repeat)	1,155
12	CBC	Royal Canadian Air Farce: Season Premiere	1,112
13	CBC	Royal Canadian Air Farce: Season Finale	995
14	CBC	Just For Laughs: New Year's	992
15	CBC	Red Green: New Year's	951

Figure 3.4 Top 20 Canadian French-Language Drama/Comedy Series Aired by Canadian Conventional Networks in 2001–2 (Quebec only)

Rank	Network	Program	Average audience (thousands)
1	TVA	Fortier	1,928
2	TVA	Le Retour	1,701
3	TVA	KM/H	1,525
4	SRC	Music Hall	1,521
5	TVA	Les Poupées russes	1,464
6	TVA	Tabou	1,444
7	TVA	Histoires des filles	1,394
8	TVA	Cauchemar d'amour	1,393
9	TQS	Lance et compte III	1,263
10	TVA	Tribu.com	1,153
11	TVA	Just pour rire	1,134
12	SRC	L'or	1,130
13	SRC	Ungars, une fille	1,101
14	TVA	Emma	1,040
15	SRC	Le dernier chapitre	1,005
16	SRC	La fureur	991
17	TVA	Arcand	989
18	TVA	Si la tendance se maintient	980
19	SRC	La vie, la vie	978
20	TVA	La poule aux oeufs d'or	962

Figure 3.5 Top 15 Canadian French-Language Special Event Programs Aired by Canadian Conventional Networks in 2001–2 (excluding Quebec)

Rank	Network	Program	Average audience (thousands)
1	TVA	Les Oliver	2,016
2	TVA	Le gala metrostar	1,955
3	TVA	Spécial le retour	1,838
4	TVA	Surprise sur prise	1,689
5	TVA	Le meilleur du festival Juste pour rire	1,686
6	TVA	Spécial KM/H	1,667
7	SRC	JO – Salt Lake : Finale Hockey	1,597
8	TVA	Histories des filles	1,528
9	TVA	Spécial bloopers	1,419
10	SRC	JO – Salt Lake : Cérémonie de clôture	1,396
11	TVA	Célébration 2002	1,307
12	TVA	Entrée des stars	1,293
13	TVA	Le meilleur da la rentrée	1,273
14	SRC	Beaux dimanche : Le Gala de l'ADISQ	1,217
15	SRC	JO – Salt Lake : Gala des champions (repeat)	1,203

Figures 3.2, 3.3, 3.4, and 3.5 list the top drama and comedy programs and special event programs in 2001–2 for French- and English-language audiences. The figures provide a sense of the popular taste of Canadians in the categories of programs reported.

CANADA'S NATIONWIDE RESEARCH AND EDUCATION NETWORK

In 1998, Canarie (Canada's Research and Innovation Network) deployed CA*net 3, the world's first national optical Internet research and education network. CA*net 3 was among the most advanced in the world when it was built, and its design has since been replicated by many network operators in the research and education as well as commercial domains. However, exponential growth in network traffic, expected growth in new high bandwidth applications, and planned extreme high bandwidth grid projects require that a new network be built to support leading-edge research in Canada. To this end, the gov-ernment of Canada committed $110 million to Canarie for the design, deployment, and operation of CA*net 4. CA*net 4, like its predecessor, will interconnect the provincial research networks and, through them, universi-ties, research centres, government research laboratories, schools, and other eligible sites, both with each other and with international peer networks. Through a series of point-to-point optical wavelengths, most of which are pro-visioned at OC-192 (10 Gbps) speeds, CA*net 4 will yield a total initial network capacity of between four and eight times that of CA*net 3.

Source: www.canet3.net.

Enter the Americans, who happen to be close by and also happen to be the world's most successful entertainment and information producers. The selec-tion they offer in such areas as television and film is too good to refuse. For one-tenth the cost of produc-ing a season of half-hour television dramas in Canada, US producers can provide a high-quality program with high ratings and ever-so-attractive stars, complete with press attention and magazine commentary. As prudent financial managers as well as liberal individu-alists, Canadian governments have been reluctant to play the role of patron in the name of cultural sover-eignty or national development. Nor have those same governments been anxious to restrict the ability of foreigners to do business in Canada. The result of a focus on technology, as well as prudent management, liberal individualism, and a lack of determination to ensure a dominance of Canadian programming, has been, for decades, a cultural low road (see Chapter 7).

CANADIAN CULTURE IN THE MEDIA, 1945–PRESENT

The history of Canadian culture in the media since the end of World War II is riddled with overwhelming struggle and a lack of policy support, followed by, more recently, significant gains and successes. For instance, in broadcasting, while ownership was restricted to Canadians (at the 80 per cent level), until the 1960s no policies were in place to ensure that radio and television content reflected Canada or was made by Canadians. Only with the invocation of Canadian content requirements did Canadian radio and television begin to have a noticeable Canadian face, and even then it was limited. No sooner were Canadian content regulations in place, which only applied to Canadian-based broadcasters, than the CRTC began to license cable companies, which took over as the main importers of foreign programming.

The story is similarly dismal in the history of other cultural media. During World War II, Canada devel-oped an admirable film production capacity in the National Film Board (NFB). After the war, as Canadian author Pierre Berton points out in *Hollywood's Canada* (1975), the Canadian government gave feature film production over to the US in exchange for the prom-ise of occasional mention of Canada in their movies. In sound recording, especially of popular music, produc-tion and distribution became established in the US and many Canadian artists journeyed to US studios to develop their careers. In book and magazine publish-ing, while little literary magazines, such as *Tamarack Review* and *Fiddlehead*, were a part of the fabric of the country, as were a few political magazines, such as *Cité Libre* and *This Magazine* (now evolved into *This*), authors of fiction looked to New York and London for affirmation of their talents and publication of their manuscripts. For non-fiction dealing with Canada, not so many looked outside the country, knowing full well that few foreign publishers would be interested. Some found Canadian publishers able to publish their work

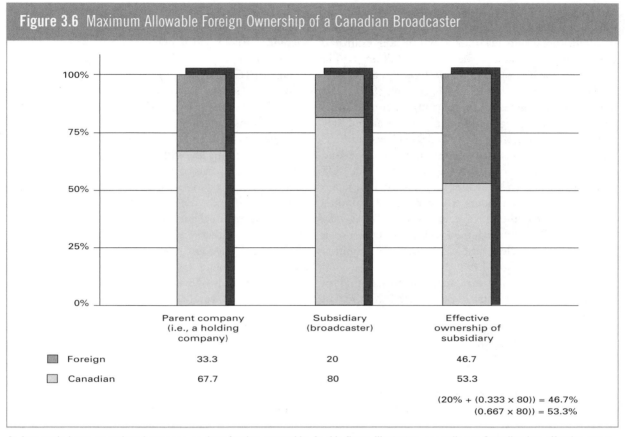

Figure 3.6 Maximum Allowable Foreign Ownership of a Canadian Broadcaster

	Parent company (i.e., a holding company)	Subsidiary (broadcaster)	Effective ownership of subsidiary
Foreign	33.3	20	46.7
Canadian	67.7	80	53.3

$(20\% + (0.333 \times 80)) = 46.7\%$
$(0.667 \times 80)) = 53.3\%$

As free trade between nations increases, so does foreign ownership. As this figure illustrates, according to Canadian law effective ownership of a broadcaster can be as much as 46.7 per cent through indirect ownership (of a holding company) and direct ownership of the broadcaster that is a subsidiary of the holding company. Any increase in allowance of foreign ownership would give majority control to a foreign owner. Within political economic theory, the role of foreign ownership looms large as a factor affecting cultural sovereignty.

by cross-subsidizing original Canadian work with revenues from educational publishing or from serving as distributors of imported foreign books. Notwithstanding these opportunities, many books were simply never written because few publishers were out encouraging potential authors to put pen to paper.

With ownership in Canadian hands and with their local market orientation, the situation for Canadian newspapers was not nearly so bleak. Canadian newspapers have always had a strong Canadian component, in spite of copious quantities of foreign wire service material adapted for their own use. The recent predominance of CanWest Global in the newspaper market, a traditional importer and distributor of foreign television programming, may weaken the Canadian content of newspapers generally.

Despite these not-so-inspiring beginnings and the spectre of CanWest looking both for cheap content

and for economies from TV/newspaper convergence, there has been a substantial turnaround in Canadian cultural media. Take, for example, sound recording. The Canadian Recording Industry Association reported a 13 per cent increase in units shipped (i.e., CDs, tapes, etc.) in 1994 as compared with 1993, with sales increasing by 16 per cent, and it appears the market has been growing ever since. Before that, according to Statistics Canada, between 1987 and 1991 record sales of material that qualified as Canadian content increased from $32 million to $53 million, an increase of 65 per cent. In book publishing significant revenue gains have been made, with Canadian firms steadily gaining small but significant market share for their own titles. Book exports have increased from their traditional level of about 10 per cent to over 30 per cent of all sales. Success has also been won in the film industry. Segments of the US film industry mount yearly campaigns to recapture 'runaway productions' produced in Canada (and other countries). In the summer of 1998, the California Film Commission estimated that every year California was losing $1 billion (US) in economic impact from film and feature film being produced in Canada (*Globe and Mail*, 26 Aug. 1998, A26). The figure has increased substantially since that time. As for television programming, in 1998, at an industry gathering in Cannes, the highly reliable Canadian Press reported that Canada had become the world's second leading producer of TV programs after the US (*Vancouver Sun*, 14 Oct. 1998, C7). This comes as no surprise to industry insiders: it is a matter of economics. For example, the average episode of *The X-Files* cost $1.7 million when filmed in Vancouver. Once it moved to Los Angeles, those costs rose to $3.2 million (*Vancouver Sun*, 26 Aug. 1998, B1).

What accounts for this apparent turnaround in Canadian cultural industries and media? Over the past three decades Canada has come a long way in the production of cultural, entertainment, and information products. Change began in the 1960s and 1970s, with public (and then government) reaction against the inundation of Canadian airwaves, bookshelves, magazine racks, cinemas, and school classrooms with American and, to a lesser extent, UK products. This negative reaction was led by intelligent, talented, young, and creative Canadians. Many of them had a vested interest: they wanted to become broadcasters, authors, magazine and book publishers, editors, filmmakers, and recording artists. And while some wanted just to be filmmakers, authors, or recording artists dealing with universal subjects for whomever might be their audience, many wanted to create work that spoke of their own Canadian experiences. However, in the 1960s, those in positions of power did not believe that Canadians could write good books, make good films, publish good magazines, or become world-famous rock stars.

In the 1970s and 1980s, although disbelief in the cultural potential of Canada continued, Canadian and provincial governments began to pay increasing attention to broadcasting and the cultural industries. They did so for two reasons: to retain these highly articulate and creative people, and because the continual importation of US entertainment products was a drain on the economy. As time progressed, and Canadians proved themselves eminently capable of creating and distributing appealing cultural products that Canadians wanted to consume, Canadian legislators

became more and more bold in putting into place policies and programs that would at least allow such activities to survive if not thrive as profitable enterprises. Such policies included the 30 (now 35) per cent Canadian content requirement in radio; Bill C-58, which created room for Canadian magazines in the Canadian marketplace; and subsidies to Canadian-owned book publishers.

Towards the end of this period, carrying into the 1990s, and, ironically, with a considerable contribution by those champions of free trade, the Mulroney Tories, cultural support programs were strengthened and various firms, if not whole industries, began to emerge as significant national and international producers of cultural goods. However, by signing first the Free Trade Agreement (FTA) and then the North American Free Trade Agreement (NAFTA), this same government sowed the seeds of weakness, if not collapse, of these industries as cultural agencies of benefit to Canadians because the trade agreements weakened the government's ability to maintain support policies.

With the election of the Chrétien Liberals in early 1993, support for cultural industries, notably book publishing, faltered. However, in due course the Liberals, too, realized the combined advantage of domestic production of cultural products (which were gaining export markets) and the opportunity for the expression of Canadian creativity and the circulation of ideas (which had been gaining international recognition). In 1998 and early 1999, policies began emerging from the Department of Canadian Heritage that appeared to embrace the cultural industries wholeheartedly. First the book publishers gained back their grants. Then, in the face of a negative ruling by the World Trade Organization (WTO), a support program for the Canadian magazine industry, led by Heritage Minister Sheila Copps, was mounted. The government put in place the Canada Magazine Fund to provide generous financial support to Canadian magazines. Copps also convened an international symposium on protecting cultural industries and promoting cultural sovereignty formally called the International Instrument on Cultural Diversity (a discussion of this initiative can be found in the international section on the Heritage Canada Web site (www.pch.gc.ca). Support for Canadian film and sound recording was also re-examined and policies put in place to assist these sectors in their growth.

These monumental changes in Canadian policy in the closing years of the century appeared to be a result of the government realizing the economic advantage, as well as the cultural and political advantages, of strong domestic cultural industries. Economically, importing cultural products supports jobs in other countries, minimizing the creation of Canadian jobs. The development of new jobs in the cultural industries creates direct and indirect employment. It also keeps Canadian dollars in the country and has important political and cultural impacts. Governments are seen as leaders by an important sector of society and Canadians get to see the world through Canadian eyes. Culturally, when Canadians see other Canadians winning international book awards (Michael Ondaatje, Margaret Atwood, Michael Crummey, Douglas Coupland, Michael Ignatieff, Wayne Johnston, Alistair MacLeod, Anne Michaels, Carol Shields), magazine awards (Tyler Brulé with *Wallpaper**, Bonnie Fuller with *Cosmopolitan*), film awards (James Cameron, Atom Egoyan), music awards (Bryan Adams, Sarah McLachlan, Alanis Morissette, Céline Dion, Nelly Furtado, Avril Lavigne), acting awards (Jim Carrey, Michael J. Fox), and even major sports championships and honours (Wayne Gretzky, Mike Weir, Simon Winchester, Donovan Bailey, Shae-Lynn Bourne and Victor Kraatz, Jacques Villeneuve, Catriona LeMay Doan, and both the Canadian men's and women's Olympic hockey teams), suddenly Canada becomes an exciting place to live. Canadians gain a certain confidence in themselves. Politically, if Canada is to remain a nation, its citizens must understand the country's distinctiveness, and that cannot happen if its cultural institutions are controlled by foreign corporations.

Nevertheless, the overall reality cannot be forgotten. While business is increasing in Canadian cultural industries, both market share and profitability depend on subsidies that support these industries. And while it may seem as if it is only a matter of time before subsidies will no longer be necessary, that may be an illusion. Also, in many industries, the nature of the increase in business is not exactly what one might expect. For example, while British Columbia has a film industry that amounts to over $800 million per year, the vast majority of that activity involves US filmmakers making films in BC locations, which masquerade as US locations (Gasher, 1995). Similarly, in book publishing, while Canadian publishers valiantly attempt to maintain their own publishing programs, they are doing an increasing business in importing and distributing US books. Furthermore, the volume of

US cultural products overwhelms the Canadian market. In spite of developments in broadcasting and the cultural industries, Canadian theatres are still crammed with US movies; Canadian magazine racks are still dominated by US magazines; Canadian bookstores still have far more foreign books on their shelves than Canadian books; over half the music played on Canadian radio is foreign; and Canadian textbooks adapted from US originals are still preponderant in schools. What the end point will be is difficult to determine; but unless we are defeated by US trade representatives who appear to wish to fight every attempt to solidify the gains we are making, whether in film, magazines, or books, the gains made in the past four decades do point to a promising future.

Politics and the Canadian Media

The traditional mass media and increasingly the new media and the interactive media participate daily in the governance of the nation. The modern nation-state is a sophisticated information apparatus, with government and the traditional mass media acting as two of its major information arms. More recently, the new mass media have provided a considerably enhanced opportunity for ordinary citizens to obtain information and to exchange it with others. The government collects and produces information to govern. The traditional mass media collect and produce information to inform the public and the state and to maintain a successful commercial venture. The interactive media allow all citizens to produce, to seek out, and to exchange information.

The desire, indeed, in the past, the necessity, of the media to carry information between people and their government makes for extremely close relations between government and the media. The media depend on the government for information. The government depends on the media to disseminate that information. The government's desire to keep from the media certain information, such as pre-decision information in cabinet documents, gives to that close relationship a certain ambivalence. The desire of the media to maintain their independence and periodically to demonstrate their separate integrity transforms that ambivalence into a love-hate relationship on the part of politicians. The dependence of the media on government for information makes that love-hate relationship mutual. (Four sources provide particularly good analyses of this relationship: Hayes,

1992; Cocking, 1980; Gratton, 1987; and the proceedings of the Canadian Study of Parliament Group,
Canada, 1980.)

In theory, the media act as a counteractive force to
potential abuse of power by the state. In pursuit of the
public good and in support of democratic theory, the
media protect individual privacy from the prying eyes
of the state, which, in the name of the community,
may venture to collect all kinds of information to ease
the job of governance. The media also help, along
with 'Her Majesty's Loyal Opposition', to monitor
government policy and action (see, for example,
Fletcher, 1981).

The parliamentary press gallery deserves some
direct attention in this context. The gallery is the sum
total of all journalists who are working on political
stories in Ottawa or the provincial capitals and
become members of the Ottawa or provincial capital
galleries. It is also, as the federal Task Force on
Government Information (Canada, 1969, vol. 2:
115–19) noted, 'the most important instrument of
political communication in the country'. The press
gallery performs two essential roles: to disseminate
government information, and to assess the wisdom of
government policy and action by reporting and analyzing House debate between government and the
opposition.

The press gallery and, more generally, the media do
not have free rein to carry out their roles. They are
generally controlled by a set of laws, standards, and
professional approaches that dictate their activities. For
instance, professional codes of ethics, press councils in
some countries, **libel** law, and limited **access to
information** are all factors in what the media report
and how. Restrictions also emerge from the manner in
which journalists operate. Political scientist Fred
Fletcher (1981) has noted the effect of the workings of
press galleries on news reporting. Until the 1960s,
when they came to be seen as compromising, press
galleries benefited from various incentives, such as
retainers paid by governments to journalists, preferred
access, and other perks. In recent decades the galleries
have emerged as independent from the control of
government, and consequently they have become
more professional. However, this independence from
government has been compromised by *pack journalism*,
just as much the result of the expectation of editors as
of the herd instinct among journalists. The term 'pack
journalism' derives from the tendency of journalists to
hang around in groups and all chase after the same

story at once. As a result, vast areas of government
activity are inadequately covered, such as the courts,
regulatory agencies, parliamentary committees, and
policy-making and adjudication within the civil service. A further shortcoming of the press gallery is that
many journalists lack the understanding necessary to
understand certain elements of government. Finally,
the size of the parliamentary press gallery is shrinking.
It is now more clearly dominated by a few larger
papers and wire services. Most noticeable is the
decreased number of regional members whose sole
function was to report on matters from the perspective of the region they represented.

In addition to the control exercised upon the
media, the media themselves can act in such a way as
to impede their role of keeping the public informed.
The public's right to know as opposed to the media's
tendency to create stories is one such issue. Access-to-
information legislation increases the power of journalists to harass the government. Every decision a government makes that involves the spending of money
can be questioned after the fact. Should the government be spending that money? Is it getting good value
for its dollar? Who is benefiting? When the media
become intent on defeating a government they need
only to ask such questions continuously to place the
government on the defensive, potentially interfering
with its ability to govern. And just as one issue is
addressed the media can move on to a new issue.
Meanwhile, the public may be ill-informed about the
intent of the government, the context of spending and
its relative prudence, and the programs that could benefit individual citizens.

There are, however, specific regulations that govern
media behaviour to ensure fair reporting—this is especially true of the media's coverage of elections.
Regulations control certain aspects of political advertising—for example, they exclude dramatization and
forbid political ads to be broadcast within 48 hours of
an election. There are also restrictions on who can
advertise what during a political campaign. For
instance, groups are restricted from advertising in
favour of one party based on their stance on one
issue—for example, abortion. Fletcher (1994) argues
that by restricting interest groups in this way, they must
strive to be heard within a political party rather than
being able to act as an outside force on its direction.
This, he maintains, strengthens political parties rather
than making them vulnerable to this or that interest
group. During elections, the electronic media must be

especially careful to provide equal coverage of all political parties. The print media, however, are free to cover elections as they choose. Interestingly, what has evolved in the print media, especially in big city newspapers, is editorial commentary supporting one party and news coverage aimed at equal coverage, but usually slightly favouring the government in the amount of coverage (see Soderlund et al., 1984, for a thorough and detailed discussion of normal press controls).

Governments and the mass media exist in continual tension. Both are the focus of the most basic and broadest public trust to act on behalf of the people in the best interest of the collective whole. A great deal rides on carrying out that public trust. But the media and the government do not always agree on what are the people's best interests. Political mechanisms have emerged that, when they come into play, indicate a serious lack of agreement between the mass media and government. In Canada, such mechanisms are rarely used but they are not unknown. These mechanisms can be directed either at journalists or at media owners.

If the federal government sees its own control and authority threatened, it can react using a variety of mechanisms, the most obvious being direct criticism. When the government's self-interest is involved, it can set up arm's-length bodies, such as **Royal Commissions**, to call the press to account. Other mechanisms include judicial harassment, setting up or encouraging others to set up competing enterprises, and withdrawing patronage. Since government is the largest advertiser in the country, the withdrawal of advertising can hurt media organizations, especially the print media. The government can also seek to control journalists by giving selective access to people or information and by exercising favouritism in its monopoly over government-created information. For example, inconsistencies in dealing with access to information can easily be exploited for political motives. Releasing news at 4 p.m. on a Friday afternoon in time for television news allows for the information to get out, but with little comment. The next morning, when the news is old, the newspapers get their shot at interpreting the event or announcement. (The soft form of this sort of manipulation by government is termed 'news management'.) Provincial governments have some, although less, power. For example, attorneys general can order probes into the interference by the media of the courts (Canadian Press, 1993c).

In recent history, political mechanisms to contain the media were used most often during the Trudeau era, in part because of the times, in part because of the Prime Minister's edgy relationship with the press. In 1970, during the Front de libération du Québec (FLQ) kidnappings, the War Measures Act was invoked along with a certain level of press and public censorship. (The War Measures Act, which has since been amended, gave the government vastly increased powers and reduced the rights of citizens. Searches and seizures were carried out in Quebec and people arrested without warrants.) In addition, as the CBC program *The Press and the Prime Minister* documents, Trudeau was continually engaged in matching wits with the press. On a day-to-day basis, he was neither an unsophisticated nor a mute observer of the role and failings of the press in Canadian society. At election times he was a master of media manipulation in his presentation of issues and persona.

At the end of the Trudeau years, the actions of a couple of press owners brought about a clear but contained confrontation between government and the

Aislin offered this version of 'press competition' in 1981 in reference to the closing on the same day of the *Winnipeg Tribune* and *Ottawa Journal* by the Southam and Thomson newspaper chains. (Aislin, *Montreal Gazette*, 1981. Reprinted by permission.)

media. One major newspaper chain, Southam, shut down the *Winnipeg Tribune* on exactly the same day (27 August 1980) as another major chain, Thomson, shut down the *Ottawa Journal*, leaving each owner with a monopoly in one of those two cities. The Liberal government responded in one week by setting up the Kent Royal Commission on Newspapers. In setting up the Commission the government subjected the newspaper chains to public examination of their operations, and by appointing Tom Kent, a former journalist, it set the journalistic community against the owners over the quality of journalism the owners were willing to pay for. The affair ended in a standoff, with ample warning given to the Thomson chain that the government would not allow it to increase its already substantial market share of newspaper holdings in Canada.

More recent examples of government control of media operations include the government's reaction to Southam's purchase of a number of weekly newspapers in and around Vancouver in the early 1990s. The House of Commons Standing Committee on Communications and Culture decided to hold hearings on the matter and, in the end, Southam was required to divest itself of certain acquisitions, such as the *North Shore News*. A spate of incidents in the 1990s that limited or forbade media access to the courts and forbade publication were brought to the attention of the public, the Homolka trial being the most well known (see, for example, Donham, 1993; Canadian Press, 1993a, 1993b; Bindman, 1993; Needham, 1993). It seems that the courts have yet to accept fully the idea of freedom of information.

When set against the powers of government, the press seems to have little more than the power of the pen (and the camera). Yet, at its most interventionist, the press can leave behind any notion of mirroring the opinions of society and become an actor-crusader. It can mount saturation coverage, exposing and arguing, coaxing and cajoling, in the hope of changing government policy or persuading the people to change government. Not incidentally, when the mass media are engaged in such a power struggle, audience ratings and readership rise.

In the most extreme circumstances, when the government feels the media are abusing their powers or impeding governance, the federal government can always invoke the national interest to impose censorship. In invoking the national interest, any attack on government can be construed as an attack on the

national community and, in the most extreme cases, tantamount to treason. When a government feels that it can no longer tolerate a free press, it can use censorship to prevent by rule of law what is otherwise impossible to prevent. Many of the devices used by government to control or manipulate the press may seem unrealistic and extreme, but they are used to effect in many countries of all political stripes around the world. The instance of 'embedded' journalists with American and British troops during the Iraq War of 2003 is a case in point. As one critic noted, they did a fine job of reporting both sides of the conflict—both sides, that is, of the soldiers protecting them. The use of manipulative and controlling devices in Canada, however, is rare. This is a tribute to the relative harmony among the various elites in Canadian society, or, if one views press ownership as far too concentrated, an indictment of the Canadian government for failing to control press owners in their search for wealth.

When rather extreme measures are taken in Canada, they often involve Aboriginal demonstrations or demonstrations against foreign heads of states. Canada has a rather volatile relationship with Native people and the exact nature of the rights of self-proclaimed First Nations peoples are not established and stable. Rules of behaviour on the part of the police, the government, the media, and First Nations peoples themselves are not clear. The situation has been similar during meetings of heads of state that take place within Canada. The functionaries surrounding many heads of state often attempt to insist that Canadian security restrict the rights of Canadians to a level that they would tolerate in their own country. The aftermath of an Asia-Pacific Economic Co-operation (APEC) meeting in Vancouver and an Organization of American States (OAS) meeting in Quebec City has taught Canada to anticipate difficulties. By 2002, at a meeting of the G-8 in Kananaskis, Alberta, the police and the politicians appeared to have learned how to behave towards all parties, including demonstrators and the media, not least by scheduling the meeting for a remote locale and keeping the media and potential demonstrators at a distance.

The Internet, with its many sources of information and capacity for information-sharing, appears to be challenging the role of the traditional mass media as the 'voice of the people'. Effectively, the people have acquired their own voice. Whether, over the long term, the power of the media will be weakened is difficult to say. It may be that the media will simply evolve and that they will maintain their role as semi-official spokespersons for the interests of societies and their citizens.

Information Needs, Communications Actualities, and the United Nations

Because of our proximity to the US and our frequent contact with American products, many Canadians equate international relations with Canadian-American relations. We tend to assume that other foreign countries behave more like the United States than they do like Canada. We also tend to believe that the US behaves in its trading relations in a manner consistent with its ideology of free enterprise and free trade. Most of the time these assumptions are wrong. We are surprised to learn that other countries are similar to Canada in their concern over the flow of American cultural products inside their borders. We are also surprised to hear that other countries have stronger restrictions on the importation of cultural goods than does Canada. As well, the US Congress is extremely protectionist. The US engages in judicial harassment by tying up foreign producers with legal challenges when it wishes and refuses to accept many negative rulings in trade disputes.

The United States is unique among nations in being the richest and most powerful nation on earth. Moreover, it has an overall ideology that reflects its position of prominence and a tenacious ideological adherence to individual freedom and freedom of enterprise. These and other factors have created a society that is materially richer than Canada's and more able to foist its products on the rest of the world. (Nevertheless, it has, at the same time, a very weak social safety net and public health-care system.)

In Chapter 5 we will explore the impact of cultural products on audiences in more detail, but for now let us advance a few simple concepts on the matter. There is little doubt that continuous exposure to American cultural products presents us with the set of attitudes, perceptions, ideas, indeed, a world view, inherent in those products. In fact, that is the basic effect in all communications, not just propaganda. It is also the reason why Jack Valenti, the president of the Motion Picture Association of America, attempts to persuade US film producers to use American rather than Japanese automobiles on their sets, when normally, Valenti spends his time trying to persuade governments not to restrict the flow of US movies into their coun-

tries (Rever, 1995). The problem with continuous exposure to foreign cultural products is that if we lack exposure to other products, other perspectives, other ways to understand the world, other alternatives for acting, then we are open to blindly adopting the values presented, which may clash with our own cultural values, whether subtly or dramatically. (In some cases, domestic cultural products, for example, pornography, may also clash with mainstream cultural values.)

The concern over the impact of foreign cultural products has been a long-standing issue for many people and communities. It arises out of a commitment to preserve, develop, and represent one's own culture and nation. The focus on American cultural products derives from the fact that the US is by far the dominant producer of cultural products. While such concern can develop into extreme protectionism, intolerance, and political self-interest, it may also be seen as a commitment to a pluralistic world society being represented in all its heterogeneity. For some time the United Nations organization, UNESCO, served as a focus for the articulation of the concerns that we have been discussing, for the desirability of nations favouring their own artists, authors, and cultural producers. With the withdrawal of the US and the UK from UNESCO in the early 1980s, and hence the loss of one-third of its budget, this agency tended to steer away from playing such a role. Their rejoining a much more timid agency in this new century signals that the US and the UK have managed to defang the agency from acting in a way that is inconsistent with their interests.

The position developed by UNESCO, more specifically by the MacBride Report, on communications problems and prospects was that *each nation needs a national informatics policy*. A nation must have the capacity to take information produced by the world community and analyze it according to its own national needs and priorities. Canada has not fully committed itself to this need, yet our investments in high technology, such as the information highway, demonstrate that neither are we entirely without commitment to this end. Canada is in the happy position of being economically able to work towards an information infrastructure oriented to its national needs and the maintenance of its independence. Being already committed, as we are, to technological development in communications, being economically well-off, and being so near and so like the US, we are in a position to lead in setting boundaries on the US cultural barrage for our own benefit and for the benefit of other nations.

Summary

The evolution of the modern mass media began around 1440 with Gutenberg's development of printing by means of movable type. Printing with movable type facilitated a social movement that saw the eclipse of feudalism and the dawning of the Age of Reason, as evidenced in the Renaissance, the Reformation, and the Enlightenment. The divine right of rulers was replaced with the notion of the consent of the governed. The printing press served an important social role from the fifteenth century onward in gathering information and informing citizens.

In making their contribution, the press and, subsequently, other communication media have been influenced by their social location, that is, the sector of society from which those who own and control the media come. No matter who owns and controls the media—the state, business, or ideologues—ownership and control bias the interests and the orientation of the media in a particular direction. The challenge to create a communication system of the greatest value to society as a whole was addressed in the design of broadcasting systems, which were based on the framework of the already established press.

Various conceptions of the relationship between the media and society exist. The notion of the media as representing a separate set of interests is contained in the concept of the fourth estate. Political economic theory stresses the playing out of the power and financial interests of those who own and control the media. Libertarian theory stresses free speech. Social responsibility theory stresses the role of the media as contributing to the evolution of the ideals of society.

In Canadian society the press and then the electronic mass media have developed under a set of liberal principles in a conservative state. Canadians have invested a great amount of public funding in the electronic media to assist in nation-building. This investment in technological infrastructure has provided Canadians with a high level of communications services. However, it has also paved the way for the distribution of foreign as well as Canadian content.

An examination of contemporary Canadian cultural industries shows that after years of subsidies and support, magazine and book publishers, filmmakers, and sound-recording artists are not only increasing their domestic market share but also making a mark on the world stage. Current difficulties lie with finding a way to encourage such activities to expand in the face of determined resistance from the US through the invoking of trade rules.

From a different perspective, the Canadian media address such basic social realities as our vast, sparsely populated, bilingual, multicultural, and regional country, which lies next to the world's most powerful nation. The United States has the world's largest economy and is the most aggressive exporter of entertainment and information products.

The role of the traditional mass media as gatherers and transmitters of information in the name of the public good is being challenged by the new mass media and the interactive media. Effectively, technological change has given a greater voice to the people not only to express themselves but also to own and control information sites that may demand greater responsiveness from both government and the traditional mass media. Whether this technological capacity will weaken the traditional mass media remains to be seen.

Canadians must remind themselves that, in taking action to regulate the mass media and to stimulate cultural industries, they are not alone. While efforts to define and protect cultural industries have weakened, especially as a result of US and UK efforts to reorient UNESCO or render it ineffective, the struggle to allow nations to maintain control over their own cultural development in the face of free trade is still being fought in various venues.

RELATED WEB SITES

Canada's Privacy Act: http://laws.justice.gc.ca/en/p-21/index.html
As you will see, the Privacy Act covers much more than Internet privacy.

Canarie: http://www.canarie.ca/canet4/
Canarie is the organization responsible for Canada's high-speed Internet backbone. This site provides information on Canarie and on CA*net 3 (and 4).

John Locke: www.orst.edu/instruct/phl302/philosophers/locke.html
Many universities have taken it upon themselves to provide texts free of charge to the world. Many are in the US. This site provides information on and texts written by John Locke.

Milton's *Areopagitica*: www.uoregon.edu/~rbear/areopagitica.html
This important work on censorship by the English poet can be found on a variety of sites that are accessible by doing a Google search on 'areopagitica'.

Department of Canadian Heritage: www.pch.gc.ca
Every Canadian student at all concerned with culture, the media, and heritage should visit the Web site of the federal government's Department of Canadian Heritage.

Canada's cultural industries: http://www.pch.gc.ca/index_e.cfm
The Department of Canadian Heritage site offers statistics on cultural industries such as film and recording.

Media Watch: www.mediawatch.ca
Newswatch Canada: http://www.sfu.ca/cmns/research/newswatch/intro.html
These are among the Canadian organizations that try to ensure that neither mainstream media owners nor governments can control the media.

Flipside Alternative Daily: www.flipside.org
Institute for Alternative Journalism: www.alternet.org
There are various alternative news Web sites, including these two.

FURTHER READINGS

Access to Information and Privacy Acts: http://canada.justice.gc.ca/en/ps/atip/ These two Acts provide a sense of Canada's legislation in these areas.

Canada. 1981. *Report of the Royal Commission on Newspapers*. Ottawa: Supply and Services. This dated but most recent Royal Commission on the press brings forward many issues. Its background papers are also extremely informative.

Siebert, F.S., T. Peterson, and W. Schramm. 1971 [1956]. *Four Theories of the Press*. Urbana: University of Illinois Press. This is a classic US view of the way in which the press works in our world.

Vipond, Mary. 2000. *The Mass Media in Canada*. Toronto: James Lorimer. This book provides a different, largely historical perspective on the mass media.

Weir, Ernest Austin. 1965. *The Struggle for National Broadcasting in Canada*. Toronto: McClelland & Stewart. As the title suggests, the author presents an account of the development of public broadcasting in Canada and of the political and cultural milieu out of which this regime was established.

STUDY QUESTIONS

1. What is the essence of the Enlightenment?
2. How are the mass media connected to enlightenment values?
3. What are the four estates of the realm in modern Canada? Is there only one answer? What perspectives might you use to answer this question?
4. What is political economic theory and why is it called by that name?
5. What are the shortcomings of libertarian theory?
6. Could you imagine the media going overboard with its sense of social responsibility and hence denying the population access to information?
7. Should a country be able to control in any way its information environment or should individual citizens have unfettered freedom of choice?

LEARNING OUTCOMES

- To describe the political/historical roots of the mass media and the connections between communication and education, our conception of human rights, and democracy.
- To introduce the beginnings of print and the social dynamics surrounding its introduction, as well as how print affected the evolution of society.
- To reacquaint students with the Enlightenment, what it represents as a world view, and how it relates to democracy and communication.
- To describe the beginnings of newspapers.
- To describe the relationship between the press and the electronic media and the democratic right to freedom of speech.
- To describe the beginnings of the electronic media.
- To introduce the concept of ownership and control of the media and the bias inherent in allowing certain sectors of society to participate as media owners.
- To introduce three models for describing how the media act in society—the political economic model, the libertarian model, and the social responsibility model.
- To place the Canadian media in their historical context.
- To provide an overview of the structure of the Canadian media and how they relate to Canadian culture and politics.
- To compare Canada's orientation to the media to that of other countries besides the United States.

PART TWO

Content and Audiences

CHAPTER 4

Media Content

Introduction

This chapter begins by introducing some terms that describe some basic characteristics of communication and media content. It then introduces a number of theoretical perspectives communication theorists use when studying content. Finally, it examines the interaction between media content and social reality.

The phrase 'in the beginning was the word' recognizes the importance of symbolic representation and the uniqueness of human beings, of all living things, in our ability to develop and use language and other symbolic systems. It also indicates the power of language as a symbolic system and its ability to serve as a medium for the creation, communication, and reception of meaning.

When we study content, we study the **representation** of ideas and images. Representation, sometimes also called **encoding** or **symbolic production**, is, literally, the construction of reality. In putting ideas into words, a painting, a sculpture, a building, a play, or any other medium of communication, a person selects certain elements to describe the object, event, person, or situation he or she wishes to represent. The person receiving or decoding that communication then uses what he or she knows of what is described and what he or she knows of the system of representation—most often language—to come to an understanding of what was encoded by the sender.

The study of content does not focus on whether a description or set of statements corresponds exactly to what it purports to describe. Communication scholars working in the social sciences are more interested in how something is described, how it is transformed by the medium in which it is communicated, the understanding the receiver develops, and the impact the communication could have. For example, a picture of a pipe is studied not for the picture itself but for the techniques used—the colour, the texture, the light, the medium, and so forth.

To put this in terms already introduced, social scientific communication scholars are more interested in a social rather than a technological model of communication. There is no ideal state of complete fidelity between what the receiver understands and what the sender meant to send. Rather, our focus is on the dynamics of the development of a message and the reception of content. This includes the bias of the various media and how the communicators, their immediate reference groups, their culture, their society, and the chosen media transform the message as it is being encoded, transmitted, and decoded. In short, a social theory of communication focuses on the transformation that occurs during the communication process.

Signification

The empirical world of objects, the 'real world' as it were, and the world of representations (e.g., language, music, text, video) exist on different planes. They are drawn together by human agency. While such a statement seems obvious today it was not until the 1970s and 1980s that representations or symbolic systems were studied for themselves, not for the degree to which they successfully approximated reality. And it was not until the late 1980s that British sociologist Anthony Giddens (1987a, 1987b) carried the study of representation one step further by emphasizing the role of human agency. Briefly, Giddens claimed that representation is derived from human agency acting on the object world. This activity—representation—is also called **signification**. Whichever term is used (i.e., representation or signification), the activity with which we are concerned involves the creation and articulation of a symbolic system for determining meaning. Human beings create symbols. Symbols order the world. Symbols transform data and experience (of the real world) into meaning.

The Indeterminacy of Representation and Its Implications

The study of representation, especially the representation of human affairs, is a study of *grounded, indeterminate systems*. They are indeterminate because there is an indeterminable number of ways of representing an object, action, or event—another original representation can always be made. Nevertheless, each representation is grounded in what is being represented, the person and/or medium doing the representing, and the audience for whom the representing is being done.

Two associated concepts for analyzing content are **intertextuality** and **polysemy**. Intertextuality (i.e., between texts) deals with grounding, referring to the fact that the meaning of something depends on how similar meanings have been communicated in texts (representations) that preceded them (see, for example, Kristeva, 1969, or Barthes, 1968). Our knowledge of any one text or interpretation depends on our knowledge and understanding of previous texts and their interpretations. Intertextuality is often connected to genres, that is, to particular kinds of literary or artistic expression. The novel is a genre, and within it are many sub-genres (the thriller, romance, sci-fi, spy novel).

Intertextuality also leads to the establishment of a genre language, of conventions that come to hold certain meanings. For example, if the action in a movie changes from one city to the next, the filmmakers may use establishing shots, such as a plane's arrival at the airport and/or mention of the city's name, to indicate the change of venue. Showing a famous building or an entrance with the name of the building also works.

Polysemy (i.e., many signs) deals with indeterminacy, referring to the notion that any message is open to a variety—but not an infinite number—of interpretations (see Jensen, 1990). For example, the simple sentence 'Anne rolled her eyes' contains two elements basic to human understanding. One is the notion of intentionality, the second is the notion of causality. Both derive from the choice of subject and verb. 'Anne's eyes rolled' has a much different meaning, an implied involuntariness. The sentence also contains less fundamental meanings: our habit of placing the agent before the verb; the popularity of 'Anne' as an Anglo-Saxon first name; the tendency for common words to be one or two syllables. As well as the expressed or **denotative** meaning of the statement— a female involved in a body movement—there exist a multitude of implied **connotative** meanings, such as the ones suggested above. There is also a cultural dimension: in one culture the action might be seen as humorous, in another it might connote exasperation.

The factors determining polysemy, or the grounded **indeterminacy of representation**, do not end here. Different systems of meaning are also derived from different media. In addition, one system of representation cannot encompass the full spectrum of the meaning of another. A painting cannot be fully translated into a prose essay, or even poetry. Nor can a sculpture be completely transformed into a photo-graph or even a hologram. Inevitably, something is lost. In short, a multiplicity of meanings can be generated within one medium, and meaning can be generated within the multiplicity of media. In general, because these representations can multiply so readily, we are dealing with a linked, or correlated, yet indeterminate system.

Polysemy, or the indeterminacy of representation, tends to lead the study of communication content away from the foundations of science and social science and more towards the foundations of interpretation we find in the humanities. In other words, it is concerned more with **rhetoric** (how things are said) and **hermeneutics** (how things are interpreted) than with truth and reason.

In the study of communication the importance of a statement is not limited to whether it predicts events, can be refuted by others, or generates other interesting hypotheses—all standards of scientific study and the social sciences. What is interesting is what and how any means of communication selects and re-presents or re-constructs something, and what gives a particular representation its force, its ability to persuade, or its attractiveness. Whatever makes one novel, painting, or film more popular or revered than another, or even a novel more powerful than a film, cannot be satisfactorily discussed by reference to the relative 'truth' of each communication. Such media and individual works are more interestingly discussed in terms of their (rhetorical) force, in terms of the nature or style of their representation. In such discussions we can compare movies with books, paintings of battles with portraits, cars with clothes, or rock music with Greek society.

For instance, if we compare media, movies quite consistently add a sense of reality that another medium, such as print, cannot provide. As well, movies often reach a wider audience. However, what they gain on those two dimensions movies often lose in subtlety, character development, and room for imaginative play on the part of audience members. In regard to other media, the discussion of abstract ideas changes when one moves from books to the popular press or to television. Television demands a necessary pluralism of sight, sound, and personage that is partially there in radio and absent in print—more than a few minutes of the same person talking, no matter what the visuals, begins to undermine the speaker's credibility or at least viewers' interest. Just the opposite seems to hold for print—a single 'voice' will more readily elicit a

A MULTIPLICITY OF MEANING

You'll notice that these two photographs of MPs Svend Robinson and Paul Martin, both in the House of Commons and taken several years apart (but by the same photographer) have quite different meanings. In themselves, they are both wonderful examples of deliberate use of polysemy (or, in more usual words, ambiguity). Together they illustrate how the same visual elements can take on an entirely different set of meanings. The photograph of Svend Robinson (a leftist looking right) was taken at the time he was introducing a petition to remove mention of God from the Constitution. Robinson's raised head, with the lights beaming down from above, creates a spiritual effect (an intertextual reference to religious paintings). The photograph of Paul Martin was taken in the context of his apparently attempting to rein in his supporters from undermining the Prime Minister, the leader of his own party. Martin's body, together with the same light effect, overplays his angelic innocence. It is up to the viewer to decide whether the photographer, in each picture, is creating a parody or glorifying the subject.

(Tom Hanson/CP)

(Tom Hanson/CP)

INDETERMINACY OF REPRESENTATION

The concept of indeterminacy of representation has roots in theoretical physics and discussions of the concept of time. Both the idea and its relation to theoretical physics can be illustrated by a quotation from an article about time: Paul Davies, 'That mysterious flow', *Scientific American* (Sept. 2002): 47. Following the quotation is a rewording of the passage in communicational terms.

. . . [A]n electron hitting an atom may bounce off in one of many directions, and it is normally impossible to predict in advance what the outcome in any given case will be. Quantum indeterminism implies that for a particular quantum state there are many (possibly infinite) alternative futures or potential realities. Quantum mechanics supplies the relative probabilities for each observable outcome, although it won't say which potential future is destined for reality.

But when a human observer makes a measurement, one and only one result is obtained; for example, the rebounding electron will be found moving in a certain direction. In the act of measurement, a single specific reality gets projected from a vast array of possibilities. Within the observer's mind the possible makes a transition to the actual, the open future to the fixed past—which is precisely what we mean by the flux (or passage) of time.

Source: Excerpted from 'That mysterious flow' by Paul Davies. Copyright © 2002 by Scientific America, Inc. All rights reserved.

Here is the parallel.

A television program (or movie, or song, or book) becomes available and garners an audience of a certain size. It is normally impossible to predict in advance how the program will be received. The quantum mechanics of society, that is, knowledge of the content, actors, effects, etc., implies that there are many potential impacts. A close examination of the program and all its variables would suggest that we could assign relative probabilities for each observable outcome, that is, each likely reaction by one or more members of the audience but that will not tell us exactly how an individual audience member is going to react (i.e., which potential future is destined for reality).

From a social framework, we tend to take note of (i.e., the equivalent of measure in physics) extreme reactions such as when a copycat crime is committed after the release of a movie. In the act of taking notice a specific (extreme) reality gets projected from a vast array of possibilities onto the social consciousness (and for that matter, the individual consciousness). The many and varied reactions of all audience members (i.e., the meaning making that goes on by all audience members) are not attended to and, in both the individual and the social consciousness, do not make the transition from the possible to the actually noticeable even though they, too, exist. Moreover, the extreme reaction of one member leads to an imputed causality (between the program and the actions of one, or a few, audience members) and a discourse on the effects of media content. Meanwhile the rich interaction among meaning generating systems—society, the media, and individuals—proceeds yet is little discussed, except as a theoretical communications concept.

---

reader's trust and understanding. Generally speaking, a book, even a textbook, by a single author or author team is more interesting than a compilation or anthology of chapters by multiple authors.

Theoretical Perspectives on the Study of Content

A number of perspectives have been developed and used to study media content: literary criticism; structuralism, semiotics, and post-structuralism; pragmatics and discourse analysis; content analysis; political-economic analysis; and media form or genre analysis. The existence of this multiplicity of perspectives underscores the importance of the notion that it is not which is correct but rather what insight each brings. Also, while it is important to understand these perspectives, it is equally important to understand that there are a variety of ways of interpreting the underlying or implicit meaning as well as the surface or explicit meaning of any message.

LITERARY CRITICISM

The roots of **literary criticism** reach back to when written records first emerged. As soon as something is recorded, it is open to interpretation and discussion. Major movements and changes in world history have focused on examinations and re-examinations of texts. For example, Martin Luther challenged the interpretation of the Bible by the Roman Catholic Church and the right of the Catholic Church to control access to, and be the sole interpreter of, the scriptures. Similarly, in China from the Sung dynasty (AD 900) forward, there existed official interpretations of classic Confucian texts and banned unofficial versions.

Literary criticism, in its modern form, is fairly recent. The discipline was established in the UK in the 1920s when English literature was recognized as a degree subject at Cambridge University. F.R. Leavis, who was involved in establishing the syllabus for English at Cambridge, stressed the independence, the autonomy, of the text. He was interested in the meaning of the text, and this required a delicate, discriminating critical act of interpretation. Interpretation meant interpreting what the author had in mind (conscious), as expressed in the text. (Freudian analysis purported to explain what the author had in his or her unconsciousness.) The text was treated as the vehicle of an individual author-creator. Thus literary studies treated texts as the products of authors—the novels of Jane Austen, the plays of Shakespeare. This approach spread to film studies (the films of Alfred Hitchcock) and became known as **auteur theory**. It focused on the creative control of the director and treated the director as the creative originator of the film.

STRUCTURALISM, SEMIOTICS, AND POST-STRUCTURALISM

In the 1960s a perspective known as **structuralism** became dominant in the social sciences and humanities, especially in the fields of linguistics, anthropology, sociology, psychology, and literature. The aim of structuralism is to discover the underlying pattern or structure of both single texts and genres. The point is to try to see beneath the surface or skin of the narrative and get to the hidden, underlying skeletal structure that holds the body of the story together.

An early and seminal work exemplifying structuralist principles was that of the Russian folklorist Vladimir Propp. In the 1920s, Propp collected over 400 traditional tales from Europe and showed how they all had a similar narrative structure. First he iden-

tified a set of basic (lexical) elements (all stories have certain, similar items): a hero or heroine, a villain, a helper. Second, he described the motifs that propel the narrative from beginning to end. Thus, something must happen to set the hero (usually male) in motion: at some point the villain will disrupt the hero's plans; and at some point the hero will receive aid from a helper (who may or may not be female) to overcome the obstacles in his way. Propp was able to reduce the apparent complexity of a great number of different stories to a simple set of underlying narrative elements that could be combined in a strictly limited number of ways (see Propp, 1970). The structural analysis of narrative has subsequently been applied to all manner of stories, including James Bond novels and films (Eco, 1982a; Bennett and Woollacott, 1987), romantic novels (Radway, 1984), and soap operas (Geraghty, 1991). Figure 4.1 illustrates structuralism at work in the romance genre.

Once narrative structures and surface elements were identified, Propp and other structuralists were able to identify common themes that recurred in stories from all over the world. The magical union of strength and beauty, power in two forms, is a good example of a myth to be found in virtually all cultures. Structuralists would attend to its basic structure. The male embodiment of spiritual and bodily strength (usually a prince) grows up in his kingdom. The female embodiment of beauty and perceptiveness (a princess) grows up in her kingdom. One or both may be disguised in a certain way (a frog prince, a pig princess) or confined (Sleeping Beauty, Cinderella), sometimes as a result of immature vulnerability (plotting by unworthy usurpers, innocence). An event, story, or intervention of some sort induces one (usually the male in a patriarchal society or the female in a matriarchal society) to set out on a quest, sometimes purposeful, sometimes not. The less purposeful the quest the more the coming union is written in the stars or blessed by the gods in the form of an unconscious urge in the seeker. The seeker finds the sought (the object of his or her dreams, again evidence of divine blessing) and recognizes her or him by virtue of her or his or both of their inner senses, inherent kindness, or nobility. This something not only confirms the union but confirms the special qualities of both seeker and sought, which befits them to rule others (divine right of kings). The children of the union are, of course, very special, since they inherit the qualities of both.

Figure 4.1 The Narrative Logic of the Romance

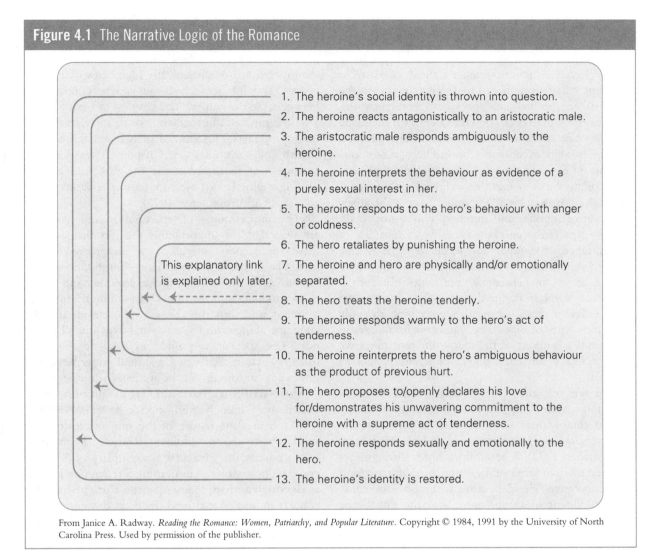

1. The heroine's social identity is thrown into question.
2. The heroine reacts antagonistically to an aristocratic male.
3. The aristocratic male responds ambiguously to the heroine.
4. The heroine interprets the behaviour as evidence of a purely sexual interest in her.
5. The heroine responds to the hero's behaviour with anger or coldness.
6. The hero retaliates by punishing the heroine.
7. The heroine and hero are physically and/or emotionally separated.
8. The hero treats the heroine tenderly.
9. The heroine responds warmly to the hero's act of tenderness.
10. The heroine reinterprets the hero's ambiguous behaviour as the product of previous hurt.
11. The hero proposes to/openly declares his love for/demonstrates his unwavering commitment to the heroine with a supreme act of tenderness.
12. The heroine responds sexually and emotionally to the hero.
13. The heroine's identity is restored.

This explanatory link is explained only later.

From Janice A. Radway. *Reading the Romance: Women, Patriarchy, and Popular Literature.* Copyright © 1984, 1991 by the University of North Carolina Press. Used by permission of the publisher.

Such myths live on. The most obvious twentieth-century example of the myth of the prince/princess ascending the throne was played out by John F. and Jacqueline Kennedy. For many people, not all of whom were American, Kennedy embodied the conquering prince bringing in a new age. So powerful are myths that US film stars have handlers who build up their mythological identity by counselling them only to accept certain roles. Some pursue a particular type of character, e.g., Arnold Schwartzenegger, others pursue versatility, e.g., Brad Pitt.

Following Propp, another influential scholar in the field of structuralism was the Swiss linguist Ferdinand de Saussure. Saussure developed what was later seen as the structural analysis of language (1974). Saussure proposed that language could be scientifically studied in the abstract, as an underlying set of linguistic structures (*langue*, in his term) that could be combined together by any native speaker to produce an utterance (*parole*). The study of the science of signs, later called **semiotics**, was founded by Saussure.

Other structuralists include anthropologist Claude Lévi-Strauss, psychologist Jean Piaget, and linguists Roman Jakobson and Noam Chomsky. Structuralism divorces the 'text' from its moment of creation and moment of reception. Anthropologist Claude Lévi-Strauss extended the structuralist formula into social interaction and meaning making and claimed to show in his work 'not how men think in myths, but how myths operate in men's minds without their being aware of the fact' (Lévi-Strauss, 1969: 12).

Semiotics, an abstracted or more formal version of

structuralism, is the science of signs. There are three basic elements to semiotics: **sign, signifier, signified**. The signified is the object—or event or person—being referred to and the signifier is the device used to represent what is signified. The signifier exists on the plane of expression (aural or visual representation), whereas the signified can be said to exist on the plane of content or reference (that to which the expression refers). The sign encompasses both. The sign is a concept meant to stand for a full and complete representation of an object or event or, as French cultural critic Roland Barthes (1968: 38) would have it, the amalgamation of signifier and signified. This is not to say that the sign is the combined totality of meaning of one instance of signifier and signified—that is, one time in which a word is used in reference to an object. Rather, it is the emergent meaning inherent in numerous signifier/signified pairs—for instance, the many different times we use the word 'pipe' to apply to various types of pipes. The sign is what emerges in our minds as a result of the many different times we come across a particular object of attention and its designation.

The semiotic analysis of popular culture has concentrated on decoding the hidden ideological meanings in things, from wrestling and striptease to the Louvre, television, popular novels, and advertisements (see Barthes, 1972). A semiotic analysis distinguishes between the two levels of meaning: the denotative and the connotative. The denotative is the obvious, natural, self-evident meaning—what you literally see or hear, for instance, in an advertisement. The connotative is what is implied, but not actually communicated explicitly.

Ads are filled with connotative meaning, as illustrated in the appendix to this chapter. For example, in an attempt to capture the 25–40-year-old age group, in late 2002 and early 2003, Cadillac ran ads stressing power and competitiveness by means of the most advanced technology (always the biggest ads and always in the best locations, such as the back cover of magazines). On the other hand, other car ads stress fun (the new VW bug) or coolness (the new BMW Mini). In each case the advertiser is trying to recapture the appeal of a brand of yesterday.

An advertisement contains a plurality of meanings (a polysemy). On the surface is a denoted image, which at first seems banal and obvious. But the image is saturated with implied or connoted meanings and values that, in combination with other saturated

images to which they refer, form the basis of a full image and lifestyle necessarily encompassing the advertised object. Barthes thought the task of the semiotician was to unmask the ideologies of a bourgeois, capitalist society, through the connections between, say, the natural attractiveness of fresh food or a well-composed photograph and the interests of capitalist producers. This kind of analysis was taken up in British cultural studies (see Chapter 5), and semiotic analysis, à la Barthes, became the preferred way of reading cultural texts (see, for example, Williamson's analysis of advertisements, 1978).

The shortcomings of structuralism and semiotics are several. Most important is the fact that each of these approaches underplays the importance of the particular in favour of the general—for instance, *langue* in contrast to *parole*. The individual speaker and listener, or producer and consumer, of communication; the moment, and thus the context of creation; and the audience, along with its situational dynamic, all disappear. The speaker is posited as a silent centre of thought, action, aesthetic, or moral judgement; the moment is universal; and the audience is untheorized.

Post-structuralism, the main proponent of which was French philosopher Jacques Derrida (1981), brings the nature of the subject-creator forward as particular to a moment. Rather than attempting to portray the particular as exemplary of the general case, post-structuralism, using a technique known as **deconstruction**, focuses on the particularity of a context in and of itself and discusses the significance of the unique and distinctive details of a particular story, told by a particular author, at a particular time, in a particular setting. This focus, as can be imagined, causes the notion of authorship as a general term to vanish in front of the eyes of the deconstructing post-structuralist.

In the same spirit as post-structuralism and in fact preceding it, Roland Barthes in his famous essay, 'Death of the Author' (1977), argued for an end to the author as the source of meaning in any text (film, novel, TV, play). ('Auteur theory' has not died but has become understood as only one window on the reality of the text.) The source of meaning, Barthes argued, is the reader, since the text only becomes meaningful in the act of being read and understood. The effect of this startling reversal was the 'empowerment' of the reader or audience. No longer chained to the dull task of trying to find out what Shakespeare 'had in mind' when he wrote Hamlet (an impossible task anyway, argued Barthes), the reader was free to create his or her own meanings, to open up rather than close down the meaning of the text. Gone was the notion of the one true and authentic meaning of the text. Texts were polysemic and had a number of different possible meanings. The conception of reading also changed from the passive absorption of the text's imposed meaning to an active exploration of the text's possibilities.

This shift in interpretation—more fancily called textual hermeneutics—parallels a shift in audience studies away from the view of audiences as passive and powerless, at the mercy of the meanings imposed by the dominant values of the culture industry. It endorses that notion of the autonomy, or independence, of the audience in the act of viewing or reading. It supports a view of the power of readers and viewers actively engaged with and exploring the meanings of cultural texts. This approach has been most vigorously touted by John Fiske (1987) with respect to television viewing (this perspective will be more fully explored in Chapter 5).

PRAGMATICS AND DISCOURSE ANALYSIS

Although pragmatics and discourse analysis have significant differences, they share two points. First, they study the interaction involved in communication. Second, they take as their starting point that part of language rejected by Saussure, namely actual utterances (*paroles*). These two approaches are part of a wider development in a number of disciplines, including philosophy, linguistics, social psychology, and sociology, in which ordinary language usage (conversation, talk) is taken as the object of study. From such studies has emerged a different view of language from that of structuralism (which, as we have seen, examines underlying, abstract linguistic structures).

The philosophy of ordinary language, first developed in the later work of philosopher Ludwig Wittgenstein and extended by the Oxford philosopher J.L. Austin, takes a pragmatic (practical) view of language. Language is almost always more than talk for talk's sake. To say something is to do something: to make a promise or an offer, to impart a refusal or an acceptance. Language as utterance is always a social act and an interaction between two or more speaker/hearers.

Philosophers, linguists, and sociologists have been intrigued by what the concept of communication

entails as a social interaction, and this has led to the reopening of a field of study called **pragmatics** (Levinson, 1985). This field of study has links to American pragmatist philosophers, such as John Dewey and C.S. Peirce, and to the interpersonal psychology of Paul Watzlawick, Janet Beavin, and Don Jackson and their seminal book, *Pragmatics of Human Communication* (1967).

Central to pragmatics is a recognition that all actual utterances are context-specific. The meaning of what is said is related to the context in which it is said. To illustrate this notion consider a simple utterance such as 'give me that'. As an abstract written sentence we understand its general meaning, but we cannot know what 'that' is, or who 'me' refers to, or in what actual situation the remark is made. In conversational context, all these things would be quite clear and obvious. Of central interest to pragmatics is the study of **implicatures** (implied meanings).

Very often, in ordinary talk there is a difference between what is said and what is meant. Or, to put it differently, we often express ourselves indirectly rather than directly. For instance, instead of saying 'Pass the salt' we normally say 'Would you please pass the salt?' Notice that this latter utterance is a request, not a question, yet it is phrased as a question. If the person to whom it is directed treated it as a question by answering yes or no (without actually passing the salt) we would be surprised. If we press our analysis further and ask why is the construction 'Would you please pass the salt?' normally preferred to 'Pass the salt', we might say because it is more polite. The notion of politeness here entails a notion of consideration for the other in the social interaction (Brown and Levinson, 1987).

A fundamental perception of pragmatics is that insofar as language is communicative (and not all utterances are), communication entails a co-operative principle or an attention to the needs, feelings, and circumstances of others in the conversation. Thus, when we talk to others we tailor the way in which we talk in order to take the other person into account. A parent talking to a child, a teacher talking to a pupil, and teenagers talking together all design not only what they say, but also how they say it. This allows them to take the other persons into account and thereby let them know that they are doing so.

Discourse analysis is another perspective with a long history, dating back more than 2,000 years to the discipline of *rhetorica*. *Rhetorica* was oriented to effective persuasiveness and dealt with the planning, organization, specific operations, and performance of speech in political and legal settings (van Dijk, 1985, vol. 1: 1). A passage, speech, or performance can succeed or fail based on the impact it makes on its audience.

Discourse analysis points to media patterns and conventions and their success in being taken for granted, as evidenced in the satisfaction and understanding of audiences. It points to what is privileged (emphasized) in such apparently natural conventions. It also provides a framework for understanding, for example, prime ministerial television appearances as discursive elements in politics. A discourse analyst might note that beyond the content itself, political debates represent a challenge mounted against the incumbent to dislodge that incumbent from a discourse of power. On the other side, it is the job of the incumbent to constrain the pretender in a discourse of questionable power-seeking. As Dutch linguist Teun van Dijk (1985, vol. 3: 8) notes, ethnographers offer up a good general approach as follows: 'People of category x (men, women, elderly, leading persons, etc.) typically use form y (intonation, pitch, lexical item, narrative form, code, etc.) in context z (with a given purpose, speaking to a specific person, and in a given social event).'

Modern discourse analysis is a mix of sociology and linguistics applied to the study of discourse: units of expression longer than a single sentence (the standard work is Brown and Yule, 1983). Thus discourse analysis looks at extended utterances, as in a conversation, a monologue on radio (Montgomery, 1991), or dialogue on TV. Modern discourse analysis is typically attentive to **deixis** (the contextual character of utterance) and topic organization and management (what is being talked about).

QUANTITATIVE CONTENT ANALYSIS

Quantitative content analysis or, more commonly, **content analysis** differs from the approaches we have outlined so far in two ways. First, it emphasizes quantitative elements, specifically, the number of occurrences of a particular category of phenomenon. For instance, how often are minorities covered in news stories (and how)? Second, it lacks a theoretical underpinning, though it has a methodology.

Content analysis works as follows. After a first overview, the researcher sets up units of analysis—phrases, sentences, nouns, verbs, adjectives, paragraphs, column inches, placement, accompanying illustrations, categories of spokespersons quoted or cited, and so

forth. The analyst then determines categories of meaning or themes that appear to be salient to a particular piece of communication. They may be salient on the basis of the focus of the author or on the basis of the interests of the analyst. With units and categories in place, the analyst counts various types of occurrences and perhaps their partnership with other types of occurrences, that is, words with pictures, long pieces with prominent placement. On the basis of these frequencies of occurrence and their relations with others, the analyst can provide a reading of an article, a newspaper, the treatment of an issue over time and by numbers of media outlets, and so on. Not just occurrences are noticed. Non-occurrences may be just as important. Content analysis can also be used for comparative purposes. Thus, during the military rivalry of the former USSR and the US, the media treatment of actions by both sides could be compared. Content studies can also show continuities and changes over time in the representation of issues, social roles, and attitudes to authority.

A content analysis focusing on the coverage of Latin America in the US press over time revealed that the dominant definition of news—what was most often reported about Latin America—was disasters, such as earthquakes and volcanoes. Over the 1970s there was a gradual shift towards a focus on dictators and banana republics. And more recently, there has been a further shift towards a broader and more accurate collection of information. Such an analysis is revealing not only in terms of the triviality of the news definition of an entire continent but also in terms of the significant absences—the failure to offer any serious account of the economic, political, or social developments of that region of the world. Likewise, content studies of social representation have pointed to the distribution of those who come to define the social order and are seen to be important social actors. In the main they are white, professional males. In contrast, black males are portrayed as criminals, athletes, or musicians.

Content analyses of media can examine anything from a set of news programs to an individual news item, story, photograph, or visual. Generally, researchers attempt to define the logic of the presentation—for instance, the positioning of the various elements in a piece or the totality of pieces being considered. The point is to work towards an articulation of the internal relations among those elements. For example, attention may be drawn to the fact that labour is usually associated with on-the-street events such as disruptive demonstrations, while management is analyzed in the context of the controlled, peaceful, quiet environment of a plush executive office. The implication of this way of using sources is that, even in a lockout, labour is shown as the instigator of the stoppage and management as the patient victim.

Other content studies of news deal with what gets included in the news and what does not. These studies then tend to turn away from content and towards the process of news-gathering and the influence of professional ideals and the goals of owners (see Gans, 1979; Tuchman, 1978; Schlesinger, 1978).

Some of the serious difficulties with content analysis are based on the lack of theorization in this approach. As such, content analysts tend to provide relatively unsophisticated readings of their findings, and baseline data of media treatment are given in very few instances as a foundation for interpreting their findings. Similarly, the role of the media as sources for the confirmation of a community's concerns and interests is rarely considered. The context of repeated mentions of particular events, actions, attitudes, and so forth is rarely fully discussed and sometimes goes unmentioned. Content analysis provides insufficient analysis of the constructed scenario, which might allow a person to determine whether further treatment of the issue outside the time period mentioned would lead to much different conclusions.

POLITICAL-ECONOMIC ANALYSIS

American communications theorist George Gerbner (1977) claimed that the reason we see so much sex and violence on television is because these provide cheap and simple ways to portray power. He who has a gun is in charge. She who has the greatest beauty holds the greatest power. Similarly, the preponderance of game shows is a matter of economics. The same is true for music videos. Political-economic analysis of media content is concerned with what sells and at what cost. For instance, what genres of movies are audiences attending? Which actors draw the greatest crowds? Which TV time slots bring in the most viewers? Political-economic analysis aims to uncover the political and economic factors that determine media production and content.

But such an analysis is never simple. Take, for instance, the success of the movie *Titanic* compared to the utter failure of the movies *Waterworld* and *Deep Impact*. Simple economics does not explain the pro-

duction of these movies—though the investors of these movies were all willing to spend about $200 million, a perfectly acceptable movie can be made for $20 million. But the makers of *Titanic*, *Waterworld*, and *Deep Impact* were playing a different game of much higher risk but with a greater potential reward. They were intent on making spectacular movies that would command so much attention and attract sufficient audiences worldwide that they would cover all costs and return a handsome profit. When James Cameron shook his Oscar in the air at the Academy Awards in 1998 and called out, 'I'm king of the world', not only was he repeating an emotional line from his movie but he was also claiming highest ground in the world of movie directors. The subtext was 'I'm the guy who can spend over $200 million and come up with a movie that works. Eat your hearts out Steven Spielberg (producer, *Deep Impact*) and Kevin Costner (producer and actor, *Waterworld*)!' Political economy combined with hubris.

In short, the political analytic equations are not straightforward. They are certainly not 'bean-counting' equations, nor are they a matter of simple economics. Rather, they encompass power; tiered markets; market positioning of stars, directors, and production houses; and much more. For instance, in filmmaking, financing through joint production agreements can account for content as well as the mix of actors and locations; and the need to fill screens and protect market share can explain dominant genres. While the political-economic framework has most often been used to talk about the influence of owners on staff hiring, the allocation of resources, globalization, and so forth, it reaches right down to the shape of productions—and not just of movies. A knowledgeable analyst can read a book, magazine, or newspaper for the economic and political dynamics involved in its production.

THE 'SUCCESS' OF WATERWORLD

Just to illustrate the difference between perspectives one might take on a movie, consider *Waterworld*. While a box-office failure, the movie can be viewed as a marvellous comedy infused with hippie values and with a special appeal to those who appreciate ganja humour.

GENRE OR MEDIA FORM ANALYSIS

Another framework of analysis that can be used as a complement to any of the above frameworks is derived from McLuhan's notion of the medium as the message. The presentation of meaning is constrained by the medium itself and how it structures and carries content. Beyond that, it is constrained by the genre within a particular medium, e.g., action movies or chick flicks as a subset of all movies.

Of the various media available, each consistently selects certain elements for emphasis, which leads to a bias about events that varies across each medium. The best comparative example (which combines both genre and media form) is the television news team of on-air reporter and camera operator versus the single newspaper reporter. The news team intrudes more on the event and operates within the constraints of a television news story, which demands good visuals. On the other hand, a newspaper story depends for its strength on various elements, including a logical presentation of the facts and thorough analysis. Each medium organizes and encourages particular elements of content and particular relations between those elements. These elements and relations are both distinct to each medium and forever shifting with the creativity of the practitioners in each: they provide the back-

---

ON ORSON WELLES

Paul Heyer has created an interesting text/audio analysis of Orson Welles's *War of the Worlds* that is a media form analysis in that it deals with the intuitive understanding Welles had of radio as a medium. Heyer's article is in *Canadian Journal of Communication* 28, 2 (2003): 149–65. Or go on-line at: www.cjc-online.ca

---

ground to the effectiveness of any individual piece. The following subsections examine a number of major media forms and their biases.

The Advertisement

The advertisement is an invention of profound significance to capitalist society. It lies at the very foundation of the commercial mass media, allowing for the production and distribution of information and entertainment across a wide segment of the population at very little cost to the consumer. For a surcharge paid on every other consumer product (the cost of ads is built into the cost of products), an advertising industry of immense size and power was developed first in the United States and then worldwide, in every country where people have disposable income.

THE LANGUAGE OF MOVIES AND TV

Part of the structuring process of each media form is that it develops a language that the audience comes to understand. The following are examples of 'languages' the audience has come to learn through TV and film content.

All police investigations require at least one visit to a strip club.

All beds have L-shaped sheets to allow the man to bare his chest and the woman to hide hers.

Ventilation systems are perfect hiding places. They reach to every part of a building, are noiseless to enter and easy to move along both horizontally and vertically, and no one thinks to look there.

German accents are sufficient should you wish to pass for a German military officer.

When alone, foreigners speak English to one another.

All women staying in haunted houses are compelled to investigate strange noises in their most revealing underwear.

Cars that crash almost always burst into flames.

Any person waking from a nightmare sits bolt upright.

All bombs are fitted with large time displays that indicate exactly when they are to go off.

You can always find a chainsaw if you need one.

Having a job of any kind ensures that a father will forget his son's eighth birthday.

Any lock can be picked easily unless it is on a door to a burning building in which a child is imprisoned.

The more a man and woman hate each other initially the greater the chance they will fall in love in the end.

Adaptation of 'A sampler of one-liners and true facts', by Gary Borders, *The Daily Sentinel* (Nacodoches). Reprinted by permission of the author.

While in the past advertising was a way to increase sales by supplementing or making known consumer satisfaction, it has increasingly become the means whereby producers create needs, launch products, and maintain sales. As numerous commentators have pointed out, we are either intimidated or tempted by advertisers into buying advertised products. The advertiser creates the need and then persuades us that the product fills that need. Advertising can also bypass product performance by boasting enough so that the boast, rather than the performance, becomes reality. For instance, you drink Gatorade because your body is a high-performance engine needing specialized products for sustenance.

In being responsible for the production of advertisements, advertising agencies have learned a great deal about the persuasive communication process. They have taught producers about consumers, showing them how to pitch their product with the audience in mind, how to layer their goods with symbols structured to persuade the consumer to purchase, and how to make the consumer feel satisfied with his or her purchase. These are the essential components and aims of advertisements.

Because so much is at stake and the constraints of space or time are so great, there is an astonishingly high investment involved in the making of advertisements. It is not at all uncommon for a 30-second television advertisement to cost more to produce than a 30-minute program. Millions of dollars of production investment in the advertised product hang in the balance. And, of course, there is the cost paid to media outlets to have the advertisement seen or heard again and again. Moreover, no surface is safe from advertising, whether the sole of a shoe, the side of a spacecraft, the sky, the walls and stall doors in washrooms, or mountainsides.

To launch an advertising campaign the producer first selects a target market. The campaign inextricably links some prized attribute of high-status members of

LOOKING FOR AD SPACE

As if the space over urinals was not enough, *Time* magazine used escalator handrails in the Metro Toronto Convention Centre to remind people of its existence. The ING bank used the floor of a major walkway serving all three of Vancouver's Seabus, Skytrain, and West Coast Express public transit systems. Some enterprising entrepreneurs, operating seemingly on the wrong side of the law, scattered ads for fake photo IDs on the streets and sidewalks in the nightclub district of Vancouver, and advertising can even be found on gas pumps.

this market, such as attractiveness to the opposite sex, to the consumption of the product. Essentially, members of the target market are presented with an idealized, supercharged image of themselves that they can connect to through the purchase of a never-ending stream of products purported to be crucial to their lifestyle and values. Consuming these articles may not only feed narcissism but also provide a means of gaining status or of maintaining it through a feeling of belonging to the group and a reinforcement of self-worth. Using this process, the producer generates sales in the target audience, as well as among people who envy and aspire to be like those who are part of the target market.

An interesting aspect of advertisements is their relation to the products, particularly when brands are essentially identical in their basic defining characteristics, such as taste and alcohol content for beer or cleaning capacity for detergent. In such cases, producers identify what image consumers have of themselves and their product and what is appealing about that image. They then design ad campaigns based on an idealized version of that image. Attributes are identified for the product—for instance, with beer, the purity of the ingredients or the esoteric technology of the brewing process—that appeal to the consumer's self-image. At the same time, advertisers attribute to the depicted consumers characteristics designed to flatter. Completely missing in this environment is the obvious distinctive attribute of the product that one might think would be the basis of choice, such as the taste of a beer.

The convergence of product attributes among competing brands gives companies both a need and a great deal of power to manipulate the image of both product and consumer in order to capture a particular market segment (Grady, 1983). It also places market share and brand control in the hands of the 'spin doctors', the advertising agencies that design the ad campaigns and the marketing managers who capture market share based on the size of promotional funds. While the market is dominated by large companies that invest heavily in marketing, two significant vulnerabilities exist for these large firms: the emergence of generic products with virtually no advertising expenses, and the emergence of small players with a genuinely different product. These vulnerabilities are very real and are constantly in play, whether the product is beer, soap, music, books and authors, or films. Once the marketing game is in play, it has a life of its own. Consumer boredom (or love of the new) keeps the advertising world turning.

Three other types of advertising are significant. The first includes advertisements for a company rather than its products—usually called *institutional advertising*. These ads are designed to propagate a favourable corporate image and promote the virtues of a corporation rather than a particular product or product line. In some cases, such as in advertisements for the energy industry, the responsible nature of the individual company or the industry as a whole is put forward explicitly with a content of concern that has either been expressed by the public or that the corporations have discerned through market research.

The second type of advertisements includes those that masquerade as pieces of reporting. They have been called a variety of names, one of which is **advertorials**. These advertisements present descriptive material on, for example, the contribution of a company to the larger economy. They are usually prepared for print publications, apparently written by a journalist, but in fact written by an employee or agent of the company or agency that is the subject of the article. A weaker form of advertorials comes in the form of material written by publishers on a subject—for example, gardening or the pleasures of an outside barbecue—that will attract producers of associated products to advertise in that issue or section. In this sense, the automobile, travel, homes, and entertainment sections of newspapers are all just advertorials. Television infomercials, half-hour programs pushing particular products, are similar to advertorials. They now account for over $1 billion in sales in the US.

The third type of advertising is called **product placement** or **plugging**. Until the last decade or so, Hollywood film producers portrayed themselves as putting out 'pure entertainment', meaning that they did not systematically attempt to promote products, take political stances, or teach public morality. However, evidence suggests otherwise. As early as 1961 product placement was in use in Billy Wilder's movie, *One, Two, Three*, which blatantly plugged Coca-Cola. Moreover, the blacklisting of persons in the industry who were purported Communists during the era of McCarthyism demonstrates Hollywood's ideological sensitivity.

Product placement is now *de rigueur*. It is part of the financing formula of filmmaking and is defended as an injection of reality into the movie world. As US media commentator Mark Crispin Miller (1990) has noted, plugsters choose projects that offer them maximum

MOVIES AND PLUGGED PRODUCTS: THE NEW HOLLYWOOD

Here is a sampling of product placements in 1997 movies:

Volcano: Land Rover
The Horse Whisperer: Calvin Klein, Land Rover
Speed 2: Chrysler, Tag Heuer watches
Men in Black: Ray-Ban sunglasses, Sprint long-distance
Hercules: General Motors, McDonald's, Nestlé
George of the Jungle: McDonald's

Batman and Robin: Apple computers, Frito-Lay, Kellogg's, Taco Bell
The Lost World: Burger King, General Mills, JVC, Kodak, Mercedes-Benz, Timberland, Tropicana
Flubber: Range Rover
Tomorrow Never Dies: BMW cars and motorcycles, Ericsson cellphones, Smirnoff vodka, Visa cards, Omega watches, L'Oréal cosmetics, Heineken beer.

Source: *Globe and Mail*, 1997.

control, even telling the film producers precisely where they want to see their clients' brands: 'The plug, in other words, must not just "foreground" the crucial name or image but also flatter it—that is, brightly reaffirm the product's advertising.' This is clearly exemplified by the plugs for Pepsi in the three *Back to the Future* movies starring Michael J. Fox, who also appeared in Pepsi commercials on TV. One of the biggest factors in plugging is how lucrative it can be for filmmakers. For instance, James Bond switched from an Aston Martin to a BMW in *GoldenEye* because BMW offered up a $15 million ad campaign to advertise the movie and the car. In

fact, agreements with eight promotional partners netted $100 million in free publicity for this film (*Vancouver Sun*, 6 Dec. 1997, E12). (For a good analysis of plugging, see Wasko et al., 1993.)

The expansion of plugging in movies illustrates how the basic relationship between content and advertisement has been distorted over the years—a change that has been underplayed by communication researchers. Advertisers buy audiences—that everyone acknowledges. What they do not acknowledge is that they purchase audiences in certain frames of mind. No advertiser is going to support a publication, broadcast-

FAVOURABLE COVERAGE AND PUFF EDITORIALS

Another part of plugging is the role newspapers have in promoting their advertisers. In fact, favourable coverage of advertisers is expected of newspapers. The number of examples of industries effectively boycotting a Canadian newspaper for a period of time as a result of unfavourable coverage demonstrates that fact.

If you look at real-estate sections, they are nothing but promotional sections for various parts of the housing industry. So accepting are most Canadians of such favourable coverage that in face of the scandal surrounding leaky condos in British Columbia, no one publicly took the newspapers to task for not having exposed this problem, which had been growing over the years through a lack of responsibility on the part of builders and building inspection codes. One journalist lost his job after writing a critical article on the subject years before it became an admitted issue. Of course

his employer denied the connection.

Not only do media shy away from critical coverage, they often supply quite positive coverage at no cost. On 3 May 1999, the *Globe and Mail* ran what it called 'A special editorial supplement on *Star Wars Episode 1: The Phantom Menace*'. Eight full pages were devoted to introducing the movie, its characters, spinoff toys, puff pieces on ticket sales, costumes, connections to real science, and so on. The cost of such advertising would have been well into the six figures.

However, it is not only commercial enterprises that are the beneficiaries of puffery. A great number of column inches were devoted to Conrad Black's attempt to gain a peerage in 1999. What importance this issue had for anyone but Black and his wife, columnist Barbara Amiel, is hard to imagine.

ing program, or Web site with content that conflicts with their products or that may cause the audience to adversely react to their products. For instance, escapes to Las Vegas are incompatible with programs exposing the human tragedy that can result from gambling. Given such constraints, the needs of advertisers can dictate the nature of content. Such advertiser interference upsets journalists, program producers, and editors, but as direct government funding continues to dry up for public broadcasting and as the need to make greater profits in film and other media increases, the influence of advertisers will continue to grow.

The News Story

The news story is a distinctive genre that differs in its structure according to the medium within which it appears. Nevertheless, all news stories share certain fundamental characteristics. Canadian sociologists Richard Ericson, Patricia Baranek, and Janet Chan (1989) developed a set of criteria to describe the characteristics that make events newsworthy. Peter Desbarats (1990: 110), former dean of journalism at the University of Western Ontario, summarizes these criteria:

* Simplification: an event must be recognized as significant and relatively unambiguous in its meaning.
* Dramatization: a dramatized version of the event must be able to be presented.
* Personalization: events must have personal significance to someone.
* Themes and continuity: events that fit into preconceived themes gain in newsworthiness.

* Consonance: events make the news more readily when they fit the reporters' preconceived notions of what should be happening.
* The Unexpected: unexpected events that can be expected within frames of reference used by reporters are newsworthy.

A more traditional description of the characteristics of the news story posits that such stories are organized according to an **inverted pyramid**. This means simply that a summary of the 'important information' is placed at the beginning, followed by a description of the development of the story and the context in which it happened. By 'important information' journalists mean the five 'w's, one 'h', and one 's-w'. That is to say, the story leads off with *who, what, when, where, why, how,* and then *so what*.

Journalism textbooks emphasize clarity and conciseness in news stories. Language must be simple and straightforward. Clarity is achieved by avoiding clichés, jargon, and excessively complex phraseology. Conciseness is partially achieved through the use of the active voice. Neither unnecessary words nor redundancies should appear. Pace and tone are crucial. Ideas must be introduced at a pace the reader can follow. The tone of the story must reflect both subject matter and treatment of the material.

Finally, news stories must have **leads**. Most often they are direct, sometimes giving the five 'w's in the first sentence. They must also serve to capture the attention of readers and orient them to the story. Delayed leads come in the second paragraph or sentence and exploit the curiosity of the reader established by an introductory delay.

NEWS TABLOIDS

The inverted pyramid has aided the development of newspaper tabloids. They gain their name from the half-sized format of the pages, which makes them easy to read en route to work by public transit. The tabloids are meant to be quick and impressionistic, often complemented by soft porn and low-level boosterism of actual and potential advertisers. More than broadsheets, they play into the predispositions of their readership, which are determined by market research. Events are often overdramatized and are interpreted as signals that things are often out of control. Headlines regularly emphasize the bizarre, as the examples cited here illustrate.

Teacher swallows live baby mice

People near death hear the same heavenly music

Psychic killed in car wreck brings herself back to life

Wife disguises self as chair to catch cheating husband

Elvis dies, again

73-year-old woman gives birth to triplets!

We've found the fountain of youth! Tomatoes, raisins and aspirin.

With the five 'w's up front, and with the constant emphasis on human interest, what the news brings us is events rather than issues. As any public interest group knows (especially Greenpeace), any amount of informed analysis about a particular issue will never bring it onto the front pages. But an event, whether it involves chaining oneself to a fence or barricading major traffic routes, can produce saturation coverage. Prior provision of information and analysis to a columnist is a good method of getting some issues discussed, but the event itself moves the issue to front and centre in the mass media.

Television versus Print: The Camera versus the Reporter

In the print medium, a journalist tells the story. This places the journalist, and indeed the paper, squarely between the event and the reader. As such the reporter and editor are seen to be interveners in the construction of the news even if they might not want to be. It is they who must tell the story. The medium itself prevents the press from removing itself from this role as intervener, interpreter, or mediator even if journalists wanted to—which is dubious in these days of the replacement of objectivity with fairness and the rise of advocacy journalism. In contrast, the camera, generally speaking, anaesthetizes the audience to the intervention of the reporter.

The most obvious difference between newspaper news and television news is the almost total reliance of television on visual presentation. The visuals are not merely moving pictures that complement a prepared text spoken by an announcer. The visual presentation actually structures the story and a text is built around the visual impact.

While a video camera is extremely intrusive for the actors of an event, it is quite invisible to the viewer, hence its anaesthetic or disarming effect. It claims, by its ability to record sound and picture, a veracity that no other medium can match. In its ability to record an event, it brings the news to us from the mouths of the participants. We think that we are seeing the actual happenings of an event, made understandable by on-the-spot observers and participants. The interviewer and his or her crew act as solicitors of information. Presenting that information and synthesizing it, television news producers are apparently removed from a primary role of interpretation. But they are not removed: they construct news products by synthesizing events and transforming them into an understandable format.

For television news producers the trick is to edit the material in such a way that the editing appears unobtrusive. The visual coverage of the event must be simple enough to orient the viewer, but it must not appear incomplete. The sentences and phrases that are recorded and subsequently used in the final piece must be succinct and directly relevant. The speakers' identities must be obvious and their involvement as observers or participants must be valid. Politicians or experts who can speak in 'clips' and who can move comfortably and vividly for the camera are often the people sought out for background to stories. What is primary in the television news story is the directing of the news-crew interviewer and interviewees to establish the elements of a story that can then be pieced together as a snippet of life.

The camera never lies, or so we are led to believe. In fact, merely by framing, the camera always lies, because it gives the audience the sense that the picture they see is the whole picture. The camera **frames**, and the story producers edit. The video production of news, or of any other material, puts some things in the picture and keeps other things out. It can emotionalize with the extreme close-up or provide a 'more objective' panorama. It can present the authoritative distance of the medium close-up against a neutral backdrop or include an entire visual environment and attendant mood. The camera only tells its own version of the truth.

Investigative Television Reporting

A common observation about investigative television reporting is that it has become a non-fiction adventure story. This construction has been applied to the US program *60 Minutes*, in which each of the permanent star investigative reporters is presented as an inveterate single-combat warrior seeking after truth in a corrupt world, exposing the liars and cheats of the world to the public eye.

Given the flexibilities and power of the television medium, investigative television reporting demands an extremely high level of trust from the audience. The credibility of the program and host is absolutely essential. For instance, the scripts of an award-winning program in which Canada's pre-eminent investigative reporter, the late Eric Malling, inquired into the safety of the highly computerized Airbus A320 (Canadian Association of Journalists, 1991) provide an illustration of the necessity of that trust, as well as indicating some of the techniques used in investigative TV reporting.

The first technique used by Malling and his producers was to set up the test pilot, Michel Asseline, as a credible witness. Asseline piloted an Airbus A320 that crashed in 1988 at the Paris air show. Malling establishes Asseline's credentials, his consistency, his reasonable tone. The program then introduces an Airbus Industrie spokesman, Robert Alizart, who states that Asseline owes his life to the plane, thus implying he is ungrateful. The effect is that the Airbus spokesperson seems harsh.

Malling then introduces further evidence that appears quite damaging to Airbus Industrie. It is intercut and called into question with commentary from Asseline. The program producers build a case of seemingly damning evidence and then show a confrontation with a second Airbus Industrie spokesman, who seems to obfuscate, to want to escape, to want to change the subject. The program then presents the Airbus spokesmen, as if cornered, building countercharges into their obfuscation.

What the program has done is intercut Airbus into a storyline with established, sympathetic characters and used them to build an accusatory dynamic. They are presented in the viewer's mind as defensive mouthpieces for a company probably all too willing to risk the lives of the general public for reasons of hubris and profit. The *coup de grâce* comes when, in response to their countercharges, Malling inserts the name of their apparently intended victim, Asseline. Immediately after naming Asseline, in a surprising move, Malling articulates the charges that Airbus officials seem to want to make directly against Asseline but dare not for reasons of libel. Malling refers to Asseline as obsessed and gives the reasons. Malling further discounts the credibility of the Airbus spokesmen by seeming to put words into their mouths, extending their counterattack to a personal vendetta against Asseline, the innocent scapegoat.

The point—and it is easy to overlook when carefully chosen words and compelling images are passing by on the television screen, and one does not have the advantage of reading slowly, checking back, and reading again—is that 'the story' is a constructed one. It is constructed from hours of tape, where interviewees know only what they are told about what their adversaries say (which is often only what the producers want them to know), and where the editors not only choose what parts of the interviews to include but also in which order and in what context.

ISOLATING ELEMENTS OF MEDIA CONTENT

A good exercise, and an excellent methodology that provides insight into the workings of some media, is to isolate one element from its context. Turn off the sound of a movie and watch the visuals; record the soundtrack of an investigative TV program and listen just to the words (a transcription is even better, as the above example shows); or read the lyrics of a song you have not heard.

The impact of the story is not at issue. Malling won a journalism prize, and, after seeing the program, many people were nervous about flying in an Airbus A320. Still, there have been no major disasters attributable to the computer control of the aircraft, the target of Malling's story. While it may well have been that the computers overrode Asseline at the Paris air show when the plane crashed and that he was wrongly scapegoated, the plane has proven to be safe.

And so we return to trust. Obviously there are limits to the distortion that producers can introduce, but television provides substantial flexibility. The audience can only rely on professional journalistic ethics and the need to maintain credibility over the long term. However, in certain situations, such as war and social unrest, those ethics may break down.

Soaps

The first soap opera, *Painted Dreams*, was developed in 1930 in the US by a schoolteacher named Irna Phillips and broadcast by radio station WGN, the station owned by the *Chicago Tribune* (Williams, 1992). In 1933 an advertising agency, Bleckett-Sample-Hummert, developed three shows for its soap company clients and went on to become a soap opera factory (LaGuardia, 1977).

The soaps were a popular cultural form designed to socialize a home-confined, female audience with disposable income into the art of consuming. In a sense, soaps represented the life of the fictitious satisfied consumer whose worldly needs were entirely taken care of by the various products that she had purchased for her family. Once these needs were satisfied, she could turn her mind to dreaming of a richer, more fulfilling life found in the Gothic and romance novels of the 1930s. However, pure fantasy was not the only powerful opiate. Not long after the soaps had established themselves in the US, a kind of realistic fantasy program was developed featuring characters who were professional people and whose lives were made of the stuff of fiction: they were important politically, became wealthy and famous, had wonderful romances, and so forth. In this manner an illusion of reality was developed that has carried through to the present-day soap opera. Our discussion of the soaps will take us through this illusion into the dominant themes of today's soaps and then into the grammar of the medium, the devices used to achieve the realistic illusion.

Along with news, soaps are the most analyzed kind of narrative genre on TV. They have been of particular interest to feminist studies because they are a preferred form of entertainment for female viewers in many countries. Analysis has concentrated on the form and content of soaps and on the pleasures they offer viewers.

A basic distinction is drawn between the narrative structure of soaps and classic narrative. In classic narrative the story has a beginning, middle, and end. The movement of the narrative is strongly organized towards the resolution of the story's riddle or enigma: the hero kills the villain (any James Bond story or Clint Eastwood western); the cop finally catches the criminal; the murderer is exposed (Agatha Christie); or the heroine gets her man. The story then focuses on one primary character (male or female) and moves to a final moment in which all is explained and everything is resolved—the end.

Soaps, however, have no sense of an ending. In sharp contrast to the 'closed' stories of classic narratives, soaps are 'open', never-ending narratives, which sometimes go on for years, even decades. In the US, the daytime soap *All My Children* has been running since the late 1930s—first on radio and then, since the 1950s, on TV. In the UK, the BBC radio serial *The Archers* has been going since 1948, while on TV, *Coronation Street* has been on continuously since 1961. (Note that *The Archers* is presented on BBC, that is, non-commercial radio. This suggests that the form has a life of its own beyond the commercial context.) Soaps have no obvious single hero/heroine. The narrative is a social world of the entwined lives of maybe a dozen or more characters, who are intermittently but continuously present in the story. While the classic narrative usually has only a single storyline, with perhaps a subplot, the soaps have several different stories that run at the same time and often overlap with each other. (See Geraghty, 1991, for an excellent early account of the structure of soaps.)

These are the most basic features of the narrative structure of soaps. In terms of their content and style—what they're about and how characters and plot are presented—some distinctions need to be made. In the US a distinction is drawn between daytime and prime-time soaps. The former are shown in the afternoon and achieve relatively small but loyal audiences of female viewers and college students. The latter are shown at peak viewing times in the evenings and often have strong family audiences. Prime-time television soaps have higher production values (are much more expensive to produce) with glossy sets, costumes, and a tendency to focus on the lives of the rich. A further distinction needs to be made between the styles of British and American soaps. British soaps are shown in the early evenings (6–8 p.m.) and achieve family audiences. They are increasingly popular with young viewers and have become part of the culture of schoolchildren (especially *Neighbours* and *EastEnders*; see Buckingham, 1987). British soaps are often described as being realistic in contrast with the melodramatic style of American soaps (or Brazilian *telenovelas*). They tend to deal with working-class life and experience, where American daytime soaps focus more on middle-class lives and prime-time soaps are about the super-rich.

British soaps are realistic in the way that the life-world of the story is organized to correspond with (to be essentially similar to) the ordinary life-world of viewers. The things that happen in the story are not implausible, and the characters have some psychological realism and depth of personality. Melodramatic American soaps are sensational, artificial, and exaggerated in terms of characters, action, and setting. Much more like a fairy tale than a realistic story, the melodrama creates a fantasy world, remote from everyday reality, into which readers and viewers escape for the duration of the tale.

Melrose Place was a classic melodramatic narrative. The appearance of the actors was stylized, the script not like ordinary talk, and a high level of emotion was always in play. The characters were continuously hating, loving, taking revenge, having identity crises, and playing havoc with each others' lives. The story often defied the logic and plausibility of realistic narrative. In one unlikely story thread, Amanda discovered she had cancer. For the sake of recovery, she left her high-powered position as president of an ad firm. Alison,

Amanda's arch-rival, was selected to take over as president—a quick climb to the top for someone who started in the mailroom only two years prior and had since been spending most of her time struggling with alcoholism. Hardly a month passed before Amanda triumphed over cancer and unscrupulously regained her position as president of the advertising firm.

The pleasures of these kinds of narratives have been much discussed. Far from being mindless rubbish for passive couch potatoes, as is the common perception, such stories create a high degree of audience enjoyment and involvement. The infamous real-life case in Brazil of an actor murdering an actress who was spurning his advances on screen is apropos. In Brazil, more attention was paid to this than to the 1992 impeachment of the president, Fernando Collor de Mello (Guillermoprieto, 1993), which was going on at exactly the same time—and not just because the actress's mother was writing the scripts.

All soaps focus on interpersonal relationships in an everyday context (usually the family, but often an institution—hospitals, schools, police stations, and prisons are favourite locations). The more you watch, the more you get out of it, because the more you know about the lives of the characters (their pasts), the more you are able to assess how they will react in their present dilemmas. Soaps create expert viewers. Regular fans remember a great deal about the past of the narrative and use that knowledge to interpret what is currently going on in the stories.

The ability to exploit these themes and convey an illusion of reality would not be possible without a cinematic code appropriate to the genre. That cinematic code for soaps is characterized by a number of techniques. Primary is the long, peering, extreme close-up, a framing technique that allows the viewer to search the face of the actor for expression of emotion. This technique also encourages feelings of intimacy. These close-ups are enhanced by their placement at eye level. The viewer becomes the eye of the camera, intimately involved, and yet quite separated from and unaffected by events. Similarly, the slow pace of the drama allows the viewer time to read in a depth of emotion and thus encourages the viewer to predict events and interpret reactions.

A prime pleasure of watching soaps is gossip—talking about the story with others (there always is, of course, a great deal of gossip going on in the soaps themselves). Watching soaps is not a solitary activity but a social and sociable act. Plenty of evidence shows that

regular viewers watch in groups—with friends, family, or schoolmates. And the story is discussed before, during, and after each episode (Hobson, 1980; Morley, 1986; Buckingham, 1987). In the UK, soaps are part of the general public discourses of daily life. The lives of soap opera stars, both in the stories and outside, are staple news items in the British tabloid press.

Over time and after much study, academic perceptions of soaps have changed. At first it was supposed that they were the essence of that common criticism of television: they were trivial, mindless entertainment. Gradually it was understood that the pleasures soaps offered were real, that they had an important socializing role in daily life, and that their narrative structure (unlike any other kind of narrative in any other medium) was linked to the character of the medium of broadcasting itself. Such a shift in attitude implied a re-evaluation of everyday life itself, and led to renewed interest in understanding the character and effect of everyday life on social relations in contemporary societies.

Music Videos

In a fashion similar to the soaps, music videos, particularly rock videos, emerged because of producers who wanted to socialize an audience into purchasing their product. The difference between the soaps and music videos is that with videos the product to be purchased is part of the promotional vehicle used to bring it to the attention of the audience. Music videos are visually enhanced versions of the CDs and tapes that the audience is intended to purchase.

As with each of the media forms discussed in this chapter, rock videos have evolved from other media forms. Movies featuring rock stars, such as Elvis Presley, Richard Lester's iconoclastic movies with the Beatles, and filmed recording sessions or concerts were the precursors of the rock video. Rock videos themselves were around in the industry for several years before they exploded onto television, first in the UK and then in North America.

The sudden explosion of music videos and rock-video television shows cannot be attributed to an ability to express something that no other medium has done quite as well. Rather, rock videos are successful because they make for cheap television, just as playing music makes for cheap radio. Suddenly, costs of a half-hour original television show dropped from $2,000–$2,500 a minute to about the same amount for a half-hour. The beauty of music videos is they assemble quite sizable, high-consuming audiences, whose attention can then be sold to advertisers. Moreover, they promote sales of music products.

In contrast to soaps, rock videos are as fast-paced as any movie or television ad. They appear to take their inspiration from the 'visual effects' of movies, providing, again in contrast to the soaps, surrealism rather than realism. They also serve to partition the music industry through easy visual identification of rock, heavy metal, rap, hip hop, country, dance music, and so forth. Insofar as they take their lead from visual effects, which require more money than imagination, they allow the purchase of market dominance. Such a situation places performers, such as Madonna, whose record companies can afford lavish extravaganzas to promote their songs at a considerable advantage over less-established artists. Carefully choreographed and staged videos guarantee heavy rotation on video playlists.

As with other communication forms, patterns of content can be seen in current rock videos. In many early music videos, bondage, especially of women, and restriction of all kinds are used, especially in the more extreme forms of heavy metal. Violence, disembodiment, chaos, explosions, and destruction are also present. Chase scenes, or their visual metaphorical equivalent, are often used. The fragmentation and fetishization of the female body are matched by aggressive phallic display. Rock videos present the necessary props for viewers to create a presentation of a stylized self by which they wish to be known. They know what clothes and accessories to buy, how to behave, what expressions to use, and so forth. In providing material for imaginative creation, music videos complement fashion photographs and magazine illustrations. Viewers thus provide individual interpretation and inject a dynamism built on popular music, ridding the pictures of their frozenness in time (see Goffman, 1974; Fornas et al., 1988). James Curran (1990: 154) has remarked that 'rock music is viewed as a laboratory for the intensive production of identity by adolescents seeking to define an independent self.'

Mechanisms of Media/Culture Binding

The media and culture are inextricably bound together through a process in which the content of the media and the lived reality of people are reflected in each other. This can be called **media/culture binding** and it involves an interpenetration of elements from the media and the real world. The task of the media is to ingratiate themselves into social life in general, and they have been quite successful in this regard. The media interact with everyday life in various ways. Catchy tunes played countless times or repeatable phrases that float through one's head at the oddest times are frequent—and intended to be. The media teach us how to kiss, how to smoke, how to rob banks, how to play with toys, how to dance. The list is endless (see Meyrowitz, 1985, and his 'effects loops'). But the interaction is not a one-way process. The media take their content out of the real lives of real individuals and groups.

While this example is rather old, it captures media/culture binding and interpenetration perfectly. In a 1986 article, the famous writer and semiologist, Umberto Eco, looked at it this way:

1. A firm produces polo shirts with an alligator on them and it advertises them.
2. A generation begins to wear polo shirts.
3. Each consumer of the polo shirt advertises, via the alligator on his or her chest, this brand of polo shirt.
4. A TV broadcast (program), to be faithful to reality, shows some young people wearing the alligator polo shirt.
5. The young (and the old) see the TV broadcast and buy more alligator polo shirts because they have 'the young look'.

- *Which is the mass medium?* The ad? The broadcast? The shirt?
- *Who is sending the message?* The manufacturer? The wearer? The TV director? The analyst of this phenomenon?
- *Who is the producer of ideology?* Again, the manufacturer? The wearer (including the celebrity who may wear it in public for a fee)? The TV director who portrays the generation?
- *Where does the plan come from?* This is not to imply that there is no plan but rather that it does not emanate from one central source.

Eco concluded:

Once upon a time there were the mass media, and they were wicked, of course, and there was a guilty party. Then there were the virtuous voices that accused the criminals. And Art (ah, what luck!) offered alternatives, for those who were not prisoners of the mass media.

Well, it's all over. We have to start again from the beginning, asking one another what's going on. (Eco, 1986: 148–50)

The mass media select markers of the human condition—people of power or position, bodies strong or beautiful, figures that are evil, infamous, or bizarre—that stand for the sacred, the profane, success, or failure, and impart them to audiences, whose attention is then sold to public decision-makers or advertisers. The media then re-express them within the confines of media productions. In drawing out certain elements and exposing them within story or narrative form, whether they are as mundane as a pink rabbit hitting a bass drum (the Energizer Bunny), or as remarkable as an insightful scientist (Stephen Hawking), they transform those markers. The markers become larger than life and as such are surrogate symbols of meaning and communication. Through story form, the media also achieve intimacy and, at the same time, socialize members to the core values of society.

In drawing content from society, not only do the mass media involve audiences, they also recognize the audience's desire to be social, to communicate. In the mass media, even though the speaker is usually only a professional talker who has little or no say in the content of the message, the impression is that the speaker is in charge of the message (as he or she would be in normal social interaction). Thus, many audience members worship speakers in the media—actors, news anchors, political leaders, and so forth. Through a trust in media speakers and a desire to 'communicate' with media figures, members of the audience are encouraged to pursue intimacy with such individuals—read books about them, wear similar clothes, become fans—and thus participate vicariously in the significant events of our time (see Pratkanis, 1992, for the propaganda implications of this phenomenon).

If Eco felt in 1986 we had to start again, goodness knows what he would say today. While the traditional mass media continue to select and present and fill the audience with envy or uncertainty, the Internet reflects us and what we have become. People develop friendships on the Internet that turn into real-life marriages. Others have personal Web sites that introduce you to their families with complete disregard for privacy. In seeming mimicry of celebrityhood, they create their own tabloid coverage. Others set up Web cameras so that you can watch them 24 hours a day. Others become addicted and create imaginary selves.

In another manifestation of media participation, at a music festival called PoMoPalooza that was held in June 2002 in Port Moody, BC, it seemed that about one-third of the audience were busy filming the event with digital movie cameras. The need for surrogate communication through identification with mass-mediated realities appears to be lessened. It has become possible to amuse and inform ourselves rather than be amused and informed by the traditional mass media institutions. As Eco foretold, this further blurs the distinction between the media and the audience. It further binds media and culture.

MEDIA PRESENTATIONS AND SOCIAL AND POLITICAL AGENDAS

The binding of culture and the media is not confined to the domain of entertainment. Political, social, and economic events also interact with the media. In November 1997, Canada hosted the Asia-Pacific Economic Co-operation forum (APEC) leaders in Vancouver, which included the rather repressive dictator of Indonesia, then President Suharto. Certain APEC meetings that took place at the University of British Columbia were targeted by student demonstrators protesting Suharto's presence. In addition to detaining certain individuals prior to the event and rather violently arresting others, the RCMP pepper-sprayed a number of demonstrators, even though they were simply exercising their right to protest. At the time, Prime Minister Chrétien joked about it, stating, 'For me, pepper, I put it on my plate.' Shortly after, however, several parts of the event were called into question. Did the government interfere with the RCMP's role? Was police action motivated by concern for safety or political image? The incident began to command headlines. In spite of a considerable amount of trying, the Chrétien Liberals were unable to remove the event from the public agenda. They attempted to control the public inquiry headed by the RCMP Public Complaints Commission, eventually forcing them all to resign; the PMO directly attacked Terry Milewski, the CBC reporter pursuing the story; and the government attempted to use polls to show that the event was not high on the public's agenda.

In the end, while the matter was effectively buried through an inquiry, the PMO and the RCMP were taught the lesson that they could not be so crude in trampling on the rights of Canadian citizens. At a subsequent international meeting of heads of state in Quebec City there was quite a standoff between police and demonstrators, but by the time the G-8 met at Kananaskis, Alberta, in May 2002, the accompanying demonstrations were peaceful (except, it seems, in Ottawa). Of course, holding the G-8 meeting on a remote mountaintop away from demonstrators and the press certainly helped in maintaining the peace.

A number of global events in the past four decades have provided opportunities to analyze the interaction of the media with governments. For instance, in 1983, the Americans invaded Grenada and sealed the island off from all travel, thereby freezing the press out entirely. The majority of the press corps sat on neighbouring islands, where they received reports of events. Following Grenada, realizing that the United States was not beyond invading a country on the pretext of protecting even one American life, Nicaragua waged what might be termed an information war against the United States. In a public manner it asked Soviet advisers to leave, did not import advanced Soviet weaponry, and generally attempted to avoid any actions that could be construed as a provocation for invasion. These very public acts were moves in a media-based information war in which the left-wing Sandinista government attempted to make it a greater embarrassment for the United States to invade than it would be a victory to oust the Sandinistas. The Sandinistas won the information war and, indeed, the military war. They could not, however, win the economic war mounted against them by the United States. In February 1990 a rival party, with $40 million in US assistance, was elected to office.

By the time the US invaded Afghanistan, subsequent to the terrorist attacks on the World Trade Center and the Pentagon of 11 September 2001, the limitations put on the media (which were even more stringent than they were in the Gulf War until after the fighting was over) were hardly discussed. In the terminology of the media, it was 'an old story', implying that it would not be of interest to readers/the audience. The US military turned the tables in its 2003 invasion of Iraq by 'embedding' journalists in various armed forces units as well as allowing some independents. The reasoning of the military appeared to be that the journalists would bond with their units and report from that point of view. With more embedded than independent journalists reporting, the overall picture presented would be favourable to the military. For the most part, it worked. (Chapter 9 provides further discussion of embedded journalists.)

Obviously, the media play a role in shaping both world and local events. An interesting aspect of this process is that though we sometimes ask whether the media should intervene in certain circumstances—to save a life or prevent violence—in other instances the question is not even asked. Nuns, monks, teenagers, and ordinary citizens have burned themselves in front of television cameras. Soldiers have murdered on camera. One US state treasurer, Bud Dwyer, committed suicide with cameras rolling. At times such actions have been obvious performances for the media, and the question has been asked: should the media intervene in such events, for instance, to stop someone from burn-

ONE PERSON'S TERRORIST IS ANOTHER'S FREEDOM FIGHTER

No doubt many in the West assume that the owners of al-Jazeera satellite television were secret allies of Osama bin Laden and al-Qaeda. Much in the same way, one might say that the US television networks were dancing to the tune of the American government when they agreed to block the transmission of al-Qaeda-made videotapes in response to the demand of the US National Security Adviser, Condoleezza Rice. (Similarly, the PMO assumed that Terry Milewski was a fellow traveller with APEC protestors when e-mail was seized in which he expressed attitudes to government apparently sympathetic to their viewpoint.) Al-Jazeera's senior producer puts the matter this way: 'It would be wild to claim that we are friends of al-Qaeda, but at the end of the day we do not answer to such

people as Condoleezza Rice. . . . We do not talk about what the king ate for breakfast or how many people kissed his hand like the rest of the Arab media. We are more likely to ask those who didn't kiss his hand why they didn't. That's why all the security chiefs in the West monitor every word of our output.'

All very well, notes Mathew Fisher (*National Post*, 28 Sept. 2002, A18). But al-Jazeera does tend to call Palestinian suicide bombers 'commandos' and Palestinians killed by Israelis 'martyrs'. One al-Jazeera journalist defended the network thus: 'After a suicide bombing even the BBC will immediately go to the Israeli government first for a reaction. We go to Hamas or Islamic Jihad first to ask them why they did it. That's logical. Our audience is Arab.'

SHOPPING FOR FUN!

In an extension of lifestyle advertising where the central idea is to transform consumption into a life-affirming experience, Canada Safeway goes to considerable length to make you a winner when you shop there. In one shopping bill in which the customer purchased 42 items for $162.49 (some of which were two and three for a certain price, bringing the total items to 68), 13 were discounted as a result of using a Club Card. The bill provided the purchaser with the total of the net savings he had achieved by using the Club Card: $21.63 or nearly 12 per cent. In addition, the bill noted, three 5 per cent discounts (which is less than 15 per cent once) were added to the end of the bill. Overall, then, his savings were approximately 25 per cent! But wait, at the bottom of the bill he was also informed him that he was a triple-added winner.

**CONGRATULATIONS (it read)
YOU'VE EARNED YOUR SAFEWAY CLUB AWARD.
YOU HAVE PURCHASED 2 OF 8 TOWARD
YOUR FIRST!!! FREE BREAD!!!.**

**YOU HAVE PURCHASED 1 OF 7 TOWARD
YOUR 1ST CLUB STARBUCKS**

**Congratulations!
(it read again, in upper and lower case)
You've been selected
to receive 5% off your eligible
purchases now through 11/28/01**

As the shopper walked giddily from the store, never having felt so lucky in his life, he may have wondered whether it might have been better to know how much he was paying for each item from the start.

ing him or herself, and, if so, under what circumstances? Interestingly, such events were more common in the 1980s than they were in the 1990s and now are in the new century. However, the same question has rarely been asked at the level of politics, global affairs, and social problems. For instance, should and could the media intervene to prevent war, perhaps by attempting to mediate or by revealing crucial information? In certain instances it is clear that the media fail to intervene although it is in their power to do so. One exception to this rule came in 2002 when an interviewer encouraged a Saudi official to make public a proposal he voiced privately in an interview. The official did and for a while it appeared that Israeli/Palestinian relations were advancing. But then, seemingly as always, they deteriorated into more violence.

Media Creating Meaning: Possibilities and Limitations

The media are constantly influencing us: they select certain events to bring forward; they create an image of those events; and they *create a discourse* within which events and issues are defined (see Mitchell, 1988). But beyond influencing our view of things, do the media have the ability to create a reality quite at odds with the facts? Such a scenario is explored in the movie, *Wag the Dog*, in which a Hollywood producer is commissioned to wage a small, bogus war to divert attention away from the domestic difficulties of the

American President. Though this movie perhaps exaggerates the lengths to which the media will go to 'create' meaning, they have at times attempted to create meaning that conflicts with common perceptions.

In the late 1980s and early 1990s, a chain of events happened in Canada in which the media attempted to create a reality that did not conform to public perception. In the late 1980s, a tentative constitutional agreement, the Meech Lake Accord, which proclaimed Quebec to be a 'distinct society' and gave that province and (de facto) the other provinces greater powers vis-à-vis Ottawa, had to be ratified by all the provincial legislatures in order to be entrenched in the Constitution. Despite the support of most politicians and pundits for the agreement, many Canadians had reservations about its contents (Coyne, 1992). In the end, the agreement failed to be ratified in time. Despite this defeat, then Prime Minister Brian Mulroney, in his determination to change the Constitution to placate nationalist sentiment in Quebec, convened a second round of negotiations. These resulted in the Charlottetown Accord, a similar but wider-reaching agreement reached in August 1992 between the provinces and Ottawa after consultation with public groups and Aboriginal leaders. The agreement was taken to a national referendum with the political and media elites of the country threatening the public with dire consequences if they failed to support it. The *Globe and Mail* ran an alarmist editorial in its 1 September edition, and on 24 and 25

October the *Financial Post* ran a letter signed by its senior executives that implored Canadians to vote in favour of the accord. On 26 October, Canadians, including the majority of Quebecers, chose not to ratify the accord, effectively banishing constitutional reform from the political agenda.

These examples illustrate just the opposite of media/culture binding. They represent a dramatic breakdown in the ability of the political and media elites to establish a reality or a discourse that is persuasive enough to command allegiance. They also illustrate the limitations on the media's ability to create meaning for their audience.

Media and Reality: Media Devices and Real Life

Few people in this era would identify so strongly with the characters and interaction in a novel that they would confuse the world of the novel with their day-to-day world. The intermingling of media realities and lived realities is more likely to happen in television, film, or even magazines. Soap opera characters, for example, regularly receive from viewers letters advising them of the intent of other characters or gifts for their upcoming television marriages. Some observers have suggested that this means the viewers do not distinguish between real life and the soaps. Or, it may be that they want to test the system. If they send gifts, will their gifts be included in what the couple receives? If they warn the character of the intent of another, will a warning be built into the plot somehow?

Comedian Rick Mercer of CBC's *This Hour Has 22 Minutes* made comic use of audience involvement and undermined credibility of the Reform/Alliance Party idea to call for public referenda on certain issues. The party was of a mind that if 3 per cent of Canadians (approximately 900,000) signed a petition asking for a referendum, then the government should be obliged to hold a referendum. Mercer asked his audience to visit a Web site and express their opinion on whether the party leader at that time, Stockwell Day, should change his first name to Doris. Over a million people visited the Web site and agreed that he should change his name. The Canadian Alliance, not surprisingly, did not ask for a referendum from the federal government on the subject.

In literature a distinction generally can be made between reality and signification, but when we consider radio, television, or film, the distance between reality and signification shrinks. In 1939, for example, Orson Welles produced a radio play mentioned earlier in this chapter called *The War of the Worlds* in which he presented, in pseudo-documentary style, an invasion of Earth by Martians. Many listeners phoned in, some as the program was being aired, to report sightings of the landings of other Martians. Some listeners seemed genuinely to fear for their lives (Cantril, 1940). After all, the program aired at the beginning of World War II, when the Nazis were mobilizing using both radio and film. And great uncertainty existed about Stalin and Communist power. Radio broadcasting was still in its infancy, and although intellectuals had been railing against it or enthusiastically

ART AND LIFE

For years, some Canadians have thumbed their noses at Americans for voting Hollywood celebrities into office, such as Sonny Bono (a mayor and then a member of the US House of Representatives), Clint Eastwood (the mayor of Carmel, California, for a time) and, best or worst of all, former US President Ronald Reagan. But in Vancouver in the fall of 2002 politics and movies were so intertwined that it was difficult to tell who was real and who was not.

First came the successful TV series, *Da Vinci's Inquest*, based on the former coroner of Vancouver, Larry Campbell. Then Vancouver's mayor, Philip Owen, became convinced that Vancouver should set up safe injection sites for heroin and other drug addicts. This stance—a bit of sand in the face of the US government of George Bush

the younger and its war on drugs, which managed to net even the President's niece, Noelle Bush, Florida Governor Jeb Bush's daughter—and perhaps other incidents caused the 'political party' Owen represented, the Non-Partisan Association (which does not canvas widely for members), to oust him. Then Larry Campbell decided to run for mayor and bill himself as the actual Da Vinci. And then came a documentary called *Fix: Story of an Addicted City*, which premiered at the Vancouver Film Festival to sold-out crowds. Finally, Philip Owen, still the mayor, asked his supporters at a fundraiser to pay $100 each to attend a screening of the film with the proceeds going to assist the filmmakers in seeking theatrical release for the documentary.

endorsing it, they certainly were not minimizing their assessments of its impact on society. In short, while the reaction of some audience members was quite real—there was considerable panic—the treatment of the reactions fed a vision of the media that is as real now as it was then: the media have the power to cause people to do things they otherwise would not do. Indeed, such programs can even encourage the setting up of research institutes. Heyer (2003) notes that *War of the Worlds* did. Hadley Cantril (cited above) became head of the Princeton University Office of Radio Research. As the following sections illustrate, the media can change our orientation towards various things by normalizing, excluding, oversimplifying.

MEDIA VIOLENCE AND NORMALIZATION

Television and movies normalize violence by making it an everyday occurrence in our lives. George Gerbner has concentrated his research over the years on the portrayal of violence on television (see, for example, Gerbner, 1977). He has argued that the frequent use of violence results from it being a cheap way to portray power. But his central concern has been the effect this constant use of violence has had on television viewers. In his studies Gerbner has pointed out how people who watch a great deal of television overestimate the amount of violence in society. They also tend to have a 'bunker mentality' to protect themselves from what they perceive to be a violent world. In spite of the broad acceptance of Gerbner's work and analysis, certain British studies (for example, Wober and Gunter, 1986) have been unable to replicate Gerbner's results.

In a variety of studies of children's play, American social psychologist Albert Bandura (1976) has shown that those children who watch a great deal of television tend to engage in more aggressive play than those who watch less or none at all. Also, following a television-watching session that depicts aggression, the amount of aggressiveness in the interactions

---

'WHAT WON'T YOU DO?'

In his book, The Highwaymen: Warriors of the Information Superhighway, *journalist Ken Auletta interviewed a number of highly placed media moguls, that is, media leaders who answer only to themselves. In Chapter 4, 'What won't you do?', Auletta asked these individuals just that—in reference to what type of material they would not allow to be aired. What is notable about these interviews is the number of media heads who apparently accept that the media have an impact on the audience and audience behaviour, but, true to the American spirit of freedom of speech, reject the notion of interfering with content.*

Auletta begins the chapter with an anecdote. In 1979 Lawrence Gordon produced a movie, The Warriors, *about street gangs. He had good reason to believe that, like his later films,* Die Hard, Predator, Field of Dreams, *and* 48 Hours, *it would be a tremendous box-office success. In the first week, three killings were linked to the movie. Gordon said to Auletta, 'People went out and pretended they were warriors.' The film was recalled. Gordon commented, 'I'd be lying if I said that people don't imitate what they see on the screen . . . I would be a moron to say that they don't, because look how dress styles change. We have people who want to look like Julia Roberts and Michelle Pfeiffer and Madonna. Of course we imitate. It would be impossible for me to think they would imitate our dress, our music, our look, but not imitate any of our violence or*

our other actions.'

Here is how some interviewees answered the question 'What won't you do?':

Rupert Murdoch, owner of the Fox Network and the British *Sun* newspaper, which publishes pictures of bare-breasted women on page three every day, replied, 'You wouldn't do anything that you couldn't live with, that would be against your principles. . . . It's a very difficult question if you are a man of conscience. If you thought that you were doing something that was having a malevolent effect, as you saw it, on society, you would not do it. We would never do violence such as you see in a Nintendo game. When I see kids playing Nintendo, and they're able to actually get their character on the screen to bite his opponent in the face, that's pretty sick violence. . . . Is the violence of *Lethal Weapon* OK? I think so. If it involves personal cruelty, sadism—obviously you would never do that. The trouble is, of course, that you run a studio, and how free are you to make these rules? The creative people give you a script and are given last cut on the movie. The next thing, you have a thirty-million-dollar movie in the can which you may disapprove of.'

Oliver Stone, director of such films as *Platoon, The Doors, Natural Born Killers,* and *JFK,* said, 'Off the top of my between children increases. University of British Columbia psychologist Tannis MacBeth Williams (1986) has conducted similar studies in Canadian communities newly exposed to television, finding an undeniable change in children's play after the introduction of television. One of the noticeable changes is an increase in aggressive play (see Williams, 1995.)

Obviously, in all of these studies, only a certain amount of control over the exposure of the subjects to the media can be achieved, and only a certain level of confidence in the results is appropriate because of other uncontrolled variables, such as socio-economic status. As well, the experimental and cultural environment may be particular to one lab in one country. Then there is interpretation. Is an increase in aggressive play a bad thing? Does it translate into increased aggressive or violent adult behaviour, or to the acceptance of violence or to a violent society? Obviously, the media did not bring about the violence of previous centuries. Do the media role models of today have a unique burden of guilt to carry?

Whatever the case, there is little doubt that Bandura's work points to effects that make sense if one takes a more analytic perspective, as we have done in this chapter by postulating persons, cultures, and the media to be meaning-generating systems in interaction with one another.

British researchers Dennis Howitt and Guy Cumberbatch (1975) have made a case for television violence having no effects. (They have also discussed pornography, claiming that while sexual depictions are sexually arousing there is no evidence to suggest that sexual crimes are caused by sexual arousal.) In spite of such arguments, the CRTC has, in recent years, moved to decrease the amount of violence shown, especially on kids' programs. The program *Mighty Morphin Power Rangers* was removed on some channels in 1994 and the producers modified the violence on the show after a five-year-old in Norway was stoned by her playmates and froze to death. (In Chapter 5 we will discuss audience impact in greater detail.)

head, I'd pretty much do anything . . . I don't view ethics from the outside, only from the inside. What you would find shocking I probably would not. For me it's a question of taste. . . . You can do anything as long as you do it well. I think Hitler would make a great movie.' Does Stone reject the notion that there is too much violence in movies? 'Yes and no', he says, 'Yes, there's too much violence when the violence is badly done. I go back to my aesthetic defense. If it's badly done it becomes obscene. It's not real. If it's well done, it has impact, it has a dramatic point, then it has meaning. It's valid.'

Michael Eisner, chairman of Disney, proffered that while he is not interested in making violent movies, 'I believe there is nothing you should not be allowed to do. . . . I don't believe, strongly, that the government has any right to be involved in anything, or almost anything [related to entertainment].' Later, Eisner added, when asked whether there is a distinction between real and cartoon violence, 'I don't think that anybody thinks that movies like *The Terminator* are real . . . I'm not sure that they don't relieve pressure more than they create it. I don't know the answer to that. I don't want to sit in judgement. I don't think about it that much.'

Michael Ovitz, chairman of Creative Artists Agency, demurred when asked the question, stating that decisions

are made on a day-to-day basis. Also, he said that seeing a violent film is a question of choice, and that violence in movies is often 'not real'. However, as to the impact of movie violence he noted, 'I absolutely think it has an impact on kids. It becomes a framework on which children build. I remember all the things of my childhood. They've been my framework for my own value system . . .'

Ted Harbert is president of the entertainment division of ABC, which broadcast a movie, *Between Love and Hate*, that ended with a youth firing six bullets into his former lover. Harbert said in justification, that a network, like a newspaper, offers choices: '. . . adults can handle that type of television. Children can't. This will sound like a paradox, but I don't believe we have to program the network and absolve parents of responsibility, as if it were our problem and not the parents' problem. Parents have to be responsible for what their kids watch.'

Auletta's interviews demonstrate that media moguls give very little serious thought to the social implications of the content they produce. When they are asked to reflect upon the subject, their responses are often simplistic, contradictory, and inconsistent with their professed personal beliefs.

Pornography and Erotica

In discussions of pornography a distinction is often drawn between pornography and erotica. The former is put forward as unacceptable, the latter as permissible. The argument usually goes something like this: there is nothing wrong with having material (literature, films, videos, music, art, Web sites) designed to be sexually stimulating; there is, however, something wrong with portraying the sexual exploitation of women, children, and men. While such a stance has obvious merit, one difficulty with the pro-erotica stance is that, in real life, erotic feelings are often a component of a private moment. The hawking of wares in which that link between the sexual and the private is broken challenges normal, personal, sexual relations.

Equally deserving of consideration is the role of erotica or soft porn in advertising. The continuous representation of ideal male and female body types in advertisements appears not only to support parts of the vast clothing, beauty, and drug industries, but also to encourage problems of individual self-worth and disease (anorexia and bulimia). We are all familiar with the use of the female body to sell products as diverse as alcoholic beverages, perfume, food, designer fashion, and tobacco products. The emergence of 'himbos' merely extends the target market from females to males: 'His erect nipples are exploited in the furtherance of fragrance and his washboard belly used to flog everything from kitchen cleanser to wrist watches' (Cobb, 1993).

CHALLENGING OTHER STANDARDS

In the same manner in which sexual portrayals and violence may challenge community standards, so do other portrayals that may not reflect a mainstream perception of the world. Some will be offended by family portrayals of same-sex parents; others by a portrayal of racially based organizations; still others by an unpatriotic satirical portrayal of their nation or their religion. The positive side of such portrayals is that they provide the viewer with another view of life besides the one he or she experiences. Such a view may encourage a striving for excellence and tolerance as well as a change in common perception. On the negative side, they may discourage an allegiance to community values in favour of the values of a world of signification.

Given the positive and negative effects of such portrayals, the question becomes whether and how much they should be controlled and by whom. Different countries address this question differently, with the most distinctive being the United States. With the First Amendment of the US Constitution stating that Congress shall make no law respecting an establishment of religion, or prohibiting or abridging the freedom of speech, control over pornography is limited indeed.

In Canada in 1992 and for some time after there was great discussion about a documentary film, *The Valour and the Horror*, which presented an unromantic view of Canada's involvement in World War II. Many veterans, some of whom were senators, wanted to have the film banned because it insulted their memories of the war. A great war of words ensued in the media about the film (available through the NFB). Most frightening were the hearings on the film conducted by the Senate Veterans' Affairs Committee. Clearly, certain senators were not in the least interested in freedom of speech and used every power they had to threaten the filmmakers, including taking them to court for **defamation** of character. This is another side of the tension between the community and the media over challenges to common perceptions and standards as well as over freedom of speech.

MEDIA REDUCTIONISM

Two phenomena are significant for consideration of media reductionism. First is the increasing power of the media to cover local, national, and world events, a power partly enabled by conglomerate ownership (explored in Chapter 8). Second is the impression this power gives the audience that it understands a world in which it does not actively participate.

To make events and issues both understandable and seemingly important to the general public, they are simplified and dramatized. This dual requirement can be handled by the creation of dichotomies. Thus we have war and peace, individual freedom and totalitarian control, free speech and censorship, pro-life and pro-choice, separatism and federalism, **liberalism** or **conservatism**, good or evil, right-wing or left-wing, progressive or traditional, sexually exploitative or reflecting family values, and so on, ad infinitum. Such dichotomies simplify by dividing the world in half instead of presenting the world as a complex multi-dimensional affair. Thus, for instance, to consider only two dimensions in the context of high unemployment—the need for community support struc-

11 SEPTEMBER 2001

If there are significant differences between the real world and the media world, it is nonetheless true that much of our experience of historical events is tied up with media accounts of those events: news reports, books, movies, popular music, radio and television documentaries. How many people recollect or know of the assassination of US President John F. Kennedy from the amateur film shot by Abraham Zapruder, resurrected by TV news clips or embedded in Oliver Stone's film *JFK*? Or the arrest of O.J. Simpson from the live CNN broadcast of the police chase along that Los Angeles freeway? Or the Persian Gulf War from the highly orchestrated Pentagon press conferences with their computerized images of 'precision bombing'?

Part of the shock of 11 September 2001 is surely tied to our ability to 'witness' the events of that day thanks to saturation media coverage, and especially the continual television coverage that provided such clear images from so many angles that many people said 'it was like watching a Hollywood movie.' Yes, it *was* like watching a Hollywood movie because it was so fantastic, so unbelievable, so unexpected, but also because we could watch it all unfold on our television screens. If we didn't see the first airliner hit the north tower, that crash nevertheless succeeded in drawing media attention to the World Trade Center so that many of us *were* watching when the second plane hit 20 minutes later, streaking across the blue sky of a spectacular late summer day, exploding into the south tower as if its hijackers were performing for the cameras.

We can relive that day through its media imagery—the twin towers burning; office workers clinging desperately to remote window ledges; the towers collapsing, almost perfectly, one by one, in a cloud of smoke and debris; monochromatic images of dust-drenched survivors; firefighters working the breached wall of the Pentagon; the smouldering crash site in a field near Shanksville, Pennsylvania. And the stunned faces of the survivors and direct witnesses to this tragedy.

That day—11 September 2001—is no longer a simple date on the calendar. The shorthand expression 9/11 refers to a brutal act of defiance against the world's sole remaining superpower, a challenge to its omnipotence and, just as importantly, a challenge to a way of life built on professed values of democracy, justice, and liberty. If the hijackers won unprecedented media coverage for their attacks on the most potent symbols of American economic, military, and political power (the plane that crashed in Pennsylvania was heading towards Washington), 9/11 remains on the media stage as we struggle to understand why it happened, what the attacks mean, and how the United States and other Western countries can or should respond, or have responded, to them. The media will continue to be heavily implicated in how we come to understand 9/11.

For students of mass communication, 9/11 is a media event in another sense. It is an opportunity to see how the media perform in a crisis situation, how the news media, particularly, live up to their professed responsibility to inform us as citizens as our democratically elected governments combat terrorism. What we have seen to date is not encouraging.

We have seen frequent examples of media reductionism, whereby any consideration of root, political causes for 9/11 are dismissed and the whole affair is framed as a simple case of good versus evil, with George W. Bush personifying the forces of good and Osama bin Laden the forces of evil. 'Either you are with us, or you're with the terrorists', as the President so succinctly put it. When Canadian Prime Minister Jean Chrétien suggested, on the first anniversary of 9/11, that such terrorist attacks were the product of a world divided between prosperous and arrogant Western nations and a humiliated 'poor world' (Canadian Press, 2002), *Globe and Mail* international affairs columnist Marcus Gee (2002) scoffed, insisting that 'evil' was the only explanation for the 9/11 attacks: 'No act of US foreign policy, no economic grievance, can explain the hate-filled ideology that led to the murders of Sept. 11. This was an act of evil perpetrated by evil men.'

We have seen the power of language to define events. When the United States captured hundreds of men during the fighting in Afghanistan and held them in a rudimentary, offshore military prison at Guantanamo Bay, Cuba, it maintained the men were 'illegal combatants' as opposed to 'prisoners of war'. POWs have rights guaranteed by the Geneva Convention. Illegal combatants have no such rights and can be tried and punished by secretive military tribunals, which maintain a lower standard of proof than US court proceedings, and which shield evidence and witnesses from all forms of public scrutiny (Thompson, 2002).

We have seen normal channels of justice derailed. More than 1,200 people of Middle Eastern descent have been detained without trial in the US, without their identities being revealed, and many without even access to legal counsel ('When violating rights', 2002). And the Patriot Act of 2001 permitted US Attorney General John Ashcroft to expand surveillance of telephone and Internet communications, increase wiretap activity, and examine financial and medical records in the interests of combatting terrorism (Lapham, 2002).

The parameters of debate in mainstream news coverage and commentary have narrowed significantly since 9/11. Describing journalists as 'security guards deciding what could and could not be seen on camera', *Harper's* editor Lewis H. Lapham (2002: 7) searched in vain for news coverage that would provide '[i]nformed argument about why and how America had come to be perceived as a dissolute empire; instructive doubts cast on the supposed omniscience of the global capital markets; sustained questioning of the way in which we divide the country's wealth; a distinction drawn between the ambitions of the American national security state and the collective well-being of the American citizenry.'

Speaking to journalism students at Concordia University in Montreal, former *New York Times* reporter Chuck Sudetic put it more simply. The news media failed to ask three basic, yet crucial, questions: Why? Why here? Why now? We are still wondering. Just as we must wonder what the real outcomes, in the ensuing years, will be of the American-British war on Iraq in 2003.

tures against the desirability of individual freedom—becomes a formidable challenge. And what about including age and ethnicity in the equation? As another example, considering the best manner to treat adolescents who have engaged in criminal activity goes far beyond getting tough or going soft on crime. It even goes far beyond understanding the youth's family history and personality. It extends into styles of child-rearing, the education system, the nature and extent of employment, the role of religion, the presence of degrading portrayals of people in the various media, and so forth. In fact, it extends to our very understanding of what an adolescent is.

Dichotomies not only simplify and stereotype, they dramatize by introducing tension, by the creation of sides battling each other for control. In media presentations, spokespeople for the environment line up against the forest companies, feminists against patriarchal society, First Nations against European immigrants, workers against employers, the poor against the rich, the taxpayers against the government, the middle class against the 'welfare bums', the government against Her Majesty's Loyal Opposition. In fact, matters are much more complex.

The media's treatment of issues creates the impression that the audience can understand all the issues. The media involve us as audience members by making the issues understandable and by introducing tension we want to see resolved. Yet when people participate in the institutions of society—helping out in a school, a soccer club, a Brownie group, even a political party—they come to understand just how difficult running social institutions can be, how full of compromise an institution must be, how challenging it is to keep people focused on the central task, and how difficult it is to maintain morale. When people do not participate in social institutions or become actively involved in issues of public concern, relying instead on the media to inform them about their community, their nation, and the world, the necessary simplification needed to tell the story and the dramatization needed to capture their attention not only provide an inadequate rendering of the complexity involved, but also, in dichotomizing, polarize public opinion into inflexible camps.

Media simplification and dramatization are reductionist, though indeed these characteristics are not solely due to media practice, as Lawrence Habermehl (1995) points out in *The Counterfeit Wisdom of Shallow Minds*. They reduce people and events into something they are not. They encourage negative and hostile reactions in those who otherwise lack knowledge of the situation and especially in those who do not otherwise participate in society. Dramatic tensions encourage us to form firm opinions on debates of which we know only what the media tell us. The media create this scenario and take no responsibility for it.

Summary

Social models of communication attempt to understand the variables or the context affecting the formation or encoding of messages and their understanding or decoding. This chapter has examined a number of different perspectives on the social elements of communication, in other words, the dynamics of meaning creation and interpretation.

The study of the creation and interpretation of

WHY TV GETS IT WRONG

In 1994, in the *Globe and Mail*, Graham Fraser wrote an article with the above title. He began the article with the following: 'Vision Statement: TV pretends to expand horizons and clarify a difficult world. Instead, it simplifies to the point of banality and ignores what it can't grasp.' He then quoted the late E.B. White, a New York writer who said (in 1938), 'We shall stand or fall by TV, of that I am quite sure.'

Fraser's points were many. He noted that TV 'frames and focuses the way Americans think about the world. Its grammar and rhetoric shape public debate' and appear to define and limit government action. Television simplifies conveying emotion, not reason: it has difficulty with abstractions such as religious beliefs and even foreign languages. At times it barely pays attention to critical issues and areas and when it does it treats them in an either/or framework. He quoted respected news commentator Robert MacNeil: 'bite sized is best; complexity must be avoided; nuances are dispensable; qualifications impede the simple message; visual stimulation substitutes for thought.' Wars must be brought to a speedy conclusion before the audience gets bored. TV can anaesthetize viewers as horrific scenes from war are shown over and over again until what is ultimately horrible becomes a visual cliché.

In times when the lives of thousands are at stake, as they have been ever since the United Nations applied economic sanctions against Iraq over a decade ago, it is truly frightening to think that we live by the dynamics of television and the understanding it is capable of delivering.

---

media content is the study of representation, or, as the semioticians would have it, signification. Such study examines how symbols, such as the words and ideas contained in language, are constructed and used to interpret the world of objects, events, persons, and even representations. This realm of making meaning is not subordinate to that of physical objects because physical objects gain their meaning through symbol systems.

The study of representation involves understanding the nature of polysemy, intertextuality, and grounded indeterminate systems. In less technical words, it involves understanding how messages are open to a variety of interpretations, how interpretations depend on other representations, and how there are bound to be a finite but unpredictable number of interpretations of the object, event, or phenomenon being represented.

A variety of approaches are used to analyze media content. The major categories are literary criticism; structural interpretations, including structuralism, semiotics, and post-structuralism; interaction analysis, including pragmatics and discourse analysis; content analysis; political-economic analysis; and genre/media form analysis. Each has particular strengths and draws out various aspects of making meaning. Literary criticism focuses on the author and the text. Structuralism focuses on the basic story and its elements. Interaction analysis focuses on the process of making meaning. Content analysis focuses on frequency of occurrences within certain categories. Political-economic analysis deals with the ideological interests of the creators and the costs of production.

Media form analysis draws attention to the biases inherent in the medium being used, while genre analysis draws attention to the biases of the genre. For example, newspaper news builds on the standard inverted pyramid. Television news is organized primarily by the intrusion of the camera as opposed to the reporter. Soap operas have developed their own set of portrayed social relations and visual techniques to present an intimate, universal world. Rock videos bombard the viewer with technological gimmicks and lavish production.

The media bind themselves to society through a process of interpenetration of media content and lived reality. Often they massage and present material from the margins of society to make it acceptable and available to the mainstream. The media are not free to create non-existent social values even though they may affect the manner in which social values are played out. The interpenetration of reality and media representation is problematic, especially with regard to violence and pornography. The simplification, reductionism, and dramatization of issues also create unacknowledged problems.

Appendix: A Semiotic Analysis of a Black Label Ad Series

The following award-winning ad series was part of a multimedia blitz on television and radio and in print in Ontario and Quebec in the late 1980s. The television and print ads had a tremendous impact. Not only did the sales of Black Label beer double, but also the world of advertising was effusive in its praise for the campaign.

Tattoos, jeans, and plain T-shirts, grainy black-and-white photographs with a single red highlight, billiards, bars, a short black leather skirt, reflective sunglasses with colourful frames, black vinyl LPs, western string bolo ties, single figures, at times no figures, a partial view of the product label, legend, black: these are some of the elements or signifiers drawn from a selection of the print ads that the agency Palmer Bonner created for Carling's Black Label. What do they mean?

Think in dyads, that is to say, opposites. Once you know the above images are from a beer ad, think of the beer ads produced during the same period for the dominant labels of Labatt's and Molson. Most often they depict groups of attractive 25–35-year-olds on the scene (and on the make). The ads spare no expense and present both human props and product in the lushest production that money can buy and video and computer technology can produce. The setting is well lit and everything is crisp, clean, life-embracing. Front and centre in the picture in full living colour is 'the product'. And if the viewer is besotted with the beauty of the actors and the set, then the music blasts the message in his/her ears.

All of this works for the mainstream. But other groups in society reject or at least do not respond to these ads and/or drink other beers. Carling Breweries and its advertising agency, Palmer Bonner, began this campaign with the knowledge that on Queen Street West in Toronto and St-Denis in Montreal there appeared to be one such non-responding group. How did they know? Because Black Label already had a high market share in those locations.

Corporations don't obtain such information out

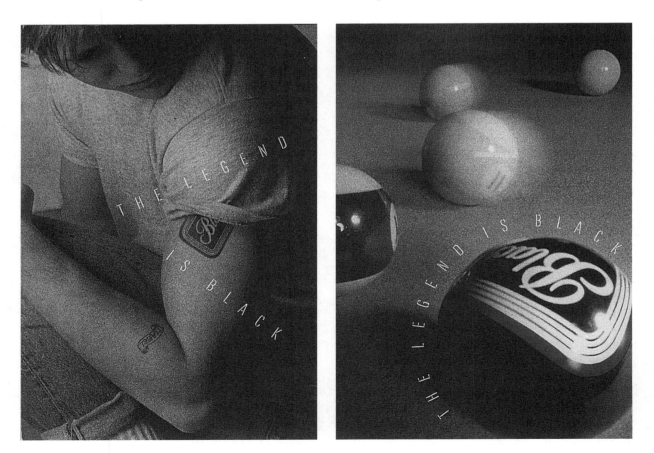

of idle curiosity only to dismiss it with a shrug. Most often, when sales figures show unusual patterns, they seek to find out why and to define, if possible, the characteristics of the consumers behaving this way (in an effort to capitalize on the trend). This is exactly what Carling and Palmer Bonner did. With this distinctive pattern of sales they set out to find who was drinking Black Label and why.

Black Label drinkers, it turned out, came from two groups. The first group contained individuals who were some or all of the following: creative, non-conformist, individualist, intellectual. As well, they tended to be anti-commercial, not inclined against homosexuals, oriented to the inner city. Their lives allowed them to play out these traits either through their employment or their unemployment. The second group of Black Label drinkers consisted of hangers-on to the first group, those who, for the most part, lived other lives but longed for and sometimes visited their ideological brethren on Queen Street West and St-Denis. What was more, it appeared that while the membership of the first group was small, the second

group was potentially large. Indeed, the agency came to believe, partly as a result of their focus group work, that a little of the focal values of the first group could be found in all of us.

The identification of the characteristics of Black Label drinkers was interesting and illuminating, but it presented a conundrum. If, as the research showed, one of the major reasons people drank Black Label was because it wasn't advertised, how could one ever hope to advertise the brand and increase sales? The agency and its client elected a strategy that seems obvious in retrospect. They would advertise the lifestyle of the drinkers; flatter those who lived it; understate the product identity; avoid too frequent exposure of any single ad; involve confirmed consumers and others in the ad by mental participation (filling in missing elements); and ensure that the creative elements of the ad reflected aspects of the lifestyle and were consistent with the values of the brand loyalists.

Why go to all this trouble if an identifiable population was already loyal to the brand and take the

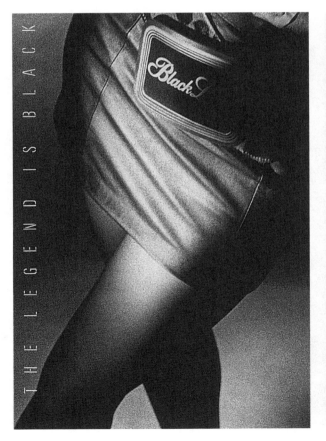

chance of alienating them? Because, the agency and the brewer reasoned, many more of the second group and perhaps some of the first group could be sensitized to the brand without alienating the brand loyalists. And, perhaps, the ads might strengthen the loyalty of the first group to Black Label.

The message of the ads was simple: 'If you look closely at this ad and you really know what is going on you'll know who we are depicting, that they are a real group in society, that they stand for something, and that they drink a certain brand of beer. You, too, can show your alliance with the values of this group by adopting elements of their lifestyle you don't already share, starting with drinking the same beer they do.'

The ads themselves are black and white, albeit with a red highlight. They are also grainy. Why? The lack of full colour immediately distinguishes the ads from all other beer ads. The graininess assists. Brand identification is obscured, not obscured enough for anyone who has been in a beer store not to know what it is, but visually obscured. Yet, by colour and

placement the brand label is the focal point of the picture. In ad number 1 the beer label is in the form of a tattoo—now there's loyalty and commitment. In all the ads no beer bottle is in sight, but what does appear, if you even notice it, in thin, white, broken letters that don't impinge on the eye, is the phrase 'The Legend Is Black'. The male and female models are in-style, 'of a type', but certainly not mainstream.

Each of these elements, led by the black-and-white grainy and red-highlighted photo, complements the others to add up to a whole-picture depiction of the brand loyalists and their preferred brand of beer. Of course, there is no one to challenge the company on whether the group it has identified actually drinks more Black Label than any other beer. No other company has identified the group and its associates as a target market.

Ad number 2 presents a grainy, black-and-white photograph of a black billiard ball in the foreground, slightly out of focus, with part of the Black Label painted on it complete with red, presented upside down with only the first four letters of the word

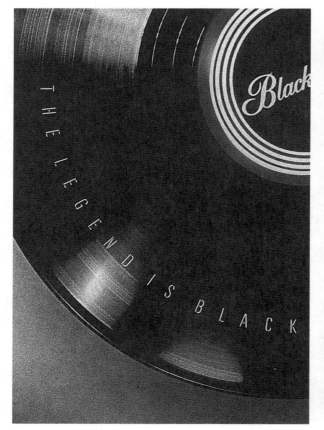

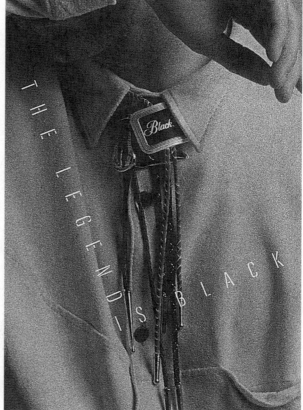

'Black' visible and with the last letter disappearing around the curve of the ball. The photograph was taken at slow speed with two balls apparently moving in the background. Around the curve of the ball, again visually understated in white, broken, sans-serif type, 'The Legend Is Black'. 'Legend'? Why 'legend'? And why not a straight-out, simple and direct, non-ambiguous, 'The Beer Is Black Label'?

Ad number 3 shows a grainy, black-and-white photograph of a woman, the photo cropped across her hip and waist. She is wearing a Black Label (sort of) belt buckle/clasp, deliberately partially obscured by a black shadow to show only 'Black L'. Her legs are crossed in a way that leads the viewer to the beer label buckle/clasp, and the miniskirt is, of course, tantalizing. Note that we have yet to see and will not ever see the full unobscured face of a model. Up the right-hand side of the picture, in horizontal, white, broken, sans-serif type is again, 'The Legend Is Black'. Legend? With miniskirts that hearken back over two decades, black-and-white graininess reminiscent of black-and-white TV, even the red, white, and black of the label in contrast to the pastels of **postmodernism** that were picked up by some of the alcoholic coolers—there is a suggestion of history—the overall style seems to echo a form of industrial art.

In ad number 4, the grainy, black-and-white extreme close-up is of a male model wearing reflective sunglasses in which 'Black' is mirrored in the telltale script of the label. The letters of 'The Legend Is Black'—which, by the way, play on 'the legend is back' (and reviving itself in the marketplace)—are at about a 45-degree angle down from left to right to the less radical off-angle of the sunglasses, which run up from left to right. The model's face is unexpressive.

Ad number 5 is the same type of photograph, this time of an LP disc with 'Black' in the place of the record label. Its minimalism and the predominance of the black of the LP lead the eye more readily to the white, broken letters that follow the curve of the LP about one-third of the way through the playing surface.

Finally, in ad number 6, we see an extreme close-up of the chest of a male model. His shirt cuff and part of his hand are coming across where the bottom of his face would be, which adds a visually interesting top border. The shirt is well worn and 'of a style', and the model is wearing three western string or bolo ties, all slightly askew. The top tie has a Black Label slide presented in a by now typical fashion, with only the word 'Black' visible. 'The Legend Is Black' is in the usual form, but radicalized somewhat by its angle of presentation and by being laid out in the form of an upper case 'L'.

The campaign—whether consciously or not—played on black as a sign (in the semiotic sense of the word), just as the brand loyalists were doing in their choice. Obviously, the whole campaign would have been different if the brand was Green Label. Black is oppositional, of the night, associated with evil, danger, rejection, rejection of colour. Our everyday language is full of allegory carried by black, as a black mood, a blackened reputation, a black mark, a black sky, a black sheep.

With black at the centre of the campaign, adding understated signifiers of the lifestyle of the brand loyalists as oppositional (in dyadic relation to) both to mainstream culture and to mainstream beer ads, Carling (later Molson) and Palmer Bonner (later Bozell Palmer Bonner) had a winning campaign. It was not based on demographics—that is, it did not try to reach as great a percentage of 25–35-year-olds as possible—and it was not intended to knock Labatt's Blue out of its top place. Rather, it was based on psychographics, designed to pick up market share by appealing to a segment of the market that possessed a certain set of attitudes. It also helped Bozell Palmer Bonner get established and, for a while, become the talk of the industry. What it 'signified' was that people who shared the values of the brand loyalists would share their beer.

(Black Label Ad. Reprinted by permission of Molson Canada.)

RELATED WEB SITES

Advertising Standards Canada: www.canad.com
A listing of Canadian advertising codes and guidelines, as well as information and reports on public complaints, can be found at this site.

Freedom Forum: www.freedomforum.org
This organization is committed to pursuing free speech and freedom of the press.

House of Commons Standing Committee Report on Communication and Culture: http://www.media-awareness.ca/english/resources/research_documents/reports/violence/tv_violence_fabric.cfm
Parts of the Committee's report, *Television Violence: Fraying Our Social Fabric*, are available at this site.

Media Awareness Network: www.medi-awareness.ca
The Media Awareness Network provides information and insightful analysis of various media issues, including violence in the media.

FURTHER READINGS

Auletta, Ken. 1997. *The Highwaymen: Warriors of the Information Superhighway*. New York: Random House. Based on a series of interviews of media managers, Auletta's book is a biting commentary on the social responsibility of the media.

Eco, Umberto. 1986. 'The multiplication of the media', in Eco, *Travels in Hyperreality*. New York: Harcourt Brace Jovanovich, 148–69. This and the other essays are delightful insights into the unrealities of representation.

Media, Culture and Society. This journal is the pre-eminent British media studies journal founded in the 1970s by five young media scholars.

Miller, Mark Crispin. 1990. 'Hollywood: the ad', *The Atlantic Monthly* 265, 4 (Apr.): 41–68. Miller is a talented journalist who continues to write insightful media commentary.

STUDY QUESTIONS

1. What is the value of a transmission model of communication? Who uses it? For what?
2. Describe the fundamentals of a social model of communication and the nature of transformation.
3. Select a major news story and perform a structural or semiotic analysis on the content. After you have completed this task, perform a content analysis on the same story (the story may be covered over a number of days, in a number of articles, in a number of publications).
4. Construct an inverted pyramid for five news stories. If any do not follow the usual model of presenting the five 'w's, one 'h', and the 's-w' in the initial paragraph, explain why.
5. Select an up-market newspaper or magazine (for example, the *Globe and Mail*) and a down-market publication (for example, one of the *Sun* chain newspapers but not the *Vancouver Sun*). Identify the major differences in treatment. Then turn to the various theoretical perspectives in this chapter and apply the most appropriate model. If done as a group, compare and discuss your selections of theoretical models and findings.
6. 'Calvin Klein is a pernicious influence on society. The ads of this company demean and exploit human beings.' Discuss. Be sure to include a consideration of polysemy.
7. The diet of violence fed to us through movies and television is steadily eroding our society. Discuss.

LEARNING OUTCOMES

- To inform students that the aim of the study of content is not to seek the one true meaning of statements but rather to illustrate how rich statements are in their possibilities for interpretation.
- To compare an engineering, technical, or mathematical model of communication to a social transformative model.
- To introduce a number of terms often used in the analysis of content, including signification, indeterminacy of representation, intertextuality, polysemy, rhetoric, hermeneutics, the semiotic triad, sign, signifier, and signified.
- To introduce, for class discussion, various theoretical perspectives including literary criticism; structuralism, semiotics, and post-structuralism; pragmatics and discourse analysis; quantitative content analysis; political-economic analysis; and media form/genre analysis.
- To expand media form analysis into genre analysis, that is, a discussion of advertisements, news stories, television in comparison to print as a news medium, investigative television in comparison to print, soap operas, and music videos.
- To explain how the media select from the social world and represent those elements, thereby binding themselves to the culture of which they are a part.
- To provide a discussion of the constraints within which the media operate or, said oppositely, the degree to which the media can manipulate.
- To introduce a framework for thinking about violence and pornography in the media.
- To draw attention to the inherent reductionism in media treatment of any issue.
- To illustrate a semiotic analysis (in the appendix to the chapter).

Media and Audiences

Introduction

Media audiences are of interest to both industry and academic researchers. Members of the industry need to know the size and the demographic characteristics (age, gender, ethnicity) as well as other attributes of audience members, such as education, income level, and purchasing patterns, so they can define the product they are selling (the audience to the advertiser). Industry members also want to know how audiences respond to audience-building techniques so they can understand how to attract larger audiences or audiences with defined characteristics. Scholars have a different agenda. They seek to understand the nature of the interaction between the media and their audiences, what audiences do with media content, how they engage with television, books, magazines, music.

This chapter explores both approaches to the audience. It begins with the academic perspective, which, in general, sees audiences as composed of active, individual, thinking, human agents who seek information, amusement, diversion, relief from boredom, family or other social bonding, confirmation of attitudes and world views, and enlightenment by means of sometimes purposeful, sometimes purposeless, consumption and interpretation. The chapter then turns to a discussion of industry measures of audiences, paying particular attention to practices in the Canadian consumer magazine industry.

A Theoretical Synthesis of Meaning-Generating Systems

Audience members do not accept all of what they see or hear—whether the facts (e.g., of a news story), the attitudes of the major protagonists (with whom they

Ever since the television became a common household item, researchers have been interested in studying how audiences interact with this medium. (Courtesy National Archives, PA-111390)

are meant to identify), or the general portrayal of society and its values that a piece may contain. Not everyone who sits down in front of the TV brings all his or her critical faculties to bear on every program watched, nor to every piece of pulp fiction. And neither is it the case that audiences are generally composed of fragile beings desperately seeking simulated social contact and meaning through the media. Watching television, reading books or magazines, listening to music, and so on are largely casual leisure activities. And no research has ever shown that the media have the power to induce audience members to act against or outside their will.

Media–audience interaction is probably best thought of as a sometimes energetic, sometimes passive engagement between audience members and the media, and, insofar as the media are part of society, also including cultures. Moreover, audience members, the media, and cultures can be usefully conceived of as **meaning–generating entities** that affect one another.

Let us take an example. A young woman, home early from classes, tunes into WWE on TV to find The Rock and Stone Cold Steve Austin throwing each other around the wrestling ring. No one is home, least of all her brother, who left the television on this channel the day before. Though normally not a fan of wrestling, she can't find the remote so she watches for several minutes. Within those few minutes she finds that the bout is nothing special. 'Boring', she thinks, and looks harder for the remote.

While it may not seem like it, this instance exemplifies many of the elements of meaning generation. That is, our protagonist collects, analyses, and synthesizes information in seconds. She immediately recognizes the scene and the characters and can sense if anything special is happening in this action soap opera directed at young men. She transforms the material on the screen by reconstructing the events in her terms and then re-expressing them, first by her implied lack of interest, and then by her renewed efforts to find the remote.

Is this interaction complex and multi-dimensional? Somewhat. Implicitly and from experience, our protagonist knows wrestling is not targeted at her. The fact that there are no ads relevant to her proves it. Were different, more interesting wrestlers in the ring, or were either of the wrestlers bellowing at the crowd, she might stay tuned for a little longer. Or were she at her boyfriend's house and he wanted to watch, she might stay with the program a while longer. The episode is also mediated by choice. What do the other channels have to offer? What is in the fridge? How soon is her next assignment due? And so on. Also, her whole frame of mind in assessing whether to watch is characterized by her degree of engagement (very small) and subject to context that is situational (as explained above) and historical (she knows what wrestling is generally about and what tends to happen). Her action in looking for the remote, her sighs of boredom, her flop down on the couch in the first place are all part of her meaning generation.

Given these media–audience dynamics, where does culture as an active, meaning-generating entity figure in this scenario? Cultural dynamics play themselves out in the woman's vision of herself and the relevance of the program to her. Also, the fact that the program is aired in the first place and commands vast audiences is part of a cultural dynamic. Finally, the very scene of these modern gymnasts/gladiators heaving each other around in an action theatre of the absurd constitutes a cultural dimension.

Because the relation between media, audiences, and cultures is based on interaction and is not predetermined, any consideration of the interaction between audience behaviour, media content, and cultural form must take place within a very broad framework—one that has the potential to encompass any and all elements of the interaction. As communications theorist Thomas Lindlof (1991) notes, audience interpretations of media content derive from at least the following factors: (a) the personality and general outlook of the audience member; (b) his/her current state of mind; (c) the social situation in which the viewing is taking place; and (d) the text or content. Given these criteria, we are able to understand the possible roots of our female viewer's behaviour. Nevertheless, a particular part of her personality or attitude in that moment might have caused her to behave differently. Also, days later she might make some comment derived from her brief exposure. The point of the analytical framework is not to predict audience reaction but rather to understand it.

In regard to cultures, they, like audiences and like media content, are meaning-generating systems. Cultures first generate identity from a host of factors, including history, laws, various institutions that mediate interaction, governing structures, and opportunities afforded by cultural and physical geography.

Through interactions based on this identity, cultures then generate meaning in a particular style and in relation to the events of the day. The actions of each culture as a totality, both domestically and internationally, and in time of plenty or in time of crisis, are derived from the wealth, history, and present-day attitudes and actions of groups and individuals. And a culture's actions can create meaning by exemplifying or violating principles of action for both itself and others to see.

Stated succinctly, lived reality at the level of the individual, the group, and the culture interacts with media realities through a constant process of mutual selection, re-stylization (or appropriation), transformation, and re-display. This interaction is a continuous process of making meaning and, as such, profoundly affects the nature of human existence in modern society.

Six Perspectives on Audiences

The study of audiences in all their manifestations and interactions can be approached in many different ways. We will examine six academic approaches to the audience: Marxist analysis and the Frankfurt School; effects research; uses and gratification research; (British) cultural studies; feminist research; and reception analysis (see also Lindlof, 1991; Jensen and Rosengren, 1990).

MARXIST ANALYSIS AND THE FRANKFURT SCHOOL

Karl Marx was a key thinker and analyst of modern societies, one of only a handful of intellectuals whose ideas have had a fundamental impact on modern life. The basis of Marx's philosophy is that if you want to understand how a society really works, you must look

A TREATISE ON FAME

Is fame a media phenomenon? Is it a produced phenomenon or an interactional phenomenon between a celebrity and an audience?

Globe and Mail columnist Doug Saunders traces it back to Goethe, who with the publication of his novel *The Sorrows of Young Werther* caused Germans to imitate the dress and mannerisms of the protagonist and become obsessed with the author's private life. Fame is probably as old as humanity. What about Jesus Christ? His wrestling with fame was featured in the musical *Jesus Christ Superstar*. What about Mohammed? What about Ulysses and, for that matter, the Greek pantheon of gods?

Saunders suggests some other historical figures who had the quality of fame. Franz Liszt, in 1841, hired Gaetano Belloni to handle his tours, perhaps the first example of agents and managers. In turn Liszt was hired by Phineas T. Barnum, a man of fame himself, for millions of dollars to tour with 'The Greatest Show on Earth'. Charles Dickens had fame in 1858 in his author tour of Britain, the US, and Canada. Florence Lawrence also had it in 1910 when she became the first actor to receive a movie credit in her own name. In 1911 the first fan magazines were launched, which helped intensify fame for such actors as Toronto-born Mary Pickford. In 1942, singer Frank Sinatra started near riots with his appearances and arguably became the first pop star. Orson Welles gained fame as a radio star with the broadcast of *War of the Worlds*. In 1948 Milton Berle became a TV star. In 1960 John F. Kennedy became as much a political celebrity as a US President. In 1968 Pierre Trudeau followed suit in Canada. In 1990, following in the footsteps of other sports celebrities such as Babe Ruth, Michael Jordan signed a $100 million contract for endorsements of other products. And in 1997 US TV networks split their coverage between two celebrities, Bill Clinton giving his State of the Union address and the verdict on the trial of O.J. Simpson.

What may be a new twist on the peregrinations of fame is its explicit exploitation.

In the second part of his three-part series in the *Globe and Mail* (18 Dec. 2000, A11) Saunders talked about the renting of fame. Bo Derek (once ranked a '10' for her beauty by her marketing manager, who was also her husband) was hired to help George H.W. Bush reach a certain segment of the voting population of the US in his run for the presidency. President Bush's son, George W. Bush, used celebrities such as Arnold Schwarzenegger and Chuck Norris, just as Bill Clinton used Barbra Streisand and Richard Dreyfuss. The stars themselves sometimes have political advisers.

Understanding the dynamics of fame is interesting in itself. Understanding the appeal of celebrity is a separate and, perhaps, an even more intriguing question.

at how it meets the material needs (for food, shelter, clothing, and so forth) of its members. In other words, you begin the study of social life by looking at production: the processing of resources and the manufacture of goods that people need to maintain themselves and others. Modern, Western societies, Marx argued, were characterized by a new and revolutionary mode of production—industrial capitalism—in which scientific techniques, applied to the mass production of an ever-increasing range of goods (or commodities, in Marx's terms), created wealth for the owners of capital (the factory owners). Modern capitalism, Marx argued, transformed all aspects of life: it changed politics, culture, and social relations. On the one hand, techniques of mass production seemed to offer the possibility of the end of scarcity. Material abundance could be available to all if the techniques of modern manufacturing were somehow regulated with everyone's interests in mind. On the other hand, Western society has not realized this possibility. It is a bitter paradox that while huge quantities of grain may sit in prairie elevators, powdered milk in storage, and butter in freezers, thousands of people live in hunger in Canada, and millions live in extreme hunger or near famine elsewhere in the world.

In Marx's analysis, the villain in the story is the capitalist—the property owner—who is motivated by a desire to accumulate an ever-increasing amount of capital and wealth. Marx argued that the system of production serves the interests of capitalists, even though capitalists are only a tiny fraction of the population: the vast majority of people are workers exploited by the capitalists. They must sell their labour to the capitalists, on whom they depend. They can be fired at any time and for whatever reason, and they have to fight to squeeze a living wage out of the owners of capital. At the heart of a Marxist analysis of modern society is the possibility of a better life that could be shared by all—a life that is blocked by the private appropriation of wealth.

Marx's analysis of modernity is based on the idea that there is a fundamental conflict of interest between the haves and the have-nots of society, between capitalists and workers. His ideas have had an enormous influence during the past century: their appeal to the poor and disinherited is obvious. They have shaped the political life of the twentieth century throughout the world. In most European democracies the development of mass parties tended to be split in two—those that represent the interests of the owners of property and those that represent the interests of workers. Experiments in socialism, more specifically communism (a political application of Marx's ideas), lasted for 70 years in Russia and continue in China, Cuba, and elsewhere in the developing world. Although so-called state socialism (as the Russian system was called) has clearly failed, having led to great misery and death for millions, Marx's ideas have not been entirely discredited. His emphasis on the fundamental importance of economic life for an understanding of how modern societies work and his analysis of capitalist societies as based on deep social divisions and conflicting interests remain a substantial and important contribution.

The **Frankfurt School** took up Marx's writings and applied them to an analysis of twentieth-century culture. The leading members of this group of intellectuals were Max Horkheimer, Theodor Adorno, and Herbert Marcuse, and their ideas were formed in the interwar period (1920–40) (see Jay, 1974, for a critical history of the work of the Frankfurt School up to the 1950s). At first they worked at the Institute for Social Research attached to the University of Frankfurt (hence the Frankfurt School), but when Hitler came to power, because they were Jews and their ideas were fundamentally out of step with fascism, they had to leave Germany, eventually settling in the US. Adorno and Horkheimer were appointed to Columbia University, where they remained until after World War II. (In the late 1940s Adorno and Horkheimer returned, with great honour, to Frankfurt, where they continued to work in the university until the 1970s.) Marcuse (1954, 1964) settled in San Franciso, where he made his major contributions, remained in the US, and became an intellectual hero of the counterculture in the 1960s.

These intellectuals argued that capitalist methods of mass production had had a profound impact on modern cultural life. Capitalist methods had been applied, in the last century, to the manufacture of the necessities of life, that is, material goods like machinery and clothing. Beginning in the 1920s, though interrupted by the Great Depression and World War II, capitalism was applied to the production of what we call consumer goods, a new range of goods, products, or commodities—the terms are more or less synonymous. Families were persuaded that the essence of modern life was the acquisition of such goods—the family car, gas and electric ovens, fridges, washing machines. In the 1950s the manufacture and sale of these items took off. They became mass-market items and transformed the character of domestic daily life. Capitalists also turned their attention to cultural goods or commodities. New forms of mass communication—cinema, radio, and photography (in newspapers and magazines)—became subject, in their development, manufacture, and distribution, to capitalist methods of mass production, replacing itinerant players and self-made entertainment.

Adorno and his colleagues argued that through such developments industrial capitalism penetrated ever deeper into cultural life, creating new forms of leisure and entertainment for masses of people on a scale that had hitherto been unimaginable. They lumped these developments together under an umbrella term: the culture industry (Adorno and Horkheimer, 1977 [1947]). Following Marx, they saw the application of capitalist methods to cultural production as exploitative. They noted the **concentration of ownership** in Hollywood cinema, in the American press, and in broadcasting. They discussed the extent to which advertising supported these new mass media. They thought of the culture or entertainment industry as creating mass-produced forms of enjoyment that were standardized and uniform. Whether the products were popular songs or soap operas, they were all the same: they were mass-produced according to standard formulas and acted as vehicles for the promotion of capitalism. Difference was destroyed, and so, too, was choice. It was impossible to resist the power of the culture industry. Mass audiences could not resist the glossy appeal of the Hollywood movie, the star system, the easy exploitation of emotions in melodramas or gangster movies (Horkheimer, 1972). They also saw these developments, along with the growth of **monopoly capitalism** (transnational corporations distributing their products all over the world) and of the strong, centralized, modern state, as increasing the domination of social institutions over individual lives. The culture industry, in their view, destroyed individuality, created uniformity and conformity, and made resistance well-nigh impossible.

The Frankfurt School members have been accused of cultural elitism and pessimism, and very few people today would suggest that the culture industry (a useful term) has the entirely negative effects that they claimed it did. Nevertheless, the members of the Frankfurt School were right to point out the importance of analyzing this industry as integral to global capitalism and to question critically the impact and effect of this industry on contemporary cultural life. The issues they addressed have a continuing relevance. We have seen, since they first developed their analysis, the continuing expansion of the cultural industries to the extent that they now circulate throughout the world. The *Lord of the Rings* movie trilogy, for instance, is not just a special effects movie; it is a marketing extravaganza. Equally, Disneyland, Walt Disney World, Disneyland Paris, and Tokyo Disneyland are part of a global process whereby tourism and entertainment converge in a marriage of the leisure and culture industries to reduce the world to a series of theme parks. Thanks to TV we've all been there and done that, and it all looks the same, partly because you can stay in the same hotels and buy the same things in the same shops in the same shopping malls around the world. The trends the Frankfurt School identified years ago today dominate the globe.

EFFECTS RESEARCH

Effects studies and uses and gratifications research developed in the US between the 1940s and 1960s. Both were heavily oriented towards content, tended to rely on quantitative measurement, and assumed a simple psychological model of human behaviour.

Imagine a person reads a newspaper article or sees a TV program related to copyright in the music industry. On finishing the article he phones a friend: 'Did you know the music industry has managed to persuade the government to tax all blank cassette tapes and writeable CDs and that the record companies are chasing after deejays and community centres to capture royalties for playing recorded music? And do you know what else? The US doesn't do it and it's not illegal to import blank CDs. So we've gotta go down to the States and buy a bunch of writeable disks. Maybe we can take orders and make a bunch of money.'

Such actions are exactly the kind of behaviour that effects researchers hypothesize and study. Imagine that his friend replies, 'Oh, sure, another one of your brilliant schemes for making money. I'm sure there's some rule against it.' However, the next day he reads in *Shift*, a magazine on technology that comes and goes from the Canadian scene, that someone else has had the same idea and has been giving CDs away in protest. **Effects research** can be applied to this scenario. For instance, effects theorists would term the sequence of effects **cultivation analysis** in that the material has affected this male's perspective on the world. Moreover, effects theorists would speak of **agenda-setting** in this situation insofar as the media have sensitized the friend to the issue and possibly increased its importance in his mind.

The conception of the interaction between the audience and the media as effects derives from early survey research into the media conducted primarily by American social psychologists, such as Elihu Katz and Paul Lazarsfeld (1965) and Joseph Klapper (1960). These psychologists were primarily interested in the influence of the media. They were working to dispel the formulations of the Frankfurt School, who, as we saw, portrayed the media as powerful instruments of social control that offered the masses false pleasures and destroyed human individuality and the possibility of critical thought (Adorno and Horkheimer, 1977 [1947]). The ideological assumption of the American psychologists who set out to counteract these notions was that the media, to the contrary, were marvellous democratic institutions that brought all people into the mainstream of the culture. They set out to document the effects of exposure to the information and entertainment the media were bringing into the homes of Americans in the 1950s and 1960s.

At first these studies assumed the media were having a strong, direct, and specific effect on individual behaviour. Researchers thought, for instance, that TV influenced people's voting patterns at election time, or that the depiction of violence on TV might have harmful consequences, especially for young viewers. But in general, and to the surprise of the researchers, they could identify only weak effects. Having found weaker effects than anticipated, they undertook the task of reconceiving the nature of effects and of the theory. They sought out longer-term, indirect, and diffuse effects.

Recent research in this same tradition focuses on phenomena such as the agenda-setting role of the media, i.e., how the media influence what issues are discussed and sometimes acted upon by the government of the day. For example, the front page of the *Globe and Mail* (and presumably, to a lesser extent, the *National Post* and the *Ottawa Citizen*) plays a significant role in what questions are asked that day in the House of Commons, as does the CBC news. The media message has also been more broadly conceived

in more recent effects studies. Thus, rather than looking for predictable voting behaviour, researchers tend now to search for positive or negative attitudes, for instance, towards a politician or a political platform, as influenced by the media. Beginning with George Gerbner (1969), researchers have examined the effects of viewing behaviour on people's conception of social reality, a perspective that has evolved into what is called cultivation analysis, wherein content is studied for its ability to encourage or cultivate a positive attitude in the viewer towards a particular person or perspective (see Morgan and Signorelli, 1990).

Effects analysis has been greatly criticized, essentially because researchers have not been able to identify clear, strong effects of media exposure. In short, it is argued that the method is too simple for the task. The links in our opening example, of media coverage of surcharges on recording media, are not usually that easy to discern. Nor, often, are they long-lasting. A week later that whole matter may be forgotten.

The major difficulty in effects research is that conceiving of the links between the media and people as effects tends to narrow the scope of questions about media–audience interaction, even when elaborations like agenda-setting and cultivation theory are introduced. Also, in any experiment or survey it is almost impossible to separate the influence of media content from the myriad of other influences that surround us. Because it is impossible to control the prior exposure of audience members to the message in question, let alone what they have made of that exposure, it is very difficult to isolate the effects of the media and their contribution to a wide selection of people's opinions or behaviour. Even in cases when one finds 'the smoking television set'—a set belonging to some individual who has committed a heinous crime and that is tuned to a channel that hours previously aired a model of the crime committed—there is always more to the story. Specifically, there is human agency. For example, what in the person's background could make him or her vulnerable to internalizing a message to act in an aberrant fashion? Obviously, discussion of the effects of media on society can be problematic.

It is interesting who gets condemned and who does not for putting forward certain media constructions. German film director Leni Riefenstahl, who reached 100 on 22 August 2002, was never forgiven for her movies *Triumph of the Will* (1934–5) and *Olympia* (1936–8), which portrayed Hitler's Nazis in a heroic light. In contrast, D.W. Griffith, whose *Birth of a Nation* (1916) portrays African Americans as ignorant and crude, is considered a pioneer of American film. Oliver Stone has also escaped condemnation for his movie *Natural Born Killers* even though copycat crimes were committed in its wake. Stanley Kubrick, on the other hand, withdrew *A Clockwork Orange* from circulation in Britain after some of its violence was re-enacted in real life (*Globe and Mail*, 22 Aug. 2002). The debate around such movies can often deteriorate into a crude effects theory discussion.

USES AND GRATIFICATION RESEARCH

Uses and gratification research (U&G) began as a reaction against effects research (Blumler and Katz, 1974). Its central question is, 'What do viewers do with the media?' Take, for example, two university students who decide to see an action movie after their last exam of the semester. They are not even at the movie yet but uses and gratification theory is already relevant. The movies are a good chance to relax, get together with friends, enjoy whatever is of interest in the movie, and go out for a coffee afterwards to socialize. Movies give people a chance to talk about other, related interests.

From the beginning, the U&G approach was more attentive to audience variables, that is, the orientations and approaches audience members brought to their selection and interpretation of media content. Given its roots in social psychology, U&G has concentrated on the micro (personal) and mezzo (group or institutional) levels of social existence, with little attention paid to the macro level—the social, ideological, cultural, or political orientations of the audience. Work during the eighties spoke of never-ending spirals of uses and effects in which audience members look to the media for certain information (Rosengren and Windahl, 1989). Having gained this information, they behave in a particular way and then return to the media for further information, and so on. In fact, the two areas—effects research and uses and gratification research—have been growing increasingly closer together and are mutually complementary.

Even given the shift in emphasis, with U&G being more aware of audience variables, the major difficulty with this approach is that it places greater emphasis on the audience member as *acted upon rather than*

acting. The nature of the research question tends to be as follows: given media exposure, what can be identified as the uses audience members make of that exposure and the gratification they obtain from that exposure? In other words, although the focus is on what individuals do with the media, the emphasis is on the impact of the media on people's lives. In the end the theory downplays human agency.

BRITISH CULTURAL STUDIES

Whereas Marx and the Frankfurt School predated effects studies and uses and gratifications research, cultural studies came after and were a critical reaction to a lack in those two approaches of any critical perspective of either the character of modern (American) society or the role of modern media therein. The impact of the growing mass culture in post-war Britain, particularly on the working class, was a concern of a number of intellectuals in the 1950s, such as Richard Hoggart (1992 [1957]), Raymond Williams (1958), and later, E.P. Thompson, who examined the formation of the English working class between 1780 and 1830 (1980 [1963]). To advance his concerns, Hoggart established a small post-graduate Centre for Contemporary Cultural Studies at the University of Birmingham, which his colleague Stuart Hall took over in the late 1960s. Hall's work in the 1970s with graduate students in what came to be called the **Birmingham School** was increasingly influential and largely defines what is today known as cultural studies.

There are many accounts of the short history of **British cultural studies** from the 1950s to the present (see Turner, 1990; McGuigan, 1992; Storey, 1993;

ON THE BIRMINGHAM SCHOOL

An article by Norma Schulman on the beginnings and impact of the Centre for Contemporary Cultural Studies at the University of Birmingham can be found on the Web site of the *Canadian Journal of Communication*: www.cjc-online.ca. For Schulman's article, follow the links through back issues to vol. 18, no. 1 and to the full text of the article.

Schulman, 1993). Two main lines of development can be identified: one focused on the analysis of working-class culture, particularly the culture of young working-class males, and then, in response to feminist critiques at the Centre, the analysis of young working-class females (Women's Studies Group, 1978). A central concern was the use of mass culture, by both sexes, to create and define gendered identities. What clothing you chose to wear, the kind of music you listened to, whether you had, for instance, a motorcycle or a scooter—these things created your image and defined your personality. Instead of individuals being manipulated by the products of mass culture—as the Frankfurt School had argued—it was the other way around. Individuals could take these products and manipulate them, subvert them, to create new self-definitions. The classic study of this process is Dick Hebdige's *Subculture: The Meaning of Style* (1979), which looked at how young, white, working-class males created identities for themselves through music: from mods and rockers in the 1950s and 1960s through to punk and beyond in the 1970s. Cultural studies paid particular attention to the ambiguous relationship between musical styles and social identities and to the embrace of black music and the culture of young, black males by young, white, working-class males. This is captured beautifully in the 1991 film *The Commitments*, based on the Roddy Doyle novel, when the protagonist, Jimmy Rabbitte, has assembled a group of working-class Dublin youth to become an R&B band and asks them to repeat after him, 'I'm black and I'm proud.'

Another important strand in the study of contemporary culture was analysis of film and television. In the 1970s the British Film Institute's journal *Screen* put forward an analysis of film that argued that how a story was told (through techniques of editing, visual images, and so forth) controlled and defined the viewer. The narrative techniques of cinema subtly but powerfully imposed their meanings on the spectator, who could not avoid being 'positioned' to see the film in a particular way. (The notion of 'position' refers particularly to the point of view constructed for the viewer through filmic techniques—how the viewer is 'put in the picture'.) In a classic analysis of Hollywood movies, Laura Mulvey (1975) argued that the pleasures of this kind of cinema were organized for a male viewer and that women (both in the storyline and as objects to be looked at) were merely instruments of male pleasure—objects of a male gaze.

Stuart Hall and his students, undertaking an analysis of television and how it worked, wanted to develop a more open kind of analysis. They argued that TV tried to impose its meaning—a preferred reading—on viewers, but that it was quite possible for viewers to refuse that meaning and develop their own interpretation of what they heard and saw (Glasgow Media Group, 1976).

The key concept, in both film and TV analysis, was that of **ideology**, a term derived from Marx's writings, in particular *The German Ideology* with co-author Friedrich Engels (1974). (The meaning of ideology has been much discussed—see Larrain, 1979, 1983; Thompson, 1980 [1963].) In essence, ideology can be understood as follows: in a neutral sense it refers to a coherent set of social values, beliefs, and meanings (for example, Catholicism, socialism, vegetarianism). In Marxist terms it is a critical concept that refers particularly to dominant or ruling-class values, beliefs, and meanings—what came to be called the **dominant ideology** (for a critique of this concept, see Abercrombie et al., 1980, 1990). In classic Marxism, the analysis of dominant values was mainly presented in terms of class. Cultural studies extended it to race (see, for example, Centre for Contemporary Cultural Studies, 1982) and gender (van Zoonen, 1991). White, Western, male values were central aspects of the dominant value system. The general idea was that through the ideological misrepresentation of social reality, subordinate social groups (workers, women, blacks) were prevented from understanding how they were exploited or oppressed because they had been lured into a false consciousness. The effect of ideology was then to maintain the status quo, to maintain the domination of the powerful over the powerless, by presenting versions of social reality that represented this process of domination as natural, obvious, right, and just—in short, the natural order or the way things are and ought to be.

The researchers argued that British television reproduced the dominant value system—loosely understood as a class-based consensus that believed in the monarchy, the Anglican Church, Parliament, and the rule of law, among other things (Hall, 1978, 1980). Television worked to maintain these beliefs and to discredit ideas and attitudes that opposed them.

One major vehicle for reproducing dominant values is news and current affairs programs, in which powerful **primary definers** (interviewed politicians, experts, the military) are routinely allowed to define the issues, express their opinions, and offer interpretations (Hall et al., 1978), while alternative or oppositional interpretations of events are seldom, if ever, allowed expression. The most extreme example of this in Britain was the banning of members of Sinn Fein (the political wing of the Irish Republican Army [IRA]) from British TV (see Curtis, 1984; Schlesinger, 1983). As discussed in Chapter 4, this sort of thing also occurs in Canada, such as when both the media and politicians threatened the Canadian public with predictions of dire consequences if they rejected constitutional reform in the 1992 referendum. Canadians did reject the Charlottetown Accord and life continued.

According to Hall, the media work to maintain the dominant value system by **encoding** dominant values in the media in complex ways. For instance, television dramas can be seen as a set of morality tales from which we are to take lessons in what constitutes desirable and undesirable behaviour. But, Hall says, media presentations can be **decoded** by viewers in very different ways (Hall, 1978). We can often articulate the intended meaning and insert left-out information that deflates (or inflates) the intended message. The media themselves expose and toy with media codes through comedy. On YTV the vain news anchorman, the miming weather woman, and a host of other characters help audiences decode television. Ken Finkleman's program *The Newsroom* was another satire of media codes.

While this perspective—of audiences decoding information in their own ways—is now taken as a given, it was not until British scholar David Morley (1980) tested it that it was really accepted by media theorists. Morley looked at how viewers of a 1970s BBC program called 'Nationwide' interpreted, made sense of, or decoded the program. He found, as Hall had suggested, three different responses: dominant, negotiated, and oppositional. Some viewers bought the values of the program, which, as its title implies, stressed national unity and strong family values, suggesting that Britain was essentially a nation of white, middle-class families living in suburbia. These viewers accepted the program's preferred meaning, this consensual, harmonious representation of British society that systematically filtered out the conflicting interests of marginalized social groups (that is, marginalized by this definition). Other viewers took a rather more critical or negotiated view of the program, while a few groups of viewers (notably young blacks) rejected it altogether.

Morley's work was very influential, and in the 1980s the cultural studies approach increasingly concentrated on how audiences made sense of the media. Audience theorist Ien Ang's (1985) study of how Dutch viewers responded to *Dallas* is a well-known example. The approach rejected the strongly deterministic view of the Frankfurt School and the journal *Screen*, stressing that viewing was an active process. James Curran (1990) has suggested that all this amounted to reinventing the wheel: after all, effects studies had discovered this negotiation process years before. While this may be so, cultural studies puts forward a much richer framework for studying both content and audiences than effects studies ever did.

FEMINIST RESEARCH

Feminist research argues that the basic inequality in society is not based on class but on gender. Women have been viewed as objects of pleasure or objects to be controlled by men. Patriarchy has been pervasive, whether through ownership of women or subordination of women's realities. These arguments, until recently, have been fairly accurate. However, in recent years, feminist researchers have been looking for and finding elements showing the empowerment of women in the media. Alanis Morissette and Chantal Kreviazuk are examples from the music world; in television *Gilmore Girls* and *Because I Said So* provide strong female characters; and in sports, Hayley Wickenheiser's hockey skill (which earned her a place in a men's hockey league in Finland) is a case in point.

Feminist studies have much in common with cultural studies (see Franklin et al., 1992). The feminist approach developed from French writer Simone de Beauvoir's book, *The Second Sex* (1957 [1952]), and the writings of Betty Friedan (1963) in the US. Like Marxism, feminism is deeply critical of the character of modern societies, which, it argues, are based on fundamental inequalities. But where Marxism locates the roots of inequality in capital ownership and class division, feminism points to the male domination (patriarchy) of women as the root of profound human inequalities and injustices. These inequalities are pervasive aspects of modern life: men have economic, political, and cultural power; women do not.

Men generally control public life, while women occupy the resigned marginal spaces of private life and domesticity.

How is it that these values (of patriarchy) continue to have such power? To answer this, critics studied how cultural products can contribute to normalizing the oppression of women. Advertisements were one obvious place to look (Williamson, 1978), and film, television, and popular fiction provided other obvious avenues. Feminist researchers developed the idea of gendered narratives (Laura Mulvey's work on film was influential here): types of stories (narrative genres) appeal or speak to male readers or viewers (adventure stories like the Western or James Bond novels are classic examples), while other types appeal to female readers and viewers (Radway, 1984, is the key text). Likewise, they looked at gendered television: feminist audience studies discovered the kind of radio and TV programs that women preferred (see, for example, Hobson, 1980, 1982). David Morley (1986) studied TV viewers in family settings and discovered a consistent profile of male and female preferences. One principal program category was TV soap operas with their largely female viewing audiences, and many studies have since examined what women enjoy in such programs (Seiter et al., 1989, reviews previous work).

In an article in Curran and Gurevitch's *Mass Media and Society*, Dutch scholar Liesbet van Zoonen (1991: 33) argues that there is a great variety in feminist discourse. She notes that feminist research is drawn together by 'an unconditional focus on analysing *gender* as a mechanism that structures material and symbolic worlds and our experience of them.' Van Zoonen also distinguishes three traditions in feminist analysis: liberal, radical, and socialist. She notes that strategies for change derive directly from each of these perspectives with the aim of either reforming existing media institutions or forming new feminist institutions.

In the same collection of essays, audience researchers Ien Ang and Joke Hermes (1991) take a much more radical approach. They criticize some of the underlying assumptions of a general feminist stance, noting that certain feminists have accepted a crude inoculation model of media effects on women derived from effects theory (i.e.: the media inject audiences with meanings). They call attention to work challenging such assumptions and urge that the discussion of the female spectator be reopened.

Noting that the notion of gender is socially constructed, essentialist, and reductionist, they underline the necessity of investigating how women negotiate with the 'texts' they encounter in the media.

RECEPTION ANALYSIS

In the 1980s cultural and feminist studies of the mass media increasingly looked at how audiences made sense of cultural products, how they interpreted what they read, saw, and heard. But it became apparent that to do this, it was necessary to attend not simply to the product itself (the novel, the film, the TV drama), but also, more generally, to the context in which the consumption of the cultural product took place. **Reception analysis** thus broadens out to take into account the social setting in which audiences respond to the products of contemporary popular culture. Reception analysis is closely related to uses and gratifications theory. However, rather than emphasizing what use or gratification an audience member gains from media exposure, reception analysis focuses on what the reader brings to the media and how he or she actively interprets all that it has to offer.

The broadening of reception analysis has been of particular interest to feminist scholars in a number of ways. For one thing, the household is a prime site for cultural consumption by women. When US researcher Janice Radway studied American women readers of romantic fiction she found that they emphasized how the activity of reading became a special moment for themselves: a moment when they took time out from domestic chores, responsibilities to husbands and children, and created a time and space for themselves and their pleasures. They saw it as a moment of self-affirmation (Radway, 1984). This discovery points to the importance of attending to what lies outside the cultural products themselves. The *meaning* of romance fiction for Radway's readers was something more than the form and content of the stories themselves. The shortcoming of such a viewpoint is that it does not speak to the significance of romance reading as a vehicle for self-affirmation.

In the same way that Radway examined romance reading, work was undertaken on how family members use radio, TV, newspapers, magazines, VCRs, and satellite dishes. It showed that these media can be used for a range of purposes that have little to do with their content. A parent may watch a TV program with a child to nourish their relationship rather than to tune in to what the program is actually about. The dynamics of power relations between males and females, parents and children, and older and younger siblings have been studied in relation to, for instance, who has access to the remote control for the TV or who can work the VCR (Morley, 1986).

In general, the attention of such research is directed towards what the audience brings to a viewing or decoding, the social context, and the act of viewing. Media researchers J. Bryce (1987), Peter Collett and R. Lamb (1986), D. Hobson (1980), and Tania Modleski (1984) have all described how various groups—women, men, families—watch television. Women, for instance, often juggle television-watching with domestic chores. Children often play while watching TV and look up when their ears tell them that the plot is thickening. Men often watch programs not of their own choosing. In some families and at some times, a switched-on television functions as a conversation stopper or mediator rather than a source of watched programming. British media scholar Paddy Scannell (1988), who assisted greatly with the original drafting of this chapter, has analyzed the manner in which broadcasting sustains the lives and routines of whole populations, while researchers Roger Silverstone (1981) and John Hartley (1987) have discussed how television provides the basis for symbolic participation in a national community, or sometimes, as in the cases of Belgium, Switzerland, and Canada, an international linguistic community.

INDUSTRY AUDIENCE RESEARCH

While academics have had their own reasons for studying mass media audiences, media institutions themselves have long been keenly interested in finding out what people read, listen to, and watch. Such information has practical value. It enables TV or radio stations, for instance, to identify their audiences and discover their listening or viewing habits and preferences. Industry-led research on audiences attends to basic issues, such as when people are available or not to listen or watch and when they are watching or listening (audience habits). Given this, they can also find out what audiences like or dislike (audience tastes). This information has obvious economic value: the more precise the information they have about their own and their competitors' audiences, the greater are the possibilities to sell these audiences to advertisers or to improve their product (to attract even more advertisers).

Traditionally, such research concentrated on audience size: the bigger the audience for a TV program, the more attractive it would be to advertisers. But since the 1970s, industry researchers have tried to provide more accurate information about what kinds of viewers are attracted to which programs. A program could have a very large audience, but a large portion of this audience may not have much disposable income. A program with a smaller audience but one with great spending power is just as valuable, if not more valuable, to advertisers as a large general audience. For instance, a program may not reach a mass prime-time audience, yet it may have a strong viewership among young, affluent professionals, and hence, can command premium prices on advertisements. The specific makeup of an audience can also attract advertisers. For instance, for the makers of Barbie, an audience of prepubescent girls and their mothers is of great value.

It is not only commercial media that conduct audience research—so do public media institutions. By 1936, for instance, the BBC had set up its own listener research department to answer questions about listener habits and preferences, such as when do people get up, go to work, return from work, and go to bed? The same department took over responsibility for television once it was established. Do people watch more in the winter than in summer? Do people in certain locations watch more or less than viewers elsewhere? As they answered such questions, media managers could schedule programs to conform to the daily habits and routines of the British people (Scannell, 1988). The BBC also undertook research into audience preferences: what kinds of music did people prefer to listen to—dance band music or orchestral music, opera, chamber music, or other? BBC audience research provided answers to such questions and helped broadcasters determine how much of each kind of music they ought to play over the air (on early BBC audience research, see Pegg, 1983; Scannell and Cardiff, 1991).

In Canada the CBC took on many of the same research tasks as the BBC but they grew out of a slightly different context (Eaman, 1994). As early as the 1920s in North America, individuals were attempting to set up procedures to measure radio audiences. There was even an early electronic device, the audimeter, designed to record the stations that were being heard in the home.

In October 1936, one month before the CBC

LEND ME YOUR EARS AND I'LL GIVE YOU WHITE BREAD

Why are radio stations as bland as sliced white bread? The answer, according to Bill Reynolds, former editor-in-chief of *eye Weekly* in Toronto, is corporate concentration and vertical integration. Reynolds (2002: R1, R5) notes, 'In 1995, for example, Clear Channel Communications (the dominant radio owner in the US) owned 43 radio stations; now it owns more than 1,200. . . . a subsidiary, Clear Channel Entertainment, . . . has become a prominent promoter, producer and marketer of live events operating out of more than 400 venues in the US and Canada.' This interpretation is really a political-economic analysis of content (see Chapter 4).

'In Canada', Reynolds continues, 'Corus radio is the largest owner with 52 stations reaching 8.4 million Canadians per week. Corus controls both the classic rock and new rock formats in two major markets—Q 107 and Edge 102 in Toronto, and Rock 101 and CFOX in Vancouver. . . . The corporate motivation is to keep those lists (playlists) as tight and familiar as possible, right across the country. . . . Research shows that tight formatting works. Stations carry only 35 "currents", or new songs, and change between three and five songs per week. . . . [For radio] losing one percentage point of market share can mean as much as $1.5 million in lost annual revenue.'

The 'research' of which Reynolds speaks is industry research on the size and nature of the audience, how long they listen, etc. Reynolds goes on to explain that it falls to the radio-promotion representatives of the record companies and, in the US, independent pro-

moters to get untried and untested songs played. The independent promoters actually pay radio stations between $100,000 and $400,000 for the right to represent them and in turn the record companies pay these promoters $800 to $5,000 for each song added to the station (depending on market size). As if that were not enough to insult the listener's right to choose, Clear Channel can charge the independent promoters up to $500,000 per year for the privilege of pitching songs to the conglomerate. Reynolds notes that most claim that pay-for-play does not exist in Canada, but he also notes that if one does not consider the 35 per cent Canadian content requirement, the playlists of Canadian and US radio stations look remarkably similar.

This side of communications businesses does not receive as much attention as it should. The vast majority of the material that audiences see in newspapers or on television, in movie theatres or magazines, as well as what they listen to on radio, is the result of major marketing efforts of producers.

Of course, in any business things never stand still. University-based radio stations, co-op stations such as CFRO in Vancouver and Radio CINQ in Montreal, and others, such as the Beat at 94.5 FM in Vancouver, are breaking the mould. And deejays at clubs also are a separate force in the music world. But like the big beer makers in contrast to the microbreweries, the availability of mainstream product will continue to dominate.

---

began operations, Montrealer Walter Elliott set up an independent market research operation with a partner, Paul Haynes, to serve both the CBC and commercial broadcasters (ibid.). Various other individuals and companies followed over the years and, while they were successful in a commercial context, they did not serve the interests of the CBC very well. The most obvious example of their failings came in the form of the ratings of a CBC radio station operating out of Watrous, Saskatchewan. Even though it was well known that this station was listened to throughout the Prairies and even into British Columbia, surveys carried out by Elliott-Haynes showed the audience share to be almost nothing. The main reason for

this inaccuracy seemed to be that the company only surveyed urban areas, and it did so within a limited time period and by telephone. Later work showed that CBC in Watrous was in fact the most listened-to station in Saskatchewan.

For years the CBC attempted to use commercial audience research services, though it realized their shortcomings. By 1954 the need for high-quality audience research for public broadcasting had become more than obvious. Moreover, the conceptualization of what information was needed had advanced beyond audience share to qualitative information. So, following the lead of the BBC, the CBC set up its own research department.

Figure 5.1 Program Supply and Viewing Share to Various English-Language Station Groups, 6:00 a.m.–2:00 a.m.

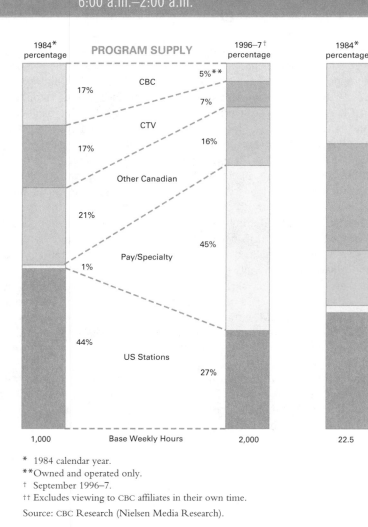

* 1984 calendar year.
**Owned and operated only.
† September 1996–7.
†† Excludes viewing to CBC affiliates in their own time.

Source: CBC Research (Nielsen Media Research).

Eaman has summarized the types of research undertaken by the CBC over the years:

- the impact of cable on television viewing;
- methodological analysis;
- critiques of other studies;
- indirect indicators of audience demand;
- program balance analysis;
- analysis of Canadian content and gender roles;
- effects analysis;
- awareness analysis;
- research on audience maximization;
- audience composition;

- special broadcasts audiences;
- audience behaviour, that is, how often people listen and/or watch, to what, when;
- habits and interests of certain age groups;
- comparisons of certain audiences to the general population;
- opinions of programs by audiences;
- opinions of what programs should be broadcast.

Figures 5.1, 5.2, and 5.3 illustrate some of the information the CBC gathers about its audiences. In Figure 5.1, bar graphs represent the amount of programming supplied by various broadcasters as a per-

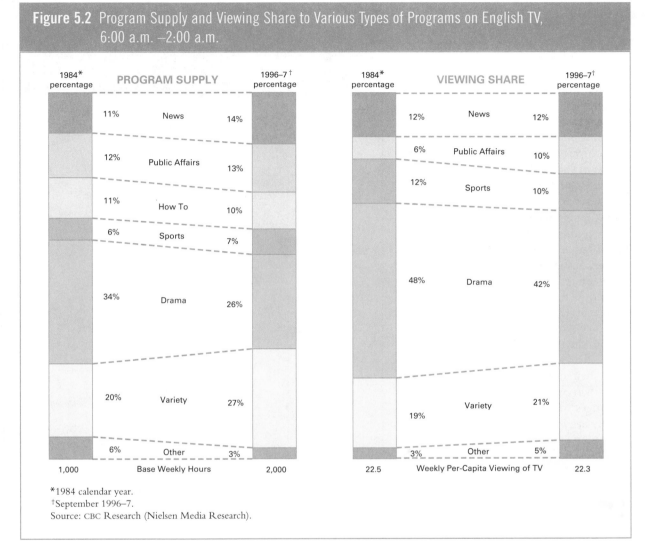

Figure 5.2 Program Supply and Viewing Share to Various Types of Programs on English TV, 6:00 a.m. –2:00 a.m.

PROGRAM SUPPLY

1984* percentage		1996–7† percentage
11%	News	14%
12%	Public Affairs	13%
11%	How To	10%
6%	Sports	7%
34%	Drama	26%
20%	Variety	27%
6%	Other	3%

1,000   Base Weekly Hours   2,000

VIEWING SHARE

1984* percentage		1996–7† percentage
12%	News	12%
6%	Public Affairs	10%
12%	Sports	10%
48%	Drama	42%
19%	Variety	21%
3%	Other	5%

22.5   Weekly Per-Capita Viewing of TV   22.3

*1984 calendar year.
†September 1996–7.
Source: CBC Research (Nielsen Media Research).

centage of the overall supply of programming and how this has changed since 1984, as well as the viewing share achieved by various broadcasters, including change since 1984. In addition, programming supply and viewing share can be compared. For instance, with 5 per cent of the program supply, the CBC has 9 per cent of the market. CBC's rival, CTV, seemingly does better, with a 20 per cent market share based on only 7 per cent of program supply. CBC managers would examine this difference and obtain a finer analysis of the data to determine if the CBC **mandate** accounted for this difference or whether, in competing head to head, they were just not as successful as CTV. Figure 5.2 indicates the CBC's most successful program areas. Note, for example, that for news, pub-

lic affairs, and variety, the percentage of viewing share is somewhat less than the percentage of program supply. In contrast, drama has a 42 per cent viewing share with only 26 per cent of program supply. Figure 5.3 removes imported programs from the mix and compares programming supply and viewing share for Canadian programs in English. Here, the CBC does well, at 25 per cent of the viewing share with only 13 per cent of programming supply. CTV does even better, with 10 per cent of supply and 26 per cent of viewing, while the specialty channels fare much worse, with 59 per cent of program supply and 28 per cent of viewing. Of course, while these general statistics give an overall sense of things, myriad details, such as program type, original programming versus reruns, and so forth, account for the observed differences, and it is in this more detailed analysis that the data can be even more useful.

Today, normal industry or institutional research (the terms are synonymous) adds information on media consumption to survey data obtained through various sampling procedures. Traditionally, media consumption has been measured by means of diaries kept by audience members, in which people log in and out as they watch or cease to watch. In 1993 the BBM (it gets its initials from its former name, the Bureau of Broadcast Measurement) introduced the **people meter**, a sophisticated electronic device to measure listening/viewing every 12 seconds (Enchin, 1993). These new devices have had a significant impact on audience data and have caused some turmoil in the industry. For instance, we now know that far fewer audience members have their eyes and minds glued to the tube than was claimed by those selling audiences. The data from the people meters has therefore caused ad rates to be readjusted.

Three important concepts basic to institutional audience research are:

1. reach: the percentage of audience members who tune in to a program for some amount of time. Program, daily, and weekly reach refer to the percentage of the audience that tunes in to some part of the program for some period of time during its showing, to the channel once in a day, or to the channel once in a week respectively.
2. share: the percentage of the average audience that tunes into a program or channel at or over any specified time period.
3. viewing time: the time spent viewing expressed over the period of a day, week, or longer period of time.

The difference between reach and share is particularly interesting. In any week a very high percentage of Canadians will tune in to the CBC, perhaps more than any other station or network. However, the share of

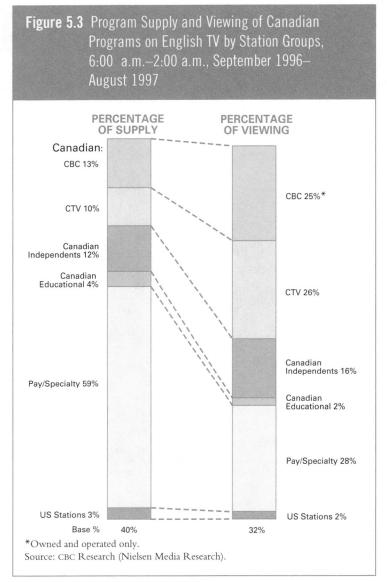

Figure 5.3 Program Supply and Viewing of Canadian Programs on English TV by Station Groups, 6:00 a.m.–2:00 a.m., September 1996– August 1997

*Owned and operated only.
Source: CBC Research (Nielsen Media Research).

the audience the CBC has at any one time is a lot lower, suggesting that the viewing time over the period of a week is relatively low.

Formative research and summative research (see Withers and Brown, 1995), much of it undertaken by TVOntario, are other approaches to measuring the appeal of TV programming. **Formative research** is undertaken during production, usually by means of focus groups, to obtain reactions to programs in the making. **Summative research** measures the effectiveness of a program after its completion.

Industry research also introduces categories within which programs are measured. Such categories

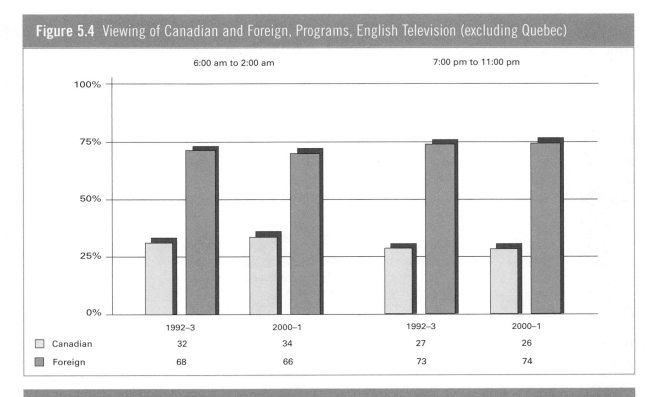

Figure 5.4 Viewing of Canadian and Foreign, Programs, English Television (excluding Quebec)

6:00 am to 2:00 am   7:00 pm to 11:00 pm

	1992–3	2000–1	1992–3	2000–1
Canadian	32	34	27	26
Foreign	68	66	73	74

Figure 5.5 Viewing of Canadian and Foreign, Programs, French Television (Quebec only)

6:00 am to 2:00 am   7:00 pm to 11:00 pm

	1992–3	2000–1	1992–3	2000–1
Canadian	68	65	69	62
Foreign	32	35	31	38

Traditionally, English Canadians have watched more foreign than Canadian content while Quebecers, partly as a result of language differences, have watched more Canadian than foreign content. Figures 5.4 and 5.5 compare viewership on two dates, in prime time and overall, and for English-language and French-language television.

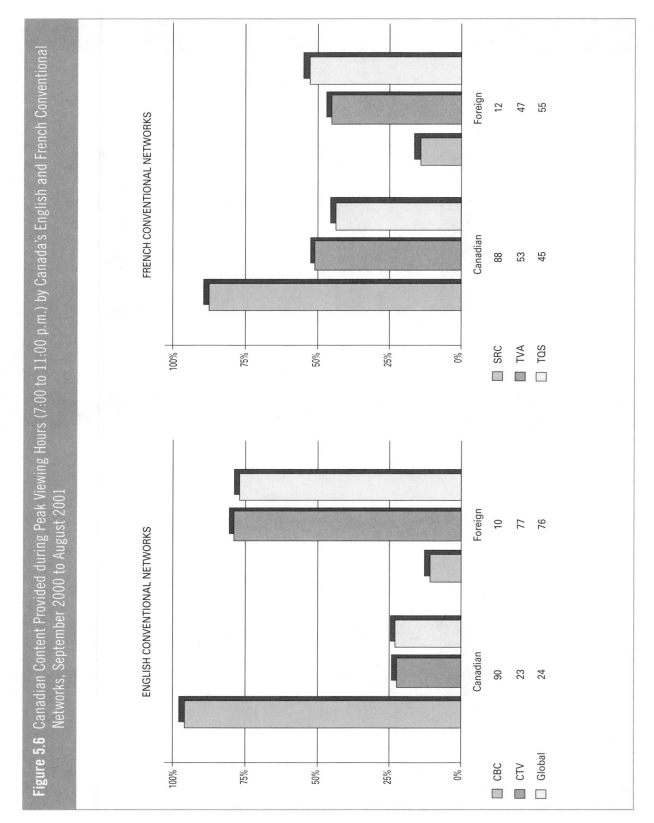

Figure 5.6 Canadian Content Provided during Peak Viewing Hours (7:00 to 11:00 p.m.) by Canada's English and French Conventional Networks, September 2000 to August 2001

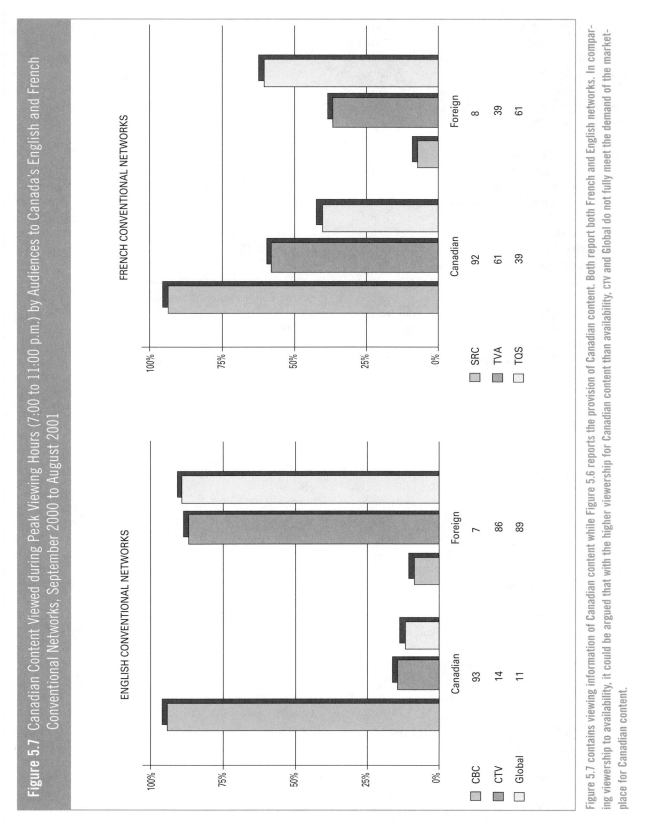

Figure 5.7 Canadian Content Viewed during Peak Viewing Hours (7:00 to 11:00 p.m.) by Audiences to Canada's English and French Conventional Networks, September 2000 to August 2001

ENGLISH CONVENTIONAL NETWORKS

	Canadian	Foreign
CBC	93	7
CTV	14	86
Global	11	89

FRENCH CONVENTIONAL NETWORKS

	Canadian	Foreign
SRC	92	8
TVA	61	39
TQS	39	61

Figure 5.7 contains viewing information of Canadian content while Figure 5.6 reports the provision of Canadian content. Both report both French and English networks. In comparing viewership to availability, it could be argued that with the higher viewership for Canadian content than availability, CTV and Global do not fully meet the demand of the marketplace for Canadian content.

allow for greater precision in assessing success, but they also demand that programs conform to the categories that are measured. For instance, commercial radio can be divided into the following categories. (Those listed here are categories revised in 2000. They are contained and elaborated on in Public Notice CRTC 1999–76.)

- Category 2 (Popular Music)
  - Subcategory 21: Pop, rock, and dance—includes all types of rock music.
  - Subcategory 22: Country and country-oriented—includes country & western, traditional country, new country, and other country-oriented styles.
  - Subcategory 23: Acoustic—music composed and performed in an acoustic style by the chansonniers and singer/songwriters of our time.
  - Subcategory 24: Easy listening—'cocktail' jazz, soft contemporary jazz, middle-of-the-road, and 'beautiful music'.
- Category 3 (Special Interest Music)
  - Subcategory 31: Concert—includes the whole spectrum of classical music traditions.
  - Subcategory 32: Folk and folk-oriented—authentic, traditional folk music as well as contemporary folk-oriented music that draws substantially on traditional folk music in style and performance.
  - Subcategory 33: World beat and international—music that draws heavily from the traditional music styles of countries throughout the world. It also includes music from the popular, folk, and classical music traditions of countries throughout the world that are played in instrumental form or sung in languages other than English and French.
  - Subcategory 34: Jazz and blues—historic and contemporary music in the jazz and blues traditions.
  - Subcategory 35: Non-classical religious—music of the church or religious faiths; gospel, hymns, contemporary Christian.

The World's Best Readership Database— PMB, A Case Study

Though our discussion on audience research has focused on the broadcast media, such research is also pursued for print media. In fact, Canada is home to the richest print audience database in the world. It is controlled by the Print Measurement Bureau (PMB), an industry organization run as a non-profit entity by Canadian magazine publishers, advertising agencies, advertisers, and other companies and organizations in the media industry. Industry members sit on the board of directors and various committees and offer guidance in many aspects of the research. PMB's annual study has grown since its first year (1983)—it now evaluates the readership of 88 print publications. Each annual PMB study reports data from a two-year rolling sample of 24,000 individuals aged 12 or more. This means that the results of 12,000 individuals interviewed in 2000 and 12,000 interviewed in 2001 would form the basis of the data reported in the year 2002.

The study's results are based on a nationally representative, stratified, random sample of Canadians. Of the 47,000 census enumeration areas in Canada, 2,000 are chosen as representative. Variables taken into account include location, ethnicity, age, socio-economic status, and language. Within each enumeration area, 10 households are selected at random and interviewers customarily succeed in getting an average of 6.5 households to agree to a one- to two-hour face-to-face interview and subsequently to the completion of a printed questionnaire. One respondent is selected from each household in such a way that each member of a household has an equal chance of being chosen.

Readership data are collected for various Canadian English-language and French-language publications such as *Maclean's*, *Reader's Digest*, *Flare*, *Alberta Report*, *TV Guide*, *L'Actualité*, *Elle Québec*, and *Chatelaine*. The at-home personal interview gathers information on reading habits: what publications respondents have scanned/read; the number of times they have read each of them; the time spent reading an issue; the degree of interest in the publication. Also compiled in the interview are the demographic characteristics of respondents (age, gender, level of education, household income and size, and personal income and occupation) and their habits with respect to other media (TV, radio, Yellow Pages, newspapers). In a questionnaire completed after the interview, respondents provide information about the products and services they use, their lifestyle and leisure activities, and their shopping habits. Examples of the areas covered are drugs, groceries, home entertainment products, alcohol, other beverages, cars, financial services, home furnishings, and so on. A PMB member can sponsor the questionnaire: in such cases, questions about the purchase and use of certain brands of products would be included (PMB, n.d.). Figure 5.8 summarizes how this information can be interrelated.

In addition to access to a comprehensive database with useful information on readers' habits, values, and attitudes on a variety of subjects/products, members of PMB can also request that previously interviewed respondents be contacted again to answer a set of specific questions tailored to the member's interests. These additional data, combined with the annual database, can provide a fuller account of people's tastes and preferences and help members of PMB— whether advertisers, publishers, or other industry organizations—know their market, improve their product/service, tailor an advertising campaign, and so on. PMB, however, does not collect all the information pertaining to readership. Additional research conducted elsewhere in the industry can tell you

what time of day people read magazines, what locations have the most number of readers (hair salons are the top), and so forth.

Magazines use PMB's annual data to understand more fully the nature of their readership. By monitoring their readership, they can, for example, mount subscription campaigns aimed at market segments attractive to advertisers. They may even complement such campaigns with a reorientation of their editorial content and approach. Magazines also use PMB data as a primary tool in selling advertising space to advertisers and ad agencies. The data also allow magazines to gain a sense of the characteristics of the readership of their competitors.

Magazines and ad agencies can carry their use of the data even further. If, for example, an ad agency is buying space on behalf of a computer company, such as Apple, it can statistically establish not only the number of people in Windsor, for example, who read a particular magazine, but also highly reliable proba-

Figure 5.8 Interrelationship of Data from PMB Surveys

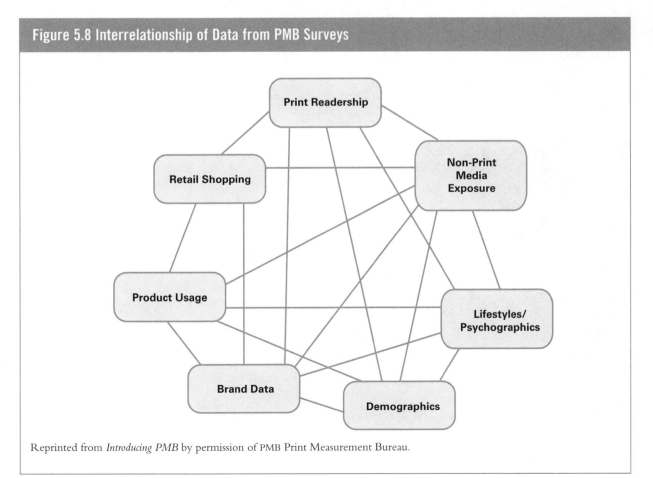

Reprinted from *Introducing PMB* by permission of PMB Print Measurement Bureau.

bilities of how many own a Macintosh, and indeed how many own a Mac, a Power Mac, an iBook, an eMac, or any other Apple product. For that matter, the ad agency can establish how many readers own other types of computers and how many do not own one at all. Given this information the agency can determine how best to access the audience and then buy, for example, a series of ads in one magazine, ads in several magazines, or some other combination.

To give a sense of the reality of the business we analyzed some of the data published in 2002. The following discussion is based on Table 5.1.

We have selected six magazines for analysis: *Canadian Geographic*, *Chatelaine*, *Flare*, *Maclean's*, *Time*, and *Reader's Digest*. We will look at readership (and make mention of circulation). From these figures,

taken from *PMB 2002 Readership Volume* (PMB, 2002), we have selected four variables to examine: age, education, region, and gender.

A few words of explanation are necessary before we start. The 'unweighted' figures (column 2) represent the actual number of respondents interviewed. The 'weighted' figures (column 4) represent an adjustment of the numbers so that they more accurately reflect the population as a whole. The 'sample' (row 1) represents the projection of the unweighted figures onto the population as a whole, while the 'population' (row 2) represents the projection of the weighted figures onto the population as a whole. So, for example, the unweighted number of readers of *Canadian Geographic* projected from the actual interviews is 4,886,000. The projection of readership

Table 5.1 Characteristics of Readership of Six Magazines Sold in Canada

					Canadian Geographic				Chatelaine			
	Unweighted	V%	Weighted	V%	000	V%	H%	I	000	V%	H%	I
Sample	29,487	100	29,487	100	4,886	100	17	100	5,374	100	18	100
Population	29,487	100	26,325	100	4,589	100	17	100	4,675	100	18	100
Age												
12–17	2,440	8	2,457	9	**706**	15	29	**165**	**474**	10	19	109
18–24	2,525	9	2,922	11	613	13	21	120	**579**	12	20	112
25–34	4,686	**16**	4,345	17	717	16	**16**	94	**751**	16	17	97
35–49	9,252	31	7,664	29	**1,288**	28	17	96	1,400	**30**	18	103
50–64	6,127	21	5,017	19	845	18	17	96	862	18	17	97
65+	4,457	15	3,918	15	429	9	11	63	608	13	16	87
Education												
No Cert. or Diploma	6,661	23	7,874	30	**1,206**	26	15	88	1,167	25	15	83
Sec./High School Grad.	6,570	22	6,697	25	1,129	25	17	97	1,263	27	19	106
Trade Cert./Diploma	3,001	10	2,905	11	547	12	19	108	480	10	17	93
University/Other Cert.	6,498	22	5,133	19	1,018	22	20	**113**	1,120	24	22	123
Bachelor's Degree.	4,213	14	2,380	9	463	10	19	**111**	422	9	18	100
Post Grad. +	2,544	9	1,336	5	236	5	18	101	222	5	17	94
Region												
Atlantic	1,617	5	2,052	8	438	10	21	122	487	10	24	**134**
Quebec	8,824	30	6,353	24	402	9	6	36	273	6	4	24
Ontario	10,201	35	10,020	38	**1,983**	43	20	113	2,240	48	22	126
Manitoba/Saskatchewan	1,666	6	1,819	7	365	8	20	115	400	9	22	124
Alberta	2,666	9	2,540	10	693	15	27	**156**	562	12	22	124
British Columbia	4,613	15	3,540	13	717	16	20	116	713	15	20	113
Gender												
Male	13,822	47	12,955	49	**2,492**	**54**	19	110	**1,116**	**24**	9	48
Female	15,665	53	13,370	**51**	**2,107**	**46**	16	90	3,559	76	27	150

Note: Highlighted data is discussed in the text.
Source: (Toronto: PMB Print Measurement Bureau, 2002). Reprinted by permission of PMB Print Measurement Bureau.

based on the weighted sample is 4,589,000. All the figures given below the top two rows of figures (sample and population) are based on weighted figures.

V% represents a percentage of the population (calculated vertically in the table) within the individual variable being examined. To take the simplest example, 2,492,000 males read *Canadian Geographic*, which amounts to 54 per cent of all readers and hence a V% of 54; while 2,107,000 females or 46 per cent read the magazine for a V% of 46. A comparison of the V% of an individual magazine to the V% of the weighted population figures indicates how much difference exists between the general population and the readership of the magazine. For instance, while women account for 51 per cent (V%) of the population, only 46 per cent of *Canadian Geographic*'s readers are women. The value I represents much the same thing as V%, only more accurately: PMB defines I as 'a measure of the relative degree of association between the two variables [for example, between readership of the publication and a demographic characteristic] relative to a base of 100' (PMB, 2002). For example, persons aged 12–17 show an I of 165 for *Canadian Geographic*, which means any sample of persons aged 12–17 would be 1.65 times more likely to be readers of *Canadian Geographic* than if the sample were selected from the population as a whole. And finally, H% is the percentage of the population calculated horizontally in the table within the individual variable being examined. Thus, for example, readers of *Canadian Geographic* aged 25–34 represent 16 per cent of the overall population of readers aged 25–34 of all magazines surveyed.

Flare				*Maclean's*				*Time* (Canada)				*Reader's Digest*			
000	V%	H%	I	**000**	V%	H%	I	**000**	V%	H%	I	**000**	V%	H%	I
1,979	100	7	100	3,647	100	12	100	3,873	100	13	100	8,094	100	27	100
1,802	100	7	100	**3,113**	100	12	100	**3,046**	100	12	100	**7,923**	100	30	100
307	17	13	**183**	271	9	11	93	328	11	13	115	776	10	32	105
404	22	14	**202**	360	12	12	104	438	14	15	130	846	11	29	96
371	21	9	**125**	498	16	11	97	510	17	12	101	1,230	16	28	94
425	**24**	6	81	861	28	11	95	836	27	11	94	2,252	28	29	98
217	12	4	63	643	21	13	108	582	19	12	100	1,585	20	32	105
77	4	2	29	481	15	12	104	351	12	9	77	1,235	16	32	105
509	28	6	95	701	23	9	75	703	23	9	77	2,076	26	26	88
507	28	8	111	745	24	11	94	736	24	11	95	2,097	26	31	104
188	10	6	95	366	12	13	107	359	12	12	107	984	12	34	113
387	21	8	110	689	22	13	113	664	22	13	112	1,749	22	34	113
158	9	7	97	356	11	15	127	371	12	16	135	682	9	29	**95**
53	3	4	58	256	8	19	**162**	212	7	16	**137**	335	4	25	**83**
135	7	7	96	246	8	12	101	237	8	12	100	943	12	46	153
75	4	1	17	136	4	2	18	282	9	4	38	373	5	6	19
901	50	9	131	1,671	50	16	133	1,384	45	14	119	3,390	**43**	34	112
175	10	10	**141**	296	10	16	**138**	221	7	12	106	778	10	43	142
236	13	9	136	398	13	16	132	401	13	16	**137**	1143	14	45	149
279	15	8	115	468	15	13	112	521	17	15	**127**	1,298	16	37	122
362	**20**	3	41	1,615	52	12	105	1,718	56	13	115	3,650	46	28	94
1,440	80	11	157	1,499	48	11	95	1,328	44	10	86	4,273	54	32	106

A sense of the variability in readership of these six magazines can be obtained from the population figures (row 2). *Reader's Digest* leads readership with 7,923,000, which is the highest of any magazine in Canada, followed by *Chatelaine* with 4,675,000, *Canadian Geographic* with 4,599,000, *Maclean's* with 3,113,000, *Time* with 3,046,000, and *Flare* with 1,802,000.

Readership alone, however, does not always tell the full story. Circulation and readers-per-copy (RPC) figures (not included in Table 5.1) can be quite different from readership. For instance, though *Time's* circulation (318,000) is much lower than *Maclean's* (501,000), it has a higher RPC (*Time* gets about 9.6 readers per copy, *Maclean's* only 6.2) (ibid., 1, 1).

Let us take a closer look at some basic characteristics of the readership of these magazines and some interesting variations from the norm. Later we will turn to readers themselves. One last thing to bear in mind is that readership is obviously affected by language, as is apparent in the figures of readership of English-language magazines in Quebec. But do not forget that there are populations of French-language speakers elsewhere in the country.

For *Canadian Geographic* the following points are of note. Examining readership by age shows that in absolute terms the largest group of readers (1,288,000) consists of those aged 35–49. In fact, the magazine has a substantial readership with those aged 25 and above. But it also is very successful with those aged 12–17—706,000 of that age group read the magazine and, as noted above, this group has an I of 165. The lower I values for age groups 18–24, 25–34, and especially 65+ indicate that the magazine is less popular among those age groups. In terms of education, again, while the magazine has a lot of readers with no certificate or diploma (1,206,000), the I values demonstrate that it is relatively more successful in attracting a healthy share of people having some university or other post-secondary certificate (113) and those with a bachelor's degree (111). In terms of region, while the main market is in Ontario (1,983,000 readers), it is relatively more successful in Alberta, with an I of 156. The magazine's stronger appeal among males compared to females can be seen in the absolute numbers, the V%, the I, and even the H%.

Chatelaine and *Flare* are most interesting if examined together. The success of *Flare* with young women is apparent in the I figures for those aged 12–34 (183, 202, and 125). But the substantial numbers of readers aged 35–49 (425,000, or 24 per cent of its overall readership) cannot be ignored. (Note: the V% and I value can be read as a rough indication of the relative appeal of the magazine to the population being described.) While *Flare* is successful in attracting young readers, *Chatelaine* actually has more readers among these age groups. The I values indicate that the appeal of *Chatelaine* is strongest among those aged 18–24, as is the case with *Flare*. In terms of numbers of readers, *Chatelaine* attracts the most readers (4,675,000). The largest share of readers (30 per cent) is comprised of those aged 35–49. The figures also show that *Chatelaine* has relatively greater appeal to those with more education. Those in the Atlantic region have the greatest tendency to be readers of *Chatelaine* while those in Manitoba and Saskatchewan have the greatest tendency to be readers of *Flare* (I values of 134 and 141); however, with both magazines they only account for 10 per cent of readers, while Ontarians account for about 50 per cent. And, surprisingly enough, 1,116,000 men read *Chatelaine* and 362,000 read *Flare*, 24 and 20 per cent of all readers respectively.

Maclean's and *Time* also make for an interesting comparison, which is made easier by the fact that the readership figures for both are near 3 million overall. Both magazines' readership data show a substantial number of readers across all age groups, with *Time* appealing to a slightly higher percentage in the 18–34 age range and *Maclean's* appealing more to those aged 50 and above. While these figures can be read in a number of ways, younger Canadians seem more inclined to stronger dollops of US content, while older Canadians prefer Canadian content. A quick look at the I figures indicates that both magazines appeal to those with more education, with the most educated being the strongest readers of both magazines (162 and 137). It is also interesting to see that *Maclean's* is strongest in Manitoba and Saskatchewan (138), while *Time* is strongest in Alberta and BC (137 and 127). Also, both publications appeal more to males than females. The reverse is true, by the way, for *Reader's Digest*.

Both absolute numbers and relative success with certain parts of the population (based on such variables as age, education, region, and gender) are important for advertisers (as well as for the magazines themselves). Reaching readers is one thing but reaching them in a particular environment is also impor-

Figure 5.9 How to Read a Cost Ranking (Crank) Report

English Adults 18+

Target: *Women Age 25–54*
Population (000): *5279*

Percent Base: *29.47%*

Media	Cost ($) 4C	Avg Aud (000)	Coverage (%)	Composition (%)	Composition Rank	4C CPM	4C Rank
Canadian Living	27220	1078	20.42	51.95	3	25.25	1
Chatelaine (Eng.)	35695	992	18.79	51.53	4	35.98	6
Reader's Digest	28610	953	18.05	30.57	7	30.02	4
Homemakers	20640	766	14.51	53.19	2	26.95	2
TV Times	61540	632	11.97	29.27	8	97.37	10
TV Guide	19775	597	11.31	33.79	5	33.12	5
Leisureways/ Westworld	37900	510	9.66	30.72	6	74.31	9
Maclean's	29995	488	9.24	27.20	9	61.47	8
Time	20530	443	8.39	27.11	10	46.34	7
Cdn. House & Home	12435	430	8.15	57.87	1	28.92	3

Source: 1998 PMB Two-Year Readership Study; Weighted by Population

Target:
A specific user-defined segment of the base population against which all magazines on this run are evaluated. It can be defined by demographics, product usage, or even psychographics.

Projected Population (000):
The projected actual population of the target (e.g., there are 5,279,000 women 25–54 living in Canada).

Cost ($):
The cost of a single insertion in a magazine. This cost can be changed to reflect ad size, colour or b/w, regional rates, or specially negotiated rates. Shown here are national, full-page, four-colour rates.

Average Audience (000):
The total number of respondents in the target market who are reached by one insertion in a magazine (e.g., 1,078,000 women 25–54 read an average issue of *Canadian Living*).

Coverage (%):
The average issue audience of a magazine as a percentage of the target population (e.g., *Canadian Living* reaches 20.42% of women 25–54—1,078,000 *Canadian Living* readers, divided by the target population of 5,279,000).

Composition (%):
The percentage of readers of a magazine's average issue who are in the target group (e.g., of all English adults 18+ who read *Canadian Living*, 51.95% are women 25–54).

Percent of Base:
The target market as a percentage of the total base population (e.g., 29.47% of all English adults 18+ are women 25–54).

Rank:
The position of each magazine in the specified category (e.g., with 1,078,000 average issue readers, *Canadian Living* ranks 3rd in composition). Rankings are also shown for CPM and can be interpreted in a similar way.

CPM (Cost Per Thousand):
The cost for each magazine to reach 1,000 women 25–54 (e.g., *Canadian Living's* CPM is $25.25—calculated by dividing the per insertion cost of $27,220 by the net reach per average issue in thousands: 1,078).

Reprinted from *PMB Media School* (Toronto: PMB Print Measurement Bureau) by permission of PMB Print Measurement Bureau.

tant. The appeal and impact of an ad will be affected by the publication in which it appears. To make the point strongly, it would be surprising to find an ad directed exclusively at the 1,116,000 male readers of *Chatelaine*. Yet if it were to appear, it would probably gain attention by virtue of its novelty. *Reader's Digest* deals with this issue all the time—in spite of its ability to deliver more readers, and across many groups, some advertisers are reluctant to advertise in the magazine because they see it as an inappropriate editorial environment. This view stems from various reasons, such as the magazine's condensation of the work of respected writers, its conservative politics, and the dentist office/barbershop/beauty parlour associations some have with the magazine.

Which brings us to a quick analysis of *Reader's Digest* figures. First, while the actual numbers are formidable, *Reader's Digest* has greater appeal to people aged 12–17 and over 50 than to those of ages 18–49. The magazine is also relatively more successful than other magazines in reaching those with less rather than more education. Note, however, that with I values of 95 and 83, it is also relatively successful with the most educated. By region, even though Ontario accounts for 43 per cent of its readership, the magazine appears to do slightly better, according to I values, in other regions (except Quebec, where the French-language edition is strong). As noted, more women than men read the magazine.

Table 5.1 only touches upon some of the variables that are of interest and that PMB monitors. For instance, the reach of publications over the past year is also calculated. For example, the net reach of *Canadian Geographic* for the past year is 8,468,000. In fact, the magazines surveyed by PMB reach 82 per cent of the Canadian population, of whom 69.8 per cent, or 18,363,000, are English-speaking and 19.2 per cent, or 5,064,000, are French-speaking (ibid., 1, 153).

The time spent reading a publication is also important, as is the frequency of a publication. Thus, while *Reader's Digest* publishes 12 issues per year, *Maclean's* and *Time* each publish 52. Readers spend 72.11 minutes digesting each issue of *Reader's Digest* (for a monthly total of the same value), while readers spend 42.45 minutes of their time with each issue of *Time* (for a monthly total of 180.42 minutes). This time per issue, the monthly calculation, and publication frequency are important for both the advertiser and the magazine in calculating how much to charge

for ad space. By calculating the levels of media exposure to radio and television, to daily, community, Saturday, and Sunday newspapers, and to a number of other variables, cross tabulations can be made and the relative salience of the magazine environment approximated.

In some of its instructional materials, PMB provides examples of how its database can be used to determine a plan for, and the cost of, reaching a certain population (Print Measurement Bureau, 1998). Figure 5.9, for example, demonstrates how to determine the cost of reaching a certain percentage of the known population of a particular target group. The various important elements of the table are explained in the boxes surrounding the central table.

Based on the data in Figure 5.9, an advertiser might choose to place ads in *Canadian Living*, *Homemakers*, and *Reader's Digest*, reasoning that these three magazines would provide good coverage of the target population with some (though not a great deal of) overlap. On the other hand, if the product were strongly home oriented, *Homemakers* and *Canadian Living* might be chosen instead. All the variables have to be assessed in order to match an advertiser's product and goals with suitable advertising venues.

In another example, Figure 5.10, a Sample Product Profile Table illustrates the power of the database to identify the amount and nature of product usage, the exact characteristics of those who are users, and, subsequently, how an advertiser might best reach the market he or she wishes.

As one can sense by the nature of the data and in the terms they are presented, the magazine industry, like most commercial media enterprises, focuses on serving advertisers and audiences. The numbers tell the important stories to advertisers and to the financial and advertising sales managers. These numbers, however, are of less or little importance to readers, contributors, and editors, who are more interested in the content of a magazine and its image.

Audience Research and the Public Interest

Industry research has its limitations, particularly when it comes to understanding the needs and desires of audiences. Ien Ang discusses such limitations in her book, *Desperately Seeking the Audience* (1991), and captures the problem with the chapter title, 'Audience-as-market and audience-as-public'. Ang notes how industry research tells producers how

Figure 5.10 Sample Products Profile Table

Personally Eat Chocolate/Candy Bars   Base: Total Canada—Age 12+

	Total		Non-User Past 6 Months				User Past 6 Months				Light (1-2)				Heavy (6+)			
	000	V%	000	V%	H%	I	000	V%	H%	I	000	V%	H%	I	000	V%	H%	I
Sample	20415	100	4889	100	24	100	4320	100	70	100	7121	100	35	100	1261	100	6	100
Population	24998	100	5876	100	24	100	17601	100	70	100	8750	100	35	100	1641	100	7	100
Male	12301	49	3198	54	26	110	8194	47	67	95	4033	46	33	94	804	49	7	
Female	12696	51	2687	46	21	90	9406	53	73	105	4717	54	37	106	837	51	7	
Age 12–17	2400	10	307	5	13	54	2019	11	84	120	890	10	37	106	355	22	15	225
Age 18–24	2857	11	459	8	16	68	2281	13	80	113	1205	14	42	120	226	14	8	120
Age 25–34	4953	20	1026	17	21	88	3681	21	74	106	1922	22	39	111	268	16	5	82
Age 35–49	7058	28	1591	27	23	96	5064	29	72	102	2609	30	37	106	447	27	6	97
Age 50–64	4139	17	1224	21	30	126	2646	15	64	91	1303	15	31	90	186	11	4	68
Age 65+	3591	14	1268	22	35	150	1911	11	53	76	822	9	23	65	159	10	4	68
EDU - No Cert or Dipl	7957	32	1883	32	24	101	5557	32	70	99								
- Sec/High Sch Grad	6208	25	1404	24	23	96	4458	25	72	102								
- Trade Cert/Dipl	2680	11	707	12	26	112	1816	10	68	96								
- University/Other Cert	4691	19	1036	18	22	94	3418	19	73	103								
- Bachelors Degree	2338	9	571	10	24	104	1635	9	70	99								
- Post Grad +	1124	4	275	5	25	104	716	4	64	91								
Married/Living Together	13888	56	3483	59	25	107	9609	55	69	98								
Single/Wid/Div/Separated	11096	44	2393	41	22	92	7980	45	72	102								
Principal Wage Earner	14757	59	3908	67	26	113	9763	55	66	94								
Principal Grocery Shopper	15558	62	3876	66	25	106	10699	61	69	98								
Professionals	1109	4	287	5	26	110	719	4	65	92								
Sr. Management/Owners	743	3	212	4	28	121	464	3	62	89								
Other Managers	2302	9	502	9	22	93	1630	9	71	101								
Tech/Sales/Teachers/Others	2014	8	440	7	22	93	1448	8	72	102								
Clerk/Secretarial	2786	11	507	9	18	77	2170	12	78	111								
Skilled/Unskilled/Prim	5879	23	1268	22	22	95	4106	23	72	103								
All Other	10364	41	2661	45	26	109	7064	40	68	97								
Employed Full Time	11682	47	2674	46	23	97	8237	47	71	100								
Employed Part Time	3011	12	545	9	18	77	2353	13	78	111								
Atlantic Region	2005	8	400	7	20	83	1553	9	76	108								
Quebec	6265	25	1483	25	24	101	4414	25	70	100								
Ontario	9388	38	2371	40	25	107	6520	37	69	99								
Manitoba/Saskatchewan	1772	7	385	7	22	92	1280	7	72	103								
Alberta	2278	9	432	7	19	81	1654	9	73	103								
British Columbia	3244	13	805	14	25	106	2180	12	67	95								
Montreal	2876	12	700	12	24	103	2028	12	71	100								
Toronto	3682	15	979	17	27	113	2550	14	69	98								
Calgary	706	3	140	2	20	85	528	3	75	106								
Edmonton	725	3	142	2	20	83	537	3	74	105								
Vancouver	1598	6	401	7	25	107	1108	6	69	98								
Comm Size Under 100M	8960	36	1984	34	22	94	6284	36	70	100								
Comm Size 100M–1MM	7881	32	1813	31	23	98	5633	32	71	102								
Comm Size 1MM +	8158	33	2080	35	25	108	5684	32	70	99								

Callout notes:

- There are 17,601,000 people 12 years of age or over in Canada who have eaten a chocolate/candy bar in the past 6 months.
- 70% of the 24,998,000 people 12 years of age or over in Canada have eaten a chocolate/candy bar in the past 6 months.
- The greatest number of chocolate/candy bar eaters is in the 35–49 age group (29%). 5,064,000 people aged 35–49 have eaten a chocolate/candy bar in the past 6 months.
- On a per capita basis, people aged 12–17 are the most likely to eat chocolate/candy bars. They have an index of 225 meaning that they are 125% more likely to eat chocolate/candy bars than their incidence in the general population.
- The absolute, unweighted, number of respondents.

Legend:

```
000 = Thousands
V% = Vertical Percentage
H% = Horizontal Percentage
I = Index
```

Source: (Toronto: PMB Print Measurement Bureau). Reprinted by permission of PMB Print Measurement Bureau.

successful they have been in reaching their audience but leaves them profoundly ignorant about the precise ingredients of their success or failure.

In an article in the *Canadian Journal of Communication*, Toronto media researcher Liss Jeffrey (1994) explores this issue in greater detail. What, she asks, are audience members? Are they individuals with particular psychological traits? Members of specific social, ethnic, age, or religious groups? Members of a society that allows for a fair amount of leisure time? Income earners? People with jobs that are repetitive and not very fulfilling? Persons who can benefit from positive role models? Commodity units to be sold to advertisers? Citizens? Obviously they are all of these. Yet only certain of these audience characteristics are served by the media. For instance, citizens are served by news and current affairs programs. People with leisure time are served by a variety of entertainment programs available at every hour of the day.

Jeffrey's main point is to underline how the bulk of audience research treats audience members as commodities whose sentience is sold to advertisers. True, their demographic characteristics may be known and their degree of attentiveness estimated, but because they are not conceived as citizens who could benefit from certain information and entertainment, they, the public and commercial sectors of programming, and the country all suffer. For instance, do the media in general impart values that reflect the ideals of society and contribute to its improvement and survival? Do they adequately inform citizens about domestic and international affairs? Do they allow us to see our own achievements? To know about ourselves so that we understand how we can make a contribution to society?

Such questions are important because the greater use society and individuals make of the media, the greater are the media's responsibilities. If audiences are seen within limited frameworks—for instance, to be entertained but not enlightened—then the media's contribution to society is very limited.

THE TRANSFORMING AND VANISHING AUDIENCE

As mentioned in Chapter 2, audiences are being transformed by the Internet from audiences and audience members into users and user groups. True, Web site owners such as newspapers, bookstores, e-mail services, and all kinds of other commercial enterprises treat users like audiences. They bombard users with all kinds of advertising, banner ads, pop-up ads, pop-under ads, animated characters, and TV-like ads with sound and motion. But when the ads interfere, users complain vociferously. This may be a function of the fact that Web users are actively involved in seeking information. They are not passive couch potatoes seeking leisure or a way to fill their time. Nor, often, do they have a Web site running as background (unless, of course, it is an audio or audiovisual stream). Rather, they are probably mentally alert, making choices, seeking certain content. It also appears that users are less annoyed by pop-ups that are thematically related to the site they are viewing, i.e., car ads on an automobile information site (Heinzl, 2002). Another factor may be that while audiences have become accustomed to advertising interruptions and they keep the remote handy to switch channels as soon as the ad appears, it is not so easy to switch out of one site to another, especially when one is looking for a particular content item. The long and short of it is that Web site users and audiences are different one from another.

As also noted in Chapter 2, the audience vanishes in certain uses of the Internet. In e-mailing, searching for non-commercial information, and participating in discussion groups or other types of messaging, the user is a creator or co-creator of content rather than an audience member. And while advertisers may not be interested in such behaviour, social scientists are beginning to study Internet users, how and why they use the Internet, what such usage represents as social behaviour, and so on. It is an obvious opening area of communications inquiry.

Summary

Media–audience interaction might usefully be conceived of as interaction between active, meaning-seeking entities and meaning-generating systems—persons, groups, the media, and cultures. Such a perspective provides a framework for explaining how media, audiences, and culture interact in an orderly but non-deterministic fashion.

The various theoretical approaches reviewed in this chapter bring out different elements of that interaction. Marx and the Frankfurt School draw attention to the production of leisure products that have the potential to advance the interests of the producers and the elites in society over those of ordinary people. Effects research highlights the direct impact of the media on the behaviour of audience members. Uses and gratification research tells us what audience members tend to do with media content. Cultural studies describe how audience members select features from the media and use them as meaningful elements in their lives. Feminist research brings forward the gendered nature of narratives and, like cultural studies, explores how the audience member is positioned by the narrative. Reception analysis emphasizes the interpretive structures of audience members, which may derive from personality, content, situation, or other variables.

All approaches to the audience offer information and insight for explaining and understanding, but not predicting, audience behaviour, which is dependent not only on what the audience brings to the text or content but also on the culturally specific references contained in the material. In academic research, the earliest analyses emphasized what the media did to the audience. More recent studies have asked what audiences do with media content. While cultural studies oriented to textual content have been dominant for some time, greater attention is now being paid to audience dynamics. Consideration of the social context of viewing, listening, and reading adds yet further elaboration to the articulation of audience variables.

Industry research generates information in precise quantitative measures on the nature of audiences, their size, age, location, education, family income, use of certain products, use of leisure time, and so on. With respect to print media, Canada has, in the Print Measurement Bureau's research, the world's best database. It is comprehensive in covering about 80 major magazines and newspapers. The sample base is large enough that reliable information is available on particular target groups. In addition, the questionnaire itself covers a vast array of consumer and leisure behaviour. However, the limitations of audience research are demonstrated by their inability to understand and meet audience needs with respect to enlightening and socially fulfilling programming.

While the literature so far is sparse, understanding Internet users and usage is an opening area of inquiry. Already, advertisers have found that certain modes of advertising are largely ineffective and others engender annoyance. How advertisers will meet with Internet users on terms acceptable to both has yet to be determined.

RELATED WEB SITES

BBM, the Bureau of Measurement: www.bbm.ca/
This site contains all kinds of interesting information on who watches TV and who listens to radio, at what time of the day they listen, how much time they spend listening, in what location, and so forth.

Print Measurement Bureau (PMB): www.pmb.ca/
The print equivalent to the BBM, this site is a bit more difficult to navigate but it does provide basic magazine circulation statistics and readership by men and women. You can also download a presentation.

Canadian Journal of Communication: www.cjc-online.ca
CJC provides links to back issues of the journal, including the Norma Schulman article cited in this chapter (vol. 18, no. 1).

Audience Dialogue: http://www.audiencedialogue.org/
As the Web site says, it 'exists to provide useful information for communicators of all kinds—broadcasters, publishers, aid agencies, arts organizations, webmasters, and anybody else who's interested in using research-based techniques to make their communications more effective.'

FURTHER READINGS

Ang, Ien. 1991. *Desperately Seeking the Audience*. London: Routledge. This book provides a very good summary of audience research.

Jensen, Klaus Bruhn, and Karl Erik Rosengren. 1990. 'Five traditions in search of an audience', *European Journal of Communication* 5: 207–38. This article provides an orientation to the various schools of thought that guide audience research.

Radway, Janice. 1984. *Reading the Romance*. Chapel Hill: University of North Carolina Press. Radway's book is a classic analysis of how women readers use romantic fiction and demonstrates the contribution scholars can make to understanding the interaction between the media and people's lives.

STUDY QUESTIONS

1. In less than 50 words, define each of the following:
   • Effects research
   • Reception analysis
   • Uses and gratification research
   • Cultural studies
   • The Frankfurt School
2. Some reception studies (for example, Radway) appear to describe the interaction between audiences and content as secondary to the tangential actions surrounding the interpretation of content. It is more the act of reading that counts over what the person is deriving from the content itself. Comment on this in relation to other methods of analysis.
3. Which of the perspectives on audiences would you use for writing an essay dealing with the impact of media violence on society? Why?
4. Which of the perspectives on audiences corresponds most closely to your own views?
5. Is there anything to be concerned about in regard to the information that industry organizations collect on audiences, which advertisers consult? Have you ever responded to a market survey? If so, have you always 'told the whole truth and nothing but the truth'? Discuss.

LEARNING OUTCOMES

- To illustrate how the interaction between media content and audience members is a dynamic interaction in which audience members selectively attend to certain elements and actively interpret content elements based on frameworks of understanding they bring to content.
- To point out that media–audience interaction is not predictable but can be explainable after the fact.
- To introduce six ways of studying how the media influence audience members: Marxist analysis and the Frankfurt School, effects research, uses and gratifications research, British cultural studies, feminist research, and reception analysis.
- To describe the types of research carried on by members of the media industries, for example, the CBC.
- To explain how industry members measure audiences and what they measure, for example, reach, share, and viewing time.
- To explain one of the ways in which the Canadian magazine industry measures its audiences and, armed with that information, sells those audiences to advertisers.
- To illustrate what industry data tell us about magazine readers and how many people read what large consumer magazines that are sold in Canada.
- To introduce the idea that industry research tends to treat audience members as consumers.

PART THREE

Major Influences on Media Functioning

CHAPTER 6

Communications Law and Policy

Introduction

Mass communication is a highly structured activity. It takes place in a built environment that includes communications technology, certainly, but also laws, policies, economic principles and pressures, and guiding ideals. Laws and policies establish the rules of the game as laid down by governments, which recognize that mediated communication is a powerful force in society and there must be rules in place to ensure that the media serve not only their owners and content creators but society as a whole. The policy realm, then, establishes both rights *and* responsibilities. If media workers have the right to freedom of expression, they also have the responsibility to respect people's privacy and laws pertaining to libel, copyright, hate speech, etc. If media owners have the right to a reasonable return on their investment, they also have an obligation not to abuse their power in the market and not to inhibit others from communicating.

Mass communication is not a frivolous activity. As earlier chapters in this book have made clear, communication plays a crucial role in defining the goals, aspirations, and values of society, and fulfills basic informational needs of a modern democratic society and the individuals who constitute that society. It is the site upon which cultures are formed. In this chapter and the next, we talk about law and policy, which, taken together, can be understood as society's answer to the question: What is communication for? Law and policy are the state's response, developed over many years and by many different governments, to the question of what Canadian society wants from its telecommunications and broadcasting systems, and from its cultural industries. Each society answers these questions in its own way, which explains why the same medium will be structured differently from country to country. All countries use the same radio technology, to take one simple example, but organize their radio systems in particular ways—who can own radio stations, how many stations they can own, over what geographical expanse they can broadcast, what kinds of programming are permitted, etc.

This chapter provides an overview of how telecommunications and broadcasting operate in Canadian society. We concentrate on the policies and principles that govern their operation, beginning with an examination of the defining laws, or, more formally speaking, statutes: the Telecommunications Act (1993) and the Broadcasting Act (1991). We then examine other statutes that affect telecommunications and broadcasting, as well as policies developed in accordance with the Telecommunications and Broadcasting Acts to ensure that these industries operate according to the goals set out in these defining statutes.

Two further points of introduction. First, the phrase 'communications law and policy' could be used to encompass all of telecommunications, broadcasting, and the cultural industries. However, we use it here to address only telecommunications and broadcasting. Chapter 7 will focus on the cultural industries, by which we mean the remainder of the communications industries: book and magazine publishing, video and film production, sound recording, newspaper publishing, and new media. Second, the terms 'regulatory' and 'regulation' generally refer to both policies and laws. However, these terms may also be used in a more restrictive sense to include only policy, creating a distinction between the regulatory framework and the legal framework (i.e., the statutes).

Governing Communications

The legal and regulatory frameworks that govern communications are founded on political, cultural, and economic considerations, which reflect the impact communication has on society. Because politics, culture, and economics may pull in different directions, tensions exist within communication policy. These tensions are derived from attempting, for example, to engage in both nation-building (a political consideration) and the construction of a viable cultural industry (an economic consideration). Or, alternatively, from trying to ensure that Canadian creative artists obtain exposure to Canadian audiences (a cultural consideration) while providing a wide range of programming to all tastes and audience sectors (a more general social consideration).

Besides the Telecommunications and Broadcasting Acts, a variety of laws and policies apply to these communications fields. They include:

- the Canadian Charter of Rights and Freedoms, which guarantees the freedom to communicate, including the right to own media enterprises and to collect and impart information;
- access-to-information legislation, designed to make government-gathered information available for public scrutiny—at both the federal and provincial levels;
- legislation protecting privacy, intended to protect individuals about whom information is collected and stored by governments and businesses;
- limits on free speech, including libel law, which is intended to protect the good name of individuals, and laws restraining the communication of hate against specific groups;
- controls over the production, dissemination, and importation of obscene material, particularly rules intended to protect children from exposure to such materials;
- copyright and patent protection, designed to protect intellectual property and increasingly used to protect electronic communications content, such as television news programs and computer software;
- requirements for public disclosure of company information, intended to protect the interests of investors or potential investors in company shares traded on a stock exchange;
- federal and provincial employment laws, which govern work conditions, training, hiring, employment equity, etc.;
- consumer protection, including rules designed to limit the market powers of large companies and monopolies; and
- contract law and company law.

Such laws in Canada may be federal, provincial, or both, depending on the division of powers described in the Canadian Constitution. They are based on legal conventions established internationally, or on common law inherited from the British system of justice.

The Legal and Regulatory Frameworks of Communications

Telecommunications policy applies to telephone, telegraph and telex, data networks, satellite communications, and the Internet. Broadcasting policy applies to radio, TV, cable TV, pay TV, and specialty TV. Both telecommunications and broadcasting policies are very much in flux. The nature of these areas of activity and the increasing overlap among them—a phenomenon known as **technological convergence**—are evolving, especially from a policy perspective. Technological convergence is leading to a need to revamp or rationalize policies developed in response to distinctive technologies, industries, and needs to bring them in line with current realities.

Also contributing to a need to rationalize policies is the general expansion of communications industries. Most notably, public ownership of communications enterprises, which has been a feature of Canadian telecommunications (e.g., Teleglobe, Telesat, Canarie) and broadcasting (the CBC), is being reconsidered. More and more, these enterprises are subjected to funding cuts as Canada and other nations open up their communications markets. Beyond the trend away from public ownership is an expanded opportunity for many different firms to compete for increasingly segmented audiences—old and young, French, English, Italian, and Chinese, sports fans, arts enthusiasts, etc.

A third major reason for rationalization of policy stems from the recent enthusiasm of developed nations, including Canada, for liberalized international trade. Canada has signed the Free Trade Agreement (FTA) with the United States, the North American Free Trade Agreement (NAFTA) with the US and Mexico, and various other general trading agreements promoted and administered by such institutions as the World Trade Organization (WTO) and the Organization for Economic Co-operation and Development (OECD). As a result, Canada and other signatory countries must abide by a common set of rules for the creation of communications products and services. These rules are most often set by those with the strongest economies (the United

FINDING LEGISLATION ON THE WEB

To access legislation currently before Parliament, go to the Canadian parliamentary Web site <www.parl.gc.ca> and click on 'Bills'. Then select 'LEGISinfo' from the box on the left-hand side. From there, you can access current House of Commons and Senate bills and search by title or bill number. To access an Act or statute, go to the Canadian Department of Justice Web site <www.canada.justice.gc.ca> and click on 'Laws' in the top right-hand corner. From there, you can access an alphabetical directory by title and search by subject or keyword.

States, Japan, Germany, the United Kingdom), which generally reject as valuable—even as legitimate—the direct intervention by governments in the market-place. At the beginning of the twenty-first century, we are seeing this dynamic play itself out in magazine legislation and media ownership restrictions. However, it is only a matter of time before the US attempts to curtail subsidies for Hollywood film companies shooting in Canada or to have some element of cable-TV policy declared unfair.

Complementing the economic and technological pressures for policy rationalization are cultural pressures to ensure that the Canadian creative community has a fair chance to be seen and heard and thereby to contribute to the cultural fabric of the country. Expressed another way, Canada and most other nations—the US is the exception—see communications as a field over which they wish to exert control to assert **cultural sovereignty**. Were governments to step aside completely, history teaches us that both the market and the airwaves would be dominated by foreign corporations and foreign content emanating primarily from the United States.

Policy Development

The aim of communications policy is not to resolve completely the tensions described above, but to balance economic opportunity with social, cultural, and political goals. For example, the Broadcasting Act states that the Canadian broadcasting system will 'serve to safeguard, enrich and strengthen the cultural, political, social and economic fabric of Canada'; that 'each element of the Canadian broadcasting system shall contribute in an appropriate manner to the creation and presentation of Canadian programming'; and that 'each broadcasting undertaking shall make maximum use, and in no case less than predominant use of Canadian creative and other resources in the creation and presentation of programming.' These goals are an attempt to strengthen Canada's cultural resources, to provide employment opportunities for Canadians, and to promote the values that Canada, as a nation, stands for.

The CRTC, which administers the Telecommunications and Broadcasting Acts, arbitrates among the social, cultural, political, and economic goals of those Acts and the economic and political interests of the organizations that provide telecommunications and broadcasting services. The CRTC sets standards, notably Canadian-content rules for broadcasters, which are designed to ensure that the goals of the Telecommunications and Broadcasting Acts cannot be circumvented.

In Canada, the process of policy-making for telecommunications and broadcasting is very much open to public participation, in part because Canada professes a strong egalitarianism and recognizes the different interests at play, in part because the CRTC is an arm's-length government agency rather than a department within a government ministry. In contrast, most European countries develop communications policy within their government structures. The public in these countries can only contribute by lobbying their elected representatives as proposed bills are in the process of becoming law, or, after the fact, by participating in determining the programming mix.

The influence of public input, however, seems to be on the decline because the CRTC has become mired in adjudicating between licensees, responding to organized interest groups, coping with international trade agreements and technological change, all while trying to abide by the goals laid out in the statutes. For instance, the CRTC has had to deal with expansion of cross-media ownership: TV companies buying newspaper chains (e.g., CanWest Global) and newspaper companies buying into TV and cable (e.g.,

Quebecor). These moves have little to do with serving the public and everything to do with personal and corporate ambition.

In addition to CRTC hearings, over the years public input has also been a feature of the various Canadian inquiries, commissions, and committees investigating telecommunications, broadcasting, and the cultural industries. Among those that engaged in public consultation are: the Royal Commission on National Development in the Arts, Letters and Sciences (chaired by Vincent Massey and Henri Lévesque, 1951); the Special Senate Committee on Mass Media (chaired by Keith Davey, 1970); the Royal Commission on Newspapers (chaired by Tom Kent, 1981); the federal Cultural Policy Review Committee (chaired by Louis Applebaum and Jacques Hébert, 1982); and the Task Force on Broadcasting Policy (chaired by Gerald Caplan and Florian Sauvageau, 1986). More recently, the Information Highway Advisory Council (IHAC) held public meetings and produced a report on economic and social opportunities that the Internet offers Canadians (Industry Canada, 1997). With the same goal in mind, the government has begun to establish Web sites to aid public discussion on policy. The CRTC's own Web site (www.crtc.gc.ca) provides a wealth of information to citizens and researchers interested in policy decisions.

In the autumn of 1998, the CRTC conducted hearings that illustrated the changing nature of public input. In those hearings, the system of regulations that govern Canadian content was reviewed. In the past, the hearings would have seen the broadcasters on one side and the regulators on the other, with members of the public given the status of interveners. As Doug Saunders of the *Globe and Mail* put it, the situation looked more like this: first were the lobby groups, such as the Friends of Canadian Broadcasting, the Canadian Association of Broadcasters (CAB), and the right-wing Fraser Institute; second came the private broadcast community within which there were substantially different positions; third were the program producers, led by Alliance Atlantis. The lobbyists argued about the overall form broadcasting should take. The private broadcasters and the right wing argued for licences free from obligation. The left wing argued for a public benefit to be derived from the granting of the opportunity (a broadcasting licence) to make money. The broadcasters also argued among themselves over

the extent of Canadian-content obligations. And the program producers argued with the broadcasters over who should own the rights to programming created in part with public subsidies. With all these various interests in the foreground, the voice of the public was difficult to discern.

Of course, part of the reason for change in the consultation process is opinion polling, especially when polling is used in tandem with fairly sophisticated and informal use of the media by government. Governments hire pollsters to poll continuously. They learn public preferences regarding all of their policies and intentions by asking representative samples of Canadians about them. They also know the political orientations of major media commentators and columnists. Thus, with major policy issues, the government puts out information with a pretty good sense of how the public will receive that information. The government also knows that commentators of various political stripes will contribute to the debate. Through the continuous process of monitoring public opinion, the government can determine where the public stands on any given question and also how best to pitch a policy initiative to engender a favourable response. Without declaring a formal public consultation process, a certain kind of informal public debate can nonetheless take place.

Telecommunications Policy

Telecommunications policy governs telephony; data communication, including the Internet; wireless telecommunications, including cellphones; and satellite communications, including links for broadcasters and for data and telephone services. More formally speaking, telecommunications is defined as 'the emission, transmission or reception of intelligence by any wire, cable, radio, optical or other electromagnetic system, or by any similar technical system' (Telecommunications Act, 1993, s. 2[1]). In strictly technical terms, broadcasting is a type of telecommunications, but in policy terms, because broadcasters control the content of their transmissions, broadcasting is treated separately and is governed by a policy section in the Broadcasting Act. Telecommunications is governed by federal statute as a result of a 1989 ruling by the Supreme Court of Canada that all major telephone and telecommunications companies fall within federal jurisdiction

TELECOMMUNICATIONS ACT, SECTION 7

The foundation for Canadian telecommunications policy is contained in Section 7 of the 1993 Telecommunications Act. It states:

7. It is hereby affirmed that telecommunications performs an essential role in the maintenance of Canada's identity and sovereignty and that the Canadian telecommunications policy has as its objectives:

(a) to facilitate the orderly development throughout Canada of a telecommunications system that serves to safeguard, enrich and strengthen the social and economic fabric of Canada and its regions;

(b) to render reliable and affordable telecommunications services of high quality accessible to Canadians in both urban and rural areas in all regions of Canada;

(c) to enhance the efficiency and competitiveness, at the national and international levels, of Canadian telecommunications;

(d) to promote the ownership and control of Canadian carriers by Canadians;

(e) to promote the use of Canadian transmission facilities for telecommunications within Canada and between Canada and points outside Canada;

(f) to foster increased reliance on market forces for the provision of telecommunications services and to ensure regulation, where required, is efficient and effective;

(g) to stimulate research and development in Canada in the field of telecommunications and to encourage innovation in the provision of telecommunications services;

(h) to respond to the economic and social requirements of users of telecommunications services; and

(i) to contribute to the protection of the privacy of persons.

---

because their networks interconnect with out-of-province carriers.

In overview, the Telecommunications Act addresses technological and economic issues, such as providing reliable and affordable services in an efficient and effective manner, nationally and internationally, and protecting the privacy of users, and the Act underlines the role of telecommunications in maintaining Canada's identity and sovereignty (see section 7 of the Act on this page). It does so by stressing Canada's social and economic particularities, by stimulating research and development in the field in Canada, by affirming Canadian ownership and control of telecommunications infrastructure, and by affirming the use of Canadian transmission facilities.

The historical core of telecommunications is the telephone industry. In Europe this business evolved from nineteenth-century state monopolies in post and telegraph (P&T) services. In Canada, privately owned monopolies have been the norm—for example, BC Tel (now Telus) in British Columbia, Bell Canada in Ontario and Quebec, Island Tel in Prince Edward Island, Maritime Telephone and Telegraph in

Nova Scotia, NB Tel in New Brunswick, NewTel Communications in Newfoundland, NorthwesTel (serving the Northwest Territories, Yukon, Nunavut, and northern BC), and QuebecTel in Quebec. These private monopolies have existed alongside provincially owned monopolies in Manitoba (Manitoba Telecom Services), Alberta (AGT, now Telus), and Saskatchewan (SaskTel). This core of telephone companies and an ever-decreasing number of smaller companies have operated as a national system and, until September 1998, presented itself to the world as the Stentor Alliance.

In addition to the provincial telephone companies are the companies that arose after the long-distance telephone markets and then the local telephone markets were opened up for competition. These alternative providers include major companies like Cantel, Call-net, AT&T Canada, and Sprint. There are also well over 200 radio common carriers providing wireless mobile radio and radio paging services as well as the personal-communications service providers. Then there is the Internet, with access either through cable or telephone (hard-wired or wireless) and local access providers as well as a growing number of satellite services.

To provide seamless service to the public, a complex set of rules and specifications has developed to allow both technological compatibility among all these providers and revenue sharing. The CRTC is the adjudicator of these rules. This includes arrangements made among Telesat Canada (the Canadian satellite communications company), the telephone companies, the cable- TV companies, Teleglobe (formerly the monopoly agency controlling transoceanic telecommunications), and those who purchase their services (e.g., the specialty and pay-TV companies).

COMMON AND CONTRACT CARRIERS

Telecommunications companies are service providers. They offer transmission services for a fee. In many cases they are **common carriers** in that they are obliged to carry any message (content) that any member of the public (company or individual) wishes to send at equitable cost. A **contract carrier** provides transmission services to specific companies or individuals, but is not obliged to provide those same services to other individuals or companies. The banks, for example, contract for telephone and data communication services and obtain bulk rates unavailable to the average citizen. Your Internet service provider is also a contract carrier. The company has a contract with its customers but is under no obligation to extend its services to others.

A carrier may not tamper with the message, nor can it be involved in creating any of the messages carried for customers (a requirement that may have to be modified as on-line services evolve). The creation of the 'content' is what distinguishes broadcasters from common carriers; broadcasters are involved in content creation and the selection of content, which they then transmit to audiences. Broadcasters, unlike carriers, are legally responsible for all the content they transmit even though much of their programming may have been purchased from third parties.

The major telecommunications issue for the past decade has been the transition from monopoly services to competing services. The major issue over the next decade may well be the challenges presented by technological convergence, which increasingly blurs the lines between broadcasting and telecommunications.

TELECOMMUNICATIONS REGULATION OVER THE YEARS

Regulation of telecommunication dates back to the nineteenth century when it was believed that only one company could provide efficient service in any given area. The rationale at that time—one that continued through to the 1980s—was that it made little sense for more than one telephone wire to be strung down every street. Telephone services were declared to be a 'natural monopoly'. To guard against undue exploitation, the monopolies were regulated by what eventually became the CRTC. Governments during the twentieth century felt that both broadcasting and telecommunications (first telegraph and later telephone) were valuable social services. They reasoned that such services ought to be provided to all Canadians at equitable prices— not necessarily the same price everywhere, but neither at prices affordable in urban areas and unaffordable in rural areas. In fact, the failure of commercial companies to commit to providing widespread telephone services persuaded the governments of Alberta, Manitoba, and Saskatchewan to create publicly owned telephone monopolies within their jurisdictions.

By the 1980s it had become apparent that technology had more to offer than telephone companies were providing. It had also become apparent that connections between competitors were possible and that it was feasible for purchasers of bulk services to resell telephone access for cheaper rates than the telephone companies were offering for individual service. Given these realities, in September 1994, in what has come to be known as Telecom Decision 94–19, the CRTC ruled that competition must be the basis for the provision of all telecommunications services, including local voice telephony service. This decision required companies to separate the costs of providing any single service (e.g., local phone service) from those for any other service (e.g., long-distance phone service), meaning that companies would no longer be allowed to cross-subsidize services. Historically, the revenue from long-distance phone services subsidized local phone service, helping to keep local phone service affordable for individuals and small businesses.

Not all aspects of Telecom Decision 94–19 were immediately implemented; the federal cabinet referred some of the rulings back to the CRTC after receiving appeals against the decision. Nevertheless, it marked a major turning point in telecommunications regulation. When Decision 94–19 was put in place, the common expectation was that the cable-TV companies and the telephone companies would compete vigorously in the marketplace. Instead, the focus of competition has been on the vast and continuing expansion of Internet services.

Competition has also led to an unanticipated outcome—the breakup of the Stentor Alliance. When telephone companies had geographic monopolies, their focus was providing service while making a reasonable rate of profit. With competition, they transformed themselves, becoming more technologically innovative and focusing on marketing their services. As competitors established themselves across the country, it became apparent that the territorial boundaries of each of the Stentor companies had become liabilities, just as it would be a liability, for example, if the *Globe and Mail* could only publish in Ontario. Stentor itself had been a cartel of companies committed not to compete with one another. Given that this cartel might be illegal and, more importantly, that its competitors were not similarly constrained, it was no longer logical for a 'no trespassing' pact to exist among Stentor members.

In overview, telecommunications has been transformed dramatically over the last two decades. Its overall function has remained constant, to allow Canadians to communicate with one another and, thereby, to build a nation. However, while in the beginning this goal seemed achievable only through territorial monopolies, with increased wealth, technological sophistication, and an existing infrastructure, the need for monopolies has passed. With the dismantling of these monopolies has come not only competition, but enhanced services.

Enhancing and expanding services costs money, of course, and in early 2003 the House of Commons Industry Committee initiated hearings to review rules restricting foreign investors to minority stakes in Canadian telecommunications companies (Chase, 2003). The law currently prevents non-Canadians from holding more than one-fifth of telecommunications operating companies and one-third of affiliated holding companies. Federal Industry Minister Allan Rock believed that permitting Canadian companies access to increased capital investment from foreign sources would lead to more innovation and competition.

SATELLITE COMMUNICATIONS

Canada has been a pioneer of non-military satellite application since the early 1960s. In 1964 Canada joined INTELSAT, the international **consortium** that operated the first satellite communications service with the mandate to provide international communications linkages. The possibility of improving trans-Canada communications links using satellites has appealed to federal policy-makers since at least 1965. A White Paper on satellite policy, issued in 1968, stated: 'A domestic satellite system should be a national undertaking stretching across Canada from coast to coast, north to Ellesmere Island and operating under the jurisdiction of the Government of Canada' (Canada, 1968).

In 1969, the Telesat Canada Act established the joint public-sector/private-sector corporation that was given the responsibility to own and operate the Canadian satellite communications system and to provide communications services to Canadian locations on a commercial basis. Telesat's first satellite was launched in 1972 and shortly thereafter the company initiated the first domestic satellite communications service in the world. By 1995, Telesat had launched five series of satellites.

Telesat is the 'carriers' carrier', a reference to the fact that most of the signals carried on satellite are transmitted on behalf of another carrier, such as a telephone or cable-TV company. Historically, the primary use for satellites was telecommunications traffic (mostly voice telephony and data communications). However, by 1987 it was apparent that broadcasting services were becoming at least as important to Telesat. The vast majority of broadcasting services consisted of the delivery of video signals across the country.

While commercial over-the-air television and radio networks in southern Canada make use of satellite transmission as part of their distribution technology, it is rare for them to abandon their terrestrial links to use only satellites, especially since the development of **optical fibre**. As well, with Telecom Decision 94–19, the door is opening for competition in providing satellite services, so that Telesat will no longer enjoy a monopoly.

Broadcasting Policy

Public policy places a heavy emphasis on being able to exert national control over the broadcasting sector, which includes radio and television in all its burgeoning forms: cable, pay, specialty, satellite. Since the late 1920s, broadcasting policy has been informed by the mandate of nation-building, and it is important to recognize from the outset that the Broadcasting Act (Canada, 1991) defines broadcasting in Canada not as an industry but as 'a public service essential to the maintenance and enhancement of national identity and cultural sovereignty' (section 3[i][b]). This distinction means broadcasting in Canada is perceived as a system of communication, not merely a medium of entertainment. This essential public service comprises three distinct sectors: public broadcasting (e.g., the CBC), private broadcasting (i.e., commercial radio and TV), and community broadcasting (i.e., non-profit, community-service radio and TV). The legal definitions relevant to broadcasting are provided in section 2 of the 1991 Broadcasting Act:

> 'Broadcasting' means any transmission of programs, whether or not encrypted, by radio waves or other means of telecommunication for reception by the public by means of broadcasting receiving apparatus, but does not include any such transmission of programs that is made solely for performance or display in a public place;

> 'program' means sounds or visual images, or a combination of sounds and visual images, that are intended to inform, enlighten or entertain, but does not include visual images, whether or not combined with sounds, that consist predominantly of alphanumeric text.

Broadcasting has been recognized since 1932 as federal jurisdiction under the Canadian Constitution, but in the 1970s it was determined that the provinces could establish educational broadcasters provided that these organizations operated at arm's length from their respective provincial governments. This led to the establishment of Radio-Québec (now Télé-Québec), TV Ontario, the Saskatchewan Communications Network, ACCESS Alberta (now privately owned), and the Knowledge Network of the West (KNOW) in British Columbia.

Policy instruments pertain to three specific aspects of radio and television broadcasting: *technological issues*, *content*, and *access*. These three areas have engendered and led to the modification of broadcasting as the needs of each have evolved.

TECHNOLOGY

The technological particularities of sending broadcast signals over the airwaves have in every country demanded some form of governing authority to assign broadcast frequencies; this was the point of entry for the state regulation of radio broadcasting in its infancy. Without getting too technical about it, radio is transmitted by waves of electromagnetic radiation at various frequencies. Radio broadcasters, therefore, need to transmit their signals at allotted frequencies in the finite broadcast spectrum in order to avoid interference with one another. Frequency allocation is assigned by national state agencies— e.g., the CRTC in Canada, the Federal Communications Commission in the United States—in cooperation with neighbouring countries.

The first regulatory authority in Canada was the Ministry of Marine and Fisheries, administering the 1913 Radio-telegraph Act. The ministry licensed both transmitters and receivers. The first Canadian radio station to obtain a licence was XWA in Montreal in 1919, an experimental broadcaster established by the Canadian Marconi Co. By 1928, there were more than 60 radio stations operating across Canada under minimal regulation, many of them affiliated with newspapers and electrical appliance dealers (see Vipond, 1992).

As the airwaves became more crowded through the 1920s, prompting disputes over both signal interference (from powerful American stations) and the content of broadcasts (especially religious broadcasts), the Canadian government recognized the need for a more comprehensive approach to broadcast policy. In December 1928 the Minister of Marine and Fisheries, P.J. Arthur Cardin, established the Royal Commission on Radio Broadcasting (known as the Aird Commission after its chairman, Sir John Aird), which was asked to 'examine into the broadcasting situation in the Dominion of Canada and to make recommendations to the Government as to the future administration, management, control and financing thereof.' The Aird Commission held public hearings in 25 Canadian cities between April and July 1929 (Canada, 1929).

Aird studied five central issues—the educational component of broadcasting, international wavelength allotment, advertising, Canadian content, and ownership—and recommended that radio broadcasting in Canada be restructured as a national public system owned, operated, and subsidized by feder-

BROADCASTING ACT, SECTION 3

Broadcasting Policy for Canada

[Declaration]

3. (1) It is hereby declared as the broadcasting policy for Canada that

(a) the Canadian broadcasting system shall be effectively owned and controlled by Canadians;

(b) the Canadian broadcasting system, operating primarily in the English and French languages and comprising public, private and community elements, makes use of radio frequencies that are public property and provides, through its programming, a public service essential to the maintenance and enhancement of national identity and cultural sovereignty;

(c) English and French language broadcasting, while sharing common aspects, operate under different conditions and may have different requirements;

(d) the Canadian broadcasting system should

  (i) serve to safeguard, enrich and strengthen the cultural, political, social and economic fabric of Canada,

  (ii) encourage the development of Canadian expression by providing a wide range of programming that reflects Canadian attitudes, opinions, ideas, values and artistic creativity, by displaying Canadian talent in entertainment programming and by offering information and analysis concerning Canada and other countries from a Canadian point of view,

  (iii) through its programming and the employment opportunities arising out of its operations, serve the needs and interests, and reflect the circumstances and aspirations, of Canadian men, women and children, including equal rights, the linguistic duality and multicultural and multiracial nature of Canadian society and the special place of aboriginal peoples within that society, and

  (iv) be readily adaptable to scientific and technological change;

(e) each element of the Canadian broadcasting system shall contribute in an appropriate manner to the creation and presentation of Canadian programming;

(f) each broadcasting undertaking shall make maximum use, and in no case less than predominant use, of Canadian creative and other resources in the creation and presentation of programming, unless the nature of the service provided by the undertaking, such as specialized content or format or the use of languages other than French and English, renders that use impracticable, in which case the undertaking shall make the greatest practicable use of those resources;

(g) the programming originated by broadcasting undertakings should be of high standard;

(h) all persons who are licensed to carry on broadcasting undertakings have a responsibility for the programs they broadcast;

(i) the programming provided by the Canadian broadcasting system should

  (i) be varied and comprehensive, providing a balance of information, enlightenment and entertainment for men, women and children of all ages, interests and tastes,

  (ii) be drawn from local, regional, national and international sources,

  (iii) include educational and community programs,

  (iv) provide a reasonable opportunity for the public to be exposed to the expression of differing views on matters of public concern, and

  (v) include a significant contribution from the Canadian independent production sector;

(j) educational programming, particularly where provided through the facilities of an independent educational authority, is an integral part of the Canadian broadcasting system;

(k) a range of broadcasting services in English and in French shall be extended to all Canadians as resources become available;

(l) the Canadian Broadcasting Corporation, as the national public broadcaster, should provide radio and television services incorporating a wide range of programming that informs, enlightens and entertains;

(m) the programming provided by the Corporation should

  (i) be predominantly and distinctively Canadian,

  (ii) reflect Canada and its regions to national and regional audiences, while serving the special needs of those regions,

  (iii) actively contribute to the flow and exchange of cultural expression,

(iv) be in English and in French, reflecting the different needs and circumstances of each official language community, including the particular needs and circumstances of English and French linguistic minorities,

(v) strive to be of equivalent quality in English and in French,

(vi) contribute to shared national consciousness and identity,

(vii) be made available throughout Canada by the most appropriate and efficient means and as resources become available for the purpose, and

(viii) reflect the multicultural and multiracial nature of Canada;

(n) where any conflict arises between the objectives of the Corporation set out in paragraphs (l) and (m) and the interests of any other broadcasting undertaking of the Canadian broadcasting system, it shall be resolved in the public interest, and where the public interest would be equally served by resolving the conflict in favour of either, it shall be resolved in favour of the objectives set out in paragraphs (l) and (m);

(o) programming that reflects the aboriginal cultures of Canada should be provided within the Canadian broadcasting system as resources become available for the purpose;

(p) programming accessible by disabled persons should be provided within the Canadian broadcasting system as resources become available for the purpose;

(q) without limiting any obligation of a broadcasting undertaking to provide the programming contemplated by paragraph (i), alternative television programming services in English and in French should be provided where necessary to ensure that the full range of programming contemplated by that paragraph is made available through the Canadian broadcasting system;

(r) the programming provided by alternative television programming services should

(i) be innovative and be complementary to the programming provided for mass audiences,

(ii) cater to tastes and interests not adequately provided for by the programming provided for mass

audiences, and include programming devoted to culture and the arts,

(iii) reflect Canada's regions and multicultural nature,

(iv) as far as possible, be acquired rather than produced by those services, and

(v) be made available throughout Canada by the most cost-efficient means;

(s) private networks and programming undertakings should, to an extent consistent with the financial and other resources available to them,

(i) contribute significantly to the creation and presentation of Canadian programming, and

(ii) be responsive to the evolving demands of the public; and

(t) distribution undertakings

(i) should give priority to the carriage of Canadian programming services and, in particular, to the carriage of local Canadian stations,

(ii) should provide efficient delivery of programming at affordable rates, using the most effective technologies available at reasonable cost,

(iii) should, where programming services are supplied to them by broadcasting undertakings pursuant to contractual arrangements, provide reasonable terms for the carriage, packaging and retailing of those programming services, and

(iv) may, where the Commission considers it appropriate, originate programming, including local programming, on such terms as are conducive to the achievement of the objectives of the broadcasting policy set out in this subsection, and in particular provide access for underserved linguistic and cultural minority communities.

[Further declaration]

(2) It is further declared that the Canadian broadcasting system constitutes a single system and that the objectives of the broadcasting policy set out in subsection (1) can best be achieved by providing for the regulation and supervision of the Canadian broadcasting system by a single independent public authority.

al government authorities, with provincial control over programming. The Aird Commission hearings prompted considerable debate between those who preferred that radio be run on the principles of a **free market** and those who saw the need for state intervention to ensure that Canadian radio was not Americanized (see Gasher, 1998). Upon release of the Aird Report, these arguments, still with us today, were taken up by the Canadian Association of Broadcasters and the Canadian Radio League, respectively. The Canadian Radio League, under the leadership of Graham Spry and Alan Plaunt, proved to be better organized and more persuasive, and the nationalist view of Canadian broadcasting won the day.

Ottawa created the Canadian Radio Broadcasting Commission (CRBC) in May 1932. The Commission was assigned the ambitious task of regulating, controlling, and conducting broadcasting throughout Canada, but in the throes of the Great Depression it was never given funding adequate to its mandate. The CRBC set up broadcast stations in only six cities—Montreal, Ottawa, Toronto, Vancouver, Moncton, and Chicoutimi—and had to rely on 14 private stations in other cities to distribute its network programs. This mixed system of public and private broadcasting was inherited by the Canadian Broadcasting Corporation (CBC) when it was established in 1936, and remains with us to the present day.

The CBC was the product of a revised Broadcasting Act, which gave the public broadcaster more money (through increased licence fees) and greater autonomy, and which accepted the role of private, commercial stations as the local broadcasting complement to the CBC's national network services. By 1944, the CBC was operating three networks— two in English, one in French—and its satisfactory performance prompted subsequent Royal Commissions to adopt CBC Radio as the model for the new medium of television in the 1950s. The Massey Commission (officially, the Royal Commission on National Development in the Arts, Letters and Sciences, 1949–51) described CBC Radio as 'the greatest single agency for national unity, understanding and enlightenment' (Canada, 1951: 279), and, with the CBC assuming responsibility for television as of 1952, the Fowler Commission (the Royal Commission on Broadcasting, 1956–7) defended Canadian broadcasting's national, public service

structure. The Fowler Commission equated the privatization of broadcasting with the Americanization of Canadian radio and television (Canada, 1957: 230–3).

Both the Massey and Fowler commissions heard complaints from the private broadcasting community about the CBC's double mandate as state broadcaster and state regulator. The new Broadcasting Act of 1958 relieved the CBC of much of its regulatory authority, establishing a 15-member Board of Broadcast Governors (BBG) to regulate both public and private broadcasting. The BBG oversaw the rapid expansion of CBC's television service and approved in 1961 a second national television broadcaster, the private, commercial CTV network, and TéléMétropole, a private, French-language station in Montreal. However, continuing regulatory disputes between the CBC and the BBG prompted the creation in 1968 of the Canadian Radio-Television Commission (renamed the Canadian Radio-television and Telecommunications Commission in 1976), with a clearer and broader mandate to regulate all of Canadian broadcasting.

Today, the CRTC's duties in the broadcasting field include:

- defining categories of broadcasting licences;
- issuing and renewing licences, up to a maximum of seven years;
- modifying existing licence conditions;
- suspending or revoking licences (the CBC licence excepted);
- licensing cable distributors and satellite delivery systems;
- hearing complaints about the broadcasting system;
- reviewing mergers of media companies.

In May 1999, for example, the CRTC reduced the length of the licence of Montreal AM radio station CKVL from seven years to three. The broadcast regulator punished the station for the insulting and vulgar remarks of 'shock jock' André Arthur and the failure of the station's owner, Metromedia CMR Montreal Inc., to take seriously numerous public complaints about Arthur (Canadian Press, 1999).

Much of the CRTC's work involves staging public hearings on licence applications and renewals. The hearings are held throughout the year, either at the Commission's head office in Gatineau or in major

A BRIEF HISTORY OF TV

1883: Paul Nipkow, a German scientist, invents a perforated spinning disk that can break down an image into a sequence of pictorial elements.

1923: Russian-born Vladimir Zworykin patents an iconoscope, an early electronic camera tube, in the US.

1926: Scotsman John Logie Baird makes a public demonstration of television by broadcasting shadow pictures; two years later he is able to broadcast colour pictures and outdoor scenes.

1928: General Electric presents the first TV drama. Sound is carried on a radio station, and the picture is seen on a three-by-four-inch screen.

1932: An RCA subsidiary begins experimental telecasts atop the Empire State Building; four years later a converted radio station feeds programs to it twice weekly.

1939: The first television sets become available to the American public. NBC begins regular service.

1940: The first official network broadcast takes place.

1941: CBS presents its first newscast, on the bombing of Pearl Harbor; war delays the construction of systems in the United States.

1950: The first community antenna TV service—the precursor to cable TV—begins in Pennsylvania.

1951: CBC initiates regular TV programs in Montreal and Toronto; CBS begins limited colour broadcasts. A videotape recorder is publicly demonstrated for the first time.

1962: Toronto is the site of a trial for closed-circuit pay-TV.

1968: The Canadian Radio-television and Telecommunications Commission is established.

1970s: Japan develops a high-definition television system.

1975: Sony launches its Betamax VCR. The VHS follows a year later.

1982: The CRTC licenses Canada's first pay-TV services.

1999: Web-TV service begins.

Source: *Globe and Mail*, 4 Feb. 1999, D5, which cited *The 1998 Canadian and World Encyclopedia; Encyclopedia Americana; Les Brown's Encyclopedia of Television*.

cities around the country. Each year the CRTC has to rule on thousands of licence applications, renewals, and amendments. For example, in May and June 1999, the CRTC held a public hearing to 'review and discuss the performance of' CBC radio and television as part of the public broadcaster's process of licence renewal (CBC, 1999).

To say that the CRTC merely regulates the broadcasting system to achieve policy objectives set by Parliament understates the extent to which the CRTC has been obliged to interpret policy. It also understates the extent to which the CRTC has established policies of its own in areas such as cable and specialty TV.

Since the 1970s there has been considerable discussion in the policy field about the degree to which the CRTC can and should initiate and resist policy action. There has also been discussion about the extent to which the federal government should maintain policy control over the CRTC. One of the controversial aspects of the 1991 Broadcasting Act is the increased scope it grants for federal cabinet direction to the CRTC. As well as making section 3 of the Act much more explicit, the statute requires the CRTC to implement stated regulatory policy (section 5) and also provides cabinet with the power to issue directions on how the CRTC is to interpret both policy sections. Since 1991, the federal cabinet has taken a much more active role in policy-making in the broadcasting field through its power of direction.

A good example of the cabinet's current powers was evident in the debate over the development of direct-to-home (DTH) satellite services. In 1994, the CRTC decided to exempt from licensing requirements any company that met specified criteria: Canadian ownership; the use of Canadian satellites for the delivery of all services; adherence to priority carriage rules already established for cable TV operators. This decision meant that only one company—ExpressVu—would be exempted, eliminating ExpressVu's principal competitor, Power DirecTV, which was partly American-owned and which intended to use US satellites for the American share of its program delivery.

ExpressVu was owned by a consortium that included BCE (Bell's parent company), Cancom, Western International Communications (WIC), and Tee-Comm Electronics (the makers of the satellite dishes required). Power DirecTV was 80 per cent owned by Power Corp. of Montreal, with the remaining 20 per cent held by Hughes Aircraft, a unit of General Motors in the US. The CRTC's decision to preclude Power DirecTV from entering the DTH satellite business prompted the federal government to establish a three-member panel to review the decision. In April 1995 the panel recommended that DTH competition should be allowed, that the CRTC should license all qualified applicants, and, in effect, that the CRTC could not use its power of exemption to avoid setting up a licensing procedure in an area of major policy significance. In July 1995 the cabinet ordered the CRTC to implement the government's policy on licensing competitive DTH pay-per-view television program undertakings. The CRTC was also required to call for licence applications to carry on DTH distribution and to issue decisions quickly on those applications. Three applications were received—from ExpressVu, Power DirecTV, and Shaw Communications—and, after a public hearing, the CRTC licensed the first two operators in December 1995.

ACCESS AND CONTENT

In recent years, a major shift in broadcasting policy has occurred pertaining to the issue of access, from an original emphasis on signal coverage to an emphasis on participation. From as early as 1936, one of the fundamental principles of Canadian broadcasting policy has been the extension of service to all Canadians, and private broadcasters' place in the national broadcasting system has been to help in pro- viding Canadians in all areas of the country access to the reception of radio, and later television, broadcast signals (see Canada, 1986: 5–14). This has been a technologically and financially challenging task given the size of the country and Canada's sparse and scattered population. Between 1936 and 1950, radio's reach in Canada expanded from 50 to 90 per cent of the population. This policy of full coverage was reaffirmed with the arrival of Canadian televi- sion in the 1950s. The federal government adopted a 'single-station policy', whereby no competing tele- vision station would be allowed in any market until a national television broadcasting system was estab- lished, thus prioritizing the extension of service rather than the encouragement of competition (Raboy, 1992: 111–14).

The notion of 'access to broadcasting' began to assume another dimension in the 1960s, once exten- sive territorial coverage of radio and television had been achieved and a private television network (CTV) had been established. Access came to mean the inclusion of all Canadians in the content and pro- duction of programming. While the issue of Canadian content has been significant since the first decade of radio, the idea of requiring a minimum percentage of broadcast time to be used for trans- mitting Canadian television productions was insti- tuted by the Board of Broadcast Governors in 1959. Today, Canadian-content regulations stem from the CRTC's obligation under the Broadcasting Act to ensure that each licence-holder makes 'maximum use . . . of Canadian creative and other resources in the creation and presentation of programming'. The CBC's programming, according to the Act, should also be 'predominantly and distinctively Canadian'.

The Canadian-content quota has never been well received by the private broadcasters, who have protested each requirement vigorously and sought to minimize their carriage of Canadian material (see

POLICY AND REALITY

Here is a simple example of a mismatch between policy and actuality in the world of the media. Canadian broad- casters are permitted by the CRTC to run 12 minutes of commercials per hour. Guess how many *Blind Date* runs? A study commissioned by the Vancouver Media Directors' Council (not a left-wing organization) and entitled *Blind Date: The 2002 Canadian Television Commercial Moni-* *toring Report* noted that the show carried up to 28.4 min- utes of non-program material. The objection of the adver- tisers who commissioned the study is that such 'clutter' makes advertising less effective and undermines televi- sion as a medium. One wonders if the movie-makers who specialize in product placement have such concerns about the medium of film.

CANADIANS LIKE THE CBC

According to a May 1999 poll done for the Friends of Canadian Broadcasting:

- Eighty-two per cent say CBC radio and TV are doing a good job; 42 per cent rate the service as either very good or excellent.
- Seven out of 10 respondents said CBC Radio serves their community better than any other broadcaster.
- Seventy-six per cent oppose the CBC getting out of regional broadcasting.
- Fifty-two per cent credited CBC and Radio-Canada with balanced reporting. In Quebec 28 per cent ranked TVA as balanced and 7 per cent ranked TQS similarly, while outside Quebec 28 per cent ranked CTV as balanced and 9 per cent ranked CanWest Global as balanced.

- Eighty per cent say the government should be committed to preserving and building the CBC.
- Twenty-three per cent say that the government is committed to preserving and building the CBC.
- More than half say that planned corporate sponsorships on CBC Radio will change the nature of programming; 40 per cent say that it will make no difference.

These findings reflect strong support among Canadians for the CBC and for continued public ownership, public funding, and a public service that is relatively independent from advertisers' priorities.

Source: Chris Cobb, *The Ottawa Citizen*, 20 May 1999. Copyright © Chris Cobb and The Ottawa Citizen. Reprinted with permission.

Babe, 1979). The CRTC requires television licensees to have at least 60 per cent of all programming hours given to Canadian productions; private broadcasters are allowed to reduce that to 50 per cent in prime time. Radio regulations will be discussed in more detail in Chapter 7, but, generally speaking, commercial AM and FM radio stations are required to play at least 35 per cent (raised from 30 per cent in 1998) Canadian musical selections, both as a weekly average and between 6 a.m. and 6 p.m., Monday to Friday.

The principal battleground for disputes over Canadian-content quotas has been English-language television, where Hollywood productions are readily available, cheap to buy, and popular with audiences and advertisers. During the 1970s a considerable amount of evidence demonstrated that, while the majority of programs aired by Canadian TV broadcasters were 'Canadian' in the regulatory definition, the English-Canadian audience showed a strong preference for US entertainment series and movies (the audiences for French-language television showed a much stronger preference for Quebec-produced programming, for both linguistic and cultural reasons). A particularly weak programming genre was English-language drama.

Since the early 1980s, several events have improved the situation significantly. The first of these

was the establishment of Telefilm Canada's Broadcast Program Development Fund, which encouraged independent producers to create high-quality TV dramas and series. These productions have, in a number of instances, shown a strong potential for export sales as well. The second event was the licensing of a number of specialty and pay-TV services, to be distributed via satellite and cable. All the new services were required to spend a portion of their revenues on programming production. While these services have not always been successful in building audiences, the trend towards specialty programming, or 'narrowcasting', is clear; the CRTC licensed 22 new specialty services in 1996. The third development was the establishment by the private sector of a number of production funds in the 1980s and 1990s, increasing the pool of capital available to production companies and making it easier for them to get airtime.

When significant numbers of Canadians began subscribing to cable television service during the 1960s, the CRTC sought to ensure that Canadian broadcasters would have priority for cable carriage. Regulations require cable-TV licensees to provide clear channels for signals in a specified order of priority, with CBC, local, and regional signals favoured over foreign (i.e., US) signals.

The federal Department of Canadian Heritage initiated a review of Canadian content in March

2002, inviting submissions from the public and interested parties in the film and television industries. In a discussion paper entitled *Canadian Content in the 21st Century* (Canada, 2002: 1), the department said 'the time has come to reassess the definition of Canadian content and ensure that the approach that is chosen is up to date and well suited to the challenges ahead.'

The notion of Canadian content has already undergone considerable refinement. In the 1970s and 1980s, there was an increasing recognition of Canada's multicultural makeup and demands were made that the broadcasting system reflect this reality. As Lorna Roth (1998: 493–502) notes, by the early 1980s one in three Canadians was of non-British, non-French, and non-Aboriginal descent, and the federal government began to enshrine guarantees of cultural and racial pluralism in the Constitution, for example, in sections 15 and 27 of the Canadian Charter of Rights and Freedoms (1982), and in legislation, for example, the Multiculturalism Act (1998).

Inclusion was one of the central themes informing discussions leading up to the adoption of a revised Broadcasting Act in 1991. Marc Raboy (1995: 457) argues that the 'transparency of public debate' between 1986 and 1991 was responsible for enshrining the rights of women, ethnic groups, Native peoples, and disabled persons in broadcast legislation. In section 3 (1) (d)(iii), the Act states that the Canadian broadcasting system should:

> through its programming and the employment opportunities arising out of its operations, serve the needs and interests, and reflect the circumstances and aspirations, of Canadian men, women and children, including equal rights, the linguistic duality and multicultural and multiracial nature of Canadian society and the special place of aboriginal peoples within that society.

Subsequent clauses call for the provision of programming that 'reflects the aboriginal cultures of Canada' and programming 'accessible by disabled persons'. When the CRTC renewed the licences of the CTV and Global television networks in August 2001, the Commission demanded from the networks a plan, to be accompanied by annual reports, to 'address a number of initiatives including corporate accountability, programming practices and community involvement as they relate to the goal of ensuring that the diversity of Canadian society is reflected fairly and consistently in CTV's and Global's programming.' The CRTC also called for the creation of a task force, to be co-ordinated by the Canadian Association of Broadcasters, to address the depiction of Canada's cultural diversity on TV screens (CRTC, 2001). As Lorna Roth (1998: 501) has stated: 'Though it still faces multiple challenges, we might say that the Canadian attempt to deal with "cultural and racial diversity" in broadcasting represents its political willingness to symbolically weave cultural and racial pluralism into the fabric of Canadian broadcasting policy and human rights legislation.'

A Future for Broadcast Regulation?

If spectrum allocation was the original premise for state intervention in the broadcasting sphere, do we still need the CRTC in the era of the 500-channel universe and the Internet? The answer would appear to be a qualified yes. In a speech to the Broadcasting and Program Distribution Summit in Toronto in February 1999, Wayne Charman, director general of the CRTC's broadcast distribution and technology division, identified three factors driving changes in the communications industry: globalization, technological change, and business consolidation (CRTC, 1999: 2). The CRTC is adapting to this new environment, Charman said, by assuming a more flexible approach to regulation. 'We have broadened our scope to include both protection [and] promotion using constraint wherever appropriate and competition wherever possible.'

Recent regulatory decisions suggest that the CRTC will not likely run out of things to do anytime soon. The Commission, for example, has been active in adopting measures pertaining to: television violence (e.g., anti-violence rules for video games, a V-chip-based classification system for programming); alcohol advertising; third-language and ethnic TV programming; Canadian content on radio; and the conversion of television broadcasters from analogue to digital services. The CRTC has expanded Canada's national television system by approving for inclusion in nationally distributed basic cable and DTH satellite packages the private, French-language TVA network (1998) and the Aboriginal Peoples Television Network (1999). In November 2000 the CRTC approved 200 new digital TV services, including 21 category-one licences, which distributors are required to carry. These include the Women's Sports Network (WSN) and PrideVision, aimed at Canada's gay and lesbian community. Two pay-per-view and four video-on-demand services were also approved, increasing both the diversity of the TV dial and the choices available to viewers (CRTC, 2000). The CRTC has also had to rule on recent corporate mergers of media companies that have resulted in considerable cross-ownership of media properties in a number of major Canadian markets (for more discussion, see Chapter 8).

While spectrum allocation may have been the original premise for broadcast regulation, scholar Robert McChesney (1999: 26) reminds us that technology was not the only reason for state intervention. 'Many of those who struggled for public broadcasting in its formative years did so not on technical grounds of spectrum scarcity as much as a profound critique of the limitations of the market for regulating a democratic media system.' If anything, concerns about a free-market approach to governing the media spectrum have intensified in recent years as a consequence of trends towards corporate concentration and media convergence, issues that will be addressed in detail in Chapter 8.

RELATED WEB SITES

Broadcasting Act: www.crtc.gc.ca/eng/LEGAL/BROAD.htm
  The full text of the current Act can be found here.
Canadian Department of Justice: www.canada.justice.gc.ca
  The Justice Department Web site includes enacted statutes.
CRTC: www.crtc.gc.ca
  The CRTC provides an excellent site with information on all aspects of regulation, as well as on upcoming hearings.

Parliament of Canada: www.parl.gc.ca
  Information on current legislation can be found at this site.
Telecommunications Act: www.crtc.gc.ca/eng/LEGAL/TELECOM.HTM
  This is where the full text of the Act can be found.

FURTHER READINGS

Babe, Robert. 1990. *Telecommunications in Canada*. Toronto: University of Toronto Press. This is a comprehensive account of the history of the technology, institutions, and government policies related to telecommunications in Canada.

Canada. 1986. *Report of the Task Force on Broadcasting Policy* (Caplan-Sauvageau Task Force). Ottawa: Minister of Supply and Services. This thorough and accessible report led to revision of the Broadcasting Act.

Gasher, Mike. 1998. 'Invoking public support for public broadcasting: The Aird Commission revisited', *Canadian Journal of Communication* 23: 189–216. This article tests the Aird Commission's claims to speak on behalf of Canadians by examining the actual testimony before the Royal Commission.

Raboy, Marc. 1990. *Missed Opportunities: The Story of Canada's Broadcasting Policy*. Montreal and Kingston: McGill-Queen's University Press. Raboy presents a thorough and readable history of Canadian broadcasting policy.

Vipond, Mary. 1992. *Listening In: The First Decade of Canadian Broadcasting, 1922–1932*. Montreal and Kingston: McGill-Queen's University Press. The brief but fascinating history of Canadian radio prior to the establishment of a national broadcaster is detailed in this work.

STUDY QUESTIONS

1. What are communication law and policy and what purpose do they serve? *146*
2. What is the fundamental policy distinction between telecommunications and broadcasting?
3. What is meant by 'rationalizing' policy, and why has it been necessary in recent years? *147*
4. What role does the Canadian public play in policy development? *148*
5. What has been the effect of telephone deregulation since the 1980s?
6. What is the significance of broadcasting in Canada being defined by the Broadcasting Act as a 'public service'?
7. What was the significance of the Aird Commission of 1928–9?
8. How has the definition of 'access' to broadcasting shifted over the past 70 years? *158*

LEARNING OUTCOMES

- To introduce law and policy as a principal structuring force in the Canadian communications environment.
- To situate law and policy with respect to other structuring forces, such as economics and technology.
- To define, and distinguish between, the telecommunications and broadcasting regimes.
- To explain the role of the CRTC and to outline its principal functions.
- To explain the policy concepts of common and contract carriage.
- To underline how the notion of public access to broadcasting has evolved historically.
- To explain the rationale behind Canadian-content regulations in radio and television.
- To consider the future of broadcast regulations in a digital environment.

CHAPTER 7

Cultural Industries Law and Policy

Introduction

Like telecommunications and broadcasting, the cultural industries—that is, film and video, music recording, and publishing (book, magazine, and newspaper)—are vehicles for the circulation of ideas. The term 'cultural industries' derives from the involvement of each of these industries in manufacturing, distributing, and retailing cultural materials. 'Culture industry', a term coined by the Frankfurt School (see Chapter 5), has a much different meaning from 'cultural industries'.

This chapter introduces the cultural industries and describes the various rationales that governments tend to use to justify their support. It examines film and video in both historical and contemporary contexts, looking at emerging trends in the industry and in film and video policy. Music recording is considered in regard to the organization of the industry, the influence of broadcasting on music recording, and the position of Canadian musicians in the context of the big five recording giants. Under book publishing we look at some history and current government support programs that have helped Canadian book publishers and Canadian authors, some of whom have become recognized around the world. The discussion of magazine publishing focuses on the legislation that has been necessary to ensure that Canadian magazines have room in the marketplace. It reviews the challenges mounted by the US and Canada's policy responses, and ends with an assessment of the future. We also describe several key elements of newspaper publishing as a cultural industry. The chapter closes by considering the new media and the kinds of policies needed for active Canadian participation in these media.

Traditionally, artistic expression relied for its survival on patrons prepared to support it and artists able to create original works. For centuries, members of the social elite—in business, politics, the church—have acted as art patrons. But in the modern era, with the establishment of democratic governments that wished to express the will of the people and encourage creativity, the state has come to share this role

more and more with the elite. Given the importance of ideas in our society, the economics of the mass market, the power of companies involved in providing cultural products, the high value placed on human creativity, and the goal of nation-building, governments have developed certain regulations and policies to support the cultural industries.

The cultural industries have in common with broadcasting and telecommunications some of the general policies and laws that regulate communications, such as copyright law, privacy laws, and the Charter's clause on freedom of speech. In addition, regulatory and funding bodies have been established to support certain cultural sectors.

In the cultural industries, the policy-making process is much less open than in telecommunications and broadcasting (with the exception of open Web sites). Basically, the industry lobbies government for supportive policies and the government responds, usually by granting something, but not everything the industry has requested. Occasionally, mechanisms are put in place to test public opinion—such as the Ontario Royal Commission on Book Publishing (1972), the Applebaum-Hébert committee on cultural policy, the Magazine Task Force (1994), and even the debate surrounding Bill C-55 on magazines (1998–9). But much more often, policy is developed by consultants undertaking investigations into the functioning of an industry and making recommendations for appropriate policy. There are many such reports at both the federal and provincial levels.

In Canada, while there were earlier attempts, such as John Grierson's report on film that led to the establishment of the National Film Board, cultural policy effectively dates back to the Royal Commission on National Development in the Arts, Letters and Sciences (1951). This Commission, chaired by Vincent Massey, led to the founding of a body, the Canada Council, with the responsibility to provide funding for artists (as well as for research in the humanities and social sciences). In the late 1960s, as the baby boomers came of age and with impetus from centennial celebrations and Expo 67, pressure increased drastically on governments to provide opportunities for Canadians to participate in both artistic expression and in the various cultural industries. The federal government and some provincial governments began to examine the cultural industries as well as their support of them—for example, funding for the National Film Board and preferential postal rates for Canadian books, magazines, and newspapers (that date back to the 1840s). Throughout the 1970s, various cultural policies were put in place and, while vibrant industries have been a long time in establishing firm financial foundations, Canada can now boast an impressive performance in film and television production and sound recording, and in writing and publishing books, magazines, and newspapers. These achievements have not been attained without considerable effort and investment from politicians, government officials, cultural industries personnel, creative artists, and support from the Canadian public.

Nevertheless, there were and still remain barriers to the sustenance of a vibrant cultural industry in Canada, particularly with respect to policy. In 1983, Paul Audley suggested in his book, *Canada's Cultural Industries*, that two major challenges faced Canadian cultural policy: financing and distribution. A proper level of financing was required to create high-quality cultural products because established, foreign-owned producers in film, music, books, and magazines could sell their products more cheaply, which made it difficult for Canadian talent and products to compete. And even if such materials were developed, access to distribution channels, that is, cinemas, bookstores, and magazine racks, was severely restricted both by business practices and by the sheer volume of imported products. In some cases, books for example, foreign companies had moved into Canada and established branch plants (wholly owned subsidiary companies) to serve the Canadian market with what appeared to be Canadian products.

Given the barriers to the Canadian cultural industries and the nature of cultural products themselves, a substantial body of research dedicated to the analysis of Canadian cultural policy has emerged (see, for example, McFadyen et al., 1994). That literature has identified a number of rationales behind the development of Canadian cultural policies. These rationales, discussed below, include democratic participation, cultural development, public service, and market failure (for a detailed review of the latter three, see Lorimer and Duxbury, 1994).

Quebec-based media scholars Marc Raboy, Ivan Bernier, Florian Sauvageau, and Dave Atkinson (1994) argue that it is the government's responsibility to enhance **democratic participation** by providing citizens with access to the ideas and creativity of their own community. To fail to do so is to prevent citizens from fully and knowledgeably participating in their community. A more local form of this model is called the community development or animation model: it emphasizes the value of self-knowledge in forming a dynamic community. Support for cultural industries is also often justified by making reference to the notion of **cultural development**. Here, it is argued, the state has a responsibility to provide citizens with access to their cultural heritage and to favour the creation of works that reflect and enrich that heritage. A public service approach stresses the role of government to assist the nation in preserving its heritage and its efforts towards human betterment—goals often left unaddressed by the constraints of business practice, such as profits. The notion of market failure is a more clearly economic justification for government inter-

POSITIONS ON CULTURAL INDUSTRIES POLICY

There is an abundant literature on the ins and outs of cultural industries policy. For example, Canadian political economist Abraham Rotstein (1988) and west-coast-based economist Steven Globerman (1983) have opposing views on market failure. Rotstein argues against using economic concepts because, he reasons, they are inappropriate for cultural and artistic activities. Applying economic concepts to culture is rather like applying religious concepts to the marketplace. Globerman, on the other hand, argues that cultural activities should, like all other activities, be made subject to marketplace realities. If audiences are too small or they are unwilling to pay enough for the service, then it should cease to exist.

ART FOR ART'S SAKE

An often-used rationale for some cultural support policies is 'art for art's sake'. This means that art should be supported by governments, or anyone else with funds, not for any motive other than for the sake of art itself. It is argued further that to do so is to celebrate human creativity and human freedom to create.

Art in the form of music or writing can be the foundation of publishing or sound recording. Filmmaking can also be the product of artistic rather than commercial motivations. In fact, in many instances, artistic aims are melded with communicational aims to create wonderful artistic works. We have not included 'art for art's sake' as a rationale for the support of cultural industries because we feel that, while it is a viewpoint related to the overall endeavour of producing cultural objects, it is one step away from being a rationale for cultural industries policy. Some would disagree.

vention and encompasses two ideas. First, there may be structural barriers to the participation of domestic businesses in domestic—and international—cultural markets. Thus the government has the responsibility to step in and assist new or 'infant industries' to establish themselves in the marketplace. Second, the market rarely reflects the true value of a work of art, which has lasting value as a public good, so it is seen as legitimate for governments to intervene to encourage production of such works.

Whichever rationale is used, cultural industries policy, like broadcasting and telecommunications policy, attempts to balance three sets of factors—the economic, the political, and the cultural (including the artistic). This balancing act, however, is difficult. First, all three sets of factors are nearly always simultaneously at work. Second, in Canada, economic interests in the cultural industries usually involve foreign businesses while cultural interests usually involve the national creative community—two parties seldom in agreement. Third, Canada is a trading nation and in recent years Canadian governments have enthusiastically pursued international trade agreements, which can often conflict with cultural goals. In the negotiations leading up to the signing of the Canada–US Free Trade Agreement (FTA) and the North American Free Trade Agreement (NAFTA), Canada managed to persuade its trading partners that the cultural industries should be exempt from full compliance with the requirements of free trade. The Canadian government insisted that Canada must retain the right to take policy and program action to support its cultural industries. The value of this exemption has been debated, particularly inside the cultural industries sector (see analysis by Carr, 1991), because of the extensive opportunities in the trade agreement for retaliatory actions by the US. In 1998 the value of that cultural 'exemption' was tested within the WTO by a US attack on Canadian magazine policy. As we will see, it was found to be lacking.

Cultural Industries Policy by Sector

The Canadian cultural industries, and the laws and policies established to regulate and support them, can be divided into five sectors: film and video, music recording, book publishing, magazine publishing, and, to a lesser degree, newspaper publishing.

FILM AND VIDEO

Federal and provincial governments in Canada have been sponsoring motion-picture production in one form or another since early in the twentieth century, and Ottawa has operated a national film production organization continuously since 1918. Canada, however, has been much more successful in the spheres of industrial and documentary film production—e.g., eight films produced by the National Film Board, founded in 1939, have won Academy Awards—than in the higher-profile domain of dramatic, feature-length film production, the kinds of movies we see in our theatres. There, Hollywood is the dominant player in the Canadian market, occupying better than 90 per cent of screen time in Canada's commercial movie theatres. Even though directors like Atom Egoyan, François Girard, Patricia Rozema, Deepa Mehta, Mina Shum, Léa Pool, and Denys Arcand have given renewed vigour to Canadian feature filmmaking since the early 1980s, domestic films have averaged only between 3 and 6 per cent of box-office revenues in Canadian cinemas. In a sense, our own domestic cinema is foreign to Canadian audiences.

Table 7.1 The National Film Board's Academy Awards

Films

Year	Title (Director)
1941	*Churchill's Island* (Stuart Legg)
1953	*Neighbours* (Norman McLaren)
1978	*Le Château de sable* (Co Hoedeman)
1979	*Special Delivery* (John Weldon, Eunice Macaulay)
1980	*Every Child/Chaque enfant* (Eugene Fedorenko)
1983	*If You Love This Planet* (Terre Nash)
1984	*Flamenco at 5:15* (Cynthia Scott)
1995	*Bob's Birthday* (Alison Snowden, David Fine)

Other Categories

Year	Award
1989	Honorary Oscar in recognition of NFB's 50th anniversary
1999	Technical achievement to NFB scientists Ed H. Zwaneveld and Frederick Gasoi and two industry colleagues for the design and development of the Film Keykode Reader

Source: National Film Board, www.nfb.ca/e/highlights/oscars.html

Although at the federal level the primary policy concern in the post-war period has been increasing the production of Canadian feature films for theatrical, home video, and television release, provincial governments—most notably in Quebec, Ontario, and British Columbia—have instituted programs to encourage Hollywood producers to locate their film and television productions in such cities as Montreal, Toronto, and Vancouver. British Columbia has become the third largest site of film and television production in North America, after the states of California and New York, with more than $1 billion in direct spending as of 2000 (Gasher, 2002a: 108).

It is important to understand that Ottawa has perceived cinema for most of its history as a medium of nation-building. The first state-sponsored films in Canada were tools to promote immigration from Britain to settle the Prairies. Motion pictures are believed to have played a key role in Canada attracting three million immigrants between 1900 and 1914. Early films were also used to lure industry and investment capital (Morris, 1978: 133–5).

The use of film as a medium of propaganda during World War I led governments to play an increasing role in film production, and Canada became the first country in the world with government film production units, although Ottawa consistently rejected calls to curtail American monopolization of the commercial film sector. A distinction was made by state officials between the purposeful films of government production and entertainment films (Magder, 1985: 86).

Having previously contracted out film projects, Ontario established the Ontario Government Motion Picture Bureau in 1917. The Bureau purchased the abandoned Trenton Studios in 1923 and ran them until 1934 (Morris, 1978: 70–1). British Columbia established its own Educational and Patriotic Film Service in 1919, becoming one of the first provinces to use film to promote immigration (ibid., 149).

In 1918, the federal government established the Exhibits and Publicity Bureau within the Department of Trade and Commerce for 'the production, acquisition and distribution of motion pictures'. This agency's *Seeing Canada* series, launched in 1919 and aimed primarily at foreign audiences, was designed to attract industry and capital to Canada (ibid., 131–5). The Exhibits and Publicity Bureau became the Canadian Government Motion Picture Bureau in 1923 and was absorbed by the National Film Board of Canada in 1941 (ibid., 161). The establishment of the NFB under the direction of John Grierson in 1939 entrenched the state as a producer of films for nation-building purposes.

Increasingly in the post-war period, the federal government has been called upon to address the commercial film sector. The aftermath of World War II demanded that the government redefine the mandate of the NFB—which during the war years was a propaganda agency—and address the American domination of feature film, particularly in the face of a balance-of-payments crisis with the United States. The

John Grierson (r), founder of the National Film Board, examines posters produced by the NFB in 1944. During World War II, the NFB was an important agency of propaganda in support of the Allied war effort—its films were distributed theatrically in Canada and the US. (Courtesy National Archives, PA-179108)

Emergency Foreign Exchange Conservation Act of 1947, which imposed import restrictions on a number of US goods, excluded motion pictures, even though $17 million of the $20 million taken out of Canada that year by the motion picture industry went to the US. A lobby group from the Motion Picture Export Association of America (MPEAA) and Famous Players Canada Corporation convinced Minister of Trade and Commerce C.D. Howe that Hollywood could help resolve the problem it had helped to create. Rather than impose screen quotas or withholding taxes, Ottawa negotiated the Canadian Co-operation Project with Washington and the resourceful MPEAA. The deal required Hollywood to: produce a film on Canada's trade-dollar problem; provide more complete newsreel coverage of Canada; produce short films about Canada; release NFB films in the United States; include Canadian sequences in its feature films; make radio recordings by Hollywood stars extolling Canada; and work with a Canadian government offi-

cer in Hollywood to co-ordinate the project (Cox, 1980: 34). Anthony D. Smith (1980: 52–3) writes:

> It is hard today to believe that Canada allowed itself to be thus fobbed off, but it is a matter of historical fact that a representative of Canada was specially appointed to reside in Hollywood and supervise small changes of dialogue and location in American films: escaping convicts would trudge their way to Canada rather than Oregon, lovers would elope to Ottawa rather than Chicago, stars would spend glamorous weekends in the Canadian Rockies.

The Canadian Co-operation Project expired in 1951 when Canada's currency reserves crisis eased (Pendakur, 1990: 141).

The first serious attempt by the Canadian government to stimulate indigenous feature-film production was the establishment of the Canadian Film Development Corporation (CFDC, now Telefilm Canada) in 1967. The CFDC was mandated to: invest in Canadian feature-film projects; loan money to producers; present awards for outstanding production; support the development of film craft through grants to filmmakers and technicians; and 'advise and assist' producers in distributing their films (ibid., 148). In sum, the CFDC was designed to ease the burden of funding feature-film production in Canada.

Private investment in film production had been encouraged by Ottawa since 1954 through a 60 per cent capital-cost allowance, a tax deduction available to investors in any film, no matter the source. The law was revised in 1974 to increase the write-off to 100 per cent, but only for investments in Canadian feature films. The impact of the capital-cost allowance is debatable in terms of the program's cultural and economic objectives. Citing figures based on tax-shelter productions from 1974 to 1986, Manjunath Pendakur (ibid., 170–3) acknowledges that the capital-cost allowance boosted film production ($660 million in eligible investment for 432 feature films) and the size of average film budgets (from $527,000 prior to 1974 to $3.5 million by 1986). But the tax shelter was less successful in increasing either the production of identifiably Canadian feature films or their distribution and exhibition. The 1985 *Report of the Film Industry Task Force* (Canada, 1985: 28–9) concluded that the capital-cost allowance, in fact, 'widened the gap between production and market'. Because the introduction of the

100 per cent capital-cost allowance coincided with the CFDC's decision to drop its demand for a distribution agreement as a funding prerequisite, the capital-cost allowance in effect reduced the importance of distributor participation in Canadian film projects. As a result, 'while the supply of Canadian theatrical properties increased considerably, many were totally unmarketable.' Investors proved to be more interested in tax savings than in cinema; when returns on investment were not forthcoming and the economic recession of the early 1980s hit, private investment in film production dried up.

Canadian governments have been reluctant to impose protectionist measures on the film industry, even though Ottawa heard repeated calls for screen quotas in Canadian movie theatres throughout the twentieth century. Part of the problem, certainly, is that the operation of movie theatres falls under provincial jurisdiction, and a nationwide screen quota would demand co-ordination among the 10 provinces. But there really is no public appetite for reducing in any way Hollywood's stranglehold on the Canadian market. Most Canadians—including francophones in Quebec—believe that going to the movies means going to Hollywood movies, and until at least the late 1980s there was probably not a large enough stock of quality Canadian features to warrant a quota.

Neither the 1984 *National Film and Video Policy*, tabled by Liberal Communications Minister Francis Fox (Canada, 1984), nor the 1985 *Report of the Film Industry Task Force* (Canada, 1985), delivered to the Conservative government of Brian Mulroney, favoured quotas, preferring instead to target the structural issues of distribution and **vertical integration**. That is, the problems Canadian filmmakers had in gaining access to Canadian theatre screens was explained by the fact that the same companies that owned major Hollywood studios also owned Canada's principal theatre chains—Famous Players and Cineplex Odeon—and the distribution companies that supplied those theatre chains with films.

Little has changed. Together, Famous Players and Cineplex Odeon control an estimated 82 per cent of the Canadian film exhibition market (McCarthy, 1997). Famous Players, with 882 screens in 101 locations across Canada, is a wholly owned subsidiary of Viacom Inc. of New York, a diversified entertainment and communications conglomerate that owns the major Hollywood studio Paramount Pictures

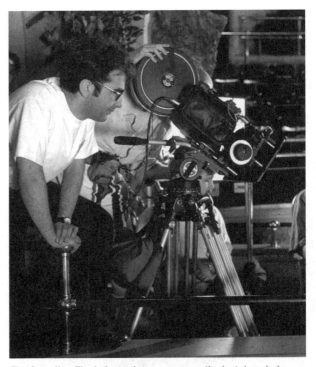

The Canadian film industry has grown over the last decade in particular. Independent filmmaker Atom Egoyan has gained critical acclaim and international recognition for his films such as *The Sweet Hereafter*, *Ararat*, *Exotica*, and *Felicia's Journey*. (Johnnie Eisen)

(Famous Players, 2002). Cineplex Odeon operates 828 screens in 122 theatres across Canada. The company merged with Sony Corp.'s Loews Theaters in May 1998 to form Loews Cineplex Entertainment (LCE), one of the largest film exhibitors in the world with 2,200 movie screens in more than 230 locations in North America, Spain, and South Korea. LCE's two principal shareholders had been the Hollywood major studios Sony Pictures and Universal Studios (Craig, 2001), but in March 2002 the near-bankrupt exhibitor was purchased by the Canadian companies Onex Corp. and Oaktree Capital (see Onex, 2002). Onex also owns Galaxy Entertainment, a chain of small-market cinemas in Canada, and Phoenix Pictures, a film production company based on a partnership with Sony Pictures and Viacom subsidiary Showtime.

In the 1980s, television became by far the largest source of revenue for private Canadian film and video companies, thanks to Canadian ownership and Canadian content regulations, the CBC's inherent interest in Canadian materials, and the licensing in the

1980s of pay-television and specialty channels devoted to broadcasting feature-length films. The CRTC expanded the market to Canadian film producers by licensing its first national pay-TV networks—First Choice and C-Channel—in March 1982 (Magder, 1993: 202). A year later, the CRTC licensed three cable services specializing in movies: SuperChannel (in western Canada), The Movie Network (in eastern Canada), and the French-language Super Écran (Canadian Cable Television Association, 1995).

Producers committed to film production on a full-time basis began to explore a variety of funding sources, specifically, co-production between the private and public sectors and hybrid film-television production. The 1981 film *Les Plouffe*, for example, received one-fifth of its budget from the CBC and was released in three versions: as a six-hour TV mini-series; as a French-language feature film; and as an English-language feature. The principal backers of the 1982 feature film *The Terry Fox Story* were broadcasters Home Box Office and CTV. Ted Magder (1993: 200–1) writes: 'Feature film producers were now more eager than ever to obtain major funding from broadcasters, who had become an important source of film capital.'

In recognition of the promise television held, the federal government in 1983 altered the mandate of the Canadian Film Development Corporation. The federal Department of Communications introduced the $35 million Canadian Broadcast Development Fund, to be administered by the CFDC, which later that year changed its name to Telefilm Canada to reflect its new emphasis on television. While the sum of money in the Broadcast Fund may not appear significant, it increased considerably the ability of production companies to access other sources of investment and it encouraged Canadian film producers to look more and more to television production. Magder (ibid., 211) argues: 'In a very real sense the Canadian government had solved the problem of distribution and exhibition by gearing production activities to the regulated market of Canadian television.'

The Chrétien government's Mandate Review Committee, chaired by Pierre Juneau, stated in its January 1996 report that Canadian movies reached their largest audiences through CBC television channels (Canada, 1996: 31). Elizabeth McDonald, president of the Canadian Film and Television Production Association, reported in July 1996 that Canadian feature films earned 40 per cent of their revenues from

pay television (Rice-Barker, 1996: 27).

Building audiences is the central theme of a new feature-film policy introduced by the federal Heritage Ministry in October 2000 (Canada, 2000). The ambitious goal of this policy, entitled *From Script to Screen*, is to capture 5 per cent of the domestic box office within five years—compared to a paltry 2.1 per cent in 1999—and to increase audiences for Canadian features abroad. 'Now that the Canadian industry has come of age and the building blocks of a vibrant industry are in place, it is time to focus on securing a larger share of our own market.'

The policy amounts to a doubling of the Canadian government's investment in the industry, from $50 million to $100 million annually. The new Canadian Feature Film Fund, administered by Telefilm Canada, supports screenwriting, production, marketing, and promotion. The biggest investment—$40 million annually—goes to the Project Development, Production and Marketing Assistance Program. A 'performance-based component' to this program allocates money to producers and distributors based primarily on their track records of success at the box office, but also recognizes the degree of Canadian content and critical acclaim achieved. A 'selective component' will fund the production and distribution of innovative and culturally relevant projects by new filmmakers. The policy will also support screenwriting, professional development, promotion, and film preservation.

Trends in Film and Video Policy

Since the early 1980s, Ottawa has been gradually ceding its leadership role in the film policy field to the private sector and the provinces. Even though Telefilm remains the single most important source of film funding, no film can be made with Telefilm money alone. Filmmakers find themselves tapping half a dozen sources of funding to get their films made.

Canada's major banks and broadcasters have become important sources of financing for both project development and film and television production. These funding sources include Astral Media Harold Greenberg Fund, Bell Broadcast and New Media Fund, Bravo!Fact, Cogeco Program Development Fund, Independent Production Fund, and Rogers Telefund (see Tiffin, 2001).

Canada's provincial governments have adopted a two-track film strategy. Every province in the country has a film office to promote it (primarily to

Hollywood producers) as a location for film and television production. In addition, British Columbia, Saskatchewan, Manitoba, Ontario, Quebec, New Brunswick, Nova Scotia, and Newfoundland provide development, production, and/or post-production support to indigenous producers through such funding vehicles as grants, loans, direct investment, and tax credits on labour costs (see Gasher, 2002a: 96–101).

MUSIC RECORDING

The music recording industry shares many of the characteristics of other cultural industries in Canada; it is comprised, on the one hand, of small domestic companies that occupy a minimal, fragile share of the domestic consumer market and, on the other hand, of a few large, multinational companies that dominate the production and distribution of recordings, mainly of foreign origin. A significant distinction, however, is the considerable exposure Canadian recording artists receive—on radio, on music television, in mainstream record stores—and the number of recognizable Canadian stars the industry can boast.

Structurally, the Canadian recording industry is dominated by five multinationals—Warner Music Group (an AOL Time Warner subsidiary that includes Atlantis, Elektra, Warner Bros. Records, Reprise, and 47 smaller labels), Universal Music Group, Sony Music, EMI, and Bertelsmann Music Group (Wallace, 2002: 211–4). The most recent statistics available indicate that for 1995–6 foreign companies captured 86.1 per cent of the Canadian sound recording market (see www.pch.gc.ca/progs/ac-ca/progs/pades-srdp/ TOC_E.htm).

With a weak market base from which to operate, Canadian recording companies find themselves in a vicious circle. Lack of profit on past productions means an inability to raise capital for future investment, which means relatively low budgets for current projects and consequently leads to an inability to attract or keep Canadian stars loyal to their labels. This results in insufficient marketing budgets to promote their products, low consumer awareness of their recordings, and low profitability on subsequent recordings. Despite this discouraging picture, the Canadian consumer market for recorded music is the sixth largest in the world with sales of $1.3 billion annually. So there is scope for larger sales if Canadian companies could increase their share.

One technique that the independent label Battle Axe Records has used to promote the music group

The latest success story in the US is Avril Lavigne, whose sales were in the Top 10 of all artists as of October 2002. (Frank Gunn/CP)

Swollen Members is to build momentum in the small Canadian market through releasing on vinyl, running a side business of providing deejays who play Battle Axe recordings, promoting clothing on stage, riding the coattails of other stars, touring, and building markets through managed appearances. In this way, in the summer of 2002, Swollen Members achieved platinum-level (100,000 records) sales. The achievement of platinum gave the band an entree into the US market, which in turn multiplied sales back in Canada.

Communications scholar Will Straw (1996) has argued that the structure of the recording industry in Canada is undergoing major changes. The international success of Canadian stars, such as Céline Dion, Shania Twain, Diana Krall, Sarah MacLachlan, Bryan Adams, and Alanis Morissette, coincided with an expansion of the domestic market for Canadian-content recordings in the 1990s, the opening up of the global market to diverse music styles (e.g., industrial noise, rap, country), and the emergence of warehouse-sized superstores that carry a range of recordings to

NAPSTER

If the Internet is celebrated for the ways in which it has liberated mass communication, it has also been derided for the way it has set free some forms of content, such as recorded music. Downloading popular music—and thus bypassing the cash register at the local music store—has become a favoured computer application, particularly among young people whose disposable income is no match for their insatiable appetite for the latest music and video clips.

MP3 technology, which allows people to share and exchange sound-recording files over computer networks, was developed by the International Organization for Standardization in Geneva in 1992. In March 1998, MP3.com began making the music of small, unknown bands available on the World Wide Web, but soon people were posting and downloading the old and new music of established artists. Not surprisingly, the music industry cried foul, citing copyright infringement and fearing a significant drop in retail sales.

Yet, at the same time the major recording companies began fighting copyright infringement, they also began searching for ways to profit from it. For example, the Recording Industry Association of America initially sent cease-and-desist letters to people posting music on-line and asked artists to support their fight against MP3. But in December 1998 the five major recording companies at that time—BMG, Sony, Universal, Warner Music Group, and Warner Bros—announced the Secure Digital Music Initiative to seek ways to work with file-sharing technology.

By 1999 two kinds of Web sites were providing music for downloading—corporate, user-pay sites such as Getmusic.com, Bugjuice.com, and Twangthis.com and free, rogue sites such as Napster.com. In June 1999, the American Society of Composers, Authors and Publishers (ASCAP) established a licensing agreement with MP3.com, selling performance rights licences to Internet sites. And in December 1999 the Recording Industry Association of America sued Napster for copyright infringement, following up a month later with a similar suit against MP3.com.

Faced with both court action and revenue shortfalls, Napster announced a partnership with the German media company Bertelsmann AG and began to transform itself into a membership service with royalties paid to songwriters and music publishers. In May 2002 Bertelsmann purchased all of Napster's assets and completed its conversion to a commercial subsidiary.

appeal to every taste. While some predicted that with the consolidation of vertically integrated multinational recording companies the global soundscape would become more homogeneous, Straw (1996: 114) concludes instead that the large multinationals are exploiting relatively autonomous music markets and directly signing artists to serve those markets. For some time, bands like the Tragically Hip, Nickelback, and the Barenaked Ladies continued to be more popular in Canada than in the US, yet they remained attractive properties to major record labels. In the case of Nickelback, their US fame eventually surpassed their renown in Canada. The latest Canadian success story in the US is Avril Lavigne, whose sales were in the Top 10 of all artists as of October 2002.

A result of the restructuring of the music industry has been the displacement of smaller, independent recording companies, which used to rely on unknown and marginal acts to develop niche markets. Straw portrays a two-tiered industry structure, divided between majors and small independents, both operating internationally:

As major firms construct global audiences from national niches, small independent firms that had hitherto dominated these niches in their own countries find their room to manoeuvre shrinking. To survive they, too, must move into international markets, licensing their own products in other territories, selling publishing and other rights on a country-by-country basis, and picking up the inventory of other small national labels for distribution. (Ibid., 104)

Historically, the most important policy development for Canadian recorded music was the CRTC's establishment in 1971 of Canadian-content quotas for radio, which required popular music stations to play a minimum of 30 per cent Canadian music. The quotas were a response to the under-representation of Canadian recording artists on Canadian radio stations; as of 1968, Canadian music accounted for between 4 and 7 per cent of all music played on Canadian radio at a time when the popular music scene was exploding (Filion, 1996: 132). A points system known as

Table 7.2 The Canadian Audio Visual Certification Office (CAVCO) Points System

For a creative series to be recognized as a Canadian production, a total of at least six points must be allotted according to the following scale. Points are allotted for each Canadian who rendered the services.	Points awarded
Non-animated productions (live action)	
Director	2
Screenwriter	2
Lead performer for whose services the highest remuneration was payable	1
Lead performer for whose services the second highest remuneration was payable	1
Director of photography	1
Art director	1
Music composer	1
Picture editor	1
Animated productions	
Director	1
Screenwriter and storyboard supervisor	1
Lead voice for which the highest or second highest remuneration was payable	1
Design supervisor (art director)	1
Camera operator where the camera operation is done in Canada	1
Music composer	1
Picture editor	1
Layout and background where the work is performed in Canada	1
Key animation where the work is performed in Canada	1
Assistant animation and in-betweening where work is performed in Canada	1

Whereas MAPL is the points system for music, CAVCO is the points system for film and video production. If a production receives six points it becomes eligible for a tax credit.

MAPL was devised to determine whether or not recordings qualify as Canadian. That is, a 'Canadian selection' must meet at least two of the following conditions:

• the music is, or lyrics are, performed by a Canadian;
• the music is composed entirely by a Canadian;
• the lyrics are written entirely by a Canadian;
• the musical selection consists of a live performance that is either recorded wholly in Canada or is performed wholly and broadcast live in Canada;
• the musical selection was performed live or recorded after 1 September 1991, and a Canadian who has collaborated with a non-Canadian receives at least 50 per cent of the credit as composer and lyricist according to the records of a recognized performing rights society.

Of course, the regulations are not universal. The quota level is lower for radio formats in which Canadian recordings are not as readily available (e.g., jazz, classi-

cal music) and higher for French-language broadcasters. The quota for English-language popular music stations was raised to 35 per cent in 1998, and the CRTC ruled that this level had to be maintained from 6 a.m. to 6 p.m. on weekdays and that selections had to be played in their entirety to qualify. At the same time, the quota for French-language music stations was raised from 50 to 55 per cent.

Although the quota system recognizes the importance of radio airplay to record sales, radio's primacy as a promotional vehicle has been challenged since the 1980s by music video stations (MuchMusic and MusiquePlus in Canada) with their attendant marketing value. Technological changes to radio—e.g., digital audio broadcasting, digital audio satellite service—also threaten to alter the economic relationship between recording companies and radio broadcasters (see Wallace, 2002).

The Canadian recording companies, represented by the Canadian Independent Record Production Association (CIRPA, www.cirpa.ca), have always insisted that the Canadian-content rules on broadcasting (radio and television) are essential to their survival. The major recording careers of some Canadian performers and composers were launched through significant airplay on Canadian radio and, more recently, on music video television. If it can be argued that Céline Dion and Bryan Adams no longer need to rely on quotas for airplay, it must also be acknowledged that less mainstream acts and up-and-coming performers do. The international success of Canadian performers like Dion, Adams, Alanis Morissette, Sarah MacLachlan, Nelly Furtado, and Bruce Cockburn has not always meant success for Canadian recording companies. As noted above, Canadian labels depend for their survival on the Canadian artists they discover and manage to hold onto.

A second significant policy measure was the establishment in 1982 of the Fund to Assist Canadian Talent on Record, which became known as FACTOR/MusicAction when a French-language component was added (www.factor.ca). With the encouragement of the CRTC, the fund was created by several radio broadcasters (CHUM Ltd, Moffatt Communi-cations, Rogers Broadcasting Ltd) in partnership with two major industry associations (CIRPA and the Canadian Music Publishers Association, www.cmrra.ca) to channel money into the Canadian music industry. The funds provided are used, for example, to produce demo tapes and promotional video clips and to organize promotional tours by musicians. In 1986, the federal government established the Sound Recording Development Program (SRDP), which provides about $5 million each year to FACTOR/MusicAction (see www.pch.gc.ca).

The 1996 Task Force on the Future of the Canadian Music Industry acknowledged that gaps in the federal government's policy apparatus compromised the effectiveness of Canadian-content regulations and the Sound Recording Development Program. Specifically, the Task Force identified three areas of future policy concern: 'grossly inadequate' copyright legislation; the absence of incentives to strengthen independent recording companies (which are responsible for 70 per cent of Canadian-content recordings); and the absence of Investment Canada guidelines for the industry.

In May 2001 the Department of Canadian Heritage announced a new Canadian Sound Recording Policy, entitled *From Creators to Audience*

'A MAJOR LABEL DEAL IS LIKE HAVING A CREDIT CARD AT 66 PER CENT INTEREST'

After enduring years of unfair contracts that caused performers such as Prince to change his name and tattoo 'Slave' on his face, in March 2002 top musicians played five venues in Los Angeles to raise money to legally transform musicians from what Don Henley of the Eagles called 'indentured slaves' to a position of greater power (*Globe and Mail*, 2 Mar 2002, R1). Journalist Doug Saunders explains the matter approximately in this way. A typical major-label contract calls for seven albums over seven years with a six-figure advance that is repaid out of royalties of 10 per cent of sales revenues. While this works smoothly for some artists—each year a record comes out—for others, a label may withhold release by months or years for 'marketing reasons', thereby extending the time span of the contract. Meanwhile, the artist cannot release a record with another label, and tours and other appearances often are determined by the release of a record. Record companies charge their entire direct operational costs, including the costs of touring, marketing, distribution, and video production against the 10 per cent royalty of the artist. As a result, the repayment of advances can take decades and top musicians can take home less than $100,000 per year. As Saunders says: 'An estimated 90 per cent of musicians fail to earn back their advances, meaning that all they have gained from their big-label contract is expensive debt. In the words of one veteran record producer, "A major label deal is like having a credit card at 66 per cent interest."'

The label can cancel the performer's contract and keep the work unreleased or sell the contract to another company. Nor are the labels scrupulously honest. Artists ranging from Peggy Lee to Meat Loaf have hired private auditors and obtained up to $10 million settlements for undisclosed sales. Perhaps the tide will turn. Mariah Carey was paid $28 million by Virgin Records to walk away from her contract. David Bowie bought himself out of his contract and finances himself with bond issues. And Billy Joel says, 'I got signed to a deal with a company that was sucking my blood for 25 years. I just don't want that to happen to nobody else, okay?'

(www.pch.gc.ca/progs/ac-ca/progs/pades-srdp/pubs/policy_e.cfm). More than the title echoes the federal government's new feature-film policy, described above. Here, too, the goal is to provide support at every level of the sound recording process—from the development of creators to the building of audiences, as its title suggests. A three-year, $23 million program to be administered, coincidentally, by Telefilm Canada, it establishes an eight-part Canada Music Fund, which absorbs the pre-existing Sound Recording Development Program and promises to:

- build community support and skills development of creators;
- support the production and distribution of 'specialized music recordings reflective of the diversity of Canadian voices';
- provide project-based support to new emerging artists;
- develop the business skills of Canadian music entrepreneurs;
- ensure the preservation of Canadian musical works;
- support recording industry associations, conferences, and awards programs;
- and monitor industry performance.

As in the film industry, federal government policy stops short of addressing structural factors that allow the major recording companies to dominate the Canadian market in the first place.

BOOK PUBLISHING

While copyright law in Canada dates back to the Imperial Copyright Act of 1841, public policy directly oriented to book publishing did not expand from that beginning until much later. In 1951 the Massey Commission allocated a scant 10 pages to publishing. The matter was not examined again by the Canadian government until 1966: at that time it was categorized as an adjunct to the pulp and paper industry. The industry was valued at $222 million (Ernst and Ernst, 1966). Within the next four years, and in the context of the positive social and cultural environment created by the Massey Commission, book publishing was recognized as a cultural endeavour.

The process of cultural self-realization that began with the Massey Commission reached fairly quickly into the arts, including writing, with the founding of the Canada Council in 1957. In 1966 a cultural consciousness of publishing began to dawn, and by the 1970s governments and the industry began to review existing laws and policies and develop support measures. In 1972 the Canada Council included publishing within its mandate and provided funding to publishers to help them meet the deficits they incurred by publishing titles of cultural significance to Canadians. That same year, the report of the Ontario

COPYRIGHT

Copyright is a form of protection for intellectual property that accrues to an author on making a 'literary work' public. It is a right that is granted for a specified time to an author (or another appointed person or body) to print, record, or perform an original creation (artistic, literary, musical). No registration is required in Canada, not even a copyright mark (©).

Copyright provides weak protection. That is to say, it protects the expression of the idea, not the idea itself, and hence allows for someone else to paraphrase and not breach copyright. But were that same person to copy what was written, word for word, then the person would be guilty of both plagiarizing and of breaching copyright.

Copyright is intended to adjudicate between the author's right to benefit from his or her intellectual work and society's right or need to know. It lasts a long time, currently 50 years after the death of the author.

Copyright has two associated rights, a moral right and a property right. Moral rights, which have nothing to do with morality, ensure that the author of a work will be recognized as the author in perpetuity—even if someone else holds the other set of rights contained in copyright, the property or economic rights. Moral rights also allow the author to retain control over the products or services with which his or her work will be associated. Moral rights also forbid mutilation or transformation of a work over the objection of the author.

Property rights for copyright are those rights that allow for the reproduction of original work, often for financial gain. They may be sold, assigned, and divided in any way the rights-holder may wish. These rights can allow someone besides the author to make money. For example, Michael Jackson, who now owns some early Beatles material, can profit from allowing this music to be used for commercial purposes.

Royal Commission on Book Publishing echoed a belief that had already been forming—that book publishing was an important cultural endeavour. In its final chapter the Commission noted:

> the Canadian book publishing industry simply makes too small a contribution to the gross national product for economic considerations to earn it any priority over many other fields of enterprise. But from the cultural standpoint, the fact that book publishing is the indispensable interface between Canadian authors and those who read their books places it squarely in the centre of our stage. . . . Government assistance (to book publishing), in whatever form, can be justified only to the extent that furnishing it will enrich and protect the cultural life of the people of Ontario and Canada. (Ontario, 1972: 219–20)

In 1977 the federal office of the Secretary of State produced a report on the book publishing industry (Canada, 1977), to be followed in 1978 by reports on English- and French-language educational publishing (Canada, 1978a, 1978b). By 1980 the Association of Canadian Publishers (ACP) had been formed (its membership was restricted to Canadian-owned firms), and it produced a strategy document in 1980 that echoed many of the findings of the Ontario Royal Commission and called for many of the same funding interventions (ACP, 1980). By the late 1980s most provinces had joined Ontario in examining the size and nature of book publishing activities within their boundaries.

From the early 1970s onward three elements of book publishing were at least tacitly recognized and they became the foundation for the development of law and policy. They were (and are):

- Book publishing is a strategic industry in that it has a substantial influence on the articulation and development of culture.
- The structure of the Canadian market, especially the English-Canadian market, makes it difficult for domestic publishers of Canadian authors writing on Canadian subjects for a Canadian reading public to survive. Survival is difficult essentially because Canadian authors and publishers must compete with run-on copies of imported books on non-Canadian or universal subjects from other

English-speaking markets, particularly the US and UK markets, where set-up costs are amortized on print runs much larger than could ever be contemplated in Canada. Moreover, set-up costs are recovered in the exporter's domestic market.
- Within the well-established Canadian framework of a mixed public- and private-sector economy, a role for government intervention has been created to avoid requiring Canadians to pay a premium for books on Canadian subjects, or not having access to books on Canadian topics and Canadian authors of comparable stature to published foreign authors.

On the foundation of these understandings, three types of interventions were considered and then implemented, and are still in effect today.

First is economic or industrial support. This financial support targets the bottom line. It is designed to assist publishing firms over the long or short term to improve their financial performance by such means as increasing market analysis and effort, choosing better-selling titles, establishing exports, co-publishing, training, selling rights, and so forth. The critical variables are: increase revenues while holding down or decreasing costs, and increase market share or establish other means for long-term survival. A review of industrial policies indicates that the focus on financial variables has not been exclusive—nor should it have been. In other words, in the same way that the strategic interests of the country are considered when government assistance is designed for the aerospace or pharmaceutical industry, or, for that matter, roads, so the cultural nature of book publishing has been taken into account in industrial programs.

By far the majority of funding for book publishing at the federal level has flowed to industrial support programs, which are directed at Canadian-owned book publishing firms, and these programs have been run directly out of government departments at both the federal and provincial levels. A commitment to stimulate a heterogeneous industry in terms of size, location, and genre orientation has evolved as an accepted feature of industrial book publishing support programs. To be specific, policy-makers have supported a variety of firms: from the very small to the large, those operating across all provinces or locally, in major cities and outside them, and controlled by a variety of individuals with a range of cultural and financial orientations.

The content of the books published is not considered in industrial support programs. This can best be seen in the objectives and current criteria on which industrial support is based. For instance, with the Book Publishing Industry Development Program (BPIDP), established in 1986 by the Department of Canadian Heritage, the objectives are to increase efficiency and long-term economic viability, to increase the competitiveness and facilitate the expansion of Canadian-owned firms, and to preserve a diversity of genres. The eligibility criteria for funding include:

- a minimum of 15 published Canadian-authored trade books with a minimum of 12 new releases published over the preceding three years; or, 10 Canadian-authored scholarly books with a minimum of six new releases over the preceding three years;
- a minimum level of eligible sales—$200,000, or $130,000 for official-language minority publishers and Aboriginal publishers;
- a sales-to-inventory ratio, for its own titles, equal to or greater than the minimum ratio established for the appropriate commercial category;
- financial viability.

This support is provided in tandem with export marketing assistance and, formerly, a postal subsidy program. Export assistance is provided by paying a portion of publishers' expenditures on export efforts.

The second type of support for book publishing is cultural. Cultural support differs from industrial support in both design and impact. Cultural support has a direct concern with specific types of publishing. As the Canada Council mandate terms it, it is support of 'artistic production in the literary arts and the study of literature and the arts'. For the Council, this includes poetry, fiction, drama, titles for children and young adults, literary criticism and literary biography, creative or literary non-fiction, CD-ROMs or cassettes with particular characteristics, and art books of certain types. Special note should be taken of the inclusion of creative and literary non-fiction. The Council has concluded that the development of a national literature of non-fiction deserves support.

Unlike industrial assistance and structural intervention, cultural support does not favour firms of a certain status, nature, size, or financial performance. Rather, once a firm is eligible and published works are deemed of sufficient professional quality, publishing firms receive support based on the number of books published and their professional quality. In fact, the program penalizes those firms that receive industrial support from BPIDP. The Canada Council reasons that this encourages small firms (which usually develop new authors) and does not overly discourage large firms to participate in bringing forward cultural titles.

Provincial support for book publishing contains both industrial and cultural elements. For example, Manitoba and a number of provinces in the Atlantic region signed regional economic development agreements with the federal government. Under the terms of these agreements, both levels of government contributed funds and services to help book publishers develop their businesses. On the other hand, in British Columbia and Saskatchewan, the main focus of support is cultural and the programs of support are modelled after the Canada Council support programs.

Structural support is the third type of support that Canadian governments have put in place for Canadian publishers. The so-called distribution right for book publishers constitutes a structural support and was incorporated in the 1997 revisions of the Copyright Act. It was designed to prevent Canadians, especially libraries and booksellers, from importing multiple copies of books for which a Canadian firm has distribution rights. **Reprographic rights**, which compensate authors and publishers for photocopying, are another structural support measure that has assisted the industry.

Each of these support measures—structural, cultural, industrial—has its own dynamic. Structural support policies usually become invisible once implemented. They become part of the environment within which publishers, book retailers, or other businesses operate: they are taken for granted just like any other principle of doing business. Industrial support encourages publishers to focus on their identities as businesses, that is, the financial elements of their enterprise—the size of markets, costs of production, distribution efficiencies, and overall performance. Cultural support programs encourage publishers to focus on the reasons for which they are in this unique business. That is, whether in New York, London, Tokyo, or Paris, book publishing companies rarely turn profits anywhere near as large as those of any other industry, cultural or otherwise. For publishers, publishing most often represents an extension of the creation of meaning. Publishers attempt to create resonance (as judged by both the critics and the market)

STRUCTURAL SUPPORT INTRODUCED THROUGH THE BACK DOOR

In the early 1990s the Competition Bureau allowed a man named Larry Stevenson to purchase and amalgamate what were then Canada's two main bookstore chains, Smithbooks and Coles. Upon being given this **effective monopoly** of the chain store segment of the market, Stevenson set out to build a series of big box bookstores called Chapters. From a public perspective his venture was a great success. More books became available in more locations throughout the country. From an industry perspective, Stevenson's operation was something between a limited success and an unmitigated disaster. While providing retail space for publishers, as the retailer of as much as 60 to 70 per cent of a publisher's books Chapters was able to dictate its own terms of payment. Thus, while publishers billed Chapters to pay within 90 days—60 days longer than in normal businesses—Chapters began to extend the payment time to 120 days or longer. To avoid paying altogether, it could ship the books back to the supplying publisher and reorder them the next day, further extending the payment time by another 90 days. Publishers were powerless to act since to do so would have meant losing the majority of their sales. This business behaviour on the part of Chapters put the ability of publishers to publish in jeopardy and in one instance, according to the monitor put in charge of restructuring General Distribution Services, led to the company's demise.

In 2001, Heather Reisman and her husband, owners of Indigo Books and Music, bought Chapters in a hostile takeover. Reisman's husband is the very rich and successful Gerald Schwartz, who owns ONEX, a diversified company with holdings in such industries as electronics manufacturing, theatrical exhibition, sugar refining, and automotive products. In 2002 ONEX had revenues of $23 billion and 98,000 employees worldwide. The two are also well-known supporters of the Liberal Party—for example, they contributed $75,000 to Paul Martin's leadership bid. While many publishers were relieved at the change of ownership, they were also concerned with the even greater concentration of ownership in book retailing. So was the Competition Bureau, which asked Reisman to sell off some of her stores. She agreed, but there were no serious buyers. Thus the Bureau let her keep the stores at the same time as it worked out a performance agreement in which she agreed to pay her bills within a certain period and to behave in a certain way towards her suppliers, the publishers. According to one perceptive analyst, the result was the beginning of a regulatory regime in book retailing, at least one governing the behaviour of Indigo/Chapters. A different way of putting it would be that the government had allowed such concentration of ownership in book retailing that it was forced to create structural support in the name of a set of rules for this national book chain monopoly.

for the meaning created by the author. Publishing is not usually conceived as a means to get rich—which is not to say that large multinational conglomerates, such as HarperCollins, Bertelsmann, Macmillan, and Pearson, are not doing exactly that.

What has been the result of these book publishing support policies? The pessimists point to the continuing low profitability of the industry and a lack of substantial increase in market share for the Canadian-owned sector. But there are definite positive signs, especially if one takes a cultural perspective. The most obvious sign is the rising profile of Canadian writers within and outside Canada. In the 1960s it was difficult to find a recently published novel set in Canada or written by a Canadian. And certainly if one could be found, the chances of it being noticed anywhere

outside Canada were almost non-existent. Canada could boast no writing community, and no authors of world stature who were recognized as Canadian writers in the same way that, say, the Group of Seven Canadian painters were recognized. Today, the field has been transformed. There are about 20 to 30 well-known and respected Canadian writers who are known in and outside Canada—and not just in English-speaking countries. They include Margaret Atwood, Alice Munro, Robertson Davies, Ann-Marie MacDonald, Anne Michaels, Michael Ondaatje, Guy Vanderhaeghe, W.P. Kinsella, Mordecai Richler, Yann Martel, Margaret Sweatman, Jane Urquhart, Douglas Coupland, Margaret Laurence, Rohinton Mistry, Antonine Maillet, and Mavis Gallant. Besides these are famous non-fiction writers such as Farley Mowat,

Michael Ignatieff, and John Ralston Saul, to mention only a few. These authors, all prize winners, many at the international level, are published in other languages and read around the world.

Another way to measure the effects of book-publishing policies is to view the growing success of Canadian book publishers. Exports have climbed to over 30 per cent of domestic sales. Canadian-owned firms are increasing their share of the domestic market. Canadian-owned, English-language firms seem to be publishing fewer titles but achieving greater sales per title. Increasing numbers of movie producers are purchasing the right to make Canadian novels into movies, and the movie version of Michael Ondaatje's *The English Patient* managed to capture nine Academy Awards in 1997. Nevertheless, while the publishing industry is culturally vibrant, it remains financially vulnerable. Without continued contributions from governments, this $4 billion industry (at the retail level) would face financial ruin.

MAGAZINE PUBLISHING

The magazine industry is interesting for a number of reasons. At a first level, magazines are powerful builders of community. Their regular, periodic publication, their specializations, their ability to provide readers with exposure to a variety of writers, and their advertiser-funded ability to provide high-quality editorial content complemented by attractive graphics for a low price all give them a significant power to build a community through loyal subscribers and purchasers. Regular readers often gradually identify with the point of view of the magazine, thereby consolidating their membership in that community.

At a second level, this community of subscribers and purchasers allows magazines to attract advertisers to buy space in their magazines. Having created a community, the magazine sells to its advertisers the passing attention of its readers, which is, hopefully, focused on the advertisement and shaped by the editorial content of the magazine. Thus, advertisers can reach their desired market—whether those interested in reading a weekly selection of Canadian news (*Maclean's*), a monthly collection of Canada's photogenic regions, flora, and fauna (*Canadian Geographic*), a monthly discussion of social issues from a left-leaning political perspective (*Canadian Dimension*), a taste of literary non-fiction (*Geist*), or a monthly look at Canadian business (*Report on Business*).

These two attributes of magazines—their creation of demographically identifiable communities and their selling of those communities to advertisers—combine to provide a third level of interest in magazines that could be termed 'the national interest'. National magazines create a national community—one that is aware of the latest changes to affect them, that engages in debate about the implications of those changes and about what other opportunities and challenges exist that might affect them. National magazines not only build a national community of authors, historians, and news junkies, but also doctors, engineers, youth, and practitioners in various fields, such as welding, small-appliance repairs, house-building, nursing, and so on. Also found on newsstands across Canada are magazines serving computer enthusiasts, cyclists, golfers, water and snow skiers, science

COPYRIGHT REFORM

In the fall of 2002, a few days following the Speech from the Throne, the federal government released a second legislative and policy agenda that, among other things, identified and prioritized new policy issues in copyright. Among the issues was linking liability, where it may be an infringement for a Web site to provide a link to another site that infringes copyright. The agenda also notes the possibility of broadening fair dealing to bring the concept more in line with the US notion of fair use. The controversial tax on blank recording media is acknowledged to be a blunt instrument. In the medium term the government notes that it will examine extending copyright protection from 50 to 70 years to bring Canadian policy in line with the European Union and the US. Over the long term, the government intends to consider a copyright attached to traditional knowledge and database protection (Geist, 2002).

In addition, in January 2003 the Canadian Private Copyright Collective (CPCC) proposed to the Canadian Copyright Board the following taxes on blank media:

Tape cassette	$0.60
Removable memory card	$0.08 per megabyte
MiniDisc, CD-R, CD-RW	$1.20
MP3 built-in memory	$21 per gigabyte
DVD-R, -RW, -RAM	$2.27 per disc

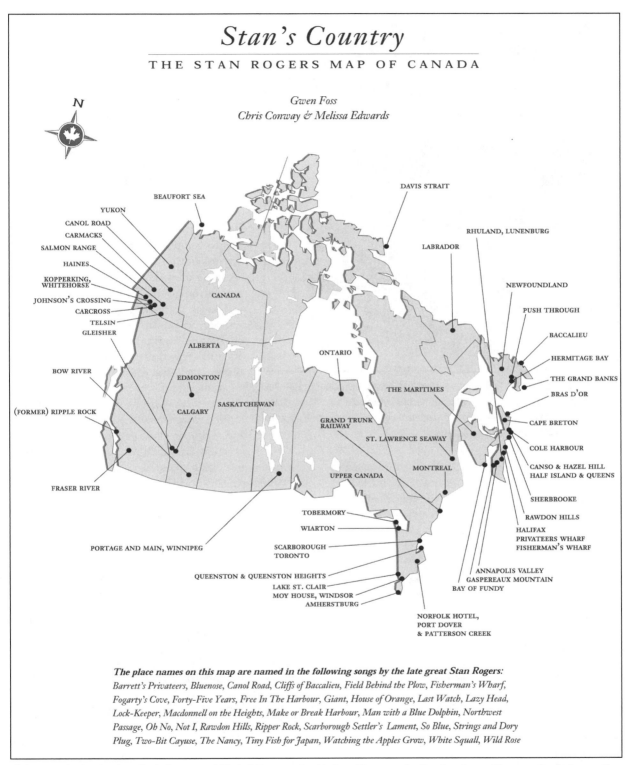

Stan's Country

THE STAN ROGERS MAP OF CANADA

Gwen Foss
Chris Conway & Melissa Edwards

The place names on this map are named in the following songs by the late great Stan Rogers:
Barrett's Privateers, Bluenose, Canol Road, Cliffs of Baccalieu, Field Behind the Plow, Fisherman's Wharf, Fogarty's Cove, Forty-Five Years, Free In The Harbour, Giant, House of Orange, Last Watch, Lazy Head, Lock-Keeper, Macdonnell on the Heights, Make or Break Harbour, Man with a Blue Dolphin, Northwest Passage, Oh No, Not I, Rawdon Hills, Ripper Rock, Scarborough Settler's Lament, So Blue, Strings and Dory Plug, Two-Bit Cayuse, The Nancy, Tiny Fish for Japan, Watching the Apples Grow, White Squall, Wild Rose

Geist magazine has been particularly successful in building a readership for a literary and cultural audience. The magazine features a thematic map in every issue, as well as a variety of other creative and engaging elements. A recent map featured locations in the songs of Stan Rogers, a wonderful Canadian musician and singer who died in a plane crash.

This cartoon, illustrating the debate surrounding Bill C-55, demonstrates how vociferously the US government pursued the market interests of its magazine companies and how much US magazines wanted access to the Canadian advertising market. (Aislin—The Montreal Gazette.)

magazines. Given that Canada's population is 10 per cent that of the US, the inevitable subordination of Canadian interests to US interests is easy to predict. While that is not so bad in magazines about water skiing, in those dedicated to social and political matters few Canadians would be happy seeing only one-tenth of the space available devoted to a discussion of Canadian issues. The inevitable shaping of Canadian opinion by American magazines has led to a national social policy concern surrounding the Canadian magazine industry.

Early magazine publishing policy consisted of copyright and postal subsidies to free up the log-jam of costly distribution for magazines. These subsidies provided a foundation to build the Canadian nation and keep Canadians in touch with one another and with the outside world. On the basis of a great deal of invested energy by authors, editors, and publishers, and assisted by lower postal rates, a Canadian magazine (and newspaper) industry was able to grow. The market never excluded foreign magazines. In fact, both readers and authors looked to foreign magazines as much as Canadian magazines for informative and entertaining material.

While postal subsidies worked well for a long time, by the 1950s and early 1960s advertising rather than circulation and subscriptions had become the driving force in the magazine industry. At that time

fiction enthusiasts, body builders, do-it-yourselfers, snowboarders, and countless other special interests.

The characteristics of the known readers and subscribers, that is, the target market, determine the structure of information created and circulated in

IS THERE AN 'O' IN O'DONNELL? IT SEEMS NOT.

O, the magazine, belongs to TV talk-show host Oprah Winfrey. Its full name is *O: The Oprah Magazine*. It seems that Rosie O'Donnell figured that if Oprah could have her own magazine, so could she, or perhaps it was someone else's idea that O'Donnell could personalize a moribund magazine and attract more readers. Whichever direction the idea came from, Rosie signed a deal with German magazine publisher, Gruner + Jahr in the fall of 2000 in which Rosie was to take over ailing *McCall's*, a women's magazine. The magazine was to be retitled *Rosie*.

By fall of 2002 Gruner + Jahr and O'Donnell were parting ways, sort of. It appears that O'Donnell felt that

the magazine had not become 'Rosie' enough. She wanted the magazine to be controversial and surprising, to cover issues about which she had strong opinions. For example, she wanted a picture of herself on the cover, without makeup, showing a bandaged hand that was recently operated on. The publishers argued that they had purchased a name and a personality, not Rosie's ideals. The magazine ceased publishing in December 2002. As Adam Sternbergh (2002) points out, only in the world of celebrity are the concepts of 'name', 'personality', and 'ideals' separate commodities.

Canada's magazine industry was dominated by foreign magazines to such an extent that no national weekly newsmagazine—only *Maclean's*, a monthly—existed. The nearest approximation was the Canadian edition of *Time*, in which a few pages of Canadian material were added to the front of the magazine.

By 1961 the relative underdevelopment of a domestic publishing industry, including magazines, had been recognized, and the Royal Commission on Publications, chaired by Gratton O'Leary, was set up to examine the situation in detail and bring forward recommendations. The O'Leary Commission identified the main difficulty of establishing a domestic magazine industry to be the unfair advantage of foreign magazines in the marketplace. Foreign magazines, such as *Time*, develop editorial content for their own market, paid for by selling ad space to advertisers in the US. They may then take this content, spruce it up a bit by adding a Canadian section, and sell a Canadian edition to readers in Canada after having collected another set of ads (from Canadian businesses) for the Canadian edition (some pan-North American advertisers always stay on to access both markets). The only added costs, because the initial costs have already been absorbed by the US edition, are the printing, the selling of ads, and the small amount of new editorial content. In contrast, Canadian magazines have to pay the whole cost of producing and editing an original magazine, the full cost of selling the ads, and the full cost of printing a short run.

In 1965, the government of Canada decided to address this unfair advantage of foreign magazines and to provide a stronger advertising base for the Canadian magazine industry (American-produced Canadian editions were 'poaching' advertising dollars away from fully Canadian magazines). It brought forward Bill C-58, which allowed Canadian advertisers to claim advertising as a tax-deductible expense only if that advertising was placed in Canadian periodicals. Two criteria determined what qualified as a Canadian periodical. The first was that ownership had to be at least 75 per cent Canadian. The second was that no more than 20 per cent of the content of a magazine could come from one or more issues of one or more periodicals that were printed, edited, or published outside Canada. This bill passed and became section 19 of the Income Tax Act.

The government enacted further legislation in 1965—Customs Tariff code 9958 (Customs Tariff, 1965, Schedule VII). This tariff forbade the importation of any split-run magazine, that is, any magazine that had been prepared for a foreign (usually the US) market and had had some or all of the advertising stripped out and replaced by advertising targeted at the Canadian market. Further, it forbade the importation of magazines that contained more than 5 per cent of advertising directed solely at the Canadian market. This legislation was silent on advertising, placed by multinational companies, targeted at both Canadians and US citizens. Thus, many multinational companies create ads with both markets in mind. The net result was that multinationals spent far less per capita on magazine advertising in Canada than they spent in the US. A study by Carleton University professors I.A. Litvak and C.J. Maule (1978), which examined the big four North American car makers, placed the per-capita value of magazine advertising in Canada at about one-fifth that spent in the US.

These two policies worked well until 1993, when Time Warner had the clever idea of beaming its editorial content by satellite, not across but above the border, to a printing plant in Canada and selling ads for the resulting magazine, a 'Canadian edition' of *Sports Illustrated*. In so doing, it was getting around the letter, though not the spirit, of the law. Time Warner was still subject to the provisions of section 19 of the Income Tax Act, that is, Canadian advertisers would not be able to declare their advertising expenses as business expenses. However, *Sports Illustrated* was able to address this problem by slashing the advertising rates that a Canadian magazine would normally charge for reaching an audience like that of *Sports Illustrated*. Canada Customs ruled that the resulting magazine was technically not a split-run.

While *Sports Illustrated* went ahead and built up its sales to 125,000 copies, the Task Force on the Magazine Industry, set up in 1993 and chaired by Patrick O'Callahan, was given the mandate 'to review federal measures to support the Canadian magazine industry [and] . . . to propose measures that will enable the government to effectively carry through on its policy objective of ensuring that Canadians have access to Canadian information and ideas through genuinely Canadian magazines' (Canada, 1994: 4). More specifically, the mandate of the Task Force was to recommend ways to bring section 19 of the Income Tax Act and Tariff Code 9958 up to date and thereby to ensure a flow of adequate advertising dollars to Canadian magazines.

A recent ad campaign of the Canadian Magazine Publishers Association included these two full-page ads of typical Canadian scenes, each with an incongruous, out-of-context, and non-Canadian element introduced to make the point that 'it's not the same if it's not Canadian'.

After reviewing the industry, the Task Force recommended ill-advisedly that an 80 per cent excise tax (payable by the printer or distributor) be placed on advertising space sold by foreign magazines to advertisers who were directing their advertising to Canadian audiences. The government looked favourably on this and brought forward Bill C-103, to apply the 80 per cent excise tax on all foreign publications.

In 1996 the US challenged this legislation, magazine postal subsidies, and the provision of Tariff Code 9958 against the importation of split-runs within the World Trade Organization. The WTO, after appeal, ruled in favour of the US. Determined to protect Canadian magazines, the Canadian government responded with alternative measures. In place of postal subsidies, the Department of Canadian Heritage now provides postal grants to qualifying Canadian-owned and -controlled magazines. These grants are deposited directly into the magazines' accounts with Canada Post. Second, in 1998 the government brought forward Bill C-55, which became the Foreign Publishers Advertising Services Act (passed into law in 1999) and would allow only Canadian magazines to provide advertising space to those seeking to reach Canadian consumers. Because advertising is defined by the WTO as a service, not a good, the same provisions do not apply. Moreover, the Act proposed fines of up to $250,000 for publication of split-runs magazines.

The reaction of the US to Bill C-55 was immediate. Knowing that it was unlikely to win if it protested Bill C-55 within WTO, the US lobbied hard and, when that failed, threatened massive retaliation, far beyond the financial restriction that US magazine firms would have to live with, in short, a trade war. In statements to the press the US challenged the legitimacy of Canada's new measures, noting that Canada should not have brought forward legitimate legislation to protect its magazine industry given that its first attempt was judged to be illegitimate by the WTO. (It is common practice for the US to interpret international agreements according to the letter, not the spirit, of the law.) The Minister of Canadian Heritage, Sheila Copps, responded in kind, saying that if the US continued to undermine legitimate cultural concerns and the development of Canadian policy, the world would see the US as a bully, which would threaten the legitimacy of international trading agreements.

Though Bill C-55 cleared the House of Commons in March 1999 and went on to the Senate for consideration, negotiations between Canada and the US continued and commentary flourished. On 26 May 1999, Trade Minister Sergio Marchi and Copps announced that a bargain had been struck, one requiring substantial amendments to Bill C-55 and, indeed, to the Income Tax Act. US magazines were given the right to create and sell split-runs in Canada. These split-runs, in which certain ads are pulled and replaced by Canadian ads, are allowed to have 18 per cent of their ad space devoted to advertising directed solely at Canadians (phased in over three years). Should US magazine owners want to increase their access to Canadian advertisers, then they would be required to get permission from the Department of Canadian Heritage, set up an office in Canada, and increase their Canadian editorial content (supposedly to at least 50 per cent). In contrast with the past, Canadian advertisers will now be able to deduct their advertising costs in split-runs of any magazine as business expenses.

Besides giving away an undetermined percentage of the advertising market to the US (with no discussion of other foreign countries), the deal also almost guts section 19 of the Income Tax Act. This legislation, which required 75 per cent Canadian ownership of Canadian publications, was also changed. Foreign owners are now able to acquire up to 49 per cent of 'Canadian' publications (magazine companies are controlled with much less than 49 per cent ownership).

What did the Canadian magazine industry get in this deal? Ministers Marchi and Copps claimed that it represented a victory for Canada: they had achieved recognition from the US of Canada's 'right in trade to protect our culture'. The fact that this is exactly what the cultural exemption in NAFTA was supposed to do was not mentioned. The ministers also promised a fund to assist the Canadian magazine industry with its anticipated loss of $98 million per year in ad revenue (Canadian Magazine Publishing Industry, various press releases). In December 1999, Copps announced a $50 million assistance fund (*Vancouver Sun*, 17 Dec. 1999, C12). By 2000 the fund had been named the Canada Magazine Fund and it had been reduced to $35 million.

The beginning of this fund was inauspicious—it really represented the government buying off the industry rather than creating justifiable policy (and potentially facing a trade war from the ever aggressive US government). However, some unexpected value

Figure 7.1 An International Instrument on Cultural Diversity: What Would It Do?

An international instrument on cultural diversity would:

- recognize the importance of cultural diversity;
- acknowledge that cultural goods and services are significantly different from other products;
- acknowledge that domestic measures and policies intended to ensure access to a variety of indigenous cultural productions are significantly different from other policies;
- set out rules on the kind of domestic regulatory and other measures that countries can and cannot use to enhance cultural and linguistic diversity; and
- establish how trade disciplines would apply or not apply to cultural measures that meet the agreed upon rules.

Figure 7.1 summarizes the five points of an international instrument on cultural diversity.

appears to be emerging. The Fund, which is being made available to associations as well as individual magazines, is encouraging national projects that otherwise would never get off the ground. For example, a proposal is being put together to make all Canadian social science and humanities journals available online, and some consideration is being given to making the journals freely available on the Internet within Canada. Also, in 2002 the Canadian Magazine Publishers Association mounted an ad campaign to draw attention to the value of Canadian-published magazines. Such national projects may inject new life into Canadian periodicals and increase the interest of Canadians in reading them.

Concern over the gutting of policy by international trading rules extends beyond magazines into all sectors of cultural policy. For nearly two years (early 1997 to early 1999), a select group of cultural and new media industry representatives met at the behest of the Department of Canadian Heritage and the Department of Foreign Affairs and International Trade to discuss and develop an overall strategy document. The group was called the Cultural Industries Sectoral Advisory Group on International Trade (SAGIT). The result was a report entitled *Canadian Culture in a Global World: New Strategies for Culture and Trade* (see www.infoexport.gc.ca/trade-culture). The report brings forward two main recommendations. The first is for the government to continue to use the strategy of exempting culture in international trade negotiations. This is really the fallback position in case the second, new, and more radical recommendation fails. That second recommendation is to negotiate 'a new international instrument that would specifically address cultural diversity, and acknowledge the legitimate role of domestic cultural policies in ensuring cultural diversity'. Such an instrument would distinguish between cultural products and policy and other trade products and policy and attempt to outline and regulate what policy measures countries can take to ensure access to natural cultural products.

Whether the international community will receive this policy initiative favourably has yet to be seen. By early 2003 there were still no clear signs. Certainly, the US will argue that it opens the door to government control as well as to interference by governments in the marketplace. Which opinion will eventually hold sway is yet to be determined.

IS *SEED* THE NEXT WALLPAPER*?

In 1996 Canadian journalist Tyler Brulé, at 28, founded *Wallpaper** magazine. It was almost an immediate success, and in 1997 Brulé sold it to AOL Time Warner. While the magazine is managing to maintain itself, it is not the media darling Brulé had foreseen. However, a replacement may be on the horizon. In 1999, then 18-year-old Montrealer Adam Bly founded the magazine *SEED*, and in 2002 he moved it to New York. The magazine combines pop culture and science and targets young professionals aged 25–40 who are making $60,000-a-year salaries. The magazine takes on big subjects, such as 'What are we going to do about the United States?' and the politics of the environment, and puts forward a personality-laden look at science. *SEED* also has connections with AOL Time Warner, which distributes the magazine in the US market.

NEWSPAPER PUBLISHING

It is not quite accurate to say that the newspaper industry in Canada is unregulated, but it is the closest thing we have to an industry that operates exclusively on market principles. Historically, the vast majority of newspapers in Canada have been organized commercially, even if their owners were political movements, trade unions, churches, or wealthy families. Beginning in the late nineteenth century, newspapers became mass media seeking to maximize readership and revenues, and as the twentieth century progressed, corporate newspaper chains were forged from previously independent family-owned newspapers. In 1967, for example, Paul Desmarais's Power Corp. bought *La Presse* from the Berthiaume family and the Montreal daily became the flagship of a newspaper group that included *Le Nouvelliste* (Trois-Rivières), *La Voix de l'Est* (Granby), and *La Tribune* (Sherbrooke). Similarly, the Southam chain expanded to eight dailies when it bought the *Montreal Gazette* in 1968 from the White family, which had owned the

Gazette for 98 years. Increased concentration and decreased competition in the newspaper industry prompted two federal government inquiries: the 1969–70 Senate Special Committee on Mass Media (the Davey Committee) and the 1980–1 Royal Commission on Newspapers (the Kent Commission). These inquiries will be discussed in further detail in Chapters 8 and 9.

Today, the newspaper industry is dominated by media conglomerates. For the most part, newspapers have become merely one sphere in a broad domain of commercial interests extending far beyond journalism as corporate owners perceive their media properties as avenues for profit and the promotion of their other goods and services. The increasingly concentrated and corporate ownership of the press in Canada, especially since the late 1990s, has prompted governments to reconsider policy measures to ensure the editorial independence of the press and a healthy range of news, information, and opinion. The ownership of Canada's community weekly newspapers, too, has

The arrival of the *National Post* on the market in the autumn of 1998 increased readers' choice for a national daily newspaper and brought greater competition among Canada's newspaper chains. (Source: *Globe and Mail*, 30 Oct. 1998. Reprinted by permission of the Globe and Mail.)

become increasingly concentrated. According to statistics compiled by the Canadian Community Newspaper Association in November 2001 (CCNA, 2002), four companies—Quebecor/Bowes (127 titles), Black Press (64), Transcontinental (62), and Metroland (60)—owned almost 30 per cent of the community weekly newspapers in the country (313 out of 1,061).

The Department of Canadian Heritage initiated a review of the concentration of ownership in the media and its relevant policies in November 1999, and continues to investigate (see www.pch.gc.ca/progs/ac-ca/progs/esm-ms/esm-ms_e.cfm). The Quebec government conducted hearings on press concentration in February and March of 2001 and produced a report in November of that year, *Mandat d'Initiative portant sur la Concentration de la Presse* (Quebec, 2001). In the fall of 2002 the Quebec government's Ministry of Communications and Culture established an advisory committee to recommend legislative measures that could be introduced as early as the spring of 2003. At the same time, the Canadian Association of Journalists established a committee to study corporate concentration and submit a policy paper at its summer 2003 convention.

During the 1990s, three companies—Hollinger, CanWest Global Communications, and Quebecor—moved to the forefront of the daily newspaper industry. Hollinger, an international company that counts among its properties the *London Daily Telegraph*, the *Jerusalem Post*, and the *Chicago Sun-Times*, launched an aggressive buying spree in 1992, quickly acquiring majority ownership of Southam Inc., which was at the time Canada's largest daily newspaper chain. By 1999 Hollinger owned 97 per cent of Southam and controlled 59 of Canada's 105 daily newspapers, including a new national newspaper, the *National Post*, which it launched in October 1998. This rapid expansion, however, overextended Hollinger, and by April 2000, Conrad Black, the company's bombastic chairman, announced his decision to sell off the bulk of Hollinger's community weekly newspapers and a number of its smaller dailies in order to reduce the company's debt. Hollinger's major dailies were initially excluded, but in July 2000 CanWest Global struck a $3.5 billion deal to acquire 13 metropolitan dailies and Hollinger's Internet properties, magazines, and community publishing operations, as well as 50 per cent of the flagship *National Post*. A year later, CanWest purchased the remaining half of the *Post*.

CanWest, founded in the early 1970s by I.H. (Izzy) Asper as an independent television company, has become the principal media conglomerate in the country with Canada's largest chain of daily newspapers (Southam), a national television network (Global Television), and an Internet portal (http://www.cana-da.com) that brings together on the World Wide Web the content of its television and newspaper divisions. CanWest, which also operates radio and television stations in Australia, New Zealand, Great Britain, and Ireland, has subsidiaries involved in film production and distribution, new media, and digital television (see www.canwestglobal.com).

Quebecor, similarly, has risen from modest beginnings to become a central player in the Canadian media landscape. Company founder Pierre Péladeau started his empire by buying the Montreal community newspaper *Le Journal de Rosemont* in 1950—with, as legend has it, money borrowed from his mother—and rapidly expanded his holdings in daily newspapers, television, and printing. When the company outbid Torstar in 1998 to take control of the Sun Media Group, Quebecor became the second-largest newspaper company in Canada with 25.4 per cent of the readership market and a major Internet portal (www.canoe.ca). In September 2000, Quebecor outbid Rogers Communications for Groupe Vidéotron, a $4.9 billion transaction that included Quebec's largest cable television distribution company and the French-language TVA television network (see www.quebecor.com).

Finally, another giant entered the newspaper market in 2000. Telecommunications conglomerate BCE Inc. (Bell Canada Enterprises) bought the country's second-largest and most prestigious daily newspaper, the *Globe and Mail*, from the Thomson Corporation. Having also acquired the CTV national television network, BCE formed a new subsidiary, Bell GlobeMedia (see www.bce.ca). The economic implications of this consolidation will be discussed in Chapter 8 and what it means for journalism specifically will be addressed in Chapter 9.

Beyond the scale of these new companies, though, what has really grabbed the attention of policy-makers is the extent to which a new generation of newspaper owners has taken to meddling with the editorial content of its newspapers. If, in the past, the owners of the Southam and Thomson chains left their editors alone to run their own newspapers—provided they were making money—Conrad Black and the

Asper family have been far more interventionist, even politically engaged. Black, for example, took great interest in the editorial content of his newspapers, to the point of writing his own letters to the editor and the occasional book review. He chose the editors of his newspapers as much for their political views as their journalistic competence, and he was constantly on the phone to them, questioning decisions, criticizing, and advising.

Black was also a newsmaker in his own right. An imposing figure with strong opinions to match his considerable intelligence, he used the platform newspaper ownership afforded to assert his right-wing views, criticizing labour unions, 'lazy' journalists, Canadian and Quebec nationalists, and especially the governing Liberal Party under Jean Chrétien (see Barlow and Winter, 1997). Black took a hard line against striking *Calgary Herald* workers during an eight-month dispute in 1999–2000, insulting their union representative and denigrating their motives

ONE PUBLISHER-EDITOR RELATIONSHIP

Journalists and newspaper readers have long laboured under the mistaken assumption that, on the whole, owners of newspapers do not interfere with the editorial stance taken in their newspapers. The actions of the Aspers, owners of CanWest Global Communications Corp., in creating national editorials flew in the face of this myth. It outraged editors working for them and journalists across the nation (and elsewhere), and moved a group of 40 former executives of Southam Inc. (the foundation of the Aspers' newspaper holdings) to take out full-page ads questioning whether the Aspers were threatening freedom of the press. Subscriptions plummeted. It also caused investors to question the wisdom of holding CanWest Global stock and their stock price fell precipitously.

David Estok has noted the Aspers' apparent backing away from the frequency of these national editorials and also noted:

> That the Aspers wanted to use their newspapers to express their opinions about current events on the editorial pages is normal and perfectly natural. That the Aspers used such a blunt instrument, bullying tactics and firing people to get their way is less so.

In other words, it is not the principle of editorial freedom that needs protection, just the finesse with which it is carried out. This is tantamount to accepting what many have argued is unacceptable: direct influence of editorial stance by an owner.

A view of a more genteel wielding of influence has been brought forward by Max Hastings in *Editor: An Inside Story of Newspapers*. Hastings is a former editor of the *Daily Telegraph*, a UK newspaper owned by Conrad Black, the man who sold the Aspers their newspapers. Hastings recounts how Black would phone him at any hour and quiz him on the *Telegraph*'s coverage of certain people, especially the rich and/or powerful, and sometimes thugs and scoundrels. He also tells of the difficulties he experienced in shaping coverage of members of the Board of Directors of the *Telegraph*. Perhaps most telling is his account of Black's real concern over the publication of a piece in another of Black's holdings, the *Spectator*, describing Hollywood as 'Jewish town'. Various Hollywood luminaries demanded space in both the *Spectator* and the *Telegraph* to denounce the author. In response to Hastings's opinion that they should be allowed space to reply, Black was reported to have said, 'You don't understand, Max. My entire interests in the United States and internationally could be seriously damaged by this.'

This one sentence captures both Black's sense of legitimacy of his role in determining editorial policy and his acceptance that his financial interests could or should be determinants of the content of his newspaper holdings. Even if Hastings is willing to soften his vision of Black—Black once wrote a note to Hastings addressed to 'Sir Max Hastings OM, CH, KBE, DSO and Cluster MA (Oxon)' from 'His Most Eminent Beatitude the Grand Mufti of the Telegraph'—the portrait of owner influence is clear. Ultimately, freedom of the press belongs to those who own one.

A final note. Newspaper proprietors are not the only ones who seek to manage content, especially when it involves them, their interests, or their close friends. Indeed, some Canadian academics suffer from the same 'Black syndrome'. For example, on two separate occasions reviews of one individual's work were to be published in the *Canadian Journal of Communication*, and both times this professor pressured for a change in content because the review was not as positive as the author would have liked. In both instances, the affair was 'managed'.

(see Ferguson, 2000; Canadian Press, 2000). When Black was offered a British peerage, after having become a British citizen for this purpose, Prime Minister Jean Chrétien cited precedent dating to 1919 that meant a Canadian could not accept a British lordship. Black then sued Chrétien and lost, renounced his Canadian citizenship, and moved to England, where he became Lord Black of Crossharbour (Arab, 2002).

Editorial interference has taken a more radical turn under Black's successors—CanWest founder and executive chairman Izzy Asper and his son, company president and chief executive officer Leonard Asper. If Black at least tolerated diversity of opinion, even criticism, in his newspapers, the Aspers have been far less respectful of contrary views, especially on their pet topics of the Chrétien Liberals and Israel. In August 2001, CanWest terminated Southam News national affairs columnist Lawrence Martin, claiming it was an effort to avoid redundancy and reduce costs and not for anything he had written. But *Maclean's* said Martin was fired for his persistent criticism of Chrétien over 'Shawinigate', an issue involving the receipt of federal funds by a resort hotel in Chrétien's Shawinigan riding (see Lindgren, 2001). Later the same month, *Montreal Gazette* publisher Michael Goldbloom announced his resignation. Though he was vague about the reasons, Goldbloom told his staff that 'CanWest has a more centralized approach to its management, and there are some aspects of the operations where we have had different perspectives' (Sweet, 2001).

The Aspers breathed new life into government inquiries into corporation concentration in December 2001 when they decided to run 'national editorials' up to three times per week in 14 of their major daily newspapers. The editorials were to be commissioned by CanWest's head office in Winnipeg. Member newspapers were not only ordered to run them, but the editorial boards of the Southam newspapers were also prohibited from publishing any subsequent editorials dissenting from the views expressed in the national editorials.

CanWest's national editorial policy was a radical departure from Southam's long-standing commitment to the editorial independence of each of its member newspapers and an attempt by head office to assume control of the editorial voice of its newspapers. The policy was met with condemnation from journalists, academics, politicians, and newspaper readers. Journalists at the *Montreal Gazette* signed and published a petition criticizing the national editorials, staged a by-line strike, and established an independent Web site to draw attention to the issue (see Gasher, 2002b). A group of 40 former Southam executives, including the company's former chief executive officer, took out a full-page newspaper advertisement in June 2002 to protest the policy (Damsell, 2002). The Féderation professionelle des journalistes du Québec called for a federal parliamentary inquiry.

With the spotlight on CanWest, the company made its own situation worse by refusing to cover the controversy it aroused—forcing people to inform themselves about what was happening at Southam by reading competing newspapers—and by providing critics with considerable evidence of its intolerance for editorial dissent. For example, four of its columnists—Stephen Kimber at the *Halifax Daily News*, Doug Cuthand at the *Regina Leader-Post,* Michael Johansen at the *St. John's Telegram*, and Lyle Stewart at the *Montreal Gazette*—subsequently quit the chain, citing continual editorial interference from CanWest managers. The issue came to a head in June 2002 when CanWest fired *Ottawa Citizen* publisher Russell Mills (Zimonjic, 2002). Mills maintained he was fired because of a four-page *Citizen* article that was critical of the Prime Minister and an editorial that called for Chrétien's resignation. CanWest's national editorials quietly disappeared after the Mills firing. No public explanation was offered for what appeared to be a change in policy in the face of significant public pressure. The national editorials quietly resurfaced in the fall of 2002. (Consult the Web site www.montreal-newspaperguild.com for an extensive collection of material written about the CanWest national editorial policy.)

While the constitutional guarantee of freedom of the press appears to leave governments little legislative latitude, the Quebec government, for one, has shown a determination to act. Quebec is particularly sensitive to the issue because two companies—Quebecor and Power Corp.—own all but one of the French-language dailies in the province (the exception is the limited-circulation *Le Devoir*) accounting for 97 per cent of circulation. Unfortunately, Quebec's November 2001 report on press concentration (Quebec, 2001) was a timid effort, calling primarily for newspaper companies to publish a statement of principles and steps they are taking to ensure editorial diversity.

Besides legal interpretations of freedom of the

press, which bind governments in their regulation of the press, there is also an ideological inhibition at play. As Enn Raudsepp, director of the Department of Journalism at Concordia University, points out, for most of the 500 years of press history, the state has been seen as the institution that the press has required freedom from and protection against. Today, however, when media conglomerates are larger and more powerful than many national governments, it is time to consider state regulation of the business practices—rather than the editorial practices—of newspaper owners in a monopolistic industry. Raudsepp (2002: 28) argues that Canadians have two choices: 'We can continue to allow the inevitable drift to a business big brother—or we can try to develop a national consensus about the quality of the news and information we expect from our media and then take steps to ensure that we get it.'

New Media

The term 'new media' is somewhat amorphous because it includes all those interactive media spawned by digitization, from CD-ROMs and DVDs to the Internet itself, and all the uses to which these technologies have been applied, from statistical databanks to entertainment, news, and information.

New media have also spawned new calls for state regulation, particularly in the domains of hate speech and pornography, which are so prevalent on the Internet. But in its *Report on New Media* of May 1999 (see www.crtc.gc.ca/ENG/NEWS/SPEECH-ES/1999/S990517.htm), the CRTC declared that it would not regulate. Operating from the simple definition of new media as 'services delivered over the Internet', the Commission conducted 10 months of hearings in 1998–9 to determine the answers to three questions:

1. Do any of the new media constitute services already defined by the Broadcasting Act or the Telecommunications Act, and if so, how should they be regulated?
2. How do the new media affect the regulation of the traditional broadcasting undertakings of radio, television, and cable?
3. Do the new media raise any other broad policy issues of national interest?

The CRTC determined that, for the most part, the Internet is not subject to either the Broadcasting Act or the Telecommunications Act. For those materials that do fall under the legal definition of 'broadcasting'—e.g., digital audio services and audiovisual signals—'the Commission has concluded that regulation is not necessary to achieve the objectives of the Broadcasting Act.' There is, for instance, a wealth of Canadian content on the Internet—an estimated 5 per cent of the world's Web sites are Canadian—and the CRTC ruled that new media have had no detrimental impact on either radio and television audiences or advertising. The Commission further determined that Web sites specializing in 'offensive and illegal content', such as pornography and hate messages, are already covered by Criminal Code provisions.

If the CRTC report kept a door open to future

THE DIGITAL DIVIDE

Canada is one of the most 'wired' countries in the world. And while it may sometimes seem that everyone we know is connected to the Internet, this is clearly not the case. Even in a relatively affluent country like Canada, Internet access is far from universal, and tends to be more common among men, English speakers, urban dwellers, those with money, and those with education. When we look at the global Internet map, the so-called digital divide is even greater.

Based on a survey conducted throughout 2000, Statistics Canada estimates that 13 million Canadians are Internet users, or 53 per cent of Canadians aged 15 and over (see table). While this figure represents little more than half of Canadian adults, it is important to note that Internet use has grown tremendously in recent years. In 1994, for instance, a similar survey indicated that only 18 per cent of Canadians aged 15 and over were Internet users (Statistics Canada, 2001).

British Columbia (61.2 per cent) and Alberta (60.3) boast the highest percentage of Internet users among Canadian provinces, while the lowest users are people in Newfoundland (43.5 per cent), New Brunswick (44.5), and Quebec (45.6). About 44 per cent of francophones in Canada use the Internet, compared with 58 per cent of anglophones. The most popular uses of the Internet are exchanging electronic mail (84 per cent), searching for information on goods and services (75 per cent), and accessing on-line news sites (55 per cent) (Dryburgh, 2001).

While the gender gap has closed somewhat, Canadian men are more likely to use the Internet than women, and this holds for every age category. Internet use tends to decrease with age, as 90 per cent of those aged 15–19 are wired, while only 13 per cent of those aged 65–9 have Internet access. Internet use is also far more common among Canadians who hold a university degree (79 per cent) than among those who never finished high school (13 per cent).

Internet use worldwide tends to be concentrated in a few industrialized countries. Leah A. Lievrouw (2000) writes: 'Though network infrastructures have extended around the world, so far virtually all new media services and content have originated in (and have served) North America and Western Europe, mainly the United States.' Of the estimated 391 million Internet users in the world, more than 43 per cent are located in the United States alone. According to the international marketing and communications company Global Reach (2001), only 10 countries in the world can boast at least 10 million Internet users: the US (169.1 million), Japan (38.5), Germany (22.5), China (22.5), Great Britain (21), South Korea (19.4), Italy (13.5), Canada, France (10.9), and Taiwan (10). In China's case, this represents less than 2 per cent of its population.

The least-wired continent in the world is Africa. As of November 2000, all 54 African countries had achieved permanent Internet access, but service in most African countries is confined to the capital cities. The estimated total number of Internet users on the continent is just three million. The most wired country in all of Africa is South Africa, with an estimated 1.8 million users, almost two-thirds of the African total. The highest number of users, according to a 2000 survey, consisted of people belonging to non-governmental organizations, private companies, and universities (Jensen, 2000). Countries such as Burundi, Liberia, and Somalia each have fewer than 200 Internet subscribers (African Internet Connectivity, 2000).

Language is one factor influencing connectivity, given that English-language content predominates on the World Wide Web. As of March 2001, 47.5 per cent of the world's Internet users were English speakers. Chinese speakers were the next highest group (9 per cent), followed by Japanese (8.6 per cent). Only 3.7 per cent of Internet users speak French as a first language (Global Reach, 2001).

Table 7.3 Percentage of Internet Users (aged 15 and over), Selected Social-Demographic Characteristics

Category	Total (%)	Male (%)	Female (%)
Canada	52.8	56.1	49.6
Age group			
— 15 to 24	84.5	85.6	83.4
— 25 to 34	66.1	68.2	63.9
— 35 to 44	60.3	62.2	58.4
— 45 to 54	50.7	52.5	48.8
— 55 and over	18.7	23.4	14.8
Education			
— University degree	79.3	83.1	75.1
— College diploma/certificate	57.5	59.8	55.4
— Some university or college	69.4	71.2	67.7
— High school diploma	41.2	44.7	38.1
— Less than high school[*]	30.9	34.3	27.4
Household income			
— Less than $30,000	32.8	33.4	32.4
— $30,000 to $49,999	49.9	50.0	49.8
— $50,000 to $79,999	65.5	65.1	66.1
— $80,000 or more	80.5	80.6	80.4
Language			
— English only	58.5	61.8	55.3
— French only	43.9	47.4	40.4
— Other language	40.0	43.6	36.1
Urban/Rural			
— Urban	55.0	59.3	50.7
— Rural	44.9	44.4	45.5

*Includes those still attending high school.
Source: Statistics Canada, 2001. Catalogue no. 56–505–XIE.

intervention, it was in the domain of public access to the Internet. While the issue of Internet access is complex—it includes questions of literacy, computer skill, and hardware affordability, which are beyond the CRTC's purview—the Commission noted that it is already studying telecommunications issues relating to access and affordability in remote, high-cost service areas such as the North. 'The Commission intends to address issues relating to whether access to the Internet should be considered as "basic" service for subsidy purposes in its decision in that proceeding.'

Summary

The cultural industries include film and video production, sound recording (sometimes referred to as music recording), book and magazine publishing, and sometimes newspaper publishing. Arguably, cultural industries also include new media, by which we mean Web site and CD-ROM production.

The beginnings of cultural industries policies can be traced back to the early 1950s and the report of the Massey Commission, but policy development began in earnest in the 1970s. At least four rationales can be identified for cultural policies: democratic participation, cultural development, public service, and market failure. In parallel with the multiplicity of reasons governments use to support cultural industries, the support policies and programs for each industry are many and varied. In film and video, investment in production and incentives for broadcasting Canadian productions are significant. In sound recording, Canadian-content regulations have been an effective policy instrument. For book publishing, structural, industrial, and cultural support measures have created a vibrant sector. In magazine publishing, ownership control through the Income Tax Act and provisions to exclude split-runs have been effective until recently. With the passage of Bill C-55, split-runs are possible but foreign publishers are limited in the amount of space they can sell to Canadian advertisers. In time, the net effect of this policy will become clearer.

Ownership and control of the distribution system is a key concern for cultural industries. In film, the tendency of movie theatres to show US movies is well documented. In bookstores, on magazine racks, and in record stores, US products dominate. Only in regard to newspapers is there clear Canadian dominance and that dominance exists only as a result of section 19 of the Income Tax Act, a section that was weakened in the aftermath of Bill C-55 in 1999. Financing has also been a problem for the cultural industries. Consequently, in nearly every field, government-sponsored subsidy programs have been required.

Canada's cultural industries are gaining acceptance within and outside Canada. A great amount of debate has been generated on whether they should continue to be assisted by government funds, and on what basis. Market economists generally believe that the matter should be left up to the marketplace. They argue that if Canadian producers can gain audiences, then they will survive. If they do not gain audiences, then such is the will of the people, and in a democracy that should be the deciding factor. On the other side, cultural and communications theorists argue that truly democratic nations should offer their citizens a full opportunity to participate in the creation and appreciation of their culture. By doing so a nation ensures its long-term survival.

Canada's participation in international trading agreements has made building the cultural industries more, rather than less, problematic. The US—and to some extent other nations, such as the UK, but notably less so other European countries—has demanded greater access beyond its already dominant position in Canada's cultural markets (which the Americans term 'entertainment markets'). As a result, the future of Canada's cultural industries and broadcasting (with spectrum scarcity becoming less relevant) is potentially threatened. In 1999 the federal government brought forward a strategy paper published in the name of an advisory group of members of the cultural industries. This paper calls for the development of a new policy instrument designed to protect domestic cultural industries from the full rigours of international trading rules. It remains to be seen whether this approach to trade in cultural products will receive international acceptance.

RELATED WEB SITES

Canada Council: www.canadacouncil.ca

The Canada Council provides information on grants made to artists and the cultural industries.

Canadian Independent Record Production Association (CIRPA): www.cirpa.ca

CIRPA is the trade organization representing the independent sector of the Canadian music and sound recording industry. For over 25 years it has been the collective voice of independent music in English-speaking Canada.

Canadian Musical Reproduction Rights Agency Ltd (CMRRA): www.cmrra.ca

The CMRAA is a non-profit music licensing agency that represents the vast majority of music copyright owners (usually called music publishers) doing business in Canada.

Department of Canadian Heritage: www.canadianheritage.gc.ca/index_e.cfm

To access information about Canadian cultural industries go to the federal government's Canadian Heritage site and follow the links to Arts and Culture and then to the cultural industry of your choice.

Foundation to Assist Canadian Talent on Record (FACTOR): www.factor.ca

FACTOR is an industry-sponsored strategy to assist the development of an independent Canadian recording industry through funding to allow Canadian songwriters and recording artists to have their work produced.

National Film Board of Canada (NFB): www.nfb.ca

As the site says: 'Created in 1939, the National Film Board of Canada (NFB) is a public agency that produces and distributes films and other audiovisual works which reflect Canada to Canadians and the rest of the world. It is an exceptional fountain of creativity, which since its very beginnings has played a crucial role in Canadian and international filmmaking. Its founder and the first Government Film Commissioner, John Grierson, wanted to make the NFB the "eyes of Canada" and to ensure that it would "through a national use of cinema, see Canada and see it whole: its people and its purpose."'

Telefilm Canada: www.telefilm.gc.ca

Telefilm Canada is a cultural investor in film, television, new media, and music. Its annual budget is $230 million.

FURTHER READINGS

Audley, Paul. 1983. *Canada's Cultural Industries: Broadcasting, Publishing, Records and Film*. Toronto: James Lorimer. Audley's book was the first to examine the cultural industries in Canada and provides an important historical perspective on the issues at that time, with particular emphasis on the production and distribution of Canadian cultural materials.

Dorland, Michael, ed. 1996. *Cultural Industries in Canada: Problems, Policies and Prospects*. Toronto: James Lorimer. Modelled on Audley's book, this edited collection reviews Canada's cultural industries with a focus on public policy and political economy.

STUDY QUESTIONS

1. Explain the four rationales for supporting cultural industries. How do they differ from one another? How might each lead to different policies?
2. Identify the main support policies for each of the cultural industries.
3. What effect has Canadian cultural industries policy had in your life?
4. What is the net impact on Canadian culture and Canada's cultural industries of international trade agreements designed to promote free trade?
5. Market economists and cultural theorists both claim that democracy is a foundation for their position on government support for cultural industries. How can this be? Outline the nature of democracy as both see it and identify which you think is the more robust use of the term.
6. You are responsible for developing a new strategy document for Canada's cultural industries, including the new media. Write a position paper.
7. How does the CRTC's decision *not* to regulate new media conform to its regulatory policies in other media, such as telecommunications and broadcasting?
8. To what extent does the 'digital divide' shape the growth of the Internet?

LEARNING OUTCOMES

- To introduce the cultural industries—film and video, music recording, and book, magazine, and newspaper publishing—and their characteristics.
- To describe the various rationales that governments use for investing in cultural industries—democratic participation including community animation, cultural development, public service, and market failure.
- To indicate that investments by government in cultural industries attempt to balance economic, political, and cultural factors.
- To review the support the federal and provincial governments provide for film and video—Ottawa's early support for documentaries through the National Film Board; Ottawa's more recent support for Canadian feature films created by Canadians; the support of the provinces for bringing US productions to Canada; and likely future directions.
- To explain how it is not quality of content that prevents Canadian movies from being seen but rather industry structures, particularly vertical integration.
- To review the nature of Canada's music recording industry.
- To describe the role of radio in Canada's music recording industry.
- To review the characteristics of Canada's book publishing industry and the nature of the support that the federal government has provided for that industry over the years.
- To introduce the concepts of copyright, intellectual property, and reprographic rights.
- To review the characteristics of Canada's magazine publishing industry, the key policies that have supported it over the years, the diminution of those regulatory policies as a result of technological development, and the resulting actions of the federal government to support the industry.
- To describe, briefly, the characteristics of Canada's newspaper publishing industry.
- To introduce new media to the policy framework, particularly with respect to the issue of public access.

CHAPTER 8

The Structure and Role of Ownership

Introduction

Though we use the term 'mass media' quite often, we can easily forget how diverse a sector this is. We could be talking about a small, family-owned community newspaper or a national television network. There is no natural or inevitable way to organize the mass media; their structures evolve through time, and different societies organize their media in particular ways. The United Kingdom, France, the United States, and Canada—all Western, liberal democracies—structure their mass media in distinct ways in response to particular social needs, desires, and pressures. Even within the same country, we see different rules applied to different media, as discussed in Chapters 6 and 7. This chapter suggests that mass media institutions are not simply products of technology, but are organized according to: the characteristics of the given medium, the resources it draws upon, and the socio-political context in which it operates.

Nevertheless, all media organizations have something in common. No matter how they are organized, they participate in the economy, that sphere of society in which, in the words of media economist Robert G. Picard (1989: 8–9), 'limited or scarce resources are allocated to satisfy competing and unlimited needs or wants.' Picard goes on to identify four groups that the media serve:

> 1) media owners, the individuals or stockholders who own media outlets; 2) audiences, those who view, listen to, or read media content; 3) advertisers, those who purchase time or space to convey messages to audiences; and 4) media employees, those who work for the firms. (Ibid., 9)

We could add to this list a fifth group: governments. Through their cultural policy apparatus, governments adopt guidelines and laws that compel media organizations to serve the needs and wants of national or regional constituencies. In the Canadian case, this has meant ensuring Canadians have access to both the cultural and economic opportunities that participation in the media affords.

It is amid these currents and countercurrents that we consider the various forms of media ownership in this chapter, and especially public ownership and private-sector commercial ownership: their goals, methods of operation, and strengths and shortcomings within the context of the interests of the society as a whole.

Allocating Resources

When we think of resources, we usually think of water, minerals, fish, or trees—things used to produce goods and services subsequently offered to consumers for a price. How such resources are managed and how they are organized economically bear closer scrutiny because similar principles apply to the resources that the mass media harness.

Water, for instance, is a resource essential to life—not only for human consumption, but also for the maintenance of plant and animal life—and is therefore considered an especially precious resource. Careless or excessive use can lead to life-threatening shortages of clean water. For this reason, governments have generally assumed control of its exploitation—how and for what purpose clean water is used. Management of this resource can take any number of forms, such as municipal governments assuming responsibility for drinking water, provincial governments taking charge of hydroelectric power, provincial governments regulating the industrial use of water by private companies. Water's inherent value also explains why governments in water-rich countries like Canada have been nervous about opening up the export of water to commercial enterprise, even though there's a market for it, and even though the United Nations estimates that one-quarter of the world's population has no access to clean drinking water (Reuters, 1998).

Resource industries like mining, fishing, and forestry tend to be in the hands of private enterprise, but the natural resources these industries draw upon are considered to be commonly owned—i.e., public property as opposed to private property. As such, these industries are regulated by governments to ensure that resource supplies are not exhausted and that the environmental impact of their extraction is minimized. Governments grant such resource companies the right to use a specified quantity of a resource, in a specified fashion, for a limited period of time.

The private ownership of resources is usually allowed when a resource is not particularly scarce. Thus private ownership by one person will not prevent private ownership by others, as is the case with land in Canada. Even agricultural land, as important as it is for the food supply, is privately owned, and agricultural producers decide what to grow based on their own best estimates of what the market will demand at harvest time.

The media use resources, too. Sometimes these resources are commonly owned, and sometimes they are privately held. For example, radio stations rely on the radio spectrum—that portion of the electromagnetic spectrum used to carry radio signals—to transmit their programs to audiences. As we discussed in Chapter 6, the radio spectrum is a finite resource and therefore requires some form of management—radio licensing—to avoid signal interference between stations. While an individual radio station may be a private enterprise operating on a commercial basis, it requires a licence to use the airwaves, which remain public property.

Television broadcasting has, historically, largely followed radio's model. Television broadcasters, whether public or private, require a licence—again, the air-waves are public property. When television signals were received exclusively via over-the-air transmission, there was a need to manage the broadcast spectrum to avoid signal interference. There was also a political-cultural imperative from the start. The regulation of the broadcast spectrum permits the federal government to ensure that Canadians have access to Canadian programming and enjoy a broader selection of programming than a free-market regime could be expected to provide. Now that most Canadians receive their television signals through cable transmission or satellite, signal delivery is less a policy issue than is the maintenance of a diverse offering of programming.

Newspapers, on the other hand, are organized on a completely different basis, in large part because the resources they employ are privately held: they buy newsprint from pulp and paper companies, print their newspapers on privately owned printing presses, and deliver them with their own trucks. Within Western democratic societies like Canada, newspapers operate entirely within a commercial marketplace and require no permission from any government to publish.

Like the newspaper industry, magazine and book publishing is organized as commercial enterprise, employing private resources. The difference is that magazine and book publishers tend to function in larger regional, national, and international markets and thus face much more foreign competition. Government subsidies—federal and provincial—have been put in place to maintain a diverse offering of Canadian magazines and books.

MARKETING

Whether or not media organizations are organized as commercial enterprises, great efforts are expended in identifying audiences, maximizing their numbers, determining their content requirements, and, in the case of media that carry advertising, matching audiences to appropriate advertisers. There is no point in offering an information service no one seems to want, just as there is no point in advertising luxury automobiles to people with limited incomes. While audience tastes remain hard to predict, media organizations leave as little to chance as possible, employing focus groups, customer surveys, and opinion polls to target their products more precisely.

The *Montreal Gazette*, for example, publishes each year a glossy, full-colour marketing brochure to distribute to potential advertisers. The brochure (*Montreal Gazette*, 1997) offers a detailed 'readership profile', which tells advertisers who reads the newspaper according to such categories as income and educational levels, occupation category, age, sex and marital status, and whether *Gazette* readers own their own home or rent. Advertisers are told, for instance, that '*Gazette* readers tend to be well-educated, high-income earners.' The brochure also positions the *Gazette* with respect to its media competitors: other newspapers and other news media in the Montreal market. Again, advertisers are told: 'Radio listeners and television viewers tend to dismiss ads as "background noise", whereas newspaper advertising is actively sought out by readers.'

PUBLIC OWNERSHIP

Public ownership is a slippery term. It can be used to mean either ownership by a government on behalf of its citizens—'the public'—or ownership by a group of self-interested shareholders. The term 'public ownership' is used in business to denote companies that make a public offering of shares in search of investment capital. It is in this sense that they are publicly owned and must make available to the public financial information about their business operations, through press releases and audited annual reports.

Of course, these two forms of ownership are fundamentally different. The government-owned institution is devoted primarily to public service, while the shareholder-owned entity is devoted primarily to generating returns for its shareholders, who are free to trade their shares at any time. The government-owned institution is answerable to all citizens, whether or not they use the service provided. The shareholder-owned company is responsible primarily to its shareholders and secondarily to the customers it serves. References to public ownership in this chapter pertain to government-owned or controlled media, and we use private ownership to refer to commercial institutions, whether they are owned by a group of shareholders or by individuals.

Much of the excitement about the Internet derives from its infinite and varied capacity for content; there is room in cyberspace for every kind of content, whether or not it has mass or narrow appeal. No one owns cyberspace, and while universal public access is a growing concern, particularly in the developing world, the costs of participation are relatively low in the affluent world. In Canada, for instance, it is far cheaper to launch an on-line publication than a printed version. In this case, the material resources employed are privately owned computers and telephone or cable lines.

Individual Freedom, Public Interest, and the Free Market

Western democracy is founded on the freedom of the individual, both as a political actor and as a participant in the economy. Western democracies, for the most part, have free-market economies, in which individuals are at liberty to produce and consume according to their own interests, although governments reserve the right to temper market forces when they feel it is in the public interest, however that interest may be defined. For instance, it was the opinion of the R.B. Bennett Conservative government in 1932 that broadcasting was an area in which public ownership should prevail. The Bennett government, in spite of its private-enterprise orientation, was not convinced that private control of radio would best serve the interests of all Canadians, particularly if it meant the American domination of Canada's airwaves.

Between the 1930s and the present, a great deal has changed. For one thing, revenue-strapped governments are eager to assign more and more areas of the economy to market forces, particularly in the cultural realm, but also in the fields of health care and education. Second, the belief in free-market economics is on the rise worldwide and even former Communist-bloc countries are keen to become part of international organizations devoted to freer trade. Third, with increased wealth and advancements in technology, the task of providing communication services across vast distances has become easier. And fourth, the globalization process, which is producing what David Morley and Kevin Robins (1995: 1) describe as 'a new communications geography', calls into question conventional notions of community; people's sense of belonging to the national community has changed. All in all, it is becoming more and more difficult for national governments to assume control of cultural production on behalf of their constituents.

The basis for private ownership derives from both classical and contemporary economic theory. In *The Wealth of Nations* (1937 [1776]), Adam Smith sought to explain how society managed to secure and produce all that was necessary for survival without any form of central planning. Smith formulated a set of basic 'laws' of the marketplace, and is perhaps best known for identifying the market's **invisible hand**, whereby 'the private interests and passions of men' are directed to serving the interests of society as a whole. As Robert Heilbroner (1980: 47-67) explains, Smith's laws of the marketplace 'show us how the drive of individual self-interest in an environment of similarly motivated individuals will result in competition; and they further demonstrate how competition will result in the provision of those goods and services that society wants, in the quantities that society desires, and at the prices society is prepared to pay.' Smith argued, in other words, that self-interest drives people to whatever work society is willing to pay for, and that this self-interest is regulated by competition. No one participant in the market can become greedy, because prices for goods and wages for workers are kept in line by competition. Similarly, competition regulates the supply of goods, preventing both overproduction and underproduction. Smith 'found in the mechanism of the market a self-regulating system for society's orderly provisioning' (ibid., 55).

While even in Smith's day there were price-fixing combines and large-scale producers who disrupted the competitive balance among producers, for the most part, eighteenth-century England conformed to Smith's model. As Heilbroner writes: 'Business *was* competitive, the average factory *was* small, prices *did* rise and fall as demand ebbed and rose, and prices *did* invoke changes in output and occupation' (ibid., 56). Contemporary society, however, does not conform to Smith's model. For one thing, market competition has given way to market dominance—hence the term 'monopoly capitalism'—as huge corporations seek to minimize, even eliminate, competition among producers and large labour unions seek to minimize competition among workers. For another, governments have entered the marketplace with their own notion of self-interest, disrupting the neat functioning of Smith's 'invisible hand'. Government intervention, that is, has been quite visible in seeking to direct the economy to serve particular government interests, whether those interests are job creation for its citizens or maximizing export opportunities for domestic producers.

While neo-classical economists appeal to societies to revive the laissez-faire credo—leave the market alone to regulate itself—Smith's model has become increasingly divorced from economic reality as his 'laws' of the marketplace have been consistently violated by all parties over the past two centuries. The idea that the mass media simply serve the needs and wants of audiences, who base their consumption decisions on universally accepted notions of merit, is an attractive one. But the evidence suggests that in the cultural sector of the economy, too, Smith's 'laws' of the marketplace have little application (see Gasher, 1992).

MARKET ECONOMICS AND CULTURAL PRODUCTION

Perhaps the most fundamental problem is the tendency of many people, and particularly economists, to apply the free-market perspective to sectors of the economy in which it may not be appropriate. Economists often argue that if films, books, TV programs, magazines, and sound recordings cannot survive in the marketplace, then they do not deserve to survive. To intervene to support what large audiences are not interested in, the argument goes, is to use the state to subsidize the tastes of the elite. While the merits of **economism**—the perception of cultural production as commercial enterprise—can certainly be debated, further consideration takes us back to the notion that private ownership is most often applied when management of a resource is not deemed critical to either the resource's or the community's survival. This is a key point because it goes to the heart of how we perceive cultural production and what role we assign the mass media in society.

In its comprehensive survey of state involvement in cultural activity in Canada, the Applebaum-Hébert Committee (Canada, 1982: 64–71) noted that governments often intervene in the cultural sphere in cases of market failure, when the market does not or cannot adequately serve the cultural needs of society. Markets, for example, do not recognize the longevity of cultural products, which may be produced by one generation and maintain their value through subsequent generations. Think of the number of artists— Van Gogh, Mozart, Gauguin, Rembrandt—who are today recognized for their genius, yet who were not adequately compensated for their creations in their own lifetimes. Markets may also fail to accommodate 'infant industries', new, domestic industries that cannot compete right away with well-established and large-scale transnational industries. The Canadian feature-film industry is a good example of an industry that continues to struggle to find a market in the context of Hollywood dominance of this country's commercial theatre screens. Cultural production, Applebaum-Hébert argued, also confounds market economics because it entails a large element of risk, requires a substantial investment of a society's resources, and the public has a 'limitless variability of tastes'. The most common instance of market failure in the cultural sphere, however, involves the market failing 'to register the full benefits conferred' by cultural activity.

. . . the fact can be demonstrated that, historically, those cultural activities that have conferred the most lasting benefits, and which have been seen, in retrospect, to have done most to illuminate their times, have more often than not served only minority interests in their own day. On grounds either of market failure or of diffuse social values, the case for [state] intervention applies with special force to the satisfaction of minority preferences. (Canada, 1982: 69)

Free-market or laissez-faire economics tends to reduce all goods and services to the status of commodities, objects that attain value through marketplace exchange. While we often believe a market economy to be especially responsive to consumer demand for choice, the cultural theorist Raymond Williams (1989: 88) reminds us that the capitalist organization of communication imposes 'commercial constraints', so that 'you can say that at times freedom in our kind of society amounts to the freedom to say anything you wish, provided you can say it profitably.' Commodities, by definition, are validated through sale. As Yves de la Haye (1980: 34–5) argues, when cultural activities are organized commercially, their purpose becomes the generation of profit. If we perceive books as, first and foremost, commodities of exchange, then their value is measured in retail sales and revenues generated. By this reckoning, the best-selling biography of a Hollywood movie star is more valuable than a critically acclaimed history of Kosovo. Yet few would deny that the book on Kosovo is more valuable in terms of its contribution to human understanding than the trivial celebrity biography; the NATO countries went to war over Kosovo, after all.

Economism confines the notion of value to exchange value, and dismisses as 'externalities' any other kinds of benefit (or liability) that may accrue from cultural production. While he was US President, Bill Clinton summoned film and television producers to the White House in the wake of the Columbine school shooting in the spring of 1999 to ask that Hollywood assume some responsibility for the harm that film and TV violence may induce. Such costs—to society, to individuals—are simply excluded from market transactions. At the same time, the benefits of educational programming can be underestimated in the marketplace.

Economism also casts individuals as consumers playing a narrow role in the economy, rather than as citizens with a larger role to play in democratic society. We may read books or watch movies for any number of reasons—entertainment or pleasure, certainly, but also for personal growth, education, insight, and critical understanding. Books, television programs, theatrical performances, and museum exhibits are not simply goods or services that we buy and sell, but crucial opportunities for the kind of communication that is fundamental to the notion of culture. In other words, cultural products are *more* than commodities. They are expressions of a culture as a way of life and as a system of beliefs and values. They are expressions of ideas and images that help a culture to imagine itself and to articulate its priorities. If excluded by the so-called 'realities' of the marketplace, certain forms of cultural expression can be marginalized, even silenced.

Historical Background: Function and Ownership

The roots of media institutions are found in two places. The first is the need of the state to circulate information about the rights, duties, responsibilities, obligations, and freedoms of the state, the community, and the individual. The second is in the social, cultural, economic, and political opportunities communication affords.

Gutenberg's printing press was an invention that responded to a social structure that created room for individual initiative, to a thirst for learning, to a growing literacy, and to an opportunity to make the Bible and other manuscripts available to a wide, literate audience. Some researchers argue that printers were among the earliest capitalist entrepreneurs in that they took risks by printing materials and tried to recoup their investments through sales (Eisenstein, 1979).

The establishment of the commercial press in Canada was a response to the opportunity to print, under contract, official government information and to make such information widely available. Taking Britain and the United States as its models, the press in Canada soon evolved into an institution capable of responding to other social and political pressures for the distribution of information and ideas. The press was by no means an isolated example; cinema in Canada, too, was originally a medium exploited by governments for political and commercial propaganda, and only later became a more independent form of art, information, and dramatic entertainment.

Given these roots, the intensive involvement of government in the press and printing is not difficult to understand. In seventeenth-century Britain, while ownership of printing facilities was not exclusive to the public domain, the government used laws and taxes to control press output so that it would reflect the interests of the ruling elites. Taxes on paper and the disallowance of type founding were two indirect mechanisms that controlled the dissemination of information. However, as printers as a group became less and less dependent on government largesse, and with the general economic and political rise of the bourgeoisie, intense, insistent pressure grew for the freedom of printers to pursue their economic interest.

FREE PRESS, FREE MARKET

From the beginning of printing to the present day there has been a struggle between 'the media' and 'the state' for control of communications. Each has compelling reasons to want control of the generation and distribution of content. The state needs to disseminate information to govern, to command allegiance from its citizens, and to generate a sense of community among its inhabitants. Reading a newspaper, for example, keeps us informed about our government's activities and offers us a depiction of our society: who our fellow citizens are, what they look like, what they think, what they value, etc. (see Anderson, 1989). The media want to speak either for their owners in pursuit of markets or for the ordinary citizen, to raise a voice against some form of mistreatment. The battle for press freedom was fought on the foundation of individual freedom and the relation between freedom of speech and democracy, with the press putting itself forward as a separate estate representative of a distinct set of interests, not those of church, business, or landowners, but those of 'the people' (see our discussion of the 'fourth estate' in Chapter 9).

Yet simultaneously, the press was fighting for the economic interests of private press owners. It would seem that the press won recognition, at least in part, on the basis of the conjoined interests of individual free speech and the generally accepted liberal theory and commercial practice of the day; intellectuals like John Milton, John Locke, and John Stuart Mill were the early proponents of the libertarian theory of the press (see Osler, 1993). Specifically, individuals—in this case, press owners—wanted to have the right to pursue their own interests, and in doing so they would create benefit to society through the workings of Adam Smith's 'invisible hand'. They would be free to pursue economic markets by participating in a free market of ideas.

Within the context of liberal-capitalist economic theory, the press asked for nothing more than any other business. But in dealing with information, which even during the Industrial Revolution was recognized as somehow different from other commodities, the press found it prudent to fight and win the battle on non-economic grounds, on the basis of the rights of individuals to free speech.

The state never did give up its right to produce and disseminate information, and, indeed, well into the twentieth century the so-called 'free press' was closely aligned with political parties (see Sotiron, 1997). In various European countries the interconnections between government and the press are still close. The most blatant example of this is Italy, where Prime Minister Silvio Berlusconi's Mediaset company owns three of the country's four national private television networks, as well as newspapers and radio stations. Berlusconi has been critical of the one major channel he doesn't own, Italy's state television network RAI. Re-elected in May 2001, Berlusconi lobbied to pack RAI's board with loyal directors, and during the summer of 2002 he caused an uproar when two RAI journalists he had publicly criticized were subsequently fired (Bagnall, 2002; Wallace, 2002).

Organizing Structures

No media industry in Canada is governed exclusively by free-market economics. Governments, both provincial and federal, are implicated in one form or another in the structure of every media industry: as proprietor (CBC, NFB); custodian (museums, galleries, theatres); patron (commissions, grants, sponsorships); catalyst (tax incentives, subsidies); or regulator (CRTC) (Canada, 1982: 72). The result is that our mass media are organized as a complex mixture of public and private enterprise.

Newspaper publishing comes closest to an exclusively private enterprise, but even here section 19 of the Income Tax Act ensures that Canadian newspapers remain Canadian-owned; the newspaper industry is protected from foreign takeover and foreign competition. Newspapers are considered by the state to be relatively untouchable because they are so closely associated with the historical struggle for freedom of mediated forms of expression. In the post-war period, governments in Great Britain, the United States, and Canada have all ignored reasoned calls to intervene in the newspaper industry to ensure a better balance between the press's freedom to publish and the citizen's right to be informed. Both the Davey Commission (Canada, 1971: 255–6) and the Kent Commission (Canada, 1981: 237) raised concerns about ownership concentration in Canada's newspaper industry and proposed legislative mechanisms to address the problem. The Kent Commission, specifically, proposed a Canada Newspaper Act to balance the rights and responsibilities of a free press and recommended legislation both to correct the worst cases of corporate concentration and to prohibit the further concentration of ownership. Magazine publishing in Canada is distinguished from the newspaper business in this regard by its dependence on both government subsidies (e.g., preferred postal rates, direct grants) and protectionist legislation (the Income Tax Act) for its survival in a marketplace dominated by American publications (see Dubinsky, 1996).

Table 8.1 summarizes the Canadian daily newspaper ownership groups while Table 8.2 provides a comprehensive summary of the holdings of these Canadian companies, testifying to the high level of corporate concentration in this segment of the economy. Southam Publications (CanWest Global), the country's largest publisher with 13 daily newspapers including the *National Post*, controls close to 30 per cent of all weekly newspaper circulation, while the top five companies together control almost 80 per cent of weekly circulation. The country's five independent newspapers together account for less than 1 per cent.

The state presence is much more apparent in the broadcasting sector. Radio, for example, has private, commercial stations operating alongside publicly owned broadcasters (i.e., CBC and Radio-Canada) and community stations. CBC and Radio-Canada compete with the commercial broadcasters for audiences, but they do not compete for advertising. Public radio in Canada has been commercial-free since 1974, leaving the public broadcaster wholly dependent on federal

Table 8.1 Daily Newspaper Ownership Groups, March 2003

Publisher	Number of Newspapers	Share of Canadian Dailies[a]	Total Weekly Circulation[b]	Share of Total Weekly Circulation[c]
Southam Publications (CanWest Global)	13	12.70	9,150,562	28.50
Sun Media (Quebecor)	15	14.70	6,813,832	21.10
Torstar Corp.	4	3.92	4,436,535	13.80
Power Corp.	7	6.86	2,995,435	9.30
Bell Globemedia	1	0.98	1,965,991	6.10
Osprey Media Group	22	21.60	1,991,122	6.20
FP Canadian	2	1.96	991,342	3.10
GTC Transcontinental	11	10.80	1,002,549	3.10
Halifax Herald	2	1.96	711,495	2.20
Horizon Operations	5	4.90	611,044	1.90
Brunswick News	3	2.94	637,400	2.00
Hollinger Canadian	10	9.80	320,888	1.00
Independents	4	3.90	290,479	0.90
Black Press	1	0.98	112,163	0.30
Annex Publishing	2	1.96	93,165	0.30
Totals	**102**	**100**	**32,124,002**	**100**

[a]Rounded to two decimal places.
[b]CNA figures as of 31 March 2003.
[c]Rounded to two decimal places.
Source: Canadian Newspaper Association, 2003 (www.cna-acj.ca).

Table 8.2 Canadian Daily Newspaper Holdings, March 2003

Owner	Region	Title	Total Weekly Circulation
Southam Publications (CanWest Global)	Quebec	*Gazette* (Montreal)	1,023,188
	Ontario	*National Post* (Toronto)	1,502,649
	Ontario	*Ottawa Citizen*	990,783
	Ontario	*Windsor Star*	458,372
	Saskatchewan	*Leader Post* (Regina)	305,871
	Saskatchewan	*Star Phoenix* (Saskatoon)	342,990
	Alberta	*Calgary Herald*	840,902
	Alberta	*Edmonton Journal*	943,320
	BC	*Vancouver Sun*	1,170,963
	BC	*Province* (Vancouver)	996,296
	BC	*Nanaimo Daily News*	51,978
	BC	*Times Colonist* (Victoria)	494,420
	BC	*Alberni Valley Times* (Port Alberni)	28,830
Group Circulation			**9,150,562**
Sun Media (Quebecor)	Quebec	*Le Journal de Montréal*	1,929,844
	Quebec	*Le Journal de Québec*	720,000
	Ontario	*Brockville Recorder and Times*	74,334
	Ontario	*Daily Miner and News* (Kenora)	17,040
	Ontario	*London Free Press*	574,757
	Ontario	*Ottawa Sun*	354,882
	Ontario	*Beacon-Herald* (Stratford)	64,584
	Ontario	*St. Thomas Times-Journal*	47,634
	Ontario	*Toronto Sun*	1,588,698
	Alberta	*Calgary Sun*	494,869
	Alberta	*Edmonton Sun*	525,205
	Alberta	*Fort McMurray Today*	22,628
	Alberta	*Daily Herald-Tribune* (Grande Prairie)	45,235
	Manitoba	*Daily Graphic* (Portage La Prairie)	19,626
	Manitoba	*Winnipeg Sun*	334,496
Group Circulation			**6,813,832**
Torstar Corp.	Ontario	*Guelph Mercury*	84,612
	Ontario	*Hamilton Spectator*	651,446
	Ontario	*Record* (Kitchener-Waterloo)	407,446
	Ontario	*Toronto Star*	3,293,031
Group Circulation			**4,436,535**
Power Corp.	Quebec	*La Presse* (Montreal)	1,426,067
	Quebec	*Le Nouvelliste* (Trois-Rivières)	258,169
	Quebec	*La Tribune* (Sherbrooke)	199,090
	Quebec	*La Voix de l'Est* (Granby)	97,706
	Quebec	*Le Soleil* (Quebec City)	618,982
	Quebec	*Le Quotidien* (Chicoutimi)	175,002

Owner	Region	Title	Total Weekly Circulation
	Ontario	*Le Droit* (Ottawa)	220,419
Group Circulation			**2,995,435**
Bell Globemedia	Ontario	*Globe and Mail* (Toronto)	1,965,991
Group Circulation			**1,965,991**
Osprey Media Group	Ontario	*Barrie Examiner*	65,550
	Ontario	*Chatham Daily News*	81,702
	Ontario	*Cobourg Daily Star*	26,820
	Ontario	*Standard-Freeholder* (Cornwall)	89,190
	Ontario	*Kingston Whig-Standard*	173,297
	Ontario	*Northern Daily News* (Kirkland Lake)	20,274
	Ontario	*North Bay Nugget*	101,058
	Ontario	*Intelligencer* (Belleville)	110,292
	Ontario	*Observer* (Sarnia)	125,394
	Ontario	*Sault Star* (Sault Ste-Marie)	117,948
	Ontario	*Sudbury Star*	129,059
	Ontario	*Daily Press* (Timmins)	58,061
	Ontario	*Sun Times* (Owen Sound)	110,808
	Ontario	*Port Hope Evening Guide*	15,558
	Ontario	*Packet & Times* (Orillia)	49,734
	Ontario	*Daily Observer* (Pembroke)	34,956
	Ontario	*Peterborough Examiner*	135,006
	Ontario	*Lindsay Daily Post*	28,596
	Ontario	*Expositor* (Brantford)	133,494
	Ontario	*Tribune* (Welland)	89,430
	Ontario	*Standard, St Catharines*	193,489
	Ontario	*Niagara Falls Review*	101,406
Group Circulation			**1,991,122**
FP Canadian Newspapers	Manitoba	*Brandon Sun*	110,022
	Manitoba	*Winnipeg Free Press*	881,320
Group Circulation			**991,342**
GTC Transcontinental	Nova Scotia	*Daily News* (Halifax)	173,861
	Nova Scotia	*Cape Breton Post* (Sydney)	150,756
	Nova Scotia	*Evening News* (New Glasgow)	48,396
	Nova Scotia	*Daily News* (Truro)	42,414
	Nova Scotia	*Amherst Daily News*	23,201
	Newfoundland	*Telegram* (St John's)	234,989
	Newfoundland	*Western Star* (Corner Brook)	47,610
	PEI	*Guardian* (Charlottetown)	124,662
	PEI	*Journal Pioneer* (Summerside)	57,660
	Saskatchewan	*Times-Herald* (Moose Jaw)	53,400
	Saskatchewan	*Prince Albert Daily Herald*	45,600
Group Circulation			**1,002,549**

Owner	Region	Ttile	Total Weekly Ciculation
Halifax Herald Ltd	Nova Scotia	*Chronicle-Herald* (Halifax)	621,537
	Nova Scotia	*Mail Star* (Halifax)	89,958
Group Circulation			**711,495**
Horizon Operations BC	BC	*Penticton Herald*	56,251
	BC	*Daily Courier* (Kelowna)	112,303
	Alberta	*Lethbridge Herald*	139,441
	Alberta	*Medicine Hat News*	84,852
	Ontario	*Chronicle-Journal* (Thunder Bay)	218,197
Group Circulation			**611,044**
Brunswick News Inc.	New Brunswick	*Times & Transcript* (Moncton)	247,832
	New Brunswick	*Daily Gleaner* (Fredericton)	157,345
	New Brunswick	*New Brunswick Telegraph Journal* (Saint John)	232,223
Group Circulation			**637,400**
Hollinger Canadian	Quebec	*Record* (Sherbrooke)	25,310
	BC	*Cranbrook Daily Townsman*	18,690
	BC	*Alaska Highway News* (Fort St John)	18,950
	BC	*Daily Bulletin* (Kimberley)	8,900
	BC	*Nelson Daily News*	16,260
	BC	*Peace River Block Daily News* (Dawson Creek)	9,445
	BC	*Daily News* (Prince Rupert)	15,350
	BC	*Trail Times*	22,790
	BC	*Kamloops Daily News*	88,566
	BC	*Citizen* (Prince George)	96,627
Group Circulation			**320,888**
	New Brunswick	*L'Acadie Nouvelle* (Caraquet)	87,840
	Quebec	*Le Devoir* (Montreal)	171,032
	Manitoba	*Flin Flon Reminder*	19,500
	Yukon	*Whitehorse Star*	12,107
Group Circulation			**290,479**
Black Press	Alberta	*Red Deer Advocate*	112,163
Group Circulation			**112,163**
Annex Publishing	Ontario	*Simcoe Reformer*	42,165
	Ontario	*Sentinel Review* (Woodstock)	51,000
Group Circulation			**93,165**

government funding for its operations. Community radio stations are run by non-profit societies with a democratic management structure, and raise money from a combination of advertising, government subsidies, and fundraising activities such as radio bingo. As discussed in Chapter 6, all radio stations—private, public, and community—are regulated by the CRTC; they are required to meet the specific conditions of their broadcast licence as well as Canadian-content quotas. The domestic sound recording industry, though owned by private interests, has of course been the principal beneficiary of Canadian-content regulations on radio.

Television, too, is a mix of private, public, and community broadcasting stations. A significant difference here is that the stations of CBC and Radio-Canada, including Newsworld and Le réseau de l'information (RDI), compete with the commercial broadcasters for both audiences and advertising. This competition for advertising has long been a sore point with the private broadcasters, who feel the CBC encroaches on their business, and the topic was raised again during the CBC's licence renewal hearings before the CRTC in 1999. Supporters of public broadcasting, too, argue that advertising competition distorts the public broadcaster's mission; advertising, they maintain, encourages the CBC to carry the same kind of programming that can be found on the commercial networks, such as professional sports and mainstream Hollywood movies. Both private and public television in Canada is regulated (e.g., licensing, Canadian-content quotas, advertising limits) and both private and public broadcasters benefit from federal and provincial subsidies for the creation of Canadian film and television programming. Specialty channels form the sector of the ownership picture that will bear closest scrutiny in the years ahead.

The film industry in Canada is a special case because it has both public and private production houses, but the distribution and exhibition sectors of the industry are organized along principles of private enterprise. As noted in Chapter 7, governments in Canada have been involved in film production—as patrons, catalysts, and regulators—since the turn of the century. Hollywood began to dominate the burgeoning commercial film industry in the 1920s and this did not sit well with Canadians in a period of strong Canadian nationalism. The federal government established the National Film Board of Canada in 1939 as a means of asserting a greater Canadian presence on cinema screens. The NFB has largely been confined to producing the kinds of films that tend not to be shown in commercial theatres—documentary, experimental, animation, and sponsored films—leaving the production of dramatic feature-length films to the private sector. If there has been competitive tension between the NFB and private-sector producers, it has been over contracts for sponsored films, which are films commissioned by government departments and corporations for educational and marketing purposes. But even the private producers of feature films in Canada rely heavily on government loans and subsidies for production, distribution, and marketing, and public television has been one of Canadian cinema's most dependable exhibition venues.

Until recently, telephone service was defined by Ottawa as a 'natural monopoly' and Canada had both private (e.g., BC Telephone, Bell Canada) and provincial state monopolies (e.g., Sasktel, Manitoba Telecom Services) operating side by side. The CRTC, however, began to deregulate the industry in the late 1980s, first opening up long-distance telephony to competition and in 1994 opening all telephone services to competition.

Even art galleries, theatres, concert halls, and museums, insofar as they can been seen as mass media, are characterized by a mix of public and private ownership, with content generated by both public-sector and private-sector sources. The international web of computer networks we call the Internet has no single owner, but it, too, counts on both public- and private-sector initiatives for its operation and its content. Cyberspace is a medium of exchange for all kinds of communication and defies any simple structural category.

Ted Magder (1993: 10–11) argues that state intervention in the cultural sphere has been motivated by two objectives: national identity and economic growth. The Canadian Pacific Railway remains a powerful symbol in Canada because it was one of the first national institutions asked to serve both goals simultaneously; the building of the railway was a private enterprise heavily subsidized by Ottawa and designed to bind a sparsely populated and vast country together. If the CPR permitted the transportation of people and goods back and forth across Canada, the federal government imagined that a national radio broadcasting network would allow for the transcontinental dissemination of ideas, values, and images. In fact, the metaphor describing the CBC as a 'railway of the airwaves' has been evoked many times.

The goals of creating a Canadian national identity and stimulating economic growth remain in perpetual tension in the communications sphere, and the various ownership structures of the media in Canada speak to Ottawa's ongoing struggle to keep both objectives in view.

Public Ownership

The central difference between public and private forms of ownership pertains to their bottom lines. Public ownership is devoted to providing communications as a public service. Private ownership is devoted to providing communications for profit. Regardless of the mix of private and public enterprise described above, this distinction is fundamental and needs always to be kept in view if we are to make the link between the ownership structure of a medium and the purpose of the communication it provides.

The idea of public service is to employ the mass media for social goals. This can mean the provision of universal and equitable service to all Canadians, as in the telecommunications, radio, and television industries. It can mean foregrounding the educational component of communication, which informs all cultural policy to some extent. Or it can mean ensuring a Canadian voice in film, radio, TV, publishing, and popular music, where there is a clear risk of being drowned out by American voices. Communication as public service is inherently inclusive, addressing audiences as citizens rather than consumers, and asserting citizens' rights to communicate and be informed.

The public service ideal, of course, is not without shortcomings when it comes to putting principles into practice. In Canada, public service has often meant *national* service—i.e., communications in the service of nation-building. As Marc Raboy (1992: xii–xiii) notes, in the broadcasting sector this has meant the subordination of other social and cultural goals to national economic and political interests, specifically, 'the political project of maintaining "Canada" as an entity distinct from the United States of America and united against the periodic threat of disintegration posed by Quebec'. It has also meant the concentration of film, radio, and television services in central Canada, creating a hierarchical distinction between the 'national' preoccupations of Ontario and Quebec and the 'regional' concerns of the other provinces and territories.

The central ethic of the public corporation is connected to the democratic ideal. More specifically, it is to provide a public service to both the users of the service and to the population as a whole. Under such an ethic, charges are sometimes levied for services rendered, and at other times costs are covered through general government revenues. In still other instances, revenue raised by general taxes is combined with user fees. On the consumer's side, user fees are often determined in part by what others must pay and in part by how much the service actually costs. For example, while rural users often pay more for telephone services, they do not pay the full amount of what it costs to bring the service into sparsely populated areas. In this way an attempt is made to provide universal and equitable access encompassed by the notion of common carriage. It is surely a national achievement to bring radio and television services to every Canadian community of at least 500 people—even if all of them cannot ever consume enough to form a market sufficiently attractive to advertisers to pay for the service. Not to provide such services would threaten the maintenance of national sovereignty; if we find ourselves unable to provide such services, another nation, most likely the United States, might. Or, some Canadians would simply be deprived.

A public service ethic also means that the object of public corporations is not to demonstrate the existence of a market or pursue profit as a primary goal. In most countries profit-making by publicly owned corporations is forbidden, and in others certain or all public media corporations are prevented from accepting advertising. These restrictions exist to ensure that the public corporation is not compromised in its ability to serve the public by its need to seek advertising revenue. It also guards against competition between the public and private sectors for advertising income.

Public service means that economics is only one factor to be considered in a larger equation. The other major element of the equation is the determination of the public interest, not in a unitary or authoritarian fashion, but in a way that reflects the many and varied interests and viewpoints that are part of any society (see McQuail, 1991, for an attempt at outlining the public interest in the context of media performance).

This public interest ethic means that the publicly owned outlet must weigh its public service mandate—such as appealing to all ages and people in all locations, training top-level journalists, or meeting the needs of audience members to be responsible and contributing citizens in society—against economic pressures. The public corporation can consider, on the merit of the case itself, whether it will carry children's programs without advertising support, develop socially oriented programs for the poor, or underwrite programming for the aged. After making this decision, it must find the means to carry it through.

PUBLIC ENTERPRISE

Public enterprise has a long and distinguished tradition in every Western country. Its most common use has been in instances when a national social need was clearly identified, yet a market was not organized or seemed incapable of adequately serving the needs of the country. In communications the establishment of a national broadcasting service such as the CBC is the classic example. Educational institutions, the postal service, and health services are others.

As Herschel Hardin (1974) points out, Canada has made extensive use of public enterprise throughout its history, with the most common form being the Crown corporation. At times, as in the case of the Canadian Pacific Railway, Canada has combined public enterprise or public support with private enterprise to produce the same end: public service. As Robin Mathews (1988) notes, we practise a brand of capitalism tempered by socialism.

Public ownership of the media has followed in this tradition. Its general purpose has been to bring information and entertainment, images, and symbols, reflective of the variety of the country and the variety of the world, to the greatest number of citizens possible, especially through broadcasting. The social value was that the audience might generally benefit from such exposure and that compatriots might see themselves as members of a single nation.

While the prime example of public ownership in the Canadian media is the CBC, there are other examples in the National Film Board of Canada, community radio stations, and the provincial educational broadcast networks. Originally a radio operation, the CBC was set up essentially because of a fear of inundation by programming from the United States. As for television, it was not apparent how Canadian production and display could be a money-making venture. The CBC extended its activities into television to bring information reflective of the variety that makes up Canada to the greatest number of Canadians, so that we might all see ourselves as members of a single and independent nation.

FORMS OF PUBLIC OWNERSHIP

The characteristic model of broadcast ownership is a national public monopoly or, in cases such as Canada, a national public broadcaster existing side by side with private-sector broadcasters. In either case, the organization and finances of the national public broadcaster may be controlled by the state. However, the broadcaster is fairly independent from government in its program policies. The CBC, for example, has a board of directors appointed by the government of the day but the board acts independently of that government. The original BBC model was adopted by France, Italy, the Scandinavian countries, and Japan, and by Commonwealth nations such as Australia, New Zealand, Zimbabwe, and India. In Belgium and Switzerland, as in Canada, each linguistic group has its own service. In Germany, where the states or Länder are responsible for broadcasting, a number of regional monopolies come together to form the national

Robert Rabinovitch was appointed president and CEO of CBC/Radio-Canada in 1999. Although CBC/Radio-Canada is funded primarily through Parliamentary appropriation, the Corporation's autonomy is assured through the authority conferred by Parliament upon its Board of Directors and the appointment of a President and CEO who cannot be fired except by Parliament. This principle of 'arm's length' is critical to CBC/Radio-Canada's role as a newsgathering orginization. (Courtesy CBC/Radio-Canada, Ottawa)

networks (Rolland and Østbye, 1986).

The dynamics of cultural identity have played a major role in the formation and design of broadcasting systems, especially of their public components. Often, when regional cultural identity is important—as it is in Norway, Germany, and France—room is created for regional productions. National cultural identity is predominant as a concern in Italy, the Netherlands, France, Finland, and Denmark. The French have seen themselves as bastions against Anglo-Saxon or English-language imperialism and are therefore strongly protectionist. They also support domestic production subsidies both in France and in the European Union. Italy has expressed its concerns in terms of 'cultural colonization'. Many European countries have established quotas governing national and imported content. Denmark and Finland have favoured variety in importation over quotas to keep foreign content from overwhelming national culture (Bakke, 1986).

The creation of public-sector institutions and their predominance over the years have ensured a firm commitment to the public service ethic. But more recently these state monopolies have been challenged by issues of fiscal constraint and economism. That is, can governments afford to promote and protect indigenous cultural activity in this manner? And, is cultural production an appropriate sphere of state activity? We have seen a shift since the early 1980s from what Colin Sparks (1995) terms a 'culturalist discourse'—which perceives cultural production as first and foremost a *cultural* activity—to an 'economistic discourse'—which defines cultural production as commercial enterprise. Among those promoting the wholesale appropriation of cultural production by the private sector are the same media proprietors who stand the most to gain from such a shift.

Private Ownership

Private-sector ownership takes two basic forms. The ownership of a company can be closely held, either by an individual or by a very small group (often family members). Or the ownership of a company can be widely held by a large group of shareholders, who buy and sell their interest in the company through the stock market. In the latter case, a company will form a board of directors answerable to its shareholders.

The general ethic of the private or commercial media outlet is survival and growth in a marketplace driven by profit. This ethic does not derive merely from the personality traits of private-sector owners. Commercial corporations are organized for the purpose of earning returns for their owners, whether those owners are individuals or groups of shareholders. Because the bottom line in the private sector is profit, private media companies have greater latitude than public media institutions in changing course to pursue more lucrative markets, whether those markets are in the sphere of communications or not. Thomson Corp., for example, was once one of Canada's two principal newspaper chains, and while its North American newspaper holdings remain substantial, Thomson redefined itself in the 1990s as an information company, identifying more promising business opportunities elsewhere, specifically in the markets of financial, legal, and scientific information (Thomson Corp., 1998, 1999).

FORMS OF PRIVATE OWNERSHIP

Even within the private sector there is a considerable variety of ownership structures. The single enterprise is, as its name suggests, a business form in which owners confine themselves to one business with no connections to other companies. It is a single, independent firm that usually operates on a small scale. Examples of this form of ownership of newspapers, radio stations, and even some television stations were quite common until media barons like Roy Thomson began acquiring them to form chain operations. Some examples still exist, particularly among magazines, community weekly newspapers, and small-town radio stations. But single enterprises are fewer and fewer as chains both large and small gobble them up or force them out of business.

Chain ownership is the linking or **horizontal integration** of a number of companies in the same business—typically, newspapers, radio stations, or television stations—occupying different markets. Chains are usually geographically dispersed, but sometimes members of the chain will occupy the same location and aim for distinct audiences. Vancouver's two daily newspapers, the *Sun* and *Province*, for example, are both part of the larger Southam chain, but they seek different readers and advertisers within the Lower Mainland of British Columbia. Member companies in a chain may have agreements to buy and sell services from each other. Southam newspapers, for instance, share editorial content (stories and pictures) among member papers and have their own wire service, CanWest News Service. In addition, chains often

IF KIDS CAN, THEN NELVANA AND CORUS CAN SURVIVE CONVERGENCE IN TORONTO

Once upon a time, there was a small publisher of children's book in Toronto called Kids Can Press. It was run by two wise women and they were successful in finding and publishing quality Canadian titles. Along the way, they published a series of stories about Franklin the Turtle™. In a neighbouring land, another Canadian company called Nelvana developed some very clever animation and visual effects technology that came to the notice of the big Hollywood moguls. Both companies were successful. Nelvana made lots of money because it was in the movie business where successful companies make lots of money. In the book business, especially in Canada, making gobs of money is extremely rare, so Kids Can made less. 'It's a living', said the wise women, 'and it's fun.'

One day, Nelvana met Kids Can. More importantly, Nelvana met Franklin the Turtle. Nelvana said: 'We can take Franklin to places he would never go in the book world. Why don't we buy your company for more money than you ever dreamed of? You can continue running the company, and we will take Franklin into the new lands of television and licensed merchandising. And we will all live happily ever after.'

So Nelvana did buy Kids Can. It paid $7 million, a sum virtually unheard of in the land of Canadian book publishing, and it took Franklin into television and licensed merchandising.

Now modern stories never begin and end that simply, because, for one thing, time passes, and, for another, the world changes. It seems that, indeed, in the land of television broadcasting and TV program distribution in Canada, changes were afoot. As a result of a decision of a queen's council of advisers (a.k.a. the CRTC), one company was able to obtain control of one of Canada's two private television networks, CTV. The triumphant company renamed itself Corus. Once the singing of joy was over, Corus thought that it would be a good idea to invest in program production to broadcast to its stations and to sell to other networks around the world from whom it purchased programs. Corus looked for a good production company to buy and it spied Nelvana. So Corus said to Nelvana, 'Why don't we buy your company for more money than you ever dreamed of? You can continue running the company.' So Corus bought Nelvana. It paid Nelvana $540 million.

All was happy in the land for about two years because Kids Can was one of Canada's leading children's book publishing companies, Nelvana was Canada's leading cartoon production company, and Corus was one of Canada's leading television-based entertainment companies. However, one morning Corus woke up to a world market filled with cartoon-based television programs. Thus it came to pass that Corus, which had declared a $100 million profit in its third quarter of 2001, declared a $190 million loss in its fourth quarter of 2002 and felt it necessary to take a further write-down of $200 million on its assets. Also, it saw its shares drop from a high in 2001 of nearly $40 to a low in October of 2002 of $20.

So, one blustery day in October 2002, the admirals from Corus said to the captain of Nelvana, 'We want Franklin to work harder. We would like to see Franklin generate about 25 per cent of revenue, not the 7 per cent he is now generating. He could do so by sailing more aggressively into the world of licensed merchandising. If Bob the Builder™, Barney the Dinosaur™, and Thomas the Tank Engine™ can generate 39 per cent profit for London-based HIT Entertainment PLC, we think Franklin can do more. Besides, as you know, we do own the rights to Babar the Elephant™ and Little Bear from the Berenstein Bears™ and they are willing to help.' The captain of the Nelvana ship pondered. Finally he said, 'Why don't I sail into port and someone else can captain the Nelvana ship. I will act as a retired admiral.' So the captains of Corus said, 'We are sorry to lose you, but maybe it would be best for all of us.'

So Corus drew up some new maps for sailing more aggressively into the land of merchandising. And they set out to find a new captain for Nelvana. As for Kids Can Press and Franklin, well, they sailed on, because, in the world of children's book publishing, there are always new authors, always new titles, and always new readers who love to fall in love with creations such as Franklin the Turtle.

Source: Keith Damsell, *Globe and Mail*, 26 Oct. 2002, B1. Reprinted with permission from the Globe and Mail.

centralize administrative resources, so that accounting and marketing services or departments responsible for technological innovation will be able to serve all members in the chain. Such sharing of resources offers chain operations tremendous cost advantages over single enterprises. Typically, chain ownership offers the advantages of reducing competition and creates economies of scale (see Rutherford, 1992).

Chain ownership is a common form of media organization in Canada. Southam Publications, owned by CanWest Global Communications Corp., runs a chain of 17 daily newspapers across Canada, including the *National Post* and major dailies in Victoria, Vancouver, Edmonton, Calgary, Regina, Saskatoon, Ottawa, and Montreal (www.cna-acj.ca). CanWest also owns the Global Television Network, which is comprised of a chain of 11 stations in eight provinces (www.canwestglobal.com).

Vertical integration is the concentration of firms within a specific business that extends a company's control over the entire process of production. A vertically integrated company, for instance, will have subsidiary companies involved in every aspect of an industry. The most common example of vertical integration is the commercial film industry, in which the major Hollywood companies not only own production studios and distribution companies, but have subsidiaries involved in theatrical exhibition, television, and home video rental to ensure their films reach audiences. The advantages inherent to vertical integration are substantial. A vertically integrated company ensures itself of both resource supplies and sales markets, and it minimizes other uncertainties related to the circuit of production (Mosco, 1996: 175–82).

Following the lead of the vertically integrated Hollywood film companies, Alliance Atlantis Communications (www.allianceatlantis.com), Canada's largest audiovisual company, creates, distributes, and broadcasts filmed entertainment. CanWest Global is primarily a chain operation with the 11-station Global Television Network in Canada and TV hold-

... Sure as night follows day:

A division of Disney Corp

A division of Westinghouse

A division of Ed's Plumbing Supplies

KRIEGER©1995 The Province

Ownership trends in the media industries as well as the contrast between well-capitalized private commercial organizations and starving public media organizations are aptly illustrated in this cartoon. (Bob Krieger, The Province)

ings in New Zealand, Australia, Ireland, and Northern Ireland. But it began to integrate horizontally in April 1998 when it acquired the Fireworks group of companies, which are involved in film and television financing, production, and distribution. Quebecor Inc. (www.quebecor.com) is a vertically integrated publishing company. Besides publishing newspapers, Quebecor has a subsidiary company in the forest products and pulp and paper business (Donohue Inc.) and another in the printing business (Quebecor Printing). However, Quebecor could also be described as a conglomerate because it has interests in business unrelated to newspaper publishing: e.g., television broadcasting (Télévision Quatre Saisons) and music retailing (Trans-Canada Archambault).

Conglomerate ownership is characterized by large companies with a number of subsidiary firms in

CONVERGENCE

Convergence is an economic strategy in which media conglomerates take advantage of the digitization of content and government deregulation to reduce operating costs and expand market share. Media content is now produced digitally, so that newspaper stories, radio programs, recorded music, and television broadcasts can be cobbled together as a content package on media companies' Web sites. At the same time, the CRTC has increasingly permitted media conglomerates to own newspapers and radio and TV stations in the same markets.

The advantages of convergence for the media conglomerate are potentially enormous. A single company can offer advertising buyers a number of media platforms from which to develop an ad campaign, as well as package deals for those who advertise in more than one media property. It offers audiences one-stop shopping for news and entertainment, creating a recognizable media brand and encouraging brand loyalty among consumers. Similarly, convergence allows media to cross-promote one another. 'In Canada, with two or three companies you can cover the country', Phillip Crawley, publisher and chief executive officer of the *Globe and Mail,* told the Canadian Newspaper Association's annual meeting in Calgary in April 2002 (Brethour, 2002).

A converged company can save costs by reducing its workforce because content created for one medium can be repurposed for use in a sister medium. Increasingly, for example, newspaper reporters are being asked to prepare news stories that can appear on the company's Web site and be twinned with a TV report on the company's local TV newscast. CanWest Global, which owns a national television network, a chain of daily newspapers, and an Internet portal, has used its convergence strategy to reduce administrative costs and to encourage content-sharing among its newspaper, TV, and Web newsrooms (ibid.).

Of course, what appears to the eyes of media executives as an advantage may be detrimental to workers and audiences. Journalists working in shrinking newsrooms are being pressured to produce more stories each day, and stories that can be used in more than one news medium. CanWest Global president Leonard Asper has been widely cited for envisioning a future in which journalists 'wake up, write a story for the Web, write a column, take their cameras, cover an event and do a report for TV and file a video clip for the Web' ('The complications of convergence', *Globe and Mail*, 4 Aug. 2001, A12). In other words, convergence strategies compel fewer workers to produce more and varied content without very much consideration for how much time and effort is required to produce high-quality news content.

But besides the qualitative implications this entails, there are quantitative concerns as well. In spite of claims to the contrary, audiences are faced with fewer distinct choices among mainstream information and entertainment sources. By pooling their production, distribution, and marketing resources, media conglomerates raise the barriers to entry for would-be competitors. Telecommunications researcher Kevin G. Wilson (2002) argues that convergence 'has produced horizontal concentration as there are fewer players in the respective telephone, cable, TV, radio, Internet and publishing industries, and vertical concentration because most of the remaining companies are now owned by one of the five convergence "champions"'—BCE Inc., Rogers Communications, Shaw Communications, CanWest Global Communications, and Quebecor Inc.

While convergence appears to be a logical economic strategy on paper, it is not at all clear that it actually generates the profits media executives have envisioned. Citing the examples of AOL Time Warner in the United States, Vivendi Universal in France, and BCE in Canada, business analyst Philip Evans (2002) has declared convergence a failure. Such a verdict is premature, however.

AOL Time Warner has been a pioneer in trying to create synergy between its media companies. Time Inc. and Warner Brothers originally merged in 1989, creating the world's largest media and entertainment company and seeking benefit—with mixed results—from its complementary properties in magazine publishing, music recording, and filmmaking. Time Warner's subsequent merger with AOL intensified this strategy, but no one knows yet whether it will pay off. Since AOL bought Time Warner in January 2001, AOL has increased traffic to Web sites associated with Time Warner properties and has added a reported 100,000 subscribers to Time's stable of magazines. At the same time, the merger has produced failures: the business news cable channel CNNfn, AOL TV, and Time Warner Cable (Manley et al., 2002).

In Canada, BCE Inc.'s chief executive officer, Jean Monty, was heralded as a 'world-beater' when his company took over Teleglobe Inc. in February 2002, becoming one of the world's largest telecommunications companies. With a presence in more than 100 countries, BCE was seen as positioned to take advantage of deregulation of long-distance telephony in the United States and anticipated Internet traffic growth in Europe (Riga, 2000). BCE continued its buying spree by subsequently acquiring the CTV television network and the *Globe and Mail*.

By April 2002, however, the Teleglobe deal had gone sour. The same day that BCE announced it would no longer support its floundering Teleglobe subsidiary—described as 'a $7 billion mistake'—Monty resigned as the company's CEO (McFarland et al., 2002). Teleglobe sought bankruptcy protection one month later. In September 2002, BCE also put CTV and the *Globe and Mail* up for sale (Ravensbergen, 2002).

CanWest Global Communications has made a concerted effort to emerge as a national player by cross-promoting its national television network (Global), its daily newspaper chain (Southam), and its Internet portal (canada.com). The portal consists of content from its newspaper and television newsrooms, and in several of its urban markets—e.g., Vancouver and Montreal—its newspaper and TV newsrooms co-operate on featured news series. For example, during the summer of 2001, the *Montreal Gazette* and the 5:30 p.m. Global television newscast teamed up on a series called 'Hot Neighbourhoods'. *Gazette* business reporter Mary Lamey appeared on Global's newscast to talk about one of Montreal's booming real estate markets, then the next morning she and *Gazette* columnist Mike Boone would write about that neighbourhood in the newspaper. Donald Babick, president and chief executive officer of Southam Publications, insists that while CanWest's convergence plan has not yet spawned short-term financial results, it is too soon to dismiss its long-term potential (Brethour, 2002).

What does convergence mean, then? Kevin G. Wilson (2002) writes: 'The stewardship of Canada's economic and cultural nervous system is literally in the hands of a handful of heavily indebted companies that have yet to demonstrate that the patchwork of companies they have assembled are capable of generating any beneficial synergies.'

related and unrelated businesses. Besides the advantages of scale conglomerates afford their owners, shareholder risk is reduced because the conglomerate is not dependent for its profits on any one industry. Convergence is the name given to the economic strategy media conglomerates employ in an attempt to create synergies among their media properties (see Table 8.3).

Tempering the Profit Motive

Because private-sector media companies operate on the basis of profit maximization, governments have seen fit to introduce policy measures—both regulations and inducements—to ensure the private sector makes a contribution to the production and dissemination of Canadian cultural products. Even the establishment of a Royal Commission can apply moral suasion to address an identified shortcoming in a particular industry.

In television broadcasting, for instance, American television programming is far more economically attractive to Canadian broadcasters than indigenous programming. First of all, it is generally 10 times cheaper for a Canadian broadcaster to buy an American show than to produce its own program. This is because American TV producers can recoup their costs of production in the huge, US domestic market, then offer their programming at bargain rates to foreign television networks. Second, there is much less risk for Canadian broadcasters in buying American programs that already have a track record of attracting audiences and advertisers than in developing their own shows from scratch. Finally, Canadian broadcasters can benefit directly from the publicity and media coverage that successful American TV shows generate. If Canadian broadcasters had to produce their own shows, they would have to market them, too.

As we discussed in Chapter 7, the vertical integration of the commercial film industry makes it difficult for Canadian feature films to penetrate exhibition markets. Because the same companies that own Hollywood movie studios have ownership ties to Canada's principal theatre chains, these companies have a vested interest in granting preference to their own films. The commercial theatres are also more inclined to book Hollywood films to benefit from both audience familiarity with what Hollywood produces and the publicity these films generate.

In other cultural industries, the private sector's reluctance to invest in Canadian cultural production is less easy to quantify. The success Canada has had in developing, with considerable state intervention, a popular music industry and a vibrant literary tradition since the 1960s seems to suggest that a certain amount of prejudice is at play in the private sector as well. That is, in spite of all evidence to the contrary, some media

Table 8.3 Converged Media Companies

Quebecor Inc.

PUBLISHING
- Newspapers: Sun Media newspaper chain with 8 metro dailies, 180 community papers
- Magazines: *7 Jours, Clin d'oeil, Dernière Heure, Échos Vedettes,* among others
- Books: Les Éditions internationales Alain Stanké, Les Éditions CEC, Éditions du Trécarré, among others

TELEVISION
- Vidéotron: cable TV provider with 1.5 million subscribers in Quebec
- TVA: owns 6 of 10 stations in TVA network; owns 49% of Global-affiliated CKMI-TV; specialty channel Le Canal Nouvelles and others
- Also owns 29.9% of southern Ontario all-news cable TV channel CablePulse 24

RADIO
- Radiomédia: group of 7 stations, including ratings leader CKAC in Montreal

NEW MEDIA
- Netgraphe: operates CANOE network of Internet properties, including canoe.ca portal
- Nurun: Web business applications
- Vidéotron: Internet service provider

RETAIL
- Archambault: retail chain of 12 book, music stores
- SuperClub Vidéotron: retail chain of video sales and rentals with 170 locations

CanWest Global Communications Corp.

PUBLISHING
- Newspapers: *National Post*, national daily newspaper; Southam Publications, chain of 11 metro dailies, 5 small-market dailies, 52 community papers

TELEVISION
- Global TV Network: 11 stations in 8 provinces; 3 independent stations (Hamilton, Victoria, Montreal); 2 CBC affiliates (Kelowna, Red Deer); Network Ten (Australia); TV3 and TV4 (New Zealand); TV3 (Ireland); UTV (Northern Ireland); specialty channels Prime TV, Men TV, Mystery, DejaView, Lone Star, Fox Sportsworld Canada, Xtreme Sports

FILM-TV
- Fireworks Entertainment finances and produces film and television programming
- Fireworks Television: program development (US)
- Fireworks International: television distribution (UK)
- Fireworks Pictures: film distribution
- Apple Box Productions: commercial production

RADIO
- 99.1 Jazz FM (Winnipeg), More FM network of 9 stations (New Zealand), Channel Z and The Breeze (New Zealand), 72% of Radioworks group with four networks comprising 27 stations (New Zealand)

NEW MEDIA
- canada.com: Internet portal for news and information
- Internet Broadcasting System
- LifeServ: Web site
- Medbroadcast
- All Sport Ventures: Internet service provider
- Faceoff.com: Web site

BCE Inc.

TELEPHONY
- Bell Canada: conventional telephone service
- Bell Mobility: wireless telephone service

NEW MEDIA
- Bell Globemedia Interactive: family of Web sites, including sympatico.ca and globeandmail.com
- BCE Emergis: e-commerce services

TELEVISION
- CTV: national television network of 21 owned and four independent affiliates
- Specialty channels: Report on Business TV, Talk TV, The Comedy Network, The Sports Network (TSN), Réseau des sports (RDS), Discovery Channel, and others
- Bell ExpressVu: satellite TV service

PUBLISHING
- Newspaper: *Globe and Mail*, national daily newspaper

Rogers Communications Inc.

TELEVISION
- Rogers Cable: Canada's largest cable TV provider, with 2.3 million customers in Ontario, New Brunswick, Newfoundland
- Rogers Broadcasting: multicultural channel CFMT (Toronto), Shopping Channel, Rogers SportsNet

TELEPHONY
- Rogers AT&T Wireless: 3.5 million wireless telephone subscribers

PUBLISHING
- Rogers Publishing: *Maclean's, Chatelaine, Flare, l'Actualité,* Canadian business and trade publications

NEW MEDIA
- Rogers Hi-Speed Internet: cable-based Internet service provider

RETAIL
- Rogers Video: chain of video sales and rentals in 260 locations

Sources: www.quebecor.com; www.canwestglobal.com; www.bce.ca; www.rogers.com (Accessed 29 Oct. 2002).

Figure 8.1 Cross-Ownership in Nine Canadian Cities by Market Share of Local Television Newscasts and Local Newspapers

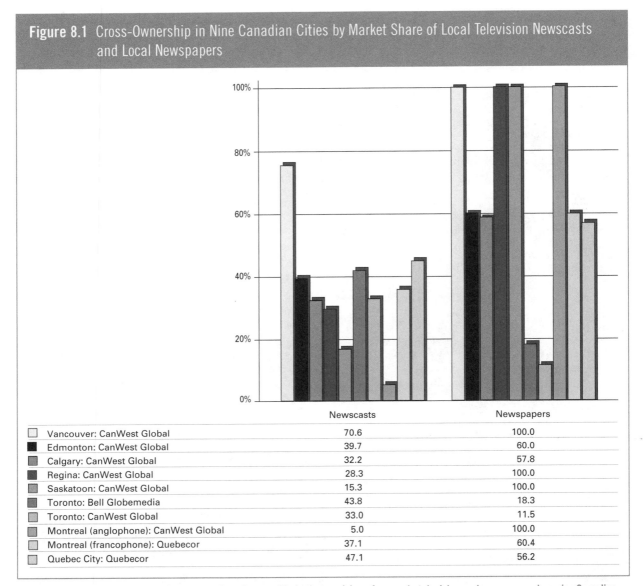

		Newscasts	Newspapers
☐	Vancouver: CanWest Global	70.6	100.0
■	Edmonton: CanWest Global	39.7	60.0
▨	Calgary: CanWest Global	32.2	57.8
▨	Regina: CanWest Global	28.3	100.0
▨	Saskatoon: CanWest Global	15.3	100.0
▨	Toronto: Bell Globemedia	43.8	18.3
☐	Toronto: CanWest Global	33.0	11.5
▨	Montreal (anglophone): CanWest Global	5.0	100.0
☐	Montreal (francophone): Quebecor	37.1	60.4
☐	Quebec City: Quebecor	47.1	56.2

Figure 8.1 is a clear illustration of concentration of ownership in the provision of news via television and newspapers in major Canadian cities. The possibility of a plurality of messages being delivered by a variety of media owners is very restricted in many Canadian cities.

owners simply do not believe Canadians can produce popular and profitable forms of entertainment.

There is no denying the tensions between the public good and the private commercial interest. The Broadcasting Act recognizes these tensions by assigning social responsibilities to all licence-holders, including minimum Canadian-content regulations and special additional responsibilities for the public sector. Section 19 of the Income Tax Act provides recognition in the form of effectively restricting ownership of Canadian newspapers, magazines, and

broadcasting stations—i.e., any medium that accepts advertising—to Canadians. It accomplishes this by denying tax deductions to advertisers in newspapers and magazines directed at Canadian consumers unless those publications have at least 75 per cent Canadian ownership. (There is currently pressure on the federal government to ease this ownership restriction to increase the pool of potential media buyers and thereby decrease the numbers of media properties held by large Canadian conglomerates.) The public goals of communication are also recognized in the form of postal subsidies to Canadian publications and in the support policies of the Department of Canadian Heritage (formerly the Department of Communications) for cultural industries, even if these subsidies are under review by a federal government committed to balancing its books. In the area of film, support policies, targeted programs, and public agencies such as the National Film Board and Telefilm Canada are recognition of public goals. Complementary provincial support policies demonstrate how deeply felt these public goals are. In telecommunications, the notion of common carriage also reflects public goals.

Policies directed at the production and broadcasting of high-quality indigenous programming have had varying success from country to country. Only in specific instances have governments and industry been able to identify mechanisms that simultaneously encourage high-quality indigenous content and either increase or maintain profits. Until the late 1980s in Canada, the private sector could not be persuaded by any form of policy to develop and sell high-quality indigenous television programming. In contrast, the United Kingdom was more successful, with Australia somewhere in between. The status of the United Kingdom as a centre of English-speaking peoples, the articulation of the notion of the public interest, and the concomitant role of export markets have contributed greatly to the ability of its private sector to produce attractive programming.

In spite of its limited abilities to pursue cultural goals, the private commercial sector is making continuous gains in its participation in media industries. One factor in this is a general reorientation underway in industrialized economies. In the post-war years, the industrialized world followed one element of Keynesian economics, that is, state spending to encourage economic growth. However, once their economies were humming, Western states never stopped spending more than their net revenues. The result was that nations saddled themselves with potentially crippling debts. A general trend in Western countries since the early 1980s has been to look for areas of state involvement that can be cut at a savings to the public purse. Publicly owned media have been one area in which public spending has been cut, while services have been expanded through increased private participation.

Another factor is that, over time, public (and existing private) corporations have identified which audiences can be served by what means to make what level of profit. Program types, employee levels, and working relationships have all been established. The knowledge infrastructure now exists and can be transferred to new firms through the hiring of qualified personnel.

As well, new technologies (specifically, communication satellites, computer applications, and fibre optics) have been developed that challenge the ability of states to control electronic communication and their legitimacy in doing so because, through innovation, limits on carrying capacity (radio spectrum scarcity) are quickly disappearing. In the case of satellites, when a signal from space can deliver programs to all homes in a country, in the context of international covenants affirming the freedom to receive information, what should be the position of the state?

In the face of insistent requests from the private sector to be allowed to engage in profit-making activity that can serve a market, if not the public good, it is difficult for states to argue that cultural goals directly contradict such activities. This is especially the case in the presence of technology able to facilitate the activities. Whenever audiences watch or listen to a program, however limited in enlightenment that program may be, cultural content is being transmitted. In addition, basic human rights to have broad access to information come into play, specifically the right of an individual to receive information.

Implications of Private Media Ownership

For those who believe that communication in all its forms involves much more than satisfying markets, the appropriation by private enterprise of a greater and greater share of the mass communication sphere is of great concern. While economists argue that the free-market organization of cultural production is the most efficient means of giving consumers what they want, political economists maintain that the commercial organization of cultural production limits choice and discriminates between those members of the public who have disposable income to spend on advertised products and those who don't. This is particularly the case when corporate concentration limits the number of, and distinctions between, producers and distributors (see Mosco, 1996: 182–205).

In the realm of the mass media, private enterprise is seen as having two particular social benefits. First, in keeping with Adam Smith's invisible hand, it is said to stimulate the provision of affordable goods and services for which consumers have expressed a need or desire through their purchasing decisions. Second, because advertising subsidizes the media, consumers are able to receive content either for free (e.g., radio) or at a minimal cost (e.g., daily newspapers).

These benefits, of course, are not as straightforward as they may seem. First of all, anticipating consumer demand is an inexact science, notwithstanding polls and focus groups. Consumers can only make choices among those already offered—supply to a large extent governs demand—and media managers have been frustrated time and again in trying to determine which new services will attract consumers. Media economists have demonstrated, for example, that most major Hollywood movies lose money, and the studios depend on their blockbuster hits to make up for their far more numerous flops (Leblanc, 1990: 287). The same applies to television series; each new fall season introduces more losers than winners, shows that are cancelled after only a few weeks. Advertising and other forms of publicity, of course, play a role in generating excitement and consumer demand around new films, TV shows, music recordings, and book releases, but consumer tastes remain very hard to anticipate.

Second, it is simply not accurate to say consumers receive some media programming for free, thanks to advertising. Instead, consumers pay for it in a roundabout way. Even if we do not directly hand over any money to a radio station to listen to its programming, we pay for that programming nonetheless every time we buy an advertised product. Advertising costs, in other words, are built into the sale price of potato chips and breakfast cereal, so that a share of the money we spend on groceries, snacks, clothing, beer, gasoline, and cosmetics is in turn used to pay for media programming.

Media economists also argue that we pay with our time—we literally *pay attention*—whenever we watch television or listen to the radio, and that time, that attention, is what advertisers seek access to (Picard, 1989). This is a key point to understanding how commercial media work within the economic system. In order to generate profits, managers of commercial media seek to attract audiences to their programming to sell those audiences to advertisers. Putting it another way, communications theorist Dallas Smythe (1994: 270–1) argues that what advertisers buy is not simply air time or newspaper space, but 'the services

of audiences with predictable specifications who will pay attention in predictable numbers and at particular times to particular means of communications'. Through increasingly sophisticated audience measurement techniques, media managers collect data on their audiences—not only the size of the audience is determined, but demographic factors such as income, education, age, and sex—and sell advertisers access to the kinds of audiences that will be interested in buying their product or service. Mass media content, then, is merely 'an inducement (gift, bribe or "free lunch") to recruit potential members of the audience and to maintain their loyal attention.' Smythe writes that 'the free lunch consists of materials which whet the audience members' appetite and thus (1) attract and keep them attending to the programme, newspaper or magazine, and (2) cultivate a mood conducive to favourable reaction to the explicit and implicit advertisers' messages.'

Private ownership of the communications media raises four particular concerns. The first is that private enterprise casts cultural production as commercial enterprise, whereby the goal of communication becomes the generation of profit. This form of organization imposes commercial constraints on communication. Communication as commercial enterprise creates pressures to maximize entertainment value and to minimize difficulty and complexity, and to provide communication in an advertising-friendly or consumption-friendly environment. In the medium of television, for example, competing programs are only a click of the remote away. Programming that is difficult, challenging, or slow-paced may have trouble holding audiences, and could be hard for broadcasters to support. This includes newscasts, which, according to the expectations of commercial enterprise, need to maximize ratings in a competitive environment even if that means sacrificing the quality and integrity of their journalism.

A second concern is that the increasing convergence of media properties reinforces the profit motive and moves owners further and further from their core areas of business. That is, conglomerates are in business to make money rather than to make movies or newspapers or books or radio programs. The goal of the conglomerate is to serve shareholders and paying customers, rather than society at large. By privileging the profit motive above all else, the creation of conglomerates weakens the owners' commitment to core areas of business; media properties may become a lesser

As this cartoon illustrates, the increase in media offerings—in this case, as provided by specialty-TV channels—is largely an illusion. (Cam/Regina Leader Post. Reprinted by permission.)

priority within the conglomerate than, for example, its real estate holdings. Managers can therefore revise the conglomerate's mandate, as Thomson has done by moving away from newspapers into more specialized media, or abandon media industries altogether for more lucrative industries.

Related to this is a third concern. The broader a conglomerate's reach, the more businesses it is involved in, the greater the chance for a conflict of interest between its media business and its other holdings. Critical themes—e.g., environmentalism, feminism, poverty—in newspaper and magazine stories, TV documentaries, or radio programs could threaten the earnings or community standing of the conglomerate's other holdings. In such cases, the conglomerate's media properties will feel pressure to avoid certain subject areas, depriving the public of a full airing of important social issues or confining their discussion within safe parameters.

Finally, the trend towards corporate concentration has reduced substantially our sources of information at precisely the same point in history when our dependence on communications media for our knowledge of the world has increased. The plethora of TV and radio channels, books, magazines, newspapers, music recordings, and video cassettes available to us is largely illusory; it disguises the fact that many of these media are the products of a mere handful of large corporations. If we are to take seriously our role as citizens in democratic society, we should be encouraging the greatest variety of information sources possible, as well as an increase in distinct media channels for us to express ourselves.

Taken together, these trends of private ownership have reduced our sources of information and narrowed the range of what can be said and how it can be expressed.

Summary

There is no natural or inevitable way to organize mass communication. The media are social institutions structured in various ways according to their technological characteristics, the resources they draw upon, and the socio-political context in which they operate. If all media organizations have something in common, however, it is that they participate in the economy by generating profits for media owners, by providing communication services to their audiences, by advertising goods and services, and by providing employment.

The mass media in Canada are owned both privately and publicly, but all operate in a mixed economy. No media industry in Canada is governed exclusively by free-market economics. Even newspaper publishing, which comes closest to an exclusively private enterprise, is subject to federal government regulations regarding ownership intended to protect newspapers from foreign takeover and foreign competition. Nor is any media organization in Canada immune to the demands of the marketplace; even the publicly owned CBC must pay attention to ratings and advertising revenues.

The critical difference between public and private forms of media ownership pertains to their bottom lines. Public ownership is devoted to providing communications as a public service, to employ the mass media for social and/or national goals. Private ownership is devoted to providing communications for the profit of media owners. These distinctions are fundamental because they speak to the role communication is assigned in Canadian society. The economistic view perceives communication, first and foremost, as commercial enterprise, subjecting all forms of cultural production to commercial criteria of supply and demand. The culturalist view regards cultural products as much more than commodities to be exchanged in the marketplace. They are expressions of a culture as a way of life and as a system of beliefs and values. They are expressions of ideas and images that help a culture to imagine itself and to articulate its priorities. As private enterprise has encroached on more and more areas of mass communication in Canadian society, concerns have been raised over the increasing commercialization of cultural production, conglomerate ownership of media organizations, conflicts of interest between media companies and other businesses owned by the same parent, and corporate concentration.

RELATED WEB SITES

Alliance Atlantis Communications Inc.:
www.allianceatlantis.com
This site provides corporate information and news about programming from Alliance Atlantis.

AOL Time Warner: www.aoltimewarner.com
The AOL Time Warner site lists its vast holdings and includes news about programming as well as corporate information.

Broadcast Dialogue: www.broadcastdialogue.com
This site offers directory and contact information for all Canadian radio and television stations.

Canadian Community Newspaper Association: www.ccna.ca
Industry news and ownership information can be found at this official site.

Canadian Newspaper Association: www.cna-acj.ca
Like the CCNA site, this official site of the CNA provides industry news and ownership information.

FURTHER READINGS

Gasher, Mike. 1997. 'From Sacred Cows to White Elephants: Cultural Policy Under Seige', in Joy Cohnstaedt and Yves Frechette, eds, *Canadian Themes* (Montreal: Association for Canadian Studies) 19: 13–29. This article traces the thematic shifts in Canadian cultural policy from the Aird Commission to the Applebaum-Hébert Report.

Heilbroner, Robert L. 1980. *The Worldly Philosophers: The Lives, Times, and Ideas of the Great Economic Thinkers.* New York: Simon and Schuster. This is a very readable reference guide to history's leading economic theorists.

Mosco, Vincent. 1996. *The Political Economy of Communication: Rethinking and Renewal.* London: Sage Publications. Mosco's theoretical work applies contemporary political-economic thought to communication and cultural industries.

Picard, Robert G. 1989. *Media Economics: Concepts and Issues.* Newbury Park, Calif.: Sage Publications. This is a useful introduction to the basic terms and concepts in media economics.

STUDY QUESTIONS

1. Why are the same media organized differently in otherwise similar countries like Canada, the US, Great Britain, and France?

2. What did Adam Smith mean by the 'invisible hand' of the market? To what extent does his economic thinking apply today?

3. What is the rationale for state intervention in the cultural economy?

4. What are 'externalities' and how are they pertinent to the discussion of media economics?

5. What are five ways in which Canadian governments are implicated in the structure of the media industries?

6. To what extent does advertising on CBC television distort the public broadcaster's central mission?

7. What are the principal distinctions between public and private forms of ownership?

8. What are three forms that private ownership of the media can assume?

9. What is media convergence and what does it imply for media content?

10. Why is it often more beneficial for Canadian television networks to buy US programs than to produce their own?

11. What does it mean to say that media sell audiences to advertisers?

LEARNING OUTCOMES

- To explain that there is no natural and inevitable way to organize media.
- To demonstrate the extent to which all media participate in the economy.
- To show that media are not simply products of technology, but are also shaped by the resources they draw upon and the socio-political context in which they operate.
- To point out that no media industry in Canada is governed exclusively by free-market economics.
- To underline the fundamental distinctions between public and private forms of ownership.
- To discuss the implications for media content of public and private forms of ownership.
- To provide a critical evaluation of the increasing privatization and deregulation of the Canadian media.

CHAPTER 9

Journalists as Content Producers

Introduction

Content producers are central to the whole media enterprise. Journalists, radio hosts, magazine photographers, television producers, film editors—all have vastly different job descriptions and work environments, but they all participate in the manufacture of the content we see in our newspapers, books, and magazines; hear on our radios; and see on our television, computer, and cinema screens. The stories and images we see, whether based on fact or fiction, are never presented simply or 'naturally', but are instead highly constructed. This process of construction involves a series of choices about what stories to tell and how to tell them. It comes into play both when content producers are trying to portray reality as accurately as possible and when they are trying to emphasize a particular point of view or style of presentation. After all, no story tells the whole story and no picture gives the full picture. This chapter posits journalism as a practice of content production and, as such, considers who Canadian journalists are and the cultural, legal, and institutional contexts of their work.

News as Content Production

Like other forms of content, news is produced, and much like other mass media—cinema, TV—news production is a form of storytelling. News items are usually referred to as 'stories', and, like other kinds of stories, they consist of characters, conflicts between characters, and temporal and geographical settings. This has implications for how we think about news and for the role journalism plays in society. News stories, while based on actual events and real people, never simply 'mirror' reality, as some journalists would contend. A mirror, after all, shows us only what is placed before it, nothing more and nothing less; the person holding the mirror may have control over where to point it, but the depiction the mirror offers is always a simple and direct, if unorganized, reflection. The mirror metaphor and the associated notion of 'reflection' do not adequately describe the role of journal-

ists as content producers. If news media were mirrors, all news reports about the same event would be identical to one another. Clearly, they are not.

Nor is news simply gathered. Such a conception of journalism underestimates the degree of selection that goes into producing a news report and the extent to which events must meet a news organization's particular standards of 'newsworthiness'. Each day news reporters and their editors or producers face an infinite number of events from which to fashion their news stories. They receive far more invitations to press conferences than they could possibly cover and they receive far more press releases than they could ever use. Journalists make choices about what to cover based on what they perceive to have 'news value', what fits within their news organization's particular areas of coverage (politics, business, sports, crime, the arts), and what they believe will interest their audience. The values journalists apply to assess newsworthiness were described in our discussion of media form in Chapter 4. To reiterate, deciding what is news is a subjective operation, involving reporters and their editors or producers in a complex process of selection. While news judgement is most often exercised intuitively by journalists under time pressure in the field, media scholars have identified a number of criteria that render some events news and others not news. Melvin Mencher (2000: 68–76), for example, identifies seven determinants of newsworthiness: timeliness (events that are immediate or recent); impact (events that affect many people); prominence (events involving well-known people or institutions); proximity (events that are geographically or 'emotionally close' to the audience); conflict (events pitting two sides against one another); peculiarity (events that deviate from the everyday); and currency (long-simmering events that suddenly emerge as objects of attention).

Figure 9.1 illustrates the process by which an event becomes news. It demonstrates that within a veritable universe of daily events going on around the world, only some are selected by journalists as worth reporting. As Jaap van Ginneken (1998: 31) makes clear, journalists' perceptions inform these decisions. 'News

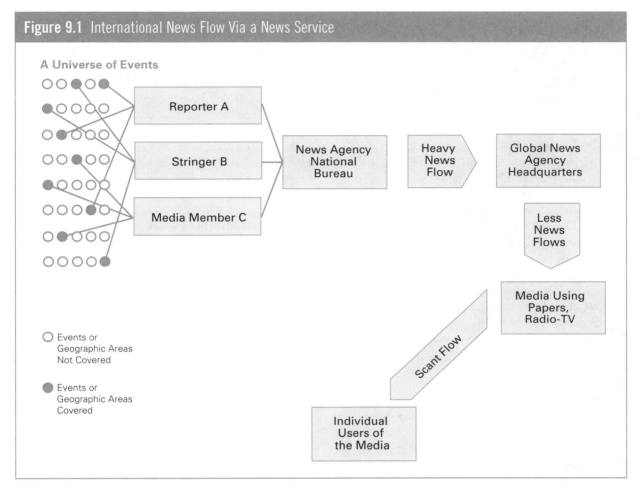

Figure 9.1 International News Flow Via a News Service

Of the many news events, only some are covered by reporters, 'stringers', or members relaying stories to the bureau of the global news agency. Editors there forward important news items to the world headquarters of the agency. Editors at world headquarters select what they think newsworthy. Finally, individual readers, listeners, or viewers decide what international news they will be attentive to. What began as hundreds of events and items has gradually dwindled to only a handful.

Source: Al Hester, 'International News Agencies', in Alan Wells, ed., *Mass Communications: A World View* (Palo Alto, Calif.: Mayfield Publishing, 1974). Reproduced with permission of the author.

is something which is (perceived as) "new" within a specific society, and not something which is (perceived as) "nothing new". It is something which is (perceived as) unexpected, extraordinary, abnormal, not something which is (perceived as) expected, ordinary, normal.' To cite a simple example, normal rush-hour traffic volume on an urban freeway is not news, while the unusual case of a seven-car pileup that kills three people and closes the freeway for an hour is.

This process of selection has compelled some theorists to perceive journalists—especially middle managers, such as editors and news directors—as **gatekeepers**, people who sift through a huge number of

events and decide which events will be covered and which stories will be broadcast or published. While gatekeeping is an evocative metaphor, it is only a *partial* explanation of the news production process, applicable only to some stages of selection. A newspaper assignment editor, for example, chooses among an assortment of scheduled daily press conferences, meetings, and speeches and decides which will be 'staffed' by a reporter and which will not. This is a form of gatekeeping. Similarly, wire editors will sort through hundreds of wire-service stories from around the world each day to select those to be considered for publication. This, too, is gatekeeping.

However, there are limitations to the metaphor of gatekeeping for describing the process by which news is produced. While it accounts for the question of *what* the news organization will cover, it leaves aside the equally important issue of *how* an event will be covered. It ignores, for example, the extent to which wire-service stories are revised by copy editors and the different 'play'—length and prominence—they receive from one news organization to the next. The same news item may occupy the first two and half minutes of the six o'clock news on one channel, complete with interviews and illustrative footage, and warrant only 15 seconds of the anchor's narration on another channel. Same event, but different news stories. Newspapers, too, assign relative importance to news stories by how they play them—whether as a front-page story with a bold headline above the fold or as a back-page brief. Again, the same event may receive completely different treatment from one newspaper to the next.

The gatekeeping metaphor also ignores the creative nature of content production. Every news organization establishes an identity for its audience and its advertisers through the style of journalism it practises—serious and thorough, entertaining and concise, etc. Developing and maintaining that identity is achieved by establishing a certain kind of editorial presence through the assignment of resources and the shaping of content. Tabloid newspapers like the *Ottawa Sun* and *Le Journal de Montréal*, for example, pay a considerable amount of attention to crime stories, covering the police beat and the courthouse quite heavily. Their news stories are relatively short and written in a lively and provocative style, and their pages are filled with bold headlines and lots of photographs. More sober broadsheets like the *Globe and Mail* and *Le Devoir*, on the other hand, pay much more attention to political, foreign affairs, and cultural reporting. They tend to feature much longer, in-depth stories and fewer photographs. These two kinds of newspapers are interested in very different kinds of stories and news presentations. Examining how this editorial style is created opens the selection process to many more factors than the notion of gatekeeping can accommodate. Nonetheless, the gatekeeping metaphor draws our attention to the refusal, or negative-selecting function, of editors and producers. In other words, we need to think about what is left out of the selection process.

A more precise way to think of journalists as content producers is through the metaphor of the frame. That is, through the use of words, images, and sounds, journalists 'frame' reality. If we think of the empty newspaper page or the blank television screen as a picture frame, it is journalists who decide how to fill that frame each day, by inserting into the frame particular stories, visuals, and graphics and by leaving out much more material. They decide not only which events to include in the news frame, but also how to depict those events: how much coverage to provide, what prominence to assign the story in the newspaper or broadcast, what aspects or angle of the story to emphasize.

The metaphor of the frame implies there are borders or limits to what a news organization can properly present as news. These limits are defined by such practical considerations as the size of the 'news hole' (the amount of editorial space available in print journalism) or 'news block' (the amount of air time available in a news broadcast), the costs involved in producing the coverage (does it involve travel and hotel accommodation?), and the availability of reporting staff. These limits are also governed by the more subjective criteria of an event's news value and how well it suits the news organization's particular areas of coverage. We would expect a news organization specializing in arts coverage to send its own reporter to the Toronto International Film Festival or the Juno Awards presentations, rather than rely on the Canadian Press wire service, just as we would expect a news organization specializing in sports to send its own reporter to the Stanley Cup final, regardless of which teams are playing. News coverage is also governed by a given news organization's various political stances, whether or not they are explicitly stated. Think about how news organizations may react differently, even if the distinctions are subtle, in their coverage of labour-management disputes, same-sex marriages, cuts in social spending, or international trade disputes. In her groundbreaking study of news practices, media scholar Gaye Tuchman (1978: 1) used the frame metaphor to emphasize the necessarily restricted view of the world journalism provides:

> Like any frame that delineates a world, the news frame may be considered problematic. The view through a window depends upon whether the window is large or small, has many panes or few, whether the glass is opaque or clear, whether the window faces a street or a backyard. The unfolding scene also depends upon where one stands, far

or near, craning one's neck to the side, or gazing straight ahead, eyes parallel to the wall in which the window is encased.

No news organization can cover every event from every possible angle. Therefore, what stories it includes and excludes can reveal a great deal about the news judgement it applies when producing its daily news package.

Ideals of Journalism

If news, then, is constructed, much like other kinds of media content, it is also subject to particular ideals that distinguish journalism from other forms of story-telling. Journalism has a fundamental guiding ideal: the quest for truth. That ideal is centred on the search for information and based on a commitment, in the words of the Kent Commission, not only to treat 'events and persons with fairness and impartiality, but also [to consider] the welfare of the community and of humanity in general in a spirit devoid of cynicism' (Canada, 1981: 23–4).

The performance of this truth-seeking function is the foundation for freedom of the press, facilitating the circulation of information and ideas for the ben-efit of all and extending the basic democratic right of freedom of expression granted to all individuals into the realm of the mass media. As scholars Robert Martin and Stuart Adam (1991: 27) note, freedom of expression can be seen as 'an essential pre-condition to the creation and maintenance of democracy itself. . . . A democratic society must not only permit, but encourage, the widest possible participation of all its members in its economic, social, and cultural affairs.' Freedom of the press is a notion that is both informed by and supportive of democracy. The flipside of the *right* to freedom of the press is the news media's *responsibility* to inform Canadians as engaged citizens—rather than consumers or spectators—in a democratic society.

The struggle for freedom of the press is ongoing and journalists are at the forefront of efforts to extend public access to information in both formal and informal ways. Journalists are often highly dependent on official sources and their own contacts for information, and the news media's role as 'fourth estate' grants journalists their moral authority to gain access to the people and institutions that populate their reportage: politicians, bureaucrats, police officers, community leaders, celebrities, Parliament, the court system, the stock exchange, and so on.

FREEDOM OF THE PRESS

Constitutional guarantees and universal declarations are important, but they define freedom of the press in largely abstract terms. The real, concrete meaning of freedom of the press is derived from its daily exercise by those journalists who push at the boundaries of what can be broadcast and what can be published.

Journalists—reporters, photographers, editors, producers, publishers—exercise freedom of the press when they report what is truly new and important to the public interest, when they broaden the range of debate, when they expand the horizons of what can be reported, imagined, revealed, criticized. Journalists also exercise freedom of the press when they hold their own news organizations to the ideals of their journalistic calling, especially when that news organization may have to pay a political or economic price for its reportage.

Freedom of the press would be meaningless as a human right if journalists never exposed scandal, if they never revealed information government officials preferred not to divulge, if they never quoted critics of powerful peo-ple and powerful institutions, if they never drew attention to hypocrisy, greed, or arrogance—if, in other words, they never gave anyone cause to restrict press freedoms. As journalism educator John Miller (1998: 115) puts it: 'Freedom is like muscle: use it or lose it.'

The right to freedom of the press is exerted not only in exceptional, headline-grabbing cases—e.g., the Somalia affair, Shawinigate, the Pentagon Papers, the Watergate scandal—but on a daily basis, in countless small ways. Journalists are giving meaning to freedom of the press every time they reveal more than their sources are willing to share with the public, every time they undermine the propaganda disseminated by corporate and political communications officers, every time they introduce factual evidence to accompany decision-makers' opinions.

To exercise freedom of the press, then, is to give it concrete meaning, even when—especially when—it means discomforting news sources, antagonizing public officials, prompting court challenges, even irritating fellow journalists.

The term 'fourth estate', which refers to the role the news media play in the governing of a democratic society, originates with the press struggle to gain access to the proceedings of the British Parliament in the late eighteenth and early nineteenth centuries. Even after the right of freedom of the press had been won in Britain—formally recognized in the Bill of Rights of 1689—journalists were prohibited from Parliament, which prevented public scrutiny of the government's affairs. Throughout the eighteenth century, however, this prohibition was repeatedly defied, until the right to report on parliamentary proceedings was recognized on a de facto basis after 1771 and legally confirmed in 1803. The role of the press in Parliament was institutionalized with the construction of a press gallery in 1831 (Osler, 1993: 61). Thomas Babington, Lord MacCauley, is believed to have coined the term 'fourth estate' in 1828, when he wrote:

> The gallery in which the reporters sit has become a fourth estate of the realm. The publication of the debates, a practice which seemed to the most liberal statesman of the old school full of danger to the great safeguards of public liberty, is now regarded by many persons as a safeguard tantamount, and more than tantamount, to the rest altogether. (Quoted in Brucker, 1981: 30)

This was a recognition of the place of journalism in representing citizens as a kind of watchdog over their governors.

The news media today fulfill the role of a fourth estate by reporting on legislative debates and other government business, and by pressuring governments to increase access to information. All legislatures in Canada have press galleries populated by print, radio, and television reporters, and journalists also regularly attend the public meetings of municipal governments. Of all the coverage the news media provide, political reportage is considered to be the most closely related to journalism's role in democratic society: providing citizens with the information they need to be independent and self-governing.

The guiding ideals of journalism are socially produced and thus evolve over time. Today's highly regarded ideals of independence and objectivity have their historical roots in the period between about 1880 and 1920, when newspapers were transformed from a partisan press supported by political patronage and subscriptions from like-minded readers into a mass, commercial press that gradually became more and more dependent on advertising revenue (see Sotiron, 1997). In this period, urbanization and increased literacy rates created sizable markets of potential newspaper readers in Canada's growing cities; technological advances in printing (for instance, faster rotary presses) made it possible to increase the size and speed of press runs; and the extension of railway lines facilitated regional delivery of both newspapers and newsprint. The result was that newspapers increased their circulations, which made them increasingly accessible to readers, more attractive to advertisers, and less beholden to political parties.

As newspapers became mass media, they could no longer afford to be seen as propaganda sheets for political parties because that would risk antagonizing both potential readers and advertisers. Historian Minko Sotiron (1997: 4) writes: 'This period in Canadian history marked the transition from the politically oriented newspaper of the nineteenth century to the corporate entity of the twentieth.' Newspapers gradually began to assert their independence from political patronage—even if they maintained a clear political leaning—by cutting their formal political ties and by making a clearer distinction in their pages between 'objective' reporting and commentary (see also Schudson, 1978).

Today, the ideal of objectivity remains central to journalism's code of conduct, even though it is undermined somewhat by the fact that news reportage is the product of the subjective processes of selection and interpretation discussed earlier in this chapter. How can any news report be objective when it has been produced by journalists who subscribe to both personal and institutional values? It may be tempting to dispense with the notion of objectivity altogether. But communications scholar Robert A. Hackett (1996: 40–3) argues that in spite of declarations that objectivity is passé and has been replaced by 'advocacy' or 'critical' journalism, 'the ethos of objectivity, broadly conceived, continues to dominate North American journalism. Audiences and sources continue to expect their news to be free from the taint of personal bias.' While notions of 'fairness' and 'balance' are often substituted for objectivity, Hackett remarks that 'very few journalists would want to be accused of lacking objectivity.'

There are, however, more sophisticated ways to think about it. Jaap van Ginneken, for one, proposes that objectivity and subjectivity be seen in relative rather than absolute terms:

> An observation report is said to be 'objective' if it is governed by the characteristics of the object, that which is being perceived; an observation report is said to be 'subjective' if it is governed by the characteristics of the subject who is perceiving. Complete objectivity or subjectivity are only extremes on a scale; they are never reached, because most observation reports are governed by varying degrees of inter-subjectivity, that is to say, by varying degrees of agreement between subjects about the characteristics of the object.

In other words, the closer a news story sticks to the agreed-upon facts of a case, the more objective it is. The more a news story deals with people's opinions, the more subjective it is. Alternatively, Bill Kovach and Tom Rosenstiel (2001: 71–9) attribute objectivity to the method journalists employ to determine what is factual.

> When the concept [of objectivity] originally evolved, it was not meant to imply that journalists were free of bias. Quite the contrary. The term began to appear as part of journalism early in the last century, particularly in the 1920s, out of a growing recognition that journalists were full of bias, often unconsciously. Objectivity called for journalists to develop a consistent method of testing information—a transparent approach to evidence—precisely so that personal and cultural biases would not undermine the accuracy of their work.

In this vein, Kovach and Rosenstiel advocate a journalism of verification—seeking multiple witnesses, checking facts, disclosing information about sources, asking many sides for comment—rather than a journalism of assertion.

Plenty of disagreement remains among journalists and scholars about the translation of journalistic ideals into practice. How well do the news media live up to their responsibility of informing the public? To what degree are the news media independent and objective? Abstract ideals are also subject to material constraints, and the extent to which we rely on the media for information about our world—the extent to which we live in 'second-hand worlds', as the

American sociologist C. Wright Mills once put it— underlines the importance of scrutinizing our sources of information. Who are journalists and under what legal and institutional constraints do they practise?

Newsmakers

Journalism is often described as a profession, even though, unlike the teaching, medical, and legal professions, it has no regulatory body and requires no mandatory formal training. Anyone who practises journalism, whether as a freelancer or as a staff member of a news organization, is a journalist. This does not mean, however, that the field is wide open. There are a limited number of news organizations in Canada and their hiring practices reveal that journalism remains an exclusive occupation. Increasingly, news organizations expect their new recruits to have a degree from one of the growing number of post-secondary journalism programs in Canada.

The most recent data available portray those who populate the newsrooms of Canada's news organizations as predominantly young, white, middle-class males with a higher level of education than the Canadian average. Canada has approximately 12,000 journalists working full-time, 30 per cent of whom work for daily newspapers, 27 per cent for radio, 22 per cent for television, 18 per cent for weekly newspapers, and about 3 per cent for news magazines and wire services. The national public broadcaster is the single most important employer of news workers; CBC/Radio-Canada alone accounts for 19 per cent of all journalists in Canada (Pritchard and Sauvageau, 1999: 15–21).

In a survey of more than 500 journalists conducted in May 1996, researchers David Pritchard and Florian Sauvageau determined that the average age of journalists in Canada is 39.7 years. Seventy-two per cent of Canadian journalists are men, with a high of 77 per cent in daily newspapers. Men outnumber women in all media, with the most equitable split in television news, where 64 per cent of journalists are men, 36 per cent women. While 56 per cent of Canadian journalists hold a university degree, this percentage ranges from 65 per cent at daily newspapers to 41 per cent at community weekly papers. One of the most remarkable observations made by Pritchard and Sauvageau in sketching their demographic profile is the fact that 97.7 per cent of Canadian journalists are white (ibid., 15–19).

In the state-regulated broadcasting sphere, inclusivity is a prominent theme of the Broadcasting Act (1991). Section 3(d)(iii) of the Act declares that the Canadian broadcasting system should:

> through its programming and the employment opportunities arising out of its operations, serve the needs and interests, and reflect the circumstances and aspirations, of Canadian men, women and children, including equal rights, the linguistic duality and multicultural and multiracial nature of Canadian society and the special place of aboriginal peoples within that society . . . . (Canada, 1991)

As discussed in Chapter 6, federal broadcast legislation has shifted its priority from the extension of radio and television services to all parts of the Canadian territory to one that enshrines the 'broadcasting rights' of three specific groups: women, Native peoples, and multicultural/multiracial communities. Lorna Roth (1996: 73) writes: 'Each has the right to be fairly portrayed on the airwaves and equitably represented on staffs throughout all broadcasting services—public,

private, and community.' Research, however, indicates that the Canadian news media remain far from attaining this goal.

Inclusivity is an important issue in a period of globalization and in a country as culturally and racially diverse as Canada, and newsmaking should bear some resemblance to the makeup of Canadian society, both in the content generated and in the people employed. Clearly, *who* reports the news has implications for both *what* gets covered and *how*.

As the preceding section of this chapter outlined, there is considerable room for interpretation in judging the news value and the appropriate presentation of a particular event or issue. Therefore, journalists' life experiences—their assumptions, their biases, their prejudices, their values—affect their reportage. In a report to the Canadian Race Relations Foundation, researchers Frances Henry and Carol Tator (2000: 169) concluded that journalists were not objective, detached, or neutral in their reporting. 'They are highly selective, in their writing. Often their own sense of social location, experiences, values and worldviews, as well as the interests and positionality of publishers and newspaper owners, act as an invisible

MEDIA BUSTERS MUFFLED

In Canada, one of the world's most concentrated print media markets, direct-action media critics are becoming the story that dares not go to press.

In January, reporter Mike Roberts of British Columbia's *Province* newspaper went to work on a story about Guerrilla Media, a covert band of Canadian culture jammers who publicize their media criticisms by wrapping mainstream newspapers in mock covers as they await sale in distribution boxes.

With research complete, Roberts sat down with his editors to discuss the approach he should take to writing the piece. 'We'd rather you didn't,' is the response he recalls.

Roberts says his editors at the paper—owned [at the time] by Conrad Black, the media titan who [controlled] 60 per cent of Canada's dailies—told him they didn't want to give publicity to an organization that breaks the law. Given that *Province* reporters regularly cover such protests as sit-ins and blockades, the reason Guerrilla Media was made an exception is 'an interesting question,' says Roberts.

Reporters tread carefully around their employers' vested interests, Robert notes. 'I was cognizant that this story

would be a tricky one to get through,' he says. 'That's the first time that situation has arisen with me at the paper. That's the first time I've been asked to not do a story.'

Adele Weder, a Vancouver-based freelancer, experienced a similar Blackout after accepting an assignment from Conrad Black's new Canada-wide daily, the *National Post*. This time, the topic was *Adbusters* magazine, including its campaign against Black, the *Post*, and corporate concentration of media ownership.

In May, Weder told *Adbusters* editor Kalle Lasn that her article had been accepted by her editors and would be published once she gathered quotes from *Post* editor-in-chief Ken Whyte and from Black himself. Shortly thereafter, Weder was told the story would not be going to press.

'They told me they killed it,' said Weder. 'I'm disappointed with the cancellation of the piece, but it's not my place to comment on what might have happened.'

In the *Post* offices, 'killed' is considered too harsh a word. Harriet O'Brien, the section editor in charge of Weder's assignment, says the piece was 'held over'—so far for three months and counting.

filter to screen out alternative viewpoints and perspectives.' A relatively young reporting staff, for example, may be less aware of, and less sensitive to, issues that pertain to an aging Canadian population, such as the future of the Canada Pension Plan or the costs of prescription drugs. A predominantly male newsroom may be less receptive to issues of particular relevance to women—e.g., child care, reproductive rights, sexism—and may be prone to patriarchal views of the issues that especially involve women, such as sexual assault, spousal abuse, pay equity, etc. (see Meyers, 1997).

Henry et al. (2000: 296–310) argue that the media are particularly important sources for information about Canada's visible minority communities. But because few Canadian journalists are non-white and because Canadians of colour are rarely interviewed by journalists unless the news item directly concerns race, minority men and women are largely invisible in Canadian newsrooms and Canadian news coverage. This invisibility 'communicates the message that they are not full participants in Canadian society.' Communications research has repeatedly determined that when people of colour are visible in news reportage, they are often depicted in negative and stereotypical ways. Henry et al. write: 'A pervasive theme of both news and [dramatic] programming is the portrayal of people of colour as "the outsiders within," reinforcing the "we-they" mindset.' People of colour lack access to the media to make their voices heard. Journalism educator John Miller (1998: 137) argues that this results in 'blind spots' in news coverage: 'If few women or visible minorities are in positions where they can determine what newspapers cover and how, issues affecting them are probably not going to receive proper attention or get on the agenda for public debate.'

The point is not to turn the news media into organs of advocacy for the disenfranchised. Instead, Kovach and Rosenstiel (2001: 108) explain: 'The ultimate goal of newsroom diversity is to create an intellectually mixed environment where everyone holds firm to the idea of journalistic independence. Together their various experiences blend to create a reporting richer than what they would create alone. And in the end that leads to a richer, fuller view of the world for the public.'

O'Brien did acknowledge that the story warranted internal discussion that went at least as high as Whyte (neither Whyte nor Black could be contacted by presstime). 'We established that *Adbusters* was launching a campaign against the *Post* and especially Conrad Black,' says O'Brien. 'There was a sensitivity there.'

Asked whether that sensitivity played a role in the piece being held, O'Brien chose to duck and cover: 'Possibly,' she said.

Noam de Plume, a pseudonymous spokesperson for Guerrilla Media, says reporters and editors seem to be taking a see-no-evil, speak-no-evil approach to Conrad Black's most confrontational critics to prevent run-ins with corporate management.

'The gatekeeping, when it has to be, is very controlling,' says de Plume. 'They're saying the criticism that we're leveling at them is something they don't want to discuss in a public way.'

Scott Uzelman of News Watch Canada, an academic research group that monitors media 'blind spots,' says the Blackout of culture-jamming critics is a blunt example of monopoly media's inability to report fairly on its own powers and responsibilities. Last year, News Watch published a study of how coverage of Conrad Black's empire in a major daily newspaper changed after that paper was bought by Black. Not surprisingly, they found the paper's coverage became far less critical; what's more, that paper took a year to acknowledge the group's study, finally printing an op-ed on the subject in the weekend magazine section.

Uzelman argues that it all points to the need to revisit the tired idea that government interference poses the greatest threat to journalists' freedom to report dissenting opinions. 'The same ideal isn't applied to the media themselves, which are increasingly large corporations,' Uzelman notes.

So Canadians shouldn't hold their breath for a Conrad Black newspaper to assign an investigative series on the effects of media concentration?

'If that happened, I would probably drop dead with surprise,' Uzelman says.

—*James MacKinnon*
Source: *Adbusters*, No. 27 Autumn, 1999: 27, www.adbusters.org. Reprinted by permission of Adbusters Media Foundation.

The Legal and Policy Contexts of News Production

Freedom of the press is one of the most fundamental rights of a democratic society, and journalism in Canada is practised in a free press environment. Section 2 of the 1982 Canadian Charter of Rights and Freedoms protects both freedom of expression and freedom of the press under the heading 'Fundamental Freedoms':

2. Everyone has the following fundamental freedoms:
    (a) freedom of conscience and religion;
    (b) freedom of thought, belief, opinion and expression, including freedom of the press and other media of communication;
    (c) freedom of peaceful assembly; and
    (d) freedom of association.

This does not mean, however, that journalists are free to report whatever they want, or that news organizations can publish or broadcast with impunity. Press freedom in Canada is constrained by laws that ensure journalists' freedoms do not compromise the security of the state or the freedoms of other Canadian citizens. As journalist and legal scholar Michael G. Crawford (1990: 3) notes: 'The danger in the term "freedom of the press" is that it implies a special right has been imparted upon the news media which is above the rights of the general public. That is not the case.' The news media have no greater privileges than the average citizen. Journalists, instead, are recognized by the Canadian courts as 'members and representatives of the public'. Journalists are also subject to constraints based on the specific conditions of their employment and the predominantly commercial organization of the news industry. In law, freedom of the press is a right of media proprietors. While it is journalists who are in the field producing stories, it is their employers who exercise the constitutional power of freedom of the press, deciding whether or not to run a particular story, deciding how any given story might be handled. Every reporter has a story to tell about a proprietor's interference in news coverage.

Freedom of the press is a core right of all modern democratic states. But this core tenet of liberal democracy is not interpreted exactly the same way by all democracies, compelling journalists to work within both national and international legal and policy frameworks. At the international level, Article 19 of the Universal Declaration of Human Rights (1949) provides the ethical foundation. It states:

> para. 1: Everyone shall have the right to hold opinions without interference.
> para. 2: Everyone shall have the right to freedom of expression; this right shall include freedom to seek, receive and impart information and ideas of all kinds, regardless of frontiers, either orally, in writing or in print, in the form of art, or through any other media of his/her choice.
> para. 3: The exercise of the right provided for in para. 2 of this article carries with it special duties and responsibilities. It may therefore be subject to certain restrictions, but these shall only be such as are provided by law and are necessary for the respect of the rights or reputation of others or for the protection of national security or of public order or of public health or morals.

Article 12 of the declaration also deals with press functioning by addressing infringement of privacy and attacks on honour and reputation. It states: 'Everyone has the right of protection of the law against such interference and attack.' These two rights, free speech and the right to privacy, always exist in tension with one another. Journalists may have rights, but they also have legal obligations and ethical responsibilities.

Canada's media laws are the product of two historical contexts, the European and the American.

THE EUROPEAN CONTEXT

The member states of what is now called the European Union have followed very closely the model provided by the Universal Declaration of Human Rights in drafting their own statements on rights and freedoms. The European Convention for the Protection of Human Rights and Fundamental Freedoms(http://conventions.coe.int/treaty/en/Treaties/Html/005.htm), adopted by the Council of Europe in Rome in 1950, included articles asserting the rights to freedom of thought, conscience, and religion (Article 9) and to freedom of expression (Article 10). The European Union's Charter of Fundamental Rights (http://ue.eu.int/df/default.asp?lang=en), adopted in December 2000, ensures the rights to freedom of thought, conscience, and religion (Article 10), freedom of expression (Article 11), as well as the related rights of academic freedom (Article 13) and the right to education (Article 14). Article 11, specifically, states:

> 1. Everyone has the right to freedom of expression. This right shall include freedom to hold opinions and to receive and impart information and ideas without interference by public authority and regardless of frontiers.
> 2. The freedom and pluralism of the media shall be respected.

Neither of these documents, however, defines these freedoms in absolute terms. Each contains qualifiers pertaining to such areas as privacy and national security, and they preserve the right of states to license radio and television broadcasters. Article 10 of the European Convention, for example, stipulates duties and responsibilities pertaining to national security, territorial integrity, public safety, the prevention of crime, the protection of health and morals, and the maintenance of the authority and impartiality of the judiciary.

Perhaps the clearest and most explicit statement pertaining to the rights of the news media in the European context comes in the Declaration of Rights and Obligations of Journalists, adopted by the European Union in Munich in 1971. The so-called Munich Charter asserts: 'All rights and duties of a journalist originate from the right of the public to be informed on events and opinions. The journalist's responsibility towards the public takes precedence over any other responsibility, particularly towards employers and public authorities.' The document lists a set of duties and rights that provide considerable insight into the meeting of journalistic ideals and day-to-day practices. In summary they are:

Declaration of duties:
1. To respect truth because of the right of the public to know the truth;
2. To defend freedom of information, comment and criticism;
3. To report only known facts and not to suppress essential information;
4. Not to use unfair methods to obtain news, photographs or documents;
5. To respect the privacy of others;
6. To rectify any published inaccurate information;
7. To protect persons who provide information in confidence;
8. Not to engage in **plagiarism**, calumny, slander, libel and unfounded accusations, nor accept bribes in any form;
9. To distinguish between journalism and advertising or propaganda;
10. To resist editorial pressure from unqualified persons.

Declaration of rights:
1. Journalists claim free access to all information sources, and the right to inquire freely into all events affecting public life;
2. Journalists have the right to refuse subordination to anything contrary to the general policies of the information organs of which they are contributing members;
3. Journalists cannot be compelled to perform professional acts or express opinions contrary to their convictions or conscience;
4. Editorial staffs must be informed or consulted about major editorial changes;
5. Journalists are entitled not only to the advantages resulting from collective agreements but also to an individual contract of employment, ensuring sufficient material and moral security to guarantee their economic independence (Clement Jones, 1980).

This 1971 document not only stipulates the basic principles upon which European journalists could reach consensus, but also identifies five areas of constraint within which journalists work: international and national law and information policy; the orientation, actions, and preferences of the government of the day; the policies, practices, and attitudes of owners; the philosophies, practices, and attitudes of colleagues, including editorial managers; and pressures from societies and subgroups within society. If, then, these rights and obligations are interpreted differently from country to country, from news organization to news organization, and from journalist to journalist, they nonetheless provide a model for the vigorous and responsible practice of news production, as well as a reference point for critics and scholars of the news media.

THE AMERICAN CONTEXT

A parallel initiative to the 1971 European statement of rights and responsibilities of journalists was long in coming to the Americas. But on 11 March 1994 the Inter American Press Association (IAPA) sponsored the

Hemispheric Conference on Free Speech in Chapultepec, near Mexico City. Out of that conference came the Declaration of Chapultepec, 'a commitment to freedom of speech and of the press, an inalienable human right and fundamental principle, to ensure the very survival of democracy in the Americas'. Several points from the Declaration's preamble are worth noting:

> Without democracy and freedom . . . justice is demeaned and human advancement becomes mere fiction.
>
> Freedom must not be restricted in the quest for any other goal. It stands alone, yet has multiple expressions; it belongs to citizens, not to governments. . . .
>
> We, the signatories of this declaration, represent different backgrounds and dreams. We take pride in the plurality and diversity of our cultures, considering ourselves fortunate that they merge into the one element that nurtures their growth and creativity: freedom of expression, the driving force and base of mankind's fundamental rights. . . .
>
> Without an independent media, assured of guarantees to operate freely, to make decisions and to act on them fully, freedom of expression cannot be exercised. . . .
>
> Even the constitutions of some democratic countries contain elements of press restriction.
>
> While defending a free press and rejecting outside interference, we also champion a press that is responsible and involved, a press aware of the obligations that the practice of freedom entails. (IAPA: http://216.147.196.167/projects/chapul-declaration.cfm.)

The principles enunciated within the Declaration follow along the same lines. Here are three of the 10 points:

- No people or society can be free without freedom of expression and of the press. The exercise of this freedom is not something authorities grant, it is an inalienable right of the people.
- Every person has the right to seek and receive information, express opinions and disseminate them freely. No one may restrict or deny these rights. . . .
- The credibility of the press is linked to its commitment to truth, to the pursuit of accuracy, fair-

ness and objectivity and to the clear distinction between news and advertising. The attainment of these goals and the respect for ethical and professional values may not be imposed. These are the exclusive responsibility of journalists and the media. In a free society, it is public opinion that rewards or punishes. (Ibid.)

The Declaration of Chapultepec excludes any state role except that of ensuring freedom. Certain statements signal the heavy hand of the US contingent, such as, 'Even the constitutions of some democratic countries contain elements of press restriction' and 'The exercise of this freedom [freedom of expression and of the press] is not something authorities grant, it is an inalienable right of the people.' The European declarations demonstrate a much better balance between responsibilities and freedoms (http://www.sipiapa.org).

As Martin and Adam (1991: 27) explain, the Canadian tradition of freedom of expression is a balancing act of the American individualistic view and the European collectivist conception. A Canadian notion of freedom of expression encompasses individuals' rights of expression to promote and encourage 'the widest possible participation of all its members in its economic, social and cultural affairs'. But it also perceives freedom of expression 'not merely as a commodity possessed by individuals, but as an essential pre-condition to the creation and maintenance of democracy itself'. That is, the right of freedom of expression is granted to individuals insofar as they are actors in a free and democratic society. This freedom is not absolute. Section 1 of Canada's Charter of Rights and Freedoms notes that the Charter's guarantees are 'subject only to such reasonable limits prescribed by law as can be demonstrably justified in a free and democratic society'.

Canadian Law and Journalism

While enjoying freedom of the press, Canadian journalists are also responsible to national and international law, and they are compelled to subscribe to a variety of ethical codes that deal with the business of news production. These codes serve as guidelines rather than laws, and while they may indeed encourage responsible journalism, their primary goal is to ward off legislative intervention.

In the electronic media, the Canadian Association of

Broadcasters has a Code of Ethics, a Sex-Role Portrayal Code for Television and Radio Programming, a Broadcast Code for Advertising to Children, and a Voluntary Code Regarding Violence in Television Programming, all of which are administered by the Canadian Broadcast Standards Council (CBSC). The Code of Ethics contains 18 clauses dealing with such issues as: the diversity of the audience; abusive and discriminatory material; the vulnerability and impressionability of children; participation in worthwhile community activities; the nature of educational efforts; the accuracy of news; the presentation of public issues; the content of advertising; subliminal devices; conformity with advertising codes; the distinction between advertising and news and public affairs programming; portrayal of each gender; and the public responsibilities of broadcasting. In addition, Advertising Standards Canada administers voluntary codes on advertising and jointly administers with the CBSC the Broadcast Code of Advertising to Children (www.mediaawareness.ca/eng/indus/advert/bcac.htm).

The Radio and Television News Directors Association of Canada (RTNDA) also has a 14-point Code of Ethics. Its preamble states: 'Free speech and an informed public are vital to a democratic society. The members of the RTNDA Canada recognize the responsibility of broadcast journalists to promote and to protect the freedom to report independently about matters of public interest and to present a wide range of expressions, opinions, and ideas.' To that end, RTNDA members follow a code pertaining to: accuracy, comprehensiveness, fairness, and authenticity; equal treatment of minority populations; independent reporting; conflicts of interest; privacy; the integrity of the judicial system; correction of errors; intellectual property rights; and confidentiality of sources. For example, Article 8 states: 'Broadcast journalists will treat people who are subjects and sources with decency. They will use special sensitivity when dealing with children. They will strive to conduct themselves in a courteous and considerate manner, keeping broadcast equipment as unobtrusive as possible. They will strive to prevent their presence from distorting the character or importance of events' (www.cbsc.ca/english/codes/rtndarevised.htm).

The written press is guided by a different set of institutions. Every province, with the exception of Saskatchewan, has a press council to address public complaints. However, press councils have no regulatory authority, relying instead on publicity and moral suasion to encourage ethical behaviour by member news-papers and their journalists.

Newspaper companies have in the past adopted their own codes of ethics, but this practice has largely been abandoned for fear that it increases publishers' legal liability. As journalism educator John Miller (1998: 115–22) has recounted, the Canadian Daily Newspaper Association attempted to abolish its Statement of Principles in the mid-1990s. Initially drafted in 1977 as a code of ethical standards for its members, this Statement was intended to be updated when the CDNA met in 1993. Instead, the CDNA's legal and editorial committees voted to abolish it altogether. Public pressure, however, compelled the CDNA's board of directors to adopt a diluted version of the statement in September 1995 (Cobb, 1995: A12). The new Statement of Principles (see Stott, 1995: A7) read as follows:

Preamble: The statement of principles expresses the commitment of Canada's daily newspapers to operate in the public interest. A newspaper is a vital source of information and a private business enterprise with responsibility to the community it serves.
Freedom of the Press is an exercise of every Canadian's right to freedom of expression guaranteed in the Charter of Rights and Freedoms. It is the right to gather and disseminate information, to discuss, to advocate, to dissent. A free press is essential to our democratic society. It enables readers to use their Charter right to receive information and make informed judgements on the issues and ideas of the time.
Independence. The newspaper's primary obligation is fidelity to the public good. It should pay the costs of gathering the news. Conflicts of interest, real or apparent, should be declared. The newspaper should guard its independence from government, commercial and other interests seeking to subvert content for their own purposes.
Accuracy and Fairness. The newspaper keeps faith with readers by presenting information that is accurate, fair, comprehensive, interesting and timely. It should acknowledge its mistakes promptly and conspicuously. Sound practice clearly distinguishes among news reports, expressions of opinion, and materials produced for and by advertisers. When images have been altered or simulated, readers should be told.
Community Responsibility. The newspaper has responsibilities to its readers, its shareholders, its

employees and its advertisers. But the operation of a newspaper is a public trust and its overriding responsibility is to the society it serves. The newspaper plays many roles: a watchdog against evil and wrong-doing, an advocate for good works and noble deeds, and an opinion leader for its community. The newspaper should strive to paint a representative picture of its diverse communities, to encourage the expression of disparate views and to be accessible and accountable to the readers it serves, whether rich or poor, weak or powerful, minority or majority. When published material attacks an individual or group, those affected should be given an opportunity to reply. **Respect**. The newspaper should strive to treat the people it covers with courtesy and fairness. It should respect the rights of others, particularly every person's right to a fair trial. The inevitable conflict between privacy and the public good should be judged in the light of common sense and decency.

The Canadian Newspaper Association adopted the same Statement of Principles when it replaced the CDNA and the Newspaper Marketing Bureau in July 1996 (www.cna-acj.ca/about/sp.asp).

In a study of Canadian journalism ethics conducted in 2001–2, researcher Bob Bergen (2002: 10–11) could identify only one daily newspaper, the *Toronto Star*, that operated according to a set of well-publicized principles. More typical, Bergen said, was the *Ottawa Citizen*, which had a 19-page Ethics and Policies manual that its journalists were expected to follow. Bergen also examined 65 collective-bargaining agreements and found that 59 contained clauses allowing journalists to take specified actions when ethical issues arose (ibid., 33).

In the present climate of increased concentration of ownership of the news media, governments are pressuring converged media companies to make public statements of their journalistic principles. For example, when the CRTC renewed the television licences of CTV and CanWest Global in August 2001, it imposed a number of conditions, including the requirement that the two networks adhere to a Statement of Principles and Practices governing the cross-ownership of TV stations and newspapers. While the CRTC conceded that better journalism could result from pooling the resources of the companies' TV and newspaper newsrooms, it was also concerned about the possibility of a reduction in editorial diversity. The CRTC demanded that CTV and Global maintain separate management of their broadcast and newspaper newsrooms and create 'independent neutral monitoring committees', which would address complaints and report to the CRTC annually. The two companies were required to spend $1 million each on promoting the committee and the Statement of Principles and Practices (CRTC, 2001).

The Quebec government, which is particularly sensitive to the high levels of corporate concentration among French-language news media, is also pressing news organizations in the province to publish ethics codes as part of a larger attempt to ensure 'the quality and diversity of information'. Minister of Culture and Communications Diane Lemieux established an advisory board in September 2002, charged with providing recommendations that could be drafted into legislation as early as the spring of 2003 (Dutrisac, 2002).

In addition to the codes of ethics and regulatory bodies that guide Canadian newsmakers to provide fair and accurate reporting, there are Canadian laws that aid or constrain the newsmaking process. These laws are designed to protect the public interest and cover areas such as access to information, libel, privacy, and contempt of court.

ACCESS TO INFORMATION

Access to information laws have recently been enacted in North America as a way of extending the right to freedom of information. The basic principle is that, in the name of democracy, most government information should be available to the people. Exceptions should be rare and are justified only when public access to information might pose a risk to national security, the privacy of individuals, or the confidentiality of certain political discussions (e.g., the advice of public servants to cabinet ministers). The reason for the existence of two terms—**freedom of information** and **access to information**—reflects two different governing traditions. 'Access to information' is appropriate to countries such as Great Britain and its former colonies, like Canada, in which information is collected and created by the government (the Crown) and is seen to be the property of the Crown unless the Crown is prepared to release it. In the United States, the same kind of information is seen to be the property of the people because 'the people' are paramount in the US Constitution. Thus, 'freedom of information' is a more appropriate label.

The federal government and all the provincial governments have access to information legislation, which outlines what kinds of government information are subject to scrutiny and how journalists and ordinary citizens can obtain access. Typically, this involves submitting an access to information request to the pertinent government department or agency and awaiting a response. Sometimes, repeated requests must be made to focus the inquiry of the specific information sought.

In 2002, the Canadian government concluded an 18-month review of its access to information legislation. While the Access to Information Review Task Force determined that the legislation was 'basically sound in concept, structure and balance', it also discovered 'an overwhelming need for more rigorous process, clearer and more widely understood rules, and greater consistency in outcomes, both for requesters and for government institutions' (www.atirf-geai.gc.ca/report/report2-e.html).

Access to information laws are important to journalists and the general public for two reasons. First, governments are ravenous collectors of information and have considerable data at their disposal. It is to governments, for example, that we submit census forms and tax returns. Second, much of a govern-ment's daily work and decision-making occurs outside of public meetings. In order for journalists to monitor government activities and report them to Canadians, they need to know what happens beyond the confines of public meeting halls.

LIBEL

While freedom of expression laws define the positive foundation of journalism, libel and other restraint laws define the negative constraints within which journalists must operate. **Libel** is defined as the publication or broadcasting of 'a false and damaging statement'. Such a statement must be seen to discredit or lower an individual, corporation, labour union, or any other 'legal entity' (Crawford, 1990: 15; Buckley, 1993: 112). The common issues surrounding libel include the determination of the nature of the libel, the damage done, those who bear responsibility, appropriate compensatory action, as well as considerations of personal privacy and the public interest.

In most countries, responsibility for libel extends beyond the author to editors and producers in their role as people who review submissions and decide what to include and not to include in putting reports together for publication or broadcast. Responsibility also commonly extends to the proprietor and can

ACCESS TO INFORMATION

Excerpt from the Access to Information Act, R.S.C. 1985, c.A-1, ss. 2, 4, 10, 13–27:

Purpose of Act
2 (1) the purpose of this Act is to extend the present laws of Canada to provide a right of access to information in records under the control of a government institution in accordance with the principles that government information should be available to the public, that necessary exceptions to the right of access should be limited and specific and that decisions on the disclosure of information of government information should be reviewed independently of government.

(2) This Act is intended to complement and not replace existing procedures for access to government information and is not intended to limit in any way access to the type of government information that is normally available to the general public.

The Act discusses right of access to government records. Right of access is granted to Canadian citizens and landed immigrants, but that right can be extended to other persons. The Act defines the circumstances under which access can be refused, requiring the government to state the reason. Exemptions are defined under 'Responsibilities of Government'. They include the non-release of documents obtained in confidence from other governments, those that could be injurious to the conduct of intergovernmental affairs, documents related to the detection or committing of crime, sensitive business information such as trade secrets, and certain financial information. Under 'Personal Information', exemptions are granted in accordance with the provisions of the Privacy Act. Under 'Third Party Information', 'Operations of Government', 'Statutory Prohibitions', and 'General', a limited set of other exemptions is included, such as the results of product testing and the possibility that the government may wish to publish the information itself (Martin and Adam, 1991).

even include distributing companies such as whole-salers and newsstand or bookstore owners.

Libel law serves to protect against falsehood the reputation of those who are the subjects of published or broadcast reports. At the same time, it seeks to ensure that journalists live up to the ideals of fairness and accuracy in their pursuit of truth.

Libel Chill

The term **libel chill** refers to the effect that the threat of libel action can have on the news media, particularly in the coverage of powerful individuals and organizations. This threat can be effective in discouraging journalists because, as analyst Nancy Duxbury (1991) points out, under British and Canadian libel law the **burden of proof** rests with the accused ('reverse onus', in legal parlance). Once a libel action is mounted, in other words, the onus is on the journalist to defend him or herself. Free comment about powerful people can exact a hefty price if those powerful people choose to contest journalists' reports about them in the court of law. Whether or not the court decides in favour of the plaintiff, the journalist must endure the anxiety associated with such an action.

The plaintiff, on the other hand, risks little from a libel suit, beyond increased publicity and general speculation about guilt or innocence. According to David Potts, a libel lawyer who served as junior counsel for the plaintiff in a case involving the Reichmann family, review commissions looking into libel law have been satisfied that the only way to protect the average citizen is to retain libel laws in their current form. The Reichmanns, extremely wealthy real estate developers, were profiled in a lengthy article in the November 1987 issue of *Toronto Life* magazine. They mounted a $102 million lawsuit, naming the author of the article, the publisher of the magazine, and the magazine's managing editor (*Globe and Mail*, 11 Dec. 1989, B1). In February 1991, the case was resolved before going to court—but only after the publisher had spent $1 million in legal costs. *Toronto Life* printed a retraction on page 1 of its March 1991 edition that stated, in part: 'Let us unequivocally and categorically say that any and all negative insinuations and allegations in the article about the Reichmann family and Olympia & York are totally false.'

The easiest way to avoid libel suits is to avoid publishing or broadcasting contentious material. While some news organizations prefer to stick to 'soft news' in order not to antagonize anyone, others continue to encourage investigative journalism as a way of both attracting audiences and fulfilling their truth-seeking mission. While libel law can be seen to work as a censoring device (hence the term, 'libel chill'), others argue that libel law contributes positively to the reporting of what would be agreed upon, by a community of fair-minded people, as the truth.

PRIVACY

Libel and personal privacy are closely connected, and often the trade-off between personal privacy and public interest is the central issue behind libel cases. Section 7 of the Charter of Rights and Freedoms states: 'Everyone has the right to life, liberty and security of the person and the right not to be deprived thereof except in accordance with principles of fundamental justice.' Section 8 protects against 'unreasonable search or seizure'. In addition, British Columbia, Manitoba, Newfoundland, and Saskatchewan all have acts that define the **invasion of privacy**: eavesdropping, surveillance, wiretapping, use of personal documents, and appropriation, to name a few.

Contempt of court is also connected closely to invasion of privacy. For instance, in Britain the media must be quite circumspect in their discussion of cases before the courts for fear of being charged with contempt. On the other hand, the royal family suffers from Britain's lack of a privacy law (witness news photographers' obsession with the late Princess Diana) and the public's seemingly insatiable appetite for 'news' about the royals. In Canada, controls on the media in commenting on cases before the courts are generally less stringent than in Britain, but much more stringent than in the United States, where the O.J. Simpson murder trial and the impeachment proceedings against President Bill Clinton resembled media feeding frenzies. In the 1990s, cameras moved into US courtrooms and made mass media spectacles of such high-profile cases as the O.J. Simpson murder trial and the William Kennedy Smith rape trial.

In Canada the courts can move in to prevent ongoing news coverage in order to protect citizens. In May 1999, for example, a Calgary court ordered *Alberta Report* magazine to stop publishing stories about genetic, late-term abortions at Foothills Hospital. The Calgary Regional Health Authority had complained to Alberta's Court of Queen's Bench that the stories were endangering the lives of hospital staff (Foot, 1999: A4).

A recent Supreme Court ruling expanded considerably the bounds of privacy legislation. The Court ruled in April 1998 that 'it is against Quebec law to publish an identifiable picture of a person no matter how harmless, taken without his or her consent, unless there is an overriding "public interest".' The Supreme Court was upholding a 1991 Quebec court decision to award $2,000 to a Montreal woman whose picture was taken without her consent while she sat in the doorway of a building. The photograph was published in the Montreal literary magazine *Vice Versa* as part of a story on urban life (Cherry, 1998: A4). The ruling means that individuals' privacy is protected even when they are in a public place. Journalists must walk a fine line between notions of personal privacy and public interest. People's lives are not fair game for journalists, unless a clear case for the public's right to know can be argued. Journalists, of course, flirt with this fine line all the time, especially in their coverage of major entertainment and sports figures, where reportage often delves into celebrities' personal relationships.

CONTEMPT OF COURT

Contempt of court refers to instances when the judicial process is interfered with and/or the courts are disobeyed (Buckley, 1993: 110). Here again, two fundamental democratic rights come into conflict: the right to freedom of the press and the right to a fair trial. Section 11(d) of the Charter of Rights and Freedoms states that any person charged with an offence has the right 'to be presumed innocent until proven guilty according to law in a fair and public hearing by an independent and impartial tribunal'. To ensure these conditions are met, the justice system has at its disposal a number of measures, some of which affect the ability of journalists to report the news in its entirety. For example, judges in Canadian courts can impose publication bans on court proceedings (for example, the Karla Homolka and Robert Pickton trials), and the press is not permitted to identify juveniles involved in court cases or to identify the alleged victim in a rape trial (see ibid., 96–111). So while journalists help to render the judicial system open and transparent, their rights in this regard are not absolute.

Making News (and Profits?)

Besides being affected by the legal and ethical imperatives described above, most journalists in Canada work for commercial news organizations and, as such, are also implicated in generating profits for their owners. Decisions about what a comprehensive news package entails will always be made in concert with the need to maximize audiences and attract advertising. Advertising, after all, pays most of the bills of mainstream news organizations and pays all of the bills in the cases of community newspapers, which are distributed free of charge, and commercial radio and TV stations. Even the CBC, a public broadcaster that receives the bulk of its funds for operation from government—60.23 per cent in 2001-2 (http://cbc.radio-canada.ca/htmen/1_10.htm)—must pay attention to audience ratings to maintain public confidence and to attract advertisers. Although its radio services are free of commercials, its television operations depend on program sales and advertising for approximately 40 per cent of costs (http://cbc.radio-canada.ca/htmen/pdf_rtf/FINANCIAL_REVIEW_ENGLISH.PDF).

Like producers of romantic fiction, news organizations target particular market segments in order to assemble an audience that will be attractive to advertisers. For example, tabloid newspapers like the *Ottawa Sun*, the *Vancouver Province*, and *Le Journal de Montréal* target younger, blue-collar readers and give extensive coverage to crime stories, popular entertainment, and sports. Their judgement of news and their writing style will be tuned accordingly. On the other hand, broadsheet newspapers like the *Globe and Mail*, the *Calgary Herald*, and *La Presse* aim for a more sophisticated readership and give much more coverage to politics, business, high culture, and world affairs.

No news organization has an unlimited budget. This means that the news value of an event must always be weighed against the costs required for coverage, particularly if the story necessitates travel. The maintenance of permanent news bureaus, whether in Beijing or Ottawa, is expensive and the coverage those bureaus produce has to warrant the costs involved, in terms of the quality of the reportage and/or the prestige that accrues to the news organization for having far-flung correspondents. At the same time, no news organization has unlimited time or space to tell its stories, and news judgement must also account for this. A television newscast is always the same length, whether it is a slow news day or a busy one. Newspapers vary in size from day to day, but this is primarily a product of how much advertising they sell. This is why newspapers are so thick during the Christmas shopping season—it is a busy time for retailers even though it is a typically slow time for news—and relatively thin in the slow shopping months of January and February.

Besides these structural factors affecting news decisions, ideological factors also come into play. Owners, managers, and journalists all subscribe to certain beliefs about how the world works and, regardless of how objective and fair a journalist tries to be, these beliefs influence what gets covered and how. During the 1988 federal election, for example, when free trade with the United States was the central issue, most daily newspapers favoured the Canada–US Free Trade Agreement and their support was evident, both in the editorial pages and in their 'objective' news reportage. The *Vancouver Sun*, to cite a specific instance, went so far as to refuse to cover an anti-free trade rally in Vancouver that attracted more than 1,000 people, denying these dissenting voices space in its pages. In a similar vein, the pro-Canada rally that preceded the 1995 Quebec referendum received very different news coverage from the federalist press (*Montreal Gazette, La Presse*) and nationalist press (*Le Devoir*) in Montreal.

More often, though, such bias in the judgement of news assumes subtler forms and may not be readily detectable to readers and viewers, many of whom may

share the bias. Jaap van Ginneken (1998: 60–3) identifies five categories of 'values' that are promoted continuously and, hence, tend to predominate in the news coverage of the Western democracies:

1. The economic values of free enterprise and a free market;
2. The social values of individualism and social mobility;
3. The political values of pragmatism and moderation;
4. The lifestyle values of materialism and autonomy;
5. The ideological values that the West's point of view is based on scientific reason, while the views of the Second and Third Worlds are based on dogma.

These values, van Ginneken asserts, are widely shared among Western journalists, with the result that they are taken for granted and through news media discourse become 'naturalized'. As these perceptions are subscribed to, particularly by those in power, they form a society's 'dominant ideology'. Alternative views, such as the belief in the necessity of market regulation or the balancing of individual with collective rights, become, by definition, deviant or 'unnatural'.

As we have been suggesting throughout this chapter, news stories are selective representations of the universe of daily events going on around us. Both the stories that are told and how they are told owe something to the prevailing values that define newsworthiness, the particular style and budget of the news organization, and the beliefs and ideas that tend to predominate in society (see Figure 9.2). In any consideration of the question, 'What is news?', a number of factors are at play. Not all events occurring in the world are considered newsworthy by journalists, and therefore only events that meet certain criteria of news value will be considered as potential stories. At the same time, not all potential news stories are of interest to all news organizations. Some newspapers carry very little coverage of sports and crime news, while others specialize in these areas. The structure of the news organization will also have an impact on the newsroom budget, which will determine what stories it can afford to cover with its own staff, especially if travel and lodging are required. Finally, all societies subscribe to certain collective beliefs and values, which form a dominant ideology, and as members of society, journalists,

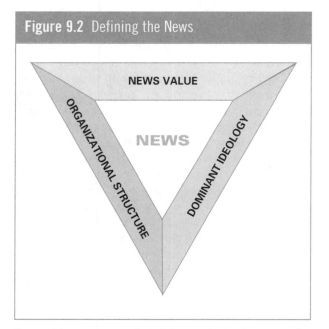

Figure 9.2 Defining the News

NEWS VALUE

ORGANIZATIONAL STRUCTURE

DOMINANT IDEOLOGY

NEWS

News can be seen as a product of the complex tension among: the factors that inform news value; the economic, time, and space constraints of organizational structure; and the beliefs that comprise the dominant ideology in society.

too, have certain beliefs about the way the world works and should work. Events that confirm such beliefs are more likely to be seen as news stories—and presented as a kind of 'proof'—than events that contradict the dominant ideology. These latter events, when covered, are often presented as sorry deviations from the norm. This distinction was clearly evident, especially in the US media but also in Canadian news reports, in the aftermath of the American-led war on Iraq in 2003. Stories highlighting the American troops as liberators received substantially greater and more favourable coverage than did those that focused on looting and anti-American protests.

Ownership and Control

A specific economic constraint in commercial news production is corporate concentration. As discussed in Chapter 8, our news comes from a handful of corporations that have media outlets in a number of Canada's major cities (or 'markets', from their perspective) and that are increasingly committed to **convergence**, or the delivery of news and information across a range of media platforms—newspapers, magazines, radio, television, Internet.

Media ownership confers control over the content of news at two levels. **Allocative control** is exercised by publishers, shareholders, and directors, who allocate resources—labour and capital—to a news organization. They determine such things as the overall mandate or philosophy of the news organization, its annual operating budget, its anticipated profit margin, and its capital expenditures for technological upgrades. They also hire senior managers who share their views on the mandate of the news organization and will ensure that it is enacted. **Operational control** is exercised by editors and producers who decide on a day-to-day and story-to-story basis how to employ the resources allocated. Such decisions include who to hire (at entry levels), who to assign to which news production tasks, and which stories to cover (Murdock, 1990: 122–3). Of course, these two levels are not mutually exclusive and some owners are more involved than others in daily news production.

NEWS ON-LINE

Today, it seems that everyone has a World Wide Web site: organizations, companies, governments, elementary school classes, our next-door neighbour, even the royal family (www.royal.gov.uk). For daily newspapers, in Canada as elsewhere around the world, the Internet is a particularly attractive medium of diffusion: it provides instantaneous global distribution and the ability to update stories constantly, offer readers hypertext links to other relevant information sites, archive past editions, and invite more immediate reader response.

Though it seems obvious that the Internet is beginning to play a significant role in the distribution of news and information, no one knows for sure how this medium will evolve, what precise journalistic role it will play, or who will develop the Internet as a news medium: established, mainstream news organizations or newcomers. What is certain is that the development of this medium will be determined by what is commercially viable rather than by what is technologically possible.

There are thousands of daily newspapers on-line, in some form or another, throughout the world. Today you can read abridged, on-line versions of most major Canadian dailies and, through their Web sites, you can submit letters to the editor, sign up for a subscription, or place a classified ad. Some Canadian newspapers have stand-alone sites—e.g., the Globe and Mail (www.globeandmail.com), Le Devoir (www.ledevoir.com)—while others are part of Internet portals—e.g., the Southam newspapers (www.canada.com) and the Sun Media newspapers (www.canoe.ca) are grouped together.

The Internet may seem to be a promised land for newspapers because it eliminates the printing and delivery costs of publishing a hard-copy edition and it opens up a potential global audience. But newspapers' experiments with this new technology have been very costly. Regrettably, the Canadian Newspaper Association does not gather this kind of financial information. In the United States, the Wall Street Journal is reported to be the only profitable on-line news site, owing to the fact that it can charge subscription fees to well-heeled clientele willing to pay for the kind of financial information this paper provides. In 2000 and 2001, a number of industry giants such as the Los Angeles Times, the New York Times, CNN, NBC, News. Corp., Dow Jones, and Knight Ridder reduced their on-line operations because of disappointing advertising revenues (see Gasher, 2002c). That news organizations nonetheless continue to absorb losses is testimony to the future commercial potential they envision for on-line news.

On-line newspaper sites from around the world can be accessed through Yahoo (www.yahoo.com).

It must be acknowledged, though, that newsrooms are complex work environments and the time pressures associated with daily journalism limit the amount of *direct* influence owners and managers can exercise over the journalists in their employ. Reporters, who spend much of their time in the field gathering information and conducting interviews, enjoy considerable latitude in generating ideas and developing their stories. Control over reporting staff is best seen as *indirect*. That is, it consists of a socialization process in which individual journalists—once hired and assigned to a particular department—learn what kinds of stories their supervisors want, and, more importantly, what kind they do not want (see Schulman, 1990). Every reporter has a tale to tell of producing a tantalizing story that was never published.

Corporate concentration is a growing concern around the media world and has attracted renewed attention in Canada in recent years. Thanks to mergers, takeovers, buyouts, and closures, fewer and fewer companies control the production of news. This has a number of implications for the process of newsmaking and the quality of information we receive. First, critics argue that as the sources of news and comment diminish, so does the diversity of such information. Alternative and oppositional voices risk being ridiculed, marginalized, or ignored altogether. Second, corporations are responsible to shareholders who are primarily interested in profit maximization. This can affect the quality of news coverage if managers are stingy with their newsroom budgets and/or their news organization avoids controversial stories for fear of antagonizing advertisers. A third concern is the potential for conflict of interest between a corporation's news business and the other businesses it owns.

Quebecor, for example, which owns *Le Journal de Montréal*, the city's most popular daily newspaper, Montreal radio news leader CKAC, the TVA television network, and the canoe.ca Internet portal, became a participant in its own news stories during the summer and fall of 2002 when 1,500 of its employees engaged in a bitter strike against Quebecor's cable television

PAPER CHAINS

The problem of corporate concentration in the media is particularly acute in the newspaper industry. The four largest newspaper companies in Canada control 74.5 per cent of the total weekly circulation of the country's daily newspapers. CanWest Global, which owns the Southam chain of 17 newspapers (among them the *Calgary Herald*, *Vancouver Sun*, *Ottawa Citizen*, and *Montreal Gazette*), accounts for close to one-third of total weekly circulation. CanWest Global also owns the *National Post*.

Quebecor became Canada's second-largest publisher of daily newspapers in January 1999, with papers in eight of the top 10 Canadian markets and more than one-fifth of total weekly circulation. Quebecor, which achieved this standing by buying Sun Media, publishes such newspapers as the *London Free Press*, *Le Journal de Montréal*, *Le Journal de Québec*, and the *Sun* newspapers in Toronto, Ottawa, Winnipeg, Edmonton, and Calgary (Lamey, 1999: F1–2). Together, Torstar Corp., which publishes four newspapers including the national circulation leader the *Toronto Star*, and Power Corp., which publishes seven French-language newspapers including *La Presse* in Montreal, account for another fifth of total daily newspaper circulation in the country.

Table 9.1 Holdings of Canada's Largest Newspaper Chains, 2002

Name of Company	Number of Dailies	Percentage of Total Weekly Circulation
CanWest/Southam	13	28.50
Quebecor/Sun Media	15	21.10
Torstar	4	13.80
Power Corp.	7	9.30

Reprinted by permission of Canadian Newspaper Association, 2003 (see **www.cna-acj.ca**).

subsidiary, Vidéotron, the largest cable supplier in Quebec. Similarly, CanWest Global media outlets found themselves compromised when pro-Palestinian activists prevented former Israeli Prime Minister Benjamin Netanyahu from speaking at Concordia University in September 2002. CanWest media properties like the *Montreal Gazette* and Global Television vigorously covered, and commented on, the low point in Netanyahu's speaking tour, a tour sponsored by the Asper Foundation. Foundation president Izzy Asper is the founder and executive chairman of CanWest Global, as well as the father of its current president and chief executive officer, Leonard Asper.

Other conflicts of interest can arise relating to ownership. For instance, the Montreal newspaper *La Presse* has long been suspected of compromise in its coverage of the federal Liberal Party because the president of the company that owns the newspaper, André Desmarais, is married to Prime Minister Jean Chrétien's daughter. In a specific instance, Chrétien's Chief of Staff, Jean Pelletier, complained directly to Desmarais about criticism of the Prime Minister by *La Presse* columnist Chantal Hébert (see Richer, 1999).

Journalist and scholar Ben Bagdikian (1990: xxii) has characterized corporate concentration as a conflict of interest between the public's need for information and corporations' desire for 'positive information'. Put another way, Peter Desbarats (1996: 61) writes: 'This concentration of ownership has created concern that the goals of media-owning corporations may at times run counter to freedom of expression and the long-term interests of society.'

Conflict between the rights and the responsibilities of the news media characterized much of the twentieth century, and governments in the UK, the US, and Canada have all conducted investigations into patterns of media ownership in the post-World War II period. As discussed in Chapter 3, the report of the Hutchins Commission on Freedom of the Press in the United States is recognized as a foundational document for what is known as the social responsibility theory of the press (Commission on Freedom of the Press, 1947). This theory extends the core democratic right of freedom of the press to include the right of citizens to be adequately informed by the news media.

Canada's Special Senate Committee on Mass Media, known as the Davey Commission (Canada, 1971: 3), concluded that media diversity defied the logic of market economics: 'More voices may be healthier, but fewer voices are cheaper.' Among the

Davey Commission's principal recommendations was a press ownership review board, 'with powers to approve or disapprove mergers between, or acquisitions of, newspapers and periodicals' (ibid., 71). But, given the federal government's refusal to regulate either Canada's free press or the free enterprise in which news organizations engage, no such panel was ever established.

In 1980 the Royal Commission on Newspapers, known as the Kent Commission, was created in direct response to a rationalization agreement between Canada's two premier newspaper chains of the period, Southam and Thomson, which left Southam the Ottawa market and Thomson the Winnipeg market. In line with the social responsibility theory of the press, the Kent Commission concluded that freedom of the press is not the owner's or editor's right to free speech, but is part of the people's right to freedom of expression and is 'inseparable from their right to inform themselves'. In the aftermath of the Royal Commission hearings, federal Consumer Affairs Minister Jim Fleming proposed a Canada Newspapers Act (1983), which would establish a national press council, offer grants to encourage newspapers to open bureaus across Canada, and impose ownership restrictions. But the legislation was opposed by the vocal publishing lobby and was never adopted by the Liberal government of the day (see Miller, 1998: 37–40). The Kent Commission's critique of the newspaper industry was sound, but to regulate the press is to redefine the legal meaning of freedom of the press, which democratic governments have so far refused to do. As discussed at length in Chapter 8, governments in Canada instigated a review of the issues raised by corporate concentration following a series of mergers between 2000 and 2002.

In their defence, news media owners assert that a wealth of information sources—print, radio, television, magazines, the Internet—makes corporate concentration less of a concern than it was when the Davey and Kent Commissions conducted their hearings. There is some merit to this argument. More newspapers, magazines, radio stations, and TV channels are available to us than ever before, and the Internet gives users access to Web sites from around the world. Alternative sources of information are available.

But in assessing this argument we need to consider two points. First, there is considerable information sharing among news media. That is, print and broadcast organizations depend heavily on the same wire services—Canadian Press, Associated Press, Agence

France Presse—for regional, national, and international news, so that frequently the same story is used by various newspapers, radio stations, television outlets, and Web sites. Chris A. Paterson argues, in fact, that convergence has resulted in the increased concentration of information delivery. Addressing on-line news specifically, Paterson cites a 1999 BBC study, which concluded that the wire services Associated Press and Reuters dominated Internet news services: 'That is, *fewer* major news providers are informing *more* people and (the BBC fails to note) doing so from *fewer* sources' (Paterson, 2001: 79).

Distinctions between print, broadcast, and on-line coverage of local stories are similarly minimized because competing news organizations often set the news agenda for each other: they monitor each other's coverage, they cover the same local events, and they cite the same sources. It is not uncommon, in other words, to read the same news story in two different newspapers and then also to hear a condensed version of the same story delivered by radio and television news readers. We may think we are benefiting from a broad range of news coverage, but all too often these media are getting their stories from the same source.

In addition, a considerable amount of Internet information comes from the same government and corporate sources used by the conventional media, and this information is often packaged by Web sites established by print and broadcast outlets. The news portal Canadian Online Explorer (www.canoe.ca), for example, was established in 1996 as a limited partnership between Sun Media, the chain that owns the Sun newspapers, and it is now owned and operated by Quebecor. As such, its content reflects it ownership connections. Similarly, CanWest Global decided in September 2001 to fold the stand-alone Web sites of its daily newspapers into a single portal (www.canada.com), bringing together the sites of the Southam daily newspapers and the Global television network. The existence of an abundance of information sources, then, does not equate with information diversity.

Corporate concentration is considered to be less of a problem in radio and television news because two important features of Canada's broadcasting industry mitigate against its domination by one or two companies. The first is the existence of the CBC as Canada's public broadcaster, for which there is no parallel in the newspaper or magazine industries. With radio and television outlets in French and English, the CBC serves Canada well with news and information programming,

even if some would argue that the CBC could do a much better job in these areas. The greatest threat to the quality of its broadcasting in recent years has been the dramatic reduction in its funding from the federal government—a drop of more than 19 per cent over the past six years, from $963.2 million in fiscal 1995–6 to $780 million in 2001–2. This reduction in funding, as noted in its annual report for 2001–2, has forced the CBC to reduce staff and to make its television programming more appealing to advertisers (http://www.cbc.radio-canada.ca/htmen/annual_report/2001-2002/pdf/cbc_2001-2002_annual_report). The second difference is that the broadcast industry is regulated by the CRTC, which, in enforcing the Broadcasting Act, can impose ownership restrictions and broadcasting standards on licence-holders. Some questions remain, however, about how much power the CRTC has

The role that journalists play in society has changed with twenty-first century war and instant communication. Journalists all around the Middle East could instantly report on the progress of the US-led war against Iraq. *Kansas City Star* photographer Jim Barcus was at Tactical Assembly Area Champion Main in Kuwait when this photo was taken in March 2003. He's wearing his desert goggles and thigh-mounted gas mask pouch. The latter is required by the 82nd Airborne, the unit in which Barcus was embedded. (The Kansas City Star)

to interfere with corporate mergers.

Corporate concentration has some supporters outside the industry. Scholar David Demers (1999) argues that corporate ownership and good journalism are not mutually exclusive. Newspaper chains, Demers maintains, benefit from 'economies of scale and superior human and capital resources', which can result in both quality reporting and industrial stability. One clearly positive result of corporate concentration is its pooling of considerable capital resources. This permits newspapers like the *Globe and Mail* and the *National Post* to establish the kind of editorial budgets that an independent news organization simply could not afford. These two dailies, for example, have permanent news bureaus across the country and around the world and they have the resources to send their reporters and columnists wherever the action is. This is important as readers expect quality newspapers to contribute independent voices to major news stories such as the 11 September 2001 terrorist attacks, the wars in Afghanistan and Iraq, and global trade agreements. Very few metropolitan dailies have foreign correspondents, relying instead on wire-service copy to supply them with both national and international news and analysis from a relatively small stable of syndicated columnists. But size does not always mean better coverage. For instance, if we compare Canada's national television networks, the CBC does a much better job than either CTV or Global of bringing a distinct, Canadian perspective to regional, national, and international news coverage.

News as Storytelling

One way of looking at journalism is as a practice of meaning production. There is always a distinction between events and stories about events, between reality and stories about reality. Journalists represent reality; they cannot reproduce it. They are thus storytellers, using words, images, and sounds to depict reality (people, places, ideas, institutions, events). As Kovach and Rosenstiel (2001: 149) put it: 'Journalism is storytelling with a purpose. That purpose is to provide people with information they need to understand

As demonstrated by this *Toronto Star* advertisement, individual media organizations, as well as individual journalists, can tell vastly different stories about the very same event. (Reprinted with permission—Torstar Syndication Services)

the world. The first challenge is finding the information that people need to live their lives. The second is to make it meaningful, relevant, and engaging.'

But what this implies is that the choices journalists make among the words, images, and sounds at their disposal will attribute particular meanings to the events they cover. A reporter covering a demonstration, for example, will define that event in different ways, depending on whether the participants in the demonstration are described as 'a small group', 'a crowd', or 'a mob'. Similarly, the specific observations and quotations cited in the story and the visuals chosen to illustrate it will define the event in a certain way. And this applies regardless of how 'objective' the reporter tries to remain. No story, after all, can tell the whole story.

In this vein, researchers Elizabeth Bird and Robert Dardenne encourage us to think of news stories as myths, stories that we tell ourselves in an effort to make sense of often complex phenomena, assert and maintain cultural values, and determine notions of right and wrong. Journalists, for example, often refer explicitly to mythical tales—Cinderella stories and battles between David and Goliath are frequently called upon—to assign meaning to events and offer the news audience a kind of shorthand to understanding. Allusions to Cinderella and the biblical David, for example, help to perpetuate and reinforce the value of social mobility, which, as we noted earlier in this chapter, has been identified by van Ginneken as one of the predominant values in the Western media's news coverage. Every time we read a real-life Cinderella story, it adds credence to the myth of social mobility. Every time we hear that another David has defeated another Goliath, it reinforces the idea that ordinary people can bring down giants, that power relations are fragile, possibly even illusory. Bird and Dardenne (1997: 346–7) write: 'While news is not fiction, it is a story about reality, not reality itself. Yet because of its privileged status as reality and truth, the seductive powers of its narratives are particularly significant.'

This is not to suggest that journalists simply make up or invent stories out of thin air. Rather, the point is to emphasize that there is always a difference between an event and a story about an event. Events are usually messy, complicated, hard to understand, with no clear beginning, middle, or end. In reporting on such events, journalists seek to impose an order on events, to render them comprehensible and meaningful, to contain the events within the 60 seconds of a television news report or the few hundred words of a newspaper article. In answering to the demands of storytelling, journalists impose a narrative structure on events—the 'who' of the story becomes character, the 'what' becomes plot,

the 'where' and 'when' become setting, the 'why' becomes motivation, and the 'how' becomes narrative (see Kovach and Rosenstiel, 2001: 156)—and this imposition runs the risk of oversimplifying complex phenomena. Any news story is merely one depiction of an event among an infinite number of other possible depictions, making it all the more important that alternative news sources remain available to us.

Summary

Journalists are content producers and storytellers (not unlike the storytellers who work in other mass media forms). News is not simply gathered; it is constructed or produced.

Journalism, as a form of storytelling, is based on real people and real events. But rather than mirroring reality, as is often suggested, the news media instead frame reality, selecting particular events, particular people, and particular aspects of a story as newsworthy while excluding many others.

Journalism shares some of the characteristics of other forms of storytelling but it is also distinguished by the following features: its guiding ideals of truth-seeking; independence and objectivity; the ethical and legal rights and obligations of the practice in a free press environment; and the institutional context of news production. Freedom of the press, one of the linchpins of news reporting, does not mean that journalists are free to report whatever they choose or that news organizations can publish and broadcast with impunity. Such constraints as privacy and libel keep news producers in line with accepted notions of integrity.

Given the selective nature of the news production process, it is important to understand where news reports come from. Journalists in Canada are not representative of the population at large. Instead, they tend to be young, male, white, and well-educated, and they work predominantly for commercial news organizations with large corporate owners. These factors have implications for both what and how news is reported, as well as for what may not be reported.

Finally, there is an argument to be made for perceiving news as myths—stories that are told over and over again and that contain reality within a culturally acceptable framework of understanding. This view originates in a tradition of study that perceives texts—all kinds of texts—as cultural constructions, as a way of creating bridges between fictional and non-fictional forms of storytelling.

RELATED WEB SITES

Canadian Association of Broadcasters: www.cab-acr.ca

The CAB represents Canada's private broadcasters. The site profiles industry sectors and highlights industry and social policy issues.

Canadian Broadcast Standards Council: www.cbsc.ca

The Canadian Broadcast Standards Council was established by the CAB and aids in the application of broadcast standards. The site contains CBSC codes, policy decisions, and annual reports.

Canadian Newspaper Association: www.cna-acj.ca

The Canadian Newspaper Association is a non-profit trade and lobby organization representing Canadian daily newspapers.

Canadian Online Explorer: www.canoe.ca

Canadian Online Explorer, the property of the media conglomerate Quebecor, is an on-line news service and Internet portal established in March 1996. A French-language version was added in September 1999 (www2.canoe.com/index.html). Both sites offer visitors a daily news package (updated throughout the day) featuring all the departments of a regular daily newspaper.

Canada.com: www.canada.com

Canada.com is a news portal that brings together news highlights from CanWest Global's daily newspapers and the Global television network.

CanWest Global Communications: www.canwestglobal.com

CanWest Global is a diversified media company with television, radio, film, and newspaper holdings in Canada, New Zealand, Australia, Ireland, and the United Kingdom.

Cyberpresse: www.cyberpresse.ca

This French-language news portal brings together news highlights from the seven Gesca-owned daily newspapers.

Globe and Mail: www.globeandmail.com

The *Globe and Mail* is Canada's leading national newspaper. Its Web site includes stories from its daily print edition as well as breaking news dispatches.

National Post: www.nationalpost.com

Canada's other 'national' newspaper, owned by CanWest Global, posts stories from its print edition on its Web site.

Quebecor Inc.: www.quebecor.com

Quebecor is a diversified media company with holdings in television, the Internet, newspaper, magazine, and book publishing, as well as book and music retailing.

Radio and Television News Directors Association of Canada: www.rtndacanada.com

The RTNDA represents Canada's broadcast journalists and news managers. It establishes broadcast standards and ethics guidelines, and lobbies on behalf of broadcast journalists.

Toronto Star: www.thestar.com

The *Toronto Star* is Canada's largest-circulation daily newspaper. The site contains a selection of stories from the print edition as well as breaking news.

Universal Declaration of Human Rights:

http://www.un.org/50/decla.htm **or**

www.un.org/Overview/rights.html

The full text of this important document can found at these sites.

FURTHER READINGS

Kovach, Bill, and Tom Rosenstiel. 2001. *The Elements of Journalism: What Newspeople Should Know and the Public Should Expect.* New York: Crown Publishers. This well-written and concise book diagnoses several fundamental problems with the state of journalism in the United States, but the problems it addresses and the recommendations it makes are quite applicable to the Canadian context.

Miller, John. 1998. *Yesterday's News: Why Canada's Daily Newspapers Are Failing Us.* Halifax: Fernwood. Miller writes from his personal experiences as a journalist and a journalism educator, pointing to Canadian daily newspapers' failure to connect with their communities.

Osler, Andrew M. 1993. *News: The Evolution of Journalism in Canada.* Toronto: Copp Clark Pitman. This concise and accessible treatment of journalism history in Canada focuses on evolving principles and themes rather than specific newspaper organizations.

Schudson, Michael. 1978. *Discovering the News: A Social History of American Newspapers.* New York: Basic Books. This oft-cited study of the transformation of journalism in the late nineteenth and early twentieth centuries, while based on American newspapers, provides an explanation of the emergence of objectivity that applies to Canadian journalism as well.

Tuchman, Gaye. 1978. *Making News: A Study in the Construction of Reality.* New York: Free Press. Tuchman's analysis of how journalists gather information and produce news is a groundbreaking study.

van Ginneken, Jaap. 1998. *Understanding Global News: A Critical Introduction.* London: Sage Publications. This critical study details how and why news circulates internationally, and includes discussion of the implications of news flows.

STUDY QUESTIONS

1. What does it mean to say that news content is highly constructed?
2. What are some of the implications of this process of construction?
3. In what sense is news production a form of storytelling?
4. What is wrong with the mirror metaphor or the reflection thesis of journalism?
5. Why is gatekeeping an inadequate metaphor for news judgement?
6. What does freedom of the press mean in the Canadian context? Is it an absolute right?
7. Does objectivity remain a viable ideal for journalists?
8. To what extent are news stories selective representations of the world?
9. In what ways do media owners and managers exercise editorial control?
10. What does it mean to say news stories define events?

LEARNING OUTCOMES

- To explain that journalism, like other forms of media content, involves the deliberate and selective production of news stories.
- To point out that events are selected as news based on specific criteria of newsworthiness.
- To propose the metaphor of the 'frame' as a better explanation for news production than the mirror or gatekeeping.
- To describe, and problematize, some of journalism's core ideals, such as the search for truth and the code of objectivity.
- To survey the demographic characteristics of journalists in Canada in order to point out that they are not representative of the population as a whole.
- To describe the legal framework of news production in Canada and to explain what freedom of the press means in the Canadian context.
- To explain that most journalists in Canada work for commercial news organizations governed by the profit motive and to explore what this implies for news production.
- To provide a more sophisticated understanding of what kind of editorial control owners and managers exercise.
- To position journalism as a narrative form that draws on a number of storytelling conventions.
- To point out that news organizations produce meaning, defining the events that they cover.

Communications Technology and Society: Theory and Practice

Introduction

There probably has been no better time since the Industrial Revolution to think about and reflect upon technology. The dot-com bubble notwithstanding, we are going through a major change in the nature and organization of society brought about by information and communications technology. Those who have been surrounded by computer/communications technology and who understand its logic and potential are working with others who understand information and communications needs and together they are creating new realities.

This chapter begins with a review of some well-established theories of technology. It provides an overview of the development of communications technology. It explores some recent technological developments in communications and reviews the categories of activity they are affecting. The chapter then concludes with some summary observations on communications technology and society.

Technology and Society

Even though some theorists have misgivings about the strength of the influence of technology on modern society (see, for example, Postman, 1993), we could hardly do without it. Indeed, some say that the distinguishing feature of Western society is its embrace of technology. From the first stick picked up and used by prehistoric human beings to the invention of the needle or even the sword, and much later the nuclear bomb and the robot, and from the printing press to the steam engine, telephone, television, computer, and satellite, technology has been inseparable from human activity. We depend on technology for the food we eat, for the homes we live in, for the work we do. The rank of nations in the world economy is profoundly affected by the great technological race. Indeed, the mental embrace of technological change is fundamental to the Western way of thinking. We simply cannot avoid thinking in a technological manner.

We depend on technology for our communications with others—whether they are just a house or two away or halfway around the world. In the second half of the twentieth century it became almost impossible to live without a television in our homes, much less without a telephone, and now we can hardly live without personal computers through which we gain Internet access and send and receive e-mail. The reality of new communications technology is that anyone is able to get in touch with anyone else, anywhere, at any time, for very little money—at least in the developed world.

As successive technologies have taken root in Western society and successive layers of infrastructure have been laid down, two highly significant developments have been occurring. First, our dependency on these systems has been growing. Second, the technological distance between developed and developing economies (and those that are not developing at all) has been increasing. This gap, which from time to time is brought forward for discussion, is often called the digital divide.

Yet another implication of the spread of technology deserves attention. The adoption and widespread use of any technology almost invariably create both negative and positive impacts on us and our environment.

Also, technology is not merely a spinoff of the pursuit of science but rather is an extension of our way of thinking. In fact, in most cases technology is a deliberate attempt to create material objects or interventions that, in changing or improving situations, can allow the developer to reap financial reward. In a sense, technological development is a business.

We are firmly in the clutches of the **technological imperative**, that is, we have convinced ourselves that we should continuously develop new technologies and apply them broadly. Therefore we must understand the fundamentals of technology—both the possible and the unavoidable consequences of its application. We must then invent laws to regulate and institutions to develop technology so that it is as generally and universally beneficial as possible. In communications, the keys to beneficial adoption of technology are patent and copyright laws, policy, regulations, and enabling legislation that cover information, education, libraries, the arts, broadcasting, and telecommunications.

Technology Defined

Technology is more than machinery. According to US communications scholar Langdon Winner (1977), technology encompasses at least three elements:

1. pieces of apparatus;
2. techniques of operation to make the apparatus work; and
3. social institutions within which technical activities take place.

Even if all these elements are present, however, the outcome is not predetermined. For instance, the same invention can lead to very different social impacts in different situations, as was the case with movable type in Europe and China. As Marshall McLuhan (1962), Elizabeth Eisenstein (1983), and others have pointed out, in Europe the introduction of movable type led to social change. In China, as David Ze (1995) has argued, it led to a reinforcement of social stability (see Chapter 1).

A substantial literature on the social impact of technology assumes Winner's broad definition. French philosopher Jacques Ellul, generally regarded as an insightful, if pessimistic, theorist of technology, discussed the nature and impact of technology in *The Technological Society* (1964). In that book Ellul's primary concern was to explore the past, present, and future impacts of technological change. Of the many conclusions and observations he drew, four, identified by technology scholar Wilson Dizard, stand out in particular:

1. All technical progress exacts a price; that is, while it adds something on the one hand, it subtracts something on the other.
2. All technical progress raises more problems than it solves, tempts us to see the consequent problems as technical in nature, and prods us to seek technical solutions to them.
3. The negative effects of technological innovation are inseparable from the positive. It is naive to say that technology is neutral, that it may be used for good or bad ends; the good and bad effects are, in fact, simultaneous and inseparable.
4. All technological innovations have unforeseen effects. (Dizard, 1985: 11)

In short, technology sets in motion powerful forces that rearrange the organizing attributes of any society. The challenge for a technological society is to invent social institutions to ensure that the technology in question is put to use for the greatest benefit for the greatest number.

A complementary viewpoint can be found in the writings of Canadian philosopher George Grant. In *Technology and Empire*, Grant argued that the foundation of all modern, liberal, industrial and post-industrial societies is to be found in technique and technology: 'the belief that human excellence is promoted by the homogenizing and universalizing power of technology is the dominant doctrine of modern liberalism, and—that doctrine must undermine all particularisms' (Grant, 1969: 69). In Grant's view, the powerful forces that Ellul identifies are homogenizing in their influence and hence are threatening the distinctive elements of societies that share the same technology.

Raymond Williams (1975) has argued that television technology is an extension of the Industrial Revolution and feeds the mass society that industrialization created. American Marxist scholar Herbert Schiller (1984) has turned this general perspective on technology around somewhat to expose a different angle. Schiller maintains that technological development and its application are an operating imperialist strategy on the part of the United States that is designed to maintain economic and political dominance, through technological prowess and technological gaps, between the US and other countries. Moreover, he sees this imperialism as steered by multinational corporations and stimulated by military research and development in communications hardware.

In contrast to these viewpoints, mainstream American scholars, like the mainstream of America and increasingly the world, have been inclined to see technology as benevolent and technological change as progressive. This optimism stems from an economic history in which the development and use of machines to create wealth has been regarded as of widespread benefit to American society over the past 200 years.

Technology and Technological Determinism

Technologically based societies affirm and embrace machinery, the social organization necessary to adopt that machinery, and the acquisition of the requisite skills needed for its operation. That embrace is so complete that both analysts (for example, George Gilder, 1991) and the general public (see media discussions of the Internet and the Web) accept projections about the future of society that are based on technological capacity. This is referred to as technological determinism—a belief that technological development equates to progress and that if technology (usually conceived of as some kind of apparatus) can do something, society will take full advantage of this technological capacity and will be shaped fundamentally by the apparatus.

For instance, technological determinism would argue that the moon landing changed society fundamentally: it was seen as the beginning of the colonization of space by humanity. Similarly, the Internet was supposed to democratize the world more completely than ever before. Of course, both technological developments have had profound impacts on society, but the extent to which they have met expectations is not borne out—mainly because this technological determinism does not account for all things.

Technological determinism fails to consider three fundamental variables. First, with reference to the idea that technology encompasses apparatus, technique, and social organization, devices that are developed emerge from a way of thinking and from the awareness of particular problems that appear in need of being solved. So it is not that the technology drops out of the clear blue sky or from the head of some unworldly genius; rather, it originates from specific efforts to address certain social realities. For example, the Internet was developed as a decentralized method of communication that could maintain itself even though parts of the network were destroyed (Leiss, 1990).

The second fundamental variable that technological determinism ignores is that the industrialized application of technology has social consequences. The Internet can as easily be a force for dictatorship or terrorism as for democracy, depending on how it is applied. In the end, at least in Western society, the matter is either or both political and/or economic. If politicians wish, they can erect policy so that a certain technology (e.g., the Internet) can only be used in certain ways (e.g., for Canadian content), and hence, with certain consequences (e.g., contributing to the cohesiveness of Canada or to massive rejection of such a policy by many Canadians). If policy is not enacted and matters are left to the marketplace or to the freedom of individuals to decide, and if a need can be created and affordable products and services developed, which, in turn, fit into existing patterns of life and are seen as beneficial, then, at least in a technological society, the particular technology will be developed and used, and society is left to adapt to the consequences.

The third fundamental variable that technological determinism ignores is that other powerful spheres of life affect the development of society. If a particular technology were to vastly distort the distribution of wealth, social action would intervene to destroy or render less powerful that technology. If a particular technology contradicted the basic values of a society then it would be ignored or, at least, not widely adopted. Stated slightly differently, technological determinism ignores the strength of the human spirit. While it is true that Soviet Communism undermined the human spirit for a period of almost 75 years, rarely can politicians prevail over the sense of survival, community, and justice that has asserted itself through history.

THE GREAT (FIRE)WALL OF CHINA

Since the advent of the Internet, the Chinese Communist government has been looking for ways to allow the economy of China to benefit but for that benefit not to threaten its hold on power. In late 2002, the Chinese government developed a high-tech device that detects illicit words such as Falun Gong. The technique the Chinese have developed produces a beep and freezes the inbox of the user's e-mail system and the computer must be rebooted. Earlier in the year, Google and AltaVista were shut down and opened, in the case of Google, with its cache function removed. The Chinese government has also found a way to block certain pages of Web sites. The irony here is that, in all probability, the US has similar technology. Its aim is not to shut down people's computers—although it would not be beyond the CIA to contract with hackers to shut down the computers of suspected terrorist groups. Of more immediate American government interest would be computer-based identification of suspected terrorist communication, an alert system, an ability to identify and decipher, at least to some extent, metaphorical speech, and computer-controlled collection of evidence (York, 2002: A14, Reprinted with permission from the Globe and Mail).

THE LIMITATIONS OF TECHNOLOGY

Implicit in technological determinism is the notion that technology can transform society. However, the consequences of the transformative dynamic of technology usually go unrealized in its initial application. And later, unanticipated problems can emerge that must then be counteracted. Take antibiotics, for example. While antibiotics have been a godsend in terms of public health, we now understand that resistant strains of bacteria have developed that the antibiotics cannot fight. Similarly, the development of monocultures, single varieties of plants that are most productive and produce the most valuable harvestable crop, makes vast food supplies extremely vulnerable to failure. The sinking of the *Titanic*, which was viewed as unsinkable because it was an example of the latest and greatest technology, was an example of technological arrogance. In communications, there are similar issues surrounding the limitations of technology. For instance, while a lot more people are able to access vast amounts of information, as economies of scale come to dominate in the preparation of information suddenly all kinds of information that has a limited audience goes missing. National, regional, and neighbourhood information ceases to reach us as we turn more and more to local and global broadcasting. Finally, elements so mundane as the number of hours one might spend sitting in front of a computer or the lack of socialization involved in working from home may have considerable negative consequences when multiplied throughout society. This is what Ellul meant by the inseparability of the good and bad effects of technology.

The Nature of Communications Technology

While Winner, Ellul, Grant, Williams, and Schiller provide some understanding of the nature of technology in general, it is in the literature on communications technology specifically that we find both a general definition of technology and a specific definition of communications technology. Shannon and Weaver, who put forward the mathematical model of communications we explored in Chapter 2, note that 'communications' includes 'all of the procedures by which one mind may affect another' (1949: 3–5). Technology theorist James Beniger (1986) maintains that information, which is the content of communications, derives from the organization of the material world, and technology is the manner in which that organization is brought about. Thus technology is 'any intentional extension of a natural process' (Beniger in Crowley and Heyer, 1991: 250), and communications technology is the intentional extension of the means to allow intelligence to move through time and/or space. For Beniger and others, the communications/information revolution (in both the evolutionary and turn-about sense of the word) is a revolution of who controls what information, generated by whom, over what geographical area. Communication and its technologies change the dynamics, the location, and the breadth of control.

The nature of control caused by communications technology has given rise to a greater separation between information about a phenomenon and the phenomenon itself. And this separation has resulted in the reorganization of space and power. Consider a few examples of the separation of a phenomenon and information. A thermostat exists in the middle of a house and a furnace in an out-of-the-way corner. The thermostat senses the pre-set temperature and turns the furnace off and on. A burglar alarm on a house sets off a signal at a police or security firm's dispatch office. A computer is programmed to monitor stock prices and alert a broker when certain stock prices rise or fall more than a set percentage. A computer monitors returning fish to a river mouth and determines how much should be caught, allocating quotas upriver.

In each case, local knowledge, sometimes of a higher quality, sometimes not, is replaced with knowledge further away from the phenomenon itself. This replacement of one kind of knowledge in the hands of one set

---

THE GREAT (FIRE) WALL OF CHINA CRUMBLES

Clever technology notwithstanding, many users have already found a way around China's firewall: wit and irony, metaphor, parody, and allusion. No machine can deal easily with plays on words. Thus, to bolster the firewall mentioned in the previous box, the official newspaper, the *People's Daily*, has taken to warning spam mailers that political rumours upset social stability. A number of articles dealing with the ineffectiveness of the Chinese firewall can be found on the Internet. Search under China+firewall. Most deal with how hackers and Internet cafés in China are circumventing the firewall.

DVDS: THE LATEST PERFECT RECORDING/PLAYBACK TECHNOLOGY

No doubt, when you first purchased your CD player, you were sold it on the basis of sound quality. In 1982, CD technology was advertised as 'perfect sound forever', that is, higher fidelity than LPs and no deterioration after each play. Though diamonds may be forever, nothing in communications technology seems to be.

In late 1998 digital audio format based on DVD home-video-disk technology was launched. What makes it better? CD technology digitizes sound by converting it into discrete electrical impulses at the rate of 44,100 per second to form a 16-bit word. Even though 44,100 is fast and it forms a reasonably accurate 'word', it is not continuous as is, for instance, analogue sound. The result for aficionados of this so-called 16/44 standard is a certain graininess, hardness, hollowness, even an excessive cleanliness. What goes missing is background information—the decay of one piano note as the other was played, the echo of a drum roll, the complete set of overtones of a Stradivarius violin.

A DVD (DVD is often thought to stand for Digital Video Disk, but instead stands for Digital Versatile Disk) contains seven times the available space of a CD. When DVDs are used for movies, most of that space is taken up by images. DVD audio provides a much richer audio signal and therefore a much more realistic sound. An industry standard had yet to emerge in 1999 but one interesting method being used was to create 24-bit words based on a higher sampling rate of 96,000 per second, a 24/96 standard. The difference in the size of the vocabulary of sound is 65,536 values as opposed to 16.8 million potential values.

The strength of DVD, its quality, its durability, is also, from a producer's point of view, a weakness. Just as second-hand CD sales are thriving, so once a person has acquired a copy of a movie or video, which will last for years, it is likely to be traded with friends, and therefore fail to generate as much profit for the producer. Enter Divx technology, a technology that allows for a DVD disk to become unplayable at a set time after it is first played. The point is to bypass rental outlets, encouraging people to purchase inexpensive, disposable Divx copies instead (consumers can upgrade, for a fee, to a version that will remain playable). In early 1999 Divx technology was being lambasted by user groups, while other commentators felt its lower-grade technology and its distribution system (through consumer electronics stores) would kill its market success.

Sources: Gerald Levitch, 'Better-than-CD sounds makes quiet debut', *Globe and Mail*, 13 Feb. 1999, C9; Gillian Shaw, 'The dawning of Divx', Vancouver Sun, 5 Nov. 1998, E1.

of people with another kind of knowledge in the hands of another set of people (or machines) can have far-reaching consequences. Particular local knowledge, based on a vast storehouse of information coded in behaviour, feelings, superstitions, and understandings that are used to retrieve the past, explain the present, and foretell the future, is set aside. Relevant variables are identified, models created, monitoring programs set in place, laws passed, and authority anointed. Such is the power of formal knowledge, communications, and information-processing. Such also is its ability to eclipse a local culture, to shift control from a multiplicity of scattered points, each in close proximity to a phenomenon, to a central location that controls activities in a far-flung hinterland. Ideally, the centralization of control improves things for everyone. However, as illustrated by the federal government's setting of a cod fisheries quota after Newfoundland fishers were argu-

ing for years that the fish were disappearing, centralization of control can also have its downside.

Once the central processing centre has gained appropriate levels of information, it can begin to replace the on-location decision-maker. The central processing centre can also introduce a further level of sophistication. It can bring in information about other locations—for instance, the state of world production, the state of markets, or even the state of government subsidies or restraints in other countries. It may even be able to predict events more accurately based on its knowledge of distant but related events.

The social and economic impact of the separation of information and entity is extensive. First, information itself becomes a separate product that can be bought and sold. Second, as noted, increased power accrues to the location of the information. Until recently, this was to be found in financial or manufacturing centres. Now, it can exist anyplace where there are sufficient technical and human resources. Third, distant homelands of indigenous peoples are turned into frontiers of industrial society, whether in the Arctic (now a source of both oil and diamonds) or the Amazon (increasingly a source of useful plant-based drugs).

Technology and the Communications Industries

Traditionally, communications industries have been differentiated on the basis of their technology. Thus, telephone systems were designed to facilitate point-to-point communications offering limited fidelity (an understandable voice) but sophisticated switching. On the other hand, broadcast technology was designed not only to carry signals from a single point to multiple points but also to have a satisfactory level of fidelity so that listening for a long time to voice and music would be an enjoyable experience. Recording technology was developed to carry the highest demands in terms of fidelity and the lowest in terms of universality of distribution, that is, available only by consumer purchase. And just as recording technology increased in its fidelity over the years from wax cylinders to 78s to LPs to tapes to CDs and now DVDs, so radio improved as stations migrated from AM (amplitude modulation) to FM (frequency modulation) and then to AM digital radio.

While no doubt many assumed that there was a technological base to this division of responsibilities, as Babe (1988, 1990) has pointed out, no such technological determinism existed. Telephones could easily have been turned into broadcast instruments as they were in the very first example of voice telephony by Reginald Fessenden (see Fessenden, 1974) and in early

radio forms, and as they have been used in some Eastern European countries.

TECHNOLOGICAL CONVERGENCE

The separation of communications functions into separate industries and the development of technology that best suited the functions of telephony, broadcasting, and sound and video recording have served society well. This industrial and technological separation has prevented the overall control of communications by one set of companies by spreading ownership somewhat broadly. Imagine if the CBC or CTV were your telephone and cable company and one of five or so major recording labels.

With digitization, cameras, computers, musical instruments, radio, television, cable, and telephones are all information machines that essentially do the same job—collect, code, and thus transform information into digital form. They are merely specialized computerized transceivers. For instance, through sampling technology, an electronic keyboard can almost reproduce any sound. Electronic drums are digital encoding pads that are quite reasonable facsimiles of the real sound of drums. Each device is a specialized computer focusing on a particular sound and/or image and/or text format. The commonality—digitization—and hence the ability for one device to send output or receive input from another is what is meant by the term 'technological convergence'.

TECHNOLOGY AND POLICY

In the beginning years of the twenty-first century, we are once again facing many of the same choices that people confronted at the turn of the last century. Just as policy, not technology, determined that telephone and broadcasting would be separated into two indus-

DIGITAL RADIO: FOREVER PROMISED, ALWAYS POSTPONED

Digital radio has been talked about for some time. Like HDTV, it was just about to hit the market in 1999. By 2002 it was once again just around the corner. In 2002 it looked as if the corner was actually being turned and that consumers might begin to invest in digital radios (2002 price: $200 to $400). Projections coming out of the US were that automobile manufacturers were getting set to

include digital radios in new cars for a surcharge of about $150 Cdn. Surprisingly, since very few own digital radio receivers, many radio stations are already sending out digital signals (on the L band between 142 and 1492 megahertz). What may persuade people to make the purchase are complementary products. The most attractive of these is the ability to record onto an MP3 device.

CROSSING THE PHOTO QUALITY BARRIER

In 2002 cameras crossed the photo quality barrier with announcements by Canon and Kodak of cameras with images built on 11 and 13 megapixels. Items on Slashdot.org noted this and referred users to the announcements. See, for example: http://www.kodak.com/US/en/corp/researchDevelopment/productFeatures/sensor2002.shtml

tries (see Babe, 1988, 1990), so policy will encourage an industrial structure that, ideally, is of the greatest benefit to Canadians. The alternative, it appears, is a totally integrated communications system controlled by a very few mega-corporations that would dwarf the largest we see now.

The challenge here is twofold: (1) to ensure that the needs of the public and of business are met, and (2) to ensure that certain businesses do not become too pow-erful and thereby thwart the participation of others and prevent further social and technological development. The attempt of Microsoft to dominate in nearly every software market is a case in point. A myriad of other similar but less noticed situations also arise. In 1997, for example, the purchase of MCI Communications by WorldCom Inc. became an issue because the combined company would control up to 60 per cent of US Internet traffic and hence would have substantial power to control pricing of access both for consumers and for small access providers (*Globe and Mail*, 2 Oct. 1997, B15). In this case the fears were unnecessary. WorldCom filed for bankruptcy in 2002.

While allowing for convergence and competition sounds like a good idea, it is difficult for the CRTC to respond with appropriate policy. For example, the telephone and cable companies provide Internet access to consumers and are known as 'backbone providers'. They also provide connectivity to small Internet service providers (ISPs), who also sell access to the public. Similarly, the cable companies now own some of the specialty channels while also providing access to their competitors—clearly a conflict of interest that the

WHEN CONVERGENCE WORKS! AND NOT!

Some people call it convergence. Others call it concentration of ownership. Still others, such as *Globe and Mail* correspondent Simon Houpt, call it synergy. In the summer of 2002, AOL Time Warner released *Goldmember*. Here is a list of what the company did to ensure the movie was a hit.

- For weeks, AOL's on-line service had been promoting the movie to its 34-million-subscriber base.
- In the week of 27 July, the AOL-owned magazine, *Entertainment Weekly*, featured Austin Powers on the cover and carried several articles inside about the movie.
- The week before, a division of Warner music, also owned by AOL, released the film sound track.
- Also in the week of 27 July, AOL-owned cable station TBS aired the previous two Austin Powers movies to help the audience get ready for the new release.
- In the week of the release (Friday, 26 July) AOL-owned Moviefone.com was awash with Austin Powers ads.
- On Wednesday, 24 July, Mike Myers received a star in Hollywood's walk of fame, an event given ample coverage by AOL media properties, CNN, *People* magazine, and numerous Web sites.

And AOL didn't pull out all the stops. It could have scheduled an appearance of Myers at its baseball franchise, the Atlanta Braves. (Its other two sports franchises at the time, the Atlanta Thrashers [NHL] and Atlanta Hawks [NBA], were both in the off-season.)

According to Houpt (2002: R5), movies such as *Goldmember* are referred to as 'tent poles'. They are event movies (in that their release is a media event) that are strong enough in their earnings to carry a season's pictures, and when they are released on video they carry ads for the other movies the company has made or is making. But in a company that does US $169 billion in business each year, smaller pictures can get lost, even good pictures, and even pictures that cost $25 to $50 million to make. They just are not big enough.

cable companies exploit to the degree that they can get away with it. It is government policy that sets the rules of the game, determining whether, for instance, cable companies can own specialty channels.

There is also an international component to policy issues. For instance, while different countries have different laws on free speech, privacy, access to information, and so forth, the Internet breaks through those laws by being universally available. Were international bodies truly out to respect the laws and cultures of member nations, great effort would be expended to find a way of building 'metatags' on information so that its flow could be controlled. However, this is on no agenda of any international body with any power. Thus, what the national laws allow in the least restrictive countries will become the norm for the world. This is certainly the case with free speech: on 27 June 1997 the US Supreme Court ruled that a law making it a crime to put 'indecent' material on the Internet was unconstitutional. The ruling went as follows:

> Notwithstanding the legitimacy and importance of the congressional goal of protecting children from harmful materials, we agree . . . that the statute (the Communications Decency Act) abridges 'the freedom of speech' protected by the First Amendment. . . . 'Regardless of the strength of the government's interest' in protecting children, 'the level of discourse reaching the mailbox simply cannot be limited to that which would be suitable for a sandbox.' (*Globe and Mail*, 30 June 1997, A17)

Of course, once barriers are broken by the Internet then it will not seem unusual for other barriers to be broken in other media. Arguably, a good example of this occurred in February 1999 with the 'Canadian edition' of *Hustler* magazine. Faced with the occasionally tough-minded Sheila Copps and her leadership in bringing Bill C-55 towards passage in Parliament, *Hustler*'s proprietor decided to run a fake naked picture of the minister, which readers were encouraged to match up to a choice of genitalia. Independent of what passes for pornography, it is doubtful that any Canadian magazine would ever think up such a scheme, let alone wish to undertake it. The Canadian media operate at a different level of decency.

It is precisely these sorts of situations that demand we create policy to address the increasingly complex issues surrounding communications technology, particularly technology that can ignore national borders.

Technological Development: Rationales and Realities

Technology has a way of propelling itself in technological societies by creating economic opportunity and by tapping into our natural curiosity with objects and the way things work. But for technology to be seized upon and heartily embraced by society requires the allocation of resources in the short term with the promise of long-term gain. The usual rationales used to encourage society's eager acceptance of technology are based on some idea that a particular technology will improve the lot of humankind. The specific areas in which that improvement is purported to arise for communications are customarily health, culture, and education. In health, the wide dissemination of preventive, diagnostic, curative, and emergency information is stressed. In culture, the inexpensive and more extensive dissemination of quality products is highlighted. In education, the availability of better information designed more effectively for the learner, with the possibility of interactivity and supplemented by motivational devices and workplace relevancy, is just a beginning. Other positive impacts are claimed in the areas of self-direction, social interaction, international and inter-ethnic tolerance, and even cognitive skills.

The realities of technological development are somewhat different, as most theorists would predict. As we all know, television and radio can open the world to people at its furthest reaches, especially now with satellite transmission and particularly to areas with low literacy rates. However, achieving the promise of universally available television—to educate, inform, empower, amuse, and enlighten—is another matter. Take, for instance, something as simple as the teaching of reading. In some societies reading is regarded as a selfish or an indulgent activity insulting to those around you because it shuts them out. Cultural barriers in the spread of technology are common. In some cultures television programs educating women on how to control their pregnancies are seen as an infringement on the male prerogative. In other cultures television programs on certain subjects break taboos on their discussion, or on their discussion in the company of certain others. This makes the possibilities for technological development more difficult to translate into a reality.

In addition to cultural barriers are economic ones. For example, education programs and educational television systems most often must be paid for by scarce public funds, which means their availability is limited.

In contrast, entertainment programs that promote consumerism and are funded through advertisements are widely available. However, such commercial programs raise expectations often beyond the ability of the recipient society to fulfill.

This is not to discount developments in communications or to claim that they cannot serve the interests of culture, education, and health. However, neither satellites nor the Internet, nor computers or any other technology, is likely to bring about a new egalitarian world. These technologies have brought about extensive efforts at distance education both in the developed and developing world—for instance, in China, India, Mongolia, Indonesia, and Thailand. In some instances they have been successful in raising the levels of skills and knowledge of students. But the efforts of people ultimately make the difference. While distance education may use computers and digital communications, because such technology can cope so easily with distance, they are not necessary components of distance education programs. Satellites (and wireless communication in general) also have the major advantage that they can help serve large, sparsely populated developed countries or developing countries that lack a land-based communications infrastructure. But again, no amount of technology of any kind will make a bit of difference without knowledgeable teachers and without a nurturing recipient society.

The introduction of computers into the classroom and access to the Internet have become symbols of modernization. The most radical rationale for their introduction has been the projected positive effects on both cognitive processes and personality development. The individualization of the learning process has also been stressed. Most importantly, and obviously, these technologies change the nature of the classroom from a closed-off laboratory of learning to a window on the world of organized and spontaneously produced information, opinion, and analysis. Nevertheless, the correlation between the rationales for technological developments and how they are manifested in reality is not always true. Nowhere is this more obvious than in situations where technology is introduced from one part of the world to another, where the knowledge of the technology is either limited or non-existent.

TECHNOLOGY TRANSFER

The export of new technologies from one country to another, especially from developed economies to developing economies, is usually referred to as **technology transfer**. Research on technology transfer reveals a number of insights. Generally speaking, direct causal correlations between the introduction of a technology into developing economies and changes in social behaviour (for example, making greater use of birth control devices and procedures) cannot be identified. Combinations of technology with other changes *can* change behaviour. For example, economically speaking (and only economically), in many rural settings it is seen as a net asset for families to have more children whereas in a city they are a net expense. Hence, birth control information with a change of circumstances may have an effect as urban dwellers gradually change their orientation to size of family.

Relatedly, technically oriented approaches to the introduction of technology (skills training, explanation of the equipment) are limited in their effectiveness. The social element is missing. Nor does manufacture of equipment in developing economies necessarily remove barriers to its adoption and maintenance. Equipment can be assembled under direction and without any understanding of its operation or any conception of how such a machine might be used to advantage. The importation of **turn-key operations**—the importing country simply opens the box and turns the machine on—often proves of limited value for lack of prior study of needs and an emphasis on the package rather than the content and the technology itself. Finally, such transfers, if they do work, often create substantial long-term dependency relationships as the receivers of the technology continue to rely on those supplying it for instruction on its use and maintenance problems.

Negotiations of technology transfers designed to increase their effectiveness are well intentioned but often get bogged down in political and economic considerations. The value of transfers is also affected by limited exploration of the differing needs and dynamics of the society receiving the technology. For instance, at a most obvious level, blowing desert sand, high temperatures, and high humidity wreak havoc on almost any electronic equipment. Massive importation of equipment may be useless until software and technologists are there to instruct users. Even attempts to create teleports, that is, self-sufficient zones of advanced telecommunications and high-tech industries to serve as springboards for industrialization, have limitations as a consequence of the technology transfer itself (Jouët and Coudray, 1991: 37, 38).

The difference in the success of technology transfer

from Europe and North America to countries such as Japan and now China can be explained in terms of the nature and organization of those societies in contrast to the societies of Africa and South America.

Regulating Communications Technology— The Fundamentals

By international covenant, countries currently have the right to participate in communications development and to protect themselves from it, a protection that has been set aside in free trade agreements such as those that apply in the European Union. For example, should an unwanted satellite signal spill over so that it is transmitting inside its boundaries, a country can object. Japan has adjusted some of its satellite footprints in response to such objections. Countries also have the power to forbid the importation or exportation of any other form of information, either material or immaterial. These rights to protect groups, which are largely dependent on national status, are termed **collective rights**.

Existing in tension with these collective rights are **individual rights**. Building from the foundation of the United Nations' Universal Declaration of Human Rights, all individuals have the right to 'seek, receive and impart information'. The challenge is this: while the collectivity has the right to act in its own interests, individuals within the collectivity have the right to do so as well, and these interests may be contrary to those of the collectivity as a whole. Thus, while Canadians as a group might want regulation to ensure a predominance of Canadian broadcast signals, many individual Canadians might want the freedom to choose what broadcast signal to tune into. Once individual rights are extended to corporations on the basis that corporations have the status of persons (in most legal respects), not only is there the force of individuals that do not want the state to interfere with individual freedoms but also that of corporations, which have an interest in promoting 'individual freedom'. This pits the political, social, and cultural interests of the collectivity against the demands for a non-interfering state by individuals and business interests. What is called for is a balancing of rights such that both can exist.

Technological developments represent a continual challenge for legal systems and policy-makers. The foremost challenge is to respect both collective and individual rights and to ensure that the greatest number gain the maximum benefit. At times and in some

countries, creating universal benefit means assisting dissemination. At other times in other countries it may mean denying people access to certain technologies and content in order to promote a more universal distribution of other content via alternative technology. For example, in Europe, cable TV has been a long time in coming. One reason it was not introduced earlier is that it would have undermined state monopolies (Collins, 1992).

Other rights enter into the picture in technological development. Personal privacy is one. The most obvious example of invasion of privacy is that which takes place when someone with a scanner intercepts a cell-phone conversation. Similarly, someone may intercept your credit card number as it is being transmitted along the Internet. But other aspects of privacy are equally important. Profiles of individual consumer behaviour gained by tracing a consumer's spending patterns potentially infringe on personal privacy. Indeed, a whole industry is developing because we have the technological capacity to monitor all sorts of information. It is commonly called **data mining** (data mining is discussed more fully later in this chapter). For now, we should note that determining the level of privacy to be protected and then protecting personal privacy are complex matters.

Protection of intellectual property has also become a salient issue in the context of the form in which intellectual property can exist and in the context of a vast increase in information products. The first question is: are patterns of electronic signals eligible for protection, and if so, over what period of time and under what regime? And what about trademarks, patents, copyright? Should vendors be allowed to sell products in which the vendor may confine the use and time period of ownership, as they now do? How should national laws be harmonized to allow international co-ordination if there are fundamentally different positions on these issues? What protection and compensation should creators receive from databases that organize information produced by them? How should financial gain be divided between the creators and the organizations or individuals that hire them? Should moral or personal rights be protected, that is, those rights having to do with who is acknowledged as the creator and who determines how the work can be used? Or should only economic rights be protected? Who has responsibility for libel in the chain of information producers, packagers, and transmitters?

Another significant issue involves **piracy**. Given the historical record, specifically of the American publishing industry, which was built on a foundation of piracy, what obligations should developing economies take on? Studies show that computer, sound, and video piracy are especially rampant. Lack of protection of intellectual property allows cheap consumption of products. However, it also stands in the way of legitimate business in intellectual property in piracy-condoning countries. In India, in the early 1990s, so many small theatres were screening pirated videos that the state introduced a licensing system to attempt to garner revenues. Although this was done, the videos shown continued to be illegal copies. However, as Urvashi Butalia (1994) notes, this should not lead to the conclusion that piracy is rampant in all media in India. On the contrary, at least in book publishing, countries such as India have come to realize that their interests are better served by enforcing copyright laws. The film industry of Egypt, for example, is severely crippled by the numerous bootleg copies made as soon as any film is finished. Nevertheless, the motivation for many countries to take decisive action is not strong—the effect of legislation would be primarily to protect the interests of US industries.

These are just some of the major issues coming forward as the information society develops. As McLuhan said: 'We shape our tools', and by inventiveness and through enacting policy, especially in the context of technological convergence and the current power of communications technology, we shape technology, its industrialization, and its impact, and 'thereafter our tools shape us.' Once in place, the logic of that technology begins to play itself out within the context of further policy. Historically, nations attempted to balance the social, cultural, economic, and technological for the benefit of the greatest number. As we move into an increasingly international arena, the technological design of our future communications system is being determined by international politics and economics. The specific institutions involved are the WTO (formerly GATT), NAFTA, the EU, and the **Berne Convention** on copyright. These international conventions set rules or **regimes** for international trade in communications products and address consumer freedoms and target audiences with shared viewing habits. However, they are weak or do not address the social and cultural needs of national and political communities and their cultures except as mediated by the marketplace.

Technology and the Special Case of the Internet

In an article on technology and the mass media written for a sociology textbook on the subject, Smith makes two points about the Internet and how different it is from most technological development (Lorimer and Smith, 2003). He calls attention to the open-source nature of the Internet, that is, how all of the elements of the Internet were developed in the public sphere by unpaid programmers, many of whom were students. Built into each new element was an RFC: a request for comment. The RFC was effectively an open peer review system where one person would have an idea for a system for exchanging messages. He would then write some lines of program and tentatively call it an electronic mail system. Another programmer might come along and build on that by grabbing the first person's idea, examining his code, and reconceiving it in a simpler and elegant fashion. Then another programmer might do that again. In such a way, various programmers, working as an electronic community, developed the basic functionality of the Internet. And that is how Eudora, the e-mail program developed at the University of Illinois, ended up as a product of a university. It was developed by students, professors, and technicians within the university. TCP/IP was a method of computers communicating with servers that developed from a doctoral dissertation. (See www.yale.edu/pclt/COMM/TCPIP.HTM for an explanation of the function of TCP and IP.)

In a way, the request for comment, the RFC, is a trivial yet profound element of the Internet that distinguishes it from most, but not all, technological development. It represents openness, a community of inquiry building a piece of technology, in this case a communication system in the public domain unencumbered by patents or other attempts to create, own, and protect intellectual property. The open Internet took the devices of Mr Gates and Mr Jobs and made them interconnectable and interoperable. This open development structure reflects the normal manner in which scientific inquiry is carried out, with no secrecy surrounding one's activities and with open publication of results. A good parallel would be the human genome project, which has scientists all over the world mapping the genes of various organisms, posting what they are doing, and posting the results for all to see. This form of open-source technological development is a dramatic contrast to the activities of Microsoft (and

LINUX

The importance of policy and of competition with regard to technology has been underlined by an operating system called Linux. Linux has been made available by Red Hat Software Inc. (www.redhat.com) and is a match for Microsoft's operating system. It is available to consumers for $50, or free on the Internet. As noted by Robert Young, Red Hat's CEO: 'My job is not to compete with Microsoft. . . . It's to lower the value of the operating sys-

tem market. Microsoft makes $5 billion in operating system sales. If I get that market, I automatically make it a $500 million market' (*Globe and Mail*, 8 Oct. 1998, C5). Had the US government or even the Canadian government brought forward policy demanding competition in operating systems for PCs, they could have lowered the cost of operating systems in the same way that Linux is doing it through competition.

all commercial companies), which goes to great lengths to protect its code and make it impossible for others to access. Doing so has made Bill Gates the richest man in the world. None of the pioneers of the Internet got rich. Effectively, they gave their intellectual property to the world.

Smith (2003) points to a second significant element of this manner of technological development. Industrial interests are not placed first and foremost. In fact, Smith argues that the open structure led to a particular technological form in which the pioneers laid down some basic rules that are reflected in the manner in which the system still operates—the RFC, the decentralized system controlled by no one, the continued evolution of open-source alternatives such as Linux.

One such project involves a group of Canadian university libraries and a number of Canadian social science and humanities journals. It is called Synergies: The Canadian Scholarly Information Network. The project involves the development of an on-line journal publication system housed at a variety of university libraries across the country, the content of which, at the beginning of the project, is intended to be the vast majority of Canadian social science and humanities journals alongside some significant cultural periodicals.

Synergies is an open-source programming project that would allow the whole system to be replicated in any other country. It will be built so that other publications will be able to be added on—cultural magazines, journals from other countries, etc. Its beginnings are to be found in the on-line capability of several scholarly journals and on-line publishing initiatives, the activities of the University of New Brunswick library, the on-line Canadian scientific journals of the National Research Council, and Project Erudit at the Université de Montréal.

Technology at the Beginning of Millennium III

The history of the tools and techniques of humanity provides a certain insight into the preoccupations of the times when they were developed and thrived. Think, for example, of the mechanical age that was captured by Leonardo da Vinci in his notebooks and of the control of the physical world at which his inventions were directed. Building on a variety of techniques of the time, Leonardo intuited the basic principles of physics and mechanical advantage. Thus, just as a gigantic threaded shaft could be used to raise a dome to the top of a cathedral, so a whirling blade could be used to lift a machine into the air. Similarly, by dissecting cadavers, Leonardo gained a deeper knowledge of the architecture of the human body and was thereby able to present it visually with greater insight than his predecessors or contemporaries.

It is true that, at all times, understanding and control of various phenomena are being advanced on a variety of fronts—the physical, the biological, the social, the philosophical. But often one or two areas predominate in certain times—for example, philosophy and mathematics in ancient Greece. Humankind has sought to control, dominate, and transcend the physical through technology from the building of the pyramids, and perhaps before, through Leonardo's time and into the modern era, where we have broken the bonds of earth, floated around it in a balloon in the jet stream (21 March 1999), and looked into the heavens with the Hubble telescope back to the beginning of time. The conquering of the physical world has captured our attention and imagination even though we have made tremendous breakthroughs in other areas, such as in medicine, where we have learned to control a variety of diseases.

The predominance of our focus on physical technology is passing. It is being replaced with two types of technology vying for our allegiance—biotechnology and communications technology. On the biological side we are moving beyond the level of the quite impressive but nevertheless fancy band-aid solutions of the past. The human genome project, together with light-sensitive drugs and a host of other developments, is taking us closer to achieving a completely new level of control over the biological realm. At the same time, communications technology is reordering our lives, forging a new integration of activities around the world and creating one very large economic, and hence social and political, system.

Marshall McLuhan was the Leonardo of the information age. Building on the existence of a number of technologies, changing times, and the initial conceptions of Harold Innis, McLuhan was able to intuit the evolving shape and the organizing principles of the information society. In examining the current state of our information society, we ask what we can do, how things are changing, and the general shape of developments now arriving, as well as those on the horizon. As enthusiasts are fond of saying, radio reached 50 million listeners after 38 years. TV took 13 years to reach the same number of viewers. It has taken the Internet a mere four years to muster the same-sized audience of 50 million. True, in each case the population base had expanded, but not by enough to account for such a vast change.

Achievements in the Information World

Over the past three or four years many new devices, services, and capacities have emerged to enhance our ability to communicate and handle information. In categorizing them according to their purpose or focus, we can see the parts of our lives that are being changed as well as the patterns of change.

INCREASED COMMUNICATION CAPACITY AND SPEED

While communications satellites are now commonplace, when they first went up in the 1960s they were very much a novelty. Newspapers provided information on what time they would pass over and where to look for them in the night sky. The idea that signals could be bounced off an orbiting satellite was stunning. Equally stunning, years later, was the technology surrounding the introduction of optical fibres. Consider this description from *The Economist* (6 July 1991: 87) of how optical fibres work:

Some scientists are dissatisfied with electrons. This seems ungrateful. Electrons have served mankind well as carriers of energy; they have become adept as shufflers of information. Some of their attributes, however, offend purists. They have mass, which makes them a bit sluggish. They have electric charges, which means they interfere with one another. Fortunately, there is something better around, something with no mass, no charge, and no rival when it comes to speed: light.

Satellites and optical fibres have changed both capacity and speed of communication. And Canada has been quick to take advantage of such technology. Not only were we the first nation to launch a domestic communications satellite but the government of Canada has maintained a surprising commitment to both speed and capacity. As mentioned in Chapter 3, Canada boasts the world's fastest data network. CA*net 3 began operations in the summer of 1999. It can transfer 40 gigabytes of data per second—the entire two and a half hours of the movie *Titanic* in just half a second. This is 20 times faster than Abilene, the American Internet 2 network. The speed of CA*net 3 is 750,000 times as fast as CA*net, set up in 1993 (William Boei, *Vancouver Sun*, 16 Dec. 1998, D5). In the fall of 2002, CA*net 4 was announced. CA*net 4's initial capacity will be four to eight times that of CA*net 3.

The social meaning of these speeds is a greater and greater erasure of distance for an increasing data-rich array of digitized information. For example, since 1997 the Children's Telehealth Network has connected various centres in the Atlantic provinces to one of the regions best hospitals, the IWK Grace Hospital in Halifax. For the hospital, it was a way of extending itself to the rural communities that had provided it with support over the years. By 2002, software together with high-speed high bandwidth connectivity allowed a surgeon in Halifax to undertake an operation on a patient in St John's, Newfoundland. He controlled a robot in St John's by high-speed data networks.

INCREASED FLEXIBILITY IN PERSONAL COMMUNICATIONS

When Alexander Graham Bell made the first phone call from Brantford, Ontario, to Paris, Ontario, on 10 March 1876, the notion that one could speak to a person in one location far distant from another inspired awe. Marconi's signalling by clicks and Fessenden's superimposing of music on radio signals anticipated Bell, but the idea of having a private conversation at a distance was some achievement. The drawbacks of the technology were never considered. First, the person you wished to reach had to be at a particular location, such as at home, at the office—anywhere there was a telephone. Second, you had to know where he or she was.

We have lived with that restriction for just over a hundred years. Only now are we moving beyond it. Pagers, cellphones, and satellite-based phones provide us with the ability to be reached anywhere and to initiate a call from anywhere to any other person, no matter their location. Whether on top of Everest, at the South Pole, sailing across the ocean, flying along in a plane, or merely eating in a restaurant, we need not lose touch with anyone—as long as we can all afford the technology.

INCREASED FLEXIBILITY IN PRODUCER COMMUNICATIONS

Communications technology is helping develop a different kind of flexibility for the producers of information. Not only can information be sent to almost anyone anywhere, but all manner of content can be sent as well. As late as 1995, broadcasting stood apart from the Internet for its capacity to generate and carry audio and visual signals. The Internet appeared to best manage text, perhaps with a few graphics. All that has changed. With Real-Audio™ and Quicktime video™, sound and moving images have become so much a part of the Internet that the whole notion of broadcasting hangs on the gossamer threads of existing (outdated) distribution and receiving technology and the organization of production to allow for high-quality content.

For example, in 1997 a video conference involving several sites across Canada would have cost the producers more than $1,000 per one-hour session. In 1999 a course on the social implications of technology was conducted out of the University of Calgary by Professor David Mitchell. It involved students and professors from McGill University, York University, Ryerson University, University of Alberta, and Simon Fraser University. Using the M-bone technology and work stations of the Sun computer company, the course was undertaken on the Internet and was carried out within the normal communications carrying capacity of the universities involved—and there were no extra telecommunications costs. By 2002 Mitchell had moved on and was able to run a half-hour video conference from a hotel Internet café in Salvador, Brazil, for the $40 it cost to rent the room and gain access to an ordinary two-megabit cable modem.

The digital foundations of computer communications technology appear to be almost as powerful as the discovery of the atom. By breaking down information into binary digits, the simplest possible code (zeros and ones), scientists and scholars have been able to rebuild

PIRACY—HISTORICALLY AND TODAY

The famous privateers of history were not unlike the pirates of intellectual property of today. Privateers were not outlaws. Rather, they were individuals with armed vessels authorized by a government to engage in hostile acts against enemies of the state, often to rob them of their property. Thus, Elizabeth I used Francis Drake and other pirates to raid Spanish galleons as they tried to bring back gold from the Americas to Spain. The history of privateers who operated on the Atlantic Ocean out of Canada stretches from 1613 to the Treaty of Ghent signed in 1815.

After the American Revolution, American printers, acting in a parallel fashion to the privateers and with the US government's full knowledge, began pirating English novelists in 1776. In fact, it was on this foundation that the US publishing industry was built. While pirating books differs from privateering in the sense that it was not the waging of physical combat to rob physical objects, it was clearly robbing English authors and publishers of their intellectual property. It was not until Canadians began to return the favour, pirating US authors and selling them back to the US, and Samuel Clemens, a.k.a. Mark Twain, started investing a great deal of time and effort to argue on behalf of his own copyright interests, that the US government considered respecting (and enforcing) copyright law.

Today, in China and other developing countries, even countries like Singapore, unauthorized copying of books, software, tapes, CDs, and videos—not to mention the production of fakes in the form of brand-name cameras, watches, and designer clothing—is common. No doubt a certain pirating in patented drugs also takes place. The US, more than any other country, makes a very large issue of this because American producers have the most to lose. Using US definitions of copyright and its own evaluation of the extent of illegal copying, losses are estimated to be in the worlds of information and communications so that electrical communication of text, sound, and image at any distance has become commonplace.

The flexibility of the emerging system and its relative low cost have led to a number of developments. In October 1998 the House of Blues—a chain of night clubs co-founded by actor Dan Aykroyd—began Netcasting (broadcasting via the Internet) three live concerts and 10 album 'listening' parties each week. The chain has also installed full digital production studios at all its locations so that it can create broadcast-quality concert videos anywhere. Also in 1998, a few on-line businesses began to offer a *legal* service whereby they customize CDs to suit a consumer's taste.

MP3 computer audio format technology began to be used extensively in late 1998 to upload and download high-quality, highly compressed (up to 12 times) music files that can easily be stored or transferred over the Internet. At the time, hundreds of sites had large selections of illegal MP3 files and encouraged users to both upload the material and make it available to others. Users claimed that the technology allowed sampling and promoted purchases among those who really like a band or artist they have listened to. Such arguments are still put forward and they have some validity. The technology also allows users to download and listen to bands or artists that do not obtain heavy rotation or exposure on radio stations. Hence it is a threat to the market control of the music companies because

it makes available music that is not under their control. In 1998, you could buy a portable player capable of downloading music from the Internet and playing it back from a memory card. In 2001, Apple purchased the rights to a whole variety of songs so that each new iMac and iBook came with a selection of songs. Users were encouraged to convert their own CDs to MP3 formats so they could have their music on their computer. Apple also introduced the iPod, a device with 5, 10, or 20 gigabytes of memory that could hold a whole library of music or equally serve as an external hard drive.

The development of MP3 and the availability of both legal and illegal material on the Internet energized SOCAN (the Society of Composers, Authors and Music Publishers of Canada) to seek to force Internet providers to pay a tariff for material distributed over their networks. In the US, the Recording Industry Association of America (RIAA) hired a company to use automated software to search the Internet for sites offering illegal songs in an attempt to force providers to pay for the material they make available. At the same time, some bands were and still are giving their music away on the Internet. Other artists are selling their albums on the Internet.

Three arguments can be made in favour of the use of MP3 technology. First, the recording industry is forever crying wolf. Tape recorders, cassette tapes, DAT recorders were all supposed to spell the end of the

billions of dollars. Of course, were those billions in **royalties** and licensing fees to be paid by the poor to the rich countries, it would only exacerbate the debt problems that already exist throughout the developing world.

With the expansion of intellectual property, and specifically the patenting of genetically modified life forms, piracy will increase. Whether this is a problem is all a matter of perspective. For instance, nations and cultures that have made plants and knowledge about the medicinal quality of plants available to Western drug and food companies have traditionally never been granted intellectual property rights for their contributions. However, the drug and food companies have benefited greatly from patenting medicines, and now foods, derived from these very same plants.

Given the inequities of such circumstances, you might ask: Why should drug companies be allowed to go to the Amazon to find out what plants are being used by Aboriginals and take them home and analyze them, identify their

active ingredients, develop patented drugs, and under patent have a monopoly to sell them for a certain time span? Why is it acceptable for medical units to test African prostitutes who seem immune to the AIDS virus to identify that immunity and not promise them a share of the millions that the drug companies will make if they can turn the active ingredient into a vaccine? Similarly, why is it commonplace for book publishers to publish fine coffee-table editions featuring Aboriginal art with no recompense going to the group from which the art came? Part of the answer to these questions lies in what is defined as proprietary knowledge and intellectual property and what is not in the public domain. Increasingly, these issues are being examined and adjustments are being made to intellectual property laws so that some rough justice is created. Nevertheless, the developed world has been having a free ride on the common resources of the earth, mainly because we have made the laws.

industry—of course, they did not. Second, with rampant piracy, producers (read rich, large companies) are forced to bring down their prices. This happened with computer software in the early 1990s. For instance, in August 1993, Microsoft's CD-ROM encyclopedia, *Encarta*, was selling at between $495 and $529. In March of 1994 its price had dropped to $189. By December of 1994 it was on sale for $79. *The Canadian Encyclopedia*, which began selling in 1994 at $79, is now available on CD in gas stations for $9.95. Third, MP3 has developed into a legitimate and extremely useful audio compression technology that can be used to distribute any kind of audio material via the Internet.

INCREASED FLEXIBILITY IN SOURCING THROUGH EASY COMMUNICATIONS

Increased flexibility has not been restricted to private communication and the production of information. The entire economic system is reorienting itself to take advantage of easy and cheap communication of all kinds of messages around the world. The best example of this is the sourcing of production offshore, where labour is cheap and restrictions are few. Designer clothes are now made in Asia; sports equipment is manufactured almost any place where cheap labour is available; data processing is done in the Caribbean; and software production is pursued in India. Often, certain areas are designated as specifically available to facilitate sourcing for foreign companies.

The views people take on such matters can vary considerably. For example, designer clothing companies can be seen as intrepid explorers who have tamed the human labour pools of the developing world for world commodity production and consumption. Or, those same corporations can be seen as rip-off artists that exploit poor people and poor countries and take advantage of human resources unavailable to small business firms. As many have pointed out, it would take a single worker about 10,000 years to earn the same amount given to a single sports celebrity for endorsing a brand of shoe.

The case of Japan is interesting. After World War II (though it started earlier), Japan began building itself into an economic powerhouse by using cheap domestic labour and producing a whole range of low-priced utilitarian products for the North American and European markets, usually under licence to US and European technology developers and manufacturers. As an economic giant, Japan increasingly developed its own brands, moved up-scale in its product mix, and began outsourcing its own manufacture to other parts of Asia, where labour costs were lower. All this was made possible and eased by communications technology, which allowed the Japanese companies to follow the North American market and develop products to meet emerging demands.

INCREASED ABILITY TO PERFORM TASKS

The number of tasks that have become less labour-intensive as well as easier continues to expand at a dizzying pace. For instance, arithmetic teaching programs are readily available for children to use along with typing programs to encourage touch typing. A scanning device that works like a magic marker is able to translate words on the fly. The translation is then displayed on the LCD (liquid crystal display) screen. The device is about the same size as a cellphone.

Wizards—small computerized programs that provide a set of predetermined alternatives for common tasks—are increasingly being made available to shorten the time required to perform certain tasks and to

WILL NAPSTER EVER DIE?

Although Napster, the site that allowed Internet users to download music they had not purchased, was closed down, other sites with slightly different technology, for example Grokster and Kazaa, have sprung up. Incorporated in Vanuatu, a South Pacific island nation, Sharman Networks makes the Kazaa software to allow copying and has an estimated 11 million users. The Recording Industry Association of America, not surprisingly, is trying to obtain a ruling making it illegal to distribute the software (*Globe and Mail*, 10 Oct. 2002, A11). Whether the government of the tiny island nation will pay attention to whatever ruling comes down will probably depend on what benefits it receives in return. Meanwhile, both the Canadian and US industries are trying to launch competitive legal sites where people can download music for a fee. The US already has MusicNet, Pressplay, and Rhapsody. Apple surprised everyone in April 2003 by creating a system (in the US) for the legal downloading of songs for $0.99 per song.

WEB OWNERSHIP AND CULTURE

Lawrence Lessig is a Stanford University professor who argues that intellectual property law is undermining fundamental freedoms of US and world citizens. Many references to his writing and speeches can be found on www.slashdot.com. He has also written two books on the subject, *The Future of Ideas: The Fate of the Commons in a Connected World* and *Code, and Other Laws of Cyberspace*, and was named one of *Scientific American*'s top 50 visionaries. In a speech called 'Free Culture' he focused on four points.

1. Creativity and innovation always build on the past.

2. The past always tries to control the creativity that builds upon it.
3. Free societies enable the future by limiting this power of the past.
4. Ours is less and less a free society.

The Recording Industry Association of America (www.riaa.com) represents the other side of the argument, as does the Motion Picture Association of America (www.mpaa.org).

Source: cyberlaw.stanford.edu/lessig/

---

enhance the ability of the user to communicate effectively. Like their more powerful brethren, the software program, and indeed in parallel with many modern conveniences, wizards encourage the user to set his or her sights higher: dress up a letter to make it appear more professional; create personal stationery rather than using blank paper; keep track of one's own financial accounts meticulously rather than haphazardly; use a thesaurus, grammar checker, and dictionary rather than let mistakes slip by.

The manipulation of text by new communications technologies is only one area of possibility. Photos and movies can be retouched to make them more attractive or, indeed, to create false impressions. Such technology was used in the movies *Forrest Gump*, in which old and new footage were merged, and *What Dreams May Come*, in which Robin Williams apparently tromps through an oil-painting heaven. As well, satellites are sent into space, guided to their destinations by computer control; computer-controlled aircraft with no persons aboard and sometimes no fuel undertake weather reconnaissance; schedules are optimized and maps are drawn using Global Positioning System (GPS) units; goods, as well as people, can be tracked; robots can even be sent into poisoned environments to retrieve, neutralize, or dispose of hazards. The possibilities for new technology seem endless.

The mother of all technologies for increasing the ability to perform tasks and decreasing the effort is database technology, specifically relational databases. We have spoken in an earlier chapter of the ONIX (Online Information Exchange) standard used by book publishers. The standard calls for the creation of

a bibliographic record of each title that a publisher publishes, which, when combined with other records, forms a bibliographic database. Its primary use is to allow publishers to send information to the computers of large bookstores such as Chapters/Indigo and Amazon.ca. But being a database, the information can be entered once and retrieved for many purposes. It can be used to provide title information for the publisher's Web site. It can also be used to flow the information into templates for the creation of catalogues. Or, it can be used to generate publicity materials. In addition, whenever any member of the company needs to obtain precise information on a title, she or he can do so simply by accessing the bibliographic record of the title in the database. In addition, by granting access to authorized persons, should data change, the book go out of print, the price change, etc., those authorized can change the information and, in certain cases, trigger a message to be sent to those who should have the information. All this may sound quite mundane to any person who is not a publisher. But when you realize that in many of the uses mentioned, the information must be re-created, and each time information is created it must be proofed, and in spite of this mistakes are still created, you can see how this fundamentally changes the nature of a publisher's operations.

NEW SERVICES AND PRODUCTS

In 1999, new Web-based services and products were emerging at a fast and furious pace. For example, a Web site matched lawyers with motorists who have received speeding tickets in the lawyers' home territory. Other

GLOBAL POSITIONING SYSTEM

The Global Positioning System, or GPS, works as follows. Twenty-four Navstar satellites orbit the earth at 18,000 kilometres and send out radio pulses—exactly the same signal at exactly the same time (within one millionth of a millionth of a second). A hand-held GPS receiver on the ground measures the time delay between when it receives signals from as few as three or four or as many as 12 satellites. By comparing time delays and satellite positions, an exact position can be calculated and the receiver plots this position on a map display or in terms of formal location descriptors coded into the GPS unit. In times of emergencies, the US military can de-scramble some of its signals from military satellites, and location and calculations can then become more feasible and accurate. As it is, the system can determine location within a matter of millimetres—if you are prepared to spend about $13,000 for a receiver, including software. If $300 is more what you had in mind, a system of this calibre can measure within about 30 metres, which is suitable for pleasure boat navigation but not for surveying.

Figure 10.1 Global Positioning

GPS Satellites

More than 20 satellites orbit the earth, of which at least four should be visible to a receiver on earth at any given time. The satellites can supply accurate location information, including real-time navigation data.

Receivers

GPS receivers, which can be the same size as a mobile phone, get and process the information provided by the satellites and can perform various location functions, such as mapping a navigational route or showing airport runway layouts. (Courtesy of Thales Navigation)

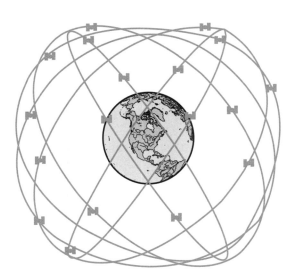

Figure 10.1 continued

Triangulation

Triangulation, a principle of geometry and trigonometry, is the system used in global positioning.

First, a circle is mapped based on how long it takes a satellite signal to reach a receiver, which allows the receiver to measure the distance to the satellite. Given this measurement, the receiver can be located anywhere along a circle around the satellite.

Next, a signal from another satellite narrows down the possible location of the receiver to two points where the circles intersect.

Finally, a third signal will determine the receiver's true location, to within about 15 metres. (Additional signals from other satellites can help determine location with greater accuracy.)

Source: Globe and Mail, 1 Oct. 1998.

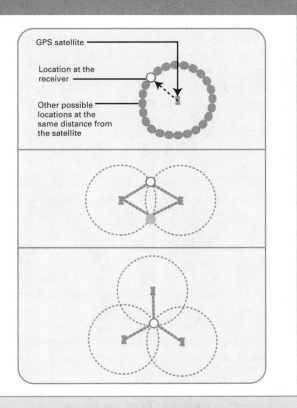

In addition to surveying, mapping, and pleasure boating, GPS can be put to other uses. For instance, by providing an exact landing location, GPS can guide a helicopter through dense fog. Satellites can also assess the state of crops and define the exact locations of infestations or of harvestable produce. The exact location of any transportation container can be known through transmitters (which can also locate stolen cars, particularly those being shipped in containers offshore). Pipeline welding joints can be mapped exactly and coded so that they can be located easily for repairs and maintenance.

Sources: *Globe and Mail*, 8 Dec. 1998; personal communication, Peter Mason, Canada Land Surveyor.

sites offered a selection of books to download—the first half of the book was free; for a fee you could download the second half of the book. And access to the Encyclopedia Britannica was available at www.eb.com. By 2002 the site had turned into a place where the owners attempt to sell users a package and the vast majority of products and services had disappeared.

In 1999, there also was much talk of the electronic book. In October 1998, Softbook Press offered its version of the electronic book (see www.softbook.com). It was followed by the Rocket e-book and others and then Microsoft itself came out with an electronic book plus e-book reader technology that could be downloaded onto one's computer. By late 2002, e-books had disappeared, perhaps to reappear when the technology is better, perhaps to be replaced by charged plastic sheets.

CAPTURING AND CHANGING BEHAVIOUR

Above and beyond the new services and products that technology has introduced and that are supposed to improve our lives, communication technology allows organizations and people to capture, analyze, mimic, and even change human behaviour.

You might not remember how speedy it used to be at the checkout in the grocery store, or indeed in any other store. Items were rung in quickly, the total was immediately available, you handed your cash to the cashier, collected your change, and were done. Now things are much slower. The slowdown is caused both by credit cards and the computerized 'cash register'—these two technological developments require that credit cards be verified, transactions registered, and your name and purchases processed in the computer. This may eat up your time but it produces valuable information for the retailer. Such information includes inventory monitoring as well as patterns of purchasing by groups and by individual consumers. Your behaviour has been captured for the benefit of the seller at the cost of your time, though we tend to believe in the speed of technology.

Every electronic transaction is recorded and the sum total of transactions creates a body of data, which, in turn, can be mined for valuable information. This information can then be used by the person who collects it or it can be sold to another party. The direct recording of information also results in a net decrease in the costs of the transactions. No longer is paying for an item one function, assessing the store's stock levels another, counting cash yet another: with electronic transactions all this and more are rolled into one.

Speed may return. Just as ATMs (bank machines) lessen the need for tellers, the grocery store cashiers' days may be numbered. For between $150,000 and $400,000, Symbol Technologies has developed a system of scanners that it can install in stores for consumers to do their own checkout (*Globe and Mail*, 9 Dec. 1997, C10). To shop is to scan; to scan is to pay. Watch for the day when you own your scanner, which is programmed by a radio wave as you enter the store. You will hear a voice greeting that will provide you with information on specials in certain categories from which you frequently buy and will ask you, after you press 'no more items', whether you have forgotten the buttermilk. Such a scenario was played out in the movie *Minority Report*.

While the above is exciting in its own way, it is important to recall that all it does is mimic human behaviour. In a small business, a one-person or one-family operation, information is constantly being processed by the person in charge. The small business often knows its customers intimately: 'The usual, Mr Wodehouse?' With all this fancy computerization we merely approximate normal, human, interactive behaviour by members of a community.

In addition to introducing new ways of doing what we already do and in offering up new work procedures and leisure pursuits, information and communications

WINDOWS AS A HORSELESS CARRIAGE

The idea of an e-book seems to exemplify Marshall McLuhan's idea that we look into the future with our eyes fixed on our rearview mirror. In other words, we desire the technologies we develop to perform tasks established technologies can already do. This rearview mirror idea recognizes the control the past exerts on the present and the future.

A similar idea can be found in McLuhan's discussion of the automobile as a horseless carriage. In that discussion, he explores the role of historically grounded metaphor for thinking about an ever-changing world. Thus, rather than seeing the automobile for what it was, people and society of the time compared the automobile to the most appropriate mode of transportation with which they were familiar, the horse-drawn carriage. Even the inventors saw it this way. For example, they put the steering at the front rather than at the rear and it took until the 1950 for Buckminster Fuller to demonstrate the greater efficiency of rear-wheel steering. In the early years of the automobile the controls society wanted to put on it were extensions of the ways in which people thought about horse-drawn carriages.

Windows, which is a not particularly high-quality adaptation of Mac OS technology, is based on horseless carriage features. It is a credit to Steve Jobs and his partner that they were able to see the value of historically grounded metaphors and so created icons of files and file folders and directories that computer users could understand. Even the trash gave people the comfort of a known environment.

Indeed, when you move a file from one folder to another, you are participating in that metaphor. What is actually going on is that you are changing the document identifiers so that when you go to a directory and a file folder you initiate a retrieval mechanism that identifies information tagged as belonging to the 'document' you wish to access. In fact, however, the information is probably stored in fragments on various parts of your hard drive. How long the metaphors of files, file folders, and trash or recycling bins will last is anyone's guess.

technology is changing our daily behaviour. For instance, in terms of leisure, according to a study done for America Online (*Globe and Mail*, 1 Oct. 1998, C6), the average family with Internet access watches 15 per cent less TV than families without such access. Our work behaviour has also changed. Working at home (telecommuting) has become much more common, with some people carrying on work for firms in other countries. As well, our information-seeking behaviour has changed. The *Vancouver Sun* (18 June 1998, D11) notes that 47 per cent of college graduates in the US go on-line to get news at least once a week (news is not defined).

CREATING VIRTUAL REALITY

While the notion of a 'true' virtual reality is overhyped, the retail world is attempting to create a shopping 'virtual reality'—an environment that has all the desirable elements required for a person to shop with confidence and enjoyment. This challenge has become quite a preoccupation in today's marketplace. If any crucial element is missing or awkward—whether browsing, payment, trying out the product, returning the product, or getting a good price—the on-line retailer will suffer. And if the respected firm Forrester Research is correct in its prediction that by 2003 $108 billion in goods and services will be sold on the Net, attentive retailers will take over the market.

The American company Amazon.com and Amazon.ca appears to be a fairly successful model of on-line book retailing, and in Canada, Chapters/Indigo is attempting to compete. The Chapters/Indigo site provides many features:

- 2.9 million listed titles (this does not mean they are in stock, only that the company is prepared to search for the book for you);
- sourcing from Canadian publishers and distributors (this means that you are supporting the Canadian publishing industry and Canadian authors);
- biographies of 20,000 authors;
- a comprehensive literary awards listing;
- editorials on the book world and reviews dating back 20 years;
- audio clips of author interviews and readings;
- on-line discussions;
- a list of literary events.

Yet to date, financially, the site has not broken even.

Nuisances, Problems, Dangers

Though plenty has been achieved in the past few decades thanks to communications technology, a number of problems have also arisen. As stated earlier, with technology the good is always accompanied by the bad. Below we explore some of the not-so-helpful effects that new technologies are having, from the bothersome to the dangerous.

SYSTEM VULNERABILITY

Moving to a computer- and communications-dominated world introduces certain vulnerabilities, some a result of human intervention, others a result of nature. For instance, it has yet to be seen whether a major cosmic event could wipe out the ever-more-delicate computer systems that are being developed. Major electronic discharges, perhaps major solar flares, could possibly interfere with computer communications. As well, gophers have been known to chew through the coatings on optical cables. Indeed, cable protection had to be developed to avoid such attacks.

In addition, satellites are vulnerable to the forces of the universe, as Canada learned when two of its communications satellites were hit with cosmic particles. This and other such events yielded extensive media coverage of the biggest non-event of 1998: scientists had predicted that the largest meteor storm in 32 years, with particles travelling as fast as 70 kilometres per second, could easily play havoc with the more than 500 communications satellites in orbit in November 1998. Called a Leonid shower because the particles came from the direction of the constellation Leo, more than $1 million was spent studying the shower and predicting its likely result. While the scientists expected the objects to vaporize on contact with the satellites—they were, after all, only about as large as a grain of sand—there was some chance that the result of the collision could be the release of an electrical charge that would disrupt or destroy service. Nothing happened. Chicken Little breathed a sigh of relief.

Beyond natural forces, human action can also expose how the technological system is vulnerable. For instance, one of the major features in Internet commerce is trust, the most obvious issue being whether or not your credit card number will be intercepted on its way to a legitimate vendor. But there are other issues as well. Will the quality of the items you purchase match what you expect? Will you be able to exchange an unsatisfactory item? Will there be prompt delivery?

Will your privacy be respected and protected?

In 1997 Ian Goldberg, responding to a challenge made by RSA Data Security Inc., broke the code of its 40-bit encryption product. At the time, RSA was an industry leader. It appears that for every encryption code, an encryption breaker code can be written. This applies to viruses as well. According to Symantec's AntiVirus Research Centre there are 19,000 different viruses. So far SAM Intercept, Symantec's anti-virus program, has been able to neutralize most of the ones that have gained any real circulation.

In January 1999 Air Miles and its customers were shocked to find thousands of 'confidential' customer files open for viewing to passing Web browsers. While the problem was fixed quickly, the vulnerability of information collected by others is well illustrated by this unintentional breach of security—and this example did not even involve outside hackers breaking into the site. Even though the files do not contain credit card numbers, to make them publicly available is an invasion of privacy.

Or is it? Consider the issue this way. Why is it not an invasion of privacy when Air Miles compiles that information and puts it to use? Has Air Miles not invaded the privacy of the consumer in the same way in which that privacy obviously seems to have been violated through its public availability? That is, does the number of people who see the information determine if the privacy is invaded? Or is there a fundamental principle involved that has no connection to the number of people who can access the information? When each magazine to which you subscribe, each charity to which you donate, each club to which you belong, or each government department with which you have dealt sells its data lists to others, is that not an invasion of privacy? These are issues that must be dealt with if we are going to address adequately the issue of system vulnerability.

On 21 October 2002 a massive denial-of-service attack was mounted on the domain-name root servers of the Internet. It pirated the use of 6,000 ordinary PCs and considerably slowed down eight of the 13 servers. The system was maintained and certain spokespeople were of the opinion that the perpetrators were attempting to demonstrate what was possible rather than bring about the collapse of the Internet (News.google.com, 23 Oct. 2002).

HYPES

Consider this statement made by Henry Blodget, analyst with CIBC Oppenheimer in New York: 'We con-

tinue to believe that Amazon.com is in the early stages of building an electronic retailing franchise that could generate $10 billion in revenue and earnings per share of $10 within five years' (*Globe and Mail*, 17 Dec. 1998, B15). Blodget could be right. Certainly the people at Amazon believe him and are determined to be a lead company in the age of on-line commerce. But Blodget could also be wrong. After all, he had only been covering the company for three months when he made the above statement. He began monitoring it when it was trading at $84. At the time of his pronouncement, the stock had reached $289. Who is to know? Who is to say that faith is all the company needs to achieve its goals? Hype seems to be a large part of the technology in the marketplace these days, often driving interest and investment. And it is becoming more difficult to assess or avoid hype.

In 2000, when the last edition of this book was written, it was reasonable to ask the question: 'Ever been spammed?' In 2003, to find an Internet user who has not been spammed would be a miracle. Anti-spam advisers recommend the following for avoiding the latest hype in advertising:

- Do not broadcast your e-mail address.
- Use filters that eliminate spams before they reach you.
- Use a code name for an on-line identity.
- Do not list yourself in directories.
- Complain to your Internet service provider if spammed.
- Do not respond.

CRIME

Then there is crime, especially fraud. As if hacking was not enough, one group extracted information from the Web site of an investment dealer and superimposed a fictitious name, Turner Phillips, on the material. It was then able to sell stock in fictitious companies and refer investors to information contained on the Web site. Numbers of investors took the bait and lost significant amounts of money.

Phreakers, the telephone equivalent of hackers, cost Canadian businesses $40–$50 million in illegitimate long-distance calls. Most phreaker fraud is carried out through Direct Inward System Access (DISA), a system that allows employees to make work-related long-distance calls from home. The fraud artist dials the DISA number, enters a security code using a computerized speed dialer until the code is cracked, and is then able to dial anywhere at no cost.

Extreme fraud involves stealing the identity of another. According to the Ontario Privacy Commissioner, Ann Cavoukian, identity theft is 'an epidemic' in the US. Identity theft involves collecting enough information on someone that the fraud artist can begin to assume that person's identity. Having set up his or her own accounts, the thief then moves in on the victim and enters his or her financial life. Knowing this to be a possibility, people who make extensive use of the Internet routinely provide false information in response to Internet queries in order to protect themselves.

In January 1999 a Canadian hacker group called the 'Hong Kong blondes', led by 'Blondie Wong', claimed to have shut down a Chinese government satellite (*Vancouver Sun*, 15 Jan. 1999, A9). Obviously, this was not confirmed by the Chinese government. Given that such a feat is possible, intelligence agencies around the world are spending resources to develop such a capability and also to develop protective measures against it. In October 1997, the US government warned that neither government nor industry has the wherewithal to protect communications and power grids (*Vancouver Sun*, 8 Oct. 1997, D2).

ESPIONAGE

Spying on the Internet is undertaken by various individuals and groups who conform to different standards of behaviour. Those who spy include governments, persons paid to use any technique to perform their task, whether legal or illegal, persons paid to operate within the law, and curiosity seekers (who merge with hackers as a group). One former CSIS employee (not a bad place to have worked if you are seeking instant credibility in this business) runs a small business intelligence agency, Ibis Research Inc. (see www.ibisresearch.com) that can keep track of businesses by using such software as Highlights 2, which is programmed to look for changes in Web sites. Price changes, personnel changes, announcements—all are pieces of a puzzle that can provide information to competitors about changes about to take place in target firms. Patent applications, e-mail contributions to discussion groups, published papers by firm personnel are all grist for the mill. They also use other Internet tools, such as search engines, and try to refine their methods, such as by logging search terms and results in order to analyze success over time (*Globe and Mail*, 26 Nov. 1998, C3).

Though Ibis Research operates within the law, a seamier side of the business definitely exists. It is to be found in the environment surrounding high-tech companies and movie stars. All kinds of digital gumshoes will hack into telephone records (or pay off someone in the phone company) to obtain access to telephone records. They will look for unexplained calls and discover secrets that celebrities would rather keep hidden. By tracking purchasing, banking, in fact, any transactions done by particular persons, all sorts of information can be gained: where they shop, where they have been on a certain day, who they are in contact with, and so forth. Such techniques are just a different, more focused, version of the data mining undertaken by companies such as Air Miles.

Much different and more serious consequences can result from communications monitoring. For instance, in a speech he gave in Vancouver in early 1999, BBC news anchor Nik Gowing reported how the BBC was now using field television production units that could be carried in two medium-sized suitcases. These units are capable of recording sound and image and beaming back information to Britain using Iridium technology. The difficulty, he noted, was that while the plight of a refugee, for example, could be documented and the footage shown around the world, those desirous of causing harm to the individual could gain valuable information not only by monitoring the programs but also by monitoring the communications and the location of those communications. As a result, journalists, in order to protect the people they report on, are having to engage in a new kind of self-censorship.

INFORMATION WARS

On the war front, when the US and its NATO allies (including Canada) waged war on Yugoslav President Slobodan Milosevic, they also declared an infowar to supplement their bombing campaign. Infowar is defined by the US Air Force as 'any action to deny, exploit, corrupt or destroy the enemy's information and its functions; protecting ourselves against those actions; and exploiting our own military information functions' (*Globe and Mail*, 24 June 1999, T2). Buoyed by its assault on Iraq's information computer system by means of viruses, hackers were employed by the US government to attack the Serbian leader's foreign bank accounts. No doubt they also made use of the Global Hawk, an unmanned infowar drone airplane that flies over enemy territory to intercept messages and inject false data into computer networks.

In late 1998 the Pentagon declared cyberspace the fourth battleground, identifying human decision-making as its primary target. To provide a sense of its scope, the Information Warfare Research Centre contains a 22-page guide to US Department of Defense infowar organizations and on-line resources, including the Information Warfare Executive Board (ibid.).

One interesting element of the Iraq War of 2003 was that once the fighting started, there was very little discussion of an information war but a great deal about the inaccuracies and insipidness of US coverage (see Mitchell, 2003). In the lead-up to the war, a certain amount of attention was paid to leaflet dropping, and during the war commentators were surprised at how long the Iraqi state television remained functioning. Also, the spirited denials during the war of Iraq's Information Minister, Mohammed Saeed-al-Sahaf (dubbed 'Comical Ali') that flew in the face of televised reality were elements of an information war.

Of course, the whole pretext for the war was information-generated rather than action-generated. The US claimed that Iraq possessed or was assembling chemical, biological, and nuclear weapons of mass destruction. The US failed to convince the United Nations but went ahead anyway. In light of the lack of evidence of such weapons of mass destruction, well after the war ceased, on 22 May 2003, US intelligence agencies began an examination of information sources, not as an act of contrition but as an attempt to determine the quality of information-gathering (Lumpkin, 2003). Such a move completely sidesteps whether invasion was justified.

The 'So-What' of Technological Developments

From the beginnings of radio to 1990 the principal debate over communications was a cultural one. The central question asked was: What are the effects of the media on society? The next question was: How can society ensure that the media speak to the full range of citizens, with their broad range of tastes and desires for entertainment as well as information and enlightenment? The guiding question appears to have changed, however. Now it is: What economic benefit can we derive from developing and applying communications technology?

This transformation is no accident. Technology has combined with the search for profit to create a juggernaut of development that, from 1999 and to 2001, was seemingly unstoppable. With the burst of the dot-com bubble, development based on information technology has not stopped, however, it has just slowed to a more realistic pace. Added to the pressure of technology and business are the efforts of the large exporting countries—the US, the UK, the leading economic powers in Asia, and certain directorates within the EU bureaucracy. They have been pushing and continue to push economics and trade in every theatre, particularly the WTO (formerly GATT), the International Telecommunications Union (ITU), EU agreements, the OECD, the G-8, and the Asia-Pacific Economic Co-operation forum (APEC)—the Vancouver meeting of which got the Chrétien government into so much difficulty for effectively denying the rights of Canadians to free assembly and expression.

Countries such as Canada and France are also enthusiastic players, except that in the name of culture these countries are attempting to secure a lasting place for domestic cultural industries—publishing, broadcasting, film, video, and sound recording. Canada's concerns for distinctive voices and for speaking to all Canadians exist within this economic context of seeking to ensure a vibrant cultural production industry.

As art and culture become, more and more, areas of commodity production, artists and cultural producers are being more fairly rewarded for the use made of their work. However, they are also becoming more involved in the exploitation of their works, and hence more conscious of markets and exploitation strategies. Today's visual artists, for example, must address several important questions. Should they sell a hundred signed prints of their work, or sign a contract for unlimited reproduction with a royalty on sales of, say, 10 per cent? Which will enhance their reputation as an artist? Which will make them richer and allow them to paint more?

At the same time, and on the less pessimistic side of things, with new technologies come new industries and new players. For every business that fell victim to the march of rail and highways, vast new opportunities were created by the new transportation. Similarly, while lots of middlemen and women will find themselves displaced, job opportunities are opening in new industries. No doubt there is and will continue to be turmoil as people are forced to change jobs, and governments certainly should be looking for ways to assist in this transition. But with each new major technological development, there is an increase in wealth, and if governments do their job of ensuring that the benefits of technology are shared, there will be increased consumption and hence increased jobs.

Reflections on Our Technological Society

As McLuhan said: 'We shape our tools. . . .' Through inventiveness and the enactment of policy, especially in the context of the evolving power of communications technology, we shape technology, as well as its industrialization. And McLuhan added: '. . . thereafter our tools shape us.' Once in place, the logic of that technology begins to play itself out within the context of further policy.

At the most general level, the major implication of information technology is it is creating a separate sector of society, the information sector. It is separating information from whole sets of actions and making that information actionable. As a result of business firms collecting our shopping patterns, we can be targeted for relevant information rather than deluged with a lot of information that is rather irrelevant to our consumer behaviour. By creating a database of book title information we decrease the work required to generate different information packages that require that information. By the establishment of Internet commerce, the purchase of goods and financial transactions from the home are facilitated. However, each of these examples has a set of unintended consequences.

While companies knowing our shopping patterns may decrease our junk mail, independent of the feeling of our privacy being invaded, we may lose touch with the general information we gain by browsing through flyers of advertised products. True, we might never buy many of these products, but the flyers tell us that such products exist and inform us about consumer culture and how others in the world live. By decreasing the number of times title data must be entered and the number of people who must enter title data in a publishing house, independent of the loss of jobs, we may find that fewer people in a publishing firm have passing familiarity with exactly what titles are being published. This may decrease the identification

employees feel with the firm's titles and authors and cause other types of unanticipated problems. By facilitating Internet commerce, independent of the opportunities for theft, we may affect socialization among various groups and thereby cause social instability.

Thus, policy is needed. Independent of the need for band-aid policy to ensure privacy and the need of severe disincentives for such non-violent crimes as identity theft, we need to understand in a very broad sense what the reorganizing consequences of a separate information sector are. We must return to Innis's notion of the bias of information. What biases will be introduced into society by the ability to collect information on just about everything or by the ability to copy easily every information package? These are difficult to imagine because most observers are either enthusiasts or resistors of new technology. The significance of commentators such as Lawrence Lessig (cyberlaw.stanford.edu/lessig/) is that they point out how, through intellectual property law, information owners are gaining an advantage to the detriment of the general social interest.

The development of new ways of doing things, new industries, and new opportunities will continue and so will the concomitant disruptions. The internationalization of markets and hence globalization, which we discuss in the next chapter, are also issues to observe. Internet-based companies will arise, but whether they will be worldwide or North American in scope, like Amazon.com, national, like Indigo.ca, or local, like your nearby independent bookseller, remains to be seen. What products will work on the Internet and how are also yet to be determined.

In terms of culture per se, as opposed to economics, it appears that in our wired world there will be increased trade and less centralized production, but only time can affirm this. In the social arena, we continue to hear about the bizarre, such as the women who create their own exhibitionist Web sites and are the inheritors of the centrally organized exploiters of

TECHNOLOGICAL THEFT PROTECTION

Weep no more for your lost computer. For less than $100 plus a monthly monitoring charge, you can buy software, for example, Computrace from Absolute Software Corp. or similar software from ADT Security Services Canada Inc., which causes your computer to periodically phone a central location and record the number from which it is calling (suppressing any indication of the activity). With the number in hand, the police can locate the computer and pick it up.

the female body, such as *Playboy*'s Hugh Hefner. Then there are the porn sites, the news sites, and so on. Unsung in our increasingly sensation-oriented media, specifically the Internet, are the wellness sites, the information sites, the medievalist sites, the research and scholarly journal sites, the social and professional organizations, and so on. Such Internet sites increase access to many for their material.

Equally as interesting as speculating on the future is looking at theories of technology. Given the rapid pace of change, are features in the interaction of technology and society emerging that are not accounted for in current theories? The theories stand up fairly well. The intended and unintended effects of technology are wrapped up together. A price is being exacted even as we 'advance'—there is, for instance, more information, but public access to information, especially on a percentage if not an absolute basis, may actually be diminishing. As well, problems are being both solved and created. For example, banking is faster and less vulnerable to human error, but banking systems are less personal and can crash or be hacked into. Many new, increasingly centralized businesses are being created—large, dynamic, national and international companies with sophisticated information systems, as well as Internet companies—while old, perfectly fine, friendly neighbourhood businesses are being destroyed. The locus of control is changing, as is the nature of control. And unforeseen consequences are constantly emerging. Who could have imagined computer viruses before they arrived (except, of course, for the hackers and companies that first created them)? Who, 20 years ago, when the largest looming problem seemed to be what we were all going to do with our leisure time, would have thought that the average professional would be working an increased number of hours per day, per week, per month, and per year? As apparatuses of technology evolve so do new professions—the best examples are the database builders and the Web site designers.

Perhaps changes in the dynamics of work have been the biggest surprise. Those who have work appear to have to work harder, even though technology seems to have facilitated our workplaces and jobs. And many are economically worse off rather than better off. Communications technology has not translated into a net increase of efficiency. Rather, it is just a new way of doing things that seems absolutely unstoppable. Along the same lines, the digital deficit is something to take very seriously as the developed world surges ahead

and developing economies do not keep pace.

Summary

This chapter began with two definitions of technology. One defined technology as encompassing apparatus, techniques, and social institutions. The other saw technology as an intentional extension of a natural process. We reviewed several complementary theoretical perspectives of technology, which emphasized how the positive and negative consequences of technology are always intertwined and unpredictable. We examined technological determinism and the limitations of the influence of technology on society.

Communications technology is closely linked to control, and in the past century this technology has been governed by policy. Indeed, at the beginning of the twenty-first century, as a result of digitalization and technological convergence, we are facing many of the same policy problems that we faced at the beginning of the twentieth century—how to provide for the greatest social benefit given the technologies and industries that are currently emerging.

The social rationales most often used in favour of technological development highlight health and education. On the other hand, the realities of technological communications systems, once they are introduced, involve commercial exploitation. Communications technology, like all technology, does not immediately transfer to developing societies. Some basic concepts in the regulation of communications technology are individual rights, collective rights, privacy, and intellectual property.

The state of communications technology at the dawn of the third millennium is nothing short of astonishing. Optical fibres can be impregnated with rare earths, which serve as natural amplifiers; cable signals can ride free of electricity lines; and dolls can have more computing power than the desktop computer of a mere decade ago.

Computers have combined with communications to make location irrelevant to the efficacy of personal communication. Video, audio, data—any kind of information—can be transmitted with ease to any location in the world and into outer space. Production need no longer be highly centralized because high-quality hardware is relatively portable and inexpensive. Indeed, so inexpensive is it and so available are transmission technologies that protection of intellectual property has become increasingly problematic. Ease of communication is creating, if not a global village, then certainly a global marketplace of producers in which dominant economies can outsource production to inexpensive labour pools.

Previously complex tasks have been simplified and aided by portable translators and macro programs or wizards. Objects can be located and maps can be drawn with ease. Vast pools of information are readily available. Behaviour of all different kinds can be monitored and patterns identified that are even a surprise to those whose behavioural patterns are being monitored. And shopping is being transformed into a virtual experience.

These developments come at a cost, however. Communications systems can be shut down by natural forces and by sabotage. No information is entirely secure because, just as computers can build walls, other computers can knock them down. Active Internet users can become unwitting victims of spams and viruses. Their whole systems can be shut down. With copying being so difficult to control, corporations are vulnerable to piracy and sabotage. Individuals can have their identities stolen and any electronic transaction can be accessed by a determined hacker. But at the same time, homing devices can be attached to private property to prevent loss.

Although communications have a cultural component, the development of communication technologies is firmly within the political and economic domain. Canada, France, and certain other nations continue to attempt to preserve cultural communication against the ravages of information and entertainment exporters led by the US. What the final balancing of interests will be remains to be seen. Indeed, the evolving shape of society as the dynamics of digital communication technologies play themselves out also remains a matter of speculation.

It is clear that the unintended consequences are rarely thought through, nor can they ever be entirely predicted. There has been very little consideration of the macro implications of the development of the information sector. This lack of prior consideration is part of the technological imperative, which assumes that any unforeseen problems can be solved in time by ever newer technological solutions. The blithe acceptance by society of technology because it means economic gain, at least for some, blinds us to considering the desirability of technological development, whether that development involves genetic or communications research and development.

RELATED WEB SITES

CA*net: http://www.canet3.net/
The CA*net Web site carries a wealth of information on Canada's data network.

Music on-line: www.musicmaker.org; www.customdisc.com; www.icebergradio.com
In 1998 the first two sites listed began providing more than 100,000 *legally* licensed song tracks by a wide range of artists. Visitors to the sites can pick out tunes and have the on-line companies create custom-compiled CDs to order. The iceberg site uses the Net to broadcast specialized music formats to interested users. Apple has now added its own system.

MP3: www.mp3.com; www.emusic.com; www.2look4.com
These are Web sites where one can download MP3 files or obtain software to transform CD tracks into MP3 files. A history of MP3 technology can be found at: www.du.edu/~bopulski/paper.htm. Technical background on the technology can be found at: www.iis.fraunhofer.de/amm/index.html

Recording Industry Association of America: www.riaa.com
The RIAA argues against the MP3 trend and has mounted a lawsuit against MP3 distributors.

Book distribution: www.amazon.com; www.chapters.indigo.ca
Competing with the huge American on-line bookseller, Amazon.com, is Chapters/Indigo.

Zero Knowledge Systems Inc.: www.zks.net
If you are really worried about people tracking your Internet activity, this outfit can make your Internet surfing a totally anonymous experience with four levels of encryption.

Infowar:

Rand Corporation: www.rand.org

Randall Whitaker's guide to infowar:
www.informatik.umu.se/~rwhit/IW.html

Terrorism Research Center: www.terrorism.com/infowar

US Air Force Information Warfare Center: www.af.mil/mediacenter/

US Army Digitization Office: www.ado.army.mil

US Assistant Secretary of Defense for Command, Control, Communications, and Intelligence: www.c3i.osd.mil
The Rand Corporation has an interesting paper on infowar, 'Cyberwar is coming', posted at its site. The other sites listed here all deal with infowar.

FURTHER READINGS

Beniger, James. 1986. *The Control Revolution*. Cambridge, Mass.: Harvard University Press. Beniger offers numerous insights on the nature of technology and demands that the reader see things from a different perspective.

Lessig, Lawrence. 2001. *The Future of Ideas: The Fate of the Commons in a Connected World*. New York: Random House. Lessig argues that established corporate interests are moving with considerable speed and force to shut down the creative and innovative space that the Internet created through such means as copyright law.

Postman, Neil. 1993. *Technopoly: The Surrender of Culture to Technology*. New York: Knopf. Postman presents a critical look at the influence of technology on modern culture.

STUDY QUESTIONS

1. Using a concrete example, such as broadcasting, radio, the Internet, or computers, outline the three elements of technology and how they interact with each other to influence society.
2. With technological convergence there are likely to be ever larger corporations attempting to take advantage of economies of scale. Working against corporate concentration on the Internet is open-source software. What is the state of open-source software development and is it a viable alternative to proprietary software?
3. If technology is developed with humanistic concerns in mind, such as serving the health and education needs of society, why does technology seem to end up serving industry? Provide examples in your discussion.
4. What communication technology developed in the past two years has affected your work or personal life?
5. Is the legitimate use of technology impinging on our personal privacy? In what ways?
6. In your opinion, which theories of technology have the most to offer?

LEARNING OUTCOMES

- To point out that some societies, particularly Western society, are more friendly towards technology than others.
- To point out that, within Western societies, attitudes and approaches to technology vary considerably.
- To explain that technology encompasses machines, professional and technical practice, and social institutions.
- To describe how, rather than solving problems, technology changes conditions.
- To discuss technological convergence.
- To review how policy, both in the past and at present, has influenced and is influencing the development of technology.
- To review rationales governments use to support technological development.
- To introduce the notion of technology transfer.
- To introduce some key areas of technology policy, specifically, individual rights and collective rights, piracy, and trading regimes governing trade in intellectual property.
- To illustrate some recent technological changes and their influence on society

PART FOUR

Our Evolving Communications World

CHAPTER 11

Globalization

Introduction

References to the term 'globalization' abound in our culture. Our political leaders mention it frequently in their speeches and globalization has become the rallying cry of the business community. But what does it mean? The term refers to a trend characteristic of the current period in world history in which social and economic relations extend further than ever before, with greater frequency, immediacy, and facility. More specifically, globalization refers to the increased mobility of people, capital, commodities, information, and images associated with: the post-industrial stage of capitalism; the development of increasingly rapid and far-ranging communication and transportation technologies; and people's improved access to these technologies. To put it simply, we are more closely connected to the rest of the world than ever before. This chapter seeks to examine globalization in broad terms and consider what globalization means for notions of community, culture, and mass communication.

Defining Terms

While globalization is often used to refer to the world's increased *economic* interdependence—formalized by the World Trade Organization (WTO), the North American Free Trade Agreement (NAFTA), the European Union, etc.—the term refers equally to political, social, cultural, and environmental interdependence. In the workplace, for example, globalization means that many of us work for companies with operations in a number of countries around the world. The specific job we do may be part of a production process organized as a transnational assembly line, and the product or service we offer is probably destined for export markets. In the political arena, globalization means that governments are increasingly implicated in events that occur well beyond their own borders. Whether it is famine, disease, war, or natural disaster, political leaders feel increasingly compelled to aid countries many of us cannot easily locate on a map. In the social sphere, globalization means that friendships and family ties extend around the

world and that our neighbours come from half a dozen different countries, speak different languages, and worship different gods. When we shop, we buy clothes made in China, wine made in Chile, and furniture made in Sweden. In the cultural sphere, globalization means that Hollywood movies are as popular in Tokyo and Madrid as they are in Los Angeles. It also means that we come into contact with more and more cultures through such activities as vacation travel and foreign-language acquisition. In the environmental sphere, we are increasingly aware that how we use natural resources—air, water, land, minerals, trees, fish—in one corner of the world has significant implications for the rest of the planet.

The term 'globalization' is somewhat unfortunate, however, because it suggests that *all* significant social relations now occur on a global scale. Clearly, this is not so. What the term more properly refers to is an intensified *interrelation* between social activity on local and global scales (Massey and Jess, 1995: 226). Once predominantly local, face-to-face, and immediate, social interactions now commonly stretch beyond the borders of our local community so that 'less and less of these relations are contained within the place itself' (Massey, 1992: 6–7). While we still talk to our neighbours when we meet them on the street, we also communicate regularly with friends, relatives, and associates—by phone, by e-mail—at the other end of the country and on the other side of the world.

Many of the features of globalization are not new. International migration is not new, nor is the mobility of investment capital or the global circulation of cultural products. What *is* new about globalization is its intensity: the expanded reach, facility, and immediacy of contemporary social interactions. The migration of people, whether regional, *intra*national, or *inter*national, whether voluntary or forced, has become a more common experience. Russell King (1995: 7) notes: 'Nowadays, in the western world, only a minority of people are born, live their entire lives and die in the same rural community or urban neighbourhood.' There is a greater circulation today of people seeking to improve their lives, whether they are refugees fleeing intolerable living conditions, youths seeking educational and employment oppor-

CANADA'S CHANGING FACE

It should be clear by now that covering Canada, with its vast geography and scattered population, is one of the greatest challenges facing media organizations, whether their content field is music, news, or dramatic entertainment. That task has become even more daunting in an era of globalization when the Canadian population is more heterogeneous than at any time in its history. In releasing its 2001 census figures, Statistics Canada (2003a, 2003b) reported that visible minorities now constitute 13.4 per cent of the Canadian population and the proportion of foreign-born Canadians is 18.4 per cent, the highest level in 70 years. There are more than 200 ethnic groups represented in Canada. Demographers predict that, if current immigration and birth-rate trends continue, visible minorities will comprise 20 per cent of the Canadian population by 2016 (Anderssen, 2003).

These figures are even higher in urban centres such as Toronto, Vancouver, and Montreal, which received almost three-quarters of immigrants to Canada in the 1990s. In Toronto, 44 per cent of the population is foreign-born, making it the most ethnically diverse city in North America. Visible minorities comprise 21.6 per cent of the population of British Columbia and 19.1 per cent in Ontario. In fact, some analysts perceive two Canadas: one in cities like Regina, where the vast majority are descendants of Aboriginal Canadians and early European settlers; the other in cities like Richmond, BC, where visible minorities (mostly Chinese and South Asians) account for nearly 60 per cent of the population

(Galloway, 2003).

But if past performance is any guide, it is unlikely that Canada's media organizations are ready to accommodate such diversity, whether in their hiring practices or in their representational strategies. As we noted in Chapter 9, an astonishing 97.7 per cent of Canada's journalists are white, and it is rare to see visible minorities occupying prominent roles in Canadian television drama. We rarely see Canadians of colour in news coverage unless the news item specifically concerns race, and non-whites remain subject to stereotypical portrayals in dramatic film and television programming and advertising.

This is a matter of great concern because, as Henry et al. (2000: 296) note, the media 'are major transmitters of society's cultural standards, myths, values, roles, and images.' Because racial minority communities tend to be marginalized in mainstream society at large, 'many white people rely almost entirely on the media for their information about minorities and the issues that concern their communities.'

It is a particularly important issue for Canadians, because the communications media have been assigned such a central role in creating a sense of national community, a theme that permeates federal cultural policy. As a socializing institution, the media of mass communication either can continue to exclude people of colour and exacerbate racism and xenophobia, or they can become more inclusive, reflecting Canada's changing face and facilitating our ongoing demographic transformation.

---

tunities far from home, or what King calls 'executive nomads' conducting business in markets around the globe.

Investment capital, too, has become increasingly mobile as companies seek business opportunities wherever they can be found and flee from regions deemed uncompetitive or hostile to free enterprise. Regions of the world are seen primarily as markets—sales markets, resource markets, and job markets—and corporate executives demonstrate less and less loyalty to their traditional places of business. American automakers, for instance, do not need to confine their operations to the Detroit area if cars and trucks can be made more cheaply with comparable quality standards in Canada or Mexico. Similarly, if Hollywood producers find the labour costs of the California film

unions prohibitive, they can seek lower labour costs in Canada or Australia. Corporations, in other words, are becoming *trans*national. They are less rooted to their 'home' bases than ever before, seeking greater productivity and improved access to international markets wherever these advantages can be found. In the economic realm, Morley and Robins (1995: 109) note that globalization 'is about the organisation of production and the exploitation of markets on a world scale.'

Nowhere has capital been more successful at penetrating world markets than in the cultural sphere. Morley and Robins (ibid., 1–11) argue that two key aspects of the new capital dynamics of globalization are, first, technological and market shifts leading to the emergence of 'global image industries', and second, the development of local audiovisual production and distribution networks. They refer to a 'new media order' in which the overriding logic of the new media corporations is to get their product to the largest possible number of consumers.

Media images also serve as a reminder of how far our social interactions stretch, the extent to which those relations are technologically mediated, and the implications of such mediation. Morley and Robins observe:

> The [television] screen is a powerful metaphor for our times: it symbolizes how we exist in the world, our contradictory condition of engagement and disengagement. Increasingly, we confront moral issues through the screen, and the screen confronts us with increasing numbers of moral dilemmas. At the same time, however, it screens us from those dilemmas. It is through the screen that we disavow or deny our human implication in moral realities. (Ibid., 141)

The screen metaphor also raises the point that globalization screens out some people, that its impact is decidedly uneven. Not all of us are in a position to reap the benefits of global interconnectivity because we don't all enjoy the same degree of mobility. In fact, many of us are hit hard by the new-found mobility of investment capital—when, for instance, sawmills are closed in British Columbia and automotive manufacturers are closed in Quebec because their owners can simply pack up and move in search of more beneficial investment climates. Zygmunt Bauman (1998: 2) argues: 'Globalization divides as much as it unites; it divides as it unites—the causes of division being identical with those which promote the uniformity of the globe.' An integral element of globalization, Bauman maintains, is 'progressive spatial segregation, separation and exclusion' (ibid., 3). The people to whom companies belong are shareholders, who are free from the spatial constraints of most workers, even nation-states. Like absentee landlords, their mobility creates a disconnect between their economic power and any sense of community obligation, whether local, regional, or national (ibid., 8–9). This means that some people are full participants in and major beneficiaries of globalization processes, while a great many others are excluded from the benefits. Indeed, if they are implicated at all, it is as victims of the instability that globalization has created.

Mass Media as Agents of Globalization

Increasingly sophisticated and accessible transportation and communication technologies have to a great extent *enabled* globalization. If you will recall our discussion of Harold Innis's theories of communication in Chapter 1, transportation and communication networks have the ability to 'bind space', to bring people and places closer together. Put more simply, they enable people to maintain close contact in spite of their geographical separation. Airline connections between major cities mean that business leaders and politicians can fly to a meeting in another city and still be home for dinner. E-mail connections mean that friends and colleagues in remote locations can communicate frequently, minimizing the implications of their actual separation.

In business, for example, it is no longer necessary to organize production based on the factory model, in which assembly-line operations take place in a single location. The particular activities involved in the assembly of a product can now be dispersed globally to take advantage of cheap labour, ready supplies of resources, and/or lax regulatory environments. Or, the production process can simply be moved closer to markets to minimize distribution costs. Through telephone contact, e-mail, fax, even video conferencing, managers can maintain two-way communication with remote operations, disseminating instructions to sub-managers and receiving from them regular progress reports. If need be, the manager can hop a plane for a brief, on-site visit.

This mobility has necessitated a whole new layer of international government since the end of World War II to co-ordinate an increasing number of integrated spheres of activity. If initially this meant the creation of the United Nations in 1945, which deals with military, economic, health, education, and cultural affairs between states, today the list of international governing agencies includes the North Atlantic Treaty Organization (NATO), the World Trade Organization (WTO), the Association of Southeast Asian Nations (ASEAN), the Asia-Pacific Economic Co-operation group (APEC), the Group of Eight (G-8), the Latin American Integration Association (LAIA), the European Union (EU), and many others. The flipside of this international co-operation, of course, is international interference in cases where states' interests conflict. As the 1998–9 dispute between Canada and the United States over magazine policy made

Computers linked to the Internet are commonplace in offices today, which permits business to be conducted on a global scale: employees can send messages that are transmitted in fractions of a second; managers at head offices can keep an eye on inventory levels and employee productivity in subsidiaries; and clients can get service through corporate Web sites that are always open for business. (PCPaintbrush PhotoLibrary)

While face-to-face interaction remains part of social relations in even the most globalized of environments—on the street, in the park, at work, at school, at public meetings, at the corner store—proximity no longer constricts our social interactions. Communications technologies like the cellular telephone, fax machine, and personal computer bind social spaces and enable people to maintain regular and frequent contact across distance. This is particularly so as these technologies have become more accessible in terms of cost, ease of use, and availability and as these media have entered the private sphere of the home. The instantaneousness with which technologically mediated conversations can be held approximates face-to-face communication. As the promoters of the digital age delight in telling us (e.g., Negroponte, 1995), such media enable us to conduct social relations over great distances, and their increasing sophistication minimizes the obstacles inherent in physical separation.

Similarly, as Harold Innis argues, communications media enable the centralized governance of a political community on the scale of the modern nation-state and the centralized administration of a transnational corporation of intercontinental scope. Both national forms of governance and global forms of capitalism require efficient means of communication to: establish a coherent agenda; disseminate instructions and information; monitor the activities of remote departments; and receive reports from local managers or governors in the field. This relationship is one of power, in which an authoritative body exercises control over social space and social order (see Drache, 1995: xlv–xlvi).

Finally, the media have themselves become a key constituent of globalization in what is called the 'information age'. This means, first, that the cultural industries are conducting a greater proportion of global trade by serving as the conduits for the

clear, globalization means that national governments no longer enjoy uncontested sovereignty within their own borders.

The mass media play three specific roles in the globalization process. First, they are the *media of encounter*, putting us 'in touch' with one another via mail, telephone, e-mail, fax, etc. Second, they are the *media of governance*, enabling the central administration of vast spaces and dispersed places. Third, they constitute a *globalized business* in and of themselves, conducting trade in information and entertainment products.

exchange of information and entertainment commodities; the communication and information sector of the world economy accounted for 18 per cent of global trade in 1980 and steadily increased its share through the 1980s and 1990s (Herman and McChesney, 1997: 38). Second, information and ideas are increasingly important to an economy that has become dependent on innovation in all industrial sectors. Ideas that can lead to new product development, greater productivity, and the expansion of markets have become an essential driving force in maintaining economic growth. Corporate management guru Peter Drucker (1993: 8) maintains that the 'basic economic resource' is no longer capital, natural resources, or labour, but knowledge. 'Value is now created by "productivity" and "innovation", both applications of knowledge to work.'

The economic role that the mass media have come to play has considerable implications for how we define communication (as commodity or cultural form, as we discussed in Chapter 8), for who gets to speak (on both the individual and the collective level), and for what kinds of messages are privileged. As Edward Herman and Robert McChesney (1997: 9) state:

> We regard the primary effect of the globalization process . . . to be the implantation of the commercial model of communication, its extension to broadcasting and the 'new media', and its gradual intensification under the force of competition and bottom-line pressures. The commercial model has its own internal logic and, being privately owned and relying on advertiser support, tends to erode the public sphere and to create a 'culture of entertainment' that is incompatible with a democratic order. Media outputs are commodified and designed to serve market ends, not citizenship needs.

By making information an exploitable resource, we have transformed the democratic ideal of free speech and freely circulating information into the media proprietors' ideal of the freedom to exploit world markets. In doing so we have also laid the foundation of the global entertainment and information industries. The problem, in a nutshell, is that these industries tend to overproduce and widely distribute specific types of entertainment and information, and neglect other, less profitable, but no less important communication products.

Global Information Trade

Like other aspects of globalization, the cultural sphere is witnessing the expansion and intensification of a trend that already has a substantial history. This history reveals that international cultural exchanges have always been uneven, with a few sources of communication serving many destinations. This asymmetry intensified dramatically in the second half of the twentieth century as large media companies exploited their increased capacity to reach far-flung markets, treating the world as 'a single global market with local subdivisions'. Herman and McChesney (ibid., 41) write:

> The rapidity of their global expansion is explained in part by equally rapid reduction or elimination of many of the traditional institutional and legal barriers to cross-border transactions. They have also been facilitated by technological changes such as the growth of satellite broadcasting, video-cassette recorders, fiber optic cable and phone systems. Also criticially important has been the rapid growth of cross-border advertising, trade and investment, and thus the demand for media and other communication services.

Terhi Rantanen (1997) points out that a handful of European news agencies—Havas, Reuters, Wolff—began to dominate global news coverage in the mid-1800s. Herman and McChesney (1997: 12) note that the development of the telegraph and submarine telegraph cables in the mid-nineteenth century meant that, for the first time, information could reliably travel faster than people.

> From the beginning, global news services have been oriented to the needs and interests of the wealthy nations which provide their revenues. These news agencies were, in effect, the global media until well into the twentieth century, and even after the dawn of broadcasting their importance for global journalism was unsurpassed. Indeed, it was their near monopoly control over international news that stimulated much of the resistance to the existing global media regime by Third World nations in the 1970s.

Herman and McChesney (ibid., 13–14) describe the film industry as 'the first media industry to serve a truly global market'. By 1914, barely 20 years after cinema was invented, the US had captured 85 per cent of the world film audience, and by 1925, US films accounted for 90 per cent of film revenues in Great Britain, Canada, Australia, New Zealand, and Argentina, and over 70 per cent of revenues in France, Brazil, and the Scandinavian countries.

Such developments have been criticized as instances of media imperialism—the exploitation of global media markets to build political, economic, and ideological empires of influence and control. If what used to be called media imperialism is now described in the more palatable language of media globalization, concerns nevertheless remain that the mass communication sphere has come to be dominated by 50 of the world's largest media companies, the majority of them based in Western Europe and North America (McChesney, 1998: 13).

The point we wish to underline here is that the interdependence characteristic of globalization is rarely symmetrical. The flow of information and entertainment products is decidedly uneven, creating a situation in which a few countries produce, and profit from, the vast majority of media content, leaving most of the world, to a great extent, speechless. The United States, for example, is the world leader in the production and dissemination of cultural products, and has since the 1940s adopted an aggressive posture in promoting the uninhibited flow of information and entertainment products worldwide. As Table 11.1 indicates, Hollywood films dominate box offices around the world. Any issue of *Weekly Variety* indicates that the theatre screens of the world have become a global market for the same Hollywood films we see in North America, although in some countries, like France, audiences support indigenous films. The US information and entertainment industry was worth $350 billion US in 1997 and had supplanted jet engines as the country's principal export (Auletta, 1997: x).

The three media industries with the most developed global markets in the 1990s were: book publishing, with global sales of $80 billion US in 1995; recorded music, with sales of $40 billion US in 1995; and film, which was dominated by the Hollywood studios owned by Disney, Time Warner, Viacom, Seagram, Sony, Philips, MGM, and News Corp. In the late 1990s, the Hollywood production studios were going through the greatest period of expansion in their history. According to Herman and McChesney (1997: 43–5), the biggest growth area among media industries at present is commercial television, thanks to satellites, cable distribution, and digital technologies, which are creating more and more specialty channels hungry for content.

Table 11.1 Top Three Box-Office Films, Selected Countries (October 2002)

Country	Title	Country of Origin
Germany	Minority Report	USA
	The Bourne Identity	USA/Czech Republic
	Bibi Blocksberg	Germany
France	Minority Report	USA
	The Pianist	UK/France/Germany/Poland/Netherlands
	Ma Femme ... s'appelle	France/Germany
Spain	Minority Report	USA
	Signs	USA
	Goldmember	USA
Australia	Lilo & Stitch	USA
	The Bourne Identity	USA/Czech Republic
	Goldmember	USA
UK/Ireland	Lilo & Stitch	USA
	Big Fat Greek Wedding	USA
	Signs	USA
Italy	Minority Report	USA
	Changing Lanes	USA
	People I Know	USA
Japan	Signs	USA
	Road to Perdition	USA
	Ashita Ga Aru-Sa	Japan
South Korea	Family Honor	South Korea
	YMCA	South Korea
	XXX	USA

Sources: *Weekly Variety*, 14–20 Oct. 2002; Internet Movie Database (www.imdb.com).

Politically, the strong trend toward deregulation, privatization, and commercialization of media and communication has opened up global commercial broadcasting in a manner that represents a startling break with past practice. Throughout the world the commercialization of national television systems has been regarded as 'an integral part' of economic liberalization programs.

Public broadcasting systems, in Canada and around the world, are under siege. Even the venerable BBC, which has come to symbolize the best of public broadcasting, has adopted a commercial strategy. The BBC launched its BBC World Service Television as a global commercial venture in 1991, seeking 'to capitalize upon the BBC brand name, considered to be the second most famous in the world after that of Coca-Cola'. In 1996, the BBC established joint ventures with two American corporations to create commercial TV channels for world markets. Herman and McChesney (ibid., 46–7) write: 'It is clear that the BBC has decided that its survival depends more upon locating a niche in the global media market than in generating political support for public service broadcasting.'

What is emerging is a tiered global media market dominated by US-based companies, which can capitalize on the competitive advantage of having 'by far the largest and most lucrative indigenous market to use as a testing ground and to yield economies of scale' (ibid., 52). These companies are moving from a predominantly US-based production system to an international production and distribution network, localizing content to some extent, but also taking advantage of lower costs outside the United States. In the 1980s and 1990s, for example, Canada became an important site of Hollywood film and television production, as American film companies took advantage of the lower dollar and comparable technical expertise north of the border (see Gasher, 2002; Pendakur, 1998). The Hollywood animation industry has similarly taken advantage of the cheap yet stable labour markets of India, South Korea, Australia, Taiwan, and the Philippines for the time-consuming and labour-intensive execution of animation projects originally conceived in Los Angeles (Lent, 1998).

Herman and McChesney (1997: 52–6) have identified the principal players in the global media market as forming two tiers. The first tier consists of about 10 vertically integrated companies with annual revenues of between $10 and $25 billion US. These companies would include News Corp., AOL Time Warner, Disney, Bertelsmann, Viacom, and TCI. The second tier comprises about three dozen companies with annual revenues of between $2 and $10 billion US.

These companies are most interested in the world's most affluent audiences, the audiences that advertisers want to reach, the audiences with the money to spend on advertised products and services. This means, for example, that the poorest half of India's 900 million people is irrelevant to the global media market, and that all of sub-Saharan Africa has been written off. '[Sub-Saharan Africa] does not even appear in most discussions of global media in the business press.' Specifically, the global media are most interested in markets in North America, Latin America, Europe, and Asia. China, with a population of 1.2 billion, is the 'largest jewel in the Asian media crown' (ibid., 64–8).

The global media market, of course, does see some two-way traffic. The Globo and Televisa television networks in Brazil, for example, have succeeded in capturing a respectable share of Brazil's domestic market, and their *telenovela* productions are major exports. Globo owns an Italian television station, has an ownership interest in an American network specializing in Latin American programming, and has joint ventures with AT&T, News Corp., and TCI. Canada, too, has begun to tap export markets in both the film and television industries, even if the financial returns are relatively modest. A renaissance in Canadian feature-film production since the mid-1980s means that directors like David Cronenberg (*Spider, Crash, ExistenZ*), Atom Egoyan (*Ararat, Felicia's Journey, The Sweet Hereafter*), and François Girard (*Thirty-Two Short Films About Glenn Gould, The Red Violin*) have made names for themselves in international film markets. And Canada has become one of the world's leading exporters of television programming. Canada enjoyed record sales at the 1998 and 1999 MIP-TV trade show in France, selling television programming to the US, Britain, Ireland, France, Germany, Australia, New Zealand, South Africa, Israel, Poland, China, Malaysia, and Zimbabwe (Vale, 1998; Binning, 1999).

THEORIES OF IMPERIALISM AND DEPENDENCY

Communication scholars developed two closely related theories in the post-war period to describe this asymmetrical trade in cultural materials: **media imperialism** and **cultural dependency**. Oliver

Boyd-Barrett (1977: 117–18) used the term 'media imperialism' to characterize the unidirectional nature of international media flows from a small number of source countries. More formally, he defined 'media imperialism' as 'the process whereby the ownership, structure, distribution or content of the media in any one country are singly or together subject to substantial external pressures from the media interests of any other country or countries without proportionate reciprocation of influence by the country so affected.' Media imperialism research grew out of a larger struggle for decolonization in the aftermath of World War II (Mosco, 1996: 75–6).

Cultural dependency is a less deterministic means of characterizing cultural trade imbalances than media imperialism. Whereas the term 'imperialism' implies 'the act of territorial annexation for the purpose of formal political control', Boyd-Barrett (1995: 174–84) maintains that cultural dependency suggests 'de facto control' and refers to 'a complex of processes' to which the mass media contribute 'to an as yet unspecified extent'.

While both approaches contributed a great deal to documenting international communication flows and drew attention to an obvious problem, neither theory offered a sufficiently complex explanation of the power dynamics behind international cultural trade, nor did they provide satisfactory descriptions of the impact of such asymmetrical exchanges. The media imperialism thesis was particularly crude, assuming too neat a relationship between the all-powerful source countries and their helpless colonies. Ted Magder (1993: 8–9) argues that the media imperialism thesis leads to two distinct questions: 'First, what are the particular social, political, and economic dynamics that establish, maintain, challenge, and modify media imperialism? Second, what effect do the practices of media imperialism have on cultural values and attitudes?' Early media imperialism studies, Magder argues, assumed that the transnationalization of cultural production led to the transnationalization of reception, that audiences around the world would get the same meanings from the same TV shows and feature films. This is not the case. Another shortcoming was its presumption that 'all power flowed from the imperial core, as if the "target" nation were an innocent and helpless victim.' Clearly, some members of the target nation stand to benefit from the economic opportunities cultural imports afford.

Magder qualifies the media imperialism thesis by underlining four points: the imperial centre is rarely omnipotent; the target nation is rarely defenceless; certain actors within the target nation may stand to benefit from media imperialism; and the effects of media imperialism are often unintended and unpredictable. He writes: 'It is not enough to document the internationalization of culture in its various forms; rather the limits, conflicts, and contradictions of media imperialism must also be evaluated.'

While slightly more nuanced, the cultural dependency thesis shared a number of the shortcomings of the media imperialism thesis. Like media imperialism, Vincent Mosco (1996: 125–6) argues, cultural dependency created homogeneous portraits of both the source and the target countries. It concentrated almost exclusively on the role of external forces and overlooked 'the contribution made by local forces and relations of production, including the indigenous class structure'. Cultural dependency also portrayed transnational capitalism as rendering the target state powerless. Like media imperialism, cultural dependency did not adequately account for how audiences in the target countries used or interpreted media messages that originate elsewhere.

Nonetheless, the clear asymmetry of globalization remains an important issue for researchers who study cultural policy and the political economy of communication from a range of perspectives. Current research seeks to account for the heterogeneity of national cultures, the specificity of particular industries and corporate practices, and varying reception practices—how cultural products are used by audiences.

A New World Information and Communication Order

Cees Hamelink (1994: 23–8) observes that two features of international communication stand out in the post-war period: the expansion of the global communication system and tensions in the system across both east-west and north-south axes. East-west tensions—i.e., Cold War tensions between the Communist bloc led by the Soviet Union and the Western democracies led by the United States—were most prominent in the 1950s and 1960s. North-south tensions—i.e., tensions between affluent, industrialized nations of the northern hemisphere and the Third World countries of the southern hemisphere—arose in the 1970s as the Third World took advantage of its new-found voice in the General Assembly of the United Nations. A number of UN initiatives led to a proposed New World Information and Communications Order (NWICO), which sought compromise between the American advocacy of the **free flow of information** and the Third World's desire for a balanced flow.

The US push for the free flow doctrine began during World War II when the American newspaper industry campaigned for the freedom of news gathering; in June 1944, the American Society of News-paper Editors (ASNE) adopted resolutions demanding 'unrestricted communications for news throughout the world'. Early in 1945, an ASNE delegation travelled around the world promoting their 'free flow' position. In February 1946, a US delegation to the United Nations submitted a proposal to UN Secretary-General Trygve Lie asking that the UN Commission on Human Rights consider the question of freedom of information. The UN held a conference on freedom of information in Geneva in 1948.

SATELLITE TECHNOLOGY

The history of communication satellites belongs to a long and continuing history of media innovations that pose fundamental challenges to national sovereignty, to the right of nations to govern their communication and cultural environment. Satellite systems, the central component in the space race between the Soviet Union and the US in the late 1950s and the early 1960s, consist of: a ground transmitter, a space-based receiver, an amplifier, a frequency switch, and a retransmitter (McDonnell, 1983: 1). In order to operate properly, satellites require **geostationary** synchronous orbit, which allows them to provide continuous coverage of the same part of the earth (Queeney, 1983: 4–5). While satellites have military, industrial, and scientific applications, our primary interest in satellites is as media of communication and entertainment that serve the private space of the home.

Satellite communication to the home follows two most common pathways: (1) satellite to cable, and (2) direct broadcasting. The satellite to cable pathway involves a relatively weak satellite downlink, which transmits signals to a large receiving dish. Cable companies subsequently redistribute these satellite signals by cable. This is a relatively simple system to license and regulate because all such signals are controlled by cable companies. Direct broadcasting, on the other hand, involves a satellite with a very powerful downlink signal, which feeds a relatively small and inexpensive receiving dish, the kind we commonly see attached to the sides of houses and apartment buildings. Direct broadcast satellite transmission is much harder to regulate because signals are received by countless numbers of privately owned dishes.

Satellite technology poses two main issues to regulators in an increasingly globalized media context. The first is signal penetration, the transmission of satellite signals across national borders, which raises questions of national sovereignty with regard to the 'information environment'. Satel-

Receiving dishes track satellites in geosynchronous orbit, capturing communication signals from around the world. While once used primarily for military and scientific applications, satellite transmission is a common medium for the news, sports, and entertainment programs we receive on our televisions. (PCPaintbrush PhotoLibrary)

lites operate through vertical space—the space above the earth. The challenge for regulators is demarcating between 'atmospheric space', which is subject to the sovereignty of states located directly beneath that space, and 'outer space', which has been defined by UN treaty as 'property common to all humanity' and not subject to national appropriation. The second major issue is orbit allotment—the distribution of orbital positions most favourable to satellite transmission. That is, to minimize signal interference from satellites using the same frequency, satellites must be spread out along the geostationary arc, limiting the number of positions available. The 1985 World Administrative Radio Conference, which governs orbit allotment, enshrined a principle of equity that sought to guarantee access to geostationary satellite orbit and to appropriate frequency bands (Meisel, 1986).

At this stage, the free flow doctrine met its stiffest opposition from the Soviet Union, which insisted on the regulation of information flows and complained that the Americans' freedom of information position endorsed, in fact, the freedom of a few commercial communication monopolies. Nevertheless, the free flow doctrine was largely endorsed by the UN and Article 19 of the 1948 Universal Declaration on Human Rights states: 'Everyone has the right to freedom of opinion and expression; this right includes freedom to hold opinions without interference and to seek, receive and impart information and ideas through any media regardless of frontiers' (ibid., 152–5).

The issue of communication flows was revisited at the behest of Third World countries in the 1970s, when it became clear that the free flow doctrine was a recipe for Western cultural **hegemony**, as the Soviets had anticipated. Herman and McChesney (1997: 22–4) write: 'By the 1970s the trajectory and nature of the emerging global media system were increasingly apparent; it was a largely profit-driven system dominated by [transnational corporations] based in the advanced capitalist nations, primarily in the United States.' The development and launching of **geosynchronous** communication satellites in the 1960s and 1970s 'fanned the flames of concern about global media.'

> Satellites held out the promise of making it possible for Third World nations to leapfrog out of their quagmire into a radically more advanced media system, but at the same time satellites posed the threat of transnational commercial broadcasters eventually controlling global communication, bypassing any domestic authority with broadcasts directly to Third World homes. (Ibid., 23)

The major global institutions dealing with communication issues at the time—the UN, the UN Educational, Scientific and Cultural Organization (UNESCO), and the International Telecommuni-cation Union (ITU)—all included majorities of Third World countries and sympathetic Communist states. The impetus for a renewed debate on international communication came from the 90-member Movement of the Non-Aligned Nations (NAM). 'The nonaligned position included a socialist critique of capitalist media and a nationalist critique of imperialist media' (ibid.).

The international debate at that time focused on three points, as it still does to some extent. First, historically, communication services together with evolved information technologies have allowed dominant states to exploit their power. Through historical patterns and enabling technology, such as communication satellites, these dominant states have assumed a presence in the cultures and ideologies of less dominant states. That presence, whether it comes from being the principal source of foreign news or from beaming satellite signals into another country, is strongly felt by developing nations.

Second, the economies of scale in information production and distribution threaten to reinforce this dominance. And any attempt to counteract a worsening situation must avoid feeding into the hands of repressive governments that would curtail freedom of expression and information circulation.

Third, a few transnational corporations have mobilized technology as a vehicle for the exploitation of markets rather than as a means of serving the cultural, social, and political needs of nations. In other words, the large corporations have seized the opportunity to develop and use communication technologies, but they have employed those technologies primarily to exploit the value of audiences to advertisers, and not to provide information, education, and entertainment to these audiences for their own benefit or for the benefit of the larger cultural whole.

Pressure from the Third World compelled the UN to broaden the concept of free flow to include 'the free and balanced flow of information'. International debate over the design of a New World Information and Communication Order coalesced around the final report of the 16-member International Commission for the Study of Communication Problems (the MacBride Commission), established by UNESCO in December 1977 (UNESCO, 1980). The underpinnings of this report are found in two principles that were accepted by a pair of intergovernmental conferences, the first held in San José, Costa Rica, in 1976, and the second in Kuala Lumpur, Malaysia, in 1979. They are:

1. Communication policies should be conceived in the context of national realities, free expression of thought, and respect for individual and social rights.
2. Communication, considered both as a means of affirming a nation's collective identity and as an

instrument of social integration, has a decisive role to play in the democratization of social relations insofar as it permits a multidirectional flow of . . . messages, both from the media to their public and from this public to the media. (UNESCO, 1980: 40, 41)

The MacBride Commission (ibid., 253–68) advocated 'free, open and balanced communications' and concluded that 'the utmost importance should be given to eliminating imbalances and disparities in communication and its structures, and particularly in information flows. Developing countries need to reduce their dependence, and claim a new, more just and more equitable order in the field of communication.' The Commission's conclusions were based on 'the firm conviction that communication is a basic individual right, as well as a collective one required by all communities and nations. Freedom of information—and, more specifically the right to seek, receive and impart information—is a fundamental human right; indeed, a prerequisite for many others.'

The MacBride Commission pointed to an essential conflict between the commercialization and the democratization of communication, and clearly favoured a movement for the democratization of communication, which would include respect for national sovereignty in areas of cultural policy and recognition that the 'educational and informational use of communication should be given equal priority with entertainment.' The report stated: 'Every country should develop its communication patterns in accordance with its own conditions, needs and traditions, thus strengthening its integrity, independence and self-reliance.'

The MacBride Report also criticized the striking disparities between the technological capacities of different nations. Recommendation 27, for example, states: 'The concentration of communications technology in a relatively few developed countries and transnational corporations has led to virtual monopoly situations in this field. To counteract these tendencies national and international measures are required, among them reform of existing patent laws and conventions, appropriate legislation and international agreements.'

Finally, MacBride described the right to communicate as fundamental to democracy. 'Communication needs in a democratic society should be met by the extension of specific rights, such as the right to be informed, the right to inform, the right to privacy, the right to participate in public communication—all elements of a new concept, the right to communicate.'

From NWICO to Now

The MacBride Report proved to be a better manifesto on the democratization of communication than a blueprint for a restructuring of international communication exchange. Even though UNESCO adopted its key principles—eliminating global media imbalances and having communication serve national development goals—the NWICO was poorly received in the West 'because it gave governments, and not markets, ultimate authority over the nature of a society's media' (Herman and McChesney, 1997: 24–6). In fact, the Western countries, led by the United States under Ronald Reagan and Great Britain under Margaret Thatcher, chose in the 1980s the more aggressive path of pursuing liberalized global trade. 'In the 1980s a wave of global "liberalization" gathered momentum, in which state enterprises were privatized, private businesses were deregulated, and government welfare initiatives were cut back.' Even Canada, which was one of the affluent industrialized nations identified by the MacBride Commission as being dominated by cultural imports, began to pursue the neo-liberal agenda of free trade and budget cutbacks in the 1980s under the successive Progressive Conservative governments of Brian Mulroney. Little changed in Canadian government policy when Jean Chrétien's Liberals assumed power in 1993. Issues like deficit reduction and freer trade continued to dominate the political agenda and the ministers of industry, international trade, and finance enjoyed as much influence over cultural policy as the minister with the culture portfolio, if not even more (see Gasher, 1995b).

International bodies like the World Trade Organization (originally, the General Agreement on Tariffs and Trade) became more important to the major cultural producers than the United Nations—the US and Britain withdrew from UNESCO in 1985—and the rules of the game for international communications were written in such treaties as the North American Free Trade Agreement (NAFTA) and the Treaty on European Union. Herman and McChesney (1997: 30–1) write: 'The political design of all these regional and global trade agreements has

INTERNAL COMMUNICATION IMBALANCES

Even within countries, communication imbalances mean that some regions communicate and others are communicated to. When we refer to the *American* television industry, for instance, we are really referring to an industry based in two media centres: New York and Los Angeles. Similarly, the American film industry might be more properly termed the Los Angeles film industry and is often simply called Hollywood.

In Canada, Montreal and Toronto serve as the country's principal media centres, responsible for most of our film and television programming and book and magazine publishing. Both of Canada's 'national' newspapers—the *Globe and Mail* and the *National Post*—are based in Toronto. Even publicly owned institutions like the Canadian Broadcasting Corporation and the National Film Board concentrate their production and administrative activities in central Canada. Statistics Canada (1998: 11) reports that in 1996–7, broadcasting consumed 80 per cent of the federal government's $1.9 billion budget for the cultural industries, the bulk of which was spent in Ontario and Quebec, 'largely as a result of the concentration of production facilities and related infrastructure located there'.

The CBC's commitment to regional production had been called into question as early as 1957 (Canada, 1957: 75–6) and in her study of the first three decades of CBC television drama, Mary Jane Miller (1987: 327) was unable to discern any coherent CBC policy on the role of regional dramatic programming. The NFB's record on regional production has been even worse. Founded in 1939, the NFB did not establish its first regional production centre until 1965, and it did not have a production presence in all regions of Canada until 1976 (Jones, 1981: 177–8; Dick, 1986: 118–21).

This concentration is especially striking in the film industry. A 1977 study commissioned by the federal Secretary of State (Canada, 1977: 154) noted that 75 per cent of Canada's production companies were located in the Montreal–Ottawa–Toronto triangle and accounted for at least 90 per cent of the country's film production. A number of provinces in Canada, excluded from the 'national' film industry, became film production centres in the 1980s and 1990s by attracting foreign film and TV production on location. British Columbia, for example, which didn't have a film industry until the mid-1970s, has become Canada's largest site of film and TV production primarily by attracting Hollywood location shoots (Gasher, 2002).

Technological factors, too, can affect the quality and equitable distribution of communication services. As much as Canada has tried to institute a broadcasting system accessible to all Canadians, the North has presented a unique challenge. Canada began experimenting with communications in the North because of the irregularity in radio signals. It seems that the same electrical disturbances that produce the northern lights also interfere with radio transmissions. When investigators concluded that reliable communications in the North could not depend on airwaves, satellites became the solution.

Early satellites were designed to enable individuals and communities to communicate with each other. Because the satellites were relatively low-powered, powerful ground stations were required to send and receive signals. Satisfactory results induced further development. The power of satellites was increased, as was their capability of transmitting larger numbers of signals, until it was possible to receive television signals with a four-foot receiving dish. Suddenly, northerners could receive at least as many TV channels as southern Canadians.

been to remove decision-making powers from local and national legislatures in favor of impersonal market forces and/or supranational bureaucracies remote from popular control.' NAFTA, for example, 'requires that government agencies operate on a strictly commercial basis, and it explicitly removes the possibility that governments can take on any new functions.'

The New World Information and Communication Order, in other words, was almost immediate-

ly supplanted by what Herman and McChesney call the 'new global corporate ideology'.

Its core element and centerpiece is the idea that the market allocates resources effectively and provides the means of organizing economic (and perhaps all human) life. There is a strong tendency in corporate ideology to identify 'freedom' with the mere absence of constraints on business (i.e., economic, or market, freedom), thus pushing political freedom into a subordinate category. (Ibid., 35)

And as the communications media have become increasingly implicated in the global economy, media policy is governed more and more by international financial and trade regimes such as the International Monetary Fund and the WTO.

Changing Notions of Place

The widespread commercialization of cultural production, communication, and information exchange raises a number of questions about the relationship between communication and culture. The perpetual flows of people, capital, goods, services, and images that characterize globalization carry significant implications for how we experience and imagine place, how we define community, and how we constitute identity. Doreen Massey (1991: 24) asks: 'How, in the face of all this movement and intermixing, can we retain any sense of a local place and its particularity?' Globalization has intensified struggles over the meaning of place. This is particularly the case in countries like Canada, whose citizens tend to be more familiar with cultural imports than the ideas and expressions of their own artists and intellectuals.

As noted above, the various flows we associate with globalization are not new. What globalization has done, however, has been both to increase the traffic—human, material, electronic, etc.—across some borders and to reconfigure others. Thus, for example, the Canada–US Free Trade Agreement was an attempt to facilitate trade across the border dividing the two countries. Although the legal boundary remains, the meaning of the border has changed, at least as far as trade relations are concerned. In fact, in the wake of the 11 September 2001 terrorist attacks on the United States, the signing in December 2001 of the Smart Border Declaration between Canada and the US, whereby the latest communications technology will be used to create a more secure shared border, has meant that the very term 'border' has taken on a rather changed and less Canadian-determined meaning for the foreseeable future. This applies to cultural exchanges as well; it has become more difficult for Canada to preserve some space within its own market for indigenous cultural products. Technologies like satellite television ignore terrestrial boundaries altogether; satellite TV is confined instead by satellite

'footprints', which mark the limits of a satellite's technological reach.

The heightened permeability of borders has been met, among some, by the desire for a more rooted, or more secure, sense of place. Gillian Rose (1995: 88–116) notes that place has been a privileged component of identity formation. 'Identity is how we make sense of ourselves, and geographers, anthropologists and sociologists, among others, have argued that the meanings given to a place may be so strong that they become a central part of the identity of people experiencing them.' Places, and the experiences we associate with places, both as individuals and as members of a group, inform memory and our sense of belonging. This sense of belonging is critical to understanding the relationship between identity and a particular locale. 'One way in which identity is connected to a particular place is by a feeling that you belong to that place.' We might, therefore, detect a very different sense of belonging between native residents of a place and migrants. Migrants such as refugees and exiles, who have not moved of their own free will, may feel little sense of belonging to their new place of residence.

Culture is another means by which identities of place are constructed and sustained. Stuart Hall (1995: 177–86) argues that we tend to imagine cultures as 'placed' in two ways. First, we associate place with a specific location where social relationships have developed over time. Second, place 'establishes symbolic boundaries around a culture, marking off those who belong from those who do not.'

> Physical settlement, continuity of occupation, the long-lasting effects on ways of life arising from the shaping influence of location and physical environment, coupled with the idea that these cultural influences have been exercised amongst a population which is settled and deeply interrelated through marriage and kinship relations, are meanings which we closely associate with the idea of culture and which provide powerful ways of conceptualizing what 'culture' is, how it works, and how it is transmitted and preserved.

At the same time, Hall explains, 'There is a strong tendency to "landscape" cultural identities, to give them an imagined place or "home", whose characteristics echo or mirror the characteristics of the identity in question.'

Our sense of place is really part of our cultural systems of meaning. We usually think about or imagine cultures as 'placed'—landscaped, even if only in the mind. This helps to give shape and to give a foundation to our identities. However, the ways in which culture, place and identity are imagined and conceptualized are increasingly untenable in light of the historical and contemporary evidence.

If one impact of globalization has been to call into question the notion of 'place' as the basis for identity and/or culture, **postmodern** thinking and improved networks of transportation and communication facilitate the imagination of communities based on gender, race, ethnicity, sexual orientation, social class, etc. Proximity, in other words, is not a necessary element of identity formation. If culture and identity are not confined to a particular place, it follows that any one place is not confined to a single culture or identity. This has precipitated localized struggles over immigration, language, urban development, architecture, and foreign investment. Mike Featherstone (1996: 66) remarks that 'cultural differences once maintained between places now exist within them.' For example: 'The unwillingness of migrants to passively inculcate the dominant cultural mythology of the nation or locality raises issues of multiculturalism and the fragmentation of identity.' Massey (1995: 48) argues: 'The way in which we define "places", and the particular character of individual places, can be important in issues varying from battles over development and construction to questions of which social groups have rights to live where.'

The conventional container of identity and culture that has come under greatest challenge from the re-imagining of community prompted by globalization has been the **nation–state**. Questions of citizenship and questions of identity have been increasingly dissociated (Morley and Robins, 1995: 19). The emergence of trade blocs in Europe, Asia, and North America and the prevalence of both international and sub-national cultural networks have undermined the primacy of the nation-state in contemporary imaginings of community, identity, and culture.

We should not overreact to these changes, however. We still have democratically elected national, provincial, and municipal governments, which continue to pass laws and pursue policies that form the basic framework within which media organizations operate in Canada. These laws and policies are responses to pressures from both the global economy and local cultures. As we discussed in Chapters 6 and 7, laws like the Broadcasting, Telecommunications, and Income Tax Acts, the funding programs of Telefilm Canada and the Canada Council, and cultural institutions like the Canadian Broadcasting Corporation remain pre-eminent in structuring cultural production in Canada. No media industry is untouched by them. Globalization alters the context in which mass communication takes place, but local conditions of cultural production remain pertinent.

Summary

This chapter began with an extended definition of globalization and showed how it was not simply an economic phenomenon, but an intensification of social relations across time and space that touches every aspect of our lives, from how we shop to what we watch on television. We then outlined three roles the communications media play in the globalization process—as media of encounter, as media of governance, and as a globalized business in and of themselves.

Having laid this conceptual groundwork, we traced the history of international communications exchanges, concentrating particularly on the period from the 1940s to the present. We discussed the doctrine of 'free flow' promoted by the United States and then explained the rise, and subsequent downfall, of the New World Information and Communication Order, whose proponents sought to alleviate communications imbalances between national communities in the 1970s and to promote the 'right to communicate' as a fundamental human right. Instead, the 1980s and 1990s were characterized by further trade liberalization and the reinforcement of the commercial view of communication as commodity exchange.

The chapter concluded with a discussion of globalization's impact on how we think about 'place', 'community', and 'identity,' given the importance of communication and cultural exchange to our sense of belonging.

RELATED WEB SITES

European Union: www.europa.eu.int

The official site of the European Union includes an institutional overview, regular news dispatches, and official report.

International Telecommunications Satellite Organization (INTELSAT): www.intelsat.com

INTELSAT provides global communications services with a 'fleet' of 20 geosynchronous satellites.

International Telecommunications Union: www.itu.int

The ITU is an international organization through which governments and private corporations co-ordinate telecommunications networks and services.

UNESCO: www.unesco.org/webworld/observatory/index.shtml

The principal objective of the United Nations Educational, Scientific and Cultural Organization is to contribute to global peace and security by promoting international collaboration through education, science, culture, and communication.

World Trade Organization: www.wto.org

The WTO governs trade between nations and seeks to promote trade liberalization throughout the world.

FURTHER READINGS

Bauman, Zygmunt. 1998. *Globalization: The Human Consequences*. New York: Columbia University Press. This book looks at globalization from a critical and human perspective, considering its political, social, and economic implications on people's daily lives.

Castells, Manuel. 2001. *The Internet Galaxy: Reflections on the Internet, Business, and Society*. Oxford: Oxford University Press. Written by one of the foremost contemporary theorists on international communications networks, this book examines the Internet from a number of perspectives, including its history and how it impacts the way people work, consume media, and interact socially.

Hamelink, Cees J. 1994. *The Politics of World Communication*. London: Sage Publications. Hamelink provides a detailed study of international communication policy formation and the central issues that continue to create conflict among national governments. The book is particularly useful for gaining a broader, international perspective on public policy issues.

Herman, Edward S., and Robert W. McChesney. 1997. *The Global Media: The New Missionaries of Global Capital-*

ism. London: Cassell. The authors present a critical assessment of the rise of concentrated and converged media conglomerates, supported by documentation on which companies owned which media during the mid-1990s.

Morley, David, and Kevin Robins. 1995. *Spaces of Identity: Global Media, Electronic Landscapes and Cultural Boundaries*. London: Routledge. This is a provocative look at how the globalization of communication has undermined and altered conventional notions of national and cultural belonging. The ideas proposed in this book remain current.

UNESCO. 1980. *Many Voices, One World: Report by the International Commission for the Study of Communication Problems* (MacBride Commission). Paris: UNESCO. The controversial MacBride Report was critical of the free-flow doctrine promoted by the US and proposed measures to ensure more equitable and balanced communications flows between nations.

STUDY QUESTIONS

1. Globalization is often used to mean *economic* globalization. Besides economics, what other globalizing forces impact the communications sphere?
2. In what ways are the mass media agents of globalization?
3. Is media globalization the same as media imperialism? Why or why not?
4. What is the argument in support of the free flow of communication? What is the basis for criticism of this position?
5. What was the MacBride Commission's position on international communication flows?

LEARNING OUTCOMES

- To define globalization in broad terms, so that it can be understood as a phenomenon that affects many aspects of Canadians' lives.
- To discuss the role of the media in enabling globalization forces.
- To point out that communication exchanges—both nationally and internationally—tend to be uneven.
- To discuss critically the theories of media imperialism and media dependency.
- To address the international communications debate, from NWICO to the present.
- To consider what globalization implies for how we think about community, place, and identity.

CHAPTER 12

Communication in a Digital Age

Introduction

Communication pervades our lives and communication media pervade all facets of modern society. Communication media encompass film, books, magazines, television and radio broadcasting, and the Internet with its associated media; professional practice in these industries and activities; and the formal institutions of communication, such as film production companies, book and magazine publishers, newspaper companies, radio stations, and Web site producers. The influence exerted by these media, including workers in the communication industries and media institutions, ranges across various realms: politics, economics, education, culture, the family, and individual lives. The media also have an enormous impact on our world view and the ability to transform it or introduce bias into it. This is not to suggest that the media cause us to lose our grip on reality. Rather, it is to acknowledge that each medium is an incomplete and imperfect tool of understanding. To study the dynamics of these tools, which we have been doing in this book, is to attempt to understand the distance between what we know and what there is to be known.

Oral discourse takes us into the world of transmitting information and mnemonics, into the character of the speaker—what we can tell and remember of him or her through choice of words, intonation, thought structure, expressiveness, and associated body language (if we can see the speaker). Literacy takes us to the printed word—to linear, sequential, and logical thought, to the analytical engine the eye represents when connected to the brain and when the mind is filled with knowledge and embraces reason. Electronic society in analogue form reopens the oral and recaptures images and sound that, when combined, are quite rich in their simulation of reality. Digital electronic society does all this and more. Specifically, it offers up textual, numeric, oral, and audiovisual representations that, given a level of investment in hardware and software, can be made instantly available anywhere in the world. In a digital society that records everything, as ours increasingly does, text and numbers are instantaneously available almost everywhere, a reality that has a binding effect on our world. As well, this instant availability of text, numbers, sounds, and images—this ubiquity—allows for the analysis of patterns. It allows for the generation of metatext, i.e., text about text, numbers, sounds, or images. With words, it is a matter of counting. With transactions, it amounts to counting and correlations. With numbers, the game gets far more complex, taking us into the realm of economics and financial forecasting.

From Mass Distribution of Symbolic Products to Mass Communication

The worldwide transmission of messages and the transformation that digital communication offers or foists upon us are the foundation for the remaking of society. As each day goes by and each new information service is offered, we smile (or frown) and accept it. It seems so insignificant. Yet, compounded, these many different small changes represent a maelstrom of change so blinding that we cannot see as far as 20 years into the future. Big box retailers, whether bookstores or hardware stores, cannot exist without electronic data interchange (EDI). The institution of EDI facilitates their development. At the same time, it challenges the existence of small suppliers and small retailers because they become exceptions to the system.

As significant as anything associated with these changes is the social struggle that digital communication has set in motion. Some might shy away from words like 'social struggle'. They might prefer 'new, open, more competitive markets' or even, as the idealists like to put it, a 'new chance for democracy'. But a social struggle it is. As with any technological change, we are not merely throwing out a bunch of old machines and bringing in some new, sleek, quieter, more effective ones—we are doing that and more. We are setting in motion revision and reformation of professional practice. We are encouraging the reorganization and perhaps the re-establishment of associated institutions. And we are opening up for reconsideration the foundations of governing policy. In doing so, we are setting in motion how our overall communication system and a separate information sector will interact with and affect society, politics, economics, community, culture, art, religion—in fact, the whole of our lives and the whole of society.

At the foundation of this massive change is the decentralization of the communication systems of the modern world. Modern electronic communications are toppling centralized mass communication—the creation of highly designed messages at one point that are meant to be received by millions. The media, practices, and institutions of mass communication are being undermined by the fragmentation of markets and by the rise of a sophisticated publicly accessible transmission system potentially available to everyone—the Internet. For example, independent recording labels and bands who sell their music via the Internet have been able to get around the control of the recording industry giants—the Sonys, the BMIs, the Universals. And unlicensed Internet radio essentially is the circumvention of the state and commercial apparatus controlling mass broadcasting. Consider, as well, open-source software, which is a concerted effort on the part of digital labourers to undermine the centralized production and market domination of software by the world's richest man, Bill Gates, a centralizer of the first order. These are but a few examples in the growing trend of decentralizing communications.

'Power to the people', as the hippies used to cry out. Well, maybe. At least there are new possibilities. For instance, software programmers may hit upon an idea that provides a product no one even thought he or she needed, but suddenly with its invention the value becomes obvious. The exploits of such programmers in 1999 and 2000 could be found on the business pages of most newspapers. With the burst of the dot-com bubble, programmers now find themselves working behind the scenes, with brick-and-mortar businesses and organizations that can benefit from communicating with other businesses and organizations by means of the Internet. The world of mergers and acquisitions, leveraged buyouts, and general 'conglomeratization' has subsided as various companies come to terms with what one company can reasonably handle.

The foundations of this change from mass distribution of centrally produced products to mass communication by people and institutions can be understood by recalling the definitions introduced in Chapter 2:

- Mass communication is the centralized production and dissemination of mass information and entertainment.
- Mass communication is also the decentralized production and wide accessibility of information and entertainment by means of public access to the Internet.
- Mass communication is the exchange of information that takes place in society among individuals and groups by means of sometimes public access to communication channels.

The latter two meanings of the term 'mass communication' are new. It is not that the processes are new. Decentralized, widespread production of content describes small literary magazines. Widespread person-to-person communication by means of the postal system is ancient. And the telephone and telegraph have been with us since 1876 and 1896 respectively. What is new in the case of widespread production of cultural products is vastly increased ease of access. The greater variation of media text, sound, and image, together with the capacity for immediate transmission, storage, and manipulation, makes electronic person-to-person communication an enterprise of far greater social significance than the telephone and data communication. The social challenge these evolved technologies present is how they can made be available in such a way that they evade capture by the global communications behemoths.

Communication and Democracy

The social change arising from developments in communication interacts with the fundamentals of democracy and society in general on at least three fronts. First is the evolving form of communication institutions and their ownership and control within society. Second is the nature of the transformative bias inherent in any medium, specifically the transformative bias inherent in publicly accessible (to message and meaning production) digital communication media. Third, the possibilities for participation

Communication pervades our lives and communication media pervade modern society. The power of both the worldwide transmission of messages and the transformation that digital communication offers is the foundation for the remaking/reordering of society. (Scott Greene, Channel Babel, oil on canvas, 1998. Courtesy of the artist. Photo credit: Damian Andrus)

in message-making are significantly expanded by what the digital media allow.

The first front on which communication engages democracy evolves from the interaction between communications institutions and society. The history of this interaction can be traced back to the printing press, which, at first, was controlled by the state or governing elite. But as the elite grew in numbers and fragmented into distinct groups— politicians, the church, landowners, business—and the provision of information and entertainment became a burden to their host institutions, the press was turned over to powerful and determined businessmen who, as a class, developed and exploited the formula of engaging content, interested audiences, and advertising revenues. As the power of the press

barons became obvious, the role of the press as an institution in society became a central question of concern. Should the press owners be allowed to use all their potential power to advance their biases in favour of business, certain political parties, and certain policies, such as free commercial speech? Should they be vehicles for inveterate seekers after truth, as the libertarian journalistic community might wish? Or should they act in a more constrained fashion, as self-aware institutions with a privileged position in society and, consequently, a responsibility to act for the social good of all? These questions exemplify the ways in which communication interacts with notions of democracy.

We saw in Chapter 3 how, particularly in Canada, the social responsibility thesis prevailed, at least until recently, not only in the press but also in the founding of broadcasting and specifically through the founding of a national public broadcasting service in the CBC. Even more than the press, broadcasting was seen as a potential harbinger of greater social coherence and responsibility in the media, offering enlightenment to individuals and encouraging the pursuit of democratic ideals. (From a slightly different perspective, public broadcasting gave the state the chance to bankroll a medium of communication on behalf of the people that would counterbalance the commercial media, which are 80 per cent or more bankrolled by the business sector through advertising.)

At the international level, the efforts of UNESCO to extend the ideals of public broadcasting through a new world order were founded on essentially the same idea of social responsibility. Dubbed fair flows of information rather than free flows (where the strongest in the market were free to dominate), this UNESCO effort was squelched by the US and the UK. The desire of these two countries to maintain their predominance as exporters of information, entertainment, and ideology to the world overrode any sense either had of social justice or of the value of celebrating diversity on a worldwide scale. Canadian policy, on the whole, decried this imperialism, and, with the help of favourable government policy, we built up cultural industries capable of carrying Canadian creative content to Canadians. Yet, no sooner had such industries been established than they became exporters, larding our cultural products on importing nations.

In the digital age the question is perhaps how extensively and quickly large corporations will move in reconsolidating their predominance and hence their control. Once we sense the extent of that reconsolidation, the next question will be to determine the consequences of that movement for democracy. Currently, production for and participation in the Internet are dispersed. At least in North America, Web site producers include virtually anyone with the desire to produce a Web site. Internet providers are often started-from-scratch small businesses. The very richness of the Internet may be the undoing of its heterogeneity. Currently, Google and certain other search engines turn up useful information. But as commercial Web site managers become more aggressive in ensuring that their sites appear in any Web search, search engines may become as cluttered with the equivalent of spam as e-mail systems. This may lead to differentiation in the Internet, with layers of information provision based on eligibility criteria thereby relegating material developed by members of the public to the margins. Or greater and greater use of portals may equally deprive the Net of its heterogeneity.

The Internet (and public communications in general) is a communication medium controlled by many rather than by a few. With the right policy in place, this trend could continue. We have the academic and research community to thank for the Internet's public-sector identity and freely available protocols and codes, which make this communication technology very accessible to both those who want to use it and those who want to create for it. Open-source programming represents a movement in the direction of public access to the tools of communication, as do mark-up languages like HTML, XML, and even PDF files. There is certainly the opportunity, if the political will exists, to create policy that will ensure that the Internet remains widely accessible and its control widely dispersed.

Even if control of the Internet and other means of publicly accessible communication does not remain dispersed and becomes more concentrated, in a digital age the dominant communication institutions may not necessarily be confined to the business sector. For example, scientists and scholars are taking back control over publication of their work. It is equally possible that a good section of the information infrastructure will remain outside the hands of corporations for some time and be controlled by governments, institutions, and individuals. This would certainly better serve democracy by avoiding the concentration of power in the hands of too few, all of whom are based in the commercial sector of society.

The dynamics of the digital age will also engage democracy through the inherent biases of each medium and its operations. For instance, the print medium encompasses newsletters, books, magazines, and newspapers; the nature and size of their publishers; the elements of their distribution systems; the developments that print has encouraged, from poetry through to the essay and scientific investigations; education, legal systems, and religions that have been built around print; and even the individualism and imperialism that is intrinsic to Western civilization. As the more varied digital age comes into greater prominence—with its capacity for sound, image, instantaneity, text, numbers, and levels of metatext—there is bound to be fundamental change in world societies. In terms of democracy, whether the electronic media and their biases will provide human beings with enhanced opportunities, and specifically, enhanced tools for governing themselves, remains an open question.

On the third front of engagement between digital communication and democracy—more potential for participation in message-making—the answer seems clearer. To the extent that democracy includes participation in our own affairs, there is little doubt that digital technology is providing enhanced opportunities for participation. Whether we speak of playing video games versus watching television, or mobilizing opinion against the latest attempt by the business community to have the world run at its convenience versus accepting the plans of our political leaders, there is little doubt that the organization of digital communications at this point in history allows for expanded public participation in formerly cloistered decision-making.

Content and Audiences

The core issue in communication is the creation and distribution of content that engages an audience. If the content does not inform, enlighten, or entertain and/or if no one tunes in, then we have, as the saying goes, a failure to communicate. Authors, publishers, filmmakers and producers, recording artists, record companies, and media moguls have nothing if no one watches, listens, or reads. Nor do advertisers have any power to reach their audiences and stimulate purchasing if no one pays attention. Without communication, politicians have no contact with their polity: they govern a figment of their imagination.

Understanding content and understanding the interaction between content and audiences are therefore high priorities. Understanding the nature of content—its ability to engage, its passing or lasting effect—is an easy matter to think about and discuss. However, defining the *exact* nature of content is much more difficult. Why? Because the manner in which an event, an object, or a person is depicted—in words, a drawing, music, a play, film, a radio broadcast, or a magazine article—is always imperfect. Moreover, there are an indeterminate number of ways in which events, objects, and persons can be depicted.

This phenomenon is termed **indeterminacy of representation**. A second level of indeterminacy is introduced when we develop approaches to understanding content. Communication researchers use a bevy of analytical stances to wrestle content into some meaningful framework so that they might better understand how it is generated and what biases it introduces into our understanding of reality. Each stance or framework contributes a piece to the puzzle of understanding content. And each framework can be deployed as the situation demands it. However, the puzzle itself, like the universe, is ever changing. Put differently, our task is not to understand variables affecting communication and remove them in an effort to attain perfect communication, as a mathematical model might lead us towards. Rather, our task is to provide a description of the event, object, or person and the manner in which the event, object, or person is depicted. In so doing, we end up describing the social process involved in the creation and transmission of meaning and the inherent transformation involved.

We can focus, for example, on the life and intent of the author, the dynamics involved in the publication of a manuscript, and the tradition in which an author created a work or body of work. Like structuralists and semioticians, we can also identify the organizational elements of a story by focusing on the terms used (signifiers), events, objects, and persons referred to (signifieds), and the foundational ideas and concepts (signs) basic to our way of understanding. Or, following the lead of the post-structuralists, we can delve into the particularities of the meaning system that has been created.

We can also examine the nature of the interaction between the players who are part of the content. Here we can emphasize their behaviour (pragmatics); the nature of their conversation, such as the implicit rules followed in speaking (conversational analysis); or the defining terms of the discussion or discourse itself, drawing on the rich foundation of discourse analysis created by linguists and others. Alternatively, or even in addition, we can simplify matters and create and count occurrences of any definable phenomenon that can be placed in a category, thereby gaining a sense of what is said, how often it is said, and how it relates to what else is said, how often, and in what context.

From quite a different perspective, we can examine the production of content in terms of the interests of the producers and those paying for production. For instance, the business sector, and arguably society as a whole, has an interest in consumerism writ large. Consumption of commercially produced products creates employment and wealth and also allows governments to take a share and influence the development of society. (The limitation in this scenario is the pace of consumption we have generated, which may not be environmentally sustainable.) The political-economic perspective, which normally focuses on the ownership and control of industries and individual corporations, can also be used to understand the nature of content. Accordingly, the portrayal of violence and sex, the creation of suspense, the telling of universal stories that pull at the heartstrings of many—all can be seen as devices to maximize audiences or to attract potential consumers and hence to maximize the profits of those involved in the production process. Knowing this gives a better understanding of why certain content exists and certain other content does not.

At quite a different level again, we can gain an understanding of the bias or nature of the organization of communication by understanding the manner in which particular forms, such as news stories, ads, soap operas, documentaries, and music videos, are used within the media: how ads are constructed to draw us in, how news presentation privileges the news anchor or one of the protagonists in a story, how investigative television can present a convincing veracity where there may be none at all, and how soap operas captivate audience members in their presentations of fictional characters. Each of these perspectives contributes to the richness of our understanding of both referents (signifieds) and the symbols (signifiers, most often words) that are used to describe them.

With the overall understanding these various perspectives make possible, we can then extend our understanding of the nature and roles of the media in society. We can understand, for example, how the media are separate from yet intrinsic to society. We can appreciate the role they play in incorporating content from subcultures and making it part of the culture as a whole, or how they can reject as legitimate perfectly normal styles of living that are a part of any culture. We can also gain a sense of how autonomous the media are in their capacity to create their own realities, what their inherent shortcomings are, and, by extension, how we must build mechanisms to ensure they cannot entrap us in a world of their own construction.

In trying to understand the influence of the media on society, we have only looked at half of the equation. Content is one thing. How it is received is another. Thus, we must also strive to understand how audience members engage with the media—what they take from the media and how. In examining what audience members take from the media we can look at systematic differences between what is presented and what is received. In searching out how audience members interpret media content we can explore their stances: are they true believers, skeptics, cynics, distracted observers, and so forth?

The first principle in understanding content–audience interaction is recognizing that it is an engagement of active systems. Audience members, even when distracted, are, as we have noted, meaning-generating or meaning-seeking entities. They seek information or entertainment; they filter it through established opinions and knowledge as well as through situational variables—fatigue, their assessment of the presentation, other pressing concerns of the day, their anticipation of certain events, their position in the workforce, and so on. Similarly, the media are active generators of meaning insofar as they create programs targeted at certain audiences, with certain intensities, designed to engage audience members in a certain fashion. Moreover, both the media and audience members interact against a background of the values and structure of their society, and this society interacts with other societies and value systems of the world.

Perceived as relatively passive, audiences can be examined for how they are affected by certain content and media exposure. In attempting to increase the precision in defining such effects, the outlooks of audiences can be defined prior to media exposure and their subsequent behaviour and outlook measured. The uses to which audience members put media content and the satisfaction and reward audience members feel they derive from media content can also be explored.

Alternatively, we can begin an examination of media–audience interaction by analyzing some fundamental dynamics of society. Such dynamics can be economic, political, or cultural. For instance, Marx's analysis of how society provides for its people and the Frankfurt School's examination of the industrialization of the production of information and entertainment provide perspectives on the audience–media relationship. The British cultural studies theorists successfully provided insight into social movements and youth subcultures, later expanding to feminist analyses. What distinguished some of this work was its emphasis on the audience members as actors rather than sentient beings acted upon. The cultural studies researchers examined the wide social context of media consumption and its meaning as framed by audience members in their actions as well as in their words.

Media audiences can also be explored from the outside, as entities to be appreciated or sought after. A political party, for example, might wish to appreciate them in planning election strategy, or media companies might see them as commodities to be sold to advertisers. Such a perspective emphasizes much different variables. At a first level, the number of people in the audience is of central importance. Then come their age, education, gender, income level, location, and so forth, followed by specific elements such as their attitudes, consumption patterns of particular products, and the time they spend listening, reading, and/or watching. Such information is valuable for the business of buying, selling, renting, and accessing audiences. Yet, it is also valuable in understanding general patterns in society. For instance, the knowledge that information technology magazines are on the upswing informs us about social change.

How the media choose to engage audiences and how audiences engage the media are diverse, and the resulting interaction creates many social issues. The various starting points and perspectives we use to gain insight into what audiences make of content reflect that diversity. True, in simple terms, media content, such as violence, may serve as an igniting spark for extreme anti-social behaviour—a good reason for us to be concerned both about content generation and about how society contributes to anti-social behaviour. But media content may also inspire lifelong ambition, grand humanitarian gestures, respect for individual freedom, social plurality, cultural values, and the building of community. This positive spark is even more important to understand.

As interactive public communication systems increase in importance in society, the content–audience equation is transformed fundamentally. In an increasingly interactive system, the media sphere is much less separated from the general social sphere. The production community is expanding both in the mass media (books, magazines, film, TV, and music production) and in public media (the Internet and the Web). The result is that the proscenium, or boundary, between the media and the audience is less physical and more temporal. Increasingly, at one time or another, we all are involved in media production of one sort or another.

Four Influences on Media Operations

Having acquired an understanding of the nature of media, their interaction with audiences, and their overall interaction with society, we can turn to four major influences on the shape and role of communication in society: (1) policy, or, more comprehensively speaking, law and policy; (2) the marketplace, specifically ownership and control of communication institutions; (3) the role and actions of professionals; and (4) technology.

POLICY

Policy provides the overall framework for how the three other factors play themselves out. Policy creates a market at the level of ownership. Various companies with access to capital compete to gain access to the marketplace, sometimes simply by setting up shop with a certain amount of capital investment, at other times by meeting certain policy criteria and/or bidding for the right to operate. For instance, broadcasters must bid for a licence, newspaper publishers must be Canadian, and while book and magazine publishers can be owned by anyone, like filmmakers and sound recording companies, they gain access to a privileged position vis-à-vis government subsidies if they are Canadian.

Policy also sets in place a market in the buying and selling of content to audiences. Once established, communication companies seek out audiences, clients, subscribers, and/or purchasers. They create content to ensure a constant market for their products for which, in certain cases such as books and movies, the customer pays, and in other cases, for example, broadcasting, audience members do not pay directly.

Policy also sets up a third market, the market in audiences. Certain communication companies—for example, broadcasters, magazine publishers, and, increasingly, filmmakers—either sell their audiences to politicians (in return for grants) or to advertisers in return for revenue. Once in play these three levels of markets operate in interaction with one another. Working at all three levels—ownership, content, and audiences—policy becomes a powerful and overriding force.

OWNERSHIP

The more successful the company is in attracting an audience (with certain characteristics), the more revenue the company can gain either from sales made directly to that audience or through advertisers. The greater the revenue from content and audience sales, the more the company can generate excess income and acquire other companies. With strategic acquisitions, economies of scale or of supply and demand can be achieved with horizontal and vertical integration. As economies are achieved, profits and revenues can increase further and be accumulated to spur on further growth until the firm becomes so large as to be unmanageable or until it loses its direction or energy for growth and is overtaken by another firm or broken up.

On the public-sector side, the impact of success in producing content and in garnering audiences, even when those audiences are large and/or demographically desirable, does not lead to greater strength or growth, expansion of services, or even a reduction in public-sector spending, replaced as it might be with commercial income in cases such as CBC TV, where advertising is utilized. Rather, at least in the case of the CBC, audience success appears to result in audience loyalty, which, at times, is trifled with through experimentation with new programs and formats. In public broadcasting, the criteria for success and the appropriate rewards for such success are, as the cultural studies theorists say, sites of contestation. This means your definition of success and its significance is no better than ours, even though the goals set out for broadcasting in the Broadcasting Act provide some guidance.

The point here is that we all understand commercial success. Our concept of public-sector success is much more nebulous and vulnerable to attack from any who care to attack it. True, in considering public broadcasting, we can speak of citizenship, participation, and reflecting the diversity that is Canada. But all that the public-sector broadcaster can trade on, and indeed, all the publishers of certain genres such as poetry can trade on, is expressions of loyalty by audience members—expressions that can always be dismissed by others. No intrinsic strength that might parallel that of successful corporations is gained from being successful in the public sector or in cultural terms.

Ownership patterns continue to evolve, whether they are public or private. There is no natural or inevitable way to structure ownership of the media. Each medium itself influences the nature of ownership, as does the socio-political context, but the laws and policies within which each medium operates comprise by far the major factor. Of course, there is also the economy. All media, public and commercial, participate in the larger economy.

It would be reasonable to expect the continuation of both public ownership, that is, media owned by the state on behalf of its citizens, and private ownership by individuals or companies. No media industry in Canada is governed exclusively by free-market economics: the industries are organized as a complex mixture of public and private enterprise. The central difference between public and private forms of ownership pertains to their bottom lines. Public ownership is devoted to providing communications as a public service. Private ownership is devoted to providing communications for profit. This distinction is fundamental because it speaks to the purpose of communications. It can be argued that the growing commercialization of communication narrows both the sources and the variety of information available to us.

PROFESSIONALISM

Policy also sets the framework for professionalism in the cultural and communications industries, even though policy in this area is quite limited. Outside journalism, only the policy of recognizing the Canadian nationality of writers, filmmakers, music composers, and recording artists has provided a foundation for the development and expansion of the cultural industries in Canada over the past three decades. Works with Canadian contributors get favourable treatment. Within journalism, the number and impact of policies are more obvious. For example, the role of journalists as seekers after truth in the name of the public interest has been recognized in various commissions of inquiry. Libel law also recognizes the role of journalists, specifically their working constraints under the supervision of an editor who, in turn, is responsible to a publisher.

Somewhat surprisingly, journalists in particular and the media in general are not specifically recognized or given any special privileges with regard to the collection and publication of information and analysis. This lack of special status was confirmed in 1961 when the courts rejected the notion that the media had a duty to publish honest communication on matters of public interest. On 5 May of that year, the Supreme Court of Canada ruled that newspapers did not have any claim to what is called 'qualified **privilege**', that is, on the basis of its duty to publish (rather than its right to free speech), a newspaper could not claim protection from libel suits (*Globe and Mail*, 6 May 1961, A1). The results of this decision have been significant. Essentially, the decision has created a greater distance between the media and such governing institutions as the courts and the government itself. While diminishing the media's privilege, the Supreme Court, by increasing the distance between the media and the governance of society, placed the media closer to the people themselves and indeed to the private sector. Since 1961, the press and the media in general have increasingly cast themselves as spokespeople on behalf of the public or commercial interests and in a more adversarial role to government.

This distance notwithstanding, journalists and other producers of cultural and information products have a recognized role in society and they make, most certainly, a dynamic contribution to the overall role of the media. Journalists are the most significant group as they attempt to serve the interests of society by informing the public in the name of freedom of speech and access to information. They engender a continuing debate over the nature and quality of the information and analysis Canadians receive and do much to limit the power of both their bosses, the media owners, and governments. Other cultural producers have been instrumental in strengthening the rights of creators through revisions to law and policies, such as the Copyright Act and the provision for public lending rights and for collecting royalties for unauthorized photocopying. In both cases, the efforts of journalists and other cultural producers have expanded their influence on the media.

Noticeably lacking in the consideration of the role of some media professionals, specifically entertainment producers, is any discussion of social responsibility. As the portrayal of violent anti-social acts in the media (as well as their manifestation in reality) reaches ever higher levels, we may see increased consideration of the social responsibility of the entertainment media. After all, if we can have physical environmental impact assessments, why can there not be parallel cultural impact assessments?

Such an effort to introduce social responsibility and thereby to expand the terms of professionalism in the cultural and information industries may be further encouraged by the quickly expanding telecommunications sector. As that sector continues to grow, there will be an increasing need to set professional as well as technical standards. Information workers at the professional level will need to have an overall understanding of the nature, dynamics, and role of their industry and its interaction with society. There is every chance that professional associations will be formed—just as they now exist in engineering, education, and the health sciences. It would be surprising if such professional societies did not define a set of ideals and principles of behaviour as well as call for a broad education to assist their members in contributing to the overall development of society.

TECHNOLOGY

Policy also sets the framework for technology. For instance, technology in world agriculture is currently being transformed by one policy—the right to patent life forms. In communication, issues such as who can use what technology for what purpose, who can control that technology, and how that control can be exploited are critical.

Because technology encompasses machines, techniques, and social institutions, technology has a substantial impact on the structure and functioning of society—not as a positive agent but, like communication itself, as a transformative agent, an agent of change that brings both negative and positive consequences. The most dramatic change communication technology brings about is a shift in the locus of control: the greater the ability to communicate, the further the control system can be from the phenomenon being controlled. As the history of communication illustrates, communication developments have generally led to increased centralization, the subordination of the local to the regional, the regional to the national, and the national to the global. Whether the decentralized Internet will lead to decentralized and pluralistic control remains to be seen. With facilitating technology in place, the strongest influencing factor will be policy.

At the level of technology, technological convergence works in the opposite direction, leading to greater centralization. Technological convergence (and permissive policy) allows any company with sufficient resources to serve the full range of communication needs of any individual or company. Consequently, the possibilities for large corporations to strengthen their dominance are considerable. Yet as we have begun to see, what technology provides, human nature may take away. The dual phenomena of an appalling lack of ethics—witness the downfall of Enron and WorldCom—and the inability of professional groups to work with one another—for example, TV reporters and newspaper reporters—appear to work against the apparent advantages of technologically based convergence. In the end, the issue comes back to the definition of technology, which encompasses not merely machines but also the social organization of professions and institutions. There is every reason for a print journalist to be disdainful of the pretty boys and girls who, with their 'beautiful people' looks and enormous egos, populate the world of television. At the same time, there is every reason why these people see print reporters as social misfits incapable of conjuring up a commanding personal presence in presenting their ideas. At the level of the institution, a newspaper newsroom and a television newsroom are wholly different places, as CanWest Global found when it attempted to merge its television empire with its purchase of newspapers, including the *National Post*.

Where current technological developments in communication are taking us is difficult to say. Certainly, on a daily basis we are increasing our ability not only to transmit information but also to collect it and turn it into communication, information, and entertainment products and services. Such products and services developed by companies like Air Miles are changing the nature of our society, primarily by collecting and circulating information about repeated behaviours of which we are currently only vaguely conscious. These same capabilities, of designing products and services based on information analysis, are allowing ordinary citizens to analyze the behaviour of corporations, institutions, and people in power to demonstrate unfairness and inconsistency. And with quantities of information being collected and hooked up to the worldwide communication system the Internet represents, certain vulnerabilities have become apparent. For instance, we are more vulnerable to being victimized by virus spreaders, identity thieves, spies, and fraud artists.

POLICY TRENDS

The challenge for policy and for society in general is to balance individual rights, such as the right to privacy, access to information, and free speech, with collective rights, such as the right of a society to allow its citizens to participate in creating and sharing information, to ensure that one foreign perspective does not dominate the means of communication within a country, to encourage communication among different subgroups within society, and to allow citizens to participate in determining the direction of development in their society.

Overall, the policy framework for the communication and information industries has changed over the past decade from a foundation in culture to one in economics. The old framework based on cultural and social goals still officially exists. It can be found in the Broadcasting Act and in the Telecommunications Act. It can be found in justifications trotted out by the federal government in its fights with the US over cultural industries such as sound recording, filmmaking, and book and magazine publishing. It can also be found in Canada Council programs.

In fact, however, the thinking behind the development of cultural, communications, and information policy is mainly economic—at times dressed in cultural language. Indeed, it can only be thus. If, in the final analysis, we are dealing with the market for cultural commodities, whether they are goods or services, policy must be directed at structuring markets so that Canadian producers can survive. The only alternative is to increase the public sector and that appears to be on no one's agenda—no group, no leading individual who has any real voice, no political party. What strictly economic thinking leads to is thinking solely in terms of business enterprises. It leads to assessing cultural contributions on the basis of market success. Thus, Margaret Atwood is taken to be Canada's top author because she sells the most books; Izzy Asper, although new to the business, is taken to be Canada's most successful newspaper proprietor because he owns the most papers. Critical evaluation of their work plays a role, but there is no arguing with market success, as the saying goes.

As the economic framework becomes ubiquitous, more and more of the cultural world is subject to its criteria for evaluation. At the level of the individual artist, if no one is buying and no gallery is showing, then how can we say that this artist is worth supporting? Or if a publisher consistently performs at a level in the market below that of other firms publishing similar materials, does this firm deserve support? If economic criteria cannot be applied to demonstrate success of institutions such as the NFB and the CBC, then do they deserve our support?

Such thinking leads to the development of what appear to be rogue policies, that is, policies that do not make sense if one examines public attitudes but that are inevitable consequences of the application of policy frameworks. The best example of such a rogue policy, which appeared to lurk in the backrooms of government when the Chrétien Liberals were in their neo-conservative spending-cuts mode, was a dramatic reduction of resources for the CBC that would have led, over a decade, to its demise, at least as we know it today. In 1999, no one would admit to such a policy—no bureaucrat, no politician, no CBC official. Luckily, the concern that this non-policy raised, together with growing evidence of imperfection in the private sector and the self-destruction of the political right as a credible federal government, saved the CBC from an ignominious fate. Still, no one yet will admit that such a policy was being considered.

Whether economics will continue to rule communications policy and culture continue to fade remains to be seen. Perhaps we are living through an economic cycle and cultural values may reassert themselves. Certainly, if one were to look at efforts at global free trade and counteractions to such initiatives, the desire of ordinary citizens to put the fabric of society before the demands of the marketplace is apparent.

Globalization

Current technological possibilities point to an ever more globalized world. Enhanced ease of information accumulation and analysis, communication, and transportation means that our lives are increasingly touched by people in distant places—who we work for, where we shop, what we eat, who makes our clothes, what we watch on television, and where our friends and family are. Bertelsmann, Sony, Disney,

News Corporation, AOL Time Warner, and Microsoft are world behemoths that rode a wave of globalization and, until 2001, expanded almost monthly. On a slightly smaller scale, other companies, such as Rogers, BCE, and International Thomson, expanded. And at a level of even smaller companies the same trend could be identified. All this came to a halt in 2001 when expansion began to fall apart. The dotcom bubble burst, convergence proved for some to be a house of cards, and accountants and bankers seemed, like Clark Kent, to emerge from their phone booths as steroid-charged, ethically challenged captains of greed and artifice.

One can argue that globalization is the monoculturalization of the world. Increasingly, Peruvians turn to Coca-Cola rather than Inca Cola (actually, Coke bought it out), Canadians to Pepsi rather than Royal Cola, Europeans to Disney, Chinese and Russians to McDonald's. Although in the greater scheme of things monoculture seems less desirable than cultural variety, when brands offer quality control, whether that quality is in a fabric, in the reliability of an electronic device, or in the purity of the water used to make a beverage, it is understandable why brand-name global products edge out locally produced products.

In the end, there are no armies behind globalization. An individual can always choose. In addition, globalization is providing increased opportunity for more producers. Countries like Canada and niche-market artists, such as those from Atlantic Canada, have increased opportunities to participate in the marketplace and to thrive. In concentrating on mass-market goods, global corporations are increasingly creating and dominating mainstream or mass commodity markets. But this, of course, leaves the margins open, and whether marginal beer producers creep into the market because all of the mainstream beers taste the same, or whether Canadian publishers creep into the book and magazine market because their authors speak with different, distinctive voices, globalization has no dictators. While global corporations may not create an ideal world, neither is it a world where plurality is forbidden.

At the personal level, globalization does not mean there is no such thing as local connection. In fact, globalization seems to have prompted a renewed desire for local attachment, rootedness to a proximate and familiar community. For instance, we watch films from around the world but we participate in local drama clubs.

Since the 1940s the global trade in information has been contested ground on the basis of two seemingly incompatible views of communication. On the one hand, communication is perceived as a site of democratization and cultural development. On the other hand, communication is seen strictly in commercial terms, as the opportunity to sell information and entertainment products to ever larger audiences. The move to stress the cultural and democratic elements of communication, led by developing countries in the 1970s, gave way to the assertion of economic interests by the industrialized world. In the 1980s and 1990s, the movement towards a balance in the global flows of information was replaced by a drive for increased commercialization, led by transnational corporations and Western governments (spurred on by a redefinition of democracy as free access for consumers to goods).

Currently, Canada appears to be benefiting from a greater globalization. In addition to our expanded view on the world, information and entertainment markets have opened up to producers other than the US, the UK, and Europe. Some developing countries, for instance, India, Brazil, and Mexico, seem also to be benefiting. But others, especially African countries, are not. Whether a plurality of active producers will be preserved in the global marketplace remains to be seen.

Globalization also carries considerable implications for how we think about 'place' and for how we situate ourselves within communities. Boundaries around places are ever more porous and communities are no longer bound by proximity. In fact, the predominance of place, in the sense of geographic location, as a foundation for community is fading. The implication for cultures, communities, and identities in our global world is beginning to be felt.

Summary

This book has examined the nature of communication in contemporary Canadian society. The final chapter has been written to provide echoes of the major themes, issues, and ideas treated in the preceding chapters. We have also gone beyond the analysis provided in the preceding chapters and attempted to discuss the significance of some of the change that digital communication is bringing to Canada and the world.

STUDY QUESTIONS

1. If the media themselves introduce a bias, a space or time bias as Innis claimed, and yet other factors exist, such as policy, ownership, and the manner in which content is produced and directed at certain audiences, how do all these factors balance out?
2. Is the world being transformed by the Internet, or will the Internet soon be largely captured by business so that we will be back to where we started?
3. Are the media a solid foundation for democracy?
4. In any medium—books, movies, TV, music, radio—it is often the case that creators slide into formulaic presentations. Does such content nullify the discussion of content dynamics to be found in Chapter 4?
5. While the media industries look at audiences in one manner, scholars tend to view them in another. Are these two approaches reconcilable?
6. Policy sets a framework within which owners, content producers, and technology act. Which factor is pre-eminent in Canada today and do you expect that the relative power of each variable will shift as we move into the future?
7. Should the Canadian government be supporting Canada's cultural industries?
8. The traditional struggle between owners and content producers is played out most obviously between journalists and management. Are Canada's laws strong enough to best benefit Canadians in this regard?
9. How will your working life be changed by communications technology over the next five years?
10. When all is said and done, is globalization a positive or negative social force?

11. In your opinion, what does the future of mass communication and media look like? Consider some of the following questions when formulating your answer:

- Who will be the large media owners and what effect will they have on shaping the industry, content, and audiences?
- How will authors and other content producers be paid?
- Will the content that is readily available to us be less or more Canadian and will we care about Canadian content?
- Will people feel they have a greater or lesser opportunity to participate in their community, their nation, their world?
- Will public broadcasters like the CBC continue to exist, and if so, will they be stronger or weaker?
- Will the economic contribution of cultural activities reign supreme or will cultural values reassert themselves?
- Are you planning a career in mass communication?

Glossary

access to information Related to the concept of freedom of information, it refers to the principle that information collected by governments belongs to the Crown and citizens must appeal to governments for access to this information; this is the operating principle in Canada. In the US, freedom of information is the more appropriate term because information collected by governments belongs to the people. See **freedom of information**.

advertorial Promotional material written in editorial form and thinly disguised as normal journalism; newspapers and magazines often provide advertorials as part of an agreement with an advertiser, and they are usually identified as 'advertising features'.

affiliate An independently owned radio or television station associated with either a private or public network of stations; a station not owned by the network.

agenda setting The process by which priorities are established; it usually refers to elite actors or media owners and managers using their influence to shape governments' priorities.

allocative control The kind of control over media operations exercised by people at the uppermost levels of management—publishers, station managers, chief executives, shareholders, directors—who assign resources of labour and capital to a media organization and determine the organization's overall mandate; it is control over the structural and philosophical context in which media content is produced. See **operational control**.

Areopagitica An essay written by John Milton in 1644 to oppose press licensing in England, expressing faith in the power of truth to prevail through free inquiry and discussion; it remains a foundational document in the libertarian theory of the press and informs discussions of freedom of the press to this day.

audience ratings See separate entries under **share**, **reach**, and **viewing time**.

auteur theory A theory of textual interpretation that assigns primary responsibility for a creative work to a clearly identified author and to the body of work produced by that author; in a complex, collective creative work like a feature film, the author is taken to be the director, as opposed to the producer, the scriptwriter, or the director of photography.

Berne Convention The basis of international copyright law, which requires, among other things, that foreign authors be treated in the same way as domestic authors and that there be a minimum number of years of protection for a copyrighted work.

Birmingham School The media scholars at Birmingham University who developed the Marxist-derived, critical school of thought that became cultural studies.

British cultural studies An approach to social analysis that began in the 1950s and was led by scholars Richard Hoggart, Raymond Williams, Edward Thompson, and Stuart Hall; it extended a Marxist class analysis to include race, gender, and other elements of cultural history, and asserted the legitimacy of popular culture forms as objects of study.

broadsheets Full-sized newspapers (as opposed to half-sized **tabloids**) that tend to be targeted at middle-class or elite readers; this is a conservative newspaper form, with much more text and relatively fewer photos than the tabloid format typically displays.

burden of proof In Western civilization, an accused is presumed innocent until proven guilty and thus the onus for establishing guilt rests with the accusers, usually the state or Crown; in libel law, however, once it has been shown that certain words were written without authorization and they could be damaging, the burden of proof that the words written are not libelous rests with the accused.

Canadian content A legal definition of material that has been either developed by Canadians and/or contains Canadian information; in broadcasting, filmmaking, and publishing, Canadian content is defined by reference to a specific set of criteria designed to encourage the production of Canadian cultural materials by Canadians.

Capital Cost Allowance (CCA) A tax provision whereby investors receive a tax deduction for investing in Canadian film production; it was used to encourage private capital investment in the domestic film industry.

carriage A policy term designed to distinguish between the simple dissemination or transmission of communication (as in telephone service provided by telephone companies) and the production or selection of content; in regulation, this distinction is drawn in order to differentiate between carriage and content activities (e.g., distinguishing between the carriage and content-production or content-selection activities of a television network).

collective rights Rights accruing to groups of people or communities that are meant to privilege the collectivity over individuals; language laws in Quebec, for example, are designed to protect and promote the language of the French-speaking majority; Canadian-content rules on radio and television are similarly meant to protect and promote the cultural expression of the Canadian community.

commercial media institutions Media outlets organized to produce profits for their owners through the sale of content and/or advertising; regardless of what kind of content the outlet produces, a primary goal of a commercial institution is to produce regular profits.

common carrier A company that provides telecommunications services to all members of the public at equitable rates; such a company is in the business of providing **carriage** services rather than content.

communication The act of transmitting and exchanging information and meaning through any form of language; while communication typically refers to exchanges through verbal, written, and electronic forms of language, clothing style, gesture, and architecture can also communicate.

concentration of ownership The consolidation of ownership of a number of media organizations by relatively few large corporations; historically, the term has referred to the concentration of the same kind of media properties—newspapers or radio stations—in a few hands, but it increasingly refers to the consolidation of cross-media ownership (e.g., the same company owning both a chain of newspapers and a network of television stations).

conductor A substance capable of transmitting an electric current.

conglomerate A company that contains within it many companies carrying on a variety of businesses not necessarily related to one another: a media conglomerate does the majority of its business in the media; a general or non-media conglomerate has its foundation in non-media firms.

connotative Implicit, suggesting, implying; a connotation is an implied meaning; in communication theory, words and messages are said to have connotative as well as denotative (or explicit) meanings.

conservatism A political stance oriented to preserving current conditions and power structures rather than

adapting to, embracing, or instigating changed conditions.

consortium A group, usually of institutions, gathered together for a common purpose such as marketing or lobbying policy-makers.

consumerism An orientation that emphasizes the role of the individual as a consumer or purchaser of goods and services.

content analysis A quantitative research method that establishes units of analysis—specified phrases, sentences, nouns, verbs, adjectives, paragraphs, column inches, placement, accompanying illustrations, categories of spokespersons quoted or cited—and counts them to indicate the meaning or perspective of a communication.

contract carrier A company that provides **carriage** to a private client, usually a firm, to transmit or communicate signals, but does not offer the same service on equitable terms to others; the opposite of **common carrier**.

convergence In media studies it refers to an economic strategy in which media conglomerates combine the resources and content of two or more different media properties to realize cost savings in content production and cross-promotional opportunities.

conversational analysis Interpretation of social interaction and communication based on a conversation or dialogue model—for example, taking turns in speaking, maintaining and changing topics, and obeying other implicit rules.

copyright The exclusive right to reproduce a work requiring intellectual labour; this right belongs to the author and constitutes: (1) a property right, which may be assigned to others, and (2) a moral right, which may not be assigned but may be waived.

cross-ownership Ownership of two or more different media in the same market—for instance, newspapers and radio stations.

Crown corporations Businesses owned by federal or provincial governments, but operating at arm's length from government.

cultivation analysis An examination of content for the way in which it may encourage or cultivate a positive attitude in the audience member towards a particular person or perspective.

cultural dependency A relationship in which one country comes to rely on the media products of stronger, exporting countries to satisfy the cultural and entertainment needs of its population.

cultural development Social change that builds on

(usually over the community); individual rights include those dealing with free speech and privacy.

information flow A description of patterns of circulation of information commodities or products, for example, movies, magazines, television programs; a summary concept describing the imports and exports of goods, specifically information and entertainment products.

intellectual property The set of rights that accrue to an author by virtue of the work expended in the creation of a literary, dramatic, artistic, or musical work; the owned expressions of intellectual work derived from copyright law; intellectual property carries two sets of rights—**moral rights** and **property rights**.

intertextuality Pertaining to the referential character of texts; the meaning of phrases, ideas, and points of view derives from the manner in which related ideas, phrases, or points of view have been explored in other intellectual works.

invasion of privacy The seeking after, obtaining, and/or publication of information about an individual that is not public knowledge and that the person has the right to keep private; in some countries this right is protected by law.

inverted pyramid The presentation of a story in a form in which the most important information—who, what, when, where, why, how, and so what—is addressed at the beginning, followed by the development of the story and the context in which it happened; the most common form of news stories.

invisible hand The notion proposed by Adam Smith that the marketplace generally works in the best interests of society by encouraging individuals to pursue their own self-interest and economic opportunity; refers to the self-regulation of a market economy.

langue In semiotics, the shared language system that we use to generate individual utterances.

lead The opening of a story.

libel (1) A published written statement that does damage to the good reputation of a person; in France and the US, libel can express true facts, while in the UK and derivative systems, truth is an absolute defence against an accusation of libel; (2) any false or insulting statement.

libel chill The threat, real or imagined, and under which authors and publishers live, that they will be accused of libel and need to expend considerable sums of money to defend themselves, especially when publishing controversial or critical material about powerful people and institutions; this threat often leads to self-censorship as a form of protection.

liberalism A political philosophy in which society is seen as composed of individuals (as opposed to social classes) and that advocates the liberty of individuals as the primary social goal.

libertarian theory A political philosophy that views the sole purpose of the state as enforcing individuals' rights.

literary criticism The analysis of literature—at times dealing with the effectiveness of the author in creating his or her intended response, at other times descriptive of the referential framework of the author when the text was created.

mandate A responsibility granted legally or via another outside authority to pursue a certain purpose—as in a cultural mandate to pursue cultural ends as opposed, for example, to economic ends.

Marxism An approach to studying society that derives from the writings of Karl Marx, who emphasized class as a fundamental dividing element in society, separating and placing in conflict the interests of workers (the class that sells its labour for wages) from capitalists (the class that owns and controls the means of production).

market failure The inability of the free market to reflect the true value of a good or service, for example, a work of art (that may be sold for a small sum during the life of the artist but for increasingly greater sums after the artist's lifetime).

mass audience A convenient shorthand term for the great numbers of people who constitute the 'mass entertainment' audience; rather than being conceived as homogeneous, vulnerable, and passive, the mass audience is better conceived as a great number of individuals of heterogeneous backgrounds who use the media for a great variety of purposes.

mass media Newspapers, magazines, cinema, television, radio, advertising, some book publishing, and popular music.

meaning-generating entity Something existing that is complete in itself and seeks information, processes it, and may act on or in relation to it.

media bias The emphasis that a particular medium places on its selection of content elements—for instance, moving pictures by television.

media/culture binding Integration of media with the culture in which they are resident or in which they display products through presentation of elements of that culture.

media imperialism The use of the media to build empires of influence and control. See also **cultural imperialism**.

monopoly Exclusive control over the supply of a particular product for a specified market; a market in which consumers have a single source for a product or service.

monopoly capitalism A form of capitalism that encourages greater and greater concentration of ownership, resulting in monopolies and thus negating market competition.

moral rights The set of rights associated with intellectual property that are deemed to be the creator's by virtue of a work being created—they are most often associated with the integrity of the work; moral rights may be held or waived but not assigned to any other person; moral rights are distinct from **property rights** and not considered to be material.

multiplier effects Indirect economic activity that results from a particular industry—for example, movie theatres generate economic activity for popcorn sellers, parking lots, gas stations, and restaurants.

narrowcasting Used in contrast to broadcasting to describe radio and television services targeted at a small or niche audience.

nation-state A sovereign political unit composed of a body of people who share linguistic, historical, and ethnic heritage.

network A group of television or radio stations that work together for mutual benefit—for example, to share programming or to extend distribution to a broader area; network stations are usually, but not necessarily, owned by the same company; increasingly used as shorthand for computer network.

operational control The kind of control over media organizations exercised by editors and producers who are responsible for day-to-day production decisions; these managers determine how best to employ the labour and capital resources assigned to them by upper management, who exercise **allocative control**.

optical fibres Thin filaments of glass made pure enough and shielded on the circumference so that many light patterns can be transmitted simultaneously for long distances (fibre optics).

parole In semiotics, the actual words used in a given utterance.

people meter Electronic device that allows audience members to record their media consumption habits.

piracy Theft of intellectual property—often of works by persons in one country by persons based in another country that does not recognize the laws of the first country.

plagiarism Using the words of another without attribution or permission.

plugging or product placement The insertion of identifiable commercial products into the content of entertainment or information media for the purpose of promoting awareness of them.

policy The set of rules, laws, and practices that govern the operation of communication sectors.

political economic theory The study of power within the social relations of production.

polysemy Openness to a variety of interpretations.

postmodernism The view that there is no rational core of meaning at the centre of modern society; a search for the integration of the historical, the contemporary, and the local; a view that no longer affirms the existence of central stories and myths that bring people of contemporary society together.

post-structuralism The theory that uses deconstruction and focuses on the unique and distinctive details of a particular story told by a particular author at a particular time in a particular setting.

pragmatics An approach to communication that deals with what people actually say and emphasizes the context-specificity of utterances; more generally, the term is taken as dealing with the relations between symbols, interpretations, and users.

primary definers Terms used to define the important elements of a news story; also used to designate those people who are first to assert a meaning to news events; primary definitions tend to be difficult to change.

privacy The right to protect certain aspects of personal life from media discussions; such rights do not exist in Britain in any formal way and are weak in the United States.

private ownership Ownership by individuals or corporations, including of publicly traded companies, as opposed to **public ownership**.

privatization The transfer of publicly owned enterprises into the hands of private individuals or corporations.

privilege Within libel law, the principle that there are occasions when it is in the public interest (in order to promote freedom of expression or public safety) to report on certain persons, even if an individual's reputation may be threatened.

probes As used by Marshall McLuhan, probes were new, original, seemingly profound ideas that may or may not have much foundation; by calling his pronouncements probes, McLuhan was indicating that such ideas were works in progress.

product placement See **plugging**.

property rights The rights pertaining to the ownership of property; intellectual property rights pertain to the ownership and material benefit one may gain from **intellectual property**.

public interest The investment that a national group or other polity has in preserving or developing the best of its values and ideals.

public ownership Ownership by arm's-length government agencies, e.g., the CBC, or by groups of individuals, e.g., co-operatives, which members of the public can join for a token membership fee. Public ownership contrasts to commercial or **private ownership** of commercial companies, some of which are publicly traded and therefore called, in business circles, public companies.

public-sector institutions Government-owned institutions operated by managers ultimately responsible to governments.

public service An orientation, usually of public-sector, volunteer, or co-operative institutions and associations, that places the interests of society above the interests of individuals or specific groups.

rare-earth doping The use of a group of chemical elements, called rare earths, in optical fibres that share the following characteristic: their electrons rise to a higher than normal energy level when stimulated by a laser and, after stimulation, emit light that can serve as an amplifier to telecommunication signals passing along the fibre.

reach The percentage of audience members who tune into a broadcast program at least once during a specified time period.

reception analysis A research method that investigates how and in what context audiences consume media products.

regime An implicit or explicit set of principles, norms, rules, and decision-making procedures in international trade, often defined in an agreement.

representation The production or construction of ideas or images in a communicative form; the depiction through language of an idea, event, person, institution.

reprographic rights The rights to reproduce, usually by means of photocopying, a copyrightable work.

rhetoric A persuasive form of communication; a research method in which communications are studied as examples of persuasive speech.

Royal Commission A high-level inquiry established by government to investigate problems and recommend solutions.

royalties A percentage of receipts received by copyright owners from those who trade in intellectual property.

satellite footprint The terrestrial area covered by a specific satellite signal.

semiotics The theory of the social production of meaning from **sign** systems; the science of signs; an abstracted form of **structuralism**.

share The percentage of the average audience that tunes into a program or channel over any specified time period.

sign (1) A physical form (a word, gesture, even an object like a rose) used in communication to refer to something else (an object, a feeling) and recognized as such; (2) the totality of associations, thoughts, understandings, or meaning brought about by the use of symbols in reference to an object, person, phenomenon, or idea.

signification The articulation of the connections of, say, an object to its referents.

signified The mental concept of what is referred to—for instance, an object as we think of it when we hear a word (image of table when we hear the word 'table').

signifier The physical form of the **sign**, for instance, symbols such as words.

social responsibility theory The notion that the media have a responsibility to make a positive contribution to society and that they occupy a privileged position of which they should be aware.

space bias An idea advanced by Harold Innis, which notes the tendency of certain communication systems and societies to privilege the extension of ideas over space or distance as opposed to time or history.

structuralism A method and theory that emphasizes the formal relations of elements in a meaning system to each other; a particular way of analyzing that attempts to identify the underlying skeletal structure that holds the body of the story together.

summative research Research that measures the effectiveness of a program after its completion.

symbolic production The systematic communication of ideas and images through language.

syndication The ability of an organization to sell material for simultaneous publication or transmission in a variety of places—for instance, a newspaper column in various papers, or a TV sitcom on different networks.

tabloids Half-size newspapers convenient for reading in limited space that often provide 'bare-bones stories'; tabloids often engage in yellow journalism, that is, the prying into the private and personal lives of the rich and famous in order to uncover scandal. See also **broadsheets**.

technological convergence The capacity of a variety of seemingly different technological devices to perform the same task.

technological determinism The notion that technology is an autonomous and powerful driving force in structuring society or elements of society.

technological imperative The perspective or way of thinking, often said to be typical of Western thought and Western society, that privileges the conceptualization and development of technology and favours the application of technology once it is developed; it perceives technology as a social force.

technology transfer The assimilation of new technologies by societies others than those involved in their development.

time bias An idea advanced by Harold Innis, which notes the tendency of certain communication systems and societies to privilege the extension of ideas over time or history as opposed to space or distance.

Toronto School Marshall McLuhan and Harold Innis lived and worked in Toronto—as such, the Toronto School is said to be composed of scholars who based their research on the ideas of McLuhan and Innis.

transmission Movement from one place to another without disturbance.

turn-key operations Technology that does not require extensive training to operate—you turn the key and it works.

uses and gratification research A theory of media focusing on how audience members use the media—for instance, for information, for entertainment, for conversation—and what satisfaction they derive from media.

vertical integration A group of companies linked by common ownership that exist in a supply-demand relation to one another, such as a sound recording company and a radio network.

videotex A technology for accessing texts and graphics from a central computer using a relatively simple home terminal.

viewing time The time spent viewing expressed over the course of a day, week, or longer period of time.

Zeitgeist The feeling of the times, the moral character of a period in history.

References

Abercrombie, Nicholas, Stephen Hill, and Bryan S. Turner. 1980. *The Dominant Ideology Thesis*. Boston: Allen and Unwin.

————, ————, and ————, eds. 1990. *Dominant Ideologies*. Boston: Unwin and Hyman.

ACP (Association of Canadian Publishers). 1980. *Canadian Publishing: An Industrial Strategy for its Presentation and Development in the Eighties*, by Patricia Aldana. Toronto: ACP.

Adorno, T., and M. Horkheimer. 1972. *Dialectic of Enlightenment*. New York: Herder and Herder.

———— and ————. 1977 [1947]. 'The culture industry', in J. Curran, M. Gurevitch, and J. Woollacott, eds, *Mass Communication and Society*. London: Edward Arnold.

African Internet Connectivity. 2000. *African Country Internet Status Summary*, Sept. www3.sn.apc.org/africa/afrmain.htm

Anderson, Benedict. 1989. *Imagined Communities: Reflections on the Origin and Spread of Nationalism*. London: Verso.

Anderson, Robert, Richard Gruneau, and Paul Heyer, eds. 1996. *TVTV: The Television Revolution, The Debate*. Vancouver: *Canadian Journal of Communication*.

Anderssen, Erin. 2003. 'Immigration shifts population kaleidoscope', *Globe and Mail*, 22 Jan., A6.

Ang, Ien. 1985. *Watching Dallas*. London: Methuen.

————. 1991. *Desperately Seeking the Audience*. London: Routledge.

————. 1996. 'Dallas between reality and fiction', in Paul Cobley, ed., *The Communication Theory Reader*. London and New York: Routledge.

———— and Joke Hermes. 1991. 'Gender and/in media consumption', in Curran and Gurevitch (1991: 307–28).

Arab, Paula. 2002. 'Black would reclaim citizenship if offered', *St. John's Telegram*, 23 May, 1.

Atkinson, J. Maxwell. 1984. *Our Masters' Voices: The Language and Body Language of Politics*. London: Methuen.

Audley, Paul. 1983. *Canada's Cultural Industries: Broadcasting, Publishing, Records and Film*. Toronto: James Lorimer.

Auletta, Ken. 1997. *The Highwaymen: Warriors of the Information Superhighway*. New York: Random House.

Babe, Robert E. 1979. *Canadian Broadcasting Structure, Performance and Regulation*. Ottawa: Economic Council of Canada.

————. 1988. 'Emergence and development of Canadian communication: dispelling the myths', in R. Lorimer and D.C. Wilson, eds, *Communication Canada*. Toronto: Kagan and Woo.

————. 1990. *Telecommunications in Canada*. Toronto: University of Toronto Press.

Bagdikian, Ben H. 1990. *The Media Monopoly*. Boston: Beacon Press.

Bagnall, Janet. 2002. 'Global concern: Media concentration has become issue in Italy, Britain and U.S.', *Montreal Gazette*, 5 July, B3.

Bakke, Marik. 1986. 'Culture at stake', in Denis McQuail and Karen Siune, eds, *New Media Politics: Comparative Perspectives in Western Europe*. London: Sage.

Bandura, Albert. 1976. *Analysis of Delinquency and Aggression*. Hillside, NJ: L. Erlbaum Associates.

Barthes, Roland. 1968. *Elements of Semiology*, trans. A. Lavers and C. Smith. New York: Hill and Wang.

————. 1972. *Mythologies*. London: Jonathan Cape.

————. 1977a. *Image-Music-Text*. London: Fontana.

————. 1977b. 'The death of the author', in Barthes (1977a: 142–9).

Bauman, Zygmunt. 1998. *Globalization: The Human Consequences*. New York: Columbia University Press.

Baumgartel, Richard. 1997. 'The Canada rack program', *Canadian Journal of Communication* 22, 2: 289–93. http://www.cjc-online.ca/~cjc/BackIssues/22.2/baumgart.html

Barlow, Maude, and James Winter. 1997. *The Big Black Book: The Essential Views of Conrad and Barbara Amiel Black*. Toronto: Stoddart.

BBC. 1987. *Handbook on Audience Research*. London: British Broadcasting Corporation.

BC Film Commission. 1999. 'B.C. film production has record year', press release, 12 Feb.

Beauvoir, Simone de. 1957 [1952]. *The Second Sex*, trans. and ed. H.M. Parshley. New York: Knopf.

Beniger, James. 1986. *The Control Revolution*. Cambridge, Mass.: Harvard University Press.

Bennett, Tony. 1982. 'Media, "reality", and signification', in Gurevitch et al. (1982).

———— and Janet Woollacott. 1987. *Bond and Beyond: The Political Career of a Popular Hero*. New York: Methuen.

Berelson, Bernard. 1972. *Content Analysis in Communication*

Research. New York: Hafner.

Bergen, Bob. 2002. *Exposing the Boss: A Study in Canadian Journalism Ethics*. Calgary: Sheldon Chumir Foundation. www.chumirethicsfoundation.calgary. ab.ca/downloads/mediafellows/bergenbob/bergen-bobindex.html

Berger, Peter, and Thomas Luckmann. 1966. *Social Construction of Reality: A Treatise on the Sociology of Knowledge*. New York: Doubleday.

Berton, Pierre. 1975. *Hollywood's Canada: The Americanization of Our National Image*. Toronto: McClelland & Stewart.

Bindman, Stephen. 1993. 'Drop review of gag order on CBC show, top court urged', *Vancouver Sun*, 14 Sept., A7.

Binning, Cheryl. 1999. 'Record sales for Canucks in France', *Playback*, 3 May, 1, 6, 9, 26.

Bird, Roger. 1997. *The End of News*. Toronto: Irwin Publishing.

Bird, S. Elizabeth, and Robert W. Dardenne. 1997. 'Myth, chronicle and story: exploring the narrative qualities of news', in Dan Berkowitz, ed., *Social Meanings of News: A Text-Reader*. Thousand Oaks, Calif.: Sage.

Blumer, H. 1939. 'The mass, the public, and public opinion', in A.M. Lee, ed., *New Outlines in the Principles of Sociology*. New York: Barnes and Noble.

Blumler, Jay, and Elihu Katz, eds. 1974. *The Uses of Mass Communications: Current Perspectives on Gratifications Research*. Beverly Hills, Calif.: Sage.

Bolan, Kim. 1995. 'Privacy chief wants access to data bases tightened', *Vancouver Sun*, 10 Jan., A1.

Boyce, George. 1978. 'The fourth estate: a reappraisal of a concept', in G. Boyce et al., eds, *Newspaper History from the 17th Century to the Present Day*. London: Sage/Constable.

Boyd-Barrett, Oliver. 1977. 'Media imperialism: towards an international framework for the analysis of media systems', in James Curran, Michael Gurevitch, and Janet Woollacott, eds, *Mass Communication and Society*. London: Edward Arnold.

———. 1995. 'Cultural dependency and the mass media', in Michael Gurevitch, Tony Bennett, James Curran, and Janet Woollacott, eds, *Culture, Society and the Media*. London and New York: Routledge.

Braham, Peter. 1982. 'How the media report race', in Gurevitch et al. (1982).

Brethour, Patrick. 2002. 'Media convergence strategy praised', *Globe and Mail*, 25 Apr., B2.

Brown, Gillian, and George Yule. 1983. *Discourse Analysis*. Cambridge: Cambridge University Press.

Brown, P., and S.C. Levinson. 1987. *Politeness: Some Universals in Language Usage*. Cambridge: Cambridge University Press.

Brucker, Herbert. 1981. *Freedom of Information*. Westport, Conn.: Greenwood Press.

Bruner, Jerome. 1978. *Human Growth and Development*. Oxford: Clarendon.

Bryce, J. 1987. 'Family time and TV use', in T. Lindlof, ed., *Natural Audiences*. Norwood, NJ: Ablex, 121–38.

Buckingham, D. 1987. *Public Secrets: EastEnders and Its Audience*. London: British Film Institute.

Buckley, Peter, ed. 1993. *Canadian Press Stylebook: A Guide for Writers and Editors*. Toronto: Canadian Press.

Butalia, Urvashi. 1994. 'The issues at stake: an Indian perspective on copyright', in Philip G. Altbach, ed., *Copyright and Development: Inequality in the Information Age*. Chestnut Hill, Md: Bellagio Publishing Network.

Campbell, Joseph. 1968 [1949]. *The Hero with a Thousand Faces*. Bollingen Series. Princeton, NJ: Princeton University Press.

Canada. 1929. *Report of the Royal Commission on Radio Broadcasting* (Aird Commission). Ottawa: F.A. Acland.

———. 1951. *Report of the Royal Commission on National Development in the Arts, Letters and Sciences, 1949–1951* (Massey Commission). Ottawa: Edmond Cloutier.

———. 1957. *Report of the Royal Commission on Broadcasting* (Fowler Commission). Ottawa: Edmond Cloutier.

———. 1968. Department of Industry, Trade and Commerce. *Report on Book Publishing* (Ernst and Ernst). Ottawa: Department of Industry, Trade and Commerce.

———. 1968. Minister of Industry. *White Paper on a Domestic Satellite Communications System for Canada*. Ottawa: Queen's Printer.

———. 1969. *Report of the Task Force on Government Information*. Ottawa: Supply and Services.

———. 1971. *Mass Media*, vol. 1, *The Uncertain Mirror: Report of the Special Senate Committee on the Mass Media* (Davey Committee). Ottawa: Information Canada.

———. 1977a. Department of the Secretary of State. *The Publishing Industry in Canada*. Ottawa: Ministry of Supply and Services.

———. 1977b. Department of the Secretary of State. *The Film Industry in Canada*. Ottawa: Minister of Supply and Services.

———. 1978a. Department of the Secretary of State. *English Educational Publishing in Canada*. Hull:

Ministry of Supply and Services.

———. 1978b. Department of the Secretary of State. *French Educational Publishing in Canada.* Hull: Ministry of Supply and Services.

———. 1980. Canadian Study of Parliament Group. *Seminar on Press and Parliament: Adversaries or Accomplices?* Ottawa: Queen's Printer.

———. 1981. *Report of the Royal Commission on Newspapers* (Kent Commission). Ottawa: Minister of Supply and Services.

———. 1982a. *Report of the Federal Cultural Policy Review Committee.* Ottawa: Minister of Supply and Services Canada.

———. 1982b. Canadian Charter of Rights and Freedoms. http://canada.justice.gc.ca/Loireg/charte/const_en/html

———. 1984. *The National Film and Video Policy.* Ottawa: Minister of Supply and Services.

———. 1985. Canadian Multiculturalism Act. R.S. 1983 c. 24. http://www.pch.gc.ca/multi/html/act.html

———. 1985. *Report of the Film Industry Task Force.* Ottawa: Minister of Supply and Services.

———. 1986. Minister of Communications. *Report of the Task Force on Broadcasting Policy* (Caplan-Sauvageau Task Force). Ottawa: Minister of Supply and Services.

———. 1988. *Canadian Voices: Canadian Choices—A New Broadcasting Policy for Canada.* Ottawa: Supply and Services Canada.

———. 1991. Broadcasting Act. http://www.crtc.gc.ca/ENG/LEGAL/BROAD_E.HTM

———. 1993. Telecommunications Act. http://www.crtc.gc.ca/ENG/LEGAL/TELECOME.HTM

———. 1996a. *Information Highway Advisory Council Report.* http://strategis.ic.gc.ca/SSG/ih01015e.html

———. 1996b. Mandate Review Committee: CBC, NFB, Telefilm. *Making Our Voices Heard.* Ottawa: Minister of Supply and Services.

———. 1999. *Report of the Feature Film Advisory Committee.* Ottawa: Ministry of Canadian Heritage.

———. 2000. *From Script to Screen.* Ottawa: Department of Canadian Heritage.

———. 2002. *Canadian Content in the 21st Century: A Discussion Paper about Canadian Content in Film and Television Productions.* Ottawa: Department of Canadian Heritage, Mar.

Canadian Association of Journalists. 1991. 'Should pilots trust Airbus?', *The Eye Opener* (Ottawa): 2–15.

Canadian Broadcasting Corporation (CBC). 1977. *The Press and the Prime Minister: A Story of Unrequited Love.* TV documentary directed and produced by George Robertson. Toronto: CBC.

———. 1999. *CBC Annual Report, 1998–99.* Ottawa: CBC.

———. 1999. 'It's Time to Talk About the CBC . . . Your Voice Matters', press release, 9 Apr.

Canadian Cable Television Association. 1995. *1994–95 Annual Report.* Toronto: Canadian Cable Television Association.

Canadian Community Newspaper Association (CCNA). 2002. *Snapshot 2002: The Developing Picture of the Canadian Community Newspaper Industry.* www.comunitynews.ca/publisher/snapshot2002.pdf

Canadian Daily Newspaper Association. 1999. *1999 Circulation Data.* Toronto: CDNA. http://www.cna-acj.ca/newspapers/facts/circulation.asp?search=a11

Canadian Journal of Communication. 1995. Special issue on media in Eastern Europe, 20, 1.

Canadian Press (CP). 1993a. 'Front-page story omits who, where, what, when', *Vancouver Sun*, 10 Sept., A8.

———. 1993b. 'Running gags courtesy of nation's courts', *Vancouver Sun*, 3 Dec., A6.

———. 1993c. 'Ontario's A-G orders probe into news coverage in case of serial-rape suspect', *Vancouver Sun*, 1 Mar., A7.

———. 1999. 'CRTC cuts CKVL's license over complaints about host', *Montreal Gazette*, 1 May, C5.

———. 2000. 'Newspaper owner, strike leader go toe-to-toe', *Ottawa Citizen*, 3 Mar., D4.

———. 2002. 'Poverty fueled 9/11 Chrétien warns UN', *Halifax Daily News*, 17 Sept., 10.

Canadian Radio-television and Telecommunications Commission. 1999. 'The means may be changing but the goals remain constant', speech by Wayne Charman to the 1999 Broadcasting and Program Distribution Summit, 25 Feb. http://www.crtc.gc.ca/ENG/NEWS/SPEECHES/1999/S990225.htm)

———. 2000. 'CRTC approves new digital pay and specialty television services—more choice for consumers', press release, 24 Nov. www.crtc.gc.ca/ENG/NEWS/RELEASES/2000/R001124-2.htm

———. 2001. 'CRTC renews CTV and Global's licences—more quality programming and services', press release, 2 Aug. www.crtc.gc.ca/ENG/NEWS/RELEASES/2001/R010802.htm

Cantril, Hadley. 1940. *The Invasion from Mars.* Princeton, NJ: Princeton University Press.

Carr, Graham. 1991. 'Trade liberalization and the political economy of culture: an international perspective on FTA', *Canadian-American Public Policy* 6: 1–54.

Centre for Contemporary Cultural Studies. 1982. *The*

Empire Fights Back: Racism in Britain in the 1970s. London: Hutchinson.

Charland, Maurice. 1986. 'Technological nationalism', *Canadian Journal of Political and Social Theory* 10, 1: 196–220.

Chartier, Roger, and Alain Boureau. 1989. *The Culture of Print: Power and the Uses of Print in Early Modern Europe*. Cambridge: Polity Press.

Chase, Steven. 2003. 'Telecom rules get spotlight', *Globe and Mail*, 29 Jan., B1, B10.

Cherry, Paul. 1998. '"A bad day," photographers say', *Montreal Gazette*, 11 Apr., A4.

Chomsky, Noam. 1968. *Language and Mind*. New York: Harcourt Brace.

Clarke, Debra. 2000. 'Active viewers and inactive Canadian scholars: the underdeveloped state of audience research in Canada', *Canadian Journal of Communication* 25, 1.

Clement Jones, J. 1980. *Mass Media Codes of Ethics and Councils: A Comparative International Study on Professional Standards*. Reports and Papers on Mass Communication. Special Issue. Paris: UNESCO.

Cobb, Chris. 1993. 'Himbo: man as sex object the new vogue: lean muscular males used to sell products', *Vancouver Sun*, 30 Nov., A1.

———. 1995. 'Newspaper group revises standards; New code reflects Charter of Rights, changing times', *Ottawa Citizen*, 28 Sept., A12.

———. 1999. 'People believe Ottawa hurting CBC, poll shows', *Vancouver Sun*, 20 May, A11.

———. 2000. 'CRTC, CBC in dogfight', *Montreal Gazette*, 7 Jan., A1–A2.

Cocking, Clive. 1980. *Following the Leaders: A Media Watcher's Diary of Campaign '79*. Toronto: Doubleday.

Collett, Peter, and R. Lamb. 1986. *Watching Families Watching TV*. Report to the Independent Broadcasting Authority. London.

Collins, Richard. 1992. *Satellite Television in Western Europe*, rev. edn. London: John Libbey Acamedia Research Monograph 1.

Commission on Freedom of the Press. 1947. *A Free and Responsible Press*. Chicago: University of Chicago Press.

Cox, Kirwan. 1980. 'Hollywood's empire in Canada', in Pierre Véronneau and Piers Handling, eds, *Self-Portrait: Essays on the Canadian and Quebec Cinemas*. Ottawa: Canadian Film Institute.

Coyne, Deborah. 1992. *Roll of the Dice: Working with Clyde Wells during the Meech Lake Negotiations*. Toronto: James Lorimer.

Crawford, Michael G. 1990. *The Journalist's Legal Guide*, 2nd edn. Toronto: Carswell.

Crowley, David, and Paul Heyer. 1991. *Communication in History: Technology, Culture, Society*. London: Longman.

Curran, James. 1982. 'Communications, power, and social order', in Gurevitch et al. (1982).

———. 1990. 'The new revisionism in mass communication research: a reappraisal', *European Journal of Communication* 5, 2–3: 135–64.

———. 1991. 'Mass media and democracy: a reappraisal', in Curran and Gurevitch (1991).

——— and Michael Gurevitch, eds. 1991. *Mass Media and Society*. London: Edward Arnold.

Curtis, Liz. 1984. *Ireland, the Propaganda War: The Media and the 'Battle for Hearts and Minds'*. London: Pluto Press.

Damsell, Keith. 2002. 'CanWest editorial policy blasted in ad', *Globe and Mail*, 6 June, A6.

Darnton, Robert. 1976. *The Widening Circle: Essays on the Circulation of Literature in Eighteenth Century Europe*. Philadelphia: University of Pennsylvania Press.

———. 1979. *The Business of Enlightenment: A Publishing History of the Encyclopédie, 1775–1800*. Cambridge, Mass.: Belknap Press.

———. 1982. *The Literary Underground of the Old Regime*. Cambridge, Mass.: Harvard University Press.

———. 1989. *Revolution in Print: The Press in France, 1775–1800*. Berkeley: University of California Press with New York Public Library.

Dayan, D., and E. Katz. 1992. *Media Events: The Live Broadcasting of History*. Cambridge, Mass.: Harvard University Press.

de la Haye, Yves. 1980. *Marx and Engels on the Means of Communication (the movement of commodities, people, information and capital)*. New York: International General.

Demers, David. 1999. 'Corporate newspaper bashing: is it justified?', *Newspaper Research Journal* 20, 1: 83–97.

Derrida, Jacques. 1981. *Positions*. London: Althone.

Desbarats, Peter. 1996. *Guide to Canadian News Media*. Toronto: Harcourt Brace.

Dick, Ronald. 1986. 'Regionalization of a federal cultural institution: the experience of the National Film Board of Canada 1965–1979', in Gene Walz, ed., *Flashback: People and Institutions in Canadian Film History*. Montreal: Mediatexte Publications.

Dizard, Wilson P. 1985. *The Coming Information Age: An Overview of Technology, Economics and Politics*. New York: Longman.

Donham, Parker Barss. 1993. 'It's no secret: what we don't know can't hurt us', *Vancouver Sun*, 15 July, A11.

Dorland, Michael, ed. 1996. *The Cultural Industries in Canada: Problems, Policies and Prospects.* Toronto: James Lorimer.

Drache, Daniel. 1995. 'Celebrating Innis: the man, the legacy and our future', in Drache, ed., *Staples, Markets and Cultural Change: Selected Essays.* Montreal and Kingston: McGill-Queen's University Press.

Drucker, Peter F. 1993. *Post-Capitalist Society.* New York: HarperCollins.

Dryburgh, Heather. 2001. *Changing our ways: Why and how Canadians use the Internet.* Statistics Canada Catalogue no. 56F0006XIE, Mar.

Dubinsky, Lon. 1996. 'Periodical Publishing', in Dorland (1996).

Dutrisac, Robert. 2002. 'Concentration de la presse—Québec demandera à l'industrie de s'autoréglementer', *Le Devoir*, 6 Sept., A3.

Duxbury, Nancy. 1991. 'Why is libel so chilling? An examination of Canadian libel law and the vulnerability of publishers', unpublished paper, Canadian Centre for Studies in Publishing, Simon Fraser University.

Eaman, Ross Allan. 1987. *The Media Society: Basic Issues and Controversies.* Toronto: Butterworths.

———. 1994. *Channels of Influence: CBC Audience Research and the Canadian Public.* Toronto: University of Toronto Press.

Eco, Umberto. 1982a. 'Narrative structure in Fleming', in B. Waites et al., eds, *Popular Culture Past and Present.* Milton Keynes, UK: Open University Press.

———. 1982b. *The Name of the Rose.* New York: Warner Books.

———. 1986. 'The multiplication of the media', in Eco, *Travels in Hyperreality.* New York: Harcourt Brace Jovanovich.

Economist, The. 1991. 'The optical enlightenment', 6 July, 87.

Eisenstein, Elizabeth. 1979. *The Printing Press as an Agent of Change*, 2 vols. New York: Cambridge University Press.

———. 1983. *The Printing Revolution in Early Modern Europe.* Cambridge: Cambridge University Press.

Ellul, Jacques. 1964. *The Technological Society.* New York: Knopf.

Enchin, Harvey. 1993. 'Audience gauge goes high-tech: electronic measurement of TV viewers, radio listeners seen as revolutionary', *Globe and Mail*, 10 Nov., B4.

———. 1996. 'Cinema chain accelerates growth', *Globe and Mail*, 13 Dec., B4.

Ericson, Richard V., Patricia M. Baranek, and Janet B.L. Chan. 1989. *Negotiating Control: A Study of News Sources.* Toronto: University of Toronto Press.

Eslin, Martin. 1980. 'The exploding stage', CBC-Radio, *Ideas* (Oct.).

Famous Players. 2002. About us. www.famousplayers.com/fp_aboutus.asp

Evans, Philip. 2002. 'A bright idea that wasn't: The E-emperor has no clothes', *Globe and Mail*, 25 Apr., A15.

Featherstone, Mike. 1996. 'Localism, globalism, and cultural identity', in Rob Wilson and Wimal Dissanayake, eds, *Global/Local: Cultural Production and the Transnational Imaginary.* Durham, NC: Duke University Press.

Ferguson, Rob. 2000. 'Protests and criticism dog Hollinger annual meeting: Black hears out appeal to end strike in Calgary', *Toronto Star*, 25 May, B1.

Fessenden, Helen. 1974. *Fessenden: Builder of Tomorrows.* New York: Arno Press.

Fetherling, Doug. 1993. *A Little Bit of Thunder: The Strange Inner Life of the Kingston Whig-Standard.* Toronto: Stoddart.

Filion, Michel. 1996. 'Radio', in Dorland (1996).

Fiske, John. 1987. *Television Culture.* London: Routledge.

———. 1989a. *Reading the Popular.* Boston: Unwin Hyman.

———. 1989b. *Understanding Popular Culture.* Boston: Unwin Hyman.

———. 1989c. 'Moments of television: neither the text nor the audience', in Ellen Seiter et al., eds, *Remote Control.* London: Routledge.

Fletcher, F. 1981. *The Newspaper and Public Affairs*, vol. 7, Research Publications for the Royal Commission on Newspapers. Ottawa: Supply and Services.

———. 1994. 'The Southam lecture: media, elections and democracy', *Canadian Journal of Communication* 19, 2: 131–50.

Foot, Richard. 1999. 'Court orders magazine to stop writing about abortion', *National Post*, 3 May, A4.

Fornas, J., U. Lindberg, and O. Sernhede. 1988. *Under Rocken.* Stockholm: Symposium.

Foundation for Media Education. 1992. *Pack of Lies: the Advertising of Tobacco* (35-minute video). Northhampton, Mass.: Foundation for Media Education.

Fowler, Roger. 1991. *Language in the News.* London: Routledge.

Franklin, Sarah, C. Lury, and J. Stacey. 1982. 'Feminism and cultural studies', in Paddy Scannell et al., eds, *Culture and Power.* London: Sage.

Fraser, Graham. 1999. 'CBC hurting private TV, Péladeau

argues', *Globe and Mail*, 2 June, A5.

Friedan, Betty. 1963. *The Feminine Mystique*. New York: Norton.

Frith, Simon. 1987. 'The industrialization of popular music', in James Lull, ed., *Popular Music and Communication*. Newbury Park, Calif.: Sage, 53–77.

Gallagher, Margaret. 1982. 'Negotiation of control in media organizations and occupations', in Gurevitch et al. (1982).

Galloway, Gloria. 2003. 'Toronto most ethnically diverse in North America', *Globe and Mail*, 22 Jan., A6.

Gans, Herbert. 1979. *Deciding What's News: A Study of CBS Evening News, NBC Nightly News, Newsweek, and Time*. New York: Pantheon Books.

Garfinkel, Harold. 1984. *Studies in Ethnomethodology*. Cambridge: Polity Press.

Gasher, Mike. 1992. 'The myth of meritocracy: ignoring the political economy of the Canadian film industry', *Canadian Journal of Communication* 17, 2: 371–8.

———. 1995a. 'The audiovisual locations industry in Canada: considering British Columbia as Hollywood North', *Canadian Journal of Communication* 20, 2: 231–54.

———. 1995b. 'Culture lag: the liberal record', *Point of View* 26 (Winter): 22–4.

———. 1998. 'Invoking public support for public broadcasting: the Aird Commission revisited', *Canadian Journal of Communication* 23: 189–216.

———. 2002a. *Hollywood North: The Feature Film Industry in British Columbia*. Vancouver: University of British Columbia Press.

———. 2002b. 'Does CanWest know what all the fuss is about?', *Media* (Winter): 8–9.

Gee, Marcus. 2002. 'Don't blame the victim, Mr. Chrétien', *Globe and Mail*, 14 Sept., A17.

Geist, Michael. 2002. 'Cyberlaw', *Globe and Mail*, 17 Oct., B15.

Geraghty, Christine. 1991. *Women and Soap Opera: A Study of Prime Time Soaps*. Cambridge: Polity Press.

Gerbner, George. 1969. 'Towards "cultural indicators": the analysis of mass mediated public message systems', *AV Communication Review* 17, 2: 137–48.

———. 1977. *Trends in Network Drama and Viewer Conceptions of Social Reality, 1967–76*. Philadelphia: Annenburg School of Communications, University of Pennsylvania.

Giddens, Anthony. 1987a. *Social Theory and Modern Sociology*. Cambridge: Polity Press.

———. 1987b. 'Structuralism, post-structuralism and the production of culture', in Giddens and R. Turner,

eds, *Social Theory Today*. Cambridge: Polity Press, 195–223.

———. 1990. *The Consequences of Modernity*. Cambridge: Polity Press.

Gilder, George F. 1991. 'Into the telecosm', *Harvard Business Review* (Mar.–Apr.): 150–61.

Glasgow Media Group. 1976. *Bad News*. Boston: Routledge & Kegan Paul.

Global Reach. 2001. Global Internet Statistics. www.glreach.com/globstats/index.php3

Globe and Mail. 1993. 'Court to hear arguments over TV mini-series', 30 Oct., A3.

———. 2001. 'The complications of convergence', 4 Aug., A12.

———. 2002. 'When violating rights becomes the routine', 19 Aug., A12.

Globerman, Steven. 1983. *Cultural Regulation in Canada*. Montreal: Institute for Research on Public Policy.

Goffman, Erving. 1959. *The Presentation of Self in Everyday Life*. Harmondsworth: Penguin.

Goody, J.R. 1977. *The Domestication of the Savage Mind*. Cambridge: Cambridge University Press.

Grady, Wayne. 1983. 'The Budweiser gamble', *Saturday Night* (Feb.): 28–30.

Grant, George. 1969. *Technology and Empire*. Toronto: Anansi.

Gratton, Michel. 1987. *'So, What Are the Boys Saying?' An Inside Look at Brian Mulroney in Power*. Toronto: McGraw-Hill Ryerson.

Guillermoprieto, Alma. 1993. 'Letter from Brazil: obsessed in Rio', *The New Yorker* (16 Aug.): 44–56.

Gurevitch, Michael, Tony Bennett, James Curran, and Jane Woollacott, eds. 1982, 1990. *Culture, Society and the Media*. Toronto: Methuen.

Habermas, Jürgen. 1984. *The Theory of Communicative Action*, trans. Thomas McCarty. Boston: Beacon Press.

Habermehl, Lawrence. 1995. *The Counterfeit Wisdom of Shallow Minds: A Critique of Some Leading Offenders in the 1980s*. New York: Peter Lang.

Hackett, Robert A. 1996. 'An exaggerated death: prefatory comments on "objectivity" in journalism', in Valerie Alia, Brian Brennan, and Barry Hoffmaster, eds, *Deadlines & Diversity: Journalism Ethics in a Changing World*. Halifax: Fernwood.

Hall, Edward T. 1980. *The Silent Language*. Westport, Conn.: Greenwood Press.

Hall, Stuart. 1980. 'Encoding/decoding', in Hall et al. (1980).

———. 1995. 'New cultures for old', in Massey and Jess (1995).

———— et al. 1978. *Policing the Crisis: Mugging, the State and Law and Order*. London: Macmillan.

————, Dorothy Hobson, Andrew Love, and Paul Willis, eds. 1980. *Culture, Media, Language: Working Papers in Cultural Studies*. London: Hutchinson.

Hamelink, Cees J. 1994. *The Politics of World Communication*. London: Sage.

Hardin, Herschel. 1974. *A Nation Unaware*. Vancouver: Douglas & McIntyre.

Hartley, John. 1987. 'Invisible fictions', *Textual Practice* 1, 2: 121–38.

Hastings, Max. 2002. 'Paint it Black', *Globe and Mail*, 19 Oct., F3.

Havelock, Eric. 1976. *Origins of Western Literacy*. Toronto: OISE Press.

Hayes, David. 1992. *Power and Influence: The Globe and Mail and the News Revolution*. Toronto: Key Porter.

Hebdige, Dick. 1979. *Subculture: The Meaning of Style*. London: Methuen.

Heilbroner, Robert L. 1980. *The Worldly Philosophers: The Lives, Times, and Ideas of the Great Economic Thinkers*. New York: Simon and Schuster.

Heinzl, John. 2002. 'Web sites, ISPs lopping pop-up ads', *Globe and Mail*, 23 Aug., B10.

Henry, Frances, and Carol Tator. 2000. *Racist Discourse in Canada's English Print Media*. Toronto: Canadian Race Relations Foundation, Mar.

————, ————, Winston Mattis, and Tim Rees. 2000. *The Colour of Democracy: Racism in Canadian Society*. Toronto: Harcourt Brace.

Heritage, John. 1984. *Garfinkel and Ethnomethodology*. Cambridge: Cambridge University Press.

Herman, Edward S., and Robert W. McChesney. 1997. *The Global Media: The New Missionaries of Global Capitalism*. Washington: Cassell.

Hobson, D. 1980. 'Housewives and the mass media', in Hall et al. (1980).

————. 1982. *Crossroads: The Drama of Soap Opera*. London: Methuen.

Hoggart, Richard. 1992 [1957]. *The Uses of Literacy*. New Brunswick, NJ: Transaction.

Horkheimer, Max. 1972. *Critical Theory*. New York: Seabury Press.

Hoskins, Colin, Stuart McFadyen, and Adam Finn. 1997. *Global Television and Film: An Introduction to the Economics of the Business*. Oxford: Oxford University Press.

Houpt, Simon. 2002. 'A lotta promotion genius?', *Globe and Mail*, 27 July, R5.

Howitt, Dennis, and Guy Cumberbatch. 1975. *Mass Media Violence and Society*. London: Elek.

Industry Canada. 1997. *Preparing Canada for a Digital World*. Final report of the Information Highway Advisory Council (IHAC). http://strategis.ic.gc.ca/SSG/ih01650e.html

Innis, Harold. 1950. *Empire and Communications*. Toronto: Oxford University Press.

————. 1951. *The Bias of Communication*. Toronto: University of Toronto Press.

Inter American Press Association/Sociedad Inter-americana de Prensa (IAPA). 1994. 'Declaration of Chapultepec', *Globe and Mail*, 7 June, A13. See also http://www.sipiapa.org/projects/chapul-declaration.htm

Jay, M. 1974. *The Dialectical Imagination*. London: Routledge.

Jensen, Mike. 2000. *African Internet Status*, Nov. http://demiurge.wn.apc.org/africa/afstat.htm

Jeffrey, Liss. 1994. 'Rethinking audiences for cultural industries: implications for Canadian research', *Canadian Journal of Communication* 19, 3–4: 495–522.

Jensen, Klaus Bruhn. 1990. 'The politics of polysemy: television news, everyday consciousness and political action', *Media, Culture and Society* 12, 1: 57–77.

———— and Karl Erik Rosengren. 1990. 'Five traditions in search of an audience', *European Journal of Communication* 5: 207–38.

Jones, D.B. 1981. *Movies and Memoranda: An Interpretive History of the National Film Board of Canada*. Ottawa: Canadian Film Institute.

Jouët, Josiane, and Sylvie Coudray. 1991. *New Communication Technologies: Research Trends*. Reports and Papers on Mass Communication, No. 105. Paris: UNESCO.

Joynt, Leslie. 1995. 'Too White', *Ryerson Review of Journalism* (Spring): 15–25.

Katz, E., and P. Lazarsfeld. 1965. *Personal Influence: The Part Played by People in the Flow of Mass Communications*. New York: Free Press.

Kesterton, W.H. 1984. *A History of Journalism in Canada*. Ottawa: Carleton University Press.

King, Russell. 1995. 'Migrations, globalization and place', in Massey and Jess (1995).

Klapper, Joseph. 1960. *The Effects of Mass Communications*. New York: Free Press.

Knelman, Martin. 1977. *This is Where We Came In*. Toronto: McClelland & Stewart.

Kovach, Bill, and Tom Rosenstiel. 2001. *The Elements of Journalism: What Newspeople Should Know and the Public Should Expect*. New York: Crown.

Kristeva, Julia. 1969. 'Le mot, le dialogue et le roman', in *Sèmiòtikè: Recherches pour une sémanalyse*. Paris: Editions du Seuil.

LaGuardia, Robert. 1977. *From Ma Perkins to Mary Hartman: The Illustrated History of Soap Opera*. New York: Ballantine Books.

Lamey, Mary. 1997. 'Merger of movie-house giants creates King Kong-sized debt', *Montreal Gazette*, 2 Oct., D2.

———. 1999. 'Sun Media to be spun off', *Montreal Gazette*, 30 Apr., F1–2.

Lapham, Lewis H. 2002. 'American Jihad', *Harper's* (Jan.): 7–9.

Larrain, Jorge. 1979. *The Concept of Ideology*. London: Hutchinson.

———. 1983. *Marxism and Ideology*. London: Macmillan.

Leblanc, Jean-André. 1990. 'Pour s'arranger avec les gars des vues, l'industrie du cinéma et de la video au Canada 1982–1984', in Gaëtan Tremblay, ed., *Les Industries de la Culture et de la Communication au Québec et au Canada*. Sillery, Que.: Presses de l'Université du Québec.

Leiss, William. 1990. *Under Technology's Thumb*. Montreal and Kingston: McGill-Queen's University Press.

Lent, John A. 1998. 'The Animation Industry and its Offshore Factories', in Gerald Sussman and Lent, eds, *Global Productions: Labor in the Making of the 'Information Society'*. Cresskill, NJ: Hampton Press.

Lessig, Lawrence. 1999. *Code, and Other Laws of Cyberspace*. New York: Basic Books.

———. 2001. *The Future of Ideas: The Fate of the Commons in a Connected World*. New York: Random House.

Levinson, S. 1985. *Pragmatics*. Cambridge: Cambridge University Press.

Lévi-Strauss, Claude. 1969. *The Raw and the Cooked*. London: Jonathan Cape.

Liebes, Tamar, and Elihu Katz. 1986. 'Decoding Dallas: notes from a cross-cultural study', in G. Gumpert and R. Cathcart, eds, *Inter/Media*. New York: Oxford University Press.

Lievrouw, Leah A. 2000. 'Babel and Beyond: Languages on the Internet', *ICA News* (May): 6–7.

Lindgren, April. 2001. 'Move to sell rest of national daily to CanWest "guarantees" its future', *Montreal Gazette*, 25 Aug., C1.

Lindlof, Thomas R. 1991. 'The qualitative study of media audiences', *Journal of Broadcasting and Electronic Media* 35, 1: 23–42.

Litvak, I.A., and C.J. Maule. 1978. *The Publication of Canadian Editions of Non-Canadian Magazines: Public Policy Alternatives*. Ottawa: Secretary of State.

Lord, A.B. 1964. *The Singer of Tales*. Cambridge, Mass.: Harvard University Press.

Lorimer, Rowland. 1994. *Mass Communication: A Comparative Introduction*. Manchester: University of Manchester Press.

——— and Nancy Duxbury. 1994. 'Of culture, the economy, cultural production, and cultural producers: an orientation', *Canadian Journal of Communication* 19, 3–4: 259–90.

Lumpkin, John J. 2003. 'US officials examine the quality of information war planners had before invasion', 22 May. Available at: www.sfgate.com/cgi-bin/article.cgi?f=/news/archive/2003/05/22/national1251ED T0637.DTL

McCarthy, Shawn. 1997. 'Cineplex deal may hinge on sale of unit', *Globe and Mail*, 3 Oct., B1, B20.

McChesney, Robert W. 1997. *Corporate Media and the Threat to Democracy*. New York: Seven Stories Press.

———. 1998. 'The political economy of global communication', in McChesney, Ellen Meiksins Wood, and John Bellamy Foster, eds, *Capitalism and the Information Age: The Political Economy of the Global Communication Revolution*. New York: Monthly Review Press.

———. 1999. *Rich Media, Poor Democracy: Communication Politics in Dubious Times*. Urbana: University of Illinois Press.

———. 1999. 'Graham Spry and the Future of Public Broadcasting', *Canadian Journal of Communication* 24, 1: 25–47.

McDonnell, Jim. 1983. 'Satellites for development, broadcasting and information', *Communication Research Trends* 4, 2: 1.

McFadyen, Stuart, Adam Finn, Colin Hoskins, and Rowland Lorimer, eds. 1994. Special Issue on 'Cultural Development in an Open Economy', *Canadian Journal of Communication* 19, 3–4.

McFarland, Janet, Jacquie McNish, and Paul Waldie. 2002. 'Look, I just want to resign', *Globe and Mail*, 25 Apr., A1, A10.

McGuigan, J. 1992. *Cultural Populism*. London: Routledge.

McLuhan, Marshall. 1962. *The Gutenberg Galaxy: The Making of Typographic Man*. Toronto: University of Toronto Press.

———. 1964. *Understanding Media: The Extensions of Man*. Toronto: McGraw-Hill.

McQuail, Denis. 1983. *Mass Communication Theory: An Introduction*. Beverly Hills, Calif.: Sage.

———. 1991. 'Mass media in the public interest: towards a framework of norms for media performance', in

Curran and Gurevitch (1991).

Magder, Ted. 1985. 'A featureless film policy: culture and the Canadian state', *Studies in Political Economy* 16: 81–109.

———. 1993. *Canada's Hollywood: The Canadian State and Feature Films.* Toronto: University of Toronto Press.

Malik, S. 1989. 'Television and rural India', *Media, Culture and Society* 11, 4: 459–84.

Manley, Lorne, Jim Rutenberg, and Seth Schiesel. 2002. 'How Does AOL Fit in the Grand Plan Now?', *New York Times*, 21 Apr., Section 3, 1, 10–11.

Mansell, Robin. 1992. 'Communication and information technologies in the new world order', paper presented at the University of Calgary, Mar.

Marcuse, Herbert. 1963 [1954]. *Reason and Revolution: Hegel and the Rise of Social Theory.* New York: Humanities Press.

———. 1964. *One-Dimensional Man: Studies in the Ideology of Advanced Industrial Society.* Boston: Beacon Press.

Martin, Robert, and Stuart Adam. 1991. *A Source-book of Canadian Media Law.* Ottawa: Carleton University Press.

Marx, Karl, and Friedrich Engels. 1974. *The German Ideology.* London: Lawrence & Wishart.

Massey, Doreen. 1991. 'A global sense of place', *Marxism Today* (June): 24–9.

———. 1992. 'A place called home?', *New Formations* 17: 3–15.

———. 1995. 'The conceptualization of place', in Massey and Jess (1995).

——— and Pat Jess, eds. 1995. *A Place in the World? Cultures and Globalization.* New York: Oxford University Press.

——— and ———. 1995. 'Places and cultures in an uneven world', in Massey and Jess (1995).

Mathews, Robin. 1988. *Canadian Identity: Major Forces Shaping the Life of a People.* Ottawa: Steel Rail.

Meisel, John. 1986. 'Communications in the space age: some Canadian and international implications', *International Political Science Review* 7, 3 (July): 299–331.

Mencher, Melvin. 2000. *News Reporting and Writing*, 8th edn. New York: McGraw-Hill.

Meyers, Marian. 1997. 'News of battering', in Dan Berkowitz, ed., *Social Meanings of News: A Text-Reader.* Thousand Oaks, Calif.: Sage.

Meyrowitz, Joshua. 1985. *No Sense of Place.* New York: Oxford University Press.

Miller, John. 1998. *Yesterday's News: Why Canada's Daily Newspapers Are Failing Us.* Halifax: Fernwood.

——— and Kimberly Prince. 1994a. *Women's By-line Study.* Toronto: School of Journalism, Ryerson Polytechnic Institute.

——— and ———. 1994b. *The Imperfect Mirror.* Toronto: Ryerson Polytechnic University, Apr.

Miller, Mark Crispin. 1990. 'Hollywood: the ad', *Atlantic Monthly* 265, 4 (Apr.): 41–68.

Miller, Mary Jane. 1987. *Turn Up the Contrast: CBC Television Drama Since 1952.* Vancouver: University of British Columbia Press.

Milner, Brian. 2000. 'New and old media merge in massive AOL deal', *Globe and Mail*, 11 Jan., A1, A8.

Mitchell, D. 1988. 'Culture as political discourse in Canada', in Rowland Lorimer and D.C. Wilson, eds, *Communication Canada.* Toronto: Kagan and Woo.

Mitchell, Greg. 2003. '15 stories they've already bungled: Mitchell on the war coverage so far', 27 Mar. Available at: http://www.editorandpublisher.com/editorandpublisher/headlines/article_display.jsp?vnu_content_id=1850208

Modleski, T. 1984. *Leaving with a Vengeance: Mass-Produced Fantasies for Women.* London: Methuen.

Montgomery, Martin. 1991. 'Our tune: a study of a discourse genre', in Scannell (1991).

Montreal Gazette. 1997. *The Montreal Gazette: In Touch with English Montreal.* Montreal: Gazette Advertising Department.

Moody's Investors Service. 1997. *Moody's Handbook of Common Stocks.* New York: Moody's Investors Service, Spring.

Morgan, M., and N. Signorelli. 1990. *Cultivation Analysis.* Beverly Hills, Calif.: Sage.

Morley David. 1980. *The 'Nationwide' Audience: Structure and Decoding.* British Film Institute Television Monographs, 11. London: BFI.

———. 1986. *Family Television: Cultural Power and Domestic Leisure.* London: Comedia.

——— and Kevin Robins. 1995. *Spaces of Identity: Global Media, Electronic Landscapes and Cultural Boundaries.* London: Routledge.

Morris, Peter. 1978. *Embattled Shadows: A History of Canadian Cinema, 1895–1939.* Montreal and Kingston: McGill-Queen's University Press.

Mosco, Vincent. 1996. *The Political Economy of Communication: Rethinking and Renewal.* London: Sage.

Mulvey, Laura. 1975. 'Visual pleasure and narrative cinema', *Screen* 16, 3: 6–18.

Murdock, Graham. 1990. 'Large corporations and the control of the communications industries', in Gurevitch et al. (1990).

Needham, Phil. 1993. 'Concerns over media ban delay ouster bid', *Vancouver Sun*, 7 Oct., B5.

Negroponte, Nicholas. 1995. *Being Digital*. New York: Alfred A. Knopf.

Olson, David R., ed. 1980. *The Social Foundations of Language and Thought*. New York: Norton.

Onex. 2002. Onex Entertainment Group. http://onex.com/cp/cp_entgp/cp_entgp.asp

Ong, Walter. 1982. *Orality and Literacy: The Technologizing of the Word*. London: Methuen.

Ontario. 1972. *Canadian Publishers and Canadian Publishing*. Report of the Royal Commission on Book Publishing. Toronto: Queen's Printer.

Osler, Andrew M. 1993. *News: The Evolution of Journalism in Canada*. Toronto: Copp Clark Pitman.

O'Sullivan, T., J. Hartley, D. Saunders, and J. Fiske. 1983. *Key Concepts in Communication*. Toronto: Methuen.

Paterson, Chris A. 2001. 'Media Imperialism Revisited: The Global Public Sphere and the News Agency Agenda', in Stig Hjarvard, ed., *News in a Globalized Society*. Göteborg: Nordicom.

Payzant, G. 1984. *Glenn Gould: Music and Mind*. Toronto: Key Porter.

Pegg, Mark. 1983. *Broadcasting and Society 1918–1939*. London: Croom Helm.

Pendakur, Manjunath. 1990. *Canadian Dreams and American Control: The Political Economy of the Canadian Film Industry*. Toronto: Garamond Press.

————. 1998. 'Hollywood North: film and TV production in Canada', in Gerald Sussman and John A. Lent, eds, *Global Productions: Labor in the Making of the 'Information Society'*. Cresskill, NJ: Hampton Press.

Picard, Robert G. 1989. *Media Economics: Concepts and Issues*. Newbury Park, Calif.: Sage.

Plato. 1973. *Phaedrus*, trans. Walter Hamilton. Toronto: Penguin.

Playback. 1998. 'Investment and Finance', 4 May, 36–50.

Popper, Karl R. 1962 [1945]. *The Open Society and its Enemies*. London: Routledge.

Postman, Neil. 1993. *Technopoly: The Surrender of Culture to Technology*. New York: Knopf.

Pratkanis, Anthony R. 1992. *The Age of Propaganda: The Everyday Use and Abuse of Persuasion*. New York: W.H. Freeman.

Print Measurement Bureau (PMB). 1998. *PMB 98 Readership Volume*. Toronto: PMB.

————. n.d. *Introducing PMB*. Toronto: PMB. http://www.pmb.ca

————. n.d. *PMB Media School*. Toronto: PMB.

Pritchard, David, and Florian Sauvageau. 1999. *Les journalistes canadiens: Un portrait de fin de siècle*. Québec: Les Presses de l'Université Laval.

Propp, Vladimir. 1970. *Morphology of the Folktale*. Austin: University of Texas Press.

Quebec. 2001. *Mandat d'initiative portant sur La concentration de la presse*. Quebec: Secrétariat des commissions, Nov. www.assnat.qc.ca/fra/publications/rapports/rapcc3.html

Queeney, Kathryn M. 1983. 'DBS: free flow vs. national sovereignty', *Communication Research Trends* 4, 2: 4–6.

Raboy, Marc. 1990. *Missed Opportunities: The Story of Canada's Broadcasting Policy*. Montreal and Kingston: McGill-Queen's University Press.

————. 1995. 'The role of public consultation in shaping the Canadian broadcasting system', *Canadian Journal of Political Science* 28, 3: 455–77.

————, Ivan Bernier, Florian Sauvageau, and Dave Atkinson. 1994. 'Cultural development and the open economy: a democratic issue and a challenge to public policy', in McFadyen et al. (1994).

Radway, Janice. 1984. *Reading the Romance: Women, Patriarchy and Popular Literature*. Chapel Hill: University of North Carolina Press.

Rantanen, Terhi. 1997. 'The globalization of electronic news in the 19th century', *Media, Culture and Society* 19, 4: 605–20.

Ravensbergen, Jan. 2002. 'BCE set to dismantle multimedia empire: After selling Yellow Pages for $3B, next to go would be CTV, Globe and Mail', *Ottawa Citizen*, 14 Sept., D1.

Reuters. 1998. 'U.S. panel on water sees it as commodity', *New York Times*, 22 Mar., 6.

Rever, Judi. 1995. 'France faces off with Rambo', *Globe and Mail*, 4 Feb., C3.

Reynolds, Bill. 2002. 'Why your local radio station sounds like this (white bread)', *Globe and Mail*, 3 Aug., R1, R5.

Rice-Barker, Leo. 1996. 'Victor victorious', *Playback*, 6 May, 1, 5, 14.

Richer, Jules. 1999. 'La presse québécoise en plein marasme: Chantal Hébert sonne l'alarme', *Le 30* 23, 3 (Mar.): 11–13.

Riga, Andy. 2000. 'BCE's Monty a world-beater', *Montreal Gazette*, 16 Feb., D1.

Rolland, Asle, and Helge Østbye. 1986. 'Breaking the broadcasting monopoly', in Denis McQuail and Karen Siune, eds, *New Media Politics: Comparative Perspectives in Western Europe*. London: Sage.

Rose, Gillian. 1995. 'Place and identity: A sense of place', in Massey and Jess (1995).

Rosengren, K.E., and S. Windahl. 1989. *Media Matters: TV Use in Childhood and Adolescence*. Norwood, NJ: Ablex.

Roth, Lorna. 1996. 'Cultural and racial diversity in Canadian broadcast journalism', in Valeria Alia, Brian Brennan, and Barry Hoffmaster, eds, *Deadlines & Diversity: Journalism Ethics in a Changing World*. Halifax: Fernwood.

———. 1998. 'The delicate acts of "colour balancing": multiculturalism and Canadian television broadcasting policies and practices', *Canadian Journal of Communication* 23: 487–505.

Rotstein, Abraham. 1988. 'The use and misuse of economics in cultural policy', in Rowland Lorimer and D.C. Wilson, eds, *Communication Canada: Issues in Broadcasting and New Technologies*. Toronto: Kagan and Woo.

Russell, Nick. 1994. *Morals and the Media: Ethics in Canadian Journalism*. Vancouver: University of British Columbia Press.

Rutherford, Donald. 1992. *Dictionary of Economics*. London: Routledge.

Rutherford, Paul. 1990. *When Television Was Young: Primetime Canada*. Toronto: University of Toronto Press.

Saunders, Doug. 2002. 'Rocking against the suits', *Globe and Mail*, 2 Mar., R1.

Saussure, Ferdinand de. 1974. *Course in General Linguistics*. London: Fontana.

Scannell, Paddy. 1988. 'Radio times: the temporal arrangements of broadcasting in the modern world', in P. Drummond and R. Paterson, eds, *Television and its Audiences: International Research Perspectives*. London: BFI.

———, ed. 1991. *Broadcast Talk*. London: Sage.

——— and D. Cardiff. 1991. *A Social History of Broadcasting*, vol. 1, *Serving the Nation 1922–1939*. Oxford: Basil Blackwell.

Schiller, H.I. 1984. *Information and the Crisis Economy*. Norwood, NJ: Ablex.

Schlesinger, Philip. 1978. *Putting 'Reality' Together: BBC News*. London: Constable.

———. 1983. *Televising 'Terrorism': Political Violence in Popular Culture*. London: Comedia.

Schulman, Mark. 1990. 'Control mechanisms inside the media', in John Downing, Ali Mohammadi, and Annebelle Sreberny-Mohammadi, eds, *Questioning the Media: A Critical Introduction*. Newbury Park, Calif.: Sage.

Schulman, Norma. 1993. 'Conditions of their own making: An intellectual history of the Centre for Contemporary Cultural Studies at the University of Birmingham', *Canadian Journal of Communication* 18, 1: 51–74.

Schudson, Michael. 1978. *Discovering the News: A Social History of American Newspapers*. New York: Basic Books.

Seiter, Ellen, Hans Borchers, Gabrielle Kreutzner, and Eva-Maria Warth. 1989. *Remote Control: Television, Audiences, and Cultural Power*. London: Routledge.

Shannon, Claude E., and Warren Weaver. 1949. *The Mathematical Theory of Communication*. Urbana: University of Illinois Press.

Siebert, F.S., T. Peterson, and W. Schramm. 1971 [1956]. *Four Theories of the Press*. Urbana: University of Illinois Press.

Silj, A., ed. 1988. *East of Dallas. The European Challenge to American Television*. London: British Film Institute.

Silverstone, R. 1981. *The Message of Television: Myth and Narrative in Contemporary Culture*. London: Heinemann Educational Books.

Smith, Adam. 1937 [1776]. *An Inquiry into the Nature and Causes of the Wealth of Nations*. New York: Modern Library.

Smith, Anthony D. 1980. *The Geopolitics of Information: How Western Culture Dominates the World*. London: Faber and Faber.

Smythe, Dallas. 1994. *Counterclockwise: Perspectives on Communication*, ed. Thomas Guback. Boulder, Colo.: Westview Press.

Soderlund, W.C., Walter Romanow, and Stuart Surlin. 1984. *Media and Elections in Canada*. Toronto: Holt, Rinehart and Winston.

Sotiron, Minko. 1997. *From Politics to Profit: The Commercialization of Daily Newspapers, 1890–1920*. Montreal and Kingston: McGill-Queen's University Press.

Sparks, Colin. 1995. 'The survival of the state in British broadcasting', *Journal of Communication* 45, 4: 140–59.

Statistics Canada. 1997. *Recent Cultural Statistics* (Highlights from *Canada's Culture, Heritage and Identity: A Statistical Perspective*). http://www.pch.gc.ca/culture/library/statscan/stats_e.htm

———. 1998. 'Focus on culture', *Quarterly Bulletin from the Culture Statistics Program* (Winter). Catalogue no. 87–004–XPB.

———. 2001. *Overview: Access to and Use of Information Communication Technology*. Catalogue no. 56–505–XIE. Ottawa: Minister of Industry, Mar.

———. 2003a. Immigration and visible minorities. <www12.statcan.ca/english/census01/products/highlight/Ethnicity/Index.cfm?Lang+E

———. 2003b. Immigration and visible minorities. <www12.statcan.ca/english/census01/products/highlight/Immigration/Index.cfm?Lang+E

Sternbergh, Adam. 2002. 'Cutie Patootie Now Kaput', *National Post*, 28 Sept., SP1, SP4.

Storey, J. 1993. *Cultural Theory and Popular Culture*. London: Harvester Wheatsheaf.

Stott, Jim. 1995. 'Today's newspapers a long leap from scandal sheets', *Calgary Herald*, 19 Nov., A7.

Straw, Will. 1996. 'Sound recording', in Dorland (1996).

Sutel, Seth. 2000. 'New media marries old', *Montreal Gazette*, 11 Jan., F1, F4.

Sweet, Doug. 2001. 'Publisher stepping down: Goldbloom cites "fundamental differences" with new owners', *Montreal Gazette*, 1 Sept., A1.

Taras, David. 1999. *Power and Betrayal in the Canadian Media*. Peterborough, Ont.: Broadview Press.

Thompson, Edward P. 1980 [1963]. *The Making of the English Working Class*. Harmondsworth: Penguin.

Thompson, John C. 2002. 'No al-Qaeda PoWs while threat looms', *Ottawa Citizen*, 23 Jan., A15.

Thomson Corp. 1998. *Annual Report 1997*.

———. 1999. *Annual Report 1998*.

Tiessen, Paul. 1993. 'From literary modernism to the Tantramar Marshes: anticipating McLuhan in British and Canadian media theory and practice', *Canadian Journal of Communication* 18, 4: 451–68.

Tiffin, Deborah, ed. 2001. *Film Canada Yearbook 2001*. Port Perry, Ont.: Moving Pictures Media.

Tuchman, Gaye. 1978. *Making News: A Study in the Construction of Reality*. New York: Free Press.

Turner, G. 1990. *British Cultural Studies: An Introduction*. London: Routledge.

UNESCO. 1980. *Many Voices, One World: Report by the International Commission for the Study of Communication Problems* (MacBride Commission). Paris: Unipub.

———. Universal Declaration of Human Rights. http://www.unhchr.ch/udhr/lang/eng.htm

Vale, Allison. 1998. 'Cdns. reap sales in France', *Playback*, 19 Oct., 1, 14–15, 19.

van Dijk, Teun A. 1985–. *Handbook of Discourse Analysis*, 4 vols. London: Academic Press.

van Ginneken, Jaap. 1998. *Understanding Global News: A Critical Introduction*. London: Sage.

van Zoonen, Liesbet. 1991. 'Feminist perspectives on the media', in Curran and Gurevitch (1991: 33–54).

Vipond, Mary. 1992. *Listening In: The First Decade of Canadian Broadcasting, 1922–1932*. Montreal and Kingston: McGill-Queen's University Press.

Wallace, Bruce. 2002. 'Mr. Showbiz comes to G8 summit: Few leaders are as colourful, powerful and controversial as Berlusconi', *Montreal Gazette*, 15 June, B1.

———. 2002. 'Recording Industry', in Paul Attallah and Leslie Regan Shade, eds, *Mediascapes: New Patterns in Canadian Communication*. Toronto: Nelson Thomson Learning.

Wasko, Janet, Mark Phillips, and Chris Purdie. 1983. 'Hollywood meets Madison Avenue: the commercialization of US films', *Media, Culture and Society* 15, 2: 271–94.

Watzlawick, Paul, Janet Beavin, and Don Jackson. 1967. *Pragmatics of Human Communication: A Study of Interactional Patterns, Pathologies, and Paradoxes*. New York: Norton.

Weir, Ernest Austin. 1965. *The Struggle for National Broadcasting in Canada*. Toronto: McClelland & Stewart.

Williams, Carol T. 1992. *It's Time for My Story: Soap Opera Sources, Structure and Response*. London: Praeger.

Williams, Raymond. 1958. *Culture and Society: 1780–1950*. New York: Columbia University Press.

———. 1974. *Television: Technology and Cultural Form*. London: Fontana.

———. 1989. *Resources of Hope: Culture, Democracy, Socialism*, ed. Robin Gable. London: Verso.

Williams, Tannis MacBeth. 1986. *The Impact of Television: A Natural Experiment in Three Communities*. Orlando, Fla: Academic Press.

———. 1995. 'The impact of television: a longitudinal Canadian study', in Benjamin D. Singer, ed., *Communications in Canadian Society*. Toronto: Nelson.

Williamson, Judith. 1978. *Decoding Advertisements: Ideology and Meaning in Advertising*. London: Boyars.

Wilson, Kevin G. 2002. 'The rise and fall of Teleglobe', *Montreal Gazette*, 18 May, B5.

Winner, Langdon. 1977. *Autonomous Technology: Technics-out-of-Control as a Theme in Political Thought*. Cambridge, Mass.: MIT Press.

Winter, James. 1997. *Democracy's Oxygen: How Corporations Control the News*. Montreal: Black Rose Books.

Withers, Edward, and Robert S. Brown. 1995. 'The broadcast audience: a sociological perspective', in Benjamin D. Singer, ed., *Communications in Canadian Society*. Toronto: Nelson, 89–121.

Wober, J. Mallory, and Barrie Gunter. 1986. 'Television audience research at Britain's Independent Broadcasting Authority, 1974–1984', *Journal of*

Broadcasting and Electronic Media 30, 1: 15–31.

Women's Studies Group. 1978. *Women Take Issue: Aspects of Women's Subordination*. Birmingham: Centre for Cultural Studies.

Woollacott, Janet. 1982. 'Messages and Meanings', in Gurevitch et al. (1982).

York, Geoffrey. 2002. 'Great Firewall of China stifles dissent on the net', *Globe and Mail*, 5 Oct., A14.

Ze, David Wei. 1995. 'Printing as an Agent of Social Stability during the Sung Dynasty', Ph.D. dissertation, School of Communication, Simon Fraser University.

Zerbisias, Antonia. 2003. 'Chaos, or just a little vase they're going through?', *Toronto Star*, 12 Apr., A14.

Zimonjic, Peter. 2002. 'CBC forum debates media ownership: Discussion organized in response to Mills' firing', *Ottawa Citizen*, 23 June, A3.

Index

NOTE: Entries in italic type refer to illustrations